LEADERSHIP

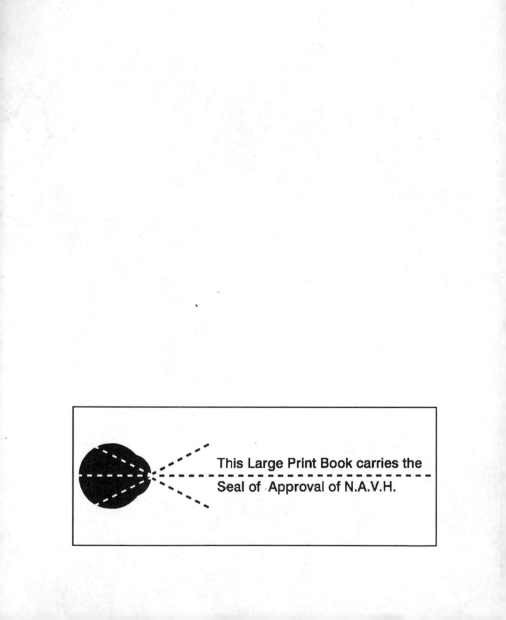

This Large Print Book carries the
Seal of Approval of N.A.V.H.

LEADERSHIP

IN TURBULENT TIMES

DORIS KEARNS GOODWIN

LARGE PRINT PRESS
A part of Gale, a Cengage Company

GALE
A Cengage Company

LIBRARY OF CONGRESS CIP DATA ON FILE.
CATALOGUING IN PUBLICATION FOR THIS BOOK
IS AVAILABLE FROM THE LIBRARY OF CONGRESS

ISBN-13: 978-1-4328-6921-2 (paperback alk. paper)

Published in 2019 by arrangement with Simon & Schuster, Inc.

Printed in the United States of America
1 2 3 4 5 6 7 23 22 21 20 19

*For my husband, Richard Goodwin,
and our best man and closest friend,
Michael Rothschild*

CONTENTS

III. THE LEADER AND THE TIMES: HOW THEY LED

FOREWORD

Abraham Lincoln, Theodore Roosevelt, Franklin Roosevelt, and Lyndon Johnson — the lives and times of these four men have occupied me for half a century. I have awakened with them in the morning and thought about them when I went to bed at night. By immersing myself in manuscript collections, personal diaries, letters, oral histories, memoirs, newspaper archives, and periodicals, I searched for illuminating details that, taken together, would provide an intimate understanding of these men, their families, their friends, their colleagues, and the worlds in which they lived.

After writing four extensive books devoted to these men, I thought I knew them well before I embarked on this present study of leadership nearly five years ago. But as I observed them through the exclusive lens of leadership, I felt as if I were meeting them anew. There was much to learn as the elusive theme of leadership assumed center stage. As

9

I turned to works of philosophy, literature, business, political science, and comparative studies, in addition to history and biography, I found myself engaged in an unexpectedly personal and emotional kind of storytelling. I returned to fundamental questions I had not asked so openly since my days of college and graduate school.

Are leaders born or made? Where does ambition come from? How does adversity affect the growth of leadership? Do the times make the leader or does the leader shape the times? How can a leader infuse a sense of purpose and meaning into people's lives? What is the difference between power, title, and leadership? Is leadership possible without a purpose larger than personal ambition?

How fondly I remember long and heated sessions over just such questions with my graduate school friends, arguing through the night with a fervor surpassing our level of knowledge. Yet, at bottom, something in these discussions was exactly on the mark, for they engaged us deeply, tapped our idealism, and challenged us to figure out how we wanted to live our own lives. I realize now that debates such as these put me on the path to find my own calling as a historian.

In Part One we see the four men when they first entered public life. In their twenties, when they set forth to forge their public identities, they appear very different from the sober, iconic countenances that have since saturated our culture, currency, and memorial sculpture. Their paths were anything but certain. Their stories abound in confusion, hope, failure, and fear. We follow mistakes made along the way, from inexperience, cockiness, lack of caution, outright misjudgments, and selfishness, and see the efforts made to acknowledge, conceal, or overcome these mistakes. Their struggles are not so different from our own.

No single path carried them to the pinnacle of political leadership. Theodore Roosevelt and Franklin Roosevelt were born to extraordinary privilege and wealth. Abraham Lincoln endured relentless poverty. Lyndon Johnson experienced sporadic hard times. They differed widely in temperament, appearance, and physical ability. They were endowed with a divergent range of qualities often ascribed to leadership — intelligence, energy, empathy, verbal and written gifts, and skills in dealing with people. They were united, however, by a fierce ambition, an inordinate drive to succeed. With perseverance and hard work, they all essentially made themselves leaders by enhancing and developing the qualities they were given.

All four men were recognized as leaders long before they reached the presidency. And like rocks in a polishing cylinder, all four were brought to shine by tumbling contact with a wide variety of people. They had found their vocation in politics. "I have often thought," American philosopher William James wrote of the mysterious formation of identity, "that the best way to define a man's character would be to seek out the particular mental or moral attitude in which, when it came upon him, he felt himself most deeply and intensely alive and active. At such moments, there is a voice inside which speaks and says, 'This is the real me!' "

Dramatic reversals that shattered the private and public lives of all four men are the subject of Part Two. They were at different life stages when forced to deal with events that ruptured their sense of self and threatened to curtail their prospects. The nature of the adversity that assailed each was unique: Abraham Lincoln suffered a blow to his public reputation and his private sense of honor that led to a near-suicidal depression; Theodore Roosevelt lost his young wife and his mother on the same day; Franklin Roosevelt was struck by polio and left permanently paralyzed from the waist down; Lyndon Johnson lost an election to the United States Senate. To draw an analogy between an election loss and the tragic reversals experienced by the others would appear, on the surface, ludicrous; but Lyndon Johnson construed rejection by the people as a judgment upon, and a repudiation of, his deepest self. For a long while, the election loss negatively changed the direction of his career until a massive heart attack and the proximity of death repurposed his life.

Scholars who have studied the development of leaders have situated resilience, the ability to sustain ambition in the face of frustration, at the heart of potential leadership growth. More important than what happened to them was how they responded to these reversals, how they managed in various ways to put themselves back together, how these watershed experiences at first impeded, then deepened, and finally and decisively molded their leadership.

Part Three will bring the four men to the White House. There, at their formidable best, when guided by a sense of moral purpose, they were able to channel their ambitions and summon their talents to enlarge the opportunities and lives of others. Specific stories of how they led will explore the riddle: Do leaders shape the times or do the times summon their leaders?

"If there is not the war," Theodore Roosevelt mused, "you don't get the great general; if there is not a great occasion, you don't get the great statesman; if Lincoln had lived in times of peace, no one would have known his name now." Roosevelt's debatable notions voice opinions heard from the beginning of our country. "It is not in the still calm of life, or the repose of a pacific station, that great characters are formed," Abigail Adams wrote to her son John Quincy Adams in the midst of the American Revolution, suggesting that "the habits of a vigorous mind are formed in contending with difficulties. Great necessities call out great virtues."

The four leaders presented in this book confronted "great necessities." All took office at moments of uncertainty and dislocation in extremis. Abraham Lincoln entered the presidency at the gravest moment of dissolution in American history. Franklin Roosevelt encountered a decisive crisis of confidence in our country's economic survival and the viability of democracy itself. Though neither Theodore Roosevelt nor Lyndon Johnson faced a national crisis on the scale of secession or devastating economic depression, they both assumed office as a result of an assassination, a violent rupture of the democratic mode of succession at a time when seismic tremors had begun to rattle the social order.

While the nature of the era a leader chances to occupy profoundly influences the nature of the leadership opportunity, the leader must be ready when that opportunity presents itself. One leader's skills, strengths, and style may be suited for the times; those of another, less so. President James Buchanan was temperamentally unfit to respond to the intensifying crisis over slavery that would confront Abraham Lincoln. President William McKinley encountered the same tumultuous era as Theodore Roosevelt but failed to grasp the hidden dangers in the wake of the Industrial Revolution. President Herbert Hoover's fixed mind-set could not handle the deepening depression with the creativity of Franklin Roosevelt's freewheeling experimentation. President John Kennedy lacked the unrivaled legislative skill and focus that Lyndon Johnson brought to the central issue of the time — civil rights.

"Rarely was man so fitted to the event," observed philosopher Ralph Waldo Emerson when eulogizing Abraham Lincoln at the Church of the First Parish in Concord, Massachusetts. One would be hard put to invent a leader who could have better guided us through the darkest days of the Civil War, a leader both merciful and merciless, confident and humble, patient and persistent — able to mediate among factions, sustain our spirits, and translate the meaning of the struggle into words of matchless force, clarity, and beauty. Yet, a similar statement might be made of Theodore Roosevelt, whose spirited combativeness was perfectly fitted to the task of mobilizing the country and the press to deal with voracious monopolies and the inequities of the Industrial Age. We could say the same of Franklin Roosevelt, whose confidence and infectious optimism restored the hope and earned the trust of the American people through both the Great Depression and World War II — or of Lyndon Johnson, whose southern roots and legislative wizardry ideally fitted him for the great civil rights struggle that altered the face of the country.

Four case studies will reveal these vastly different men in action during defining events of their times and presidencies. These four extended examples show how their leadership fit the historical moment as a key fits a lock. No key is exactly the same; each has a different line of ridges and notches along its blade. While there is neither a master key to leadership nor a common lock of historical circumstance, we can detect a certain family resemblance of leadership traits as we trace the alignment of leadership capacity within its historical context.

There is little question that the first three leaders studied here — Abraham Lincoln, Theodore Roosevelt, and Franklin Roosevelt — rank among our greatest presidents. Despite flawed decisions and mistaken judgments, all have been accorded a stable and honored place in communal memory.

The case of Lyndon Johnson is more problematic. I have wrestled with his place in history since the days when I worked with him in the White House as a twenty-four-year-old

16

White House Fellow. That White House fellowship nearly came to an unceremonious end before it had even gotten started. Like many young people in my generation, I had been active in the anti–Vietnam War movement. Several months before my selection, a fellow graduate student and I had written an article, which we sent to *The New Republic,* calling for a third party candidate to challenge Lyndon Johnson in 1968. *The New Republic* published the article days after my selection as a Fellow had been announced. I was certain I would be dismissed from the program, but surprisingly, President Johnson said: "Oh bring her down here for a year and if I can't win her over no one can!" I stayed on after the fellowship and when his presidency was over accompanied him to the Texas ranch to assist him with his memoirs.

While Johnson's conduct during the war will continue to tarnish his legacy, the passing years have made clear that his leadership in civil rights and his domestic vision in the Great Society will stand the test of time.

Lyndon Johnson entered Congress as a protégé of Franklin Roosevelt. From his desk in the Oval Office, Johnson gazed directly across to a painting of his "political daddy" whose domestic agenda in the New Deal he sought to surpass with his own Great Society. As a young man, Franklin Roosevelt had daydreamed of his own political ascent molded step by step upon the career of Theodore Roosevelt. From childhood, Theodore Roosevelt's great hero was Abraham Lincoln, whose patient resolve and freedom from vindictiveness blazed a trail that Theodore Roosevelt sought to follow all his life. And for Abraham Lincoln, the closest he found to an ideal leader was George Washington, whom he invoked when he bade farewell to his home in 1861, drawing strength from the first president as he left Illinois to assume a task "greater than that which rested upon Washington." If George Washington was the father of his country, then by affiliation and affinity, Abraham Lincoln was his prodigious son. These four men form a family tree, a lineage of leadership that spans the entirety of our country's history.

It is my hope that these stories of leadership in times of fracture and fear will prove instructive and reassuring. These men set a standard and a bar for all of us. Just as they learned from one another, so we can learn from them. And from them gain a better perspective on the discord of our times. For leadership does not exist in a void. Leadership is a two-way street. "I have only been an instrument," Lincoln insisted, with both accuracy and modesty, "the antislavery people of the country and the army have done it all." The progressive movement helped pave the way for Theodore Roosevelt's "Square Deal," much as the civil rights movement provided the fuel to ignite the righteous and pragmatic activism that enabled the Great Society. And no one communicated with people and heard their voices more clearly than Franklin Roosevelt. He absorbed their stories, listened carefully, and for a generation held a nonstop conversation with the people.

"With public sentiment, nothing can fail," Abraham Lincoln said, "without it nothing can succeed." Such a leader is inseparably linked to the people. Such leadership is a mirror in which the people see their collective reflection.

I
Ambition and the Recognition of Leadership

One:
Abraham

"Every man is said to have his peculiar ambition"

Lincoln was only twenty-three years old on March 9, 1832, when he declared his intention to run for a seat in the Illinois state legislature. The frontier state had not yet developed party machinery to officially nominate candidates. Persons desiring to run simply put forward their own names on a handbill expressing their views on local affairs.

"Every man is said to have his peculiar ambition," Lincoln began. "I have no other so great as that of being truly esteemed of my fellow men, by rendering myself worthy of their esteem. How far I shall succeed in gratifying this ambition is yet to be developed. I am young and unknown to many of you."

For many ambitious young men in the nineteenth century, politics proved the chosen arena for advancement. While Lincoln's ambition was as central to his makeup as his backbone, it was, almost from the start, twofold. It was not simply for himself; it was for the people he hoped to lead. He wanted to distinguish himself in their eyes. The sense of community was central to the master dream of his life — the desire to accomplish deeds that would gain the lasting respect of his fellow men.

He asked for the opportunity to render himself worthy: "I was born and have ever remained in the most humble walks of life. I have no wealthy or popular relations to recommend me. If the good people in their wisdom shall see fit to keep me in the background, I have been too familiar with disappointments to be very much chagrined."

Where did this ambition come from, his "strong conviction," as one friend described it, "that he was born for better things than seemed likely or even possible"?

When asked later to shed light on his beginnings, Lincoln claimed his story could be "condensed into a single sentence: The short and simple annals of the poor." His father, Thomas, had never learned to read, and, according to his son, never did "more in the way of writing than to bunglingly sign his own name." Trapped in an exitless poverty, Thomas cleared only sufficient land for survival and moved from one dirt farm to another in Kentucky, Indiana, and Illinois. While traces of the life of Lincoln's mother, Nancy Hanks, are sketchy, those who knew her agreed "she was superior to her husband in Every way." She was described as "keen — shrewd — smart," endowed with a strong memory and quick perception. "All that I am or hope ever to be I get from my mother," Lincoln later said.

When Abraham was nine, Nancy Hanks died from what was known as milk sickness, a disease transmitted by way of cows that had eaten poisonous plants. After her burial, Thomas abandoned his young son and his twelve-year-old daughter, Sarah, for a period of seven months while he returned to Kentucky to find a new wife. They were left on their own in what Lincoln described as "a wild region," a nightmarish place where "the panther's scream filled the night with fear and bears preyed on the swine." When Abraham's new stepmother, Sarah Bush Johnston, returned with Thomas, she found the children living like animals — "wild — ragged & dirty." She was stunned to find that the floorless cabin lacked even a door. Inside, there were few furnishings, no beds, and scant bedding. From the store of goods she had brought with her in the wagon, the industrious Sarah created a "snug and comfortable" home. A floor was laid, door and windows hung, and she provided clothing for the children. How, within the confines of this desolation, did Lincoln develop and sustain a grand, visionary ambition, a belief that he was meant for higher and better things?

The springboard to the development of Lincoln's ambition can be traced to his recognition, even as a young boy, that he was gifted with an exceptionally intelligent, clear, and inquisitive mind. Schoolmates in the ABC school in rural Kentucky where he was taught to read and write at the age of seven recalled that he was able to learn more swiftly and understand more deeply than others. Though he was able to attend school only sporadically, when his father didn't require his labor on their hardscrabble farm, he stood without peer at the top of every class. "He was the learned boy among us unlearned folks," one classmate recalled. "He carried away from his brief schooling," his biographer David Herbert Donald observes, "the self-confidence of a man who has never met his intellectual equal." A dream that he might someday be in a situation to make the most of his talents began to take hold.

In the age-old debate about whether leadership traits are innate or developed, memory — the ease and capacity with which the mind stores information — is generally considered an inborn trait. From his earliest days in school, Lincoln's comrades remarked upon his phenomenal memory, "the best," the most "marvelously retentive," they had ever encountered. His mind seemed "a wonder," a friend told him, "impressions were easily made upon it and never effaced." Lincoln told his friend he was mistaken. What appeared a gift, he argued, was, in his case, a developed talent. "I am slow to learn," he explained, "and slow to forget what I have learned. My mind is like a piece of steel — very hard to scratch anything on it, and almost impossible after you get it there to rub it out." His stepmother, who came to love him as if he were her own son, observed the arduous process by which he engraved things into his memory. "When he came upon a passage that Struck him, he would write it down on boards if he had no paper & keep it there until he did get paper," she recalled, "and then he would rewrite it" and keep it in a scrapbook so that he could preserve it.

While his mind was neither quick nor facile, young Lincoln possessed singular powers of reasoning and comprehension, unflagging curiosity, and a fierce, almost irresistible, compulsion to understand the meaning of what he heard, read, or was taught. "When a mere child," Lincoln later said, "I used to get irritated when anybody talked to me in a way I could not understand. I do not think I ever got angry at anything else in my life." When he "got on a hunt for an idea" he could not sleep until he "caught it," and even then was not able to rest until he had "bounded it north and bounded it south, and bounded it east and bounded it west."

Early on, Abraham revealed a keystone attribute essential to success in any field — the motivation and willpower to develop every talent he possessed to the fullest. "The ambition of the man soared above us," his childhood friend Nathaniel Grigsby recalled. "He read and thoroughly read his books whilst we played." When he first learned how to print the letters of the alphabet, he was so excited that he formed "letters, words and sentences wherever he found suitable material. He scrawled them in charcoal, he scored them in the dust, in the sand, in the snow — anywhere and everywhere that lines could be drawn." He soon became "the best penman in the neighborhood."

Sharing his knowledge with his schoolmates at every turn, he soon became "their guide and leader." A friend recalled the "great pains" he took to explain to her "the movements of the heavenly bodies," patiently telling her that the moon was not really sinking, as she initially thought; it was the earth that was moving, not the moon. "When he appeared in Company," another friend recalled, "the boys would gather & cluster around him to hear him talk." With kindness, playfulness, wit, and wisdom, he would explain "things hard for us to understand by stories — maxims — tales and figures. He would almost always point his lesson or idea by some story that was plain and near as that we might instantly see the force & bearing of what he said." He understood early on that concrete examples and stories provided the best vehicles for teaching.

He had developed his talent for storytelling, in part, from watching his father. Though Thomas Lincoln was unable to read or write, he possessed wit, a talent for mimicry, and an uncanny memory for exceptional stories. Night after night, Thomas would exchange tales with farmers, carpenters, and peddlers as they passed along the old Cumberland Trail. Young Lincoln sat spellbound in the corner. After listening to the adults chatter through the evening, Abraham would spend "no small part of the night walking up and down," attempting to figure out what they were saying. No small part of his motivation was to entertain his friends the next day with a simplified and riotous version of the arcane adult world.

He thrived when holding forth on a tree stump or log captivating the appreciative attention of his young audience, and before long had built a repertoire of stories and great storytelling skills. At the age of ten, a relative recalled, Abraham learned to mimic "the Style & tone" of the itinerant Baptist preachers who appeared irregularly in the region. To the delight of his friends, he could reproduce their rip-roaring sermons almost word for word, complete with gestures of head and hand to emphasize emotion. Then, as he got older, he found additional material for his storytelling by walking fifteen miles to the nearest courthouse, where he soaked up the narratives of criminal trials, contract disputes, and contested wills and then retold the cases in lurid detail.

His stories often had a point — a moral along the lines of one of his favorite books, *Aesop's Fables* — but sometimes they were simply funny tales that he had heard and would retell with animation. When he began to speak, his face, the natural contours of which gave off a sorrowful aspect, would light up with a transforming "winning smile." And when he reached the end of his story, he would laugh with such heartiness that soon everyone was laughing with him.

Not all his humorous gifts were filled with gentle hilarity, and he would learn to muzzle his more caustic and mocking rejoinders. An early case in point was one Josiah Crawford who had lent Lincoln his copy of Parson Weems's *Life of Washington.* During a severe rainstorm, the book was damaged. Crawford demanded that Lincoln repay the value of the book by working two full days pulling corn. Lincoln considered this unfair, but nonetheless set to work until "there was not a corn blade left on a stalk." Later, however, he wrote a verse lampooning Crawford's unusually large, ugly nose, reciting "Josiah blowing his bugle" for the entertainment of his friends.

If he was the hub of his young circle's entertainment, he was also their foremost contrarian, willing to face their disapproval rather than abandon what he considered right. The boys in the neighborhood, one schoolmate recollected, liked to play a game of catching turtles and putting hot coals on their backs to see them wriggle. Abe not only told them "it was wrong," he wrote a short essay in school against "cruelty to animals." Nor did Lincoln feel compelled to share in the folkways of the frontier — a harsh culture in which children learned, for survival and for sport, to shoot and kill birds and animals. After killing a wild turkey with his father's rifle when he was eight years old, he never again "pulled a trigger on any larger game."

These attitudes were not merely moral postures. The young boy possessed a profound sense of empathy — the ability to put himself in the place of others, to imagine their situations and identify with their feelings. One winter night, a friend remembered, he and Abraham were walking home when they saw something lying in a mud hole. "It was a man, he was dead drunk," and "nearly frozen." Abe picked him up and carried him all the way to his cousin's house, where he built a fire to warm him up. On another occasion, when Lincoln was walking with a group of friends, he passed a pig caught in a stretch of boggy ground. The group continued on for half a mile when Lincoln suddenly stopped. He insisted on turning back to rescue the pig. He couldn't bear the pain he felt in his own mind when he thought of the pig.

Lincoln's size and strength bolstered his authority with his peers. From an early age, he was more athletic than most of the boys in the neighborhood, "ready to out-run, out-jump and out-wrestle or out-lift anybody." As a young man, one friend reported, he "could carry what 3 ordinary men would grunt &

sweat at." Blessed with uncommon strength, he was also favored with robust health. Relatives recalled that he was never sick. Lincoln's physical dominance proved a double-edged sword, however, for he was expected, from the age of eight to the age of twenty-one, to accompany his father into the fields, wielding an axe, felling trees, digging up stumps, splitting rails, plowing, and planting. His father considered that bones and muscles were "sufficient to make a man" and that time in school was "doubly wasted." In rural areas, the only schools were subscription schools, so it not only cost a family money to give a child an education, but the classroom took the child away from manual labor. Accordingly, when Lincoln reached the age of nine or ten, his own formal education was cut short.

Left on his own, Abraham had to educate himself. He had to take the initiative, assume responsibility for securing books, decide what to study, become his own teacher. He made things happen instead of waiting for them to happen. Gaining access to reading material proved nearly insurmountable. Relatives and neighbors recalled that Lincoln scoured the countryside to borrow books and read every volume "he could lay his hands on." A book was his steadfast companion. Every respite from the daily manual tasks was a time to read a page or two from *Pilgrim's Progress* or

Aesop's Fables, pausing while resting his horse at the end of a long row of planting.

Some leaders learn by writing, others by reading, still others by listening. Lincoln preferred reading aloud in the presence of others. "When I read aloud," Lincoln later explained, "two senses catch the idea: first, I see what I read; second, I hear it, and therefore I remember it better." Early on, he possessed a vivid sensibility for the music and rhythm of poetry and drama; he recited long stanzas and passages from memory. When the time came to return the borrowed books, he had made them his own. As he explored literature and the history of the country, the young Lincoln, already conscious of his own powers, began to imagine ways of living beyond those of his family and neighbors.

When his father found his son in the field reading a book or, worse still, distracting fellow workers with tales or passages from one of his books, he would angrily break up the performance so work might continue. On occasion, he would go so far as to destroy Abraham's books and whip him for neglecting his labors. To Thomas, Abraham's chronic reading was tantamount to dereliction, a mark of laziness. He thought his son was deceiving himself with his quest for education. "I tried to stop it, but he has got that fool idea into his head, and it can't be got out," Thomas told a friend.

At times, when the tensions with his father seemed unbearable, when the gap between his lofty ambitions and the reality of his circumstances seemed too great to bridge, Lincoln was engulfed by sadness, revealing a pensive, melancholy side to his temperament that became more pronounced as time went by. "His melancholy dript from him as he walked," said his junior law partner William Herndon, an observation echoed by dozens of others. "No element of Mr. Lincoln's character was so marked," recalled his friend Henry Clay Whitney, "as his mysterious and profound melancholy." Yet, if melancholy was part of his nature, so, too, was the life-affirming humor that allowed him to perceive what was funny or ludicrous in life, lightening his despair and fortifying his will. Both Lincoln's storytelling and his humor, friends believed, were "necessary to his very existence"; they were intended "to whistle off sadness."

In the end, the unending strain with his father enhanced, rather than diminished, young Lincoln's ambition. Year after year, as he persevered in defiance of his father's wishes, managing his negative emotions and exercising his will to slowly master one subject after another, he developed an increasing belief in his own strengths and powers. He came to trust "that he was going to be something," his cousin Sophie Hanks related, slowly creating what one leadership scholar calls "a vision of an alternative future." He told a neighbor he did not "intend to delve, grub, shuck corn, split rails and the like. I'll study and get ready, and then the chance will come."

Opportunity arrived the moment he reached twenty-one, the age of majority, releasing him from his near-indentured lot in his father's home. "Seeing no prospect of betterment in his condition, so long as his fortune was interwoven with that of his father," one friend recalled him saying, "he at last endeavored to strike out into the broad world." Bundling his sparse possessions on his shoulders, he headed west, walking more than one hundred miles to reach New Salem, where he had been promised a job as a clerk and book-keeper in a general store. A bustling small town, recently sprung up along the Sangamon River, New Salem boasted a gristmill that "supplied a large section of the county with its meal, flour and lumber." The entire settlement consisted of a few hundred people, fifteen log cabins, a tavern, a church, a blacksmith, a schoolmaster, a preacher, and a general store.

To the villagers of New Salem, the tall young stranger struck them as odd and unappealing. "Gawky and rough-looking," with dark weathered skin, great ears, high cheekbones, and black quill-like hair, he was dressed in "the most ludicrous character. His long arms protruded through the sleeves of a coat," and his pantaloons were "far better adapted for a man of much less height, which left exposed a pair of socks."

From this unprepossessing start, how was Lincoln able to establish himself so quickly in the minds of the residents that within eight months they encouraged him to run for a seat in the state legislature? The answer, one local man explained, lay in Lincoln's sociability, his "open — candid — obliging & honest" good nature. "Everybody loved him." He would help travelers whose carriages were mired in mud; he volunteered to chop wood for widows; he was ever ready to lend a "spontaneous, unobtrusive" hand. Almost anyone who had contact with him in the little community spoke of his kindness, generosity, intelligence, humor, humility, and his striking, original character. Rather than golden mythmaking tales spun in the wake of Lincoln's historic presidency, these stories, told by the score, join into a chorus of the New Salem community to form an authentic portrait of a singular young man.

Working as a clerk in New Salem's general store provided Lincoln with an ideal foundation upon which to build his political career. The general store "filled a unique place" on the frontier. Beyond the sale of groceries, hardware, cloth, and bonnets, the village store provided "a kind of intellectual and social center," a place where villagers gathered to read the newspaper, discuss the local sporting contests, and, mainly, argue about politics in an era when politics was a consuming, almost universal concern. For the farmers, who might ride fifty miles to grind grain into flour at the village gristmill, the store offered a common meeting place to unwind, exchange opinions, share stories.

Within weeks, a fellow clerk recalled, Lincoln's gregarious nature and cornucopia of funny stories had made him "a Center of attraction." The townspeople regarded him as "among the best clerks" they had ever seen. "He was attentive to his business," one villager remembered, "was kind and considerate to his customers & friends and always treated them with great tenderness." At the same time, his "unabashed eagerness to learn" deeply impressed the people of New Salem. A volume of poetry or book of prose was always kept behind the counter so he could read during a lull in the general store's business. In discussions about politics, he revealed an intimate familiarity with the issues of the day. Clearly, this was no ordinary clerk. The local families were attracted by his reflective, gentle, meditative temperament. They wanted him to prosper. They felt part of his upward climb. They lent him books.

The village cooper kept "a fire of shavings sufficiently bright" so that Lincoln could come into his place at night and read.

"When he was ignorant on any subject," one friend recalled, "no matter how simple it might make him appear he was always willing to acknowledge it." When he told the schoolmaster he had never studied grammar and wanted to do so, the schoolmaster agreed that if he ever wanted to speak in public this was something he had to learn. While no one in New Salem had a proper grammar text, the schoolmaster knew of a volume in a house six miles away. Lincoln rose from the table and started out on foot to procure the book. Returning with a treasured copy of Kirkham's *English Grammar,* he began at once to sort through the complicated rules governing the structure of sentences and the use of adverbs and adjectives. He worked hard to develop a simple, compact style of speaking and writing, with short, clear sentences that could be "understood by all classes."

The handbill Lincoln published announcing his candidacy stretched to two thousand words. Clearly, he labored over the statement to let people know how he stood on public issues and to declare something of his nature and character. He ran as a member of the Whig Party in a county that was predominantly Democratic. He stood for four central ideas — the creation of a national bank, protective tariffs, governmental support for internal improvements, and an expanded system of public education. A state representative could do little to promote national banking or high tariffs. The call for public education and for infrastructure projects to improve roads, rivers, harbors, and railways was not simply a matter of Whig boilerplate, however, but an expression of deeply urgent needs involving his own aspirations and those of his little community.

The Sangamon River was New Salem's lifeline. Upon it, settlers sent their produce to market and received necessary goods. Unless the obstacles to its navigability were surmounted, unless channels could be dredged and drifting logs removed, New Salem would never develop into a full-fledged community. The previous year Lincoln had piloted a flatboat on the river, gaining first-hand knowledge. He spoke with competence and confidence about a subject closely entwined with his own ambitions. If rivers and roads could be improved, if the government could aid in economic growth and development, hundreds of small hamlets like New Salem would thrive. "If elected," Lincoln pledged, any law providing dependable roads and navigable streams for "the poorest and most thinly populated" communities "shall receive my support."

On the topic of education, he declared, "I can only say that I view it as the most important subject which we as a people can be engaged in." He wanted every man to read the history of his country, "to appreciate the value of our free institutions," to treasure literature and the scriptures. Lincoln spoke of education with the passion of a young man who had made ferocious efforts to educate himself in the hope of building a bridge between "the humble walks of life" and his dreams of an expansive future. The education he continued to seek for himself was one he wanted available for every man.

In this first foray into politics, Lincoln also pledged that if his opinions on any subject turned out to be erroneous, he stood "ready to renounce them." With this commitment, Lincoln revealed early on a quality that would characterize his leadership for the rest of his life — a willingness to acknowledge errors and learn from his mistakes.

The pact Lincoln offered the people — the promise of unremitting labor in return for their support — was for him a covenant. The business of a vote or an election expressed a bond of affection that united people together; it was a question of trust. From the start, the destiny he sought was no simple craving for individual fame and distinction; his ambitions were, first and always, linked with the people.

While uncertain about his prospects in this first election, Lincoln made it clear that failure did not intimidate him. Should he lose, he had said when declaring his intention to run, he had been "too familiar with disappointments to be very much chagrined." And yet, he forewarned, only after being defeated "some 5 or 6 times" would he deem it "a disgrace" and be certain "never to try it again." So, along with the uncertainty of whether his ambition would be realized was the promise of resilience.

His campaign had scarcely begun when he volunteered to join the Illinois militia to fight against the Sac and Fox Indians during what became known as the Black Hawk War. To his surprise, he later said, he was elected captain of his company. No later "success in life," he told a journalist a month after he had been nominated for president, had provided him "so much satisfaction."

When he returned to New Salem after three months of service, he had only four weeks to campaign before the August election. Traveling by horseback across a sparsely populated county the size of Rhode Island, Lincoln spoke at country stores and small village squares. On Saturdays, he joined his fellow candidates in the largest towns, where farmers gathered at auctions, "vandoos" — "to dispose of produce, buy supplies, see their neighbors and get the news." The speaking would start in mid-morning and last until sunset. Each candidate was given a turn. Lincoln, one contender recalled, "did not follow the beaten track of other Speakers." He set himself apart by the candid way in which he approached every question and by his habit of illustrating his arguments with stories based on observations "drawn from all classes of Society" between men and women in their daily lives. At times, his language was awkward, as were his gestures, but few who heard him speak ever forgot "either the argument of the Story, the Story itself, or the author."

When the votes were counted, Lincoln found he had lost the election. His lack of success, however, "did not dampen his hopes nor sour his ambition," a friend recalled. On the contrary, he gained confidence from the knowledge that in his own town of New Salem, he had received an overwhelming total of 277 of the 300 votes cast. After the election, Lincoln worked several jobs to procure bread and keep "body and soul together." He served as New Salem's postmaster, and then, after teaching himself the principles of geometry and trigonometry involved in determining boundaries of land parcels, he was appointed deputy surveyor for Sangamon County, a position that allowed him to travel from one village to another. So swiftly did his reputation for storytelling precede him, a friend of Lincoln's recalled, that no sooner had he arrived in a village than "men and boys gathered from far and near, ready to carry chains, drive stakes, and blaze trees, if they could hear Lincoln's odd stories and jokes."

In 1834, now twenty-five, he ran for the state legislature once again, making good on his seriocomic warning that he would keep trying a half-dozen times before giving up. Once again, he traversed the district on horseback, delivering speeches, shaking hands, introducing himself, joining in local activities. Seeing thirty men in the field during a harvest, he offered to help, taking hold of the scythe "with perfect ease," thereby winning every vote in the crowd. His ungainly appearance initially put people off. "Can't the party raise a better candidate than that," a doctor asked upon first seeing Lincoln. Then, after hearing him talk, he changed his mind: "Why, he knows more than all of them put together."

This time, having expanded his contacts throughout the county, Lincoln easily won. As he prepared to leave for the capital to take up his seat in the legislature, his friends chipped in to help him buy "suitable clothing" that would allow him "to maintain his new dignity." They recognized a leader in their midst just as surely as he had begun to feel the makings of a leader within himself.

■ ■ ■ ■

The rookie assemblyman was, in the words of his friend William Herndon, "anything but conspicuous" during the opening session of the state legislature. He remained "quietly in the background," patiently educating himself about how the Assembly operated, acquainting himself with the intricacies of parliamentary procedure. He carefully monitored debates and discerned the ideological rifts between his fellow Whigs and the Democrats. Aware that he was in the presence of an unusually talented group of legislators (including two future presidential candidates, six future United States senators, eight future congressmen, and three State Supreme Court justices), Lincoln was neither bashful nor timid. He was simply paying close attention, absorbing, readying to act as soon as he had accumulated sufficient knowledge to do so. A finely developed sense of timing — knowing when to wait and when to act — would remain in Lincoln's repertoire of leadership skills the rest of his life.

Between legislative sessions, Lincoln began to read law, knowing that a legal education would nourish his political career. An autodidact by necessity, he "studied with nobody," he later said, poring over cases and precedents deep into the night after working long days as surveyor and postal clerk. He borrowed law books, one at a time, from the set of John Stuart, a fellow legislator who had a law practice in Springfield. After finishing each book, he would hike the twenty miles from New Salem to Springfield to secure another loaner. An unwavering purpose supported him. "Get the books, and read and study them," he told a law student seeking advice two decades later. "Always bear in mind that your own resolution to succeed, is more important than any other one thing."

At the commencement of the second session, the transformation of Lincoln's demeanor and activity was clear. He was suddenly conspicuous, as if something in him had awakened. So thoroughly had he mastered both the legalese required for writing legislation and the intricacies of parliamentary procedure that his colleagues called on him to draft bills and amendments. The clear, legible handwriting he had perfected as a child proved invaluable when public laws and documents were initially written in longhand. More importantly, when he finally rose to speak on the Assembly floor, his colleagues witnessed what the citizens of New Salem had already seen — a young man with a remarkable array of oratorical gifts. "They say I tell a great many stories," Lincoln told a friend. "I reckon I do; but I have learned from long experience that *plain* people, take them as they run, are more easily *influenced* through the medium of a broad and humorous illustration than any other way." As people read his speeches in the newspapers or heard about his lively metaphors and analogies through word of mouth, awareness of Lincoln's signal ability to communicate spread throughout the state.

Heralded for his leadership in moving the state capital from Vandalia to Springfield, Lincoln, the second youngest member of the Assembly, was selected by the full Whig caucus as their minority leader. Their choice signified not only their deference to Lincoln's language skills and his mastery of parliamentary procedure, but what became known as his "crowning gift of political diagnosis" — his ability to intuit the feelings and intentions of his fellow Whigs and the opposing Democrats as well. After silently considering his colleagues' strategy and opinions, he would stand and simply say: "From your talk, I gather the Democrats will do so and so." If we want "to checkmate them," here are the maneuvers we should take in the days that follow. So clear was his recommended course of action that "his listeners wondered why they had not seen it that way themselves." It was "his thorough knowledge of human nature," one fellow legislator observed, that "made him an overmatch for his compeers and for any man that I have ever known."

"We followed his lead," a Whig colleague recalled, "but he followed nobody's lead; he hewed the way for us to follow, and we gladly did so. He could grasp and concentrate the matters under discussion, and his clear statement of an intricate or obscure subject was better than an ordinary argument." Democrats, of course, felt otherwise. How Lincoln responded to attacks directed against him and his party reveals much about his temperament and the character of his developing leadership. Such was the lure of politics in the antebellum era that discussions and debates between Whigs and Democrats regularly attracted the fanatic attention of hundreds of people. Opponents attacked each other in fiery, abusive language, much to the delight of raucous audiences, inciting an atmosphere that could burst into fistfights, even, on occasion, guns being drawn. While Lincoln was as thin-skinned and prickly as most politicians, his retorts were generally full of such good-humored raillery that members of both parties could not help but laugh and relax in the pleasure of his entertaining and well-told stories.

So memorable were several of Lincoln's counterattacks that citizens could recite them afterward word for word. The "lightning-rod" episode is a case in point. A crowd was beginning to disperse from a spirited rally at which Lincoln had spoken, when George Forquer stood up. A prominent Whig who had recently shifted to the Democratic Party after receiving a lucrative appointment as land register, Forquer had lately built a fancy house, complete with a newfangled lightning rod. Standing on the stage, Forquer declared that it was time for someone to take young Lincoln down, which he attempted to do with ridicule. Though the attack had "roused the lion within him," Lincoln remained quiet until Forquer finished, silently preparing his rejoinder. "The gentleman commenced by saying the young man would have to be taken down," Lincoln began, drolly admitting, "I desire to live, and I desire place and distinction; but I would rather die now than, like the gentleman, live to see the day I would change my politics for an office worth three thousand dollars a year, and then feel compelled to erect a lightning-rod to protect a guilty conscience from an offended God." The outburst of laughter provoked from the audience was thunderous.

On certain occasions, however, Herndon recalled, Lincoln's humor ran amok, his light mockery turning vindictive, even cruel. After Democrat Jesse Thomas had "indulged in some fun" at Lincoln's expense, Lincoln displayed an aspect of his great theatrical skill, resorting to mimicry, at which he had no rival. "He imitated Thomas in gesture and voice, at times caricaturing his walk and the very motion of his body." As the crowd responded with yells and cheers, Lincoln "gave way to intense and scathing ridicule," mocking still further the "ludicrous" way Thomas spoke. Seated in the audience, Thomas broke down in tears, and soon the "skinning of Thomas" became "the talk of the town." Realizing he had badly overstepped, Lincoln went to Thomas and gave him a heartfelt apology, and for years afterward, the memory of that night filled Lincoln "with the deepest chagrin." Increasingly, though not always, he was able to rein in his impulse to throw a hurtful counterpunch. He was after something more significant than the gratification of an artfully delivered humiliation.

Even early on, Lincoln's moral courage and convictions outweighed his ferocious ambition. At the age of twenty-six, he made a public statement on slavery that threatened to drastically diminish his support in a state that was then largely settled by southerners. The rise of abolitionism in the Northeast, coupled with the refusal of some northern states to return fugitive slaves, had led legislatures in both South and North to pass resolutions confirming the constitutional right to slavery. The General Assembly in Illinois fell in line. By the disproportionate vote of seventy-seven to six, the assembly resolved that "we highly disapprove of the formation of abolition societies" and hold "sacred" the "right of property in slaves." Lincoln was among the six who voted no. Registering a formal protest, he proclaimed that "the institution of slavery is founded on both injustice and bad policy." He had always believed, he later said, that "if slavery is not wrong, nothing is wrong." Lincoln's protest stopped well short of abolitionism. Until such time as the Constitution empowered Congress to eliminate slavery, he felt that his hands were tied against interfering where slavery was already established. Fearing anarchy above all, he believed it essential to abide by a law until that settled law be lawfully changed. Though carefully worded and "pruned of any offensive allusions," the protest was, nonetheless, writer William Stoddard observed, "a bold thing to do, in a day when to be an antislavery man, even at the North, was to be a sort of social outcast and political pariah."

Remaining true to his original promise to do everything he could to secure governmental aid for infrastructure improvements, however, was more personal and pressing to Lincoln in these early years of his political career than the issue of slavery. He used the power of his leading position in the Assembly to mobilize support behind a series of bills authorizing millions of dollars for a spectacular range of projects to widen rivers, build railroads, dig canals, and create roads. From prairie and first-growth forest, from clogged creeks and rivers, from black earth perfect for farming but untenable for road and train beds during the spring melts and fall rains, Lincoln envisioned a massive infrastructure system. Drawn from his firsthand knowledge of the land, his plan would provide the vital connectors to create a circulatory system of people and their products — a living social body necessary to build and sustain a growing economy. His dream, he told a friend, was to be known as the "DeWitt Clinton of Illinois" — invoking the celebrated governor of New York who had vastly spurred economic development and left a lasting imprint on his state when he secured legislation to support the building of the Erie Canal. In like fashion, Lincoln hoped that with the completion of these projects, markets would develop, bustling towns would spring up, living standards would rise, new settlers would come, greater opportunities would open for more people. Those born in the lower ranks would rise as far as their talents and discipline might take them, and the promise of the American dream would be realized.

When a sustained recession hit the state in 1837, however, public sentiment began to rear up against such expensive and still unfinished internal improvement projects. As the state debt rose to monumental proportions, Lincoln continued to stoutly defend the infrastructure system against the surge of condemnation, likening the abandonment of the new canal system to stopping a small boat "in the middle of a river — if it was not going up, it would go down." To relinquish the program of improvements, he repeatedly warned, would leave behind only failure and debt, resilted canals, obstructed waterways, half-built roads and bridges. Adamantly, he refused to give ground, abiding by his father's old maxim: "If you make a bad bargain, hug it the tighter." His dogged resistance to abandon the policies he had so passionately advocated seemed to some a sign of stubbornness, but he held fast to his vision, as if his innermost hopes, personal dreams, and ambitions were under direct assault. Which was exactly the case.

Six years after first declaring his own "peculiar ambition" to his new neighbors in New Salem, the twenty-nine-year-old Lincoln elaborated on the nature of ambition and the thirst for distinction in an address to the Young Men's Lyceum of Springfield. He opened his address with a warning that "something of ill-omen," was developing among the people — a tendency to substitute violence, murder, and lynching for the rule of law, the courts, and the Constitution. Two months earlier, the entire North had been rocked when a proslavery mob in Alton, Illinois, killed the abolitionist editor Elijah Lovejoy. In Mississippi, a group of Negroes, suspected of inciting insurrection, were hanged, as were a group of whites suspected of aiding the Negroes. If this moblike spirit continued to spread, Lincoln cautioned, the "good men, men who love tranquility," would become alienated from a government too weak to protect them. The country would then be vulnerable to the imposition of order from above.

While the ambition of the hallowed framers had been "*inseparably* linked" with building up a constitutional government allowing the people to govern themselves, he feared that in the chaos of moblike behavior, men of the likes of "an Alexander, a Caesar, or a Napoleon" would likely seek *distinction* by boldly setting themselves "to the task of pulling down." Such men of "towering" egos, in whom ambition is divorced from the people's best interests, were not men to lead a democracy; they were despots.

To counter the troublesome ambition of such men, Lincoln called upon his fellow Americans to renew the framers' values and to embrace the Constitution and its laws. "Let reverence for the laws, be breathed by every American mother," taught in every school, preached in every pulpit. The great bulwark against a potential dictator is an informed people "attached to the government and laws." This argument takes Lincoln back to his first statement to the people of Sangamon County when he spoke of education as the cornerstone of democracy. Why is education so central? Because, as he said then, every citizen must be able to read history to "appreciate the value of our free institutions." And reading about the Revolution and the making of the Constitution was more urgent, for time had passed and remembered scenes of the Revolution were fading. Indeed, Lincoln declared that the story of America's birth should "be read of, and recounted, so long as the bible shall be read." The founding fathers' noble experiment — their ambition to show the world that ordinary people could govern themselves — had succeeded, and now, Lincoln concluded, it was up to his generation to preserve this "proud fabric of freedom."

Still in his twenties, Abraham Lincoln had already developed a conception of leadership based upon the leader's shared understanding of his followers' needs for liberty, equality, and opportunity. In less than half a dozen years, seemingly from nothing and from nowhere, he had risen to become a respected leader in the state legislature, a central figure in the fight for internal improvements, an instrumental force behind the planting of the new capital, and a practicing lawyer. Given his beginnings, he had traveled an immense distance; yet, given the inordinate nature of his ambition to render himself worthy of his fellow men, he had hardly begun.

Two:
Theodore

"I rose like a rocket"

Theodore Roosevelt, like Abraham Lincoln, was twenty-three years old when he made his first foray into the political world — but there the similarities end. In Lincoln's rural environment, anyone who wanted to be a candidate could step up and nominate himself, "run on his own hook," and speak on his own behalf. Since voters came to encounter candidates firsthand in general stores and village squares, personal impressions mattered more than party affiliation. Lincoln's two-thousand-word statement announcing his aspiration for a seat in the state legislature revealed his deepest personal ambitions as well as his stand on local issues. In contrast, Roosevelt's thirty-three-word statement — devoid of promises, pledges, and personality — was a simple acknowledgment of a nomination already secured: "Having been nominated as a candidate for member of Assembly for this District, I would esteem it a compliment if you would honor me with your vote and personal influence on Election Day."

In the half-century span between Lincoln's and Roosevelt's beginnings in public life, the means of entry into politics had radically changed. While Lincoln had stepped forward on his own, young Roosevelt was chosen to run by the local boss, Joe Murray, a burly red-haired Irish immigrant. The 21st Assembly District where Roosevelt dwelled embraced both the elegant brownstones along Madison Avenue and the crowded tenements on the West Side of Manhattan. Known as the Silk Stocking District, it was one of the few reliably Republican districts in the city. Young Roosevelt was not widely known. The boss "picked me as the candidate with whom he would be most likely to win," Roosevelt later granted. "I had at that time neither the reputation nor the ability to have won the nomination for myself."

In selecting Roosevelt, a second-year law student at Columbia, the Irish boss recognized the allure of the Roosevelt name. Theodore's father, the late Theodore Roosevelt Sr., had been a highly respected philanthropist who had worked to improve the lives of poor children through his work with the Children's Aid Society, Miss Sattery's Night School for Little Italians, and the Newsboys' Lodging House. Indeed, when the nomination of Theodore Roosevelt was announced, the *New York Daily Tribune* suggested that in voting for the son of "one of the most loved and respected" figures in the history of New York, voters would have the opportunity "to show their regard for an honored name." The boss also understood that Roosevelt had the means to contribute to his own campaign. So while Lincoln, as he conceded in his opening statement, had "no wealthy or popular relations" to recommend him, it was precisely those relations and that wealth that brought young Roosevelt to the attention of the Republican boss.

Looking back, Roosevelt credited "the element of chance" — the demographics of the assembly district and the power of his family name — as the chief instrument behind his first opportunity. He also understood, however, that when an opportunity comes, a person has "to take advantage" of that opportunity. "I put myself in the way of things happening, and they happened." Indeed, it was young Roosevelt himself who had taken the initiative to become a member of the local Republican Association, which held its meetings at Morton Hall at the corner of 59th Street and Fifth Avenue. Morton Hall was a large smoke-filled room over a saloon with shabby benches, cuspidors, and poker tables. To join the party then was "no simple thing," Roosevelt later recalled. "The party was still treated as a private corporation, and in each district the organization formed a kind of social and political club. A man had to be regularly proposed for and elected into this club, just as into any other club."

When he began inquiring about the local Republican organization, he was warned by his privileged circle, "men of cultivated taste and easy life," that district politics were "low," the province of "saloon-keepers, horse-car conductors and the like," men who "would be rough and brutal and unpleasant to deal with." Their disdain did not dissuade Roosevelt, who turned their condescension on its head: "I answered that if this were so it merely meant that the people I knew did not belong to the governing class, and that the other people did — and that I intended to be

60

one of the governing class; that if they proved too hard-bit for me I supposed I would have to quit, but that I certainly would not quit until I had made the effort and found out whether I really was too weak to hold my own in the rough and tumble."

So, once again, questions emerge: What attracted this abundantly privileged, sheltered young man to the alien and contemptible world of local politics? Where did his ambition come from?

When Roosevelt sat down at the age of fifty-three to trace the narrative that led from this first run for office to the White House, he provided his own useful, albeit sometimes misleading, answers to some of these questions. In order to frame the discussion, he methodically distinguishes two types of success — whether in the arts, in battle, or in politics.

The first success, he argues, belongs to the man "who has in him the natural power to do what no one else can do, and what no amount of training, no perseverance or will power, will enable an ordinary man to do." He cites the poet who could write the "Ode on a Grecian Urn," the president who could "deliver the Gettysburg Address," and Lord Nelson at Trafalgar as manifestations of genius, examples of men assigned extraordinary gifts at birth.

The second and more common type of success, he maintains, is not dependent on such unique inborn attributes, but on a man's ability to develop ordinary qualities to an extraordinary degree through ambition and the application of hard, sustained work. Unlike genius, which can inspire, but not educate, self-made success is democratic, "open to the average man of sound body and fair mind, who has no remarkable mental or physical attributes," but who enlarges each of those attributes to the maximum degree. He suggests that it is "more useful to study this second type," for with determination, anyone "can, if he chooses, find out how to win a similar success himself."

It is clear from the start of Roosevelt's story of his leadership journey that he unequivocally aligns himself with this second type of success. His story is the tale of a sickly boy with a timid temperament who, believing in "the gospel of will," transforms his body and emboldens his spirit. Through great effort and discipline, his weak body becomes strong; through visualization and practice, he confronts fear and becomes brave. "I like to believe that, by what I have accomplished without great gifts, I may be a source of encouragement to Americans."

This picture of a young boy building his character, brick by brick, until he develops a moral concept of leadership based upon that character, is simplistic and incomplete; yet, remarkably, however, it contains large elements of truth. "Teedie" Roosevelt was, indeed, a nervous, unhealthy, fragile child, whose boyhood was shaped by terrifying attacks of bronchial asthma. Generally stealing on him in the middle of the night, these attacks created the sensation of suffocating or drowning. Hearing his son coughing, wheezing, and struggling for breath, Theodore Senior, known as Thee, would rush into the bedroom. Taking his son into his arms, he would carry him around the house for hours until he could breathe and fall asleep. If this ritual proved inadequate, he would call for the servants to bring the horse and carriage round. Wrapping the gasping child in a blanket, he would drive the horse at a good clip through the gas-lit streets, believing that the bracing night winds would stir the child's lungs. "Nobody seemed to think I would live," Roosevelt later recalled. "My father — he got me breath, he got me lungs, strength — life."

While asthma weakened young Roosevelt's body, it indirectly spurred the development of an already precocious mind. "From the very fact that he was not able originally to enter into the most vigorous activities," his younger sister, Corinne, noted, "he was always reading or writing" with a most unusual "power of concentration." There was nothing ordinary about his intellectual vitality, his curiosity, or his ambitious dream life. Under the guiding eye of his father, who ceaselessly encouraged his son's intellectual and spiritual development, Teedie became a ferocious reader, transporting himself into the lives of the adventurous heroes he most admired — men with extraordinary bodily strength, who were fearless in battle, explorers in Africa, deerslayers living on the edge of the wilderness. When asked years later whether he knew the characters in James Fenimore Cooper's *Leatherstocking Tales,* he laughed: "Do I know them? I have bunked with them and eaten with them, and I know their strengths and weaknesses."

Few young children read as broadly or had such access to books as young Roosevelt. He had only to pick a volume from the shelves of the vast library in his family's home or express interest in a particular book and it would magically materialize. During one family vacation, Teedie proudly reported that he and his younger brother and sister, Elliott and Corinne, had devoured fifty novels! Thee read aloud to his children in the evenings after dinner. He spiced learning with family games and competitions. He organized amateur plays for them, urged them to recite poetry, and encouraged each of them to follow their particular interests. Above all, he sought to impart didactic principles of duty, ethics, and morality through stories, fables, and maxims.

Leaders in every field, Roosevelt later wrote, "need more than anything else to know human nature, to know the needs of the human soul; and they will find this nature and these needs set forth as nowhere else by the great imaginative writers, whether of prose or of poetry." The effortless way Teedie secured hundreds of books provides stark contrast with the six-mile trek of Abraham to borrow Kirkham's *English Grammar,* a comparison made brutal by superimposing Thee's constant endeavors to feed Teedie's reading with the image of Thomas Lincoln tearing books from Abraham's grasp. Yet, however dissimilar their upbringings, books became for both Lincoln and Roosevelt "the greatest of companions." Every day for the rest of their lives, both men set aside time for reading, snatching moments while waiting for meals, between visitors, or lying in bed before sleep.

Roosevelt's insistence that he had no great gifts is contradicted not only by his remarkable mental vitality but also by his prodigious memory. When talking about books he had read years before, the pages would appear before him, as if he were able to read anew with his mind's eye. In contrast to Lincoln's mind, which he himself likened to "a piece of steel — hard to scratch anything on it," though "almost impossible thereafter to rub it out" — Roosevelt's mind, one friend observed, was "wax to receive and marble to retain." It seemed as if he could "remember everything he read," the friend marveled; he had only to read something once and it was his to retrieve forever, allowing him to summon not only whole passages, but the feelings evoked in him when he first encountered them.

Young Roosevelt, unlike Lincoln, did not identify himself early on as a leader. Nor was he identified as such by those around him. Teedie's precarious health kept him from public school and from natural relationships with boys his own age. He and his siblings (his older sister, Bamie; younger sister, Corinne; and younger brother, Elliott, all suffered from a range of serious physical ailments) were taught the fundamentals of reading, writing, and arithmetic by tutors at home. Their only playmates were members of their extended family, all from the same patrician class.

Within this small circle of children, however, Teedie occupied the center, organizing their play, directing their games, entertaining them with his talent for telling stories. Corinne treasured the episodic narratives her eight-year-old brother would spin, stories drawn from both his imagination and the books he had read. Storytelling played an integral role in the Roosevelt family life. Teedie's mother, Martha Bulloch (Mittie), an "unreconstructed" southerner, who had grown up in a stately mansion in Georgia, regaled her son with romantic, chivalric tales of life in the antebellum South.

The precocious Teedie, one biographer noted, displayed not only "a purposeful, determined personality" but also "an almost ruthless single-mindedness where his interests were concerned." By the age of ten, he had developed a passionate interest in nature and the ambition to become a famous ornithologist like J. J. Audubon. As he roamed the woodland trails surrounding his family's summer retreats, searching for freedom to clear his lungs, he began to observe birds, listening to their songs, discerning their various shapes and plumage. He collected bugs, insects, and reptiles, which he kept in his bureau drawers. Noting his son's absorption in birds and mammals, Thee bought him a collection of volumes on natural history and provided private taxidermy lessons with one of Audubon's assistants. The same aggressive focus Teedie had given to his reading, he now directed toward skinning, dissecting, and mounting hundreds of meticulously labeled specimens which he assembled in what he proudly called the "Roosevelt Museum of Natural History." Oblivious to the mess he created in the bedroom — fetid containers filled with dissected creatures stood in every corner — he drove Elliott to beg for a separate room.

The uniquely extensive education Thee provided his children, so different from the intensive education Lincoln crafted for himself, stretched far beyond the boundaries of their winter and summer homes to include two separate yearlong journeys abroad — the first to Europe, the second to the Middle East, the Holy Land, and Africa. They stayed in exclusive hotels and inns, in tents, and private homes. They spent two months in Rome, three weeks in Greece, two weeks in Lebanon, three weeks in Palestine, and an entire winter in Egypt. And always at night, Thee — solicitous father, mentor, minister, and tour guide — would read aloud the poetry, history, and literature of the region they were visiting. In Dresden they lived for two months with a German family. Thee had made arrangements to hire the host's daughter to immerse the children in the German language, literature, music, and art. Teedie was so intrigued with his lessons, which lasted six hours of the day, that he pleaded to extend them further. "And of course," Elliott complained, "I could not be left behind so we are working harder than ever in our lives."

While Abraham, gifted with physical agility and uncommon athletic prowess, had to *make* his mind, Teedie, privileged beyond measure with resources to develop his mind, had to *make* his body. By the age of ten, his chronic asthma required more and more days of bed rest. Thee feared that his son was becoming too familiar with illness, timidity, and frailness, following in the footsteps of his mother, who had become increasingly fragile after the destruction of her family's Georgia home during the Civil War. Plagued by palpitations, intestinal pain, debilitating headaches, and depression, she regularly withdrew to her room. Worried that Teedie, like Mittie, was becoming an invalid, Thee took his son aside: "Theodore, you have the mind but not the body, and without the help of the body the mind cannot go as far as it should. You must *make* your body. It is hard drudgery to make one's body, but I know you will do it." Teedie responded enthusiastically, promising his father: *"I'll make my body."*

With the help of his father, who hired the owner of a nearby gym to build a fully equipped gymnasium on the back porch, Teedie lifted weights and hoisted himself on horizontal bars, slowly, ever so slowly, expanding his physical capabilities and refashioning his body. That his bodily self-esteem remained vulnerable was apparent the following summer when he encountered two bullies while traveling alone on a stagecoach to Moosehead Lake in the north woods of Maine. "They found that I was a foreordained and predestined victim," he remembered years later, "and industriously proceeded to make life miserable for me." Finding he was unable to fight back, he resolved that he would "not again be put in such a helpless position." When he told his father he wanted to learn how to box, Thee hired the services of an ex-prizefighter to train his son.

Even when Teedie began studying for Harvard's entrance examinations, he continued his rigorous exercise regime. "The young man never seemed to know what idleness was," observed Arthur Cutler, a recent Harvard graduate who had been hired to prepare Teedie for the exams. "Every leisure moment would find the last novel, some English classic or some abstruse book on natural history in his hands." Working long hours every day, Teedie studied Latin, Greek, literature, history, science, and mathematics, completing in two years what normally took three years of preparation. His ability to concentrate, one contemporary recalled, was such that "the house might fall about his head," and "he would not be diverted." When given an assignment, he rarely waited until the last moment. He regarded procrastination as a sin. Preparing ahead, he recognized, freed him from anxiety — a habit of mind that would set an example for his colleagues in the years ahead. Easily passing all eight examinations, he was admitted to Harvard, eager to leave his mark on the world, though not knowing exactly how.

"The story of Theodore Roosevelt," one biographer has suggested, "is the story of a small boy who read about great men and decided he wanted to be like them." There is a decided accuracy to this statement; but more than the fictional characters he admired, young Roosevelt found in his own father the most powerful exemplar of the heroic ideal. "My father was the best man I ever knew," Roosevelt later said. "He combined strength and courage with gentleness, tenderness, and great unselfishness." He was a public figure of great accomplishment in the philanthropic world, committed to "every social reform movement"; yet, "I never knew any one who got greater joy out of living than did my father." Roosevelt considered Thee not only "his best and most intimate friend," but a beloved mentor whose advice he heeded above all others. "It seems perfectly wonderful in looking back over my eighteen years of existence," he told his family, "to see how I have literally never spent an unhappy day, unless by my own fault!"

While more than intellectually prepared for his studies at Harvard, Theodore lacked the social skills of many of his fellow students. One classmate remembers him as "studious, ambitious, eccentric — not the sort to appeal at first." The shelves in his room were filled with dead lizards and stuffed birds. If academic nonchalance was in style, Theodore was strident and zealous, prone to interrupt class in order to barrage professors with objections and questions. He disdained fellow students who drank or smoked, and kept his distance from classmates until he could determine if their families shared his own station in life.

If young Roosevelt lacked the empathy and kindness that won Lincoln affection wherever he went, his original personality eventually captivated his classmates, who marveled at his irrepressible energy and lack of self-consciousness. Though he "never conquered asthma completely," suffering spasms at irregular intervals for decades, he had strengthened his body sufficiently so that he could participate in a wide array of sports. He wrestled and sparred, ran three or four miles a day, took up rowing and tennis, and continued to work out in the gym. Though he failed to excel in any of these activities, he derived immense satisfaction from the sheer fact of overcoming his earlier invalidism. While posting honor grades every semester, he organized a whist club and a finance club, joined the rifle club and the arts club, and was elected to the most prestigious social club of all, the Porcellian. Nor did he abandon his interest in birds, tramping miles from Cambridge to observe them, shoot them, and stuff them. In the midst of all this activity, he managed to teach Sunday school and take weekly dance classes. Of course he danced awkwardly — "just as you'd expect him to dance," a class-mate recalled; "he hopped." His life at Harvard "broadened every interest," Corinne noted, "and did for him what had hitherto not been done, which was to give him confidence in his relationship with young men of his own age."

Theodore would need all the confidence he had developed at Harvard to withstand the single greatest sorrow he could possibly have imagined. In December of Theodore's sophomore year, his forty-six-year-old father fell ill with colon cancer. Earlier that fall, Thee had been nominated by President Rutherford B. Hayes to be collector of customs for the Port of New York, the most powerful federal post beyond the cabinet. Thee's nomination, which had to be approved by the Senate, was considered a triumph for civil service reformers and a blow to the corrupt politicians who, over the years, had treated the post as a private treasure chest. For weeks, the Senate was consumed by a battle between the reform element of the Republican Party and the machine politicians. The machine element won; Thee's nomination was turned down. "I fear for your future," Thee wrote his son. "We cannot stand so corrupt a government for any length of time" — a warning that would long reverberate in young Roosevelt's mind, helping to shape his embattled style of leadership.

Thee's death, three months after his diagnosis, brought Theodore unbearable sorrow. "I felt as if I had been stunned, or as if part of my life had been taken away," he recorded in his diary. "If it were not for the certainty, that, as he himself has so often said, 'he is not dead but gone before,' I should almost perish." In the days that followed, Theodore filled his diary with thoughts of his father. "Every now and then it seems to me like a hideous dream," he wrote. "Sometimes when I fully realize my loss I feel as if I should go wild," for "he was everything to me; my father, companion, friend."

"The death of Mr. Roosevelt was a public loss," stated the *New York Times.* "Flags flew at half-mast all over the city. Rich and poor followed him to the grave." As Theodore contemplated his father's legacy, he began to take the measure of his own life. "Oh, how little worthy I am of such a father," he wrote in his diary. "How I wish I could ever do something to keep up his name."

For Theodore, who had been blessed with a positive temperament, it was only a matter of time before he recovered his spirits. In late June, he confided in his diary the surprising recognition that he was "leading the most intensely happy and healthy out of doors life," spending his days "riding on horseback, making long tramps through the woods and fields after specimens." In frenetic movement he found relief as well as an understanding of his fundamental character. "I could not be happier, except at those bitter moments when I realize what I have lost. Father was so invariably cheerful that I feel it would be wrong for me to be gloomy, and besides, fortunately or unfortunately, I am of a very buoyant temper, being a bit of an optimist."

"No one but my wife, if ever I marry," Theodore wrote in his diary, "will ever be able to take [my father's] place." The following fall, his junior year at Harvard, he fell in love with Alice Hathaway Lee, the seventeen-year-old daughter of a wealthy Brahmin family in Chestnut Hill, Massachusetts. "It was a real case of love at first sight," Theodore told a friend, "and my first love too." With the same single-mindedness he had given to his books, his specimen collections, and the building up of his body, he launched a crusade to make Alice his wife. He escorted her to parties and to dances, took her skating and sledding, on horseback rides over trails and long hikes through the woods. He introduced her to his friends at Harvard and brought her to meet his mother and siblings in New York. He laid siege to her family, playing whist with her parents, entertaining her younger brothers with ghost stories and tales of adventure. He made "everything subordinate to winning her." He asked her to marry him six months after they met. She turned him down, fearful of taking such a big step at such a young age. Her rejection made him "nearly crazy," unable to study or sleep at night. He refused to give up, however, and eight months later, "after much pleading," she finally consented to be his wife. "I am so happy that I dare not trust my own happiness," he recorded the night she accepted. "I do not believe any man loved a woman more than I love her," he rejoiced two months later.

Privilege can stunt ambition, just as the lack of privilege can fire ambition. Privilege had not hampered the fierce drive that led Theodore to master every activity, from his voracious reading to the creation of the Roosevelt Museum of Natural History, from the rigorous workout regimen he maintained to the intense concentration that produced excellence at every stage of his education. Yet, under the sheltering wing of his father, privilege had allowed him to indulge his wide-ranging interests without the need of practical focus. Thee was the one who had provided his son with his own library, a private gym, a personal trainer, tutors in taxidermy and college preparation, and the means to collect specimens from around the world to fill his personal museum. During his freshman year at Harvard, his father had told him that if he were still committed to becoming a naturalist, he could do so. He explained "that he had made enough money to allow me to take up such a career and do non-remunerative work of value if I intended to do the very best work there was in me; but that I must not dream of taking it up as a dilettante." That Theodore Roosevelt did not become a naturalist he attributed to the curriculum at Harvard, where biology was treated "as purely a science of the laboratory and the microscope," ignoring the study of birds, animals, trees, and the outdoor world. For a young man who craved continual motion, who had methodically increased his physical endurance and strength over the years, the idea of a sedentary career, studying tissues under a microscope, held no allure.

Theodore's recognition that he was not suited for science revealed a growing self-awareness — a deepening understanding of his own temperamental strengths and weaknesses — that would become an essential tool in his leadership arsenal. Though he abandoned the prospects of a naturalist career, he never stopped pursuing outdoor adventures or his passion for the natural world. In the eighteen months after his father's death, he went on three expeditions into the deep wilderness regions of Maine, each sojourn further stretching the horizons of his cramped social world and bringing him in close quarters with people whose lives he had encountered only through books.

The first trip had been arranged through his Harvard tutor. "I want you to take that young fellow under your special care," Cutler told the Maine guide, Bill Sewall. "He is not very strong and he has got a great deal of ambition and grit. . . . Even if he was tired, he would not tell you so. The first thing you knew he would be down, because he would go until he fell." Cutler's assessment proved on the mark. While Theodore suffered from a serious asthma attack during the trip, he never once lost his good nature or seemed "out of sorts," whether canoeing five miles on the river, tramping thirty-five miles in the forest, helping to pitch the tents, or missing numerous shots at loons, ducks, and pigeons.

The thirty-four-year-old Maine guide, who would become Roosevelt's mentor and life-long friend, was the first to see in the young man the makings of a leader. "He was different from anybody I had ever met," Sewall said. "Wherever he went, he got right in with the people," connecting with them, talking with them, enjoying them, without the slightest trace of condescension. The boy who had begun college leery of commingling with lower social echelons now bunked in a lumber camp with a large crew of woodsmen who did not know anything but the woods. "I doubt if they could have written their names," Sewall recalled. "But they knew the woods, the whole of them, and they knew all the hardships connected with pioneer life." That young Roosevelt could open himself up to such men, relate to them, and learn from them suggested that in the aftermath of great sorrow he was beginning to chip away at the inherited elitism of his privileged background. He told Sewall he was thrilled to get "firsthand accounts of backwoods life from the men who had lived it and knew what they were talking about." Even at this early age, Sewall marveled, "he was quick to find the real man in very simple men." He listened intently to their stories: he told stories himself from the adventure books he had read; he connected with them. He was learning, Sewall said, what it meant to be an American, the idea that "no man is superior, unless it was by merit, and no man is inferior, unless by his demerit." The profound pleasure Theodore had discovered in a different kind of social life would lead to a reassessment of his future prospects.

He had thought for a time to follow his father's footsteps, carrying on the philanthropic work Thee had so successfully undertaken to improve the lot of the poor. "I tried faithfully to do what my father had done," he told a friend, "but I did it poorly." After joining "this and that committee" and assuming several board positions formerly held by his father, he found the work uncongenial. He could no more sit in meetings for hours on end than he could sit in a laboratory, staring into a microscope. He concluded that he had "to work in his own way" to carry forward the moral ardor his father had displayed. The noblesse oblige he had inherited from his privileged class felt too removed from the action of life, too indirect. Moreover, he began to suspect that charitable work would be less necessary if the political order provided remedies for the underlying social conditions. "I'm going to try to help the cause of better government in New York City," he told a friend during his senior year in college; "I don't know exactly how." He decided to go to Columbia Law School, not because he wanted to be a lawyer, but because he considered it a first step toward involvement in some aspect of public life.

He found the courses at law school ill-suited to his temperament, noting critically that the professors were more concerned with "what law is, not what it ought to be," emphasizing legal precedents rather than justice. In college, he had deliberately stayed away from debating societies, believing it wrong to train young men to "talk glibly" on any given side of a proposition, regardless of their convictions or moral principles. He worried that as a lawyer, he would be required to do precisely that. He wanted to win arguments because they were right, not because he had skillfully marshaled an array of one-sided facts. His energies not fully engaged in his classes, he began spending more and more time at Morton Hall, immersed in the blood sport of working-class politics.

"When I went into politics," Roosevelt later conceded, "I was not conscious of going in with the purpose to benefit other people but of getting for myself a privilege to which I was entitled in common with other people." Unlike Lincoln, who held a double ambition from the start (not solely for himself, but also for the people he wanted to lead), twenty-three-year-old Roosevelt intended simply to exercise his right of citizenship, with small consideration toward embarking upon a career. Deploring the "lack of interest in the political questions of the day among respectable, well-educated men, young men especially," he sought to set an example.

Who's the "greenhorn"? the people of New Salem had asked upon first encountering the awkward, poorly dressed, ill-educated Lincoln. "Who's the dude?" the local politicians inquired upon first seeing young Roosevelt. With his hair parted in the center, short whiskers on his cheeks, a monocle over one eye held in place by "a gold chain over his ear," a waistcoat and trousers "as tight as a tailor could make them," he looked the embodiment of a dandy, overly concerned with appearance and manners.

Yet, for Theodore and young Abraham, once the oddity of first impressions faded, perspectives shifted and people strongly connected with both of them. Week after week, Theodore visited Morton Hall, relaxing with working-class Irish and German immigrants, with butchers, carpenters, and grooms as they drank beer and smoked cigars, listening to their stories, joining them in games of cards, thoroughly enjoying the convivial, masculine atmosphere.

"I went around often enough to have the men get accustomed to me and to have me get accustomed to them," he later said, "so that we began to speak the same language and so that each could begin to live down in the other's mind what Bret Harte has called 'the defective quality of being a stranger.' " In time, the men at Morton Hall recognized they were in the presence of an exceptionally good-natured, earnest, appealing, intelligent young man, who fought for what he believed but accepted defeat with good humor. Watching Roosevelt over a period of months, local boss Joe Murray began to take "a paternal interest" in him, and finally concluded that this twenty-three-year-old son of privilege could make a credible run for the state legislature.

The time between the November first nomination and the election occupied but a single week, magnifying the vital role of the party organizations in bringing out the vote. To open the campaign, the boss planned to take Roosevelt on "a personal canvass through the saloons along Sixth Avenue." Saloonkeepers in those days played an instrumental political role, drawing up checklists of the "right" voters in the ward, making sure those voters got to the polls. The first stop was Valentine Young's bar. No sooner had Roosevelt been introduced to Mr. Young than trouble began. The saloonkeeper told Roosevelt that if he won, he expected him to vote for lowering the cost of the liquor licenses, which were much too high. Roosevelt replied that while he would treat all interests fairly, on the contrary, liquor taxes were "not high enough," and that he would vote to raise them. The boss swiftly shepherded Roosevelt away, deciding that he and his colleagues would henceforth take care of the Sixth Avenue vote, leaving Roosevelt to solicit votes among his neighbors and friends.

In the few statements he made, Roosevelt proclaimed that he was "owned by no man" and would enter the legislature "untrammeled and unpledged." With no sense of irony, he proclaimed that despite his friendship with and key obligations to Joe Murray, he "would obey no boss and serve no clique." His pledge of independence struck a chord with the residents of the Silk Stocking District, who detested machine politics and rarely bothered to get involved in local elections. The strategy of running as an independent widened Roosevelt's appeal. Two days after the nomination, a list of twenty prominent New Yorkers, including future secretary of state Elihu Root and Columbia law professor Theodore Dwight, published a vigorous endorsement of young Roosevelt's candidacy. "We take much pleasure in testifying to our appreciation of his high character," the manifesto declared. "He is conspicuous for his honesty and integrity." That same day, Joseph Choate, the future ambassador to Great Britain, organized a circle of Thee's friends to contribute to Republican campaign coffers. "Men worth millions solicited the votes of their coachmen," journalist Jacob Riis reported, "and were glad to get them." On Election Day, the "brownstone vote" came out in much larger numbers than usual. Roosevelt won the Assembly seat with a margin almost twice the size of the typical Republican vote.

"My first days in the Legislature were much like those of a boy in a strange school," Roosevelt recalled. "My fellow-legislators and I eyed one another with mutual distrust." Not only was Roosevelt the youngest member, but the Democrats held a commanding majority, and he was a Republican from "the wealthiest district in New York." While Lincoln kept quietly in the background throughout his first session, watching and figuring, Roosevelt charged into action, often irritating his colleagues, violating the rules of parliamentary procedure.

With abrasive and manic energy, he interrogated his fellow assemblymen, aggressively soaking up everything they knew about how the Assembly operated. "How do you do this in your district and county," he would ask. "What is this thing and that thing?" Within a short period of time, "he knew more about State politics" than "ninety percent" of the veteran members did. In short order, he had divided the members into three groups: a small circle of fellow reformers, those he labeled "very good men;" another circle of "very bad men" beholden to Tammany Hall, New York's political machine, and susceptible to bribery; and a majority, "neither very good nor very bad," who could be swayed in either direction, depending on the strength of public opinion.

After scarcely two months in office, he seized the spotlight, displaying what would become a characteristic penchant for brash maneuvering. Newspaper reports had accused state judge Theodore Westbrook of using court proceedings to help the Wall Street financier Jay Gould gain control of New York's elevated railway system. After investigating the matter further, Roosevelt was convinced that Westbrook had forged a corrupt alliance with the notorious robber baron. Rising from his seat, the rookie assemblyman delivered a fiery indictment of the judge that produced banner headlines, making Theodore Roosevelt "the most talked about man in the State." In an era of "subserviency to the robber barons of the Street," the *New York Times* editorialized, "it needs some little courage in any public man to characterize them and their acts in fitting terms."

At this introductory stage of his career, Roosevelt viewed politics in a puritanical light, as an arena where good battled evil. He had seen his father's dreams of high office undone by corruption; he had absorbed his father's warning that the country could not much longer stand "so corrupt a government." He was a knight embarked on a crusade to uncover corruption at the highest levels, jousting against the "black horse cavalry" of machine politicians. "There is nothing brilliant or outstanding about my record, except perhaps for one thing," he told a reporter, "when I make up my mind to do a thing, I act."

Even as his political star was beginning to rise, Roosevelt insisted that politics was not a proper occupation. As a citizen, one might intermittently engage in political activity, but it would be "a dreadful misfortune for a man to grow to feel that his whole livelihood and whole happiness depend upon his staying in office. Such a feeling prevents him from being of real service to the people while in office, and always puts him under the heaviest strain to barter his convictions for the sake of holding office."

Yet, it was already clear after this first year in the Assembly that Theodore Roosevelt had found his calling. Politics encompassed the activities he found most enjoyable and fulfilling: speaking, writing, connecting with people, assuming center stage. A fuse had been lit that would keep him in politics and public life for the rest of his days.

"I rose like a rocket," Theodore Roosevelt recalled of his ascent. Notwithstanding a statewide Democratic sweep, he had gained a second term, and despite his youth, he had been chosen by his Republican colleagues as their minority leader. But as his friend Jacob Riis shrewdly warned, "if they do shoot up like a rocket they are apt to come down like sticks." In the wake of these triumphs, Roosevelt lost perspective. His head "was swelled"; he became indulgent and self-absorbed. He began to think that he alone had cornered the market on honesty and integrity. "There is an increasing suspicion," one observer noted, "that Mr. Roosevelt keeps a pulpit concealed on his person." The small circle of reformers who had idolized him at the start watched with growing concern as he became "a perfect nuisance," constantly interrupting Assembly business, yelling and pounding his desk with his fist. "He was just like a jack coming out of a box," one member recalled. When criticized by Democrats, he fired back venomously, castigating the entire party as "rotten." His friends pleaded with him "to sit on his coat-tails," warning that he was ruining himself and "everybody else" with his "explosive" and "indiscreet" attacks, but he "would listen to no argument, no advice," self-infatuated as he reveled in the headlines his colorful language generated.

After failing to mobilize support for several projects, however, he realized that he "was absolutely deserted," even by his friends. "My isolated peak had become a valley; every bit of influence I had was gone. The things I wanted to do I was powerless to accomplish." The "bitter experience" was a blow to his ego, to the dogmatic and self-righteous aspect of his nature that prevented him from working with others and learning to compromise. He began to see, he conceded, that he "was not all-important," and "that cooperation from other people" was essential, "even if they were not so pure as gold." And he learned that "if he could not get all he wanted, he would take all he could." He turned to help others, and they, in turn, gave him a hand. The world was far more complicated and nuanced than his categorical moral vision had led him to believe. The ability to learn from the excesses of his egocentric behavior, to alter course, to profit from error, was essential to his growth.

Roosevelt further revealed that capacity for growth when a union-sponsored bill to prohibit the manufacture of cigars in tenement houses was referred to one of the committees on which he sat. When the bill was first introduced, he presumed he would vote against it, as he had voted against minimum wage legislation and bills to limit the hours of the working day. Both his membership in the privileged class and the laissez-faire economics he had learned in college had "biased" him, he later said, "against all governmental schemes for the betterment of the social and economic condition of laborers." In the case of the cigar bill, he believed that tenement owners, who were also the manufacturers, had a right to do as they wished with their own property.

After meeting with labor leader Samuel Gompers and hearing his description of the dreadful conditions in the tenement apartments where thousands of families lived and worked stripping, drying, and wrapping cigars, he agreed to make a personal inspection. Roosevelt was so stunned by what he found that he made a turnabout and agreed to become the bill's champion. Thirty years later, he would still remember one noxious tenement in which five adults and several children, all Bohemian immigrants who could barely speak English, were enclosed in a single room, compelled to work sixteen hours a day, with tobacco crammed in every corner, next to the bedding, mixed in with food. The investigation persuaded him "beyond a shadow of a doubt that to permit the manufacture of cigars in tenement-houses" was "an evil thing from every standpoint, social, industrial, and hygienic."

The incident suggests Roosevelt's developing sense of empathy. While Lincoln's seems to have been his by right of birth, Roosevelt slowly expanded his understanding of other people's points of view by going to places that a man of his background typically neither visited nor comprehended. "The real things of life were getting a grip on him more and more," Jacob Riis observed. In an essay on "fellow-feeling," written a decade and a half later, Roosevelt maintained that empathy, like courage, could be acquired over time. "A man who conscientiously endeavors to throw in his lot with those about him, to make his interest theirs, to put himself in a position where he and they have a common object, will at first feel a little self-conscious, will realize too plainly his aims. But with exercise this will pass off. He will speedily find that the fellow-feeling which at first he had to stimulate was really existent, though latent, and is capable of a very healthy growth." Indeed, he argued that a "very large part of the rancor of political and social strife" springs from the fact that different classes or sections "are so cut off from each other that neither appreciates the other's passions, prejudices, and, indeed, point of view."

By his third term in the Assembly, Roosevelt had begun to soften his abrasive self-righteousness. Working with Democrats, whom he had previously labeled as "rotten," he brought the two parties together to pass civil service reform and a host of bills to benefit the city of New York. He had taken his weaknesses, his physical liabilities, his fears, and the brash and self-centered aspects of his leadership style, and had carefully worked to overcome them.

At twenty-five years old, happily married and awaiting the birth of his first child, he now felt, he told his wife, that he "had the reins" in his own hands.

THREE:
FRANKLIN

"No, call me Franklin"

No fixed timetable governs the development of leaders. While Abraham Lincoln, Theodore Roosevelt, and Franklin Roosevelt all possessed inherent leadership capacities, the period of time when they first perceived themselves as leaders and were considered leaders by others occurred at different stages of their growth.

Hardship quickened Abraham Lincoln's self-reliance. Early on, he revealed a number of traits associated with leadership — ambition, motivation, resoluteness, language skills, storytelling gifts, sociability. The people who knew him from boyhood to young manhood saw the makings of a leader, just as he was beginning to feel that same potential within himself.

Theodore Roosevelt came later to the sense of himself as a leader, though others had clearly seen flashes of a unique nature — a remarkable willpower, intellectual vitality, irrepressible liveliness, wide-ranging interests, and a growing gratification connecting with people from different backgrounds and stations in life.

Franklin Roosevelt, reared without siblings at Springwood, a country estate on the banks of the Hudson, was the latest bloomer of the three. The fierce ambition to succeed, so apparent in young Abraham and Theodore, was largely concealed, just as he concealed so much else in his life. There was little evidence of exceptional motivation or focus. Though he was the most conventionally handsome of the three, he lacked the physical strength and competitive athletic skill that lent young Abraham standing among his male companions; nor did he seem to possess the torrential energy that amused and overwhelmed everyone who met young Theodore. An indifferent student at Groton, Harvard College, and Columbia Law, Franklin ostensibly was following an expected path for a member of the privileged class by joining an old, conservative Wall Street law firm.

At the age of twenty-eight, when both Lincoln and Theodore Roosevelt had already evidenced striking leadership attributes, Franklin had not impressed the partners of his law firm with either his native intelligence, his work ethic, or his sense of purpose. Yet, when fortune shone on him in the form of a wholly unexpected offer from the top Dutchess County Democratic bosses, John Mack and Edward Perkins, to run for a safe Democratic seat in the State Assembly with the full backing of the party, Franklin hastened to accept, revealing a great eagerness to jump into politics. He knew something about himself that others did not — that beneath his complacent demeanor, he craved adventure, a desire for freedom from the confines of his insulated world. In all likelihood, he felt the promptings of ambition within himself long before others detected it. Some impulse told him that the political world might provide the best fit for his gregarious temperament, natural abilities, and undeveloped talents.

It is not clear whether John Mack had even met Franklin before the late spring day in 1910 when he called upon the young law clerk at Carter, Ledyard & Milburn. As a pretext for the visit, Mack carried some documents that required the signature of Franklin's mother, Sara. After concluding the business part of the meeting, Mack turned to the real reason for dropping by — to sound out Franklin on the possibility of running for an Assembly seat from the district that included Poughkeepsie and Hyde Park, the village where Roosevelt had grown up and where his mother still lived. Mack explained that the incumbent Democratic assemblyman, Lewis Stuyvesant Chanler, had decided to retire. For generations, Democrats had held the seat, based largely on the Irish and Italian vote in Poughkeepsie. But the party hoped to reach out as well to the traditionally rural Republican areas within the district, and Mack thought Franklin might be "the right person for the job."

That Mack and Perkins considered Franklin the best choice had little to do with their perception that the young law clerk had within him the makings of a leader. The key to their interest lay in the resonance of the Roosevelt name in Republican circles. In 1910, after serving nearly two terms in the presidency, Theodore Roosevelt, Franklin's fifth cousin, remained the most dominant figure on the national scene. Mack also understood that Sara Roosevelt's wealth would allow her son not only to pay his own campaign expenses but to contribute to the general Democratic coffers. So, while Abraham Lincoln took the initiative on his own to run for his first elective office and Theodore put himself in a position to gain the nomination by mingling with politicians at Morton Hall, Franklin Roosevelt was simply chosen to run.

What proved more compelling than why Franklin was chosen was the manner in which he responded to the proffered opportunity. "Nothing would please me more," he enthusiastically replied, "just tell me what to do, where to go, whom to seek out." What to do? Mack told him to spend time in the district, make the acquaintance of local Democratic activists. Franklin said he would start at once. He would spend as many summer weekends as he could in Hyde Park and Poughkeepsie, leaving his Wall Street firm on Friday afternoons, returning on Monday mornings. Whom to seek out? He should start with the Democratic committeeman from his home village — Tom Leonard.

Consequently, at three o'clock one August afternoon, he searched out Leonard, a house painter currently at work inside one of the houses on the Roosevelts' country estate. The estate resembled an English country manor, "with class lines separating the close little family of three at the top from the nurses and governesses, and these in turn from the maids and cooks indoors, and these in turn from the stable boys and farm hands outside." As a child, Franklin, seated on his pony, had ridden with his father every morning to survey the plantings and the various construction projects under way on the estate. As they rode by, employees "tipped their hats."

Never having been formally introduced to the house painter, Roosevelt rang the bell. "There's a Mr. Franklin wants to see you," the housekeeper told Leonard. "I thought for a moment," Leonard said, but after searching his memory, he concluded, "I don't know any Mr. Franklin." Nonetheless, he stepped out to meet the gentleman, surprised to find none other than Mr. Franklin Roosevelt. "Hello, Tom," said the young patrician, smiling warmly and extending his hand in greeting. "How do you do, Mr. Roosevelt?" asked the puzzled painter. "No, call me Franklin. I'm going to call you Tom," he declared, telling him that he had come to ask his advice about getting into politics. That Roosevelt was able to extend his hand and seek counsel with such good-natured spirits and without a trace of affectation or pomposity won over Tom Leonard as it would soon win over thousands in Dutchess County. His manner, his affability, and his sincerity conveyed something authentic. With this first foray into politics, he had bridged, emblematically at least, a lifetime of social distance.

Everywhere he went, people were immediately struck by young Franklin's warmth and charm. He made arrangements for a driver with a horse and two-wheeled wagon to meet him at the Hyde Park train station on Friday evenings. On Saturdays and Sundays he traversed the district, attending political meetings, talking with people in general stores, stopping in village squares, standing outside manufacturing plants, shaking hands. He made a good impression, Tom Leonard recalled, "because he wouldn't immediately enter into the topic of politics"; instead, he encouraged people to talk about their work, their families, their lives. He had always loved to talk, but now he learned to listen, and to listen intently, his head nodding in a welcoming way, with an air of sympathetic identification, an attentive posture and manner that would become a lifelong characteristic.

With the assurance from the bosses that he would be nominated for the Assembly seat at the convention scheduled for early October, Franklin delivered his maiden political speech at the annual policemen's clambake on September 10. "On that joyous occasion of clams and sauerkraut and real beer," Roosevelt later recalled, "I made my first political speech and I have been apologizing for it ever since." Introduced by John Mack, Franklin began with a favorite phrase of Theodore Roosevelt's. "I'm dee-lighted," to be here, he said, summoning with phrases, gestures, and pince-nez glasses an identification with his famous relative, "and next year promise to be here again with all my relatives." No further record of the speech exists, though people who heard him speak in the weeks ahead remarked on his relaxed, conversational style. He mingled easily with crowds, pumped hands with enthusiasm, made friends everywhere he went. To the surprise of John Mack and other veteran officeholders, it was beginning to seem, unaccountably, that this twenty-eight-year-old son of privilege, upon diving into the water for the first time, could swim like a seal!

How, one wonders, was this possible?

"Temperament," Richard Neustadt argues in his classic study of presidential leadership, "is the great separator." Four days after Franklin Roosevelt took the presidential oath on March 4, 1933, he paid a call on former Supreme Court justice Oliver Wendell Holmes, who was celebrating his ninety-second birthday. After Roosevelt left, Holmes famously opined: "A second-class intellect. But a first-class temperament." Generations of historians have agreed with Holmes, pointing to Roosevelt's self-assured, congenial, optimistic temperament as the keystone to his leadership success.

If temperament is the key, the answers to our questions take us back to Springwood, the rural estate in Hyde Park, where the very bedrock of Franklin Roosevelt's temperament was formed. "All that is in me goes back to the Hudson," Roosevelt liked to say, meaning not simply the tranquil river and the big country house but the atmosphere of love and affection that enveloped him as a child. The boy's personality flourished in the warmth of his environment. Those who knew him as a child invariably use the same adjectives to describe him — "a very nice child," "bright and happy," radiant, beautiful, uncommonly poised.

For his first eight years, Franklin enjoyed a childhood of extraordinary stability and balance. From all accounts, James and Sara Roosevelt had a genuine love marriage despite the difference in their ages; James, courtly, well-educated, and gentle, was fifty-two when Franklin was born; Sara, beautiful, strong-willed, and confident, was but half his age. The Roosevelt money had been made years before in real estate and the sugar trade, allowing Mr. James, as he was known, to lead the life of a country gentleman, adopting the habits and hobbies that imitated the English landed gentry. Franklin's still vigorous father introduced him to the masculine outside world while his mother supervised the inside world of books, hobbies, and governesses. "Never," Sara claimed, did Franklin observe conflict between his parents regarding his upbringing, for at all times they presented "a united front" in dealing with him. With but a single child, Sara suggested, "the problem of juvenile squabbles virtually dispensed with itself." Franklin alone was the focus of his parents' lives, their joint vocation, heir and hub of the place that was both a landed estate and a state of mind, a place from which all unpleasantness and discord seemed banished.

In casting back her thoroughly idealizing light upon Franklin's upbringing, Sara failed to appreciate, as her great-grandson John Boettiger Jr. later observed, that "pain-killing can itself be a lethal act." Children are strengthened through sibling relationships; they learn to play, bicker, fight, and play again, to accept criticism and bounce back from hurt, to tell secrets and become intimate. "If there remained in Franklin Roosevelt throughout his life," Boettiger Jr. continued, "an insensitivity towards and discomfort with profound and vividly expressed feelings it may have been in part the lengthened shadow of his early sheltering from ugliness and jealousy and conflicting interests."

Yet, when Franklin was young, the impression that he was the center of the world produced a remarkable and lingering sense of security and privilege. For the rest of his life, Roosevelt remembered the peacefulness and regularity of his childhood days with great affection. Each passing season brought its unique cluster of outdoor activities. In winter, father and son went sledding and tobogganing down the steep hill that stretched from the south porch of the estate to the wooded bluffs of the river far below, maneuvering every curve with perfect ease. "We coasted!" Franklin needled his mother. "Nothing dangerous, yet, look out for tomorrow!!" With his father by his side, Franklin learned to ice-skate and ice-boat on the frozen Hudson. Then, with the first signs of spring, Franklin rode with his father each morning to survey the various constructions under way on the estate (he graduated from a donkey when he was two to a pony at six and a horse at eight). "Went fishing yesterday after noon with papa, we caught a dozen of minnows," Franklin enthusiastically wrote his mother when he was only six. Beyond lessons on how to fish, Mr. James taught his son how to observe birds and identify trees and plants in the woods, fostering a lifelong love of nature. In summers, the family went to the island of Campobello off far Downeast Maine, where Franklin learned to sail on Passamaquoddy Bay and to navigate the massive tides of the Bay of Fundy. In the fall, father and son went hunting together. With few playmates his own age, Franklin viewed his indulgent and protective father as a companion and friend.

While James nourished Franklin's love of the outdoors, Sara organized a carefully scheduled indoor regimen of regular mealtimes and specified hours for study and hobbies. Once, when Sara saw her five-year-old son uncharacteristically melancholy, she asked him why he was sad. He refused to answer at first, so she repeated her question. "Then," Sara recalled, "with a curious little gesture that combined entreaty with a suggestion of impatience, he clasped his hands in front of him and exclaimed: 'Oh, for freedom!' "Worried that her rules and regulations were cramping her son's spirit, she proposed a day without rules so he could meander the estate as he chose. Straightaway, she reported, "quite of his own accord, he went contentedly back to his routine."

"We never subjected the boy to a lot of unnecessary don'ts," Sara maintained. "We were never strict for the sake of being strict. In fact, we took a secret pride in the fact that Franklin never seemed to require that kind of handling." If the young boy's independence was compromised by the protective care of both his parents, if there was little of the spontaneous explorations that enlivened Theodore's childhood, the disposition and temperament of Franklin Roosevelt would

103

bear the indelible stamp of his optimistic spirit — a general expectation that things would turn out happily, testament to the immense self-confidence developed during this perfectly balanced time of his life.

Roosevelt's ability in later years to adapt to changing circumstances, to alter his behavior and attitudes to suit new conditions, proved vital to his leadership success. Adaptability was forced upon him at the age of eight, when the tranquil world of Springwood was shaken to the core. In November 1890, Mr. James suffered the heart attack that left him essentially an invalid for the remaining decade of his life and forever disrupted the family equilibrium.

The outdoor activities the father and son had shared were necessarily curtailed, pulling Franklin and his mother into a conspiracy to keep the father's life untroubled, free from anxiety. Ever after, Franklin's innate desire to placate, to mollify, and to please by being "a very nice child," was intensified by the fear that if he appeared sad or troubled he might be responsible for damaging further his father's heart. When a steel curtain rod fell on him, producing a deep gash on his scalp line, Franklin insisted that his father not be told. For days, he simply pulled his hat down over his forehead to hide the wound. The need to navigate the altered dynamic of

Springwood required new measures of secrecy, duplicity, and manipulation — qualities that would later prove troubling but were at this juncture benign, designed only to protect a loved one from harm.

Consequently, in the absence of his father's companionship, and with the lack of nearby playmates, Franklin spent more and more time inside the house, devoting hours each day to what became an impressive assembly of collections: stamps, maps, model ships, birds' nests, coins, naval prints. His stamp collection came to be his central hobby. Sara started him off with the collection she had built up as a child, and then his uncle Frederic Delano, seeing how earnestly the boy pursued his hobby, gifted Franklin with his own valuable collection. In an essay on the nature of genuine collectors, Walter Benjamin suggests that collecting is a way of ordering a disordered world. He notes that collecting holds a special meaning for children, offering a small corner of the world where the child is in charge, experiencing "the thrill of acquisition" and the pride that comes with unifying and mastering a hodgepodge of assorted items. The quiet time Franklin spent each day poring over stamp catalogues, selecting and arranging his stamps into albums, furnished a haven, a protected space where he could be on his own, free from the demands of a mother who had developed an increasing dependence on her son in the aftermath of her husband's diminished state. Mr. James had been their protector; together, she and her son were now responsible for protecting him.

Roosevelt's childhood hobbies would serve in later years as invaluable tools nourishing his leadership — providing a meditative state, a space in which he could turn things over in his mind, the means by which he could relax and replenish his energy. On a visit with Roosevelt during World War II, Winston Churchill recalled sitting by the president's side one evening as Roosevelt sorted and arranged his stamps, placing each one "in its proper place," forgetting "the cares of State." Roosevelt's secretary Grace Tully recalled the "feeling of calm" that invariably descended on her whenever she saw her boss, "a magnifying glass in hand, Scott's Stamp Catalogue, scissors, and packages of stickers," for she knew that for a short of period of time, at least, he could escape "the problems that beset him."

Compared to the philosophical and poetic depths of Lincoln's mind or the scintillating breadth of Theodore's intelligence, Franklin's intellect might seem, as it did to Oliver Wendell Holmes, "second-rate." That presumption is seriously misleading. An uncommon intuitive capacity and interpersonal intelligence allowed him as a child to read the intentions and desires of his parents, to react appropriately to shifting household moods — gifts that he would nurture and develop in the years ahead. While he did not learn as a fledgling academic often does — by mastering vast reading material and applying analytical skills — he possessed an incredibly shrewd, complicated, problem-solving intelligence, coupled with a supple, and often jaunty, verbal capacity.

All his life, Franklin learned more from listening than from reading in solitude. He was able to absorb great quantities of information by hearing people talk. When he was young, his mother regularly read to him. One night, Sara recalled, she was reading to him while "he lay sprawled on his tummy, sorting and pasting" his beloved stamps. Thinking that he was not listening, she put the book down. "I don't think there is any point in my reading to you anymore," she said. "You don't hear me anyway." He looked up, "a whimsical smile on his face," and "quoted verbatim the last paragraph of the essay." With "a mischievous glint in his eye," he said, "Why, Mom, I would be ashamed of myself if I couldn't do at least two things at once." Years later, Roosevelt told his cabinet secretary Frances Perkins that as he grew older, he much preferred to read aloud to someone than to read by himself. "There was something incurably sociable about this man," she observed, "he was sociable in his intellectual as well as his playful moods." Instead of reading documents or memos, White House counselor and speechwriter Sam Rosenman observed, Roosevelt "generally preferred to get his information orally; he could interrupt and ask questions: it was easy for him to get the gist right away."

In contrast to the vigorous education Thee had given Theodore and his siblings both at home and during their sojourns abroad, Franklin's education was casual and haphazard. A series of governesses tutored him in childhood, but even this intermittent instruction was interrupted by three lengthy stays in Europe, where James and Sara sought the healing powers of mineral spas at Bad Nauheim, Germany. Focused entirely on restoring his health, James could not take his son on the expeditions to battlefields and famous literary landscapes that Thee had chosen to enliven both history and literature for his children. Franklin attended a local German school for a short time, where his acutely receptive ear allowed him to pick up the German language with remarkable ease. When Franklin turned twelve, Mr. James wrote to Endicott Peabody, headmaster at the Groton School, asking if he could recommend "a gentleman" tutor who could also "be my boy's companion." Mr. James finally found the young man he wanted in Arthur Dumper, a Latin and mathematics master at St. Paul's prep school.

Franklin, Arthur Dumper later remarked, went about learning in a curiously "unorthodox" manner. He preferred to engage his tutor in conversation, talking over what he was learning, spending more time with his stamps than with his books. Through that passionate interest in stamps, however, Franklin assimilated a great deal of knowledge, cobbling together bits and pieces of information to form a complicated tissue of associated interests. Each stamp told a story — beginning with the place and date of issue, the image represented on the front, postmarks providing the time and location of its travels — stories as alive in Franklin's fantasy life as the adventure tales of James Fenimore Cooper had been for Theodore Roosevelt or *Aesop's Fables* for Abraham Lincoln. Sara's original collection had been assembled during her family's protracted sojourn in Asia. Other stamps came from Europe; still others from South America. When asked years later how he had gained such familiarity with obscure places in the world, Roosevelt explained that "when he became interested in a stamp, it led to his interest in the issuing country." Digging through the encyclopedia, he would learn about the country, its people, and its history. Finding words he didn't understand, he carried Webster's unabridged dictionary to bed at night, at one point telling his mother he was "almost halfway through."

He was learning in his own way, revealing a unique transverse intelligence that cut naturally across categories, a characteristic mode of problem solving, and a practical mastery of detail that would last a lifetime. A fascination with maps and atlases developed next, fixing in his mind an astonishing range of facts about the topography of countries, their rivers, mountains, lakes, valleys, natural resources — information that would prove invaluable when he was called upon in future years to explain to his countrymen how and where two wars would envelop the entire world.

Franklin's ability to adapt to changing circumstances was put to a punishing test when he was sent to boarding school at Groton at the age of fourteen. Most boys started at twelve, but Sara, unable to part with him, had kept him back for two years. "The other boys had formed their friendships," Franklin later told Eleanor. "They knew things he didn't; he felt left out." Unaccustomed to the ordinary give-and-take of schoolmates, the studied charm and mannered gentility that had impressed adults struck fellow students as stilted, foppish, affected, insincere. Nor did he possess the athleticism to shine or even participate in varsity team sports. He later confessed that he "felt hopelessly out of things." He fiercely desired to be popular but had no idea how to court the favor of his fellow students, mistakenly assuming that he would be respected if he had no black marks for minor infractions.

Never once, however, did the lonely boy divulge his true feelings to his mother. On the contrary, in a string of cheerful letters, he insisted he was adjusting splendidly "both mentally and physically," that he was "getting on very well with the fellows," receiving good marks in his classes. Sara was relieved and thrilled. She had feared that arriving so late he might be seen as "an interloper," but "almost overnight," she proudly noted, "he became sociable and gregarious and entered with the frankest enjoyment into every kind of school activity." The image he projected was meant to placate his mother but also to hearten himself, blurring the distinction between things as they were and things as he wished them to be.

The ingrained expectation that things would somehow turn out positively allowed him to move steadily forward, to adjust and persevere in the face of difficulty; and in time, he found his own niche as a member of the debate team. In keeping with Groton's mission to educate young men for public service, all students were required to participate in debates before an audience. Franklin prepared hard and long for each of his debates, asking his father for advice, information, and pointers. His excellent memory put him in good stead, allowing him to speak directly to the audience without notes. Unlike Theodore Roosevelt, who shunned debating societies, believing they encouraged insincerity by training young men to take a position counter to their own feelings and beliefs, Franklin enjoyed considering an issue from different points of view, demonstrating a persuasive reasoning to express whatever side he was given. He connected emotionally with his audience and reveled in victory. "Over 30 votes were cast out of which our opponents received three!" he gloated to his parents. "I think it is about the biggest beating that has been given this year." He began to relax more with his classmates, and by his final year, he had made some good friends. Though failing to distinguish himself in his academic studies, he achieved high scores on the entrance examinations for Harvard, making his parents "immensely proud."

Nonetheless, these accomplishments did little to mark him as a leader among his schoolmates. It was not until the end of his first year at Groton that he realized how little he gained from being a well-behaved, well-mannered young man. "I have served off my first black-mark today [for talking in class] and I am very glad I got it," he told his parents, "as I was thought to have no school-spirit before." Three decades later, after Roosevelt's election as president in 1932, headmaster Endicott Peabody observed: "There has been a good deal written about Franklin Roosevelt when he was a boy at Groton, more than I should have thought justified by the impression that he left at school. He was a quiet, satisfactory boy of more than ordinary intelligence, taking a good position in his form but not brilliant. Athletically he was rather too slight for success." Ostensibly accurate, such an assessment failed to recognize that upon his entry to Groton, the cosseted young boy had never experienced the jostle of relationships with boys his own age. He had been accorded the center of attention wherever he went, simply by being Franklin Roosevelt. Not yet a leader of the boys, not even accepted as one of the boys, he was learning to project a confident good cheer, to mask his frustrations, which, at this stage of his development, was a great achievement in itself.

The ambitious striving for achievement that had served as powerful catalysts to both Abraham Lincoln and Theodore Roosevelt was not visible in Franklin Roosevelt's behavior when he entered Harvard College. In later years, when Sara was asked if she ever imagined that her son might become president, she replied: "Never, no never! That was the last thing I should ever have imagined for him, or that he should be in public life of any sort." Both she and her son, she insisted, shared a far simpler ambition. "It might even be thought not very ambitious, but to me, and to him, too, it was the highest ideal — to grow to be like his father, straight and honorable, just and kind, an upstanding American."

Sara could not fathom that her eighteen-year-old son was beginning to form dreams of his own, visions of a life beyond that of a country squire, who would lead a regular seasonal existence, managing the estate, summering in Campobello, dabbling in local affairs. Beneath his insouciant exterior, the young man who had held center stage the first decade of his life harbored desires to replicate that experience in the world at large, to accomplish something worthy of attention.

During his first semester at Harvard, the elements that had held Franklin's life in compliant balance careened out of joint when his father suffered a fatal heart attack. Suddenly, Franklin was forced to take stock of his position, desires, and ambitions. The college student was now expected to be the man of the family. He had already developed a profound, reciprocally dependent bond with his mother. Without the focus and buffer of the father/husband, they were alone together. Unable to bear the "unthinkable" idea of living by herself at Hyde Park, Sara rented a townhouse in Boston to be near her son. "She was an indulgent mother," observed a family friend, "but would not let her son call his soul his own." Franklin's quest to achieve autonomy without wounding his mother required new levels of manipulation, nimbleness, and guile, a deeper resourcefulness, persistence, and willfulness — self-preserving qualities he would add to his developing capacities.

For the first time, he began to chart his own course, seeking a place where he could shine on his own, free from parental imposition and expectation. He found that place at the *Harvard Crimson.* He began at the lowest level, one of seventy freshmen vying for a position on the staff. "The competition was tough," a classmate recalled, "the drain on the candidate's thought and time exhausting." The challenge demanded his full attention, providing legitimate reasons to decline his mother's constant invitations for dinner or the theater. He worked harder than he had ever worked before, harder than he did on his studies, where he settled into a gentleman's C average. "My Dearest Mummy," he wrote, "I am working about 6 hours a day on [the *Crimson*] alone and it is quite a strain." Though he failed to make the first group of five freshmen selected in February, he refused to give up.

A combination of luck, initiative, boldness, and privilege opened the door two months later. After reading in the Boston newspapers that Theodore Roosevelt, who was then vice president, was coming into town, he contacted his famous relative to see if they could get together. Franklin had met Theodore a number of times during family outings at Oyster Bay. He had reveled in the stories Roosevelt told at a Groton chapel lecture about his days as police commissioner — stories that "kept the whole room in an uproar for an hour." Having developed a special fondness for Franklin, Theodore arranged to meet him directly after his guest lecture scheduled for Professor Lawrence Lowell's class the following morning. The lecture, intended only for the students in the class, had not been made public. Franklin hurried to the *Crimson* to break the news.

"Young man," the managing editor told him, "you hit page one tomorrow morning." Professor Lowell was livid when the front-page article brought two thousand people clamoring to get into the hall, but Theodore Roosevelt, never one to slight publicity, took it in stride. Weeks later, Franklin was elected to join the *Crimson* staff. Flush with his first electoral success, a more independent Franklin wrote his mother as summer approached:

"I don't want to go to Campo; neither do you." It would be too sad. Instead, he suggested a trip abroad. "We both will enjoy seeing new places & new things and it will quite take us out of ourselves." Landing back in New York in September, they learned that President William McKinley had been assassinated and that cousin Theodore Roosevelt was now president of the United States.

Returning to Harvard, Franklin slowly worked his way up the *Crimson* ladder — his sophomore year he was elected secretary, then assistant managing editor, then managing editor, and finally, his senior year, to editor in chief of the newspaper. Franklin's ascent at the *Crimson* was such a landmark in his developing sense of himself as a leader that he chose to take graduate courses in order to extend his position at the paper's helm. While many of his editorials reflected typical college concerns with flagging school spirit and athletics, in one revealing piece he recommended that students interested in politics would learn more "in one day" by venturing into Boston to observe ward politics — "the machinery of primary, caucus, convention, election and legislature" — than by listening to abstract lectures on government. Though he had "read Kant and a little of Rousseau," he confessed that in neither philosopher had he found "the decisive leader." Experience, he believed, was the "best teacher."

Roosevelt would look back in later years with prideful nostalgia on this first leadership position, much as Abraham Lincoln considered his first election as captain in the Black Hawk War the success that had given him more pleasure than any other in his life. While a few fellow editors found Franklin "conceited" and "cocky," more self-assured than his writing skills deserved, the majority agreed that he was "quick-witted and capable as an editor" and "a very good companion," with an optimistic spirit and an infectious sense of humor. "There were traits of his, which, as one looks back on them, become significant," one colleague recalled. "He had a force of personality . . . he liked people, and he made them instinctively like him. Moreover, in his geniality there was a kind of frictionless command."

At Groton, he had managed to survive; at Harvard, he had begun to thrive.

The first hint of a signature component of what would characterize Franklin Roosevelt's fundamental style — the ability to make decisions without hesitating or looking back, coupled with a propensity to keep the process of determination hidden from view — emerged during his clandestine courtship of Eleanor Roosevelt. Early on, Franklin had sensed and been wary of even the appearance of competition between his interest in other girls and his mother's love. In letters and conversation, he would exhaustively share with his mother details of his daily activities, skillfully omitting his innermost feelings, the intimacies she might consider a trespass upon the primacy of their own relationship. In the wake of his father's death that need for concealment intensified.

No one, not a single friend, and surely not his mother, knew that he had fallen in love with his plain cousin Eleanor in the spring of his junior year at Harvard. They had been together at horse races, house parties, sailing trips, dances, and family events, but Sara had no inkling they shared other than a friendship when, the following Thanksgiving, Franklin delivered the shocking news: he had asked Eleanor to marry him; she had accepted.

"I know what pain I must have caused you, and you know I wouldn't do it if I really could have helped it," he wrote Sara after returning to Harvard. "I know my mind, have known it for a long time and know that I could never think otherwise. Result: I am the happiest man just now in the world; likewise the luckiest — and for you, dear Mummy, you know that nothing can ever change what we have always been & always will be to each other — only now you have two children to love & to love you."

In saying that he knew his mind, had known it for a long time and could never think otherwise, Franklin declared that his decision was not up for discussion. His mother recognized this conclusiveness. As would be true the rest of his life, once he made a decision, he rarely second-guessed himself: In the end, he had sought his own counsel until the inner struggle between filial devotion and love for Eleanor had been resolved. Thereafter, he refused to squander energy by raking over and reexamining whether he had made the right choice. He would marry Eleanor and that was that. He would always love his mother. His identity and future course were the issues at stake here.

Eleanor was unlike any girl Franklin had met. She was highly intelligent, free from affectation, deeply absorbed in social causes, wholly uninterested in the privileged world of debutante balls. Eleanor's early years had been as fraught with sorrow as Franklin's were filled with joy. She was eight when her mother, Anna, died from diphtheria and ten when her father, Elliott, Theodore Roosevelt's younger brother, died gruesomely from alcoholism. When she began seeing Franklin, however, she had just returned from three triumphant years at a girls boarding school in England. At Allenswood, she had started "a new life," free from the conventions and traditions of her social class. Basking in the maternal love of the legendary feminist headmistress, Mlle. Marie Souvestre, Eleanor became "everything" in the school, the most popular and respected student among faculty and students alike. "She is full of sympathy for all those who live with her," the headmistress reported to Eleanor's grandmother, "and shows an intelligent interest in everything she comes in contact with."

"The surest way to be happy," Eleanor wrote in an essay at school, "is to seek happiness for others." When she returned to New York, at the urging of her headmistress, she became involved in social work, teaching classes to immigrant Italians at the Rivington Street Settlement in the Lower East Side. She joined a group of female activists who were investigating working conditions in factories and department stores. "I had a great curiosity about life," she wrote, "and a desire to participate in every experience."

In the subterfuge of their betrothal, Franklin and Eleanor shared their unfolding dreams to leave a mark on the world. Eleanor's social consciousness and urgent sense of social justice — the awakening of a caring for the other, a championing of the underdog — far preceded and exceeded his. He admired her distaste for the debutante world she was about to enter, her rebellious desire to find something meaningful to do. She was a serious person, and so was he, despite the "featherduster" impression he sometimes left. He, too, was going through a rite of passage. The life he might lead, as reflected and encouraged in Eleanor's eyes, was a life involving a "broad human contact" with all manner of people. One afternoon, when he picked her up from the settlement house, she enlisted his help in carrying home a young girl who had fallen ill. "My God, I didn't know anyone lived like that," he told Eleanor when they reached the decrepit tenement where the girl's family lived. He was as dumbfounded and astounded as his cousin Theodore Roosevelt had been when he witnessed the squalor in which the dwellers of the cigar tenements were forced to live.

With Eleanor by his side, Franklin believed "he would amount to something someday." After a weekend together in New York, Eleanor wrote: "It is impossible to tell you what these last two days have been to me, but I know they have meant the same to you so that you will understand that I love you dearest and I hope that I shall always prove worthy of the love which you have given me. I have never known before what it was to be absolutely happy."

Eleanor knew, she later said, long before Franklin's run for the State Senate, that he wanted to go into politics. The impulse, she believed, had been stimulated by his admiration for her uncle, Theodore Roosevelt, whose every activity he followed with great attention. When their engagement was announced, President Roosevelt wrote Franklin: "We are greatly rejoiced over the good news. I am as fond of Eleanor as if she were my daughter; and I like you, and trust you, and believe in you. . . . You and Eleanor are true and brave, and I believe you love each other unselfishly; and golden years open before you." Franklin and Eleanor went to Washington together on March 4, 1905, to celebrate Theodore Roosevelt's inauguration, joining the inner circle at an intimate lunch, sitting with the family at the reviewing stand during the parade, and then attending the inaugural ball. Eleven days later, President Roosevelt, standing in his deceased brother's place, gave the bride away. "Well, Franklin," the president said with a smile, "there's nothing like keeping the name in the family."

Just as Theodore Roosevelt had recognized that when opportunity comes, a person has "to take advantage" of it, so Franklin, who seemed to be adrift when he entered his second year as a junior law clerk at Carter, Ledyard & Milburn, was simply waiting for the right moment to make his move. During a slack time at the office, he and his fellow clerks "fell into discussion" about their hopes and plans for the future. When Franklin's turn came, he disclosed that "he wasn't going to practice law forever, that he intended to run for office at the first opportunity." Indeed, he had already visualized and privately rehearsed the steps that he would in all likelihood take: election to the State Assembly would come first, leading to an appointment as assistant secretary of the navy, before becoming governor of New York and then, with good fortune, president of the United States. No mockery greeted young Roosevelt's hypothetical ascent, despite the fact that the twenty-five-year-old had never held a single public position. Franklin "seemed proper and sincere," one fellow clerk recalled, "and moreover, as he put it, entirely reasonable." After all, the career trail Franklin intended to follow was identical to the one Theodore Roosevelt had blazed to the White House.

The matter-of-fact manner in which Franklin had laid out his career course explains why he immediately embraced John Mack's suggestion that he run, with the party's full backing, for the Assembly seat from Hyde Park and Poughkeepsie. Even more revealing is Franklin's reaction when, only five weeks before the election, he learned that he was no longer the party's choice. The incumbent assemblyman, Lewis Chanler, had changed his mind, informing the Democratic chieftains that he had decided to retain his old seat in the Assembly after all. Feeling "snakebitten,"

Franklin told John Mack and Edward Perkins that he had come too far to stop; he just might have to run as an independent. The local bosses responded with a counteroffer. The convention had not yet decided on a Democratic candidate for the State Senate seat — clearly, a far more prestigious position. They conceded, however, that winning in the larger and mainly rural district was a long shot. Republicans, with a single exception, had held the Senate seat for almost half a century. The incumbent Republican, John Schlosser, had beaten his Democratic opponent by a two-to-one margin in the last election. The chances for victory, Mack surmised, were one in five, but if Roosevelt wanted the nomination, he could have it. How could he be certain he would get the nomination, Franklin asked. "It was made by a committee of three," Mack replied. He "was one," and he "was sure of another and quite sure of the third."

"I'll take it," Franklin said, with "absolutely no hesitation," and "I'll win the election." His immediate response revealed the decisiveness and sublime confidence that mark his mature nature. The acceptance speech he delivered after the nomination was longer than Theodore's thirty-three-word statement, but equally devoid of content and far removed from Lincoln's substantial and poignant introductory circular. By saying he did "not intend to sit still," however, he made it clear that he would give his all to the campaign.

From the start, Franklin "had a distinct feeling that in order to win he must put himself into direct personal touch with every available voter." The horse and wagon he had hired earlier in the summer had been sufficient when he was running for the Assembly, but the three-county Senate district was thirty miles wide and ninety miles long. Furthermore, only five weeks remained before the election. As he thought the problem over, he devised an innovative strategy. He would be the first candidate to crisscross the district in an automobile instead of a horse and buggy. Veteran advisers cautioned him. "The automobile was just coming into use," Mack recalled. "Get a horse!" farmers jeered when passing frequent automobile breakdowns. Furthermore, Mack explained, "horses were terrified of the new 'contraption' and, when meeting one on the highway, would bolt, frequently upsetting the farmer's wagon with occasional injuries."

Despite such hazards, the idea of breaking precedent captivated Franklin, as it would again and again in the years ahead. Locating a driver and a splashy red Maxwell touring car, he invited two fellow Democrats running for different offices to accompany him on what turned into a rollicking circuslike adventure. People were drawn to the sight of the newfangled gadget, festooned with flags and campaign banners, traversing the rough country roads at a startling speed of 20 mph. Meanwhile, Franklin turned the potential liability into an advantage. He ordered the driver to bring the car to an immediate stop whenever they encountered a horse and buggy or wagon. Such deference not only impressed the farmers but afforded Franklin the occasion to introduce himself and shake hands.

Every aspect of the barnstorming process excited Franklin. He designed his own posters and buttons; placed ads in county newspapers; and, most importantly, reveled in direct contact with people. At crossroads, train stations, general stores, saloons, and front porches, he delivered short speeches, sometimes as many as ten a day. Franklin "spoke slowly" then, Eleanor recalled, "and every now and then there would be a long pause, and I would be worried for fear he would never go on," but he always did, and when he finished, Democratic committeeman Tom Leonard recalled, he moved easily and naturally among the crowd, flashing "that smile of his," introducing himself as Frank, approaching every person "as a friend."

This was his first political campaign, a local politician recalled, "but none of his later campaigns were entered with more will to win than was this Senatorial campaign of 1910." He promised voters that if they elected him, he would "be a real representative," giving his full energies to their concerns "every day of the 365, every hour of the 24. That is my promise. I ask you to give me the chance to fill it." He pledged to return regularly to the district, traveling from one end to the other, listening to voters' concerns. Over and over, he stressed his independence, vowing to stand against "the bosses" in either party. "I know I'm no orator," he liked to say. "You don't have to be an orator, Roosevelt," someone in the audience yelled back. "Talk right along to us on those lines, that's what we like to hear." When the votes were tallied on Election Day, Franklin learned that he had vanquished his opponent, winning by the largest margin of any Democratic candidate in the state.

In analyzing Roosevelt's victory, one can cite the fortuitous historical moment, the split in the Republican Party between progressives and conservatives that produced Democratic victories across the nation; one can point to the reflected glow the presidential surname lent the aspiring state senator (along with the substantial funding made possible by the family's wealth); or summon the novelty of that red Maxwell barnstorming the country roads. But what was evident in the end was the fact that the cheerful, gregarious, disarmingly glamorous young man had out-worked, out-traveled, and out-strategized the Republicans by simply listening to the hopes and needs of whoever crossed his path. Long-visualized ambition and directed energy had finally brought him to the place where he wanted to be.

No sooner had Franklin entered the State Senate than he charged into battle against the entrenched Tammany machine that held a grip on the state Democratic Party. Just as Theodore Roosevelt had found in Judge Westbrook a vehicle to fight corruption, so Franklin found his instrument in Tammany boss Charlie Murphy's personal choice for the United States Senate — "Blue-Eyed" Billy Sheehan, a machine politician who had made millions through collusion with the streetcar industry. Hearing that a rebel group was forming in the Assembly to block Sheehan, Franklin became the first senator to sign the manifesto pledging the insurgent band to boycott the caucus as long as it took to foil Boss Murphy's choice.

Luck — the proximity of his dwelling to the Assembly, which made it the perfect place for the insurgents to convene — combined with Roosevelt's personal charm and celebrated name to make the novice senator the spokesman for the twenty-member group. "I never had as much fun in my life as I am having now," a beaming Roosevelt told reporters. Late at night, the esprit de corps among this fraternity was palpable. The "good fellowship" of his twenty comrades provided "the most pleasant feature." With cigar smoke curling in the air, "we sit around and swap stories, like soldiers at the bivouac fire," he said.

Invigorated by the battle and emboldened by the headlines, Roosevelt refused to compromise, even after Murphy withdrew Sheehan's name. The substitute Murphy put forward, Roosevelt declared, was equally unsuitable. Frances Perkins, then an Albany social worker lobbying on behalf of unions, recalled how "disagreeable" and conceited young Roosevelt struck her during this period. "I can still see 'that' Roosevelt now, standing back of the brass rail with two or three senators arguing with him to be 'reasonable' — his small mouth pursed up and slightly open, his nostrils distended, his head in the air, and his cool, remote voice saying, 'No, no, I won't hear of it!' " Years later, Roosevelt admitted to Miss Perkins that he was "an awfully mean cuss" when he first entered politics.

Like young Theodore, Franklin had developed a grandiose sense of his own importance — and, like his cousin, he was heading for a fall. By the end of March, nearly three months after the battle had begun, the ranks of the weary insurgents finally began to break. When Murphy put forth yet another name, that of Justice James Aloysius O'Gorman, a Tammany man with an independent streak, enough insurgents decided to go along to bring the battle to an end. Though some critics contended that "O'Gorman was no better than Sheehan," Roosevelt "converted defeat into victory simply by calling it a victory," declaring that Murphy had been taught moderation and shamelessly maintaining that the party had "taken an upward step."

Recognizing, however, that his actual power within the chamber had dimmed even as his political star rose brightly, Franklin began to moderate his approach. He learned, in much the same way as Theodore Roosevelt had, to work together with different factions and strike bargains. He reached out to individual Tammany members, no longer categorically assuming that all of them were corrupt. On the contrary, many of them had forged enduring ties with the common men and women in their districts, dispensing aid, jobs, and comfort, working around the clock to satisfy their constituents' immediate needs. Indeed, it was Bowery boss "Big Tim" Sullivan and the Tammany organization that had taken the lead in sponsoring much of the progressive social legislation that Franklin eventually supported, including workman's compensation, the fifty-four-hour workweek, and women's suffrage. Franklin had been a quick study in learning the art of compromise in order to get things accomplished.

In hindsight, the most enduring impact of the Sheehan battle lay in the fact that the widespread coverage of this young Democratic crusader against Tammany had caught the eye of the newly elected Democratic president, Woodrow Wilson. Within two weeks of his inauguration, Wilson offered the state senator the coveted post of assistant secretary of the navy. "How would I like it: I'd like it bully well," an excited Roosevelt replied. "It would please me better than anything in the world. All my life I have loved ships and have been a student of the Navy, and the assistant secretaryship is the one place, above all others I would love to hold." Sara believed that her son's deep attraction to the ocean was hereditary. Her Delano grandfather had captained American clipper ships, renowned for their beauty and speed, to the Orient. As a boy, Franklin "always thrilled to tales of the sea." At the age of thirteen, he had told his father he wanted to go to the Naval Academy in Annapolis, but Mr. James persuaded him "man-to-man" that it would be too hard on his parents for their only son to be away as much as a naval career would demand. While at Harvard, he had kept his interest in the Navy alive by trolling secondhand bookstores to build a collection of books and manuscripts on naval history that eventually comprised some 2,500 volumes. Little wonder that the proffered post was the one he desired above all others.

Moreover, the post as assistant secretary of the navy placed Franklin on the next rung on the ladder to the presidency he had uncannily visualized as a twenty-five-year-old, when he confided his vaulting ambitions to his fellow law clerks. Observers noted when the appointment was announced that he was following, lockstep, Theodore Roosevelt's path. Indeed, Theodore recognized the parallelism in his congratulatory note to Franklin. "It is interesting that you are in another place which I myself once held. I am sure you will enjoy yourself to the full."

As assistant secretary of the navy, working for seven years under Secretary Josephus Daniels, a former newspaper publisher with long experience in Democratic Party politics, Franklin had to learn for the first and last time in his political career how to operate as a subordinate. The situation proved challenging for the young man, who, despite his unfolding leadership skills, remained deficient in one essential quality — humility.

Josephus Daniels, two decades older than Franklin and a neophyte in naval protocol and language, approached his new job tentatively. A courtly southerner, able to swap yarns and relax with colleagues, Daniels worked with deliberation to build solid relationships with key congressmen and senators. Franklin, an activist by nature, and a passionate believer in an expanded Navy ready for action in an increasingly volatile world, considered Daniels "an old fuddy duddy," who, he told Eleanor, "was too damn slow for words." One evening at a dinner party, Franklin made several derogatory remarks about Daniels. "You should be ashamed of yourself," Secretary of the Interior Franklin Lane cautioned. "Mr. D is your superior. And you should show him loyalty or you should resign." Franklin heeded Lane's advice. He held his tongue in public and eventually came to appreciate the great value of the warm relationships Daniels had managed to cultivate with members of the appropriations committees responsible for the Navy's funding.

As secretary of the navy, Daniels was responsible for overall naval policy, the disposition of the fleet, and congressional relations. While Daniels handled policy, Franklin, his sole assistant secretary, was charged with administering the giant Navy Department, which employed 65,000 men, with a budget representing 20 percent of federal expenditures. He was responsible for procuring supplies and equipment, supervising docks, navy yards, and personnel. And beyond the daily bureaucratic tasks under his purview, he was determined to move the entrenched bureaucracy forward, to build bigger and better-equipped ships, and to reorganize the work of the civilian personnel to strengthen the Navy's readiness for battle should the necessity arise.

What enabled this thirty-one-year-old with virtually no management experience to meet the double challenge of administering the department he inherited, while initiating a transformative process of moving it forward in a different direction? To be sure, having the vision to know where he wanted to go, to see a different future for the organization, was the essential first step. But how did he actually succeed in making it happen? And how, despite his contentious start with his superior, Daniels, was he able to forge a productive working relationship and lifelong friendship that eventually benefited both men?

For answers, one cannot resort solely to Franklin's celebrated "first-class temperament," but rather confront the speed and rule-bending originality of his intellect, which, at work within a complex organizational arena for the first time, proved anything but "second-rate." All his life people had underestimated (and would continue to misjudge) Franklin's native intelligence. The academic yardsticks used at Groton, Harvard College, and Columbia Law failed to measure his distinctive, problem-solving capacity, to gauge his aptitude for seeing how disparate things connect, or to credit the quickness with which he absorbed information. These unique aspects of his mind were often camouflaged by his outward geniality and the easy charm of his demeanor, leading members of his social circle to consider him a lightweight.

Those who witnessed young Roosevelt in the Navy Department, however, clearly understood that they were in the presence of a striking intelligence. "A man with a flashing mind," was how one rear admiral described him. "It took my breath away," he said, "to see how rapidly he grasped the essentials of a situation," how thoroughly he absorbed "the details of the most complicated subjects."

To gain a dynamic up-to-date picture of the size and capacity of the current fleet and the disposition of the 65,000 military and civilian personnel, Franklin had fixed to his office wall a large map of the world. Colored pins denoted the position of every ship in the fleet. Whenever a ship moved, the pins were moved. Other pins indicated the numbers of people employed at various navy yards, docks, and supply centers, allowing him to see what was transpiring. From the start, he formed a mental image of the Navy as a living organism rather than a moribund bureaucracy filled with "dead wood"; he envisioned a vast organization comprised of people working in places and working in jobs that could be grown into a Navy "second to none."

With a glance at his wall map, Roosevelt noted dozens of useless navy yards, originally designed for the maintenance of sailing vessels presently operating at great loss due to patronage and political pressure. Rather than closing these obsolete yards, he conceived of a new plan. He would convert each one into a specialized industrial plant for the manufacture of vessels and equipment needed for an expanded modern navy. The old Brooklyn Navy Yard would specialize in radios to outfit the fleet. Ropes and anchors and chains for battleships would become the province of the Boston yard. Cruisers would be built in Philadelphia, submarines and destroyers in Norfolk. This new mode of reorganization gave Roosevelt a reputation as an "economizer." More importantly, such consolidation was a necessary step to ready a peacetime navy for a potential war.

From the start, Roosevelt assembled a personal staff to assist him not only to manage the existing bureaucracy but, at the same time, to introduce new ideas and methods. Aware that he needed an assistant to whom he could entrust the routine aspects of the job, he kept Charles McCarthy as his private secretary. McCarthy, who had served in several previous administrations, embodied the traditions and rituals of the naval status quo. Within short order, Roosevelt secured McCarthy's respect and affection. "It is only a big man and real executive," McCarthy told Roosevelt, "who can distinguish between the minor details of such an office, which you have properly left to those in whom you have had confidence, and the bigger problems which you have so ably handled yourself." Winning the veteran bureaucrat's admiration made it easier for Franklin to gain the co-operation of the traditional bureaucratic cadre as he moved to change and reform the institution.

To help implement the transformative agenda of putting the Navy on a new readiness footing, Roosevelt brought in his own man, forty-year-old Louis Howe, an out-standing reporter for the *New York Herald,* whose strange appearance inspired a range of hyperbolic descriptions as a "gnome-like" creature, "a singed cat" with thinning hair and "luminous eyes," clothed in wrinkled suits perpetually covered with cigarette ashes. Howe had first encountered Roosevelt during the campaign to boycott Sheehan's appointment to the U.S. Senate. Such was the immediate attraction between the two men that they would become not merely the closest of friends but indispensable to one another.

Thereafter, Howe dedicated his life to Roosevelt. For the next quarter-century they seldom spent more than a couple days apart. While the genial and optimistic Roosevelt was generally averse to confrontation, Howe was tough and cynical by nature, happy to battle opposing people head-on. Never shy about his opinions, Howe could "deflate Roosevelt's pride, prod his negligence," and tell him flatly when and where he had gone astray. Remaining largely behind the scenes, he let Roosevelt absorb credit when things went well and readily accepted blame when they did not.

The methods Roosevelt used to propel a sluggish bureaucracy toward a more expansive and prepared status would become his characteristic way of dealing with constraints in the years ahead. He insisted that when something had to be done, there was always a way to do it, whether it involved bypassing regulations, cutting through red tape, or breaking precedent. "He was a great trial and error guy," Admiral Emory Land recalled of Roosevelt during this period. He would fling things against the wall, seeing if they would stick; if they didn't, he would acknowledge his mistake and try something else. When regulations prevented the government from selling naval guns to merchant ships, for example, he devised a scheme for loaning them with "a suitable bond" instead of offering them for sale, a seed that would germinate into the historic Lend-Lease program during World War II.

In addition to the fertility of his imagination and the suppleness of his techniques for circumventing strictures was his willingness at times of urgency to employ questionable means to achieve his goals. He placed official orders for millions of dollars' worth of guns, supplies, and equipment prior to congressional approval of the funds. He persuaded manufacturers to commence filling the orders on the basis of his word alone. Indeed, he once theatrically declared that if his brash maneuvers proved illegal, he was willing "to go to jail for 999 years," for he was certain that his insistence on preparedness would ultimately save his countrymen's lives.

His readiness proved of paramount importance. Not unlike his cousin Theodore's preparation for conflict with Spain (contrary to the policy of President McKinley and his naval superior, John Davis Long), Franklin had laid the foundation for America's entry into the Great War years in advance. After the sinking of the *Lusitania* in 1915, and the entrance of the United States into the war two years later, however, he no longer risked the charge of insubordination but rather basked in the status of a visionary. Indeed, so successful had he been in stockpiling supplies for the Navy that an admiring President Wilson brought him into a meeting with the

Army chief of staff and, "with a twinkle in his eye," said: "I'm very sorry, but you've cornered the market for supplies. You'll have to divide up with the Army." In the end, the foresight that led Franklin to fight for his preparedness campaign redounded not only to the credit of his boss, Josephus Daniels, but to the entire Wilson administration as well.

As a training run for his later leadership roles, Roosevelt's administrative experience in the Navy Department proved invaluable, developing not only his management skills, but his abilities to deal with labor. Within weeks of taking office, he visited civilian workers in the Washington Navy Yard who had felt neglected by the Navy brass and the government over the years. "We want to get down and talk across the table with you," he told them, assuring them they could come to him at any time "with complaints," or simply to "talk things over." He delivered the same message to workers in every yard and every dock he visited, telling disgruntled American Federation of Labor machinists that his door would always be open. During his tenure as assistant secretary, there was not a single strike by the thousands of civilian workers in the Navy Department.

With the Allied victory in the war, Roosevelt's tenure in the Navy Department came to a close. "My dear chief," he wrote Daniels in warm acknowledgment of the mentoring role he had played in his political education. "You have taught me so wisely and kept my feet on the ground when I was about to skyrocket."

Just as chance had intervened a decade earlier when the bosses chose him to run for the state legislature, so chance played a central role in the selection of thirty-eight-year-old Franklin Roosevelt as the Democratic nominee for vice president in 1920.

Roosevelt's name had not even appeared among a list of thirty-nine potential vice presidential candidates printed in the *New York Herald* on the day the Democratic National Convention opened in San Francisco. By the summer of 1920, public opinion had turned against the Democrats. Woodrow Wilson had suffered a stroke and lay incapacitated in the White House. Weary of both war and progressive reform after eight years of the Democratic administration, Americans were anxious to return to the simpler way of life promised by Republicans in their campaign slogan: "Return to normalcy." Needless to say, a cheerless mood engulfed the party faithful. Aware that 1920 was not likely to be a Democratic year, the major figures in the party had declined to enter the fray. With no clear front-runners, forty-four ballots were taken before Governor James Cox of Ohio finally secured the presidential nomination. At this point the vice presidential nomination seemed of small concern; the delegates were impatient to get home. Having chosen a candidate from Ohio, the bosses sought geographical balance. Franklin Roosevelt was from the critical state of New York, had carved a reputation for independence, carried a famous name, was young and energetic, and might be used to muster those still faithful to the stricken Woodrow Wilson. He was nominated by acclamation.

Though his party had little hope of victory, Roosevelt "had everything to gain and nothing to lose" in terms of his own future prospects. As the vice presidential candidate, he would not be blamed for defeat; by campaigning day after day with unflagging energy and exuberance for his party, however, he could build an account of goodwill that could be drawn upon in the future.

Franklin gave everything he had to the campaign. Traveling by train to nearly forty states, he worked eighteen hours a day. "We really had trouble holding Franklin down on that trip," Louis Howe recalled. "His enthusiasm was so great that we were after him constantly to keep him from wearing himself down to his bones." Refusing to listen, he insisted on speaking wherever the train paused, explaining to Howe that if he were elected someday, these people would be his "bosses," and "they've got a right to know what they're hiring." A reporter on the train with Franklin marveled that "once he met a man along the road who wielded any political influence whatever, he never forgot him." Nor did he forget "the particular circumstances" of the man's connection with the party.

In the course of delivering nearly eight hundred speeches, he polished the ease of his delivery, speaking so simply and directly, one reporter noted, that he managed to keep "the driest subjects from seeming heavy." No longer did Eleanor watch with dread when he hesitated, fearing that he might never continue. On the contrary, she told Sara, "it is becoming almost impossible to stop F. now when he begins to speak. 10 minutes is always 20, 30 is always 45 & the evening speeches are now about two hours!" Members of his staff "all get out & wave at him in front, and when nothing succeeds I yank his coattails!"

Inexperience, hubris, weariness, and a penchant for improvisation led inevitably to mistakes along the campaign trail. In Montana, talking about Latin America, he boasted that as assistant secretary of the navy he "had something to do with running a couple of little republics. The facts are that I wrote Haiti's Constitution myself, and, if I do say, I think it a pretty good constitution." Not only was this a gross exaggeration, but it gave

Warren Harding, the Republican presidential candidate, ammunition for a blistering counterattack. The story faded quickly, however, providing but a small dent in an otherwise splendid campaign. Franklin Roosevelt had emerged a national figure.

Prepared from the start for defeat, Roosevelt was not in the least depressed when the Democrats lost by an overwhelming majority. "A darn good sail," he characterized the abysmal loss. "Curiously enough," he told a friend, "I do not feel in the least down-hearted. It seems to me that everything possible was done during the campaign."

Of all the strengths Roosevelt displayed during the campaign, none was of greater significance than his ability to assemble and sustain a remarkably talented and staunchly loyal team that would remain together in the years ahead. For his advance man, he selected Stephen Early, a young wire service reporter who would become his White House press secretary. As his speechwriter, he chose another newsman, Marvin McIntyre, who would become his appointments secretary in the White House. To head his New York office, he hired Charles McCarthy, the veteran bureaucrat who had helped him negotiate the intricacies of the naval bureaucracy and who would eventually serve in the Justice Department during his presidency. And, of course, there was Louis Howe, the indispensable figure who would remain by Roosevelt's side until he died. Such was the atmosphere on the long train rides that storytelling, cards, and drinks regularly alleviated the pressure of preparing itineraries, studying local issues, and drafting speeches. Roosevelt long treasured recollections of the train trip, "a fraternity in spirit." To each of these men, Roosevelt presented a pair of gold Tiffany cuff links with FDR engraved on one side and the recipient's name on the other, binding them together in what became known as the "Cuff-Links Club," an extended family that expanded over the years to include Missy LeHand, his private secretary; Eleanor Roosevelt; Harry Hopkins, the head of the New Deal relief program; and Sam Rosenman, his counsel and chief speechwriter.

That Franklin Roosevelt had the weight and breadth to lead the nation was already established to all the members of this original team. They were not simply devoted to him; after months of intimate contact, they had come to revere and love him. No one identified Franklin Roosevelt as a potential president earlier and with more certainty than Louis Howe, one of the few people who always called him Franklin. "At that very first meeting," Howe told a reporter, "I made up my mind that he was Presidential timber and that nothing but an accident could keep him from being President of the United States."

FOUR:
LYNDON

"A steam engine in pants"

Lyndon Johnson was a gangly twenty-two-year-old college senior in July 1930, when he delivered his first political speech on behalf of former governor Pat Neff, who was running for railroad commissioner — a performance that would set in motion a mysterious chain of events that would eventually lead him to the height of power in Washington, D.C.

His speech concluded the annual picnic outside the small community of Henly. This picnic was a signal event in South-Central Texas and one Lyndon had attended with his father, Sam Johnson, since he was ten years old. All the candidates for state and local offices were generally present at the daylong "speaking." As hundreds of citizens milled about, enjoying the barbecue and the outdoor festivities, the candidates were summoned one by one to the makeshift speaker's stand to make the case for their election. A similar brand of humor and bombast, of folkloric shrewdness and local pride might have been heard a century earlier at the vandoos, where Abraham Lincoln and his fellow aspirants spoke before gatherings of farmers who had come into the village square to auction off their stock, gossip, and especially talk politics.

At dusk, the master of ceremonies called Pat Neff's name. When no one responded, he called again to see if someone wanted to speak for him. Still, no one stepped forward. State representative Welly Hopkins remembered vividly what happened next. The master of ceremonies was about to declare a default when suddenly, "I saw coming through the crowd a young fellow, kind of waving his arms about, calling out: By God, I'll make a speech for Pat Neff!" As the tall young man with black curly hair was hoisted upon the tailgate of the wagon bed, which served as a speaker's platform, he was introduced as "Sam Johnson's son." Sam had served in the state legislature for eight years and was widely known and well-liked in the region. Lyndon's speech, according to Hopkins, was a ten-minute "stem-winding, arm-swinging talk on behalf of Pat Neff."

"I'm a prairie dog lawyer from Johnson City, Texas," Lyndon began. By identifying himself as a prairie dog lawyer he employed a vernacular perfectly tailored to his audience. Prairie dog lawyers had little training in the law; they relied upon passionate advocacy rather than legal precedent to defend their clients before a jury. So young Lyndon, with a self-mocking yet assertive tone, let the picnickers know that while he was not an experienced politician, he intended to throw himself into the task of representing the missing Pat Neff. His style of speaking was "so wrapped up in youthful enthusiasm and sincerity of purpose," Hopkins recalled, "that his audience came along with him." While "it wasn't a rich oratorical style," there was "a timber in his voice that was pleasantly received." When he finished his testimony for Neff, the crowd responded with whistles and sustained applause. Indeed, his speech was considered "the hit of the Henly picnic."

From the time Lyndon was a small boy, he identified with his father's political ambitions. In the evenings, when Sam sat in the brown rocker on the porch swapping tales and jokes with three or four political cronies, the boy stood in the half-darkness of the doorway, straining to overhear the comings and goings of people in the legislature. He liked the animated, crude way the men spoke, the deep knowledge they had of the different families in their region.

"I loved going with my father to the legislature," Johnson remembered. "I would sit in the gallery for hours watching all the activity on the floor and then would wander around the halls trying to figure out what was going on." Sam Johnson was a popular figure in the statehouse. "If you can't come into a room full of people and tell right away who is for you and who is against you, you have no business in politics," he told his son. Sam "was very friendly," one colleague recalled, "a very down to earth man, a man who attracted people and knew how to deal with people." He was known to have an "explosive" temper, "but it was like a sunshine thing," a neighbor recalled. "It was gone in a minute and then he was always going about doing something nice." He was a progressive Democrat, speaking up for the people against the interests, supporting bills to establish an eight-hour workday, regulate public utility companies and tax corporations. He championed the underdog, using his office to help poor farmers, Army veterans, and soldiers' widows. "We've got to look after these people," Sam told a friend, "that's what we're here for."

Lyndon was his father's shadow and replica. They shared the same long arms, large nose, enormous ears, and hard squint. Lyndon learned to envelop people in the same fashion. "They walked the same, had the same nervous mannerisms," recalled Wright Patman, who served with Sam in the state legislature and later became a congressman, "and Lyndon clutched you like his daddy did when he talked to you." And like his father, gregarious young Lyndon struck up conversations with everyone he met. He became a favorite of all the older women in town, inquiring how they were feeling, how things were going. If he heard a group of men talking politics on the street, he would stand on the sidelines, smitten. At ten, he took a job after school shining shoes at Cecil Maddox's barbershop, the place where politics and the latest items of news were discussed.

The only thing Lyndon loved more than accompanying his father to the statehouse was traveling along with him on the campaign trail. "We drove in the Model T Ford from farm to farm, up and down the valley, stopping at every door. My father would do most of the talking. He would bring the neighbors up to date on local gossip, talk about the crops and about the bills he'd introduced in the legislature, and always he'd bring along an enormous crust of homemade bread and a large jar of homemade jam. When we got tired or hungry, we'd stop by the side of the road. He sliced the bread, smeared it with jam, and split the slices with me. I'd never seen him happier. Families all along the way opened up their homes to us. If it was hot outside, we were invited in for big servings of homemade ice cream. If it was cold, we were given hot tea. Christ, sometimes I wished it could go on forever."

This campaign idyll offered a welcome, albeit temporary relief for both father and son from the discord of the Johnson family household — a place often filled with the severe tensions that contributed to Lyndon's excitable temperament. All his life, he would vacillate between security and insecurity, assertiveness and obsequiousness, charm and taunting cruelty, a desire to please and a need for control. In contrast to the balanced, secure, and placid childhood upon which Franklin Roosevelt's genuinely confident and optimistic nature was anchored, Lyndon had to negotiate between his father and mother, each representing very different and clashing worlds of values.

"My mother told me the first year of her marriage was the worst year of her life," Johnson remembered. Having grown up in "a two-story rock house, with a fruitful orchard of perfectly spaced trees, terraced flower beds, broad walks," and a white picket fence, she was utterly unprepared for the disorder and isolation of Sam Johnson's small cabin on a muddy stream with neither electricity nor indoor plumbing. The daughter of a college-educated lawyer, and herself a graduate of Baylor University at a time when few women attended college, Rebekah Baines had aspired to be a writer when she interviewed the "dashing and dynamic" Sam Johnson for her family newspaper during his first term in the state legislature. A "whirlwind courtship" ensued, leading to marriage and "the problem of adjustment to a completely opposite personality," as well as "a strange and new way of life."

Accustomed to culture, books, and intellectual discussions about philosophy and literature, Rebekah found that the man she had fallen in love with enjoyed nothing more than sitting up half the night with his political cronies, drinking beer, sharing gossip, swapping stories. She had originally hoped that Sam would run for national office and carry her away to the nation's capital, where ideas and ideals would be discussed, but he soon made it clear that he had no interest in leaving home. Meanwhile, her own days and nights were consumed in the tedium of drawing water from the well, feeding chickens, boiling clothes, and scrubbing floors on her hands and knees, leaving insufficient time for the unread books "piled high" in her bedroom, and no time at all for writing. She was miserable. "Then I came along," Lyndon said, "and suddenly everything was all right again. I could do all the things she never did."

Lyndon seemed at first the perfect instrument for Rebekah to realize her ambitions. Relatives and friends claimed they had "never seen such a friendly baby," nor one as inquisitive and intelligent. He learned the alphabet before he was two, learned to read and spell before he was four, and at three could recite long passages from Longfellow and Tennyson. "I'll never forget how much my mother loved me when I recited those poems," Johnson said. "The minute I finished she'd take me in her arms and hug me so hard I sometimes thought I'd be strangled to death." Even after she gave birth to four other children, Lyndon remained Rebekah's favorite. "I remember playing games with her that only the two of us could play. And she would always let me win even if to do so we had to change the rules. I knew how much she needed me. I liked that. It made me feel big and important. It made me feel I could do anything in the world."

But opposite the bright and beaming side of the moon was an equally dark side — an insecurity that would plague Lyndon Johnson for the rest of his life. When he failed to fulfill his mother's ambitions for him — when he became a sluggish student or resisted continuing violin and dancing lessons — she withdrew her love and affection. "For days after I quit those lessons she walked around the house pretending I was dead," Johnson glumly said. "And then," he added, "I had to watch her being especially warm and nice to my father and sisters." Love was alternately lavished and snatched away, a quid pro quo for obedience and achievement. In later years, Johnson would exhibit a similar pattern in dealing with friends, colleagues, and members of his staff. He would blanket someone with generosity, care, and affection, but in recompense, expect total loyalty and sterling achievement. Failing this standard was perceived by him as a betrayal. His affection would be withdrawn, a pattern of behavior so pronounced it earned the epithet, the Johnson "freeze-out."

Storytelling played a central role in young Lyndon's life, just as it had in the lives of young Abraham, Theodore, and Franklin. When tensions in the Johnson household flared, Lyndon found the "perfect escape" down the road at his grandfather's house. There, the two of them could share an hour or more while Sam Ealy Sr. elaborated upon his cowboy days driving a herd of fifteen hundred cattle from ranches in Texas up the Chisholm Trail to Abilene, Kansas. "I sat beside the rocker on the floor of the porch," Johnson recollected, "thinking all the while how lucky I was to have as a granddaddy this big man with the white beard who had lived the most exciting life imaginable."

Sam Senior possessed a narrative gift able to shape those early adventures into a vast trove of seminal tales that would form the building blocks of Lyndon's heroic conception of leadership. Central to such stories was the image of the lead cowboy driving cattle through icy rivers, ever vigilant to avoid the ultimate horror of the stampede.

Lyndon's idealization of the bold cowboy in his beloved grandfather's cattle-driving tales shaped his concept of manhood, just as the perilous tales of hunters and deerslayers living on the margins of wilderness informed Theodore Roosevelt's ideal of the heroic male. The extravagant oral tradition of the Old West infused Johnson's language. Only Abraham Lincoln, who had actually endured physical danger and the bitter hardships of wilderness life, never romanticized his family's past.

Lyndon's classmates recognized the superiority of his intelligence. He was "very brilliant," one schoolmate recalled. The boys his age were simply not in "his class mentally." Even the older boys "saw that he talked — and thought — faster than they did." He was too restless to sit still or concentrate in class, however, and recoiled from completing his homework. His mother tried to remedy his lack of preparation by reading his assignments out loud while he ate breakfast, but he felt "smothered" by her "force feedings." Consequently, he was held back and forced to complete a summer session before graduating high school. Nor, despite his mother's best urgings, did he ever become a reader. "Is it true?" he would ask her when she handed him a book, agreeing to open its cover only if it were about history or government. If Abraham Lincoln carried away from his standing at the top of his class "the self-confidence of a man who has never met his intellectual equal," Lyndon Johnson remained forever plagued by a sense of academic inferiority. "My daddy always told me that if I brushed up against the grindstone of life, I'd come away with more polish than I could ever get at Harvard or Yale," he said years later, a wistful tone in his voice. "I wanted to believe him, but somehow I never could."

■ ■ ■ ■

"The way you get ahead in the world, you get close to those that are the heads of things," Lyndon told his college roommate when he finally arrived at Southwest Texas State Teachers College in San Marcos. "Like President Evans, for example." Cecil Evans had served as the college president for fifteen years and was well respected by faculty and students alike. Aware of the demands on the president's time, Johnson concluded "there was only one way to get to know Evans, and that was to work for him directly." It was school policy to give students part-time jobs in the library, cafeteria, bookstore, administrative offices, or maintenance department. Lyndon's first job was on the janitorial crew, picking up papers and trash. Most students did the minimum work necessary to keep their jobs, but Lyndon labored with extravagant enthusiasm, making a game of collecting the largest trash pile in the shortest time. His eagerness garnered a promotion to the janitorial crew that worked inside the administration building. Assigned to mop floors, Lyndon focused on the hallway outside the president's office, allowing him to strike up conversations as President Evans passed by. Like Lyndon, Evans was enamored of politics from his earliest days; in fact, Evans still harbored the hope that someday he might run for office. With Lyndon, as with no other student or even most faculty members, he could enjoy conversations about doings in the legislature or share stories about various political figures. When Lyndon asked if he could work in his office running errands and delivering messages, Evans promptly agreed.

What began as an inconsequential position soon became, in Lyndon's hands, a generator of actual power as he expanded the limited function of messenger by encouraging recipients to transmit their own communications through him. Occupying a desk in the president's foyer, he would announce the arrival of visitors as if he were the appointments secretary rather than the office messenger. In time, faculty members and administrative officials, whose names Lyndon always remembered, came to think of the skinny young Texan with black curly hair as a direct channel to the president. Increasingly impressed by Lyndon's perceptive observations about state politics, Evans brought him to Austin when committee hearings were held on appropriations for state colleges and other educational matters. Soon, he began relying on his young messenger to work up reports on the hearings, which Lyndon did with flair, analyzing the inclinations of individual legislators as well as the mood and atmosphere of the legislature as a whole. Before long, Lyndon was handling the president's political correspondence, drafting reports for various state agencies, and taking up residence in a room above the garage in the president's house. In time, he almost seemed the son President Evans never had — a son who not only provided affection and companionship but whose organizational skills and attention to detail allowed him to assume burdensome tasks and responsibilities belonging to the older man.

Without a doubt, many students perceived Lyndon's flagrant consolidation of power as repellent. They considered his ingratiating attitude toward administrators and faculty "kowtowing," "suck-assing," "brown nosing." Several of Lyndon's classmates regarded him as "ruthless," prepared "to cut your throat to get what [he] wanted." They "didn't just dislike Lyndon Johnson," one said, "they despised him."

"Ambition is an uncomfortable companion," Lyndon conceded in a college editorial. "He creates a discontent with present surroundings and achievements: he is never satisfied but always pressing forward." This personification of ambition lacks comprehension of the impression he made on others. He failed to understand when to ease up and was often blind to the collateral cost of his own compulsive energies.

■ ■ ■ ■

Lyndon's need to achieve this self-aggrandizing and self-serving ambition was harnessed in the service of a larger purpose for the first time when, during a yearlong break from college, he became the principal of a six-teacher Mexican American elementary school in Cotulla, Texas, a dusty, impoverished town not too far from the border with Mexico. Most of the families lived in dirt hovels, engaged in a continual struggle to wring a living from the dry and treeless land.

As principal, Lyndon occupied his first true position of authority and employed every leadership attribute he already possessed — indefatigable energy, ability to persuade, willingness to fight for what he wanted, intuition, enterprise, and initiative — to enlarge opportunities for his students and to improve their lives. The students adored him, his fellow teachers came to admire him, and he left an enduring impression upon the little community as a whole. At last, biographer Robert Caro observes, Lyndon was "the somebody he had always wanted to be." He was neither trying to absorb power by accommodating an older mentor nor savagely competing with peers. He was simply trying to elevate the hopes and conditions of the marginalized and dispossessed of this South

Texas town.

Empathy fired Lyndon's efforts at Cotulla. "My students were poor and they often came to class without breakfast, hungry," Johnson later recalled. "And they knew, even in their youth, the pain of prejudice." Because there was no school funding for extracurricular activities, he used half his first month's salary to buy sports equipment, and then badgered the school board to include track and field events, baseball games, and volleyball matches in the school budget. In addition to his administrative responsibilities as principal, this one-man band taught fifth, sixth, and seventh grade classes, coached debating, and served as the softball coach, the drama coach, and the choir leader. At first, he had the children practice and compete against one another. Soon, however, he arranged field days with a dozen other regional schools.

A chorus of voices decades later testifies to the enormous impact Lyndon left on the school. "He respected the kids more than any other teacher we ever had," said Manuel Sanchez. "He put us to work," another student remembered. "But he was the kind of teacher you wanted to work for. You felt an obligation to him and to yourself to do your work." He was strict, they all agreed; he made them stay after school if they hadn't done their homework. But he was "down-to-earth and friendly," and years later they were grateful so much had been demanded of them.

And no one worked more fiercely than Lyndon Johnson. The first to arrive in the morning and the last to leave at night, "he didn't give himself what we call spare time," a fellow teacher said. "He walked so fast, it was like seeing a blur," one townsman recalled. His unflagging energy, his ferocious ambition, and his compulsive drive to organize were now linked to something larger than himself. The success he sought was coupled with an equally powerful desire to transform the lives of his students. "I was determined to spark something inside them, to fill their souls with ambition and interest and belief in the future. I was determined to give them what they needed to make it in this world, to help them finish their education. Then the rest would take care of itself."

The year Johnson spent teaching the Mexican American children in Cotulla was a pivotal experience, one to which Johnson returned again and again. "I can still see the faces of the children who sat in my class," he said years later. This was the display of a different kind of leadership, one based on empathy and generosity he had never exercised before.

Among the seasoned political eyes trained upon young Lyndon Johnson on the occasion of his first political speech at the Henly picnic of 1930 was the gaze of Welly Hopkins, who was about to launch a campaign for the State Senate. On the spur of the moment that day, Hopkins had cannily invited Lyndon to take a leading position in his campaign, a chance encounter that would have a far-reaching impact on Lyndon's future.

"Even in that day," Hopkins recalled of young Lyndon, "politics was in his blood, just by inheritance and by training, and by general aptitude." Not only was he "steeped in political lore," but he was "gifted with a very unusual ability to meet and greet the public," and to organize. Within days, Lyndon had mobilized a half-dozen of his college friends into a tightly-knit machine.

"We worked Blanco County in and out," Hopkins recalled of his travels with Lyndon. "I was up every branch of the Pedernales," following Lyndon's judgment "almost completely," because he knew the area so well and "had a favorable standing with the local people." No matter how tired they were, Lyndon scoured the countryside for votes, even if the car had to travel to a single farm at the end of an unpaved road. "On one occasion," Hopkins laughingly recalled, Lyndon had him stand in a dry creek bed to deliver a ten-minute speech to a group of three — a man, his wife, and a relative. Such attention to detail paid off. Hopkins secured a surprising victory. "I always felt he was the real balance of the difference as to whether I'd be elected," a grateful Hopkins said. Word spread that there was a "wonder kid in San Marcos who knew more about politics than anyone in the area."

Lyndon was poised for entry into a political career, but the times said otherwise. The Depression offered no opportunity for a government job. Fortunately, his uncle George Johnson, longtime head of the history department at Sam Houston High, found him a position as a teacher of public speaking and debate. The moment Lyndon arrived at Sam Houston High he set a dramatic goal for the debate team: though they had never "won anything" in competition with neighboring schools, Lyndon told them that for the first time in the history of the school, the team would win not only the city and district competitions, but would go on to the state championship. Straightaway, he had set a psychological target to elevate the team's ambitions before the debating season even got under way.

At Houston High, as at Cotulla, Lyndon channeled his ravenous drive for success to benefit others, deploying his headlong leadership style to mobilize funding for the debate club. Luther Jones, one of the club members, recalled overhearing a "rather vigorous argument Johnson had with the principal," who told him that money for the debating team had never been part of the school budget. "Yes, but you've never had a teacher like me!" Johnson countered. "By some people's standards," Jones observed, "you would say he was very conceited," and surely his attitude was "extremely aggressive," but he "could get people to do things they would under ordinary circumstances never think of doing."

Lyndon appeared to his students "a human dynamo," "a steam engine in pants," driven by a work ethic and an unlimited enthusiasm that proved contagious. His first day on the job, he had students stand before their mates and make animal noises, anything to slough off nervousness and self-consciousness. "He had a variety of ways to get you going," debate club member Gene Latimer recalled. He'd either "make you feel ashamed" that you hadn't seemed to invest sufficient time in the library studying the topic at hand, or "he'd brag on you and make you want to go do some more." And always, "he liked to pit one against the other." These techniques "came to him instinctively," Latimer believed. "No one before or since has ever motivated me like he could. If he told any of us to go get up on a roof of a building and jump off, we'd all pile up there and do it."

Storytelling, Johnson taught his students, was the key to successful debating. In contrast to the previous public speaking teacher who came from the "old school," and trained his debaters to "be bombastic and loud," Lyndon urged a conversational style that illustrated points with concrete stories. "Act like you're talking to those folks," he counseled his students. "Look one of them in the eye and then move on and look another one in the eye." During competitions, he utilized all his supple array of gestures and facial expressions to cue and prompt — now frowning, narrowing his eyes, creasing his brow, shaking his head, gaping in wonder — creating a silent movie to steer and goad his charges to victory.

From the start, Johnson sought to create an aura around the debate club that had previously been reserved for the football team. At the first competition, only seven people attended, but as the undefeated team's victory tally mounted, excitement began to build. By the time the team clinched the city championship and began competing at the district level, every seat in the auditorium was taken. He had transformed debate into a community-wide campaign complete with pep rallies, cheerleaders, and team sweaters. Indeed, an amalgam of his father's coarse politicking and his mother's prim scrutiny of appearance and demeanor when she taught elocution at Johnson City High can be clearly traced in their son's pedagogy. When the team clinched the district level championship, pictures of the two star debaters, Gene

Latimer and Luther Jones, were splashed across city newspapers. Though the state championship was lost in the final competition by a single vote, by the time the school year ended, Latimer proudly noted, "we were more important than the football team."

The services Lyndon rendered to Welly Hopkins's campaign were remembered and repaid with Welly's recommendation to Richard Kleberg (who had just won an election to fill a vacancy in the 14th Congressional District) that Lyndon Johnson was just the man he needed as his legislative secretary — in essence, his chief of staff. After meeting Lyndon, Kleberg promptly offered the job. A few days later the two men set off on a Pullman train for the two-day trip to Washington. "All that day I'd gone about feeling excited, nervous, and sad," Johnson recalled. "I was about to leave home to meet the adventure of my future. I felt grown-up, but my mind kept ranging backward in time. I saw myself as a boy skipping down the road to my granddaddy's house. I remembered the many nights I had stood in the doorway listening to my father's political talk. I remembered the evenings with my mother when my daddy was away. Now all that was behind me."

If ever a destination seemed a destiny for Lyndon Johnson, it was Washington, D.C. — a city whose intricacies he would master and for a while dominate as completely as he had dominated his college in San Marcos, Cotulla, and Houston High. Upon seeing the Capitol dome for the first time, Johnson vowed that someday he would become a congressman in his own right. "I would not say I was without ambition ever," he recalled. "It was very exciting to me to realize that the people, many of them that you were passing, were probably congressmen at least, maybe senators, members of the cabinet. And there was the smell of power. It's got an odor you know. Power I mean."

Such was the nature of Johnson's driven temperament that he had no sooner settled into the Dodge Hotel, where the majority of congressional secretaries lived, than he began his quest to determine the sources and relationships of power in the nation's capital. There was no time to waste — the scale of inquiry was so much greater than ever before. His adaptation of rural friendliness to his competitive city lodgings made for bizarrely comic tactics: he took four separate showers in the shared bathroom his first night to engage as many people as possible; the next morning he brushed his teeth every ten minutes — all to winnow out the most useful informants in the lot. "This skinny boy was as green as anybody could be," an older congressional secretary said, "but within a few months he knew how to operate in

169

Washington better than some who had been here twenty years."

Managing a staff for the first time, Johnson filled his two positions with young men whose work ethic he had already formed and tested — his star debaters from Houston High, Latimer and Jones. Johnson was "a hard man to work for because he insisted on perfection," Jones recalled. The Chief, as he was known to them, "wanted to answer every day's mail every day." And every letter "had to be just right," which meant typing and retyping the same letter over and over again, until it was exactly "the way he wanted it." One Saturday evening, Johnson came back to work after dinner to find Latimer and Jones gone. A note on the desk said they had gone to a movie and would be back at nine. Shuffling through the mail stack, he spied what he was searching for: an unanswered constituent letter! Seizing it, he raced to the local theater, found the two men, and brought them outside, only to learn that in compliance to his earlier directive, the letter in question had been put aside. Anxious to mollify matters, Johnson invited them to dinner at a local restaurant. No sooner had the first drink arrived than up he jumped. "We've been relaxing long enough," he said, "there's still three more good working hours until we fold."

When critics wrote about Johnson's ruthless manner in dealing with the members of his staff, Latimer insisted that his boss was "extremely sentimental about the people close to him." And yet, increasingly, the price for admission into his select extended family had grown from dedication and unquestioned loyalty to devouring all of the subordinate's personal time and space. "If he caught you reading a letter from your mother," Jones said, "or if you were taking a crap, he'd say, Son, can't you please try a little harder to do that on your own time?"

Within a matter of months, Kleberg's office had developed a reputation as one of the most efficient on Capitol Hill. For Congressman Kleberg, "a bluff and good natured, multi-millionaire," the situation was ideal. Preferring to spend his time playing golf, poker, or polo, he was happy to let Lyndon run the show, and Lyndon, in turn, was delighted with the vacuum Kleberg afforded him. From the start, Johnson gave first priority to constituent requests, understanding the central importance of strengthening Kleberg's elected base at home. Through prompt and helpful answers to the hundreds of petitioners who wrote each month — veterans with claim of injuries sustained during World War I, desperate farmers hoping for aid from the agricultural administration, unemployed men and women in need of a government job — word of Kleberg's reflected zeal began to spread across the district; on the inside,

171

Lyndon's reputation as a doer was established.

Since most of the constituent case work involved problems with one bureaucracy or another, Johnson had to spend hours each day penetrating the bureaucratic maze, figuring out where the power lay, identifying and targeting the person who would make the ultimate decision. Then his bombardment commenced — hectoring pressure combined with contagious enthusiasm, flattery mingled with threat, until the determination he sought was finally made. He believed that "every problem had a solution," Jones marveled. He refused to take no for an answer, and when the constituent received what he was hoping for, Johnson was jubilant, treating each successful case as a major victory for the team. With stunning audacity and speed, Lyndon Johnson had become a congressman in all but name.

By the age of twenty-five, Lyndon Johnson was on the path to a political career. He had come a long way in the three short years since that moment at the Henly picnic when he raced through the crowd to deliver his first political speech. Earlier than the three men we have studied, he had laid out an elaborate blueprint for a different kind of leadership, an executive competence and a distinctive, grinding pattern of behavior that would mark his management style the rest of his days.

Already he had become a consummate political animal, a man with a dowsing rod inexorably drawn to every reservoir of power. The instinctive ability to locate the gears and levers of power in any institution, to secure wise and faithful mentors, and to transform minor positions into substantial founts of influence would accompany every stage of his upward climb.

In contrast to Abraham Lincoln, who was able to relax with poetry and drama; or Theodore Roosevelt, who was interested in birds, the mating habits of wolves, and the latest novels; or Franklin Roosevelt, who spent happy hours sailing, playing with his stamps, enjoying poker and genial social chatter, Lyndon Johnson could never unwind. Luther Jones never remembered him reading a novel, or, indeed, reading anything other than the newspapers and current magazines he obsessively devoured. He rarely went to movies or plays, for he disliked sitting in the dark for three hours unable to talk. At baseball games, he would insist on talking politics between innings and even between pitches. At social events, he danced with the wives of congressmen and government officials rather than with single girls, discussing the latest news and political gossip as they twirled across the floor. All his life, he would continue to work at this same compulsive pace, as if victory and success might somehow reclaim the steady love and affection he had been denied as a child.

The same qualities Lyndon brought to every stage of his climb — single-minded determination, contagious enthusiasm, flattery mingled with threats, indefatigable energy, and an overwhelming personality — were conspicuous in his successful endeavor to win the hand of Claudia "Lady Bird" Taylor in marriage. If Theodore Roosevelt waged a concerted yearlong campaign to woo his wife and her family, Lyndon, with not a second to spare, accelerated the process, reaching his goal in a matter of weeks.

The daughter of a wealthy businessman, Lady Bird had recently graduated from the University of Texas with a degree in journalism. After a single date in Austin, Johnson, to his credit and good fortune, decided not to let this intelligent, reserved, sensitive, and shrewd woman go. During their first conversation, she later remembered, he told her all manner of "extraordinarily direct" things about himself — "his salary as a secretary to a congressman, his ambitions, even about all the members of his family, and how much insurance he carried. It was as if he wanted to give a complete picture of his life and of his capabilities." She thought he was "very, very good-looking, with lots of black, wavy hair," but considered it "sheer lunacy" when on their second date he asked her to marry him.

"I'm ambitious, proud, energetic and madly in love with you," he declared. "I see something I *know* I *want* — I *immediately exert efforts* to get it." On his next visit to Austin two months later, he issued an ultimatum: "We either get married now or we never will." When she agreed, he released a "Texas yip," and then drove straight to San Antonio, where they were married in a simple ceremony that same day. "I don't think Lady Bird ever had a chance once he set eyes on her," Latimer observed three decades later. She was his "balancing wheel," Jones said. He was constitutionally impatient; she was constitutionally calm. He was abrupt and profane; she was gentle and gracious. Without such forbearance and devotion, without a love steadily given and never withdrawn, the course of Lyndon Johnson's ascent amid the most complicated intrigues of the political world becomes inconceivable.

Furthermore, the home Lady Bird established in Washington proved instrumental not only to Lyndon's stability but to his enlarging ambitions. Lady Bird offered a welcoming hospitality to Lyndon's guests at any time of day or night. He might call her as late as six or seven to say he was bringing home a half-dozen people, and by the time they arrived, the table would be set, drinks ready, the supper cooking.

Among the many guests, none played a larger role in Lyndon's future than Sam Rayburn, the Democratic congressman from Bonham, Texas, who had served with Lyndon's father in the state legislature and would go on to become speaker of the house for seventeen years. Without a wife or family of his own, "Mr. Sam" was often lonely in the hours when the House was not in session. Sensing this, Lyndon more and more frequently began inviting him for dinner, invitations that soon extended to breakfasts on weekends so the two men could read the Sunday papers together. The warmth and informality of the atmosphere engendered a genuine companionship, providing Lyndon with a wise, trusted, and most useful mentor and Mr. Sam with the affectionate and loyal son he never had. And soon, Mr. Sam's exercise of brute political force would prove indispensable to Lyndon's attainment of the next way station of his political rise.

On a Tuesday morning in June 1935, by executive order, President Franklin Roosevelt created the National Youth Administration. The NYA was designed to save "a lost generation" of young people by providing part-time work for students from needy families who could not otherwise afford to stay in school, as well as full-time jobs for thousands of unemployed youths between the ages of sixteen and twenty-one. That very Tuesday, Lyndon approached Mr. Sam and proposed himself as the perfect candidate for director of the Texas NYA. Straightaway, Rayburn asked an uncharacteristic favor of Texas senator Tom Connally: "He wanted me to ask President Roosevelt to appoint Lyndon Johnson," Connally recalled. "Sam was agitated." That this was a matter of significant personal import for Rayburn was so apparent and persuasive that Connally agreed at once. Connally was unable to convince Roosevelt, however, that the twenty-six-year-old Lyndon, with no administrative experience, was qualified to run a statewide agency. In truth, the largest staff Lyndon had ever managed consisted of three people. Furthermore, another man had been announced for the post before Rayburn appealed to the president. Nonetheless, Roosevelt heeded Rayburn's wish. In short order, the White House acknowledged that "a mistake had been made." The post would go instead to Kleberg's congressional secretary, Lyndon Baines Johnson.

Concerns about Johnson's youth and inexperience were soon put to rest as it became increasingly clear that the youngest state director in the United States possessed a rare cluster of executive skills. "I'm not the assistant type," he rightly told a friend upon leaving Kleberg's office. "I'm the executive type." Recruiting a staff that would eventually comprise nearly fifty people posed the first hurdle. He began by summoning the same young men he had teamed with since college, at Sam Houston High, and in Kleberg's office. They were familiar with his driving leadership, they had witnessed his modus operandi in smaller arenas, and they were ready for a larger challenge. Most of them were poor, like himself; they, too, had found it necessary to scavenge for jobs in the depressed time in order to stay in college. For them, as for Johnson, the mission of the NYA — to provide education, training, and jobs for young people — was personal. "We gathered that dream in ourselves and agreed to be a part of it and go to work," one staffer recalled.

The enormity of the statewide undertaking overwhelmed Johnson until he came up with an ideal plan to "start the ball rolling" with an all-important inaugural project. He would put thousands of out-of-school youth to work building roadside parks along state highways where travelers could stop to rest, have something to eat, and go to the bathroom. Within a matter of weeks, Washington approved the paperwork and the plan was put into operation. While the NYA paid for the labor, the State Highway Department provided the supervision, the trucks, and the material. State engineers trained the young men to mix concrete, build driveways off the roads into the parks, lay bricks for barbecue pits, construct picnic tables and benches, plant shade trees and curbside shrubs. Johnson was "beside himself with happiness" when the first project was up and running, for he knew that it would create an atmosphere of success. When the roadside parks project proved successful, he made sure it was publicized throughout Texas, and in a short time it actually became "a model for the nation."

Lyndon's performance during this first undertaking opened the door to supplementary funding and scores of additional projects. Within six months, Johnson had convinced officials in 350 agencies — schools, hospitals, libraries, recreational facilities — to provide the material and supervision for their particular project. Eighteen thousand young people were at work repairing school buses, surveying land, and building arbors, swimming pools, school gyms, and basketball courts. It was as if the recreational and extracurricular projects he had once furnished out of his own pocket for recess and after-school activities at Cotulla could now be expanded with federal monies across all of Texas. When Eleanor Roosevelt came to Texas in 1936, she asked to meet the youthful state director about whom she had heard so much.

As the pressure increased, however, accounts of the Chief's frantic, harsh, even abusive behavior toward his staff multiplied. "Everything had to be done NOW," one staffer recalled. "And he could get very angry if something couldn't be done immediately." Seconds after dictating a letter, he "couldn't wait" to see the finished product. "Where's that letter?" he would shout to his secretary; if his howl didn't produce the desired result, he would pull the letter midstream from the typewriter. "The hours were long and hard," recalled Bill Deason, another old friend Johnson had recruited. The team worked six days a week, from 8 a.m. to midnight. Sundays were reserved for staff meetings to go over what had been done and outline plans for the week ahead. The lights and the elevators in the government building were supposed to be turned off at 10 p.m., but Johnson persuaded the building manager to leave them on until midnight, and sometimes 1 a.m., until the building owner intervened. There were no "clockwatchers" on the staff; indeed, it seemed as if Johnson had simply "never heard of a clock."

He instilled fear; he kept everyone on edge. "He would pair us off, or there'd be one or two or three of us and you were always behind somebody else," recalled Ray Roberts, a member of the staff. He'd go to one person and tell him how great the other was doing and "that he ought to try to catch up";

then the next day he'd reverse the process. "I don't care how hard I worked," one staffer lamented, "I was always behind." Staffers never knew what might trigger an outburst. "God, he could rip a man up and down," one humiliated team member remembered. It could be a cluttered desk, which he took as a sign of disorganization, or a clean desk, which signified idleness. More often than not, his blistering outbursts were followed by indulgent affection, tactile sentimentality, effusive praise, or contrition. For some team members, Johnson's oscillating behavior proved too much to bear. A few broke down physically, others quit, but the majority stayed.

Why did the team members stay on? Leadership studies suggest such behaviors undermine internal motivation, that pitting workers against one another rarely succeeds in the long run, and that public humiliation crushes an employee's spirit, autonomy, and production. Yet Johnson's team, by and large, performed magnificently. Aubrey Williams, the national NYA director, publicly declared that the NYA program in Texas was paramount in the entire nation. How did the team accomplish so much, so quickly, and for so long?

The answers require an appreciation of Johnson's unsurpassed work ethic, the feeling among staff members that they were learning important skills, and the sense of shared engagement in a significant mission. No matter how late they stayed, nearly all the staff members agreed, Johnson closed the door behind them. No matter how early they arrived, he was already there. "Now, fellows, we can do this," Johnson exhorted his team, "if you all put your shoulders to the wheel and pitch in." Here, as in Washington, Lady Bird proved an indispensable ally. By making her home an extension of the workplace, she softened the often inconsiderate harshness of Lyndon's compulsive pace. Various staff members lived with the Johnsons in a room on the second floor. They ate breakfast and often dinner at the house. "We weren't like boarders," Bill Deason recalled, "we had the run of the house and I felt like a member of the family." Mind-numbing meetings going over NYA rules and regulations, "paragraph by paragraph, page by page," were often held on the Johnson porch. "This was usually pretty late at night," William Sherman Birdwell recalled. "Lady Bird always had coffee and cake for us."

For the young men, Johnson (though hardly older than they) proved an inspiring mentor, motivating them not only "to work harder," observed one staffer, but "to be more imaginative, to think of new approaches that we could take to stretch the boundaries or the limitations under which we operated, to be more effective." They considered him "the greatest organizer" they had ever seen; they marveled at his ability "to put first things first and more or less take them one at a time." And yet, while focused on the present, he seemed to know what was coming next; they believed he could actually "see around corners." Working so closely with the most forceful and unusual leader they had ever met, they felt they were daily learning something new. And "we made no bones about it," Ray Roberts acknowledged. They all knew then, even before Lyndon was thirty, that he was "going somewhere," and that it would be great to go along with him.

More than anything else, however, what allowed the staff to endure Lyndon's overbearing behavior was the sense they were joined together in an incredibly exciting new organization that promised to change the lives of thousands of young people who had lost hope during the early years of the Depression, providing them with jobs, keeping them in school, teaching them marketable skills, renewing their faith in the future. By hitching their lives to Lyndon Johnson, his staffers knew they were riding the momentum, breadth, and meaning of a larger story.

The swiftness with which Lyndon Johnson made life-altering decisions was prominently displayed when an opportunity suddenly arose to run for the House of Representatives. On February 23, 1937, not eighteen months into his directorship of the Texas NYA, Lyndon was conducting the fellow director of the Kansas NYA on a tour of several of his work projects when his eyes fell on the headline of a newspaper left on a park bench: *Congressman James P. Buchanan of Brenham Dies.* "I just couldn't keep my mind on my visitor," Johnson later said. "I kept thinking that this was my district and this was my chance. The day seemed endless. She never stopped talking. And I had to pretend total interest in everything we were seeing and doing. There were times when I thought I'd explode from all the excitement bottled up inside." Not seven weeks later, in a special election conducted against eight far better known and more experienced opponents, the twenty-nine-year-old Lyndon Johnson was elected Buchanan's successor. How was victory accomplished against older, veteran politicians, all prominent, well-established citizens in a district where, at the outset, Lyndon Johnson was hardly known?

For a start, Lyndon's almost instantaneous decision to run cleared the most important obstacle to victory. While the other eight candidates put off their decision until Buchanan's widow determined if she would run, Lyndon publicly declared three days after the funeral. Buchanan had represented the district for nearly a quarter of a century; it might have been deemed inappropriate to challenge his fifty-seven-year-old widow, who had publicly hinted that she desired the seat. "She's an old woman," Sam Johnson shrewdly counseled his son. "She's too old for a fight. If she knows she's going to have a fight, she won't run. Announce now — before she announces. If you do, she won't run." Sam's prediction hit the mark; after Lyndon announced, she resolved not to run.

Lyndon had consulted a very small circle before making his decision. Most important was a man who had become a trusted mentor in Austin — Alvin Wirtz, an influential lawyer and politician who was serving as chair of the advisory board of Texas NYA. "Wirtz had a wife and daughter," his secretary Mary Rather said. "But he would have loved to have had a son. And he loved him [Lyndon] as a son." When Wirtz told him he would need at least $10,000 to make a run, Lady Bird called her father to ask for the money. "Ten thousand dollars," her father asked. "Isn't that a great deal? What about five thousand or three thousand?" "No," Bird said, "we've been told it must be ten." "All right," he replied, "ten thousand will be transferred to Lyndon's bank by tomorrow morning." And, Lyndon remembered, "I was at the bank at 9 a.m. the next morning and there it was." As soon as "the die was cast," Luther Jones recalled, before he had publicly announced, before he had even sent in his resignation from the NYA, Johnson "walked out on the street, and he immediately, first person we passed, stuck his hand out and said, 'I'm Lyndon Johnson. I'm running for Congress.' I bet he shook hands with fifty people before we got to his car."

Johnson read his official announcement from the porch of the Johnson City home. After Lyndon spoke, Sam Johnson, stricken the year before by a massive heart attack, rose to embrace his son. "My father became a young man again," Johnson recalled. "He looked out into all those faces he knew so well and then he looked at me and I saw tears in his eyes as he told the crowd how terribly proud he was of me and how much hope he had for our country if only his son could be up there in the nation's capital with Roosevelt and Rayburn and all those good Democrats. When he finally sat down, they began applauding and they kept applauding for almost ten minutes. I looked over at my mother and saw that she, too, was clapping and smiling. It was a proud moment for the Johnson family."

Johnson's strategy left the competitive field flat-footed. To stand out from the better-known pack, he presented himself as a "total Roosevelt man," trumpeting his support not only for the popular aspects of the New Deal but for the president's recent court-packing plan which had aroused strong opposition. "I don't have to hang back like a steer on the way to the dipping vat," Johnson declared in his best Hill Country vernacular. "I'm for the president. When he calls on me for help I'll be where I can give him a quick lift, not out in the woodshed practicing a way to duck." While several of his competitors eventually backed the court-packing plan, Johnson had already fashioned himself FDR's man in the race.

From the start of the campaign, Johnson believed he could win so long as "he could get up earlier and meet more people and stay up later than anybody else." The youngest man in the contest, Lyndon would simply out-campaign his rivals. He would stop "in every store, every fire station, every place of business," a campaign worker recalled, and he would personally meet every person in there all the way to the back door where the janitor was sitting. He would "press the flesh" and "look them in the eye," as his father had advised him so long ago, and as he had reiterated to the members of his debate team. While his competitors focused on population centers in large cities and towns, Lyndon ventured to every small village and crossroads, searching out far-flung homes and farms. If he spied the glow of a kerosene lamp in the distance, he would back up his car and head for it. With his long legs, he could climb over barbed-wire fences to talk with farmers plowing their fields. He kept his speeches short. "A five minute speech," he pointed out, "with fifteen minutes spent afterward is much more effective than a fifteen minute speech, no matter how inspiring, that leaves only five minutes for handshaking."

He seemed to have "a phenomenal memory not just for names and faces, but for the people behind those names and faces," a historian remarked. What seemed an inborn trait, however, was a deliberately nurtured talent, as it was for Lincoln. Johnson's driver Carroll Keach described the ritual the candidate would follow after each encounter on the campaign trail. He would murmur to himself, meditating out loud. "It was like he was going over his mental notes," Keach recalled. "Who the people were, and little things about them, and who their relatives were," as if he were making "a mental imprint in the back of his mind." Even more importantly, though generally not self-reflective, Lyndon conducted "discussions with himself about what strategy had worked and hadn't worked, and what strategy he should use the next time." If things hadn't gone well, he would scold himself. " 'Boy, that was dumb!' 'Well, you'll just have to do better, that's all.' "

So great was Lyndon's anxiety two days before the special election that perspiration poured down his face as he solicited votes door-to-door in Austin. Severe pains racked his stomach and he felt nauseous. After delivering a speech at a big rally that evening, he collapsed. Rushed to the hospital, doctors found that his appendix was on the verge of rupturing. An emergency operation was necessary. His campaign came to a dead halt. Left in a state of limbo with nowhere to go, no flesh to press, no one to persuade and charm, Lyndon agonized. But his long days of relentless, unstoppable effort had paid off. From his hospital bed he learned that he had won the election, beating his nearest opponent by more than three thousand votes.

Soon after the election, Lyndon met President Franklin Roosevelt. Returning to the port of Galveston, Texas, after a fishing cruise in the Gulf of Mexico, the president greeted the young congressman-elect at the dock and invited him to join his special train as it traveled through the state. Though neither a tarpon fisherman nor a devotee of naval matters, Lyndon, nonetheless, made the most of his opportunity. "I've just met the most remarkable young man," Roosevelt later told White House aide Tommy Corcoran. "Now I like this boy, and you're going to help him with anything you can."

So Lyndon Johnson entered the House of Representatives as a protégé of President Roosevelt, the supreme of a long lineage of fatherly mentors who had abetted his climb: San Marcos president Cecil Evans, Welly Hopkins, Sam Rayburn, Alvin Wirtz. While there is a measure of truth to the criticisms of those who thought that he drew close to older men only to facilitate his rise, Johnson's search for mentors also represented his own emotional need and provided an occasion to learn. "He was very much of a hero worshipper," one New Dealer observed. "He had people he looked up to and depended on." He listened intently to their stories, absorbed their expertise, valued their guidance, and performed whatever tasks they outlined. If he utilized them for his advancement, his devotion to them was authentic, his loyalty to and performance for them without equal.

As Johnson settled in Washington to take up his new position, he recognized once again, as he had during his first days as NYA administrator, the importance of making a striking and dramatic impression before the workaday tasks of the job inundated him. During the campaign, he had promised the people that if elected, he would bring electricity to the Hill Country; that if he had to lobby the president to make it happen, he would do just that. Now, he intended to keep that pledge.

When Franklin Roosevelt took office, nine out of ten American farms had no electricity. "The lack of electric power divided the

United States into two nations," one historian notes, "the city dwellers and the country folk." Farm wives enjoyed none of the conveniences of twentieth-century life — refrigerators, washing machines, irons, vacuum cleaners. Farmers had to rely on hand labor to draw water from a well or milk the cows. For decades, private utility companies had refused to install power lines in rural areas, maintaining that the rate of return in thinly populated areas precluded a profit. With the creation of the Tennessee Valley Authority in 1933 and the Rural Electrification Administration in 1935, the New Deal had brought electricity to millions of farm families, but the needs of the people of the Hill Country had been ignored. Though two government-sponsored dams were being completed in Texas to control floodwaters and potentially generate hydroelectric power, the REA guidelines for building lines and wiring houses required a population density of at least three farms per mile — a requirement the Hill Country could not meet by half. After failing to persuade the REA administrator, John Carmody, to make an exception to the population density requirement, Johnson prevailed upon Tommy Corcoran to arrange a meeting with President Roosevelt.

The story of the two White House meetings between two of the wiliest politicians of the age finally resulted in a triumph for Lyndon

Johnson, a testament to his great salesmanship skills. But the meetings also served as a testament to Roosevelt's humor, judgment, and ability to cut through the rigid parameters of bureaucratic restrictions. The first meeting was congenial but Johnson came away stymied. Roosevelt, as was his habit when not wanting to directly refuse someone, simply filibustered. "Did you ever see a Russian woman naked?" Roosevelt deflected. "And then he started telling me," Johnson remembered, "how their physique was so different from the American woman because they did the heavy work." Johnson entered into the conversation with Roosevelt but "before I knew it," he lamented, "my fifteen minutes was gone . . . and I found myself in the West Lobby without ever having made my proposition. So I had to go back and make that damn appointment all over again."

Before returning, however, Johnson sought Corcoran's advice. Roosevelt liked demonstrations, presentations, pictures, drawings, and maps, Corcoran told him, "the bigger the better. That's where you made your mistake. Don't argue with him, Lyndon, show him." So Johnson assembled an exhibition of three-foot pictures of the two recently constructed dams and a map of the transmission lines that showed the power flowing to the "city big shots" while neglecting the poor folk in the countryside — represented by pictures of old tenant farmer houses. Aware that he was about to be solicited, Roosevelt focused keenly on the pictures of the dams. "I have never seen better or more marvelous examples of multiple-arch construction. It's real ingenuity." This time, Johnson knew enough not to be sidetracked into a conversation about engineering marvels. He hit upon the tactic of absolute silence, until finally, Roosevelt lifted his gaze from the pictures. "Lyndon, now what in the hell do you want? Just why are you showing me all these?"

"Water, water everywhere, not a drop to drink! Power, power, everywhere but not in a home on the banks of these rural rivers!" Johnson began explaining that the people in his district could not get power because of a population density requirement in the REA guidelines. He then, as he later told Lady Bird, painted "a mental picture of all those women out there, old before their time, bending over the wash pot, and all those men getting up on a cold winter morning to milk those cows, where there could have been electric washing machines and milking machines." This aspect of the story was not confined to facts and figures; it was grounded in emotional memories of his mother hauling water from a well, washing clothes on a corrugated washboard, forced to heat the iron on a red-hot wood stove even at the height of summer, scrubbing floors on her hands and knees, consumed by backbreaking chores that left her too exhausted to read the books piled high beside her bed.

Roosevelt was enthralled by the gifts of a fellow storyteller. In the end, he surrendered to the conviction of the young man himself. He asked his secretary to get REA head John Carmody on the line. "John, I have a young congressman in here, Lyndon Johnson. Carmody said yes, he knew me and had turned me down. The REA could not afford to build transmission lines where there were only one and a half customers per square mile." Roosevelt listened, and then turned on the charm. "John, I know you've got to have guidelines and rules and I don't want to upset them, but you just go along with me — just go ahead and approve this loan and charge it to my account. I'll gamble on those folks because I've been down in that country and those folks — they'll catch up to that density problem because they breed pretty quick." Johnson was exultant. "I walked out of there with a million dollar loan," he remembered, savoring the successful meeting as "one of the happiest moments of my life."

To Johnson's lasting regret, his father did not live to witness and share in his son's achievement. The summer after Lyndon took his seat in the House, Sam suffered another heart attack. For two months, he remained in the hospital, kept inside an oxygen tent. When

Johnson returned home that fall, Sam pleaded with his son to bring him "home to that little house in the hills where people know when you're sick and care when you die." Johnson resisted at first; the doctors had told him that his father needed oxygen and that no oxygen tent was available in Stonewall. "You have to help me, son," Sam said. Johnson understood. "I brought him his clothes, helped him dress, and I carried him home." In his own room, surrounded by family and friends, his father seemed to improve, but two weeks later, shortly after his sixtieth birthday, Sam Johnson died.

The same sense of purpose that fueled Johnson's dedication to rural electrification animated a series of kindred New Deal projects. Not long after he took office, Congress passed a bill providing federal funds to cities for slum clearance and public housing projects. In early 1938 the first three grants were awarded: New York, New Orleans, and Austin. How did a small southern city like Austin end up as one of the three successful applicants? "Because," the general counsel of the U.S. Housing Authority, Leon Keyserling, explained, "there was this first-term congressman who was so on his toes, and so active and so overwhelming."

Johnson had been present when Roosevelt signed the public housing bill. Acting with his usual dispatch, he set up a meeting with Austin's mayor and the members of the City Council. "Now, look, I want us to be first in the United States," he told them. "You've got to be willing to stand up for the Negroes and the Mexicans." After taking a walking tour through the city's slum district, Johnson described his findings on a radio broadcast: a hundred Mexican and African American families were crowded into a five-block area, each family confined to "one dreary room where no single window let in the sun. Here they slept, they cooked and ate, they washed themselves in a leaky tub after hauling the water two hundred yards. Here they raised their children, ill-nourished and sordid." When realtors and owners of the slum apartments charged that the government was competing unfairly with private enterprise, Johnson shot back: Yes, indeed, "the government is competing with the shacks and hovels and hogsties and all the other foul holes in which the underprivileged have to live." Once the application was in, Keyserling recalled, Johnson "was up and down our corridors all the time. It was his go-getterness that got the first project for Austin. That's how."

Such was the clamor and din that surrounded Lyndon Johnson when he first took his seat in the House that "a consensus about the boy" and his bright future soon developed among the inner circle of young New Dealers who served in the administration, including Tom Corcoran and Jim Rowe in the White House and Arthur Goldschmidt and Abe Fortas at Interior. Johnson became not simply a member of this group but, as he so intensely craved, the central pin around which the group wheeled. Jim Rowe's wife, Elizabeth, remembered the "marvelous stories" he told and the way he told them, striding around the room, mimicking the voices and mannerisms of the people he was describing. But his "greatest stories," bequeathed by his grandfather, were about the Old West in the days of the cattle drives, about the cast of folkloric personalities who had once sat in the governor's chair in Texas, about his beloved Hill Country. "If Lyndon Johnson was there a party would be livelier," New Deal attorney Abe Fortas said. "The moment he walked in the door, it would take fire."

President Roosevelt's "special interest" in the young congressman also sharpened. There was something he saw in Lyndon Johnson that made him think that "if he [Franklin] hadn't gone to Harvard, that's the kind of uninhibited young pro he'd like to be." Roosevelt went so far as to predict that "in the next generation the balance of power would shift south and west, and this boy could well be the first Southern president."

■ ■ ■ ■

II
ADVERSITY AND
GROWTH

■ ■ ■ ■

FIVE:
ABRAHAM LINCOLN

"I must die or be better"

By the time they were in their late twenties, all four young men knew that they were leaders. In public service, they had found a calling. They had chosen to stand before the people and ask for their support, to make themselves vulnerable. Already, these young men resembled sketches of the leaders we would recognize in the years that followed.

201

For these sketches to become fuller portraits, however, would require the ability to transcend both public and private adversity.

Scholars who have studied the development of leaders have situated resilience, the ability to sustain ambition in the face of frustration, at the heart of potential leadership growth. "Why some people are able to extract wisdom from experience, and others are not," Warren Bennis and Robert Thomas write, remains a critical question. Some people lose their bearings; their lives are forever stunted. Others resume their normal behaviors after a period of time. Still others, through reflection and adaptive capacity, are able to transcend their ordeal, armed with a greater resolve and purpose.

Soon, each of these four men would experience dramatic setbacks. All of them would fall into depression and consider leaving public life.

During a bleak winter in 1840, thirty-two-year-old Abraham Lincoln fell into a depression so profound that his friends feared he might kill himself. They confiscated all knives, razors, and scissors from his room. As the Prairie State entered the third year of recession, the legislature, despite Lincoln's passionate pleas to the contrary, had little choice but to halt work on half-finished railroads, canals, bridges, and roads. As one of the chief architects and advocates of the state's expansive dreams, Lincoln received the lion's share of the blame for the ensuing catastrophe. The crushing debt crippled the state, destroyed its credit rating for years, and deterred new pioneers from settling in Illinois. Land values plummeted, thousands lost their homes, banks and brokerage houses closed down. "Lincoln's roseate hopes of becoming the De Witt Clinton of Illinois," a friend noted, "faded away like the mists of morning." Acknowledging that he was "no financier," Lincoln shouldered responsibility for the crisis and paid a heavy price for that admission. His belief in himself shaken, he announced his retirement from the state legislature at the end of the current term.

Most troubling to Lincoln was the realization that his reputation had been compromised. He had promised the people during his first run for office that if elected, he would support any law providing dependable roads and navigable rivers so the poorest and most thinly populated communities could thrive. That pledge, which he considered binding upon his honor, reputation, and character, had not been fulfilled. The burdens he had sought to lift from the people had instead been multiplied.

The blow to Lincoln's conception of his public integrity coincided with a blow to his private sense of honor, occasioned by his anguished decision to break off his engagement to Mary Todd, the well-educated, intelligent daughter of a wealthy Whig Party member who had served in both the Kentucky House and Senate. The couple had been drawn together by their shared love of poetry and politics. Lincoln's idol, Whig Party leader Henry Clay, had been a frequent guest at the Todd family home; Mary considered herself a passionate Whig; she took pride in her "unladylike" zeal for politics. Her faith in Lincoln's destiny spurred his aspirations and drew them together.

As the courtship moved toward marriage, however, Lincoln began to question the strength of his love for the mercurial young woman who could be affectionate and generous one day and depressed and irritable the next. His best friend Joshua Speed recalled that "in the winter of 40 & 41, he was very unhappy about his engagement to Mary — Not being entirely satisfied that his heart was going with his hand — How much he suffered on that account none Know so well as myself."

Beyond Lincoln's vacillation concerning Mary, he was also anxious, a relative suggested, about "his ability and Capacity to please and support a wife." His work in the legislature and on the stump had taken a toll on his fledgling legal practice. "I am so poor, and make so little headway in the world,"

Lincoln acknowledged, "that I drop back in a month of idleness, as much as I gain in a year's rowing." How could he expect to support a wife and children? Would the responsibilities of family life prevent his continuing pursuit of education and his political ambitions? He possessed no template of a successful family life, no foundation on which to construct his own family. He had seen glimpses of family life — people sitting together at meals, fathers serving as providers — but had never shared in it. Riddled by agitation, Lincoln ended the engagement.

The "breach of honor" soon became common knowledge in the small town of Springfield, magnifying Mary's humiliation. Feeling Mary's sorrows as intensely as his own, Lincoln could not bear the idea that he was responsible for her unhappiness. It "kills my soul," he said. Most damaging of all, he confessed to Speed, he had lost confidence in his ability to keep his "resolves when they are made. In that ability you know, I once prided myself as the only or at least, the chief gem of my character; that gem I lost," and until it is recovered, "I cannot trust myself in any matter of much importance."

That very winter, Joshua Speed was preparing to leave Springfield to return to his family's plantation in Kentucky. His father had died and he felt a responsibility to care for his widowed mother. For seven years,

Speed's general store had been the hub of Springfield's political and social life. He and Lincoln had lived together in a large upstairs room. The two men had traveled together to political events, dances, and parties. The anticipated departure of Speed represented the loss not simply of a friend but of the sole human being with whom Lincoln had shared his private self at a time when he needed companionship the most. Lincoln loved Speed "more than any one dead or living," William Herndon believed. "I shall be verry [*sic*] lonesome without you," Lincoln told Speed. "How miserably things seem to be arranged in this world. If we have no friends, we have no pleasure; and if we have them, we are sure to lose them, and be doubly pained by the loss."

These central events of his personal life combined with the public collapse of the improvement projects he had so wholeheartedly espoused plunged Lincoln into what soon became an incapacitating depression. Lincoln had suffered from bouts of melancholy before. Six years earlier, when his first love, Ann Rutledge, died, he had seemed "indifferent" to life, taking his gun and ominously wandering into the woods. His friends feared that unless he quickly gained equilibrium, "reason would desert her throne." By openly sharing his sorrows with his neighbors in the closely knit New Salem community, however, he had soon been able to return to his law studies and his legislative duties.

This breakdown, when he was thirty-two, was the most serious of his lifetime, with more lasting ramifications. "I am now the most miserable man living," Lincoln wrote his then law partner. "If what I feel were equally distributed to the whole human family, there would not be one cheerful face on the earth. Whether I shall ever be better I can not tell; I awfully forebode I shall not. To remain as I am is impossible; I must die or be better, it appears to me." The letter ended abruptly with the simple statement "I can write no more."

Day after day, he remained bedridden, unable to eat or sleep, unfit to carry out his duties in the legislature. "Lincoln went Crazy," Speed said, "it was terrible." Fellow Illinois lawyer Orville Browning recalled that Lincoln was "delirious to the extent of not knowing what he was doing" and that he "was so much affected as to talk incoherently." He no longer looked "like the same person," one friend remarked. "He is reduced and emaciated in appearance," another friend observed, "and seems scarcely to possess strength enough to speak above a whisper. His case at present is truly deplorable."

The doctors in Springfield believed that Lincoln was "within an inch of being a perfect lunatic for life." Joshua Speed remained with Lincoln throughout this harrowing time. The conversation that passed between them branded both men for the rest of their lives. When Speed warned Lincoln that he must somehow revive his spirits or he would assuredly die, Lincoln replied that he was more than willing to die, but that he had "done nothing to make any human being remember that he had lived." The greatest passion he harbored, he confessed to Speed, was "to link his name with something that would redound to the interest of his fellow man."

The same powerful thirst — the elemental desire to engrave his name in history — that a dozen years before had empowered "a friendless, uneducated, penniless boy, working on a flatboat" to present himself to the settlers of New Salem and ask for their support that he might represent them in the state legislature would rescue him now from the worst personal disintegration of his life.

First, Lincoln had to repair what was lost, to reconstruct both his private and his public life. Step by step, this was to become the task of better than a decade. After leaving the legislature, Lincoln formed a new partnership with Stephen Logan, the leading lawyer in the county, and "one of the finest examples of the purely legal mind" in the West. Logan knew that Lincoln had little methodical understanding of the principles and precedents of law, but he had seen Lincoln's clarity, humor, and speaking skills in dealing with juries, and believed the younger man "would work hard." The partnership turned out well for both men. Lincoln found in Logan a mentor who guided his general reading in the law and became, Lincoln said, "almost a father to me." Logan taught Lincoln "how to prepare his cases" and, most importantly, bolstered the confidence of the self-made lawyer when he occasionally despaired of ever catching up to his college-educated colleagues. "It does not depend on the start a man gets," Logan told him, "it depends on how he keeps up his labors and efforts until middle life." Working together, the two men built up a reliable practice, and finally, Lincoln began to make a decent living.

As doubts about his ability to support a wife began to fade, Lincoln resumed his courtship with Mary. He realized that he had been held back not only by financial insecurity but, as he told Speed, by untenable imaginings of love, by "dreams of Elysium far exceeding all that anything earthly can realize." By committing himself once again to the engagement he had broken, he began to restore his sense of honor; he had proved to himself that he could, indeed, keep his "resolves" — "the chief gem" of his character. While his marriage to Mary proved troublesome at times, Lincoln made great efforts to be a good husband and a kindly, playful father, forging a relationship with his children he had never experienced with his own father. "It is my pleasure that my children are free — happy and unrestrained by paternal tyranny," he noted. "Love is the chain whereby to lock a child to its parent." The life he was leading may have seemed commonplace, but to him it was no small thing to have built, for the first time, a firm foundation of domestic and financial security, without which little else would have been possible.

That chance plays a master role in the fortunes of leaders is vividly illustrated by Lincoln's experience. As the Illinois economy began to revive, so, too, did Lincoln's inert political ambitions. "Now if you should hear any one say that Lincoln don't want to go to Congress," he instructed a Whig friend shortly after his marriage, "I wish you as a personal friend of mine, would tell him you have reason to believe he is mistaken. The truth is, I would like to go very much."

In the years since Lincoln's first election to the state legislature, when aspirants simply stepped forth and nominated themselves, both Whigs and Democrats had developed a convention system to nominate candidates for public office. That the Whigs enjoyed a strong majority in the 7th Congressional

District, which included Sangamon County, boded well for Lincoln. If he gained the nomination, victory was certain. To buffer potential dissension among potential rivals, however, the Whigs in the 7th District had recently adopted the principle of rotation: each nominee agreed to serve a single term and then give way to the next. Thus John Hardin, the son of a U.S. senator, would be nominated in 1842; Edward Baker, a member of the State Senate, in 1844; then, lastly, Abraham Lincoln in 1846. The rotating system promised each candidate united support when his turn came, but such brief congressional tenure hardly offered time for even the most striking among them to make a lasting impression. Given this single-term system, the Congress of the 1840s seemed an unlikely place to further the fierce aspirations of a man like Abraham Lincoln, thought by one friend to be "as ambitious of earthly honors as any man of his time" and by another as "the most ambitious man in the world."

Hardly two weeks after Lincoln's arrival in Washington, the freshman congressman introduced an eye-catching resolution on the House floor that called into question the legitimacy of the recently completed Mexican-American War. He charged that President James K. Polk had deliberately provoked Mexico into war, "trusting to escape scrutiny, by fixing the public gaze upon the exceeding brightness of military glory." He proceeded to contrast the president's war message to "the half insane mumbling of a fever dream," revealing a guilty mind "running hither and thither, like some tortured creature on a burning surface." This was a far cry from the careful, step-by-step analysis that would later characterize Lincoln's public reasoning. His impatient need for widespread recognition had managed only to inflame Democrats, vex Whigs, and lose support in Illinois, where patriotic zeal over the victorious war ran high.

The 1848 presidential race provided Lincoln with an opportunity to distinguish himself among his colleagues in a more effective manner, one based upon his unique charisma and storytelling gifts. Speaking on the House floor on behalf of the Whigs' candidate, war hero General Zachary Taylor, Lincoln won high praise from fellow Whigs and reporters alike for a thoughtful, yet humorous speech. He impressed them, one reporter noted, as "a very able, acute, uncouth, honest, upright young man." The *Baltimore American* rated the highly original performance "the crack speech of the day," observing that "Lincoln's manner was so good-natured and his style so peculiar that he kept the House in a continuous roar of merriment." As he spoke, he roamed up and down the aisle, continually "talking, gesticulating," in a fashion so electrifying and entertaining that Hannibal Hamlin (who would later serve as Lincoln's vice president) inquired as to the identity of the young man. "Abe Lincoln," the colleague marveled, "the best story teller in the House." Whig Party chieftains were so taken by his speech that they invited Lincoln to stump for Taylor that fall in New England.

Years later Lincoln vividly recalled that first visit to Massachusetts. "I had been chosen to Congress then from the Wild West and with hayseed in my hair, I went to Massachusetts, the most cultured state in the union, to take a few lessons in deportment." Self-mockery aside, he required no instruction to connect with eastern audiences, who found his droll storytelling style novel, diverting, and unique. His speeches in a dozen different cities, reporters noted, were "replete with good sense, sound reasoning, and irresistible argument, and spoken with the perfect command of manner and matter which so eminently distinguishes the western orators."

Far more important than the popularity he excited from the partisan Whig audience was the greater consciousness, sensitivity, and emotional understanding Lincoln gained concerning the issue of slavery. The vast new territories acquired from Mexico had reignited the slavery issue. While slavery was protected by the Constitution in the states where it already existed, that protection did not apply to the newly acquired territories. Before the war ended, Pennsylvania congressman David Wilmot had affixed an amendment to a war appropriations bill, which stipulated that "neither slavery nor involuntary servitude shall ever exist in any part of said territory." While this Wilmot Proviso passed the House over and over again, it was repeatedly blocked in the southern-dominated Senate. Though Lincoln later claimed he had voted for the Wilmot Proviso "at least forty times," he had not spoken a single word about slavery on the House floor.

During his swing through Massachusetts, unlike in Illinois, the oxygen was sucked from every room he entered by passionate discussions about slavery. This experience would quicken Lincoln's evolving views on the issue that would rend the country in the decade ahead. At Tremont Temple in Boston, he heard a passionate keynote speech by William Henry Seward, the former governor and future senator from New York. Seward argued that "the time had come for sharp definition of opinion and boldness of utterance." Lincoln and Seward shared a bedroom the following night and stayed up long past midnight engrossed in a discussion about slavery. "I reckon you are right," Lincoln told Seward in the early morning hours. "We have got to deal with this slavery question, and got to give much more attention to it hereafter than we have been doing."

After Taylor won the election in November 1848, Lincoln returned to Congress for the final three-month rump session, resolved to make his voice heard on the slavery issue. Working for weeks, he crafted what he considered an equitable, almost mathematically balanced proposal. He began by conceding that the Constitution protected slavery in the states where it already existed, but proceeded to argue that Congress had the right, under its authority to control affairs in the nation's capital, to address slavery within the District of Columbia. Accordingly, on the one hand he called for the gradual emancipation of slaves within the District; on the other, he insisted that the government compensate slaveholders for the full value of their slaves. Furthermore, he argued that local authorities be equipped to arrest and deliver up fugitive slaves from the South who were attempting to find sanctuary in the District and that the people of the District should have a chance to vote on his proposal. However logically balanced his formulaic proposal, it failed to fathom the irreconcilability of sentiments in the North and the South. The abolitionist Wendell Phillips chastised Lincoln as "that slave hound from Illinois," while proslavery forces refused to contemplate any form of emancipation that opened the door to abolishing slavery in the country at large. Without sufficient endorsement from either side, Lincoln withdrew his carefully measured compromise.

Historians generally consider Lincoln's single term in Congress a failure, an assessment with which Lincoln himself would likely concur. He had served the Whig cause with strident fidelity, but the scope of his ambition was higher than party and wider than geographic section.

Upon returning to Illinois, he had expected that his vigorous advocacy on Taylor's behalf would gain him an important presidential appointment. He had focused his fondest hopes upon securing the position of commissioner of the Land Office, a powerful sub-cabinet post that would oversee all federal lands in the western states, allowing him the opportunity to redress the pledge he had made when he first ran for office — to do all that he could to promote economic development in the poorest communities by providing government aid for roads, railways, and navigable rivers. He reckoned his failure to deliver on that promise not merely a political failure but a moral one. The commissionership would provide a rare opportunity for reparation; but in the end, the post was given to another Whig politician who had prudently kept silent on the probity of the war's origin, when Lincoln had scathingly impugned the president for a popular war already waged and won.

Upon learning that he had been bypassed for the position he coveted, Lincoln "despaired of ever rising in the world," Herndon recollected. Lincoln voiced a sentiment that would become a refrain in his troubled passage to middle age: "How hard — Oh how hard it is to die and leave one's country no better than if one had never lived." Years later, after he had become president, the emotions of this moment remained so intense, Lincoln remembered, that "I hardly ever felt so bad about any failure in my life."

The half-decade that followed Lincoln's brief and unhappy tenure in Congress is often depicted as a period of withdrawal from public life. He himself claimed that he "was losing interest in politics." Although one might suspect his claim, it is undeniable that he "practiced law more assiduously than ever before." Furthermore, this waiting period was anything but a passive time; it was, on the contrary, an intense period of personal, intellectual, moral, and professional growth, for during these years he learned to position himself as a lawyer and a leader able to cope with the tremors that were beginning to rack the country.

What fired in Lincoln this furious and

fertile time of self-improvement? The answer lay in his readiness to gaze in the mirror and soberly scrutinize himself. Taking stock, he found himself wanting. From the beginning, young Lincoln aspired to nothing less than to inscribe his name into the book of communal memory. To fulfill what he believed to be his destiny, a different kind of sustained effort and discipline was required, a willingness to confront weakness and imperfection, reflect upon failure, and examine the kind of leader he wanted to be.

The diligence and studiousness he exhibited during this period of introspection would have been remarkable in a young student; in a man of forty, it was astounding. Lincoln's avid self-improvement commenced with a fresh reexamination of and rededication to his chosen profession. Upon resuming his legal practice after returning to Illinois, he noted with matter-of-fact candor: "I am not an accomplished lawyer." Lincoln had already practiced law for twelve years and was earning sufficient money to support his family. But after a long hiatus politicking, he felt that his legal prowess had atrophied while the profession had grown more complex and sophisticated in his absence, requiring greater powers of reasoning and "a broad knowledge of the principles" beneath the statutory law. No sooner had Lincoln returned to his law practice than William Herndon observed a decided change in his partner's demeanor. Acknowledging "a certain lack of discipline — a want of mental training and method" — Lincoln began to apply himself mightily and, in Herndon's experience, "no man had greater power of application. Once fixing his mind on any subject, nothing could interfere with or disturb him."

In Lincoln's day, the judges, lawyers, witnesses, and bailiffs traveled together on "the circuit" eight weeks every spring and fall. Covering some 150 miles, the traveling bar, like a theater troupe, moved from one county seat to another, holding court and trying cases in dozens of sparsely settled villages and towns. Villagers came from miles around to witness the courtroom drama as hundreds of cases were tried, ranging from murder, assault, and robbery, to disputed wills, collection of debts, and patent challenges. With the arrival of the circuit, the county seats bustled with excitement and anticipation, much like a fair coming to town. The itinerant troupe would settle in the overcrowded local tavern for the night, always forced to share rooms and often beds.

Lincoln relished this convivial setting; but more importantly, it was on the circuit that he managed to create the time and space needed to conduct his intensive course of study — a curriculum that extended well beyond the practical parameters of the law.

He studied philosophy, astronomy, science, political economy, history, literature, poetry, and drama. He struggled to work out mathematical theorems and proofs. From his earliest years, when unable to understand what someone had said, he would turn the phrases over in his mind, battering his brow against them until he could capture their meaning. So now, with mathematics, he persisted "almost to the point of exhaustion," until he could proudly claim that he had "nearly mastered the Six Books of Euclid."

Lincoln "would read and study for hours," Herndon recalled, long after everyone else had gone to sleep, "placing a candle on a chair at the head of his bed," often remaining in this position until 2 a.m. "How he could maintain his mental equilibrium or concentrate his thoughts on an abstract mathematical proposition" while the snores of his roommates rumbled the air was a puzzle, marveled Herndon, "none of us could ever solve." Not only did Lincoln stay up later than colleagues, but "he was in the habit of rising earlier." One circuit rider recalled how Lincoln would "sit by the fire, having uncovered the coals, and muse and ponder, and soliloquize." A stranger entering the room and hearing Lincoln "muttering to himself," might have imagined "he had suddenly gone insane." But these fellow circuit riders knew Lincoln, so they only "listened and laughed."

What might have seemed to an outsider a picture of leaden dejection was rather Lincoln's peculiar manner of figuring things out — a form of mental wrestling. Then, once the breakfast bell rang, Lincoln hurriedly dressed, joined his cohorts at breakfast, and readied himself for the cases he would try over the course of the day. So successful did Lincoln become in defending his clients and speaking before juries, that he soon developed "the largest trial practice of all his peers in central Illinois."

The key to Lincoln's success was his uncanny ability to break down the most complex case or issue "into its simplest elements." He never lost a jury by fumbling with or reading from a prepared argument, relying instead "on his well-trained memory." He aimed for intimate conversations with the jurors, as if conversing with friends. Though his arguments were "logical and profound," they were "easy to follow," fellow lawyer Henry Clay Whitney observed. "His language was composed of plain Anglo-Saxon words and almost always absolutely without adornment." An Illinois judge captured the essence of Lincoln's appeal: "He had the happy and unusual faculty of making the jury believe they — and not he — were trying the case."

When the courtroom closed, the lawyers, who had fought one another during the day, would come together as friends in the tavern at night, eating supper at the same long table with Judge David Davis presiding. Once the meal was done, everyone would gather before a blazing fire to drink, smoke tobacco, and engage in conversation. Neither a smoker nor a drinker, Lincoln nevertheless commanded respect and attention with his never-ending stream of stories, whether the crowd was ten, fifty, or several hundred. "His power of mimicry," Herndon noted, "and his manner of recital, were in many respects unique, if not remarkable. His countenance and all his features seemed to take part in the performance. As he neared the pith or point of the joke or story every vestige of seriousness disappeared from his face. His little gray eyes sparkled," and when he reached the point, "no one's laugh was heartier than his." There are myriad accounts of Lincoln's stories and tales, but the common denominator is that long after the laughter ended, they provoked thought and discussion. Small wonder that Lincoln drew crowds from the countryside eager to be regaled and entertained by a master storyteller.

Despite his blossoming reputation, incessant striving, and self-imposed scholastic regime, Lincoln treated everyone, high or low, without a trace of affectation, with the same tenderhearted patience, the same generous and helpful kindliness and empathy that had drawn the protective affection of the settlers of New Salem to him when the twenty-three-year-old first appeared on the banks of the Sangamon River. "No lawyer on the circuit was more unassuming than was Mr. Lincoln," a fellow lawyer recalled. "He arrogated to himself no superiority over anyone — not even the most obscure member of the bar." The seating arrangements at the tavern table reflected the hierarchy of the court. Judge Davis would preside, surrounded by the lawyers at the head of the table. On one occasion when Lincoln had settled himself at the foot among the common clientele the landlord told him: "You're in the wrong place, Mr. Lincoln, come up here." Lincoln queried: "Have you anything better to eat up there, Joe? If not, I'll stay here."

As Lincoln became a leader in his profession, he assumed responsibility for mentoring the next generation. "He was remarkably gentle with young lawyers," his colleagues noted. Henry Whitney was deeply affected by how "kindly and cordially" Lincoln treated him when he first arrived at the bar. If a new clerk appeared in court, "Lincoln was the first — sometimes the only one — to shake hands with him and congratulate him on his election."

The art of communication, Lincoln advised newcomers to the bar, "is the lawyer's avenue to the public." Yet, Lincoln warned, the lawyer must not rely on rhetorical glibness or persuasiveness alone. What is well-spoken must be yoked to what is well-thought. And such thought is the product of great labor, "the drudgery of the law." Without that labor, without that drudgery, the most eloquent words lack gravity and power. Even "extemporaneous speaking should be practiced and cultivated." Indeed, "the leading rule for the lawyer, *as for the man of every other calling,* is diligence. Leave nothing for tomorrow that can be done to-day." The key to success, he insisted, is "work, work, work."

Lincoln's mind was his "workshop," a fellow lawyer recalled. "He needed no office, no pen, ink and paper; he could perform his chief labor by self-introspection." During this waiting period, he was not simply enlarging his grasp of law and his growing practice, nor was he *generally* educating himself to fulfill the constitutional need and intellectual curiosity of his nature. For although he eschewed politics and professed no great interest in returning to the national fray, his pursuit of knowledge was anything but random. It was directed toward understanding the role and the purpose of leadership.

Two eulogies delivered during this time of introspection, the first for Zachary Taylor, the second for Henry Clay, cast light into that workshop, revealing Lincoln's evolving thoughts on leadership. The first eulogy

224

argued that while Zachary Taylor's military leadership was not distinguished by "brilliant military manoeuvers," he succeeded "by the exercise of a sober and steady judgment, coupled with a dogged incapacity to understand that defeat was possible. His rarest military trait was a combination of negatives — absence of excitement and absence of fear. He could not be flurried, and he could not be scared."

The 1852 eulogy for Clay struck a far more personal note, for the Kentucky statesman had been a major figure and mentor in Lincoln's life. Early on, the young Lincoln had identified with the image of the self-risen, self-educated lawyer and politician who had been elected speaker of the house in his early thirties, served multiple terms in the Senate, and been nominated for president three times by the Whigs. For Lincoln, that Henry Clay had dined on numerous occasions with Mary's family in Lexington lent a luminous quality to the Todd household.

In his lengthy address, Lincoln identified three leadership attributes in Clay that accounted for the "enduring spell" he had cast on the American people. To start, Clay possessed an unsurpassed eloquence, which proceeded not from an "elegant arrangement of words and sentences" but "from great sincerity" and "thorough conviction." Eloquence without judgment, however, counts

225

for nothing, and without the will to sustain both, leadership would fail. What made Clay, in Lincoln's mind, "the man for a crisis," was the fusing of these leadership qualities with crucible moments in the country at large. "In all the great questions which have agitated the country," Lincoln pointed out, most particularly those surrounding the issue of slavery, Clay had been able, decade after decade, to quell rancor and bring opposing parties together in compromise. Time and again, he resisted "extremes of opinion" in both North and South. "Whatever he did, he did for the whole country."

While the slavery issue had been a source of division between North and South from the beginning of the nation, every expansion of territory reignited the smoldering embers. When Missouri, part of the vast territory acquired by the Louisiana Purchase, "knocked at the door" for admission as a slave state, an angry struggle ensued between North and South. Constructed under Clay's leadership, the Missouri Compromise of 1820 brought an end to the escalating tensions. It granted Missouri's request for statehood, admitted Maine as a free state, and drew an imaginary line: territories north of that line would enter the Union as free states; those below would be slave states. For the following three decades, the Missouri Compromise kept that peace until Congress was called upon to decide the fate of the territories acquired by the Mexican War. Speaking for many southerners, Robert Toombs of Georgia warned: "If by your legislation you seek to drive us from the territories of California and New Mexico, purchased by the common blood and treasure of the whole people, *I am for disunion.*"

Once again, Lincoln said, the nation turned to Henry Clay and once again, the seventy-three-year-old senator forged a compromise that promised to keep the Union intact. The Compromise of 1850 admitted California as a free state but brought Utah and New Mexico into the Union with no restrictions on slavery; it called for an end to the slave trade in the District of Columbia, but asked Congress to strengthen the old Fugitive Slave Law, empowering federal officials to draft citizens to hunt down escapees in free states. For his role in these two critical compromises, Lincoln regarded Clay, as did a grateful nation, as "The Great Pacificator."

While the 1850 Compromise seemed to end the crisis, the new, more strenuous provisions in the Fugitive Slave Law sparked the fury of antislavery activists in the North. Violent disturbances broke out when slaveholders tried to recapture runaway slaves who had settled in Boston and New York. While Lincoln, too, was dismayed about the provision bolstering the Fugitive Slave Law, his unhappiness was superseded by the fact a solution had been reached. "Devotion to the Union," he maintained, "rightfully inclined men to yield somewhat, in points where nothing could have so inclined them." William Herndon, who now considered himself an abolitionist, was frustrated by Lincoln's "apparent conservatism when the needs of the hour were so great." The issue of slavery began to dominate discussion on the circuit, as the lawyers argued over the various journals they were reading — the antislavery papers in the North and the proslavery papers in the South. The center was being drained while both extremes were hunkering down with rampant animosity. "The time is coming," a fellow lawyer told Lincoln, "when we shall have to be all either Abolitionists or Democrats." The 1850 Compromise lasted only four years.

Lincoln was on the circuit when he heard the news that Congress, after prolonged debate, had passed the controversial Kansas-Nebraska Act. Designed by Stephen Douglas of Illinois, the popular leader of the Democratic Party (presently in his second term in the Senate and a presumptive contender for president), the bill would allow settlers in the new territories of Kansas and Nebraska, both of which stood above the dividing line created by the 1820 Missouri Compromise, to decide for themselves whether they wanted to enter the Union as slave or free states.

"Popular sovereignty" — the simplistic evasion at the heart of the bill — would release slavery from its southern cage and allow it to aggressively spread. In one stroke, the three-decades-old Missouri Compromise had been obliterated. No longer was slavery on the path to ultimate extinction, as Lincoln had hoped and believed. Lincoln grasped at once the meaning, ramification, and gravity of the new law. The situation of the slave was now "fixed, and hopeless of change for the better." Before speaking out, Lincoln withdrew to the State Library, where he investigated the slavery issue and the debates at the time the Constitution was framed, searching and researching logically and methodically until, as Herndon once remarked, he knew his subject "inside and outside, upside and downside." As a boy, when Lincoln was on "such a hunt for an idea," he could not sleep until he had "caught it." He was on a hunt now, and would not sleep until he caught what he was after — a way of hammering the issue of slavery into the story of our country and the impasse of the present moment.

Fragmented notes penned during this period reveal Lincoln's attempt to boil down the slavery argument into its elemental components. "If A. can prove, however conclusively, that he may, of right, enslave B,"

Lincoln began, "why may not B. snatch the same argument, and prove equally, that he may enslave A? You say A. is white, and B. is black. It is color, then; the lighter, having the right to enslave the darker? Take care. By this rule, you are to be slave to the first man you meet, with a fairer skin than your own. You do not mean color exactly? You mean the whites are intellectually the superiors of the blacks, and therefore have the right to enslave them? Take care again. By this rule, you are to be slave to the first man you meet, with an intellect superior to your own." To Lincoln, this fragment was more than an exercise in logic. By extension, A. and B. were dramatic personifications of antagonistic points of view. Each exercise of logic was a small drama of contention and persuasion, a kernel of full-blown argument and debate as yet enacted only in Lincoln's mind.

It would not be long before Lincoln's scattered thoughts would dramatically unfold as full-blown arguments and debate with his old rival, Stephen Douglas. Lincoln and Douglas had met nearly two decades earlier during nightly sessions around the fire in Joshua Speed's general store. "We were both young then," Lincoln later wrote. "Even then, we were both ambitious; I, perhaps, quite as much so as he. With me the race of ambition has been a failure — a flat failure; with *him* it has been one of splendid success. His name fills the nation."

In the fall of 1854, Douglas returned to Illinois to defend the Kansas-Nebraska Act, which had fomented mass protest meetings throughout the North. Appalled by the hostility he encountered, even in his own Illinois, Douglas chose a series of public forums where he might champion the inviolable principle of self-government. After a preliminary skirmish with Lincoln at the Springfield State Fair, the two men engaged in a highly publicized joust in Peoria. While Douglas rode into the second largest city in Illinois "at the head of a triumphal procession, seated in a carriage drawn by four beautiful white palfreys and preceded by a band of music," Lincoln arrived without fanfare sometime after midnight. By early afternoon, an enormous crowd, seated in chairs, standing, or sprawled on the grass, had spilled over the public square; hundreds of farmers had traveled long distances to hear the two men speak. Speaking from the courthouse balcony, the "Little Giant," as the short, stocky Douglas was called, stripped off his jacket and, like a spirited pugilist, inflamed the crowd with a speech that ran three hours long.

By the time Lincoln's turn came, it was past five in the evening. "I wish you to hear me thro," he said. "It will take me as long as it has taken him. That will carry us beyond eight o'clock at night," well past suppertime.

So he suggested that everyone take a break, enjoy dinner, and reassemble in the cooler evening air at seven. He further told the crowd that he had agreed to let Douglas have an additional hour to reply after his own three-hour rejoinder. This gesture, he acknowledged, "was not wholly unselfish," for it assured that the Douglas Democrats would return and stay to the end, "for the fun of hearing him skin me." Then, turning to the audience, he asked: "What do you say?" And "immediately, a cheer went up," one attendee recalled, "accompanied by the throwing of hats in the air, and other demonstrations of approval."

Even in this brief, lighthearted negotiation for a supper delay, Lincoln had established an intimacy of tone as between friends who agree on a date later in the evening. That the members of the audience readily returned, and indeed, swelled in number, for a torch-lit evening session that would last until the hour before midnight, demonstrates the high level of citizen interest and participation in politics in the 1850s. With few public entertainments available in rural America, villagers and farmers regarded the spoken word and political debates as riveting spectator sports.

It was an age when the gift for oratory was essential to political success, when audiences listened with rapt attention to lengthy, well-researched speeches. Indeed, at Peoria, the audience was asked to give seven hours of concentrated thought broken only by a supper intermission. Following such debates, the dueling remarks were regularly printed in their entirety in newspapers and then reprinted in pamphlet form to reach distant villages and farms, where they provoked discourse over a wider space and prolonged time. Such circumstances were ideally suited for Abraham Lincoln — a natural storyteller with an exceptional range of oral and written skills of communication. He could simultaneously educate, entertain, and move his audiences with recognizable tales replete with such accessible, humorous, everyday images that they were remembered and repeated far and wide.

True to the storyteller's art, Lincoln began his speech by explaining the situation that had brought the people together — the looming expansion of slavery begotten by the Kansas-Nebraska Act. He then took his listeners back to their common beginnings, to the founding of the nation, unraveling a narrative to demonstrate that when the Constitution was adopted, "the plain, unmistakable spirit of that age, towards slavery, was hostility to the *principle,* and toleration, *only by necessity,*" because slavery was unhappily knit into the origin of America's social and economic life. Stressing the fact that the word "slavery" was deliberately omitted from the

Constitution, Lincoln claimed that the framers concealed it, "just as an afflicted man hides away a wen or a cancer, which he dares not cut out at once, lest he bleed to death; with the promise, nevertheless, that the cutting may begin at the end of a given time."

In recent decades, Lincoln argued, with the line of the Missouri Compromise firmly in place, slavery had seemed to be on the wane; the time for excising the wen — returning to the ideals set forth in the Declaration of Independence — was in sight at last. "But now," with the line of compromise rescinded by this disastrous law, slavery had been "transformed into a 'sacred right,' " suddenly placed "on the high road to extension and perpetuity; and, with a pat on its back, [the law] says to it, 'Go, and God speed you.' "

To demonstrate the thorny problem created by removing the imaginary line that had separated the country North and South and had prohibited expansion of slavery north of latitude 36°30', Lincoln had developed a string of metaphors drawn from the worlds of farming, pastures, fences, and livestock. Imagine, Lincoln suggested, two adjacent farms with a dividing fence between them. Suddenly, one farmer, whose prairie grass had dried up, removed the fence so his famished cattle could feed on his neighbor's meadow. "You rascal," protested the neighbor. "What have you done?" The farmer replied: "I have taken down your fence; but nothing more. It is my true intent and meaning not to drive my cattle into your meadow, nor to exclude them therefrom, but to leave them perfectly free to form their own notions of the feed, and to direct their movements in their own way." No person in the audience failed to comprehend the analogy between this parable and Douglas's deceitful claim that by removing the line there was no intent to bring slavery into northern territory.

The figurative language Lincoln used was designed to let the people see for themselves the profoundly threatening aspects of the Nebraska law, just as he had sought to make each jury believe that "they — and not *he* — were trying the case." Having brought his listeners to understand the impasse created by the new law, he was then able to suggest a way forward. The Nebraska Act must be repealed; the Missouri Compromise must be restored. "The doctrine of self government," as set forth in the Declaration of Independence, "is right — absolutely and eternally right," declared Lincoln, but to apply it, as Douglas proposed, to extend slavery, perverted its very meaning. To allow slavery into new territory where it did not already exist by the original bargain of the Constitution would spark an open war with the "spirit of concession and compromise" that had marked the history of the Union. "Let us

235

return [slavery] to the position our fathers gave it," Lincoln implored.

This was no abolitionist credo; first, and last, the credo was containment. In arguing against the Nebraska Act, Lincoln made it clear that he had "no prejudice against the Southern people. They are just what we would be in their situation. If slavery did not now exist amongst them, they would not introduce it. If it did exist amongst us, we should not instantly give it up." But if empathy allowed Lincoln to comprehend the difficulty of dealing with slavery where it already existed (and with all humility, he confessed that he had no easy solution to resolve that dilemma), he considered the annulment of the Missouri line a violent act that, if not reversed, might well lead to the destruction of the Union. The choice we face, he told them, is all of ours together. If we allow the Kansas-Nebraska Act to stand, if we allow slavery to spread, then the hope of America and all that it means to the whole world will be extinguished. But if we join together, "we shall not only have saved the Union; but we shall have saved it, as to make, and to keep it, forever worthy of the saving."

"The whole house was still as death," the *Springfield Journal* observed, "and when he finished, the audience approved the glorious triumph of truth by loud and continued huzzas." Contemporary accounts considered

Lincoln's speech the most accessible, persuasive, and profound argument ever made against the extension of slavery. He penetrated his subject with deep insight and carried his listeners along to his way of thinking. What persuaded and changed minds was the sincerity, clarity, conviction, and passion of the story he told. "The inspiration that possessed him took possession of his hearers also," a young reporter noted. "His speaking went to the heart because it came from the heart. I have heard celebrated orators who could start thunders of applause without changing any man's opinion. Mr. Lincoln's eloquence was of the higher type, which produced conviction in others because of the conviction of the speaker himself."

Even those who had heard Lincoln speak over the years were taken aback. "When," they asked one another, "had he mastered the history of the slavery questions so completely?" The answer lay in the long period of work, creative introspection, research, and grinding thought that emerged in the wake of his dispiriting time in Congress and his failure to secure the high-ranking position he thought he deserved after sustained party politicking. From that crucible of self-doubt had come an accelerated striving, a self-willed intellectual, metaphysical, and personal growth. Never again would he assume that his side of the aisle held a monopoly on righteousness; never again would he deploy satire as a means to vindictively humiliate another.

"Nothing so much marks a man as bold imaginative expressions," Ralph Waldo Emerson wrote in his diary, speaking of Socrates and the golden sayings of Pythagoras: "A complete statement in the imaginative form of an important truth arrests attention and is respected and remembered." Such oratory "will make the reputation of a man." The way Lincoln had learned to use language, the collective story he told, and the depth of his conviction marked a turning point in his reputation as both a man and a leader.

"A great storyteller will always be rooted in the people," essayist Walter Benjamin writes. "It is granted to him to reach back to a whole lifetime," culling from "his own experience" as well as "the experience of others" to unfold narratives that provide counsel, advice, and direction. Such storytellers are "teachers and sages," he remarked. "Counsel woven into the fabric of real life is wisdom." This was the leadership voice Abraham Lincoln had developed during his long waiting period.

Everyone who had known him in earlier years remarked upon changes that had begun to transform him from a local politician and country lawyer into the personage connoted today by the name of Abraham Lincoln. People observed that something large and lasting had happened during this introspective crucible period, something that could be gauged in his appearance and demeanor, his manner of delivery, and his profundity of thought.

In the antislavery struggle, he had found the great purpose that would thrust him back into public life, and that purpose, larger by far than his large personal ambition, would hold him fast until he died.

Two giant strides toward Lincoln's ascension to the presidency were, ironically, his two failed efforts, in 1855 and 1858, to become the U.S. senator from Illinois.

In 1855, in a clear-cut surrender of personal ambition to moral principle, Lincoln orchestrated his own defeat to ensure victory for a fellow antislavery man over a pro-Nebraska candidate. In January, when the 100-member state legislature convened to choose a new senator, Lincoln was the clear "first choice" of 47 of the anti-Nebraska Whigs; the candidate of the Douglas Democrats had 41 votes; and a small band of five independent Democrats, who had broken from Douglas after the passage of the Kansas-Nebraska Act, held the balance of power. Led by Norman Judd of Chicago, this little band supported Democratic congressman Lyman Trumbull for senator. A deadlock went on into the night, until Lincoln instructed his Whig supporters to vote for Trumbull, fearing that the Douglas Democrat would win. Lincoln's supporters were heartbroken, claiming the unfairness of "the 47 men being controlled by the 5," but they followed Lincoln's directive and Trumbull was elected senator. "The agony is over at last," the chagrined Lincoln wrote a friend, but the defeat of the Douglas Democrat "gives me more pleasure than my own [defeat] gives me pain."

When Lincoln ran in 1858 for the U.S. Senate he represented the new Republican Party, assembled from the disparate opponents of the Nebraska bill — antislavery Whigs, bolting Democrats, Free Soilers, abolitionists. As the leader who had fused this fragile coalition in the Prairie State, Abraham Lincoln was the overwhelming choice of Illinois Republicans to oppose the incumbent Democrat, Stephen Douglas. Recalling the generosity Lincoln had exercised three years earlier in his first run for the Senate, when he had maneuvered his own defeat to ensure victory for an antislavery Democrat, hundreds of party activists stood ready to commit their energies to ensure Lincoln's victory.

Lincoln's opening campaign statement offers a clear glimpse into his general blueprint for orienting his followers by gentle education and persuasion. "If we could first know *where* we are and *whither* we are tending, we could then better judge *what* to do and *how* to do it." With this simple statement, he launched upon a communal storytelling voyage with his audience so they might collectively address a problem and together set about to forge a solution. "A house divided against itself cannot stand," he began, echoing the gospels of Mark and Matthew, invoking an easily approachable image of the Union as a house in danger of collapse under the pressure of slavery advocates who, by repealing the Missouri Compromise, had jeopardized the integrity of the entire structure. Despite the ominous metaphor of a collapsing house, the tone of Lincoln's speech was positive, exhorting Republicans to recapture control of the nation's building blocks by restoring the laws that prevented the extension of slavery. If slavery were again on a course to eventual extinction, people in all sections could once more live peaceably in the revered house their forefathers had built.

All was now in readiness for the historic convergence of the Lincoln-Douglas debates, seven face-to-face encounters that attracted tens of thousands of people and fastened the attention of tens of millions more who read the full transcripts in leading papers across the country. If it was Douglas, the leading Democratic candidate for president in 1860, who drew the public and national journalists to the debates, it was Lincoln, then barely known outside his state, who made the lasting impression. "Who is this man that is replying to Douglas in your State?" an eastern political figure asked an Illinois journalist. "Do you realize that no greater speeches have been made on public questions in the history of our country; that his knowledge of the subject is profound, his logic unanswerable, his style inimitable?" When voters went to the polls that November, Republicans won a popular majority of the statewide vote, for which Lincoln received a great share of the credit. Nonetheless, by means of an unfair and outdated reapportionment scheme, the Democrats retained control of the state legislature, which promptly reelected Stephen Douglas to the U.S. Senate.

Once again, Lincoln's personal aspirations were dashed, but he accepted loss with equanimity. Days later, while "the emotions of defeat" were still "fresh" upon him, he wrote dozens of consoling letters to his supporters. Characteristically, it was he who consoled them rather than the other way around. To his friend Dr. Anson Henry, he wrote: "I am glad I made the late race. It gave me a hearing on the great and durable question of the age, which I could have had in no other way." After hearing that another friend was despondent, Lincoln promised, "You will soon feel better. Another 'blow-up' is coming; and we shall have fun again." The serenity and composure he exhibited were not simply to hearten his followers. Lincoln was in dead earnest. He trusted that this was a temporary loss. The antislavery fight not only would continue; it *must* continue until it was won.

"No man of this generation has grown more rapidly before the country than Lincoln in this canvass," editorialized the *Evening Post* as the Senate race came to a close. The knowledge of Lincoln's leadership capacities was rapidly spreading. When a friend suggested that he might well be considered a formidable presidential candidate, however, Lincoln protested, noting that William Henry Seward, Salmon Chase, and others "were so much better known." They were the men who had "carried this movement forward to its present status." Seward had been New York's youngest governor before his election to the Senate, where his fiery speeches won a passionate following among northern liberals and marked him as the nation's most celebrated antislavery politician. Chase, now the first Republican governor of Ohio, had been the Senate leader in the fight against the passage of the Kansas-Nebraska Act and was one of the founders of the Republican Party. Judge Edward Bates, a widely respected native Virginian who had migrated to Missouri and joined the antislavery cause, had a natural constituency among conservatives throughout the North and within the southern tier of the mid-western states.

While recognizing that he had only an outside chance, Lincoln quietly pursued the nomination. From the start, he understood, with a raw political instinct as keen as his ambition, that the only path to his nomination against three celebrated opponents required a combination of relentless determination and self-effacing humility. By holding back, by not thrusting his own candidacy forward, he gained the goodwill of tens of thousands of fellow Republicans by speaking solely on behalf of the party and the Republican cause. In dozens of rousing speeches, delivered in cities and towns throughout the North, from Kansas, Missouri, and Ohio to New York, Connecticut, and Rhode Island, he beseeched Republicans to put differences aside and unite behind the movement that was their new party. Aware that beyond his home state he was not the first choice of any, he sought to become the second choice of many. Refusing to disparage his rivals, he aimed to leave their supporters "in a mood to come to us if they shall be compelled to give up their first love."

As his national renown began to build, so his estimation of his own chances improved. Even as he cast a humorous and skeptical eye on suggestions that he might successfully aspire to the nomination, he had begun to visualize himself as a legitimate contender. In all likelihood, he had been turning over the prospect of a presidential bid long before he made his candidacy known. "No man knows," Lincoln said years later, "when the presidential grub gets to gnawing at him, just how deeply it will get until he has tried it." As the possibility of success became more conceivable, Lincoln redoubled his efforts, working harder than all his opponents combined. While Seward, confident that the nomination was his, traveled through Europe for eight months prior to the convention, Lincoln labored daily, researching and deepening his speeches, keeping them fresh. As he crafted each speech, he would withdraw into a cocoon, finding a corner in the State Library or a back room or small chamber wherever he was speaking. There, he could be alone to focus his research, thought, and feeling. At times, he employed his closest friends as sounding boards, but the more he traveled the country, the more he relied upon his own perceptions of what he should say and exactly what it would take to win the nomination.

Nowhere did the product of such relentless discipline reap greater rewards than at Cooper Union in New York, where he accepted a lecture invitation which Salmon Chase had earlier declined. Understanding the importance of making a strong impression on an audience in Seward's home state, Lincoln spent many weeks extensively researching the attitudes toward slavery of each of the thirty-nine original signers of the Constitution, allowing him to demonstrate that a close reading of their writings and statements revealed that a clear majority had marked slavery "as an evil not to be extended, but to be tolerated and protected only because and so far as its actual presence among us makes that toleration and protection a necessity." Accordingly, the new Republicans, Lincoln claimed, were the authentic conservatives, the party closest to the words and intentions of the framers. He reached out to the South, speaking as a mediator, calling for calmness and deliberation as the shrapnel from explosions (the brutal assault on Massachusetts senator Charles Sumner by a southern congressman, the Supreme Court's *Dred Scott* decision claiming Negroes were not citizens, and John Brown's raid on Harpers Ferry) severely lacerated the country. Yet beneath the well-documented, crystalline logic of his argument and the moderate tone he preached, there surged an ardor so profoundly felt that even the more radical members of the audience were shaken.

Two major tenets ran through every public statement Lincoln had made since he reentered public life in 1854: no extension of slavery into the territories; no interference with slavery where it already existed. While Seward, in the months leading up to the convention, endeavored to soften the fiery rhetoric that had delighted abolitionists, and Bates sought to win liberal support by proposing equal constitutional rights for all citizens, Lincoln remained steadfast. His adherence to the two central party tenets placed him precisely on the intersection of the two lines that marked the perfect mean of the extreme elements of the Republican Party. Nor was his "avoidance of extremes" the result of calculation; it was, the *Chicago Daily Press and Tribune* pointed out, "the natural consequence of an equable nature and a mental constitution that is never off its balance."

As the convention opening drew near and support for Lincoln's candidacy grew stronger, Lincoln himself took nothing for granted. Realizing that a successful bid would require the unanimous support of the Illinois delegation, he worked to bridge the divisions within the state party, openly asking for help from delegates representing different factions in the party. "I am not in a position where it would hurt much for me not to be nominated on the national ticket; but I am where it would hurt some for me to not get the Illinois delegates," he wrote to a politician in the northern part of the state. "Can you not help me in this matter, in your end of the vineyard?" When the state Republicans met in convention ten days prior to the National

Convention, they passed a resolution instructing the delegates to "vote as a unit" for Abraham Lincoln. By contrast, Chase did not lift a finger to ensure a united Ohio delegation, having mistakenly assumed that every delegate would automatically vote for him, given all he had done for the party and the state.

No team in Chicago worked harder than Lincoln's team. While some of the intimate circle had political ambitions of their own, "most of them" Henry Whitney observed, "worked *con amore,* chiefly from love of the man, his lofty moral tone, his pure political morality." Indeed, two of the key members of Lincoln's team were former Democrats Norman Judd and Lyman Trumbull, whose refusal to cross party lines in 1855 had cost Lincoln his first Senate election. Lincoln's magnanimity (in contrast to the enemies Seward and Chase had created in their climb to power) had brought both men to his side in abiding friendship.

When the balloting began, Seward was considered the front-runner, followed by Chase and Bates. On the third ballot, however, to the surprise of many, Abraham Lincoln emerged as the nominee. Over the years, people have debated the factors that led to Lincoln's victory. Some have argued that the verdict represented "the defeat of Seward rather than the nomination of Lincoln." Others have pointed to luck — that the convention was held in Chicago and that Illinois was a key battleground state. While happenstance played a role, in the end, Lincoln's victory was due predominantly to his leadership skills — his shrewd comprehension of the lay of the land, growing confidence in his own judgment and intuition, unmatched work ethic, rhetorical abilities, equable nature, and elevated ambition. He never allowed his ambition to consume his kindheartedness or to modify his allegiance to the antislavery cause. While the delegates may not have recognized the true measure of Lincoln's leadership strengths, events would soon prove that they had chosen the best candidate to lead their new party to victory.

From the start, Lincoln discerned that his first task was to unite the candidates he had defeated into a single Republican movement. To that end, he wrote a personal letter to Chase humbly asking for his "especial assistance" in the campaign; he dispatched a close friend to St. Louis to beseech Judge Bates to write a public letter on his behalf; and most importantly, he secured Seward's willingness to act as his chief surrogate on the campaign trail. Pursuing a strategic policy of self-restraint, he remained in Springfield throughout the entire campaign. Aware that anything he said or wrote would be taken out of context to inflame sectionalism for partisan purposes, he simply pointed to the party platform and his many published speeches when asked about an issue; these carefully crafted documents, he maintained, fully represented his opinions on the central issues of the day.

By the fall of 1860, the slavery issue had smashed the Democratic Party much as it had shattered the Whigs. John Brown's raid on Harpers Ferry had hardened southern attitudes; no longer supporting Douglas's popular sovereignty, the southern wing demanded explicit protection from Congress to bring slaves into the new territories regardless of the vote of the people. Accordingly, when Douglas became the nominee of the Democratic Party, southern Democrats walked out and nominated their own candidate, Kentucky senator John Breckinridge. Before the split, Lincoln told a friend, Republican "chances were more than equal"; now, with a divided party, the Democratic chances seemed "very slim." Nonetheless, he understood that nothing must be left to chance.

Lincoln even agreed, after much hesitation, to write a short autobiography to put some muscle, sinew, and fat onto the bare bones of his scanty résumé and help construct a campaign persona. While he refused to sentimentalize the extreme hardships of his frontier childhood, he supplied memories of building his log cabin and splitting the rail fence that surrounded its ten acres. Soon rails purportedly split by young Lincoln began surfacing at public gatherings. The emblem caught fire: Rails were embossed on campaign medals, went zigzagging across newspaper cartoons, were motifs in campaign slogans and jingles. While Lincoln never claimed he had split a particular rail presented to him with great fanfare, he acknowledged that he had indeed been "a hired laborer, mauling rails, at work on a flat boat, just what might happen to any man's son!" The story of his life and his laborious efforts to educate himself made Lincoln into "a man of the people," the American dream made flesh.

On Election Day, Lincoln was understandably restless. Struggle had been his birthright, adversity his expectation. When his youthful dream of becoming the DeWitt Clinton of Illinois had been dashed with the spectacular demise of his internal improvement projects, he had fallen into depression. A period of doubt and self-assessment had followed his disappointing congressional term. Yet, neither of his two Senate losses had triggered personal doubt or depression. On the contrary, he considered both defeats positive steps in the advancement of the antislavery movement. By then, he was "so thoroughly interwoven in the issues before the people," his law partner William Herndon observed, that "he had become part of them." The inner voice that anticipated defeat had been stilled by the strength of his belief in the antislavery cause. When the returns came in, a jubilant fifty-two-year-old Lincoln learned that he had won.

This victory was the culmination of a different ambition than that of a twenty-three-year-old who had striven to bolster his self-worth by the esteem in which he was held by his fellow men. He now emanated the quiet sense of responsibility he had found in his role model, Henry Clay, regarded by all as the "man for a crisis." His spoken and written words were pared down, leaner, more measured, cautious, centered, more determined, displaying a rhetoric less hectic yet no less impassioned than the poetry he had delivered half a lifetime earlier at the Lyceum. He had found his mature voice.

SIX:
THEODORE ROOSEVELT

"The light has gone out of my life"

On the floor of the Albany legislature, Theodore Roosevelt received the joyful telegram that he was now father to his first child, a healthy baby girl. When shortly afterward a second telegram was delivered, all liveliness drained from his being. He rushed from the floor and caught a train to New York City, where his family had congregated to support his wife, Alice, and celebrate the birth of their child. In the next six hours, Roosevelt would be plunged into such an excessive nightmare of grief as to be found only in grand tragedy.

"There is a curse on this house," his brother, Elliott, told him upon his arrival. "Mother is dying and Alice is dying too." By midnight, both women were in a semiconscious state. His forty-nine-year-old mother, Mittie, still a youthful-looking, beautiful woman, had been suffering from what was considered to be a severe cold, but which turned out to be a lethal case of typhoid fever. Theodore was at his mother's bedside at 3 a.m. when she died. Less than twelve hours later, as he enfolded his young wife in his arms, Alice died from what was later diagnosed as acute kidney disease, its symptoms masked by her pregnancy. In his diary that night, the twenty-six-year-old Theodore placed a large X, along with the simple words "The light has gone out of my life." Two days later, he recorded: "We spent three years of happiness greater and more unalloyed than I have ever known fall to the lot of others. For joy or sorrow my life has now been lived out."

In Albany, the legislature voted unanimously to adjourn until the following Monday night, a marked tribute to the popular assemblyman, "wholly unprecedented in the legislative annals." At the double funeral service held at the Fifth Avenue Presbyterian Church, party bosses and dozens of assemblymen were present, along with members of New York society and scores of people who had attended Roosevelt Senior's funeral six years before. During the service, Theodore appeared to his former tutor, Arthur Cutler, "in a dazed stunned state. He does not know what he does or says." The pastor nearly lost command of his voice as he noted the "peculiar" circumstances that made the service especially sorrowful. "Two members of the same family, of the same home were on the same day taken from life and were to be buried together," he said. He did not remember anything like it in the course of his long ministry.

In a rare introspective reply to a condolence from his Maine friend, Bill Sewall, Roosevelt revealed what would become a full-blown stoic fatalism. "It was a grim and evil fate, but I have never believed it did any good to flinch or yield for any blow, nor does it lighten the blow to cease from working." Two days after the funeral, Roosevelt returned to the Assembly, telling a friend: "I think I should go mad if I were not employed." He seemed "a changed man," remarked his colleague Isaac Hunt; "from that time on there was a sadness about his face that he never had before. He did not want anybody to talk to him about it, and did not want anybody to sympathize with him. It was a grief that he had in his own soul." To his sister Bamie, to whom he had bequeathed total responsibility for the care and well-being of his newborn daughter, he wrote: "We are now holding evening sessions and I am glad we are; indeed the more we work the better I like it."

He had always applied himself at a pace governed by inordinate energy. Now, driven by the need to mitigate his misery, he lashed himself into a legislative frenzy, pushing one reform bill after another onto the floor, heedless of parliamentary procedure, failing to weigh criticisms of colleagues. It did not take long to squander the political capital which the goodwill and sympathy of the old machine politicians and the young reformers had bestowed upon him after his grievous losses. Before the session came to an end, he made the determination that he could not bear returning to Albany for another legislative term. His career in the state legislature was over.

There remained one crusade left to fight — one that gave Roosevelt a temporary sense of purpose but would ultimately worsen his depression. At the Republican National Convention in June, he led a small but vocal independent group supporting reformer Vermont senator George Edmunds for president against James G. Blaine, the choice of the party bosses. With good reason, reformers identified Blaine as an emblem of the corrupt moral standards of the post–Civil War Republican Party. While Roosevelt's refusal to support Blaine earned him "the bitter and venomous hatred" of the political bosses, it gained him widespread admiration among the ranks of reformist Republicans. To many young men, Charles Evans Hughes recalled, Roosevelt "seemed to incarnate everything that was noble and worthwhile in politics." He was like "a splendid breeze" that made "everyone feel brighter and better."

Roosevelt's reformist zeal failed to carry the delegates. When the votes were finally counted, the bosses prevailed. Blaine trounced Edmunds. "Our defeat is an overwhelming rout," Roosevelt told Bamie. "Of all the candidates, I consider Blaine as by far the most objectionable, because his personal honesty as well as his faithfulness as a public servant, are both open to questions." That he was victorious "speaks badly for the intelligence of the mass of my party." Veteran Republican reformer George William Curtis, who had joined Roosevelt's fight, lamented: "I was at the birth of the Republican Party and I fear I am to witness its death." The nomination of Blaine led scores of Republican independents to abandon the party. Calling themselves "mugwumps," they pledged not only to vote but to advocate for the Democratic nominee.

The independents were certain that Roosevelt would join their ranks. In a state of fury when he left the convention, Roosevelt told a reporter that he could never vote for Blaine and would give "hearty support" to any upright Democrat. In the weeks that followed, however, he backslid, announcing that "by inheritance and education" he was a Republican, a party man who believed in party government. He had acted with the party "in the past," and felt obliged to act with it "in the future." Not wanting to burn his bridges, he resolved that he would "abide by the outcome of the Republican convention." Roosevelt's fellow reformers were stunned. Reform newspapers, which had championed the young legislator, now considered him a traitor to the cause.

"Theodore Beware of Ambition: By that sin has fallen many another young man as promising as you," warned the *Boston Globe.* By his actions, Roosevelt had initially angered the bosses. Now he enraged the independents, betrayed by his reversal and subsequent support for Blaine. "I have very little expectation of being able to keep in politics," he told a New York journalist. "I can not regret enough the unfortunate turn in political affairs that has practically debarred me from taking any part in the fray," he admitted to his friend Massachusetts representative Henry Cabot Lodge. "I think it will be a good many years before I get back into politics," he despaired in a letter to his sister Bamie.

Feeling the need to escape from the catastrophe that beset his private life and the untenable political crisis in which he had bound himself, Roosevelt headed for the Badlands, where he had purchased a ranch the previous year. "I am going cattle ranching in Dakota for the remainder of the summer and a part of the fall," he told a reporter who was harassing him. "What I shall do after that I cannot tell." Even then, jilted reformers were not appeased. "No ranch or other hiding place in the world" can shield a man who backs a man like Blaine, the *Evening Post* scornfully observed. "Punching cattle is the best way to avoid campaigning" was Roosevelt's unhappy rejoinder.

So began a sojourn on the western frontier he would come to regard as "the most important educational asset" of his entire life. When asked two decades later which chapter of his life he would choose to remember, including the presidency, he said: "I would take the memory of my life on the ranch with its experiences close to Nature and among the men who lived nearest her." During this western interlude, Roosevelt would gather material for the most accomplished writing ventures of his life — *Hunting Trips of a Ranchman, Ranch Life and the Hunting Trail,* and *The Winning of the West.* But by far the greatest and most enduring of the projects during these months and years of reaction to the trauma he had experienced was the work of his own healing, growth, and self-transformation.

In selecting the four-member team to manage his ranching operations, Roosevelt revealed the characteristic sure touch with which he would choose associates in the years ahead. After spending only two weeks with Bill Merrifield and Sylvane Ferris during his hunting trip the previous fall, he had determined on the spot to trust them with $40,000 (one-third of the money his father had bequeathed him) to buy and tend a thousand head of cattle. To partner with him in the daily operation of the ranch, he chose his Maine guide, Bill Sewall, and Sewall's nephew, Will Dow. Neither man had prior experience with cattle ranching. That made small difference to Roosevelt. Astutely reading the character of both men, he guaranteed them "a share of anything" the new enterprise might earn, while promising that he would absorb any losses. He also invited them to live with him in the ranch house they would together design and build. "He never was a man to hesitate to make a decision," Sewall recalled years later. Once he could discern "a streak of honor" in a man, that man could be trusted.

When Roosevelt first got to the Dakotas, Sewall recounted, he "was very melancholy — very much down in spirits." The landscape of the Badlands — its lonely plains, open spaces, and haunting beauty — mirrored the desolation of his inner landscape. With Sewall, as with few people, Roosevelt expressed his feelings, confessing "that he felt as if it did not make any difference what became of him — he had nothing to live for." Sewall suggested he had his daughter to live for, but Roosevelt countered that his sister was better positioned to take care of the child. "She would be just as well off without me."

Just as he had driven himself to exhaustion in Albany in the weeks after Alice's death, so now, with reckless abandon and headlong intensity, he punished himself with the hardest and most dangerous work of the cowboys, as if, through excitement and fear, he might retrieve the possibility of feeling alive once again. He rode his horse sixteen hours a day, galloped at top speed over rugged terrain, hunted blacktail deer, antelope, elk, and buffalo, and joined in the frenzied five-week roundups when the cattle were branded and gathered for market. By flinging himself into every aspect of the daily lives of the cowboys, Roosevelt "was not playing cowboy — he was a cowboy." The daily work of the ranch, companionship with his fellow cowboys, and the sustained pursuit of his writing endeavors distracted him from overthought, and he was finally able to sleep at night. "Black care," he wrote, "rarely sits behind a rider whose pace is fast enough."

The young reformers in the East, who had once idolized Roosevelt, knew nothing about this immersion in the West. "We only knew that the man who seemed to have the brightest opportunity and the most splendid career opening had disappeared," Charles Evans Hughes said, "and apparently had disappeared in absolute failure. He was out of politics altogether, he was no longer apparently available for anything. He had gone away, and it seemed like a candle light that had been snuffed out, mistaken for some luminary which was ever to be the guide."

But Theodore Roosevelt was neither a snuffed candle, nor had he altogether abandoned politics. He had retreated west seeking in a state of nature not gentle balm but a test, a strenuous challenge where he might confront his deadened heart and fear of intimacy and somehow renew confidence in himself and in a future where he might become a genuine luminary, guide, and leader.

And as the seasons passed, his depression slowly began to lift. By the end of his two-year hiatus, Roosevelt had emerged from his traumatic ordeal stronger in body and resurgent in spirit. Though he would periodically suffer from asthma the rest of his life, he had improved his lungs in the cool mountain air and developed a more muscular chest. When he first arrived, Sewall recalled, "he was a frail young man," troubled by bouts of breathlessness and chronic stomach pains. "When he got back into the world he was as husky as any man I have ever seen who wasn't dependent on his arms for his livelihood." He had gained thirty pounds "and was clear bone, muscle and grit." The falsetto voice which "failed to make an echo" in the legislative chamber was "now hearty and strong enough to drive oxen."

Transforming his body was but one step in the psychological struggle to overcome what Theodore still considered his own "nervous and timid" nature. When he arrived in the West, he acknowledged, "there were all kinds of things of which I was afraid at first, from grizzly bears to 'mean' horses and gunfighters, but by acting as if I was not afraid I gradually ceased to be afraid." While some men, he observed, were naturally fearless, he had to train his "soul and spirit" as well as his body. So, "constantly forcing himself to do the difficult or even dangerous thing," he gradually was able to cultivate courage as "a matter of habit, in the sense of repeated effort and repeated exercise of will-power." Though only a mediocre horseman, he volunteered to ride "mean" horses, those liable to buck. As the owner of the ranch, he wanted to set a leadership example, even at the cost, on several risky occasions, of breaking his ribs. Similarly, while poor eyesight prevented his becoming a crack shot, he nevertheless joined professional hunters in the hazardous pursuit of bear, antelope, and buffalo.

"Perseverance," he insisted, was the key to his success as both a hunter and a cowboy. With endless practice, he learned to shoot at a moving target with the same accuracy as at a stationary one. Years of studying animals allowed him to identify, track, and anticipate the behavior patterns of his prey. He hoped his example of acquired courage would prove instructive, persuading other men that if they could consider danger "as something to be faced and overcome," they would "become fearless by sheer dint of practicing fearlessness." So completely was he able to surmount his own fears that in the years ahead, countless observers made reference to "the indomitable courage" that seemed to them clearly "ingrained in his being."

In this two-year interval, Roosevelt had recast himself as a new kind of American man, a hybrid of the cultivated easterner and the hard-bitten westerner. Without his extended stay in the Badlands, his sister Corinne suggested, "he would never have been able to interpret the spirit of the West as he did." For the rest of his life, countless countrymen regarded him as a man of the West, a romantic figure far removed from his upper-class background. He reveled in the knowledge that opponents could no longer describe him as a dude or a dandy. A cult of personality had taken root. Simply put, Roosevelt later said, "I would not have been president had it not been for my experience in North Dakota."

There are points of likeness in the seminal disasters that befell both Abraham Lincoln and Theodore Roosevelt in the early stages of their careers. Both crucibles were precipitated by a combination of intimate, personal crises and public repudiation that seemed to crush their core ambitions. Both swore off politics or at least paid lip service to deserting politics forever. Both suffered severe depressions. Healing change had to come from within while they waited for the historical kaleidoscope to turn.

Yet the two men dealt with their depressions in contrasting manners, ways congruent with their very different dispositions. Lincoln opened to grief and melancholy, sharing his feelings with neighbors, colleagues, and friends. Roosevelt closed down completely. He repressed his emotions, abandoned his daughter, and refused even to speak her given name, Alice, the name of his deceased wife. He referred to her simply as "Baby Lee," confessing, "there can never be another Alice to me." Nor could he bear reminiscing about his courtship and brief marriage. He destroyed almost all the pictures, letters, and mementos of their shared past. It was "both weak and morbid," he insisted, to dwell on loss.

As Roosevelt's spirits revived, his thoughts returned eastward to the home and friends left behind. On a short visit to New York in the fall of 1885, he encountered Edith Carow, the highly intelligent, intensely private young woman who had once been his closest childhood friend. As a five-year-old, Edith had joined Theodore and his sister Corinne in the home school Theodore Senior had established in the family's 20th Street household. In the summers, she had been a frequent guest at the family's Long Island estate. There, she and Theodore had become inseparable buddies; together they discovered a first love of literature, explored nature, rode trails on horseback, and sailed in the bay. As adolescents, they were dancing partners at cotillions and familiar companions at social events. In the summer before Theodore met Alice, however, the young couple had an enigmatic "falling out." What Theodore termed their "very intimate relations" were suddenly terminated. Edith later confessed that she had loved Theodore "with all the passion of a girl who had never loved before," and that when he married Alice, she was certain she would never love again. The chance meeting in 1885 revived long-hidden feelings in the conflicted widower as well, and in the ensuing months they met whenever he was in New York and regularly wrote when they were apart. If Theodore's devotion to Edith Carow lacked the churning romantic sentimentalism of his passion for Alice, his marriage to Edith provided his tempestuous nature with a life-sustaining stability and sanctuary.

By the summer of 1886, two years after he had fled to the West, Roosevelt was ready to reenter the political world. Life as a literary cowboy had been a formative respite, but it was never able to gratify his grand ambitions. "I would like a chance at something I thought I could really do," he told his friend, Massachusetts representative Henry Cabot Lodge. He was ready to test himself again in the public arena, the world for which he was born and bred.

The loss of his wife and mother on the same day became more than a catastrophic landmark in Theodore Roosevelt's personal life: The brutal twist of fate reshaped his philosophy of leadership as well. It underscored the vulnerability, fragility, and mutability of all his endeavors, political and personal. Career objectives now seemed air-drawn, subject to dissolving or reversing in a moment's time. Following that gruesome February day, chance — good luck and bad — would be deemed the trump card in his deck. This basic fatalism helps explain what might otherwise seem a haphazard choice of career opportunities during the next decade.

Shortly after returning home, he entered and lost a race for mayor of New York, despite his belief, given the city's overwhelming Democratic majority, that it was "a perfectly hopeless contest." After campaigning vigorously for the victorious 1888 presidential campaign of Republican Benjamin Harrison, Roosevelt had hoped to be appointed assistant secretary of state, but was finally offered a relatively minor federal post as one of three members of the Civil Service Commission. Roosevelt's friends urged him to decline, worried that the obscure position, far beneath his standing and reputation, "would bury him in oblivion." To their bewilderment, however, Roosevelt eagerly accepted and, furthermore, remained at the post for an astonishing total of six years. When the opportunity to return to his home state was presented, Roosevelt resigned to become one of four New York police board members, a thankless job fraught with political peril. Three years later, after stumping for the victorious Republican candidate, William McKinley, in the fall of 1896, he was offered assistant secretary of the navy, a post his friends again felt "below" what he deserved. Yet, once again he accepted, remaining at the Navy Department until the outbreak of the Spanish-American War, at which point, yet again counter to friends' advice, he resigned to volunteer in the Army.

What had become of the singular ascending ambition that had driven young Roosevelt from his earliest days? What explains his willingness, against the counsel of his most trusted friends, to accept seemingly low-level jobs that traced neither a clear-cut nor a reliably ascending career path? The answer lies in probing what Roosevelt gleaned from his crucible experience. His expectation of and belief in a smooth, upward trajectory, either in life or in politics, was gone forever. He questioned if leadership success could be obtained by attaching oneself to a series of titled positions. If a person focused too much on a future that could not be controlled, he would become, Roosevelt acknowledged, too "careful, calculating, cautious in word and act."

Thereafter, he would jettison long-term career calculations and focus simply on whatever job opportunity came his way, assuming it might be his last. "Do what you can, with what you have, where you are," he liked to say. In a very real way, Roosevelt had come to see political life as a succession of crucibles — good or bad — able to crush or elevate. He would view each position as a test of character, effort, endurance, and will. He would keep nothing in reserve for some will-o-the-wisp future. Rather, he would regard each job as a pivotal test, a manifestation of his leadership skills.

Roosevelt's crucible experience had heightened his awareness of mortality, drastically reducing the span he felt remaining for him to live and fulfill his ambitions. His intensified sense of passing time, his awareness that life could turn on a dime, made him impatient, sometimes unbearably so, to get things accomplished. The hectic speed with which he had introduced dozens of bills in the legislature following Alice's death became a lifelong pattern, a confrontational and often abrasive mode of leadership that put him at odds with the established procedures and the sluggish metabolism of any bureaucratic institution.

When Roosevelt was later asked how he was able to successfully lead such disparate departments as the Civil Service Commission, the New York Police Department, and the Navy Department, he insisted that the challenges he faced did not necessitate administrative "genius" or even "any unusual qualities, but just common sense, common honesty, energy, resolution, and readiness to learn." While this analysis may sound banal or disingenuously modest, Roosevelt's leadership style was, in actuality, governed by just such a series of simple dictums and aphorisms: *Hit the ground running; consolidate control; ask questions of everyone wherever you go; manage by wandering around; determine the basic problems of each organization and hit them head-on; when attacked, counterattack; stick to your guns; spend your political capital to reach your goals; and then when your work is stymied or done, find a way out.*

Friends who had urged Roosevelt to turn down the unheralded post of Civil Service commissioner failed to comprehend what Roosevelt himself instinctively grasped — that the fight to enforce the controversial new Civil Service Law represented a signature battle in the war against corruption, a battle ideally suited for this son of a reform-minded philanthropist with his own outsized crusading temperament. The Pendleton Civil Service Reform Act, passed in the wake of President James Garfield's murder (the assassin, a disappointed patronage seeker), was designed to replace the reigning spoils system with a merit system based on competitive examinations. Roosevelt regarded the spoils system as a cynical corruption of the democratic idea that every man should be judged on his merits. "It treats all offices," he argued, "as prizes to be scrambled for by the smirched victors in a contemptible struggle for political plunder, as bribes to be parceled out among the most active and influential henchmen of the various party leaders." He vowed to make the commission "a living force." He intended to enforce the new law to the fullest, to thwart anyone, including leaders in his own party, who were doing "everything in their power" to halt "the progress of reform and hamper the execution of the law." Roosevelt understood from the start that he would have "a hard row to hoe." The spoils system was the heartbeat of machine politics.

No sooner had he arrived at the Civil Service Commission than he signaled that business as usual no longer applied. To hit the ground running, to dramatize the change in direction, he launched an unexpected raid on the powerful New York Custom House, where, rumor suggested, violations of the new law were rampant. Questioning employees, he gleaned that government clerks were selling examination questions to favored party candidates for fees of $50 to $100. After hearing testimony, taking affidavits, and examining documents, Roosevelt demanded the immediate dismissal of three guilty employees, serving unmistakable notice in the press and before the public that the new law was "going to be enforced, without fear or favor."

His investigation also uncovered that party leaders continued to extort "so-called voluntary contributions" from Custom House employees as the price for retaining jobs.

He walked the corridors to directly engage with low-level officeholders — clerks, copyists, letter carriers, and the like. They disclosed how hard it was to meet the party leaders' demand for 2 percent of their salary. The winter assessment, he dramatically noted in a blistering report summarizing the investigation, might mean "the difference between having and not having a winter overcoat for himself, or a warm dress for his wife." To see the problem in terms of the concrete seasonal needs of the poor provided the public with an immediate comprehension of the real meaning of civil service reform. Less than a month later, having heard that postmasters in several cities were manipulating examination scores to appoint favored party members, he set forth on an investigatory tour of post offices.

This change in direction, hampered by interminable wrangles among a three-headed commission, prompted him to consolidate power. He seized leadership, took responsibility directly on his shoulders, and executed what was essentially an unacknowledged coup — not the last time he would make an inaugural move to strengthen his authority. "His colleagues were quiet men," the *Philadel-*

phia Record observed of his fellow Civil Service commissioners. It was Roosevelt "who did the fighting in the newspapers and before Congress and everywhere else and of course bore the brunt of the consequent attack." Swiftly, he became the public face of the commission. "My two colleagues are away and I have all the work of the Civil Service Commission to myself," he crowed to his sister Bamie. "I like it; it is more satisfactory than having a divided responsibility; and it enables me to take more decided steps."

Not surprisingly, Roosevelt's seizure angered Republican Party bosses, produced friction with colleagues, and elicited sporadic criticisms in the press. "He came into official office with a blare of trumpets and a beating of gongs, blared and beat by himself," the *Washington Post* observed. "He immediately announced himself the one man competent to take charge of the entire business of the Government." Another critic recommended that he "put a padlock on his restless and uncontrollable jaws." But he kept talking. "Mr. Roosevelt is a young Lochinvar," the *Boston Evening Times* remarked. "He isn't afraid of the newspapers, he isn't afraid of losing his place, and he is always ready for a fight. He keeps civil-service reform before the people and as the case often is, his aggressiveness is a great factor in a good cause."

By the time Roosevelt left the commission,

his leadership had stoked such public support for the new Civil Service Law that open violations were no longer tolerated; a true merit system was actually in the process of being born, so that, as Jacob Riis summarized, "the fellow with no pull should have an even chance with his rival who came backed; that the farmer's lad and the mechanic's son who had no one to speak for them should have the same show in competing for public service as the son of wealth and social prestige."

Any man who has been successful, Roosevelt repeatedly said, has leapt at opportunities chance provides. In the fall of 1894, a series of exposés, most notably involving Tammany's unscrupulous relationships with the city's police department, had compromised the Democratic Party's traditional hold on city politics. A defiant mood of reform was in the air. In the wake of the scandals, a reform-minded Republican businessman, William Strong, was elected mayor. Not long after he was sworn in, he offered Roosevelt the most challenging job in his administration: police commissioner, chief of the four-man police board. Roosevelt accepted without hesitation. "I have the most important and the most corrupt department in New York on my hands," Roosevelt wrote about the difficulties ahead, the note of excitement loud and piercing.

Using many of the same leadership techniques he had devised and utilized in his "Six Years' War" as Civil Service commissioner, Roosevelt wasted no time heralding the fact that regime change had transpired. He literally hit the ground running, racing up the steps of the Mulberry Street police headquarters in order to dramatize for the reporters in his wake that accelerated activity would henceforth mark the Police Board. "It was all breathless and sudden," one reporter recalled. Still jogging along, Roosevelt fired off questions: Which higher officials should be consulted, which ones ignored, which ones punished? What were "the customs, rules, methods" of the police board? "What do we do first?"

In truth, Roosevelt needed no suggestions on what to do first. On the police board sat two Democrats and two Republicans. Roosevelt had agreed to accept Strong's offer on the condition that he be made head of the board. His preordained election was the first order of business. To Roosevelt's mind, the structure of the four-member board portended "unmitigated mischief." Power "in most positions," he believed, should be concentrated "in the hands of one man." This might signify the fairly bold credo of a dictator except for the major caveat Roosevelt added: "so long as that man could be held fully responsible for the exercise of that power by the people." While his election as chief helped Roosevelt to consolidate power, this time, in contrast to his experience with the Civil Service Commission, board members proved less pliable. "Thinks he's the whole board," complained Democrat Andrew Parker. "He talks, talks, talks, all the time. Scarcely a day passes that there is not something from him in the papers." Politically at odds and filled with personal animosity, Parker failed to understand that for Roosevelt publicity was not merely the craving to bask in the focused glare of public attention; public sentiment was his single most potent instrument for driving change.

Roosevelt clearly understood that he had much to learn about the machinations of the police department and he had to learn at once. He turned for guidance to veteran police reporters Jacob Riis and Lincoln Steffens. Roosevelt could not have found two more valuable mentors. Roosevelt had read Riis's first book, *How the Other Half Lives,* a devastating depiction of the daily struggles of the poor in the immigrant ghettos of New York. So shaken was Roosevelt by this pathbreaking tour-de-force that he set out to find Riis in his office. Riis was absent, but Roosevelt left a card with a scribbled message, saying, "I've come to help." Thus began a lifelong friendship between the two men that blossomed during Roosevelt's tenure as police commissioner. "For two years," Riis recalled, "we were to be together all the day, and quite often most of the night, in the environment in which I had spent twenty years of my life. And these two were the happiest by far of them all. Then was life really worth living." While Roosevelt's relationship with the immensely ambitious, self-confident Steffens was both less profound and less durable, he benefited greatly from this talented reporter who had covered the state legislature's stunning probe of police department corruption for the *Evening Post* and was now the head of the *Post*'s police bureau. With solid information and advice provided by Riis and Steffens, the new police commissioner felt equipped to launch his new venture.

The first massive task that presented itself was to analyze the basic problems of the organization and assault them head-on. The notorious investigation by the state legislature had revealed ubiquitous corruption "from top to bottom"; the police force was found to be "utterly demoralized." It had been revealed that Tammany required new police recruits to pay a fee for their appointments, with the understanding that as they rose in the ranks they would participate in the blackmail fund Tammany accrued by their multifarious extortion schemes. For a monthly fee, gambling houses and brothels were guaranteed protection from raids, grocery stores could display their wares on the sidewalk, and compliant saloons could remain open on Sundays. With each higher rank a policeman or a politician attained, his percentage of the blackmail fund grew.

Roosevelt's diagnosis of the situation led to the formation of a three-pronged strategy. He had to purge leaders at the top, change the culture in which the individual policemen worked, and deal a fatal blow to the widespread system of graft and bribery that enveloped the police, the politicians, and the managers of thousands of small businesses.

Within three weeks of his swearing in, Roosevelt forced the resignations of the powerful superintendent of police, Tom Byrnes, and his chief inspector, Alec "Clubber" Williams. Questioned under oath during the hearings conducted by the state legislature, neither man could adequately account for how they had accumulated hundreds of thousands of dollars in their bank accounts. The sudden firings generated headlines in every city paper, signaling that the new Police Board "would spare no man" in its drive to weed out corruption. In the future, merit alone would guide appointments of recruits and determine every level of promotion. Roosevelt's assertive action provoked anxiety on the part of the Republican bosses. They feared he was moving too far too fast and creating uproar wherever he went. So long as Roosevelt could count on the full-throated support of the public, he would stick to his guns.

Despite the changes he had made in the top leadership, Roosevelt recognized that lasting reform would be determined by the behavior of the patrolman on the beat. Accordingly, he initiated the second prong of his strategy — to patrol the patrolmen. He resolved to learn firsthand the nature of the patrolman's work and to lay down the values of a new culture for the entire force. Following the advice of Riis, he made a series of unannounced "midnight rambles." Disguising his identity with an oversized coat and a floppy hat drawn down over his forehead, he roamed the streets of a dozen or more patrol areas between midnight and sunrise to determine whether the policemen assigned to those zones were carrying out their duties. With Riis by his side to help him navigate parts of the city he barely knew existed, Roosevelt found policemen relaxing in bars, eating at all-night restaurants, entertaining women on street corners. In each case, Roosevelt summoned the officer to appear at headquarters the following morning for disciplinary action. In one instance, he found a patrolman eating oysters at a Third Avenue bar. Without revealing his identity, he inquired why the officer was not on the street at his post where he belonged. "What is that to you, and who are you anyway," the officer asked. "I am Police Commissioner Roosevelt," came the reply. "Sure you are," the patrolman mocked. "You're Grover Cleveland and Mayor Strong, all in a bunch." "Shut up, Bill," the bartender said, "it is his Nibs sure! Don't you see his teeth and glasses?"

Stories of Roosevelt's unprecedented midnight rambles captivated reporters and the public alike. After his initial foray, seasoned reporters and writers often accompanied him (including Lincoln Steffens, Hamlin Garland, Stephen Crane, and Richard Harding Davis). Within short order, these nocturnal forays produced headlines across the country. "Sly Policemen Caught by Slyer Roosevelt," one headline read. "Roosevelt on Patrol: He Makes the Night Hideous for Sleepy Policemen," blared another. Cartoonists had a field day. Cartoons of policemen crouching in fear at the sight of an enormous set of teeth, metal-rimmed spectacles, and a mustache entertained the country and ushered Roosevelt into new national prominence. The *Chicago Times-Herald* dubbed him "the most interesting man in America." But as one reformer noted, "However amusing to the public, Roosevelt's purposes were entirely serious." The prospect that the commissioner might suddenly appear in the dark of night made individual patrolmen more accountable for their actions. To reformers, these reconnaissance missions were emblematic of "the beginning of a new epoch."

Even as Roosevelt disciplined individual policemen who were shirking their duties, he insisted that the majority of the police force were "naturally first-rate men" caught in a bad system that had to be changed to reward merit, not wrongdoing. When he came upon an officer on proper patrol, he offered encouragement and thanks. If he found a designated area where every patrolman was on his scheduled watch, he sought out the officer in charge. "You are to be congratulated, sir," he told the sergeant with effusive goodwill, "this precinct is well-patrolled." Maintaining that it was as important to recognize good behavior as to punish bad conduct, he established a system to award certificates and medals to officers who exhibited "courage and daring" — men who risked their lives to catch criminals, struggled with runaway horses, saved children from drowning, and performed countless other heroic deeds in the course of their everyday duties. Recognition ceremonies, promotions based solely on merit, professional training, a new school of pistol practice, and the formation of a popular bicycle squad: Such a combination of programs provided incentives to the "men with the nightsticks." An innovative bureaucrat, Roosevelt introduced a range of technological improvements to the police department, including a Rogue's Gallery of photographs, the use of fingerprinting, and an expansion of telephone communications. The morale of the police force began the slow process of healing and restoration.

At the same time, Roosevelt recognized the importance of building a police force that represented the diversity of the city. By the end of his tenure, all the dominant ethnic strains were included — Irish Americans, German Americans, African Americans, Jews, Scandinavians, Italians, Slavs, and many other nationalities. Seeking to weld them into "one body," he acted swiftly when signs of prejudice or discrimination became visible. "When one man attacked another because of his breed or birthplace, I got rid of him in summary fashion," Roosevelt claimed.

As police commissioner, Roosevelt proudly noted, "my whole work, brings me into contact with every class of people in New York as no other work possibly could." His position on the Police Board included membership on the Board of Health, authorizing him to scrutinize sanitary conditions in the slums in a more systematic and comprehensive way than afforded by the single eye-opening visit under the auspices of Samuel Gompers he had made a decade earlier to the cigar tenements. Together with Riis, he conducted inspections of overcrowded, unsanitary tenements with crumbling staircases, peeling walls, insufficient air, and unlit hallways. "One might hear of overcrowding in tenements for years," Riis later remarked, "and not grasp the subject as he could by a single midnight inspection." After midnight, the slum is "caught off its guard," Riis remarked, "the veneering is off and you see the true grain of the thing," especially on sweltering summer nights. The reports Roosevelt made to the Board of Health forced owners to make improvements, to light dark hallways and fix unsafe stairways. In several cases, the worst tenements were razed.

No action Roosevelt took during these months required more strength and resolution and, in the end, took a greater personal and political toll than the third prong of his headlong assault — his mission to sever "the tap-root" of corruption — the Sunday closing law. Over the previous decade, the law had been warped into a colossal sluiceway of political and police graft. Owners and managers of the more than ten thousand saloons operating in the city understood that so long as they continued making a monthly dole to police and politicians, they were free to remain open on the most profitable day of the week. Those who refused payment were summarily shut down and arrested for violating the law. "The result," Roosevelt argued, "was that the officers of the law, the politicians, and the saloon-keepers became inextricably tangled in a network of crime." By enforcing the law "fairly and squarely" against all establishments instead of imposing it "against some and not others," he hoped to eliminate the central source of the city's corruption.

Personally, Roosevelt did not agree with the Sunday closing law, which the state legislature had passed as a concession to rural constituents. For the working class, on the job six days a week, the local saloon was a place to relax with friends on their one day off, to drink beer, play cards, shoot pool, and talk politics. But the law was on the books, and as police commissioner, Roosevelt felt he had "no honorable alternative save to enforce it." He had "never been engaged in a more savage fight," Roosevelt told Cabot Lodge.

The months of warfare had begun to show results, however. Surveying the battlefield with his comrade-in-arms, Jacob Riis, "driving and walking around for nine hours to see for ourselves exactly how the law was enforced, I had no idea how complete our success was; not four percent of the saloons were open and these were doing business with the greatest secrecy and to a most limited extent." Though he had fully expected the "furious rage" of the saloonkeepers and their political allies, he was ill-prepared for the venomousness of the messages that flooded his office from members of the working class. "You are the biggest fool that ever lived." "You are the deadest duck that ever died in a political pond." "What an ass you have made of yourself." A box sent to his office containing dynamite detonated before reaching its destination. "A less resolute man" would have backed down, observed Jacob Riis, "but he went right on doing the duty he was sworn to do."

Refusing to take "the howl" of criticism personally, Roosevelt astonished his critics when he accepted an invitation to attend what turned out to be a massive parade protesting the new enforcement policy of "the Police Czar." Escorted to the reviewing stand on Lexington Avenue, he stood for two hours, smiling and waving as decorated floats and more than thirty thousand marchers paraded by carrying scornful banners and placards. Sighting one large banner inscribed with the words "Roosevelt's Razzle Dazzle Reform Racket," he asked the men carrying it if he could keep it as a souvenir. His good-natured embrace of criticism captured the imagination of the crowd. "Bully for Teddy!" marchers shouted. "Teddy, you're a man!" The *Chicago Evening Journal* summed up the day's event: "Cheered by Those Who Came to Jeer."

Although Roosevelt's self-mockery won the day, his war against the saloons was politically untenable. With the next election cycle approaching, Mayor Strong pressured Roosevelt to "let up on the saloon," threatening to fire him if he balked. "He was terribly angry," Roosevelt told Lodge, but "I would not change." The results of the election confirmed the worst fears of Republican leaders. The Democratic Tammany machine roared back into power, regaining all it had lost two years earlier. "Reform was beaten," Lincoln Steffens lamented, and the blame was squarely affixed to Roosevelt. The systematic reform he had tried to institute by enforcing the Sunday closing law had been perceived as a curtailment of personal liberty. Roosevelt had failed to frame the narrative as a necessary battle against corruption in such a way as to gain the people's confidence and support.

In Albany, the state legislature debated various ways to legislate Roosevelt out of office. A noose was tightening. "Just at present I am a special object of censure on every side," Roosevelt admitted to Bamie, acknowledging that he now suffered from "hours of profound depression." Lodge also worried about his friend and told Bamie, "He seems overstrained & overwrought — that wonderful spring and interest in all sorts of things is much lowered."

Where had Roosevelt's leadership gone astray? "I do not deal with public sentiment.

I deal with the law," Roosevelt had repeatedly insisted. But every leader must deal with public sentiment, as Abraham Lincoln had learned from the negative reaction to his intemperate maiden speech before the Congress, when he had failed to take into account the widespread popularity of the Mexican-American War. It was one thing for Roosevelt to earn the ire of the political bosses and the saloonkeepers, quite another to have become the scapegoat and antagonist of the working class he had worked so hard to understand and befriend. While he had anticipated trouble from the public when he first began to enforce the Sunday law, he had underestimated the intensity of the outcry from working-class immigrants. In contrast to his experience as Civil Service commissioner, where he had no doubt that his meritocratic efforts were entirely positive, he belatedly realized that there were other times (and the complicated saloon brawl was one) where there was a little of right and wrong "on each side, and then it becomes mighty puzzling to know the exact course to follow."

So virulent had the personal animosity toward Roosevelt grown that his innovations, policies, and programs risked being diluted or even undone if he stayed longer. He needed to find a way out. He rationalized that his work was accomplished — he had prepared the ground for those who would come after him. And there was truth to his rationalization, for a difficult reform had begun and it would impact the police department for years to come.

William McKinley's 1896 campaign for president provided Roosevelt with the perfect exit. Taking temporary leave from the Police Board, he stumped far and wide for the Republican nominee and swiftly became one of the most sought after speakers on the campaign trail. However unpopular he was as police commissioner in New York, his corruption and crime-fighting exploits had made him a compelling figure across the country. Already, Theodore Roosevelt had become a symbol and leader in the war against corruption that in the next decade would win the widespread support of his countrymen. Everywhere he went, he attracted great crowds, the venues "jammed, people standing in masses in the aisles." By giving "all of his time, all of his energy, and all his towering ability to the work of the campaign," he once again earned the plaudits of the Republican bosses.

Returning to the Police Board after McKinley's victory, Roosevelt waited expectantly for a high post in the new administration. While numerous friends lobbied on his behalf, hopeful for his appointment as secretary of the navy, McKinley hesitated. "I want peace," the new president told one Roosevelt ally, but "Theodore — whom I know only slightly — is always getting into rows with everybody. I am afraid he is too pugnacious." Roosevelt's supporters refused to relent. And finally, McKinley made an offer to Roosevelt — the post of assistant secretary of the navy. As so often before, friends cautioned Roosevelt not to settle for this lesser post, but in what had become a familiar pattern, he snatched up the offer.

As assistant secretary to Navy Secretary John Davis Long, Roosevelt was relegated to an actual subordinate role for the first time, directly answerable to a superior. Potential minefields surrounded the relationship from the start. Two decades older than Roosevelt, Long, cautious by temperament, personified the status quo of the McKinley administration. Having experienced the horrific years of the Civil War, Long, like McKinley, was committed to preserving the peace. Roosevelt was convinced that a looming war with Spain over their treatment of the Cuban freedom fighters was on the near horizon, and that the Navy must be transformed to address that likelihood.

How then, did Roosevelt manage this subordinate position? For a start, Roosevelt built up "a reserve of good feeling" through repeated acts of courtesy, kindness, and helpfulness that secured the trust and confidence of Secretary Long. Recognizing that Long, who had no prior experience with the Navy, was uncomfortable with talk of "dry docks, gun turrets, blueprint specifications, or the frailty of torpedo boats," Roosevelt swiftly mastered the technical details involved in overseeing the Navy — the schedules for inspection, repair, and maintenance, the numbers of inactive vessels, the construction of new ships — which he then translated into clear, readable reports delivered to Long's desk every morning. As ever, Roosevelt's voracious scientific and historical reading and writing served him well. In this case, his statistical understanding and expertise, begotten as a fledgling naval historian when he wrote his first published work, on the naval battles in the War of 1812, enabled him to easily master telling details that held no interest for his superior Long.

Long was delighted with his industrious young assistant. "He is full of suggestions; many of which are of great value to me," Long remarked, "and his spirited and forceful habit is a good tonic for one who is disposed to be as conservative and careful as I am." Just as Roosevelt had instituted hands-on inspections in the Civil Service and extended his rambles to the sidewalks of New York, so now he left his desk to investigate, inspect, and review various aspects of the Navy. He was on hand during an investigation of a torpedo accident; spent five days reviewing the Naval Reserve Militia in the Midwest, accompanied the First Battalion on a practice cruise, and went aboard the *Iowa*, the Navy's state-of-the-art battleship. When he met with the crew that had designed the ship, he "broke the record asking questions," leaving the shipbuilder in a state of amazement at the combination of his "theoretical knowledge" of construction and his command of "the details of bolts and rivets." And just as he had commended policemen on the beat, so he now praised members of the Second Battalion after witnessing a field exercise on parade grounds.

Even as he surveyed the current readiness of the Navy and appeared to Secretary Long a dutiful and solicitous son, Roosevelt was carefully formulating his agenda to build an expanded, war-ready Navy. Sensitive to the administration's reticence regarding war, he cloaked his plans in the sheep's clothing of preparedness. In a well-publicized speech at the Naval War College, he drew upon the wisdom of the country's first president. "A century has passed since Washington wrote, 'To be prepared for war is the most effectual means to promote peace,'" he began. "In all our history there has never been a time when preparedness for war was any menace to peace." The speech garnered widespread praise, making Roosevelt a leading proponent of preparedness and war-readiness.

While pleased with the response, Roosevelt craved action. "I have always had a horror of words that are not translated into deeds," Roosevelt frequently charged. And that summer presented the opportunity for action when the fatigued Secretary Long retreated to Massachusetts for an eight-week vacation. This was not remarkable in the days before air-conditioning; government officials, including presidents, regularly escaped Washington during the summer. Furthermore, prior to the hot weather setting in, Roosevelt had graciously promised Long that he would give up his family summer at Sagamore Hill to accommodate his superior's schedule.

Long's protracted hiatus left Roosevelt the acting secretary of the navy and he made the most of his temporary elevation. "The Secretary is away, and I am having immense fun running the Navy," Roosevelt reported to a friend in August. "As I am given a free hand when alone, I am really accomplishing a great deal," he told Bamie. Indeed, under Roosevelt's "hot-weather" acting secretaryship, ports and coastal fortifications were improved, numerous shakedown cruises were taken, and Congress was lobbied to expand the fleet. Most importantly, Roosevelt's awareness of the disposition of fleets around the world persuaded him that the Pacific sector, where the bulk of the Spanish fleet was stationed, could play an instrumental role if war broke out in Cuba. Consequently, he pulled every string to get the man he wanted appointed commander in chief of the Asiatic Squadron — Admiral George Dewey. Though they had met but several times, Roosevelt instinctively recognized in Dewey the right leader for a crisis. "I knew that in the event of war Dewey could be slipped like a wolfhound from a leash; I was sure that if he were given half a chance he would strike instantly and with telling effect; and I made up my mind that all I could do to give him that half-chance should be done."

Simultaneously, he conducted an extended, informative, and affectionate correspondence with Secretary Long, assuring him that all was under control. "You must be tired and you ought to have an entire rest," he wrote in early August. "If things go on as they are now there isn't the slightest reason to you to come back for six weeks more," he reiterated a week later. "I am very glad you have been away," he followed up, "for it has been the hottest weather we have had." He could not have pressed harder against the bounds of duplicity and not broken them.

The relationships Roosevelt had long cultivated with the press aided his quest to build up the Navy. Invited to participate in several cruises, reporters praised the current state of the Navy but indicated what still needed to be done. On occasion, Roosevelt's comfort with the press led to the publication of overtly bellicose statements that countered the administration's agenda and drew the ire of Secretary Long. In such instances, Roosevelt immediately apologized to Long, accepted his reprimand with grace, restored obedience by promising that his spirit was "chastened," and then proceeded exactly as before. He succeeded in keeping Long's trust by remaining "beguilingly honest and open" about their differences of views. Of paramount importance was simply to acknowledge who was in charge.

When a potentially troublesome article appeared in the *Boston Herald,* charging that Roosevelt was trying to seize for himself the functions and responsibilities of the man in charge, Roosevelt instantly notified Long about the piece and confessed that it greatly discomforted him. He understood, Roosevelt added, that the idea that he would not be a loyal subordinate "was just what you were warned against before I came," and he "flattered" himself to believe that aside from a few "infernal" statements, he had done nothing of which Long would have disapproved. While he would continue to present his own views as "strongly" as possible, "when you have once determined on your policy I shall carry it out in letter and spirit."

That both men were truly fond of each

other smoothed such occasional tensions. After Long highly praised his subordinate in an interview, Roosevelt wrote to thank him for his "generous" statements. "It has been an entirely new experience for me to serve under a man like you. Of course, you will never have any friction with me, excepting from wholly unintentional slips on my part, for the excellent reason that I should regard myself as entirely unworthy to hold such a position as I do hold if, now that I have a chief like you, I failed to back him up in every possible way."

Dramatic reports of Spanish treachery against the Cuban rebels in the winter of 1898 (many luridly exaggerated by war-mongering newspapers) sparked widespread humanitarian outrage, ratcheting up Roosevelt's sense of urgency about the possible need for intervention. If war should come, "it should come finally on our initiative," he beseeched Long. "If we drift into it, if we do not prepare in advance, and suddenly have to go into hostilities without taking the necessary steps beforehand, we may have to encounter one or two bitter humiliations, and we shall certainly be forced to spend the first three or four most important weeks not in striking, but in making those preparations to strike which we should have made long before."

Roosevelt's warning proved prescient. On

February 15 the USS *Maine,* stationed in Havana Harbor as "an act of friendly courtesy" to the Cuban people, exploded, killing 266 Americans. Though the cause of the explosion was never determined, widespread rage and a call to declare war swept the country. Still, President McKinley, who had fought at Antietam, the bloodiest battle of the Civil War, hesitated. "I have been through one war; I have seen the dead piled up; and I do not want to see another." While the president was plagued with indecision, Roosevelt took a series of unwarranted actions that under any boss other than John Davis Long might well have caused his immediate firing for insubordination.

On February 25, Long left the office for a day's rest. "Do not take any step affecting the policy of the Administration without consulting the President or me. I am not away from town and my intention was to have you look after the routine of the office while I get a quiet day off. I write to you because I am anxious to have no unnecessary occasion for a sensation in the papers." Despite this warning, Roosevelt's months of preparatory work burst into coordinated execution. He launched a series of "peremptory orders" — "distributing ships, ordering ammunition," purchasing tons of coal, "sending messages to Congress for immediate legislation authorizing the enlistment of an unlimited number of seamen," and finally, ordering Admiral Dewey to "keep full of coal" and be prepared if war comes to take offensive action "to see that the Spanish squadron does not leave the coast."

Long discovered these orders when he returned to the office the next morning. "Roosevelt, in his precipitate way, has come very near causing more of an explosion than happened to the Maine," he confided to his diary. "He means to be thoroughly loyal but the very devil seemed to possess him yesterday afternoon." Reacting more from compassion than in anger, Long rationalized that Roosevelt had lost his head as a consequence of grave troubles at home: Edith suffered from what doctors would finally diagnose as a massive abscess in a muscle near the base of her spine, requiring a long and dangerous operation to remove; at the same time, Long knew that their ten-year-old son, Theodore Jr., was "just recovering from a long and dangerous illness." This combination, Long wanted to believe, "accentuated" Roosevelt's "natural nervousness" and prompted him to take action which he otherwise would not "for a moment have taken." Long's supposition that Roosevelt's sensitive nature had resulted in a man overburdened by family crises was the opposite of the well-meditated, if transgressive, case at hand on February 25.

Nonetheless, neither Long nor McKinley

revoked a single one of Roosevelt's orders. Accordingly, when Congress finally declared war on Spain nearly nine weeks later, Commander Dewey was well-positioned to strike. Two hours after the Battle of Manila Bay commenced, seven weeks before the invasion of Cuba, the Spanish Pacific fleet was decimated, giving the American forces a decided advantage. "If it had not been for Roosevelt we should not have been able to strike the blow we did at Manila," the chairman of the Senate Committee on Foreign Relations remarked. "It needed just Roosevelt's energy and promptness." American army officer Leonard Wood later observed that "few men would have dared to assume this responsibility, but Theodore Roosevelt knew that there were certain things that ought to be done and that delay would be fatal. He felt the responsibility and he took it." For Roosevelt, being a subordinate was never confused with being subservient.

No sooner had Congress declared war on Spain on April 25, 1898, than Theodore Roosevelt proclaimed that he would resign his Navy post and volunteer for the Army. Not a single friend agreed with what seemed to them an impulsive decision. "I really think he is going mad," one remarked. "The President has asked him twice as a personal favor to stay in the Navy Dept., but Theodore is wild to fight and hack and hew. It really is sad, of course this ends his political career for good." Both his intimate political friend Cabot Lodge and his old mentor William Sewall emphatically concurred that he had far "more important work to do in the Navy Department." Secretary Long worried that he had "lost his head in this unutterable folly of deserting his post where he is of most service and running off to ride a horse and probably, brush mosquitoes from his neck on the Florida sands." While "his heart is right, and he means well," he added, "it is one of those cases of aberration — desertion — vainglory of which he is utterly unaware."

Roosevelt's decision was, in fact, anything but rash. His "usefulness" in the Navy Department, he suspected, would "largely disappear in time of war." Not only would the military advisers take center stage, but Secretary Long would steadfastly remain at his post. War would close the doors on his decisive and eventful days as acting secretary. The time had come to find a way out. "My work here has been the work of preparing the tools," he told Sewall. "They are prepared, and now the work must lie with those who use them. . . . I would like to be one of those using the tools."

The chance to volunteer in war touched a raw nerve in Theodore. He considered his father's decision to avoid service in the Civil

War a stain on his family's honor, even though the decision was made to avert the utter breakdown of his southern wife within a badly strained family dynamic. So, now, in the spring of 1898, despite the fragility of his own family — Edith had not yet recovered from her operation and young Theodore seemed to be suffering a nervous collapse — Roosevelt felt compelled to serve in Cuba. "You know what my wife and children mean to me," he later told his military adviser, Archie Butt, "and yet I made up my mind that I would not allow even a death to stand in my way; that it was my one chance to do something for my country and for my family and my one chance to cut my little notch on the stick that stands as a measuring-rod in every family. I know now that I would have turned from my wife's deathbed to have answered that call."

Among our four leaders, only Theodore Roosevelt would command men in the heat of a military operation. Only Roosevelt would face an actual enemy with his life and the lives of his men in the balance. When he took command of his troops in Cuba, he was directly responsible for them, an experience that altered and vastly enlarged his confidence in himself as a leader.

When the original call for three volunteer regiments to supplement the Regular Army was issued, it was to be "composed exclusively of frontiersmen possessing special qualifications as horsemen and marksmen." Here was the fortuitous conjunction of precisely the skills Theodore Roosevelt had honed during his years in the Badlands. He had willed himself to become an indefatigable hunter, a reasonable marksman, a cowboy able to stay in the saddle for a dozen hours at a time, inured to extremes of weather, equipped to tolerate all manner of unexpected hardships. Yet, when Secretary of War Russell A. Alger offered Roosevelt the top leadership post — colonel of the first of these three volunteer regiments — he declined.

Why, when Roosevelt had the opportunity to actualize a lifelong fantasy of the knight on horseback, the heroic martial figure leading a charge at the forefront of his men, would he decline and instead defer to his younger friend Leonard Wood? The answer reveals a critical leadership attribute — the self-awareness to soberly analyze his own strengths and compensate for his weaknesses. He declined the offer and recommended Wood solely because he knew that he lacked the experience and technical knowledge to speedily outfit and provision a regiment — the knowledge possessed by Wood, who had served in the Regular Army and been awarded the Medal of Honor. "I told [Alger] after six weeks' service in the field I would feel competent to handle the regiment, but that I did not know how to equip it or how to get it into action." If Wood were made colonel, however, Roosevelt said he would happily, without the slightest reservation or competitiveness, accept the subordinate post of lieutenant colonel. "Alger considered this an act of foolish self-abnegation on my part," Roosevelt later said, "instead of its being what it was — the wisest act I could have performed." Central to Roosevelt's decision was not the title he would enjoy, but the ultimate success of the regiment in which he would share command.

Colonel Wood and Lieutenant Colonel Roosevelt formed an effective and complementary team. While Wood requisitioned horses, saddles, tents, blankets, boots, and the like, Roosevelt so successfully promoted the concept and public perception of the regiment, which eventually became known as the Rough Riders, that twenty thousand applications were received within five days for fewer than eight hundred places. Projecting a vision of a unique fighting force that would represent a microcosm of the country itself, Roosevelt persuaded the authorities to enlarge the regiment to include a troop of easterners who "possessed in common" with the cowboys, Indians, hunters, and miners "the traits of hardihood and thirst for adventure." He found such qualities among Ivy

League football stars, polo players, oarsmen, sportsmen from the Knickerbocker Club and the Somerset Club, and policemen from their beats in New York City. This glamorous mosaic of the country's diversity would form any journalist's dream of a melting pot, and Roosevelt was just the figure to supply sufficient heat to melt these heterogeneous elements into a cohesive unit. In the men he gathered into his regiment, he had quilted together the broad episodes of his life: his willed athleticism, body building, Harvard education, engagement with hunters and woodsmen in Maine, ranching and riding in the Far West, and working with the police force in New York.

How was he able to pull these disparate men, regions, and social climes together — westerners and easterners, cowboys and the "swells," educated and noneducated? To stimulate the "fellow feeling" he believed essential to the success of the mission, he deliberately arranged the tents at the training ground in San Antonio in such a manner that cowboys and wranglers slept side by side with the scions of financiers. He assigned Knickerbocker Club members to wash dishes for a New Mexico company and brought easterners and westerners together in the daily chores of washing laundry and digging and filling in latrines. Eventually, a common denominator emerged throughout the entire regiment — a leveling of money, social status, and education under the aegis of teamwork.

Roosevelt understood from the start that leadership had to be earned; it was not something to be granted by rank or title. The frontiersmen who made up the majority of the regiment were individualists, possessed of a disparaging attitude toward entitlement and hierarchy. As he had learned on the cattle drives in the Dakotas, being the one who issues orders and pays wages was not sufficient to becoming a bona fide boss; he had to lead by sharing his life with the men, by his own willingness to do anything he asked them to do, by never asking them to suffer anything he wouldn't suffer first. "When we got down to hard pan, we all, officers and men, fared exactly alike as regards both shelter and food," Roosevelt later wrote. Grumbling ceased "when all alike slept out in the open."

The crash training course which provided a formidable learning experience for Roosevelt and his men was not without mistakes on his part. He had to learn how to be one with his men without overstepping the line of familiarity to the point of diminishing their respect for him. After a successful day of mock drills in the oppressive heat of San Antonio, he announced to his troops: "The men can go in and drink all the beer they want, which I will pay for!" Later that evening, Colonel Wood summoned Roosevelt to his tent. He described the various disciplinary confusions and dilemmas that inevitably surfaced when an officer relaxed with his recruits. Wood's admonition was taken to heart: "Sir, I consider myself the damnedest ass within ten miles of the camp." Chastened, he realized that while he had gained the affection of his troops, he had not established the proper space between himself and his men. "When things got easier I put up my tent and lived a little apart," Roosevelt recalled, for "it is the greatest possible mistake to seek popularity either by showing weakness or mollycoddling the men. They never respect a commander who does not enforce discipline." Experience taught him to strike the right balance between affection and respect.

In the boiling chaos of the removal from the drill grounds in Texas to Port Tampa to Cuba, Roosevelt revealed a sure-handed improvisational ability and the administrative initiative to quell confusion, impose order, and skirt protocol to protect his troops. When trains to transport the heavy equipment for his regiment could not be secured, he paid from his own funds. When the canned beef they were fed proved rancid, he demanded and obtained edible provisions. When the boat to convey his men was not available, he occupied another regiment's assigned boat with a combination of stealth and dispatch. Despite filthy, cramped quarters on board, he imposed inspections and roll calls. In a matter of weeks, he had established the kind of leadership that is bonded by two-way trust. He had taken command of his men by assuming responsibility for them. He had shown his men that he was prepared to do anything he could to provide for them; they, in turn, were prepared to give everything he asked of them.

The master chord of Theodore Roosevelt's temperament was displayed in the battles and skirmishes of the Rough Riders' engagement in the Spanish-American War: "Forward to the charge," "straight ahead," "charge into the open." Once the order was set in motion, there was no reverse. "Instead of falling back, they came forward," one Spanish soldier recalled. "This is not the way to fight, to come closer at every volley." Yet, even as dozens of men were killed and wounded along the way, Roosevelt, time and again, propelled his troops toward the enemy.

The first battle, at Las Guasimas, began in confusion. As the Rough Riders made their way through the tall grass and twisted brush, they encountered fierce fire from an unseen enemy. Beset by great difficulty, unable to determine what was happening around him, Roosevelt seemed overwrought, jumping "up and down" with tension, bewilderment, and excitement. "What to do next I had not an idea," he later confessed. When they came upon a cut in a barbed-wire fence indicating the route the Spanish had taken, however, Roosevelt's uneasiness vanished. Leading his men across the wire, heading straight toward volleys of rifle fire, he suddenly became, according to a witnessing journalist, Edward Marshall, "the most magnificent soldier I have ever seen. It was as if that barbed-wire strand had formed a dividing line in his life." Leaving indecision behind, Marshall observed, Roosevelt found on the other side of the thicket "the coolness, the calm judgment, the towering heroism which made him, perhaps, the most admired and best beloved of all Americans in Cuba." Under Roosevelt's lead, the outnumbered Rough Riders charged uphill and drove back the Spanish soldiers.

What Roosevelt termed the "great day" of his life — the day that ended with the triumphant charges up Kettle Hill and San Juan Hill — began with him exhibiting to the Rough Riders the most placid morning-time demeanor, calmly shaving and knotting a blue polka-dot bandanna around his neck. Rough Rider Arthur Crosby found it heartening "to see our commanding officer on the dawn of a great battle performing an everyday function as though we were on an enjoyable camping trip." When orders came to march on Kettle Hill while the regulars attacked San Juan Hill, Roosevelt immediately mounted his horse and mustered his men, shouting, "We must advance. Rough Riders forward. Come on." With Roosevelt in the colonel's customary position at the rear of the column, the troops advanced hesitantly under a hail of bullets. To inspire his troops to move at an accelerated clip, Roosevelt, the only mounted man, suddenly charged up the lines, rallying his men as he made his way to the front of the regiment. "No one who saw Roosevelt take that ride expected he would finish it alive," Davis reported. Seated high on his horse with his blue polka-dot bandanna floating "out straight behind his head," he was "the most conspicuous object in the range of the rifle pits."

Ascending the hill, Roosevelt's troops were blocked by another regiment that had not yet received the official order to attack. "If you don't wish to go forward, let my men pass, please," Roosevelt addressed the captain. "Up, up they went in the face of death," one reporter marveled, "men dropping from the ranks at every step. The Rough Riders acted like veterans. It was an inspiring sight and an awful one." Roosevelt remained erect on his horse all the way, "shouting for his men to follow," until at last they forced the Spanish to retreat and reached the summit, "cheering and filling the air with cowboy yells." Within short order, the city of Santiago was captured and the Spanish surrendered.

In newspapers, magazines, and journals

across the country, Roosevelt was melodramatically portrayed as the man who "had single-handedly crushed the foe." Although Roosevelt effusively credited his regiment in multiple military reports and numerous conversations with journalists, carefully citing individuals he felt warranted special recognition, it was the iconic image of the man on horseback, the face so amenable to caricature, that became the emblem of American valor.

"You are the next governor of New York!" reporters shouted at Roosevelt when his regiment arrived at Montauk Point, Long Island. The situation was not so simple, however, as Roosevelt well understood. While he might be the choice of the people at large, the political machine controlled the nomination, and the powerful old boss Thomas Platt had no desire to see a reformer like Theodore in the governor's chair. In this instance, fate smiled upon Roosevelt. Once again, the Republican Party's prestige had been besmeared by an exposé of corruption in the current Republican administration in Albany. Believing the hero of San Juan the only candidate who could rescue the party from defeat, Platt reluctantly agreed to support him for the nomination. On September 15, 1898, the Rough Riders disbanded. Two days later, Theodore Roosevelt entered the governor's race.

The war veteran who ran for the highest office in New York State was not the same man who had volunteered to fight in Cuba. A more deepseated, durable confidence in his leadership capacities had been earned. "In my regiment," he told his son, "nine-tenths of the men were better horsemen than I was and two-thirds better shots than I was, while on the average they were certainly hardier and more enduring. Yet after I had them a very short while, they knew, and I knew too, that nobody else could command them as I could." After the experience of leading his men in combat, earning not only their trust but their devotion, Roosevelt had come to believe that leadership itself constituted the chief of his talents.

Perhaps due in some measure to the heroic image disseminated by the press, the returning colonel projected a newly minted charisma that enabled him to emotionally connect to his audiences. Though candidates in those days rarely campaigned on their own behalf, relying instead on the political machine to whip up voters, Roosevelt "stumped the State up and down and across and zigzag, speaking by day from the end of his special train and at night in mass meetings, in the towns and cities." He had an aura, one observer noted, "electrical, magnetic." Audiences discovered "that indefinable 'something' which led men to follow him up the bullet-swept hill of San Juan." Less than three months after returning home, Theodore Roosevelt was elected governor of New York.

Casting an eye over the improbable Cuban Summer, the campaign, and the election, he wrote to a friend, Cecil Spring Rice: "I have played it in bull luck this summer. First, to get into the war; then to get out of it; then, to get elected. I have worked hard all my life, and have never been particularly lucky, but this summer I was lucky, and I am enjoying it to the full. I know perfectly well that the luck will not continue, and it is not necessary that it should. I am more contented to be Governor of New York," he added, invoking a refrain psychologically necessary to him throughout his career, and always ending with "I shall not care if I never hold another office."

Roosevelt's newfound composure, patience, and maturity were immediately apparent in his adroit handling of the traditional undertow and riptides of New York politics. To reestablish his reputation as a reformer, he had to prove his independence; to get anything accomplished, he had to work with Boss Platt and his political machine. Within days of taking office, he announced that he would make weekly pilgrimages from Albany to New York City to meet with Boss Platt for breakfast or lunch. To reformers who complained that he was belittling "the dignity of the office" by "running down" to confer with the conservative, business-oriented Platt, Roosevelt countered that he had no sympathy for those who found it essential "to preserve their dignity by asserting their right to enter a room first, or to sit on a red instead of a green chair."

When he was younger, Roosevelt acknowledged, he was too prone to quarrel over trivial matters. The more he read about Abraham Lincoln, the more he valued Lincoln's willingness to yield lesser issues for more important ones. "No man resolved to make the most of himself, can spare time for personal contention," Lincoln was wont to say. A conciliatory tone with Platt cost the new governor nothing and could well enhance future endeavors. Moreover, Roosevelt was sensitive to the old man's pride. Despite the appearance of capitulating to the Boss, he was happy to meet on Platt's home ground.

In Albany, Roosevelt scheduled every moment of his day with quick military precision, allotting the scores of daily petitioners specific time slots of five or ten minutes. No sooner had the visitor entered the room than the governor jumped up from behind his desk to greet him. "I am delighted to see you," he began, warmly clasping the visitor's hand. During these sessions, Roosevelt remained "ever on his feet," pacing restlessly back and forth, encouraging immediate discussion of "the meat" of the subject. Listening intently, he rapidly absorbed whether he would accede to the request, take it "under advisement," or regret that he had to say no. Once the decision was rendered, the visitor was gently ushered out of the office with hardly a slack moment before the next visitor entered.

During his tenure as governor, Roosevelt liked to reference an old African proverb: "Speak softly and carry a big stick." If a leader "continually blusters," "lacks civility" or likes to quarrel, Roosevelt cautioned, he would not go far. Nor would he succeed by speaking softly if "strength" and "power" did not lay "back of that softness." As always, a good leader must make it clear that if negotiation fails, as a last resort he would be willing to turn his back and walk away.

Two struggles during his governorship — the fight over a franchise tax and the reappointment of an insurance commissioner with suspected illicit ties to the insurance industry — best illustrate how Roosevelt successfully navigated his contentious relationship with the political machine.

Roosevelt discovered that for decades past the New York legislature had granted exclusive franchises worth tens or even hundreds of millions of dollars to corporations to operate electric street railways, telephone networks, and telegraph lines. Such lucrative franchises were regularly awarded with no attempt to secure tax revenues in return. Recompense came in the form of campaign contributions to fuel the Platt machine — funds which were then distributed to candidates for the state legislature with the "gentlemen's understanding" they could be counted upon for important votes, particularly those related to corporate interests.

"It was a matter of plain decency" that corporations receiving great benefits from the public should "pay their fair share of the public burden," the new governor flatly concluded after thoroughly researching the franchise issue. He sent a special message to the legislature indicating his support for a franchise tax bill. The bill's surprise passage just before the legislature adjourned set off a "storm of protest" from the business world. Overnight, the stock market plunged. Angry corporate representatives descended upon Roosevelt, threatening to move their operations to a more accommodating state. Platt, in a bitter letter, promised an ugly confrontation unless Roosevelt summoned the courage to correct "the big mistake" of his life by declining to sign the bill.

Refusing to be bullied, yet understanding that a break with the machine would be politically fatal, Roosevelt agreed to hold a hearing with corporate representatives in order to solicit suggestions for improvements in the bill. So long as the kernel of the bill remained intact, he considered everything else the husk which he was willing, if necessary, to discard. Persuaded by these conferences that sections of the law were carelessly drawn, he consented to call the legislature back into a special session to modify the bill. If the ultimate product weakened the principle of taxation in any essential way, however, he was fully prepared to restore and sign the original bill. The final legislation both protected the core principle of taxation and made minimal concessions allowing Platt to save face with his constituents in the business community.

Roosevelt's inclination to "speak softly and carry a big stick" brought an even more troubling dispute with the Republican organization to a desirable outcome. He had heard rumors that Platt's "right-hand" man, superintendent of insurance Lou Payn, had "intimate" dealings with companies he was assigned to regulate. Roosevelt decided to conduct his own inquiry. Preliminary evidence was sufficient to persuade him that Payn should not be reappointed once his three-year term ended. Platt met Roosevelt's decision with an "ultimatum": By law, the incumbent could remain in office until a successor was confirmed. Since the machine controlled the Senate, Platt effectively had the power to veto any replacement the governor chose. The boss made it clear to Roosevelt that he intended to use that power as long as necessary.

"I persistently refused to lose my temper, no matter what he said," Roosevelt recalled. "I had made up my mind," he simply explained to Platt, "that the gentleman in question would not be retained." To ease the matter, he gave Platt "a list of four good machine men" and told the Boss to select any one of the four. Platt refused to budge. Reformers abused Roosevelt for negotiating at all with Platt. They wanted him to wage open warfare. The impasse dragged on for weeks until further investigation disclosed a $400,000 loan Payn had received from a trust company controlled by an insurance firm under his own jurisdiction. To prevent a scandal, Platt quietly capitulated, agreeing to the nomination of one of the men on Roosevelt's list.

If he had "yelled and blustered" in public, Roosevelt told a friend, he would not have mustered "ten votes" in the Senate; by the same token, if he had not wielded "the big stick," the organization would not have gotten behind him. He had preserved his relationship with Platt "by the simple process of telling him the truth, of always letting him know before anyone else when [he] was going to do something that I knew would be disagreeable to him." Platt respected Roosevelt's personal candor: "I have ever preferred that a man should tell me face to face

317

that he will or will not do a thing, than to promise to do it and then to not do it."

Despite the governor's ostensible truce with Platt, the business corporations "served notice" on Platt's political organization that if Roosevelt were renominated they would refuse to contribute to the Republican Party's campaign chest. Since it was risky to flagrantly deny the popular governor a second term, the organization devised a perfect solution. They would promote Roosevelt to "the most dignified and harmless position in the gift of his country — the Vice-Presidency." Exiling him to the vice presidency would kill two birds with one stone: The chronic irritant of his presence would be excised from New York politics; at the same time, the Republican Party and McKinley would be invigorated by Roosevelt's charisma and energy on the national campaign trail.

Boss Platt's scheme attracted the support of all the party bosses in the Republican Party save one — Mark Hanna, Republican Party chair. "Don't you know that there's only one life between that madman and the White House?" he warned. Even Hanna eventually concluded, however, that Roosevelt would add more traction to the national ticket than any other candidate. At first, Roosevelt strongly resisted the so-called promotion. He had no desire to be the "figurehead" in a job then considered a graveyard for political ambitions. Not a single vice president had been elected to the presidency in over sixty years. He understood, however, that if he refused the nomination, people would say, "Roosevelt has a big head and thinks he is too much of a man to be Vice-President." When the convention nominated him by acclamation, he felt he had no choice but to accept with gratitude and grace. "His enemies triumphed," Jacob Riis wrote, "at last they had him where they wanted him."

For the first time in a decade and a half of focusing his full concentration on the job at hand, Roosevelt occupied a job where his active temperament could gain no hold. Frustration, depression born of inactivity grew by the day in that "useless and empty position," where he was bereft of the spotlight he craved as a plant craves sunshine. The president gave him no responsibilities, nor did he seek Roosevelt's advice. Roosevelt grew so bored that he contemplated returning to law school. Wistfully, he told his close friend William Howard Taft, then fully engaged as governor-general in the Philippines, "I am not doing any work and do not feel as though I was justifying my existence. More and more it seems to me that about the best thing in life is to have a piece of work worth doing and then to do it well."

Friends counseled patience. They remained fully confident that the White House would be his future home. But Roosevelt reasoned that by the time McKinley's second term ended, his window upon the presidency might be shut forever. Life had shown him that logic and step-by-step planning hardly controlled events. Before an opportunity might arise to attain the presidency (the position he could scarcely bring himself to mention aloud), he knew "the kaleidoscope will have shifted completely and the odds are that an entirely new set of men and set of issues will be at the front. Moreover, to change the metaphor, the chances are strong that the pendulum will have swung back and that a Democratic victory will be in order."

Kaleidoscopes and pendulums — Roosevelt's images connoted an abiding belief in the hard lesson of his crucible philosophy: All one can do is to prepare oneself, to wait in readiness for what might come.

Chance had placed him in the catapult and now it was up to the vagaries of history to cut the catapult's rope. On September 6, 1901, an assassin's bullet brought McKinley's life to a slow end, and at forty-two years of age, Theodore Roosevelt was "shot into the presidency," the youngest man to occupy the White House in the history of the country.

SEVEN:
FRANKLIN ROOSEVELT

"Above all, try something"

On a late August day in 1921 at Campobello, the family's island retreat off Downeast Maine, Franklin Roosevelt awoke with a mild sensation that something was wrong. His back ached and he felt oddly enervated. Nothing serious, he assumed; physical activity would surely shake off this peculiar torpor.

From youth, Roosevelt took keen pleasure in a large range of physical exertion. His earliest letters expressed the thrill of sledding, skating, and fishing with his father. He developed into an avid golfer, tennis player, sailor, and horseback rider. While neither strong nor muscular, he was agile and graceful. A family friend never forgot the vision of young Franklin leaping "like some amazing stag" across a brook; an observer at the 1920 convention was struck by the moment he hurdled four or five chairs in order to make a motion: "It was the most wonderful athletic feat," she recalled.

So, rather than surrendering to his weariness by remaining in bed, he had launched upon a day of strenuous physical activity. First, he embarked on a long sail with Eleanor and their two oldest sons. On their return home, they spotted a brushfire on one of the islands. Bringing the boat close to shore, they jumped out and spent an hour slapping down smoldering flames. Eyes "bleary with smoke," they no sooner had reached their "cottage" when Franklin challenged the boys to jog a mile and a half to their favorite swimming spot, a freshwater pond on the other side of the island. Still unrefreshed and uncomfortable after swimming, he raced the boys back home and plunged into the ice-cold Bay of Fundy. Then, suddenly so lethargic he was unable to take off his wet bathing suit, he slumped on the porch and tried to sort through mail. Abruptly, he announced that he had a severe chill and would go straight to bed. "I'd never felt quite that way before," he recalled.

Within forty-eight hours, paralysis had spread to his limbs, thumbs, toes, back, bladder, and rectal sphincter. Pain shot up and down his legs. Misdiagnosis by the first attending doctors accelerated his dire condition. Fear, confusion, and persistent agony followed. Finally, a specialist was summoned who correctly diagnosed his condition — poliomyelitis, a virus that attacked the nerves controlling muscular activity. In the days that followed, Eleanor, with the support of Franklin's assistant, Louis Howe, a guest at Campobello, lifted him off the bed onto a bedpan. She administered enemas and learned how to use a catheter. The doctor mandated complete bed rest, save a daily tub of soothing warm water.

For weeks, Franklin lay in bed, unable to perform the most basic bodily functions on his own. He had sustained a fundamental blow to his body, to his identity as a man and a human being. Until the acute phase passed, no predictions could be made about the subsequent course of his illness. Some muscles might return; others would recover only partial strength or remain totally paralyzed. In mid-September, he was transferred from Campobello to New York Presbyterian Hospital, where he remained for six weeks. While his bladder and sphincter muscles returned, his shoulders remained remarkably weak, his back could not support a seated position, and his legs showed no response at all. The physicians generally concurred that he would not walk or stand on his own power. Neither Eleanor nor Louis Howe believed he would ever be able to use his legs again. Upon discharge the chart read: "Not improving."

The poet Koltsov, referenced by Turgenev in the story "Death," asks:

What if a falcon's
Wings are tied?
What if all ways
Are to him denied?

It was this dreary future of dependency and obstruction that this graceful falcon of a man was now forced to contemplate: loss of uprightness, deprived of the stamina and appearance of strength which political leadership seemed to demand.

Franklin Roosevelt's ordeal provides the most clear-cut paradigm of how a devastating crucible experience can, against all expectation and logic, lead to significant growth, intensified ambition, and enlarged gifts for leadership. The trajectory he had envisioned as a twenty-five-year-old, the large figure he longed to cut in the world — climbing from the state legislature to assistant secretary of the navy, up to governor of New York, and then to the presidency itself — had in all likelihood been derailed. Months and years of striving lay ahead of him, accompanied by fear, anxiety, and concealed bouts of depression; but eventually, the sustained effort Roosevelt directed toward spiritual, mental, emotional, and physical recovery led him to a spectacular, albeit risk-filled return to public life.

Roosevelt's irrepressible optimism, his tendency to expect the best outcome in any circumstance, provided the keystone strength that carried him through this traumatic experience. From the outset, he set an objective: a future in which he would fully recover. Although necessity forced him to modify the timetable for attaining this goal, he never lost his conviction that he would eventually succeed.

Roosevelt's physician, Dr. George Draper, feared that his remarkably upbeat patient would be unable to cope once he fully understood the gravity of his situation. During his hospital stay, Roosevelt was always smiling and cheerful, casting a genial glow of positive jocularity onto his visitors. In letters and conversations with friends, he predicted that he would be upright on crutches by the time he left the hospital, walking without a limp by the following spring. Then, it was simply a matter of time before he could resume playing golf. "The psychological factor in his management is paramount," Draper told a fellow doctor. "He has such courage, such ambition, and yet at the same time such an extraordinarily sensitive emotional mechanism, that it will take all the skill which we can muster to lead him successfully to a recognition of what he really faces without utterly crushing him."

Dr. Draper was not the first to miscalculate the resourceful depths of Roosevelt's character. Appearing "bright and happy" had been the expected pattern of behavior in the Roosevelt household in the wake of the heart attack that left his father an invalid. The changed dynamic at Springwood — a defense fashioned to protect Mr. James from worry or anxiety — had demanded secrecy and duplicity. Franklin's letters from Groton sparkled with reports of how splendidly he was getting along with his classmates, when in reality he was lonely, ill at ease, and having difficulty fitting in.

Now, in the face of traumatic illness, Roosevelt brought these old patterns of behavior to bear in a more powerfully nuanced way than ever before. The positive image he projected, so starkly incongruous from the ordeal he was confronting, was not simply to protect others but to buoy his own spirits. Some days were harder than others. In time, however, the steadfast affectation of good cheer begot real cheer. If there was something contrived and theatrical about the relentless sunniness he conveyed — a willful whistling in the dark — he radiated warmth, hope, and confidence that would, in the end, prove contagious.

Fueled by resolution, perseverance, and newly acquired patience, he set forth on the tortuous journey to reclaim his "rebellious" body. Told that his upper body had the greatest likelihood of recovery, Franklin endured punishing exercises to salvage and remake his chest, shoulders, neck, arms, and back. In a manner more grueling than any body building of Theodore Roosevelt, Franklin did everything possible to solidify the intact remnant of his physical core. Hour after hour he pulled himself up on a set of rings installed in "a trapeze-like contraption" above his bed, slowly and painfully strengthening his muscles until his upper body came to resemble that of a champion boxer or wrestler. With powerful arms, he could finally manipulate a wheelchair, and push himself into a sitting position. Everything below the waist, however, remained "a goner," according to one of his doctors, preventing him from getting into or out of the wheelchair without assistance. Day after day he would ask to be lifted from the wheelchair and set down on the library floor so that he could further exercise his back and arms by crawling around the room. He then proceeded to tackle stairs, grabbing railings on either side with his hands, hoisting up his body step by step to the top, sweat pouring from his face. He insisted that family members be on hand to witness and cheer on each of these triumphs.

And with every small "win," Eleanor observed, Franklin felt stronger than before. "He regained his joy in living," she later wrote, "his hearty laughter, his ability to be happy over little things." The day he was at last able to move one of his frozen toes called for a grand celebration, creating a shared mood of joy and happiness. When asked during his presidency how he dealt with continuing problems, he half-jokingly observed: "If you spent two years in bed trying to wiggle your big toe, anything would seem easy!" Each increment of increased mobility led to the possibility of new progress. After being fitted with heavy steel braces to keep his legs rigid, he met the laborious challenge of learning to totter awkwardly on crutches. Through it all, he adamantly refused to relinquish his ultimate goal of walking on his own.

In his never-ending search for treatment, Roosevelt deployed a "trial and error" method, an indelible fingerprint of his leadership style. In the Navy Department, he had flung ideas against the wall to see which ones might stick; during the New Deal he would experiment with one program after another, swiftly changing course if the present one proved ineffective. Now, he enthusiastically embraced dozens of novel contraptions: an electric belt, an oversized tricycle, a specially designed shoe, a children's double-swing. Over time, he invented his own devices to deal with "a number of mechanical problems" that obstructed his mobility. He designed a small wheelchair without arms to exercise his quadriceps and fastened pincers to a stick to reach his library books. He had the first hand-operated throttle and brake installed in his motor vehicle.

And all the while, he carried out an extensive correspondence with his "fellow polios," as he addressed them, comparing ideas for overcoming common dilemmas. The shared vulnerability revealed in these letters represented the first flowering of a new humility of spirit, a concern for the pain and suffering of others that would later grow to maturity during his years at Warm Springs, Georgia.

Far more than the sum of its parts, the unorthodox, fiercely loyal, and intimate team that Franklin assembled during his seven-year convalescence — comprised of Eleanor Roosevelt, Louis Howe, and Missy LeHand

— became an extension of Roosevelt's body. Together, they functionally diminished the isolating impact of his paralysis. We have seen how Abraham Lincoln and Theodore Roosevelt reassembled and reinvented themselves in the wake of their crucible experiences. The nature of Roosevelt's paralytic polio was such, however, that he had to depend on others as he fought to recover his physical and mental strength. This highly talented team dedicated their lives to "serving his purposes," as Eleanor once said. Simultaneously, he manifestly served their purposes. For Franklin's long period of recovery and transformation was also a time of metamorphosis for all three members of the core team, a time of realignment and growth, a time when they discovered previously undeveloped interests and talents of their own.

Both Eleanor Roosevelt and Louis Howe recognized from the outset that Franklin's spirit would be destroyed if his political ambitions were throttled. "If he didn't have political hope," they believed, "he would die spiritually, die intellectually, and die in his personality." Working side by side, they mobilized a strenuous campaign to sustain his political dreams. Anxiously at first, and then with genuine enthusiasm, Eleanor took on the task of keeping her husband's name alive in political circles. She served as his surrogate at public events, joined various Democratic Party committees, volunteered for the victorious gubernatorial campaign of New Yorker Al Smith, and spoke at luncheons and dinners. Having little experience in public speaking, her son James recalled, she gave more than a hundred practice speeches to an audience of one — her mentor and coach, Louis Howe. Howe taught her to restrain her nervous giggle, lower her high-pitched voice, say what she wanted to say, and then sit down. When she began to speak before packed audiences, Howe would sit in the back row, using a series of hand signals (similar to those Lyndon Johnson would employ with his debate students) to indicate where she was reaching her audience, and where she had fallen into nervous mannerisms. Before long, she was recognized as a powerful speaker.

Entering public life proved a liberating force for Eleanor. Her marriage had foundered three years earlier upon her discovery of a packet of love letters to her husband from a young woman named Lucy Mercer. When Franklin pledged never to see Lucy again, Eleanor agreed to remain in the marriage. From that moment on, she later told friends, she no longer loved him in the same way, though they remained joined by unbreakable ties and retained "a deep and unshakeable affection and tenderness" toward one another.

Now, in the wake of Franklin's paralysis, she could serve her husband's initiatives and simultaneously forge a role for herself. In the course of her political activities for Franklin, she joined a circle of progressive feminists dedicated to abolishing child labor, passing protective legislation for female workers, fighting for the minimum wage and maximum work hours. She further developed the leadership traits she had exercised during her days as a star student in boarding school: organizing people, inspiring them to loyalty, articulating their goals. She was stirred once again by the ambitions that had been curbed by the responsibility to care for a husband and five children. With his paralysis, new opportunity had opened up whereby she might aid him and realize her own dreams of leaving a mark on the world.

Franklin's paralysis transformed Louis Howe's world in equally dramatic fashion. For nearly a decade, while married with two children, Howe had served as Franklin's secretary, adviser, and friend. Franklin's illness, Howe told an interviewer, "changed everything." From the moment his boss was stricken, Howe never lived with his family again, choosing instead to make the Roosevelt family his own, visiting his wife and children only on occasional weekends. He had his own room at the Campobello cottage, the New York townhouse, the Governor's Mansion, and ultimately, the White House. "He had one loyalty in life and it was a kind of religion," White House speechwriter Sam Rosenman said: "Franklin D. Roosevelt." He courted politicians on Franklin's behalf; held private conferences with Democratic governors, mayors, and congressmen; attended local and state party conventions; and put together a twice-weekly roundup of interesting articles and gossip about politics, business, and world affairs — creating in effect a newspaper designed for a readership of one — Franklin Roosevelt. "Father was too busy with his fight for his life to think of his political future," Roosevelt's son James said. According to his biographer, "Howe's solution to balance the two priorities — Roosevelt's physical well-being and the resumption of his public life — was to lift one of them off of his shoulders." Howe's belief in Roosevelt's destiny was a matter of faith. Soon after Franklin was stricken by polio, when Eleanor queried Howe as to whether her husband could navigate the rough-and-tumble world of politics, Howe assured her that nothing had altered his belief that one day Franklin would be president of the United States.

Meanwhile, Roosevelt continued to pursue his own consuming vision of full recovery. While grudgingly he agreed to wear the cumbersome twenty-pound braces and practice using crutches, he never stopped searching for a cure that would allow him to regain the power of walking, the necessary condition, he believed, for him to fulfill his political ambitions. He continued the arduous task of experimentation to figure which treatments worked most effectively. He found that his "leg muscles responded more quickly" when he could sit outside in the summer sun; on cloudy days they would "freeze up from about 5 p.m. on." In swimming he found the most promising therapy of all, one allowing him to exercise his legs without the weight of gravity.

Roosevelt held an almost mystical belief in the healing power of sun and water. He had been enraptured from early childhood by sea tales of his grandfather's clipper ship days, thrilled at learning to sail with his father, and considered his model ships and naval prints among his most prized possessions. Not surprisingly, his relentless search for a cure led to the halcyon waters off Florida, where he spent the winter months cruising on the *Larooco,* a spacious houseboat, in the company of the third member of the team, twenty-five-year-old Missy LeHand. "Water got me into this fix," he mystically quipped (referring to his dip in the ice-cold Bay of Fundy), "water will get me out again!"

Unexpectedly, Missy LeHand would play as vital a role in Franklin's restoration as either Eleanor or Louis. Eleanor had accompanied Franklin on his first Florida cruise, but she detested the listless days occupied by fishing, entertaining guests, and simply relaxing. Far better for everyone, Eleanor believed (and, in some large part, rationalized) that Missy should remain with Franklin in Florida while she herself returned to New York to cultivate prospective political allies and pursue the network of new friendships that had grown central to her own social and intellectual existence. Thus, Missy became Franklin's other "wife." Over the next four years, Roosevelt spent a total of 116 weeks in the South. Of that total, Missy accompanied him for 110 weeks, Eleanor for four weeks, his mother, Sara, for two. Missy gave "Effdee," as she called him, unconditional devotion. Like Louis, she was absorbed into the Roosevelt family and would live in both the Governor's Mansion and the White House.

The early months spent on the *Larooco* allowed Franklin to evade the martial rigor of the exercise regime prescribed by his doctors, giving him time to explore his own idiosyncratic routines. Holding the boat's tiller, he could feel the surge of control. He floated in the warm waters, lowered from the side of the boat by a contraption of his own contrivance, and bathed in the sun. Missy sat by his side as he fished from the deck, served as his hostess when guests regularly came aboard, and shared his "sense of nonsense" in a way Eleanor never could. Storytelling, fun, and humor were as central to Roosevelt's well-being as to Lincoln's. But even more important than the role Missy played in sustaining Franklin's high spirits was the fact that he was able to reveal to her his darker fears. "There were days on the *Larooco,*" she later told his secretary of labor Frances Perkins, "when it was noon before he could pull himself out of depression and greet his guests wearing his light-hearted façade." Slowly, but surely, those bad days began to dwindle.

Roosevelt would replicate the strengths of this inner circle in the years ahead, as he expanded his working team as governor and president. There was not a yes man/woman among this original triumvirate. They offered Roosevelt a range of opinions, delivered in widely different ways. From the earliest days of their relationship, Louis Howe had never hesitated to argue with Franklin. According to Rosenman, Howe "probably said No to Roosevelt more frequently and loudly than anyone else, and stuck to his position longer." Missy handled dissent in a more fun-loving but equally effective manner. In addition to her various gifts as typist, companion, and hostess, she was an astute reader of Roosevelt's moods and needs, "never hesitating to tell him unpleasant truths or express an unfavorable opinion about his work," yet always with a deft sense of timing, and always in a way he could handle. During one of his campaigns, she was in the room while Roosevelt read aloud from the draft of a tedious speech on finance to be delivered at Pittsburgh's Forbes Field. Before he reached the second page, Missy stood up: "By this time the bleachers are empty and the folks are beginning to walk out of the grandstand." Everyone burst into laughter and the speechwriters started over from scratch.

Eleanor, of course, added the most essential dimension to the progressive strain and moral gravity of Franklin Roosevelt's leadership. "He might have been happier with a wife who was completely uncritical," she observed in her memoirs, adding, "That I was never able to be." She was more uncompromising, more straightforward, more deeply involved with activists whose thoughts challenged conventional boundaries. His political timing and overall comprehension of public sentiment was far more astute than hers. If he balked at something she wanted, she would return to try again. If he would not meet with someone she thought it imperative for him to meet, she would take it upon herself to invite that person to dinner. "I sometimes acted as a spur even though the spurring was not always wanted or welcomed," she later wrote. Her constant pressure and lack of humor made it difficult for him to relax. "We're not going to do that now," he would often cut her short. "I don't want to hear about that anymore." And yet, invariably, he would return to her unwanted suggestion, realizing before long that her persistence might well have been warranted.

This remarkable team, locked together in a complicated dance around the same center, succeeded so well in keeping Roosevelt's spirits up and his political name alive that in 1924, three years after the onset of polio, Governor Al Smith proffered Franklin Roosevelt the New York chairmanship of his pre-convention campaign for the presidency. Roosevelt hesitated at first, feeling far too vulnerable to appear in public, but when told they simply needed his name, not his body, he agreed to become titular head of the campaign. Two months later, Governor Smith presented Roosevelt with a far more unnerving and challenging proposition: Would he consent to place Smith's name in nomination at the Democratic National Convention to be held at Madison Square Garden in late June?

If ever there were an example of political courage, of an enormous risk taken, of great personal and public stakes wagered, it was Roosevelt's acceptance of Al Smith's offer — given the looming prospect of a pratfall in front of twelve thousand delegates.

That Franklin had not yet mastered the technique of walking with braces and crutches had been made clear months earlier when he ventured forth for the first time since the polio attack to meet with business colleagues at a private luncheon on Wall Street. An elevator would carry him upstairs; but first, he had to cross a slippery marble lobby to reach the elevator bank. With his chauffeur's assistance, he had reached the halfway mark when a crutch skidded out from under him. He collapsed in a heap, his hat rolling off to the side. Appalled spectators gathered round as he tried to prop himself into a seated position. "Nothing to worry about," Franklin announced to placate the onlookers, bursting into a sudden peal of laughter. "We'll get out of this all right." He then called for help from two young men who eventually pulled him to a standing position. "Let's go," he said to his chauffeur. Someone put his hat on his head. Cheerfully, he acknowledged the crowd, and made his way toward the elevator.

The convention speech was to be his first public appearance in three years. It was one thing to fall in a lobby, quite another to risk humiliation and jeopardize one's political ambitions at a national party convention that would be broadcast nationwide for the first time on radio. To minimize the immense risk, he carefully rehearsed and trained. "Nobody knows how that man worked," Eleanor's suffragist friend Marion Dickerman recalled. "They measured off in the library at the 65th Street house just what the distance was and he struggled, and struggled and struggled." With the support of his sixteen-year-old son, James, he alternately shifted his weight from his son's arm on the left to the crutch under his right arm. James remembered how his father's fingers dug painfully into his arm "like pincers" as he hoisted and dragged his legs, locked in heavy steel braces, along the narrow line between potential pity and awe toward the imaginary podium.

On the night of the actual performance, Franklin directed a friend to shake the rostrum in order to assure him of its weight-bearing stability. When his moment of introduction came, he replaced his son's arm with another crutch and approached the lectern alone. "There was a hush and everybody was holding their breath," Frances Perkins recalled. After what seemed a long-drawn moment of tension, he reached the rostrum, handed off his crutches, gripped the lectern edges with his powerful, viselike grip, tilted back his head, and "across his face there flashed a vast, world-encompassing smile." Twelve thousand voices exploded with admiration for the courage he epitomized even before his speech had begun. This was a far cry from the "unfortunate habit" of throwing his head back when he was in the state legislature, a gesture that had seemed condescending to Perkins, the unconscious mannerism of a handsome and entitled youth. Now, by contrast, his stiffened legs and strained shoulders supported a head thrown back with hard-earned pride and perhaps a touch of theatrical confidence; rather than vanity, this was the confidence of having overcome fear of humiliation, a confidence born of making a great effort, of taking a great risk — and overcoming.

His rich tenor voice had a musical quality as he asked delegates "from the great cities of the East and the plains and hills of the West, from the slopes of the Pacific and from the homes and fields of the southlands" to close divisions between city and country, wet and dry, Catholic and Protestant, and unite behind Governor Al Smith, "the 'Happy Warrior' of the political battlefield." This epithet, drawn from a Wordsworth poem about how one confronts life's difficulties, how one "doomed to go in company with pain/turns his necessity to glorious gain," would from that moment forever affix itself to Al Smith; with striking force, however, it succinctly described Franklin Roosevelt himself. Seated in a front row, Perkins observed that he was "trembling" and "shaking" from the "extreme pain and tenseness with which he held himself up to make that speech," but his delivery "was strong and true and vigorous." He stood as the living emblem of a man who had truly transformed his own pain and necessity into glorious gain.

When he finished, according to Eleanor's friend Marion Dickerman, the crowd "just went crazy," igniting an hour-long demonstration. "They howled, yelled, screamed and sang from densely crowded galleries," the Hagerstown, Maryland *Morning Herald* reported. "I have witnessed many heroic deeds in my lifetime," the reporter for the *Syracuse Herald* wrote, "but I never was present at so fine a display of mental courage." It little matters, the New York *World* editorialized, if Governor Smith gains the nomination (he would lose on the 103rd ballot), for "the real hero" of the convention is Franklin Roosevelt. "Adversity has lifted him above the bickering, conflicting personal ambitions and petty sectional prejudices." Indeed, the hard-boiled Kansas City boss, Tom Pendergast, opined that if Roosevelt had "been physically able to withstand the campaign, he would have been named by acclamation . . . he has the most magnetic personality of any individual I have ever met." Later that evening, Eleanor hosted a reception at their New York house. Exhausted but exhilarated, Franklin kept to his room. When Marion Dickerman went to see him, "he held out his arms and he said, 'Marion, I *did* it!' "

Though four years would pass before Franklin returned in earnest to his political vocation, this speech was a vital way station. That he had made great progress was evident by this trial balloon, but his greatest growth as a man and as a leader lay ahead — on a road that led through Warm Springs, Georgia.

The story of Warm Springs, the pioneering rehabilitation center Roosevelt built from a ramshackle resort, begins with his "discovery of a place" where he believed he would learn to walk again. Instead, he experienced a different kind of recovery, developed a more profound level of humility, and provided inspiration for (and was inspired by) the vibrant community he created with his fellow polios.

Told about a spa in Georgia where a young man had restored strength to his legs by swimming in a giant pool fed by mineral water that gushed from the hillside at a soothing 86 degrees, Roosevelt journeyed to the Meriwether Inn to find out for himself. His initial impression of the once popular resort was not heartening. "Almost everything was falling to pieces," Roosevelt later recalled, the turreted wooden hotel dilapidated and the roofs of the surrounding cottages leaking. But the buoyant water of the T-shaped thermal pool delivered on its promise, allowing him to exercise his muscles for an extended period of time without throbbing fatigue. "Every morning I spend two hours in the most wonderful pool in the world," he told a friend. "There is no question this place does more good than all the rest of the exercising put together."

Within a matter of weeks, he had "a hunch" that "a great 'cure' for infantile paralysis and kindred diseases could well be established here." He envisioned a renovated hotel with bright, sunny rooms, spruced-up cottages, a medical staff of doctors, nurses, and physical therapists, along with a host of recreational and social activities designed to let the patients "live normal lives and at the same time receive the best treatment known to science at the time." Furthermore, the place he imagined held out the curative promise of the great European spas he had known so well as a child without the trappings of wealth — here was therapy within a rustic and democratic simplicity. Meditating years afterward on Roosevelt's leadership strengths, Frances Perkins marveled that "there were times when he could truly see it all," when he instinctively understood how one decision or one undertaking related to another. Warm Springs was such a time.

That he was able to turn his initial vision into a combined resort and treatment center that would accommodate hundreds of patients and their families revealed a surprising entrepreneurial flair. Against the advice of his wife, mother, and friends, he decided to invest $200,000 (roughly two-thirds of his fortune) to buy the hotel, the springs, and the cottages along with twelve hundred acres of land. This would be the first major project he administered completely on his own.

Deploying a hands-on, dogged leadership, he worked with architects to build a completely accessible campus, dispensing advice on remodeling the hotel and the surrounding buildings. In addition to his role as "consulting architect," Roosevelt served as "landscape engineer," provided suggestions for manicured lawns, oversaw the planting of trees and flowering garden arrangements. He designed the layout of golf courses, riding trails, a dance hall, and a movie theater. During the construction phase, he drove around encouraging the crew with a contagious zeal, just as he had made the rounds with his father surveying the various construction projects at Springwood. He staffed the facility with great care. Recognizing the importance of support from the medical establishment, he persuaded the American Orthopedic Association to create "a research protocol" to measure outcomes and deliver a report. When the report proved positive, he placed the entire enterprise into a nonprofit foundation. This allocation allowed him to raise additional funds to carry out improvements and to make provisions for those who could not afford the full fare, making a reality of his initial democratic impulse.

He became known as old Doc Roosevelt, head counselor, spiritual director, "Vice-President in charge of picnics," and therapy pioneer "all rolled into one." He directed morning exercises in the therapy pool and then led patients to a separate pool, where they laughed and shouted as they engaged in swimming contests, played tag and water polo. During the afternoons and evenings, "there were bridge tournaments and poker games, classes, movies, excursions, amateur theatricals," as well as festive cocktail parties and dinners. He aimed not merely to restore the bodies of the patients but to return the possibility of joy and pleasure to their lives. "We mustn't let the fun go out of our program," he insisted. "We've got to make these patients more alive every day." He took pride, he told a reporter, in having created "a remarkable spirit of cooperation and competition among the patients to see who can improve the most," adding that "the spirit of the place has an extraordinary effect on the progress they make. Here they find people just like themselves. They get over their self-consciousness."

While micromanaging this grand scheme for almost four years, Roosevelt underwent what Perkins has called a "spiritual transformation." An "old priest" had once told her that "humility is the first and greatest of virtues. If we don't learn it on our own, the Lord will surely teach it to us by humiliation." The humility Roosevelt learned at Warm Springs was of a different order than merely accepting one's limitations. By sharing those limitations with his fellow polios, by listening and learning from them, he had, Perkins believed, "purged" the elitist aura that had once surrounded him. He emerged from the experience "completely warm-hearted, with humility of spirit and with a deeper philosophy."

He had developed a powerful new empathy, allowing him to connect emotionally with all manner of people to whom fate had also dealt an unkind blow. He had inspired the entire Warm Springs community with his optimistic spirit, infusing his fellow polios with his own indomitable courage. "It was," one patient recalled, "a place which changed forever our feelings about ourselves and the man who made this . . . possible." And he, in turn, had experienced the intense fulfillment of linking his ambitions to the betterment of others, of creating an institution from the ground up that would serve for generations as a model for the treatment of people with disabilities.

At Warm Springs, he had found a cure different from what he had initially sought. He had come to restore his ability to walk (a condition he thought requisite to run for public office). He knew that no one so paralyzed had ever been active and successful in politics. Could a propped-up leader, a wheeled or carried leader, lead and uplift? Were crutches antithetical to American command? He knew the answers to those questions now. He had developed a different concept of leadership. The deep affection and respect accorded him from the shared community he had created at Warm Springs made it clear that a polio victim who needed help to walk was fully able to exercise leadership of the highest order. He had made a separate peace with his recovery and in his heart was ready to recommence with a life fully in the public glare.

Opportunity knocked in 1928, when Al Smith, having won the Democratic nomination for president, pressured Roosevelt — as a service to both the party and himself — to run for governor of New York. The Roosevelt name, Smith figured, would boost voter turnout in a state that had to be won. All the Democratic Party hoped from Roosevelt, Smith assured him, were four or five radio addresses to strategically punctuate the month-long campaign. As soon as the campaign was done, Roosevelt could turn over the heavy lifting to the lieutenant governor and return to Warm Springs and recuperation.

While Al Smith had rightly calculated the impact of the Roosevelt name in New York, he had badly miscalculated the man himself. Once Roosevelt had agreed to be drafted and assumed the responsibility of running for governor, he was in it for keeps. "When you're in politics you have to play the game," he told a friend. He resolved to prove to himself and to the public that he had the physical vigor and the capacity for sustained hard work that would outstrip any ordinary campaign effort. Often speaking fourteen times a day, he delivered thirty-three major speeches in thirty different venues, together with scores of informal talks and clusters of meetings.

"It was a dreadful physical business to make this campaign," Perkins observed. "He really was kind of scared." As she watched him being carried up a fire escape to enter a third-floor hall, "a perilous, uncomfortable" ordeal, she said to herself, "My God, he's got nerve." Moreover, he accepted his "humiliating entrance" with grace and dignity. He was "good-natured" with everyone, "conserving his strength" by never complaining about small things or wasting time over trifles: "If you can't use your legs and they bring you milk when you wanted orange juice, you learn to say, 'That's all right,' and drink it."

Roosevelt eked out a narrow victory in the gubernatorial race, but in the national election Smith went down to defeat when a Republican wave swept Herbert Hoover into the White House. Stunned by the devastating loss, Smith retreated to Albany, determined to be the power behind the governor whose nomination he had engineered at the Democratic State Convention.

Just as Roosevelt had not waged a token campaign, however, so he made it clear during the transition that he would not be a proxy governor. Shortly before Christmas, Roosevelt later recounted, "Al came to see me and told me that Mrs. Moscowitz [Belle Moskowitz, Smith's political manager and chief aide] was preparing my Inaugural Address and Message to the Legislature. Honestly I think he did this in complete good faith . . . but at the same time with the rather definite thought that he himself would continue to run the Governorship. His first bad shock came when I told him that I had already prepared my Inaugural Address and that my Message to the Legislature was nearly finished."

Roosevelt faced a second challenge to his independence when Smith strenuously recommended that he appoint Belle Moskowitz his chief secretary. Brilliant, dynamic, and domineering, Moskowitz had been as indispensable to Smith as Louis Howe was to

Roosevelt. Roosevelt promised to consider her appointment, but in the end, after much waffling, patter, and calculated delay, he balked. "I realized that I've got to be Governor, and I've got to be myself," Roosevelt explained to Frances Perkins, who would serve in his cabinet in Albany and as his labor secretary in Washington. When he first agreed to run, he recalled, he wasn't sure if he could handle the rigors of the campaign, "but," he proudly noted, "I made it." Nor had he been certain that he was "sufficiently recovered to undertake the duties of Governor of New York, but here I am." Roosevelt's rejection provoked an irate response from Smith: "I created you and now what are you doing to me!" This brutal, personal struggle at the start of Roosevelt's term as governor, Eleanor recalled, "ended the close relationship between my husband and Governor Smith."

Formulating his own team in his own way was particularly important for Roosevelt because, as he had realized early on, his team would be a vital extension given his restricted mobility — its members serving as his "eyes and ears" — going forth into the field to localities he could not easily traverse, gathering information in the form of stories and human anecdotes that would animate issues and problems. When the narrow corridors and stairways of state institutions for the blind, the aged, the insane, and the deaf made it difficult for him to navigate, he encouraged Eleanor to go as his surrogate, to glean information and return with insights on how well the institutions were carrying out their stated missions.

"At first my reports were highly unsatisfactory," Eleanor acknowledged. "I would tell him what was on the menu for the day and he would ask, 'Did you look to see whether the inmates were actually getting that food?' " She learned to sample pots on the stove, notice if beds had been folded up and placed behind doors to hide overcrowded sleeping quarters, observe the patients' interactions with the staff. These were the details her husband craved and taught her to discern. Before long, under Roosevelt's mentoring, Eleanor became a first-rate investigative reporter, becoming so adept it was as if he had secured the data firsthand.

Roosevelt sought team members whose experiences and specific knowledge amplified his own far-flung curiosity. He was endlessly "educable," said Frances Perkins, at the time his commissioner of industry. He filled the Governor's Mansion with a steady stream of visitors from all walks of life who joined him at lunch, dinner, and frequently stayed overnight. If he couldn't go out into the world, he would funnel the world into him. Having been away from state politics for a decade and a half, he asked Sam Rosenman (a young lawyer who had recently served three terms in the state legislature) to be his counselor. While Rosenman was considering Roosevelt's offer, the story of his appointment appeared on the front page of an Albany newspaper. "I made up your mind for you," Roosevelt gleefully informed him. Rosenman was not offended. How could one resist such affability? Soon he became one of Roosevelt's closest advisers, so intimate that Franklin and Eleanor invited him to move into the Governor's Mansion. Long afterward, Rosenman asked of his boss why he had been willing to place such a young man whom he barely knew into such a "close and confidential relationship." Roosevelt replied, "I get to know people quickly and I have a pretty good instinct about them," adding, "Sometimes that instinct is better than a long and careful investigation."

To shore up Roosevelt's knowledge in various pertinent fields affecting his prospective agenda, Rosenman recruited three Columbia professors, Raymond Moley, Rexford Tugwell, and Adolf Berle, to form the nucleus of what would become known as the "brain trust." This inner circle, in turn, reached out to experts in various fields — business, agriculture, labor — who then filled the Governor's Mansion with a parade of interesting and useful guests. Soon, expanding circles of experts revolved around the governor as a little Ptolemaic universe around the earth.

"The routine was simple," Ray Moley recalled. The atmosphere at dinner would be pleasant and casual. Roosevelt encouraged his visitors to talk about their work, their families, and themselves, making each person feel that "nothing was so important to him that day as this particular visit, and that he had been waiting all day for this hour." Dessert done, they moved to the governor's small study where "random talk came to an end." There Roosevelt would throw questions to the experts "at an exciting and exhausting clip." As the night wore on, the questions became "meatier, more informed — the infallible index to the amount he was picking up" in the course of the evening. Moley marveled at "the amount of intellectual ransacking Roosevelt could crowd into the evening." From hindsight, it was clear to Moley that Roosevelt "was at once a student, a cross-examiner, and a judge."

The Depression did not fall upon the land like a moonless night. Even as the stock market was thriving, there were signs of a darkening and protracted twilight. The very operating method Roosevelt had devised from the beginning of his governorship — sending people out to inspect and retrieve information while simultaneously bringing in a stream of selected experts — sensitized him early on to the fact that something was fundamentally wrong. From Perkins he learned of a puzzling "irregularity" in the labor market — "many people were out of work for longer periods than was comfortable." When an inspection of the State Public Employment Service revealed many of its undermanned offices were overwhelmed by applicants, he called for an overhaul of the system — a small but important step before the October 1929 stock market crash.

As usual, Roosevelt was galvanized into action by way of the stories of specific needs and grievances. He could understand a problem, Perkins realized, "infinitely better" when baffling statistics and facts could be translated into a human story. Upon visiting a sweater mill in a small village near Poughkeepsie, he found both the owner and the workers "frightened and confused." Before the crash, the mill had employed 150 people making high-quality knitted sweaters. The workers received good wages, the owner made a good profit, and the community thrived. As the Depression deepened and demand fell, the owner was forced to halve his work, reduce wages, and use a lower-quality yarn to produce cheaper sweaters. He kept the mill going as long as he could, even to the point of forgoing any personal profit. He lived in the village; his employees were friends. Still, demand continued to plummet and was soon insufficient even to cover costs. This small sweater mill, which was eventually forced to close, served as an emblem and an allegory to lend a human dimension to the abstract economic term "the descending spiral."

Roosevelt had no overarching remedy for handling the Depression. He began with piecemeal solutions, trial-and-error methods to spread available jobs to a greater number of people: part-time work, a shortened workweek, a reduced workload, small make-work community projects. "What was clear to Roosevelt," Perkins recalled, "was that we must find *some* answers and stimulate *some* immediate activities." Although he mobilized charities to respond, coordinated local relief efforts, and called on local towns and cities to use their borrowing capacity to the fullest, the growing magnitude of the Depression burst the bounds of all these institutions.

After waiting through the winter and spring of 1931 for federal initiatives from President Hoover and the Republican administration, Roosevelt resolved in late summer to "assume leadership for himself and to take action for the State of New York." He summoned the Republican legislature into an extraordinary session to pass what was then considered a radical idea — a state-sponsored comprehensive program of unemployment insurance.

He knew from the start that the Republican majority would block his proposal. Like President Hoover, the state Republican leaders believed that private enterprise, charity, and local governments were the sole institutions capable of meeting the economic challenge. Relief brought from the distant level of the state or federal government, they insisted, would only impair the enterprise of the American people and worsen the problem.

Roosevelt spent several days preparing his message to the legislature. He had schooled his speechwriters Rosenman and Moley on how to communicate to the people at large in order to circumvent the legislators: Avoid dull facts; create memorable images; translate every issue into people's lives; use simple, everyday language; never use big words when small words will do. Simplify the concept that "we are trying to construct a more inclusive society" into "we are going to make a country in which no one is left out."

"What is the State?" Roosevelt began. The State was created by the people for their "mutual protection and well-being." One of its central duties is to care for its citizens who are unable, through adverse circumstances, to maintain their lives without help. In normal times, such aid would be provided by private or local contributions. But these were not normal times. The prolonged unemployment had exhausted the savings and credit of millions of families; the state had a responsibility to do its share, *not out of charity, but out of duty.* He called on the state, through a tax on citizens fortunate enough to be able to pay, to "provide public work for its unemployed citizens," and "if no work could be found," to provide unemployment insurance in the form of "food, clothing and shelter from public funds." The Republican leaders rejected the bill. They substituted what the governor termed a "wishy-washy" measure and prepared to adjourn. Roosevelt threatened to veto the bill and to call the legislators back into a second extraordinary session until an effective bill was passed. Finally, the Republican leaders yielded.

First in the country, New York's comprehensive relief program became a model for other states, establishing Governor Roosevelt as the leading spokesman for the progressive wing of the Democratic Party. In a celebrated radio address in April 1932, Roosevelt called on the country to rebuild its lost prosperity from "the bottom up and not from the top down," to "put their faith once more in *the forgotten man* at the bottom of the economic pyramid." For Roosevelt, that image was "not merely an oratorical abstraction," as Sam Rosenman had directly witnessed; the forgotten man "was a living person" — a farmer facing crushing debt; a small businessman unable to compete against monopoly; a housewife incapable of making ends meet. Roosevelt's hands-on leadership style, tireless search for information, and demand for stories that enlivened statistics with the flesh and blood of a shared humanity had acquainted him with the suffering and distress of individuals and afforded him a visceral understanding of the impact of the Great Depression.

Cast as a voice for the common man, Roosevelt sought the nomination for president at the Democratic National Convention in Chicago. Despite a substantial majority of the delegates on the first ballot, Roosevelt fell 104 votes short of the two-thirds total then required for nomination. His opponents represented the old-guard conservative wing of the Democratic Party. Standstill prevailed through two additional ballots, but after much wrangling, the Roosevelt forces finally broke the deadlock. It was agreed that John Nance Garner of Texas would be nominated as the vice presidential candidate. In return, both the Texas and the California delegations would switch to Roosevelt, pushing him over the magic two-thirds number.

No sooner had he received word that he had won on the third ballot than Roosevelt took the unprecedented action of traveling to the Coliseum to accept the nomination in person. Tradition had dictated that a committee chosen by the convention visit the winning candidate in a leisurely month or six weeks to deliver official notification. Roosevelt decided to break with what he later called the "absurd" idea that he should remain for weeks "in professed ignorance"; instead, he provided a novel, bold, activist approach to leadership. At a time when airplane travel was still uncommon, he flew from Albany to Chicago in a tri-motor plane. Conventional methods and old remedies would not help the country now. He had come in person to show that he was ready and eager to lead the battle against inaction, timidity, and hidebound thought. "I pledge you, I pledge myself, to a new deal for the American people," he concluded. "This is more than a political campaign; it is a call to arms."

The battle between Herbert Hoover and Franklin Roosevelt illuminated how strikingly different characters, temperaments, and leadership styles responded to the enormous stress and uncertainty of the country. Both men had been progressive protégés of Woodrow Wilson. As assistant secretary of the navy, Roosevelt had urged the Democratic Party to nominate Hoover for president in 1920. An enlightened businessman who had served with spectacular success as head of the Commission for Relief of Belgium during World

War I, Hoover was deeply respected by both parties. In 1928, the Republicans nominated him for president. In his acceptance speech, delivered at the height of prosperity, Hoover proclaimed that Americans were "nearer to the final triumph over poverty than ever before in the history of any land."

His profound belief in individualism, voluntarism, and the fundamental strength of the American economy blinded him from realizing, until too late, that government had to exert a primary role in helping people through what was fast becoming the worst Depression the country had ever known. At the slightest uptick in the stock market, Hoover believed and summarily proclaimed that the worst was over. When the economy continued to flounder, he came under blistering assault. Still, he would not admit that voluntary activities had failed. He adopted a bunker mentality, refusing to countenance the worsening situation.

By contrast, Roosevelt had adapted all his life to changing circumstances. The routine of his placid childhood had been disrupted forever by his father's heart attack and eventual death. Told he would never walk again, he had experimented with one method after another to improve his mobility. So now, as Roosevelt campaigned for the presidency, he built on his own long encounter with adversity: "The country needs and, unless I mistake its temper, the country demands bold, persistent experimentation. It is common sense to take a method and try it: If it fails, admit it frankly and try another. *But above all, try something.*"

On Election Day, by an overwhelming majority, the people chose Franklin Delano Roosevelt as their president. In a time of national duress, it was Roosevelt's confident cheer and powerful shoulders — symbols of his resilience — that made it possible for the common people not only to believe and trust him but to identify with him. As a young man, Franklin had daydreamed of ascending step by step to the presidency, but that narrative had been disrupted by paralysis and Warm Springs. There can be found the unlikely fulcrum point of both his ascent to the White House and his activist, experimental, and empathetic leadership. He had come through a dark time. And so would they all.

EIGHT:
LYNDON JOHNSON

"The most miserable period of my life"

From his early twenties, Lyndon Johnson had operated upon the premise that if "he could get up earlier and meet more people and stay up later than anybody else," victory would be his. For a decade he had toiled nonstop. He had no hobbies and had developed no ways to relax. His goal was simply and solely to win. As debate coach, he had led his team to the championship; as secretary to Congressman Richard Kleberg, he had earned a reputation as the best secretary on Capitol Hill; as the youngest director of any state's NYA, he had instituted projects that served as models for the entire nation; as a freshman congressman, he was touted as a "wunderkind" for bringing rural electricity to the Hill Country.

In his run for a Senate seat in 1941, the most important campaign of his life, he lost. Abraham Lincoln's loss in his first election had neither diminished his hopes nor stifled his ambition. On the contrary, as one "familiar with disappointments," he had been heartened by the nearly unanimous vote he had received from those who knew him best — the voters in his own small hamlet of New Salem. Franklin Roosevelt considered his lost vice-presidential run "a darn good sail," an experience that had expanded his contacts and reputation across the nation.

But elections for Johnson were fraught with extra meaning: He felt the Senate loss as a bodily blow, a referendum on his self-worth. He had been weighed by the public and been found wanting. This defeat that should have been merely an obstacle in his political career became, for Johnson, a life-altering ordeal, changing the nature of his ambition and setting in motion a protracted depression he later described as "the most miserable period of my life."

How had Lyndon Johnson, Franklin Roosevelt's protégé, a man willing and able to work with greater focus and intensity than any of his opponents, failed to secure the Senate seat he coveted with every fiber of his being?

Death had once again opened the door to opportunity and advancement. Four years earlier a headline spied on a park bench announcing the death of Congressman James Buchanan had led to the start of his congressional career. Now, on April 9, 1941, a brain hemorrhage would strike down the senior senator from Texas, Morris Sheppard, calling forth another special election. Johnson's aide, Walter Jenkins, remembered that when he called Johnson at home to deliver the news early that morning, Lyndon was "immediately interested."

A cleverly staged scene signaled Lyndon Johnson's launch into the race. On April 22, Johnson met privately with Roosevelt, allowing reporters gathered for the president's scheduled press conference to observe the young congressman's entrance and departure from the Oval Office. Shortly afterward, on the White House steps, Johnson formally announced he was running for the Senate. When reporters were ushered into the Oval

Office, a genial Roosevelt awaited them. "Lyndon Johnson just announced he is a candidate for the Senate in Texas," one reporter began. "Any comment on that?" With a laugh, the president replied, "He told me, too." "You don't mingle in these State primaries," the reporter said, "but I would like to ask if you look with favor upon Mr. Johnson?"

"Wouldn't that be mingling if I said yes or no? Have you stopped beating your wife, yes or no?" Roosevelt queried. Laughing along with the president, the reporter countered, "She's away. That's the answer to that," at which point the entire press corps burst into laughter. High spirits prevailed as Roosevelt laid out a three-part recipe: "Now it is up to the State of Texas to elect their own Senator, that is number one. Number two, I can't take part in the Texas primary. Number three, if you ask me about Lyndon Johnson himself, I can only say what is perfectly true — that he is a very old and close friend of mine. Now don't try to tie those things together!"

From the very start of the campaign, Johnson sought to fuse his image with that of FDR, as if his mentor had not only schooled but hatched the protégé. "If you really want to continue and help Roosevelt," Johnson reiterated, "there's only one way to do it, and that's to elect me." Four years earlier, at Lyndon's first meeting with Roosevelt in

Galveston, a picture had been taken showing him reaching over Texas governor James Allred to shake hands with the president. This photo, with the governor erased from the frame, became the signature image of the campaign, the sloganeering jingle of which was "Franklin D. and Lyndon B." Johnson would need all the presidential boost available, for he faced three formidable opponents, all far better known statewide than he — popular governor Lee "Pappy" O'Daniel, five-term congressman Martin Dies, and Attorney General Gerald Mann.

The enormous scale of Texas, vaster than all the New England states combined, proved challenging for Johnson, whose gifts of persuasion hinged upon making connections on a human scale. In a statewide race, attempt as he might to shake every hand (as if touch alone could convey conviction and extract a vote), the shortness of the special election and the distance he had to cover worked against him and required a frenetic pace that made his speedy handshakes seem mechanical. In his first congressional campaign in the 10th District, he had spoken extemporaneously before hundreds of small groups, winding up presentations in five minutes in order to leave fifteen minutes for direct talk and contact with individual voters. The 10th Congressional District was one of twenty in which he would now have to campaign and in the majority of those districts he was a virtual unknown. Necessity demanded that in each district he speak before the largest audiences possible, separated from the people by a stage.

In such formal settings, Johnson betrayed a crippling incapacity to speak naturally. His conception of senatorial dignity compelled him to give hour-long speeches, strike an elevated tone, and steer clear of the raw figures of speech that so enlivened his improvisational delivery. Invariably, the crowds began drifting away before his lackluster speeches drew to a close. The same man whose "tremendously commanding presence" could dominate any room he entered seemed ill at ease when framed by the proscenium of the stage, frozen in place.

Lyndon's confidence was further rattled when a series of early polls showed him badly trailing the four-man pack. Apprehension that he might lose began to take its toll upon his body. "When my mother and wife told me that I was the last man in the race," he recalled, "my throat got bad on me, and I had to spend a few days in the hospital." Those two days grew into two weeks, then worsened into "nervous exhaustion," a condition that the campaign sought to conceal. "He was depressed and it was bad," Lady Bird recalled. Once before, a collapse during his first congressional campaign had been followed by appendicitis, setting a clustered pattern of ailments — rashes, colitis, ulcers, inflamed bowels — that political stress would wreak upon his anxious body.

His spirits began to lift when a strategy was devised to draw more people to his rallies and minimize his speaking deficiencies. During his time as debate coach he had created a carnival aura around the events, providing pep rallies, songs, and cheerleading normally associated with athletic contests. What if traditional political rallies were turned into circuslike entertainment, as if the Henly picnic of his youth exploded into a full-blown variety show and revue?

Such a plan would require a massive infusion of money, which Johnson had access to through wealthy Texans introduced to him by Alvin Wirtz, a group including George and Herman Brown, founders of Brown and Root Construction Company. The Brown brothers put together tens of thousands of illegal corporate dollars, which they categorized as "legal fees" or "bonuses" to their employees, who then made individual contributions to the Johnson campaign. The money allowed the campaign to hire a charismatic radio personality and successful advertising executive to produce and market the theatrical/musical events, write the scripts, hire the talent, and transport the twenty-four-piece jazz band and the cast of singers and dancers from place to place. The evenings, billed as patriotic pageants in a time of war, began with selections from a jazz band attired in white dinner jackets, followed by "America the Beautiful" and other patriotic songs.

With the audience appropriately stirred, Lyndon appeared onstage. Standing in front of a towering image of himself shaking hands with Roosevelt, he "shed his coat, rolled up his sleeves and launched into an extemporaneous talk in which he let his hair down and talked turkey." He promised to be a senator who could get things done; he pledged to do the job President Roosevelt wanted him to do — had indeed asked him to do. The well-advertised climax followed, the foremost reason no one left their seats: Upon entry, every person had been given a raffle ticket; the numbers drawn from a giant bowl on the stage corresponded to defense bonds and stamps, worth anything from $1 to $100 for the lucky winners.

As Johnson's crowds swelled in size and enthusiasm, his poll numbers followed suit. From a mere 5 percent at the bottom of the four-man race, Johnson climbed to 20 percent and then to 30 and finally, in the last week, he pulled slightly ahead of front-runner Governor O'Daniel. But polls only told a piece of the story. Texas politics at the time was rife with corruption. In certain counties in South and East Texas, the local bosses could "deliver" whatever votes were needed in a close election. With the money flowing into his campaign, Johnson had easily outbid the others to secure the controlled votes in South Texas. By Election Day, Johnson was confident of victory. Early returns gave him such a healthy lead that a photograph appeared in the press showing him being carried aloft by campaign workers.

It was at this moment that an ebullient Johnson let down his guard and released the purchased precincts that were traditionally withheld until all the official votes were in. The early release widened his margin still further and by the end of the evening, Johnson was ahead by five thousand votes, though paper ballots from rural precincts were still trickling in. "Lyndon Johnson Captures Senatorial Election," headlined the *McAllen Daily Press*. The *Dallas News* suggested, "Only Miracle Can Keep FDR's Anointed Out." The next day, that "miracle" came to pass. A large swath of O'Daniel votes suddenly materialized from counties in boss-controlled East Texas. And because Johnson had revealed the hand he held, the O'Daniel campaign knew precisely the hand they needed to win the election. When all the votes were "counted," O'Daniel was declared the victor by a margin of 1,311 votes.

As he prepared to return to his seat in the

House, Johnson feared a diminution of the respect and affection he had gained over the years in Washington. From his vantage, the psychic landscape of the House he had left was not the same he returned to now in defeat. He felt he had disappointed, even embarrassed, President Roosevelt, who had gone out of his way to support his candidacy. "We gave him everything we could, everything," Roosevelt adviser Tommy "the Cork" Corcoran recalled, but "he didn't win." So disquieted was Johnson, feeling he had lost favor with the White House, that he refrained from calling on the president. "I felt that I had written too many checks on my rather wobbly account," he confided to Governor Allred. "I had overdrawn, and I did not want a check to bounce back in my face." Eventually, Roosevelt reached out to Johnson and, in a private meeting at the White House, tried to lift Johnson's spirits with a teasing remark: "Lyndon, apparently you Texans haven't learned one of the first things we learned up in New York State, and that is when the election is over, you have to sit on ballot boxes." Despite Roosevelt's continued support, Johnson remained despondent. He was no longer the boy wonder; he no longer saw a limitless future before him. He was simply one of 435 congressmen consigned to remain in a place where everyone, including his overburdened staff, knew he had failed.

To consider Lyndon Johnson's 1941 electoral loss as a catalyst for a crucible event on the order of the debilitating depression that led Abraham Lincoln's friends to remove all knives, scissors, and razors from his room, or the deaths of a wife and mother that confronted Theodore Roosevelt on the same day in the same house, or the polio that left Franklin Roosevelt a paraplegic and threatened all his dreams, seems an exercise in hyperbole — unless Lyndon Johnson's insecurity and the fusion of his public and private life are taken into account.

Politics had consumed Johnson from earliest childhood when he had eavesdropped on the political stories his father swapped with cronies on the side porch. The boy trailed his father through the statehouse and blissfully accompanied him on the campaign trail. While he momentarily and gratuitously considered leaving public life after his Senate defeat, he had no political alternative but to keep the congressional seat he still retained after the special Senate election loss. Nor could he find solace in his private life, which essentially existed to propel his public life. He had cultivated few pastimes that did not overlap with public affairs. Even the act of eating was essentially gobbling nutrition to move from place to place. Lyndon Johnson ate, drank, and slept politics.

In the months after the collapse of his

dream of making Illinois an economic model for the country, Abraham Lincoln was able to resume the practice of law, a profession that provided the camaraderie for which his gregarious nature yearned while also giving him time and space to read books, to listen and learn and hone his storytelling skills. Inherited wealth allowed Theodore Roosevelt to purchase land and cattle and build a comfortable ranch in the Badlands, where his depression gradually lifted as he rode his horse sixteen hours a day, joined in the five-week roundups, hunted game, explored the natural world, and transformed his body. Sara Roosevelt provided the means for Franklin to purchase and develop the treatment center at Warm Springs, where he found the healing he sought in the persona of "Doc Roosevelt," head counselor and spiritual director of a unique therapy program that combined work with play, restoring in polio patients the optimism and the sense of fun that he himself had never lost.

Each of these three men emerged from a catastrophic turn of fortune with an enlarged capacity for leadership. But what if adversity leads to a darkening of temperament, to mistrust and anger? What if grief and loss result in a shrinkage of genuine empathy and give way to a single-minded drive to accumulate power and wealth? Such was the case with Lyndon Johnson. The loss exposed and magnified negative aspects of his nature that would compromise his leadership until a massive heart attack renewed old priorities, reset his course, and reestablished the determination he had first shown at Cotulla to use the power he accumulated to better the lives of others.

The tailwind Franklin Roosevelt supplied young Lyndon in his first congressional term had obscured a fundamental mismatch between the institutional structure of the House of Representatives and the leadership gifts Lyndon Johnson possessed. President Roosevelt's interest, access, and tutelary spirit had bestowed upon the freshman congressman an opening to be productive in a deceptively swift and impactful way. Upon his return to Congress after the failed Senate bid, with the president increasingly preoccupied, distracted by the ever-enlarging world war, Johnson was left adrift in an organization that proved increasingly uncongenial to his temperament.

The Congress of the 1940s rewarded a slow and steady accretion of power within a seniority system based solely on longevity. Key congressmen had invested years, even decades, to facilitate their rise to leadership positions. In such an institution, one requiring an extended period of resigned waiting, Johnson's strengths (his instinctive ability to seize an opportunity, his capacities to work harder and faster than anyone else) were neutralized.

Simply put, the House was no institution for a young man in a hurry. Sam Rayburn had been in the House for a quarter of a century before becoming speaker at the age of fifty-eight. Fear of dying young exacerbated Johnson's characteristic sense of urgency. Johnson men shared a history of heart disease. Lyndon's father's health had begun to decline when he was in his mid-forties. He had suffered his first heart attack in his mid-fifties and died days after his sixtieth birthday. His uncle George, who had secured Lyndon's teaching job at Sam Houston High, had died from heart disease at fifty-seven. If family history held true, Lyndon could not afford to spend decades moving upward at a snail's pace.

The size of the House also played against Johnson's strengths. The membership, which continually changed after biennial elections, made it difficult for Johnson to build the network of personal relationships that had always been the nucleus of his power. His physical size, his encroachment and determined force of will had given Johnson an insuperable advantage in the context of face-to-face relations. "I always believed," he said, "that as long as I could take someone in the room with me, I would make him my friend."

The greater the distance from his audience, however, the more diluted, stifled, and ineffective he became. His ability to fathom people's desires and motivations depended upon repeated, informal exchanges that were not the norm in a body of 435 representatives, separated into different office buildings, protected by ever-enlarging staffs.

Nor, given Johnson's discomfort in addressing large audiences, was he able to establish a national reputation by speaking out on various issues and participating in floor debates. "Some of us were on the floor all the time, fighting for liberal causes," a representative from California recalled, "but he stayed away from the floor, and while he was there, he was very, very silent." Johnson did, of course, continue to service his constituents, but these routine duties no longer gratified his relentless ambition. "I always had the feeling he was a little restless," his fellow congressman O. C. Fisher recalled, "looking for bigger worlds to conquer." Indeed, Johnson viewed the seven years spent in the House between 1941 and 1948 as a kind of purgatory.

Not surprisingly, Johnson's enervation and diminished interest in the job adversely affected his relationship with his staff. "Fits of depression were punctuated by angry outbursts in which he blamed anybody or everybody for his loss," historian Randall Woods writes. His abusive behavior worsened. "One day I didn't get a telephone number fast enough for Mr. Johnson and he threw a book at me," recalled a female staffer. "I was a little afraid of him after that." Even before the Senate run, Johnson's two longest-serving aides, Luther Jones and Gene Latimer, had quit. Jones knew after less than a year on the House staff that he simply "had to get away" or be "devoured" by Johnson. Latimer lasted exactly a year to the day of his arrival. "I was literally working myself to death," he recalled. "I never took a breath." Johnson quickly replaced Jones and Latimer with able men, but without the inspiration of Johnson's intensely focused energy, without the thrill of shared engagement in important, beneficial projects, the new team never achieved the camaraderie that had bound the older team together despite their volatile and oppressive "Chief."

Though never driven before by the dream of amassing wealth, Johnson began to devote more and more of his time and energy to its acquisition. After a stint in the Navy in the wake of Pearl Harbor, he bided his time in Congress, relegated constituent matters to his staff, and spent his days pursuing the accumulation of what would, before a decade had passed, become a massive fortune. Money, its erratic comings and goings, had been a significant player in Lyndon Johnson's family from the beginning. The vicissitudes of his father's business dealings had brewed dissension and insecurity from Lyndon's childhood years, influencing the sometimes humiliating figure the Johnson family cut in town.

Lyndon Johnson's multimillion-dollar empire was planted by Lady Bird in 1943 with the purchase of KTBC, a shabby radio station operating on the verge of bankruptcy in Austin, Texas. No sooner had Lady Bird secured this tiny station for the sum of $17,500 from her trust fund than the Federal Communications Commission rained its blessings upon the enterprise, permitting an increase in transmitting power, expanding its hours of broadcast to a full twenty-four hours a day, disallowing all competition, and granting network affiliations. The sum of all these advantageous rulings led finally to a lucrative television contract that begot further investments in bank securities, real estate, and cattle. "Like two young oaks springing up side by side," a *Wall Street Journal* reporter summarized, "LBJ's careers in government and business grew mightily — their trunks rising parallel and branches intertwining."

To juxtapose Lyndon Johnson, the principal of the elementary school at Cotulla who had spent a significant amount of his meager salary in order to buy athletic equipment and furnish a playground for his Mexican American students, with the congressman whose rightward political drift accelerated as his wealth increased, underscores the loss of bearings he had experienced in the traumatic aftermath of his Senate loss. The ambition to better the lives of others that had given his life direction and meaning during his early years in politics — his work with the NYA, his fight for slum clearance and rural electrification — was now focused solely on himself. He had lost the sense of purpose that had accompanied his drive for power, the doubleness of ambition so central to genuine leadership.

Lyndon Johnson's loss of bearings grew more marked upon the death of his greatest political mentor, Franklin Roosevelt. When a U.S. Senate seat opened in 1948, he resolved to make one last try to reach the upper house. As he prepared for the statewide run in an increasingly conservative Texas, he shifted still further to the right, even repudiating his former allegiance to the New Deal. "I think the term 'New Dealer' is a misnomer," he told a reporter. While he still believed in the "development of water power" and in some of the programs Roosevelt backed, he said: "I believe in free enterprise and I don't believe in the government doing anything that the people can do privately. Wherever it's possible, the government should get out of business."

Though he had waited seven years for this opportunity, the forty-year-old Johnson was filled with trepidation. This time there was no safety net of a special election. It was all or nothing; a loss would forfeit his congressional seat with its decade of accrued seniority and lock him out of official Washington for the first time since his twenties. "I just could not bear the thought of losing everything," he confessed, as if his identity was contingent upon his position and standing. Friends and relatives prodded him to enter, but he remained indecisive. Tired of waiting, a group of his associates suggested that he convince his former congressional aide John Connally to make a bid. That afternoon, Johnson announced that he was running for the United States Senate.

Once again, the elevated stress that elections invariably brought Lyndon began to surface in an array of physical ailments — fevers, chills, stomach pains, headaches, depression, even kidney stones. "You have to realize that a politician — a good one — is a strange duck," Johnson told campaign worker Joe Phipps. "Anyone who periodically has to get down on hands and knees to beg voters to prove they love him by giving him their vote is really sick. Depending on how obsessed he is, he could be very, very sick. . . .

Try to think of me as a seriously ill, dear relative or friend who needs all the care, compassion, comfort and love he can get in order to get well, knowing that in time he will get well. The illness . . . won't come back till the next election rolls around."

Johnson's chief antagonist, Coke Stevenson, a celebrated two-term Texas governor, was, at the beginning of the race, the prohibitive favorite. In the one-party state of Texas, however, where the winner in the Democratic primary was assured of victory in the fall, the campaign revolved around personalities. And no personality was more original than Lyndon Johnson. On the trail, he worked twenty hours a day, shaking hands, making short speeches, giving radio interviews. He "even worked in the bathtub," his secretary Dorothy Nichols recalled. "You'd be in a little hotel in this little town, and you'd get a summons to come into the bathroom to talk to the Congressman. You'd go in and he'd be in the tub, and he would talk to you and two or three secretaries would come in and take letters. He never stopped."

Understanding the importance of flamboyantly seizing the attention of the electorate, Johnson crisscrossed the state in a helicopter, something no candidate had previously done. The helicopter — dubbed the "Johnson City Windmill" — was just the vehicle to draw astonished voters from far-flung corners of

Texas. Much as young Franklin Roosevelt had stormed from barns to hayfields in a bedecked red Maxwell in his first campaign for the State Senate, so now Lyndon Johnson combined fun, hokum, and excitement with the techniques of a modern campaign, complete with advance men, sophisticated polling, and radio advertising. Circling the town square or the local football field, he would blast his arrival over the PA system attached to the helicopter runners. "This is Lyndon Johnson, your next United States senator, and I'll land in just a minute. I want to shake hands with all of you." If the town lacked a proper landing site he would consult a list of voters from the different small towns and villages who had written him over the years. "Hello there, Mr. Jones," his voice would boom overhead. "This is your friend Lyndon Johnson. I'm sorry we can't land today, but I want you to know that I'm up here thinking of you and appreciate your kind letter and comments. I just want you to be sure and tell your friends to vote for me at election time."

On Election Day, the results were so close that neither candidate was able to declare victory. Both held back, playing the same game of undercounting, overcounting, withholding, and opportune releasing. This time, however, the Johnson campaign played the shrewder hand. In 1941, an overconfident Johnson, anxious to capture headlines of victory the next day, had released the votes in his "bought" precincts prematurely. "In 1948, we learned better," Johnson's aide Walter Jenkins recalled. While the cocksure Stevenson campaign released their votes early, "we didn't rush the people in the counties where we had strong votes. We rather hoped they would hold back" until the very last moment. That way, if "any sort of fraud" was involved, it would be too late for the Stevenson campaign to retaliate.

"They were stealin' votes in east Texas," Johnson supporter and Austin mayor Tom Miller recalled, "we were stealin' votes in south Texas, only Jesus Christ could say who actually won it." But Jesus wasn't counting, and, by an eighty-seven-vote margin, "Landslide Lyndon" attained the Senate seat he had coveted for so long.

By that mere eighty-seven votes, Lyndon Johnson had gained entry to a wholly different institution with different dynamics of power than the House, one far more contoured to his temperament and formidable leadership gifts. Smaller, more intimate, less procedure-bound, and more stable (given the six-year tenure in the Senate rather than the two-year turnover in the House), the Senate was ideally adapted to a leader whose ability to persuade, charm, subdue, and overwhelm depended upon intimate encounters, engaging people face-to-face or in small groups. The Senate's "folkways" and "unwritten rules of the game" called upon freshman senators to serve a period of apprenticeship, show deference to their elders, refrain from speaking too often on the floor, concentrate on learning the expected "norms of behavior" — habits of mind Johnson had long cultivated.

Had he become a senator in a different era, he might not have been able to exercise his unique leadership talents to full effect. His diminished ability to speak effectively in formal settings, for example, would have made it challenging to achieve recognition during the Senate's "golden age," the decades leading up to the Civil War, when the upper chamber debated the central issues of the day and great orators became the nation's eminent figures — Daniel Webster of Massachusetts, John C. Calhoun of South Carolina, and William Henry Seward of New York. The Senate Johnson now entered was perfectly suited to his trademark leadership style; as aide George Reedy said, Lyndon was "the right man in the right place at the right time."

No sooner had Johnson arrived than he set about figuring out the structural machinery of the institution. It quickly became apparent to the freshman senator that power resided in an informal coalition, an inner club of southern Democrats and conservative Republicans. A bargain had been struck whereby the conservative Republicans would vote with the South against civil rights legislation and, in return, the southern Democrats would oppose liberal social and economic measures. Conceived in the struggle to defeat Roosevelt's court-packing plan (which ironically catapulted Johnson into Congress), this coalition had solidified its authority over the years by securing strategic committee chairmanships and displaying a keen and imperious parliamentary acumen. The undisputed leader of this inner club, commanding the respect of almost every member of the Senate, was Richard Russell.

From the beginning, Johnson recognized Russell's mentorship would be the linchpin to his hopes of gaining influence in the Senate. He was, of course, not alone among his freshman colleagues in recognizing Russell's unique position in the Senate hierarchy, but he alone set in motion a strategy to ingratiate himself with the courtly senior senator. "The way you get ahead in the world, you get close to those that are the heads of things," Johnson had told his college roommate when he took a job mopping floors in the hallway outside the president's office. Shortly after his Senate entrance Johnson realized "there was only one way to see Russell every day, and that was to get a seat on his committee. Without that we'd likely be passing acquaintances and nothing more. So I put in a request for the

Armed Services Committee — and fortunately, because of all my work on defense preparedness in the House, my request was granted." Though the two men were wildly dissimilar in temperament and style, they shared a consuming devotion to work. The Senate was the bachelor's entire existence; Russell embodied the Senate much the way Rayburn embodied the House.

Lyndon Johnson respected, loved, dutifully served, and thoroughly exploited both mentors. He understood the anxiety and loneliness both men experienced when they were away from work. "Russell found in the Senate what was for him a home," Johnson explained. "With no one to cook for him at home, he would arrive early enough in the morning to eat breakfast at the Capitol and stay late enough at night to eat dinner across the street. And in these early mornings and late evenings I made sure there was always one companion, one senator, who worked as hard and as long as he, and that was me, Lyndon Johnson. On Sundays the House and Senate were empty, quiet, and still; the streets were bare. It's a tough day for a politician, especially if, like Russell, he's all alone. I knew how he felt for I, too, counted the hours till Monday would come again, and knowing that, I made sure to invite Russell over for breakfast, lunch, or brunch or just to read the Sunday papers. He was my mentor, and I wanted to take care of him."

The central decision an aspiring senator makes is how to spend time and resources, to determine what kind of role he might choose to fill — a spokesman on national issues, a regional leader, an expert in a specific field. Johnson aimed to secure a leadership post in the operation of the party itself, beginning with the admittedly insubstantial post of assistant party leader, known as the party whip. With effort and luck, he might transition to party leader. Most senators in the late 1940s and early 1950s shunned these official positions, which, given the entrenched power of the inner club, were largely symbolic. Moreover, the time-consuming duties of corralling votes kept party leaders trapped in Washington, vulnerable to opposition at home. It was not coincidental that in 1950, both the Democratic Party whip and the Democratic minority leader were defeated for reelection.

Acting with his usual dispatch, Johnson sought to seize upon the opening chance provided and thrust himself forward for party whip. Recognizing a potential others had overlooked, he extravagantly beseeched Russell for the job he called "one of the most urgently desired goals of his life." In 1951, with Russell's support, he became the youngest party whip in history; two years later, when the post of minority leader opened through yet another reelection defeat, he launched a characteristic quicksilver campaign, and, despite initial opposition from liberals, was unanimously elected.

In every leadership position thus far attained, Johnson had understood the importance of achieving a bold and eye-catching beginning. This time, he inaugurated a dramatic shift in the way committee assignments were awarded. Sensing a building resentment on the part of freshman senators who were prevented by seniority from important committees, he persuaded Russell and his fellow coalition members to promise each new senator at least one choice committee assignment. While this required a slight modification of the seniority rule, Johnson convinced the inner circle that the present system stifled energetic young talent that could benefit the Senate as a whole. With this single change, Johnson promptly gained the favor and gratitude of all the freshman senators, who henceforth considered him their patron.

Having made inroads to win the backing of junior senators, he was careful not to slight the seniors. On the contrary, he catered to the older senators as he had always catered to his elders. He assisted them with committee preparations, provided concise summaries on issues, showed overt and lavish respect. As age slowed them down, "they feared humiliation, they craved attention. And when they found it, it was like a spring in the desert;

their gratitude couldn't adequately express itself with anything less than total support and dependence on me. And besides, I always liked to spend time with older people."

In the months following his election as party leader, Johnson exponentially expanded his ability to convert operating and procedural tasks into sources of genuine power. Intuitively, he had fathomed the potential in the commonplace functions of messenger, gatekeeper, and appointment-maker. According to rules, the party leader was responsible for scheduling bills for floor debate. Johnson assumed this taxing task with alacrity. If a colleague required prompt action on a pet bill or wanted to delay a controversial vote, he would seek Johnson's assistance. Another workaday job he transformed into an influential resource was discovered in a loophole in the Senate rules that enabled him to transfer the responsibility of assigning office space from the Senate Committee on Rules and Administration to the party leader's office. Before long, a marked hierarchy of choice accommodations in the new Senate office building belonged to Johnson's allies; those antagonistic to him were relegated to the smaller, older office building.

At the core of Johnson's success in the Senate, however, was his celebrated ability to read character, to gauge the desires, needs, hopes, and ambitions of every individual with whom he interacted. If Theodore Roosevelt's speed of learning in the state legislature had astonished witnesses, those who watched Lyndon Johnson in his early years in the Senate were positively boggled. In short order, Johnson was able to memorize the entire institution, its people, its rules, its traditions. "When you're dealing with all those senators," he explained, "the good ones and the crazies, the hard workers and the lazies, the smart ones and the mediocres — you've got to know two things right away. You've got to understand the beliefs and values common to all of them as politicians, the desire for fame and the thirst for honor, and then you've got to understand *the* emotion most controlling that particular senator."

And whatever Johnson learned of his cohorts, he never forgot. Over time, he was able to create a composite mental portrait of every Democratic senator: his strengths and vulnerabilities; his aspirations in the Senate and perhaps beyond; how far he could be pressured and by what means; how he liked his liquor; how he felt about his wife and family, and, most importantly, how he felt about himself — what kind of senator he wanted to be. As Johnson's mental profiles of his colleagues became more intimate and expansive, his political instincts became nearly unerring. Knowledge of the minutiae of the needs and desires of his colleagues on both sides of the aisle enabled him to assign places in senatorial delegations, gratify one senator's wish for a trip to Paris and another's desire to shore up his foreign policy credentials by attending the NATO Parliamentary Conference. Senators incurred debts large and small to Johnson, debts that would be owed for future collection.

At every step of his drive for power within the Senate, Johnson was aided by what one reporter called "the biggest, the most efficient, the most ruthlessly overworked and the most loyal personal staff in the history of the Senate." Working with Johnson was never easy, George Reedy recalled. He could be "a magnificent, inspiring leader" at one moment, "an insufferable bastard" the next. "He was cruel, even to people who had virtually walked the last mile for him. Occasionally he would demonstrate his gratitude for extraordinary services by a lavish gift — an expensive suit of clothes, an automobile, jewelry for the women on his staff," but such gifts were often prelude to an additional outpouring of invective. And, as always, the staff members "were required to drop everything to wait upon him and were expected to forget their private lives in his interests." At regular intervals, Reedy would contemplate resigning, but then Johnson would do something so "superb" that he "forgot his grievances."

■ ■ ■ ■

When Democrats, by a single vote, gained a majority in the upper chamber in 1955, the forty-six-year-old Lyndon Johnson was elected the youngest majority leader in the history of the Senate.

With a quiverful of arrows — unflagging energy, guile, single-minded determination, a politician's ability to link names, people, and events, executive drive, entrepreneurial flare, beguiling storytelling gifts — he had reached the summit of congressional legislative posts. Newspaper reporters painted a picture of a surpassing political mechanic, capable of starting what was stalled, keeping the whole legislative machine humming without rancor and without overheating.

If at last Lyndon Johnson was "sitting on the top of the world," the road to get there had taken a drastic toll. During a press conference summing up the Senate's work in the first half of the year, he "blew his stack completely." He screamed, "Goddamn you," at a reporter who had asked a question he resented. "You can get the hell out of here." The press conference was shattered; members of the press corps left stunned. Though members of his team had witnessed Johnson's fabled irascibility behind closed doors, he had generally been able to tamp down his temper in public venues.

Plagued with an odd lethargy, indigestion, and accelerating stress, Johnson finally decided to take a rare hiatus from work to spend the 4th of July weekend at the Middleburg, Virginia, country estate of his good friend and benefactor, George Brown. On the two-hour ride to Middleburg, "my chest really began to hurt," Johnson recalled, "as though I had jacked up a truck and the jack had slipped and the truck had crushed my chest in." Fortunately, another guest, who himself had suffered a heart attack, recognized the symptoms: "My God, man, you're having a heart attack." An ambulance transported Johnson to Bethesda Naval Hospital in Washington, the nearest major cardiac unit. A long-term friend of Johnson's, Posh Oltorf, rode with him in the ambulance. "It was a very hectic ride, it hurt him desperately," Oltorf recalled. "I think he definitely felt there was a possibility that he'd die before we got there," but throughout the ordeal, Johnson remained "extremely courageous and brave," adding, "if he had a toe ache, he'd complain" and "expect a great deal of sympathy. He was just the opposite with this serious thing."

Lady Bird awaited his arrival at the hospital, where he went into shock, hovering between life and death. Each passing day greatly increased his odds for survival, but the doctors told the press that the majority leader's immediate return was absolutely out of the question, that he could not "undertake any business whatsoever for a period of months." An Associated Press headline blared: "Heart Attack Drops Johnson from White House Hopefuls." Political chatter speculated that the heart attack had not only extinguished the prospect of his running for the presidency but that he might not be able to resume the burdensome role of majority leader. The upward trajectory of his career was interrupted, and perhaps brought to an end.

Johnson fell into a depression so consuming that it appeared he was grieving over his own death. The depth of his despondency was measured by the crushing descent from the eminence he had achieved. Everything he held dear was at hazard — his present attainments, his future ambitions. This was different in degree from the depression one might expect after a heart attack. "He'd just sort of lie there," Reedy recalled. "You'd feel that he wasn't there at all, that there was some representation of Johnson alongside of you, something mechanical."

"Then one day he got up and he hollered to have somebody come up and give him a shave, and just in a matter of minutes the whole damned hospital started to click. He took over the corridor, installed a couple of typewriters there, he was dictating letters, he was just going full speed." What had reanimated him from his corpselike state? The crucial tonic, it soon became clear, was not administered by the doctors and the nurses, or even by the round-the-clock ministrations of Lady Bird. What animated him was the spate of more than four thousand letters of concern, condolence, and love. "He'd read them over and over and over again," Reedy remembered, "oh, he was just basking in those letters." Finally, it "got to the point where we couldn't let them all in his room: there wouldn't have been enough room for him." The letters, Johnson exulted, showed that "everybody loves Lyndon," and they kindled in him a fierce need to reciprocate that love. Just as he would answer constituents immediately, so he rose to action now to reply to every single letter. He needed reconnection to these people. Stenographers were installed in the physicians' station in the hospital corridor, the typewriters were going nonstop, the seventeenth floor became a hive of activity. The letters did not merely occupy his time, entertain, or distract him. They invigorated him as would life-giving transfusions.

"Time is the most valuable thing you have; be sure you spend it well" had been a favorite, oft-repeated adage of Johnson's. Now, however, it took on a sharper urgency. He had always been a most excessive, immoderate man. Ceaseless striving, a chronically strained metabolism, an appalling diet of whatever he was able to consume in the gaps of his maniacal schedule, could now be fatal. It was necessary that he curb a lifetime of habits. In his six-month period of convalescence at the ranch, a healthy diet replaced breakfasts of four cigarettes and black coffee, dinners of fried steaks and fried potatoes. He exercised daily in a newly built swimming pool, drank less bourbon, lost forty pounds, and took regular naps. He endeavored to walk more slowly and somewhat assuage the excitable tempo of his speech. He spent more time with his wife and children and even behaved in a gentler, or at least less demanding, fashion toward his staff.

To counter the gossip in the press that he might not have the stamina to return to the political cauldron of the majority leadership, he launched a campaign for public consumption, spinning the narrative of a man whose entire mode of living had been altered. This included a thoroughgoing philosophical change most succinctly expressed in a magazine article: "My Heart Attack Taught Me How to Live." He portrayed himself as a new man, leading a well-rounded and meditative life, reading Plato and American history, listening to classical music, taking pleasure in the natural world of the Pedernales, his ranch and its animals. When reporters and interviewers came to the ranch, they found him "sprawled on a hammock," holding a book, as "Strauss waltzes floated into the air" — a stage set, complete with soundtrack and arranged props.

Yet, beneath this contrived projection, a bona fide metamorphosis was taking place. Death had brushed hard against him, and beneath the calculations of a public relations machine, he was struggling mightily within himself. Johnson's New Deal friend Jim Rowe had sent him a recently published biography on Lincoln, which detailed the profound change Lincoln had undergone during a waiting time when he was out of politics. This was Johnson's waiting time, a time of gathering strength and direction.

When Lincoln had suffered his deep depression he had asked himself: What if I died now? What would I be remembered for? Coming back from "the brink of death," Johnson asked himself a similar set of questions. He had laid the foundation of a substantial fortune, but what purpose did that serve? He had learned to manipulate the legislative machine of the Senate with a deftness and technical expertise without parallel in American history. But to what end did one accumulate such power? Regardless of one's impressive title, power without purpose and without vision was not the same thing as leadership.

■ ■ ■ ■

As the January opening of the new congressional session drew near — the date doctors
designated for the convalescent's earliest
return to Washington — Johnson made plans
to deliver a major public speech that would
display his physical and mental readiness to
resume full command of the Senate. The time
and site for his formal reemergence in the
public eye were chosen — the late November
dedication of the Lake Whitney Dam at the
National Guard Armory in the lakeside community of Whitney, Texas. Though the town
itself was tiny, the armory had a seating
capacity of five thousand, which the advance
team intended to pack with people from all
over the state, making it "a matter of honor
for everybody" to show their joy that Lyndon
was back.

All through November, with George
Reedy's help, Johnson nervously worked on
the speech. Though fully aware of his dis-
abling inability to deliver an effective formal
speech, he was determined to show that he
was "back in the saddle again" — indeed that
was the song chosen for his introduction. Of
even greater importance, he had decided to
use the speech as an occasion to rededicate
himself to the values that had originally
drawn him into public service: the idea that

government should be used to help those who needed help — the poor, the undereducated, the ill-housed, the elderly, the sick. "We've got to look after these people," his father had repeatedly told him, "that's what we're here for." He had returned from this crucible of a massive heart attack with a renewed allegiance to his father's plainspoken counsel, resolved to act upon it while he had the time and if he had the chance.

Just as Franklin Roosevelt had obsessively rehearsed and trained before the 1924 convention speech that would mark his first public appearance since he had been stricken with polio, so Johnson called Reedy "every three minutes to switch 'and' to 'the' or 'the' to 'and' . . . just the most incredible nit-picking stuff. It had to be retyped each time. My poor secretary retyped that goddamned speech so much" that "her fingers were still flying" when she went to bed at night. "He even rewrote it as we drove from the Ranch to Whitney," Mary Rather recalled, "and I had to type it again at the last minute."

In the speech, the man who had renounced his allegiance to the New Deal and soft-pedaled his views on civil rights in order to remain viable in an increasingly conservative Texas, laid down a powerful "call to arms," a boldly progressive agenda that set a clear direction for the approaching congressional session and would mark the national dimension of his leadership for the first time. He demanded enlarged Social Security coverage, increasing tax exemptions for low-income groups, federal subsidies for education and housing, a constitutional amendment to eliminate the poll tax, liberalization of immigration, public roads and water conservation, and, embedded in the midst of this liberal barrage, a single reactionary thorn — a natural gas bill for moneyed Texas conservatives.

Billed as a "Program with a Heart," the speech showed that the resurgent Johnson advocated a social vision beyond anything the likely Democratic presidential nominee Adlai Stevenson was proposing. "I had never before seen him take such complete command of an audience," George Reedy remembered of that electric moment. On several occasions the audience "leapt to their feet, clapped their hands, stamped their feet, beat on the tables and whistled to show their approval." The compassion he felt for the marginalized, the badly educated, the badly housed fueled his delivery in such a way that he "sounded like Joshua ordering the trumpets blown at Jericho." Once he was done with his prepared text, he stepped away from the rostrum and with renewed assurance addressed the audience extemporaneously. "People walked out of that speech dazed," Reedy said, stunned by "the amount of emotion that he put into it and the fire."

Since the entire national press corps was present for the majority leader's first public appearance, the speech received widespread coverage. On this single speech he had rolled the dice and his emotional charge had "affected every newspaperman that was there." Liberal icon Hubert Humphrey declared: "Twelve home runs and one strike out" — "A very fine batting average." Humphrey especially noted the call for elimination of the poll tax, which would "give some forward action at last" in the civil rights struggle. Johnson had not only demonstrated his physical readiness to lead through the impassioned conviction of his delivery, he had shown a deep resolve to move both his state and the country forward on a more progressive path.

With clarified purpose, the prodigal son of the New Deal had returned.

Lyndon Johnson had no sooner resumed his role as Senate majority leader in January 1957 than he committed himself to the passage of a civil rights bill. For eighty-two years, since the passage of the 1875 Enforcement Act, though various civil rights measures had survived the House, the southern bloc in the Senate had used the filibuster to keep the door to the passage of any civil rights bill firmly shut.

A sequence of events had created a new

urgency for legislative action. The Supreme Court's 1954 *Brown v. Board of Education* decision prohibiting racial segregation in public schools had quickened the civil rights movement, incited a violent reaction in the South, and prompted the Eisenhower administration to send a bill to Congress expanding federal authority to protect black citizens in a wide range of civil rights, including voting rights. Passed by the House the previous year, the bill landed on Johnson's desk for consideration in early January. Despite the long historical track record of failure, he told friends that before summer's end, he would carry a civil rights bill safely through the Senate for the first time in more than three-quarters of a century.

As he studied the initial Republican bill passed by the House, he understood at once that as written (like every other bill sent to the Senate over the past decades), it was dead on arrival. According to witnesses, he "ran his pen twice through one section, and made certain alterations in other sections" before predicting: "This will be it in the end!"

The plot line, he understood at once, had to unfold in three acts.

In Act One, Johnson had to convince Richard Russell, his mentor and the leader of the southern bloc, that a filibuster would gain a Pyrrhic victory for the South. The growing momentum of the civil rights movement sug-

403

gested that it was only a matter of time until a two-thirds vote could be gathered to secure cloture and then, "there'll be no way of putting a brake on all sorts of wild legislation." Moreover, a successful attempt to kill the bill would plunge the Senate into paralysis and prevent action on the South's most fundamental problem — economic stagnation. If the South accepted the inevitability of small, incremental progress on civil rights, it might well become one of the most prosperous regions in the country. If it refused to move forward, it would remain an economic backwater.

He promised Russell he would remove any mention of social or economic integration, limiting the bill solely to the protection of voting rights. He pledged to remove the part giving the president power to send federal troops to the South to enforce the bill's provisions. And he would work to secure a jury trial for any southerner indicted for violating black rights, a gambit that stacked the deck heavily in favor of the accused. For the time being, Russell agreed to hang fire and let the debate proceed, knowing that if Johnson failed to deliver on his promises, the filibuster would commence.

Act Two featured the Mountain States in the West, where the minuscule black population exerted scant sway. While most of these senators supported civil rights, they had less to lose than their colleagues in the North by working toward a compromise. It was in this region that Johnson hoped to find sponsors for the amendments he needed to reshape the bill. And for this objective he was willing to barter. For nearly a decade, western Democrats had struggled to secure federal support for a dam at Hells Canyon near the Idaho-Oregon border that would supply inexpensive public power for the entire region. The Eisenhower administration and their conservative allies in the South had opposed the bill, asserting that private industry should finance the project and control the rates. In an overtly political deal, Johnson persuaded the southerners to vote for the Hells Canyon Dam if the Mountain State senators worked with him to delete the most objectionable provisions of the pending civil rights bill.

All the while Johnson remained in the cloakroom or on the floor, moving from one group of senators to another, correcting, mollifying, blunting extreme statements, preventing the conflict from being cast in irreconcilable terms, ensuring that bargains made were bargains kept. No sooner had the bill for the Hells Canyon Dam passed than the Mountain State senators, to the surprise of their northern colleagues, took center stage in the civil rights debate. Senator Clinton Anderson of Wyoming stood on the floor to offer an amendment that limited the bill to voting rights and excised the president's power to send federal troops to enforce the bill's provisions. "I want to see a civil rights bill passed by the Senate," Senator Anderson said. "This may be the last clear chance the Senate will have in a long time."

The moment Anderson offered his amendment, the ever-vigilant majority leader knew he had attained the necessary coalition. Immediately, he called for the vote and the amendment passed. A few days later, Wyoming's junior senator, Joseph O'Mahoney, and Idaho's Frank Church took to the floor to introduce an amendment providing defendants accused of violating voting rights the right to a jury trial. With the passage of that additional amendment, Johnson had the only bill that had a chance of soldering the three regions of the country together.

There still remained Act Three — the challenge of persuading northern senators that an admittedly diluted bill was preferable to no bill at all. To be sure, the *New York Times* editorialized, "by the standards of all those who had hoped for conclusive Federal action to enforce the whole range of civil rights," it was "a weak" bill. Nonetheless, it was "the beginning of a curative process in an old national wound." No one understood more clearly than Johnson that the bill was only a preliminary step, but by dealing, however moderately, with the right to vote, it was a necessary and vital step. Speaking on the floor of the Senate, he said: "A man with a vote has his destiny in his own hands." Although people spoke of how toothless the bill was, Johnson knew that the fact of the passage was more important than its content. "We've shown we can do it," he said. "We'll do it again in a couple of years."

On September 9, 1957, the Civil Rights Act of 1957, in almost precisely the form Johnson had envisioned seven months earlier, became the law of the land. The brand burned into that bill was LBJ's. It was LBJ, newspapers noted, who had stitched together an improbable coalition of westerners, easterners, liberal Democrats, and conservative Republicans. It was LBJ who had brought the Senate to pass the bill "without the Democratic bloodletting that had been expected," shaping a compromise that persuaded five moderate southern senators "to leave the Confederacy voluntarily" to vote with their northern and western colleagues. It was LBJ who had opened the door of the legislature to black Americans for the first time since the Civil War era.

Newspapers across the country considered the passage of the bill "the most dramatic moment" in Lyndon Johnson's career, testimony to the widespread agreement that he had become the most powerful majority leader in the history of the Senate. "The Democratic Party owed Johnson the [presidential] nomination," Massachusetts senator John F. Kennedy declared the following year. "He's earned it. He wants the same things for the country that I do. But it's too close to Appomattox." Former presidential nominee Adlai Stevenson agreed on both counts, judging Johnson "the best qualified Democrat for the presidency from the standpoint of performance and ability, but plagued with a great weakness: he was a Southerner."

Twenty years earlier, when Franklin Roosevelt first laid eyes on Lyndon Johnson, he foresaw in the wiry and loquacious congressman the stuff of a future president. But with his political prescience, Roosevelt also understood that first "the balance of power" would have to "shift south and west." That requisite shift had not sufficiently happened when Democrats convened in mid-July 1960. They chose John F. Kennedy as their nominee for president.

As a shrewd act of political calculation, Kennedy offered the second spot on the ticket to Lyndon Johnson. To the bafflement of many, Johnson accepted. Why, they wondered, would Johnson relinquish his inordinately commanding position as majority leader to accept a historically insignificant position, a snare of talent and ambition, and agree to work as a subordinate to a man who, he claimed, had "never said a word of importance in the Senate"? The answer lay in the multiple occasions during his career when Johnson had been able to mine riches unseen by others in overlooked, unpromising positions.

That he was unable to transform the vice presidency into a significant position of power was not for lack of trying. Immediately after Kennedy's victory (made possible by the Democratic win in Texas), Johnson devised a radical proposal to enlarge the breadth of the vice presidency itself. When the Senate Democrats convened in caucus in January, the new majority leader, Mike Mansfield, introduced a motion to elect the new vice president chairman of the Democratic Conference, which would make him the presiding officer at all formal meetings of the Senate Democrats. While a substantial majority of forty-six senators voted yay, seventeen voted nay, arguing that the move strained the constitutional division of powers. Interpreting the vote as a severe personal rejection, Johnson told Mansfield to let the motion die, abandoning any hope of leading the Congress from the chair of the vice presidency. Indeed, so wounded was Johnson that from that day forward he withdrew from the Hill and abstained from active participation in legislative strategy, the arena in which the president most needed his help.

"A vice president is generally like a Texas steer," Johnson opined. "He has lost his social standing in the society in which he resides." With insufficient outlet for his energies, deprived of center stage, he plunged into profound depression, finding temporary fulfillment only in his work as chairman of the President's Committee on Equal Employment Opportunity, created to eliminate racial discrimination in hiring by the federal government and by companies with federal contracts. In meetings on civil rights, Johnson came to life, speaking in an "evangelical" tone, according to historian Arthur Schlesinger, that was "extremely effective" — more so "than the President or the Attorney General." By contrast, in meetings on other subjects, Johnson was so quiet and reclusive that he "appeared almost a spectral presence."

Like Theodore Roosevelt, Johnson found he simply wasn't "made to be Vice President." He, too, felt adrift, shrunken, bereft of the kind of meaningful work that provided justification for his existence. The ceremonial aspects of the office — "trips around the world, chauffeurs, men saluting, people clapping" — meant "nothing." He "detested every minute of it." If Theodore Roosevelt contemplated law school, anything to alleviate the tedium of the subordinate office,

Lyndon Johnson had no other life he could imagine. "He felt," one friend recalled, "he had come to the end of the political road."

One could hardly find two more dynamic men, twin "engines in pants," to suffer more volubly from the structural constrictions imposed by the vice presidency. Then, for both men, the prison cell of the vice presidency was violently opened. President William McKinley moved toward a receiving line at the World's Fair, where an anarchist's revolver hidden under a handkerchief awaited him; and Kennedy's black limousine rounded the corner past the Texas School Book Depository Building into Dealey Plaza.

■ ■ ■ ■

III
THE LEADER
AND THE TIMES:
HOW THEY LED

■ ■ ■ ■

NINE:
TRANSFORMATIONAL
LEADERSHIP

Abraham Lincoln and the Emancipation Proclamation

When Abraham Lincoln entered the presidency on March 4, 1861, the house was not merely divided; the house was on fire. In the four months between his election and inauguration, seven southern states had passed resolutions to secede from the Union. At a meeting in Montgomery, Alabama, representatives from these seven states formed a new government with a new constitution, selecting former Mississippi senator Jefferson Davis as provisional president of the Confederate States of America. Meanwhile, a growing rancor threatened to tear apart the Republican Party. On one side stood conciliators convinced that with the proper compromises, the remaining slave-holding states could be kept in the Union; on the other, hard-liners who believed compromise would further agitate the recalcitrant South.

From the start, Lincoln correctly identified the full gravity of the challenge that secession posed to the continued existence of his country's communal life, its shared experiences, its memories, its role as a beacon of hope to the world at large. "I consider the central idea pervading this struggle is the necessity upon us of proving that popular government is not an absurdity," he told his secretary John Hay. "We must settle this question now, whether in a free government the minority have the right to break up the government whenever they choose. If we fail it will go far to prove the incapability of the people to govern themselves."

To meet the terrible burden he faced, Lincoln pieced together the most unusual cabinet in American history, representing every faction of the new Republican Party — former Whigs, Free Soilers, and antislavery Democrats, a combination of conservatives, moderates, and radicals, of hard-liners and conciliators. "I began at once to feel that I needed support," he later noted, "others to share with me the burden." Where President James Buchanan had deliberately chosen like-minded men, adherents who would not question his authority, Lincoln created a team of independent, strong-minded men, all of whom were more experienced in public life, better educated, and more celebrated than he. In the top three positions, at the State Department, the Treasury, and the Justice Department, he placed his three chief rivals — William Seward, Salmon Chase, and Edward Bates — each of whom thought *he* should be president instead of the prairie lawyer from Illinois.

When asked why he was doing this, Lincoln's answer was simple: The country was in peril. These were the strongest and most able men in the country. He needed them by his side. Furthermore, Lincoln had sufficient confidence in his leadership that he would be able to meld this contentious, personally ambitious, gifted, yet potentially dysfunctional group into an administrative family whose loyalty to the Union was unquestionable.

As the president-elect began his journey from Illinois to the nation's capital, he bade farewell to friends gathered at the train station. "No one, not in my situation, can appreciate my feeling of sadness at this parting," he said. "I now leave, not knowing when or whether ever, I may return." Later, considering the trials and tensions he would endure those first weeks in office, he confessed to a friend: "They were so great that could I have anticipated them, I would not have believed it possible to survive them."

The life Lincoln had led, a life marked by perpetual struggle, provided the best preparation for the challenges the country faced. His temperament was stamped with melancholy but devoid of pessimism and brightened by wit. He possessed a deep-rooted integrity and humility combined with an ever-growing confidence in his capacity to lead. Most of all, he brought a mind tempered by failure, a mind able to fashion the appalling suffering ahead into a narrative that would give direction, purpose, and lasting inspiration.

No episode more clearly reveals the unique chemistry between the particular configuration of leadership within its particular historical context than Abraham Lincoln's first unveiling and subsequent implementation of the Emancipation Proclamation.

On July 22, 1862, Abraham Lincoln convened a special session of his cabinet to reveal — not to debate — his preliminary draft of the Emancipation Proclamation. He understood that there were "differences in the Cabinet on the slavery question" and welcomed their suggestions after the confidential reading was concluded. At the outset, however, he "wished it to be understood that the question was settled in his own mind" and that "the responsibility of the measure was his." The time for bold action had arrived.

What enabled Lincoln to determine that the time was now right for this fundamental transformation in how the war was waged and what the Union was fighting for? And how did he succeed in persuading his fractious cabinet, the Army, and his divided countrymen in the North to go along with him?

Acknowledge When Failed Policies Demand a Change in Direction.

In the last week of June 1862, General George B. McClellan's Army of the Potomac suffered a crushing defeat in its first major offensive. In a series of brutal battles, General Robert E. Lee's forces had repulsed McClellan's advance up the Peninsula to attack the Confederate capital at Richmond, driving the Union Army into retreat, decimating its ranks, and leaving nearly sixteen thousand dead, captured, or wounded. At one point, the capitulation of McClellan's entire force had seemed possible. Northern morale was at its nadir — lower even than in the aftermath of Bull Run. "We are in the depths now," New York businessman George Templeton Strong admitted, "permeated with disgust, saturated with gloomy thinking."

"Things had gone from bad to worse," Lincoln recalled of that midsummer, "until I felt that we had reached the end of our rope on the plan of operations we had been pursuing; that we had played our last card and must change our tactics."

Gather Firsthand Information, Ask Questions.

No sooner had the crippled Union Army arrived back at Harrison's Landing on the James River than Lincoln resolved to visit the troops — to comfort the wounded, talk with them in small groups, bolster their morale, and sustain his own spirits. The stimulant of the president's unexpected visit on the enervated regiments was instantaneous.

Equally important, Lincoln's accessibility to his soldiers afforded him the chance to gather information and ask questions — questions and observations that led to a major revision in his thoughts about the role of slavery in the war. From the beginning of the struggle, Lincoln had stressed that the North was fighting solely to preserve the Union, not to interfere with slavery. Though he had long despised slavery, as we have seen, he felt compelled to muzzle his abhorrence in deference to both public sentiment regarding the primacy of restoring the Union and the constraints of the Constitution that protected the institution of slavery in states where it already existed.

Through firsthand inquiries at the encampment with commanders and soldiers, however, Lincoln came to realize a fortifying link between slavery and the Confederate war effort. Slaves dug trenches and built fortifications for the Confederate Army. Slaves served as teamsters, cooks, waiters, and hospital attendants. On the home front, they tilled fields, raised crops, and picked cotton. Slave labor kept farms and plantations in operation. The toil of slaves liberated Confederate soldiers to fight. "The slaves," Lincoln understood, "were undeniably an element of strength to those who had their service, and we must decide whether that element should be with us or against us." If the rebels were divested of their slaves, the beleaguered North would thus gain a desperately needed military advantage.

Find Time and Space in Which to Think.
As Lincoln began to survey the darkening landscape of the war and consider a new strategy regarding slavery, he needed time to reflect upon both the constitutionality and the ramifications of issuing an emancipation order. Yet, amid the crush of hundreds of visi-

tors and office seekers who poured into the White House as soon as the morning doors were opened, Lincoln scarcely had time to relax much less contemplate the complexities of the issue. Wherever he moved, "he had literally to run the gantlet" through throngs in the hallways and lining the stairs leading up to his second-floor office.

That pivotal summer, he found refuge at the Soldiers' Home, a three-hundred-acre complex in the hills three miles north of the city. Within the government-run compound, which included a main building that could accommodate 150 disabled veterans, an infirmary, and a dining hall, were a number of smaller residences, including a two-story brick cottage where Lincoln and his family settled from June until mid-October. Rising before seven in the morning, Lincoln rode his horse to the White House, returning to his country cottage in the evening when the cooling breezes brought relief from the oppressive swelter and tumult of Washington.

The Soldiers' Home provided sanctuary. There, Lincoln recalled, he was able to dwell thoroughly and "earnestly on the gravity, importance, and delicacy" of the subject of slavery. Since the first shot at Fort Sumter, two issues — the legal/constitutional issue and the moral issue — had been at loggerheads. In the tranquil setting of the Soldiers' Home, he was able to resolve at last the chasm between the constitutional protection of slavery and the moral abomination of slavery.

The worsening context of the war, which threatened the survival of the Union and the Constitution itself, provided a suitable resolution to this dilemma. Given the manifold advantages the slaves supplied the Confederacy, an executive order freeing the slaves could be considered "a military necessity absolutely essential for the salvation of the Union." Emancipating the slaves, "otherwise unconstitutional," might therefore become a lawful action. The constitutional protection of slavery could be countermanded by the constitutionally warranted war powers of the commander in chief. Thus, Abraham Lincoln was able to come to the decision that would define both his presidency and his place in history.

Still, Lincoln dreaded unleashing "the weapon of emancipation" as a unilateral military decree. A quarter of a century earlier, he had warned his Lyceum audience against men the likes of an Alexander, a Caesar, or a Napoleon who exploited times of chaos to impose order from above. The irony burned deep that to save the Union required suspension of constitutional law upon which the Union had been founded. To rescind his inaugural pledge of noninterference with slavery by a sweeping executive fiat was a resort predicated upon the failure of all other options.

Exhaust All Possibility of Compromise Before Imposing Unilateral Executive Power.

Four months earlier, Lincoln had sent a message to Congress calling for federal aid to the four loyal border states — Missouri, Kentucky, Delaware, and Maryland — if they were willing to adopt a plan for the gradual abolition of slavery. In return for voluntarily relinquishing their slaves, slave owners would be compensated at an average price of $400 per head. It was Lincoln's conviction that nothing would shorten the war faster than compensated emancipation. If the rebels were deprived of hope that the border states might join the Confederacy, they would lose heart. The plan depended upon the approval of the border state legislatures. To the citizens of those states Lincoln appealed directly: "You can not if you would, be blind to the signs of the times — I beg of you a calm and enlarged consideration of them, ranging as it may be, far above personal and partisan politics. The proposal makes common cause for a common object, casting no reproaches upon any. . . . The change it contemplates would come gently as the dews of heaven, not rending or wrecking anything. Will you not embrace it?" The appeal to Congress had foundered on the sweeping and disruptive change that would be unleashed on an economic and social system dependent upon slavery.

In the aftermath of the Peninsula disaster, Lincoln called a meeting of the twenty-eight border state representatives and senators to renew his proffer of compensation. To his great dismay, they once again refused, arguing that "emancipation in any form" would fan the spirit of secession in the loyal border states and would further consolidate the spirit of rebellion in the seceded states, lengthening, not shortening the war.

"I am a patient man," Lincoln told one of the group, "but it may as well be understood, once for all, that I shall not surrender this game leaving any available card unplayed." That final card was the unveiling of his first draft of the Emancipation Proclamation.

So the situation stood on July 22, 1862, when the president gathered the cabinet to read his proclamation. As depicted in Francis Carpenter's famous painting of the occasion, Lincoln is seated in the center. The radicals — Edwin Stanton and Salmon Chase — are to Lincoln's right. The conservatives — Caleb Smith, Montgomery Blair, and Edward Bates — are grouped on Lincoln's left. The moderates — Gideon Welles and, seated in the foreground, William Henry Seward — surround Lincoln, who is presented as the nucleus and fulcrum of the composition. Battlefield maps and books are strewn everywhere — tilted against the walls, spread on the floor, rolled in standing racks. It was the young artist's goal to bestow enduring fame on "that band of men, upon whom the eyes of the world centered as never before."

Silence prevailed as the president unfolded two lined foolscap sheets from his pocket, adjusted his glasses on his nose, and began to read what amounted to a legal brief for emancipation. He enumerated the various congressional acts regarding confiscation of the property of rebels, repeated his recommendation for compensated emancipation, and reiterated his purpose to preserve the Union. And then he came to the single sentence that would change the course of history:

As a fit and necessary military measure for effecting this object, [preservation of the Union] I, as Commander-in-Chief of the Army and Navy of the United States, do order and declare that on the first day of January in the year of our Lord 1863 all persons held as slaves within any state or states, wherein the constitutional authority of the United States shall not then be practically recognized, submitted to, and maintained shall then, thenceforward and forever, be free.

By setting the effective date for the Proclamation nearly six months hence, Lincoln offered the rebellious states a last chance to end the war and return to the Union before permanently forfeiting their slaves. At a moment when one would have expected an elevated language commensurate with this historical turning point in the narrative of the nation, Lincoln deployed a language that was pedestrian, remarkable for its flat precision, devoid of a single spark of figurative or poetic language. In vain, one searches for a stirring phrase, a moral endorsement of emancipation — not taking into account that the Emancipation Proclamation was not an oration at all, but a legal notice, a document subject to future court examination and ruling. Furthermore, no one knew better than Lincoln that words have consequences. In a world of tinder, he was determined to hold his rhetorical gifts in abeyance in order to reach across factions and avoid a single spark that could set loose an avoidable conflagration.

Restrained language aside, the scope of the Proclamation was stunning. For the first time, the president yoked Union and slavery into a single, transformative, moral force. Some three and a half million blacks in the South who had lived enslaved for generations were promised freedom. Eighty words in one sentence would supplant legislation on property rights and slavery that had governed policy in the House and Senate for nearly three-quarters of a century. To the confusion of some, the executive order did not cover the nearly half a million slaves in the loyal border states. Since these states had not joined in the insurrection, the president's war powers could not be used to liberate their slaves. Yet, if emancipation posed no immediate threat to the border states, it concealed a latent warning of a legally impending mandate should they choose, in the future, to join the rebel Confederacy.

Anticipate Contending Viewpoints.
Though Lincoln had signaled that his mind was already made up before reading the Proclamation, he welcomed reactions from his cabinet, whether for or against. So clearly did he know each of the members, so thoroughly had he anticipated their responses, that he was prepared to answer whatever objections they might raise. He had deliberately built a team of men who represented the major geographical, political, and ideological factions of the Union. For months past, he had listened intently as they wrestled among themselves about how best to preserve this Union. At various junctures, diverse members had assailed Lincoln as too radical, too conservative, brazenly dictatorial, or dangerously feckless. He had welcomed the

wide range of opinions they provided as he turned the subject over in his mind, debating "first the one side and then the other of every question arising," until, through hard mental work, his own position had emerged. His process of decision making, born of his characteristic ability to entertain a full carousel of vantage points at a single time, seemed to some painfully slow, but once he had finally come to a determination to act, it was no longer a question of WHAT — only WHEN.

Like bookends seated at opposite ends of the council chamber, Secretary of War Edwin Stanton and Attorney General Edward Bates — the most radical and the most conservative of Lincoln's family — were the only two who expressed strong support for the Proclamation. That Stanton recommended its "immediate promulgation" was understandable. More intimately aware than any of his colleagues of the condition of the hard-pressed Army, he instantly grasped the massive military boost emancipation would confer. As for the constitutionalist Bates, though portrayed in Carpenter's rendering in a pose of resistance, warding off Lincoln's reading with folded arms and fixed expression, he unexpectedly and wholeheartedly concurred — albeit with the condition that a deportment plan be put in place for all the emancipated Negroes.

Secretary of the Navy Gideon Welles, his curly wig perched on his head, kept silent, later admitting that the Proclamation's "magnitude and its uncertain results," its "solemnity and weight," mightily oppressed him. Not only did it seem "an extreme exercise of War powers," but he feared that "desperation on the part of the slave-owners" would likely lengthen the war and raise the struggle to new heights of ferocity. Standing behind Welles, Interior Secretary Caleb Smith, a conservative Whig from Indiana, remained silent as well, though he later confided to his assistant secretary that should Lincoln actually issue the Proclamation, he would summarily "resign and go home and attack the Administration."

Late-arriving Montgomery Blair, the postmaster general, forcefully opposed the Proclamation. As a spokesman for the border states (he had practiced law in Missouri before moving to Maryland), Blair predicted that emancipation would push loyal Union supporters in those states to the secessionists' side. Furthermore, it would cause such an outcry among conservatives throughout the North that Republicans would lose the upcoming fall elections. Lincoln had considered every aspect of Blair's objections but had concluded that the importance of the slavery issue far exceeded party politics. He reminded Blair of his persistent and multiple efforts to find a compromise. He would, however, willingly allow Blair to lodge written objections.

That Salmon Chase, the most ardent abolitionist in the cabinet, recoiled from the president's initiative was irksome. "It went beyond anything I have recommended," Chase admitted, but he feared that wholesale emancipation would lead to "massacre on the one hand and support for the insurrection on the other." Far better to deal with the dangerous issue piecemeal, in the incremental fashion General David Hunter had employed earlier that spring when he issued an order freeing the slaves within the territory of his command, which encompassed South Carolina, Georgia, and Florida. Although Chase and his fellow abolitionists had been sorely tried when Lincoln summarily annulled Hunter's order, Lincoln had held firm: "No commanding general shall do such a thing, upon my responsibility," he had said. He would not "feel justified" in leaving such a complex issue "to the decision of commanders in the field." A comprehensive policy was precisely what executive leadership entailed.

Secretary of State Seward had an internationalist perspective and, consequently, transatlantic worries. If the proclamation provoked a racial war interrupting the production of cotton, the ruling classes in England and France, dependent on American cotton to feed their textile mills, might intervene on behalf of the Confederacy. Lincoln had also weighed the force of this argument, but he believed that the masses in England and France, who had earlier pressured their governments to abolish slavery, would never be maneuvered into supporting the Confederacy once the Union truly committed itself to emancipation.

Despite the cacophony of ideas and contending voices, Lincoln remained fixed upon his course of action. Before the meeting came to an end, Seward raised the sensitive question of timing. "The depression of the public mind, consequent upon our repeated reversals is so great," Seward argued, that the Proclamation might be seen as "our last shriek, on the retreat." Far preferable to wait "until the eagle of victory takes its flight," and then "hang your Proclamation around its neck."

"It was an aspect of the case that, in all my thought upon the subject, I had entirely overlooked," Lincoln told Carpenter afterward. "The result was that I put the draft of the proclamation aside, as you do your sketch for a picture, waiting for a victory. From time to time I added or changed a line, touching it up here and there, anxiously watching the progress of events."

For two months, Lincoln bided his time,

awaiting word from the battlefield that the "eagle of victory" had taken flight. At last the tide turned with the retreat of Lee's army from Maryland and Pennsylvania. This battle at Antietam, with some 23,000 dead, was "the bloodiest single day of combat in American history." Overwhelming carnage left both sides in a paralytic stupor. This nightmare was not the resounding victory Lincoln had hoped and prayed for, but proved sufficient to set his plan in motion. No sooner had the news of Antietam reached Lincoln at the Soldiers' Home than he revised the preliminary draft of the Emancipation Proclamation and, only five days after the "victory," once again summoned the cabinet to convene on Monday, September 22.

Tension in the room could not have been more tautly drawn, yet, unaccountably, to the disapproval of the grimly serious Stanton, Lincoln commenced with an Artemus Ward anecdote, a ludicrous tale of how a wax representation of Judas had been dragged from a diorama of the Last Supper, beaten and broken by a Utica, New York, resident, a battery resulting in "arson in the third degree." Ward's silly legalese briefly lanced tension for Lincoln, as humorous stories and pointed jokes often eased and distracted him. Except for Stanton, the members chuckled and smiled along with Lincoln's boisterous laughter, the darkly playful moment letting off pressure as they stood on the verge of a moment from which there was no return.

Assume Full Responsibility for a Pivotal Decision.

The time for taking the action he had postponed in July had come. "I wish it were a better time," he said, abruptly launching into the grave matter of emancipation. "I wish that we were in a better condition." However, he divulged, as witnessed by Chase and recorded in his diary, "I made the promise to myself and (hesitating a little) to my Maker" that if Lee's army were "driven out" of Maryland, the Proclamation would be issued. The decision was "fixed and unalterable," Lincoln declared. "The act and all its responsibilities were his alone." He had "pondered over it for weeks, and been more confirmed in the rectitude of the measure as time passed on." That clearly established, he read his slightly amended version of the proclamation.

After making a "very emphatic speech sustaining the measure," Stanton suggested that "the act was so important, and involved consequences so vast that he hoped each member would give distinctly and unequivocally his own individual opinion." The response to the reading of the first draft had been very troubling. In the subsequent two months, however, Lincoln had talked individually with each member of his cabinet.

His views were not subject to change; emancipation, he was certain, was indispensable to victory in the war.

While Chase considered graduated emancipation by the generals a safer course, he was now "fully" satisfied, he told the president, "that you have given to every proposition which has been made, a kind and candid consideration. And you have now expressed the conclusion to which you have arrived, clearly and distinctly." Therefore, "I am ready to take it just as it is written, and to stand by it with all my heart." Welles remained vexed that the Proclamation was "an arbitrary and despotic measure," even if promulgated in "the cause of freedom." If the president was ready to take the full weight of responsibility for the decision, however, then Welles, too, was ready "to assent most unequivocally to the measure." In like manner, Caleb Smith gave his approval. He abandoned his earlier threat to attack the administration if the Proclamation were issued. In December, after the judge of the U.S. District Court of Indiana died, Lincoln granted Smith's long-held wish for a federal judgeship.

Montgomery Blair acknowledged he remained "afraid of the influence of the Proclamation on the Border States and on the army." Lincoln agreed that danger lay in this direction, "but the difficulty was as great not to act as to act"; a "forward movement" had to be made. Blair once again asked to file his dissent and Lincoln once more gave his approval; but in the end, Blair never lodged his filing. His loyalty to the administration was freely given, neither imposed nor coerced.

As for Seward, such was his dogged allegiance to the president that he had no thought of opposing a decision so categorically made. He had but one substantive proposal. Wouldn't it be more powerful, he asked, if Lincoln deleted his reference to sustaining emancipation during his incumbency, and instead pledged all future executive governments "to recognize and to maintain" the freedom of slaves. This way the government itself rather than this particular administration would be the guarantor of the pledge. Lincoln hesitated to make a promise he himself could not fulfill, but in the end, he embraced the importance of Seward's suggested alteration.

When the proclamation appeared in newspapers the following day the entire cabinet, unlikely as it had first appeared, had banded behind the president. If the members of this most unusual team — a microcosm of the disparate factions within the Union itself — had not coalesced at this critical juncture, there was small chance of holding together the country at large.

How had Lincoln been able to lead these

inordinately prideful, ambitious, quarrelsome, jealous, supremely gifted men to support a fundamental shift in the purpose of the war? The best answer can be found in what we identify today as Lincoln's emotional intelligence: his empathy, humility, consistency, self-awareness, self-discipline, and generosity of spirit. "So long as I have been here," Lincoln maintained, "I have not willingly planted a thorn in any man's bosom." In his everyday interactions with the team, there was no room for mean-spirited behavior, for grudges or personal resentments. He welcomed arguments within the cabinet, but would be "greatly pained," he warned them, if he found his colleagues attacking one another in public. Such sniping "would be a wrong to me; and much worse, a wrong to the country." The standards of decorum he demanded were based on the understanding that they were all involved together in a challenge "too vast for malicious dealing." It was this sense of common purpose that had originally guided the formation of the cabinet and would now sustain its survival. What can be learned from Lincoln's success in keeping this disparate team together?

Understand the Emotional Needs of Each Member of the Team.
An ongoing attentiveness to the multiple needs of the complex individuals in his

cabinet shaped Lincoln's team leadership. From the start, Lincoln recognized that Seward's commanding national and international reputation warranted the preeminent position of secretary of state and required special treatment from the president. Not only attracted by Seward's cosmopolitan glamour and the pleasure of his sophisticated company, but also sensitive to his colleague's hurt pride in losing a nomination widely expected to be his, Lincoln frequently crossed the street to pay a visit to Seward's townhouse at Lafayette Park. There, the two men spent long evenings together before a blazing fire, talking, laughing, telling stories, developing a mutually bolstering camaraderie. An equally intimate though less convivial bond was formed with the high-strung, abrasive Stanton. "The pressure on him is immeasurable," Lincoln said of "Mars," his affectionate nickname given to his war secretary. Lincoln was willing to do anything he could to assuage that stress, if only sitting by Stanton's side in the telegraph office, holding hands as they anxiously awaited bulletins from the battlefield.

Reliant above all on Seward and Stanton, Lincoln was aware of the jealousy engendered by the specter of favoritism. Accordingly, he found exclusive time for each individual team member: whether flagging down Welles on the pathway leading from the White House to the Navy Department, suddenly dropping in at Chase's stately mansion, dining with the entire Blair clan, or inviting Bates and Smith along to converse with him on late afternoon carriage rides.

"Every one likes a compliment," Lincoln observed; everyone needs praise for the work they are doing. Frequently, he penned handwritten notes to his colleagues, extending his gratitude for their actions. He publicly acknowledged that Seward's suggestion to await a military victory before issuing the Proclamation was an original and useful contribution. When he had to issue an order to Welles, he assured his "Neptune" that it was not his intention to insinuate "that you have been remiss in the performance of the arduous and responsible duties of your Department, which I take pleasure in affirming had, in your hands, been conducted with admirable success." When compelled to remove one of Chase's appointees, he understood that the prickly Chase might well be resentful. Not wanting the situation to deteriorate, he called on Chase that evening. Placing his long arms on Chase's shoulders, he patiently explained why the decision was necessary. Though the ambitious Chase often chafed under Lincoln's authority, he acknowledged "the President has always treated me with such personal kindness and has always manifested such fairness and integrity of purpose, that I have not found myself free to throw up my trust . . . so I still work on."

Refuse to Let Past Resentments Fester; Transcend Personal Vendettas.

Lincoln never selected members of his team "by his like, or dislike of them," his old friend Leonard Swett observed. "If a man had maligned him, or been guilty of personal ill-treatment and abuse, and was the fittest man for the place, he would put him in his Cabinet just as soon as he would his friend." Guided by the "principle of forgiveness," Lincoln insisted he did not care if someone *has* done wrong in the past; "it is enough if the man does no wrong *hereafter.*"

Lincoln's adherence to this rule opened the door to Edwin Stanton's appointment as secretary of war, despite a troubled early history between the two men. They had first crossed paths on a major patent case in Cincinnati. Stanton, a brilliant and hard-driving lawyer, had already earned a national reputation; Lincoln was an emerging figure only in Illinois. One look at Lincoln — hair askew, shirt stained, coat sleeves and trousers too short to fit his long arms and legs — and Stanton turned to his partner, George Harding: "Why did you bring that d — d long armed Ape here . . . he does not know anything and can do you no good." And with that, Stanton dismissed the prairie lawyer.

He never opened the brief Lincoln had laboriously prepared, never consulted him, nor even spoke a word with him.

Out of that humiliation, however, came a powerful self-scrutiny on Lincoln's part, a savage desire to improve himself. He remained in the courtroom the entire week, intently studying Stanton's legal performance. He had never "seen anything so finished and elaborated, and so thoroughly prepared." Stanton's partner recalled that while Lincoln never forgot the sting of that episode, "when convinced that the interest of the nation would be best served by bringing Stanton into his cabinet, he suppressed his personal resentment, as not many men would have done, and made the appointment."

"No two men were ever more utterly and irreconcilably unlike," Stanton's private secretary observed. Where Lincoln would give "a wayward subordinate," such as McClellan, too many chances "to repair his errors," Stanton "was for forcing him to obey or cutting off his head." Where Lincoln was compassionate, patient, and transparent, Stanton was blunt, intense, and secretive. "They supplemented each other's nature, and they fully recognized that they were a necessity to each other." Before the end of their partnership, Stanton not only revered Lincoln; he loved him.

Set a Standard of Mutual Respect and Dignity; Control Anger.

When angry at a colleague, Lincoln would fling off what he called a "hot" letter, releasing all his pent wrath. He would then put the letter aside until he cooled down and could attend the matter with a clearer eye. When Lincoln's papers were opened at the turn of the twentieth century, historians discovered a raft of such letters, with Lincoln's notation underneath; "never sent and never signed." Such forbearance set an example for the team. One evening, Lincoln listened as Stanton worked himself into a fury against one of the generals. "I would like to tell him what I think of him," Stanton stormed. "Why don't you," suggested Lincoln. "Write it all down." When Stanton finished the letter, he returned and read it to the president. "Capital," Lincoln said. "Now, Stanton, what are you going to do about it?" "Why, send it of course!" "I wouldn't," said the president. "Throw it in the waste-paper basket." "But it took me two days to write." "Yes, yes and it did you ever so much good. You feel better now. That is all that is necessary. Just throw it in the basket." And after some additional grumbling, Stanton did just that.

Not only would Lincoln hold back until his own anger subsided and counsel others to do likewise, he would readily forgive intemperate public attacks on himself. When an unflattering letter Blair had written about Lincoln in the early days of the war unexpectedly surfaced in the press months later, the embarrassed Blair carried the letter to the White House and offered to resign. Lincoln told him he had no intention of reading it, nor any desire to exact retribution. "Forget it," he said, "& never mention or think of it again."

Shield Colleagues from Blame.

Time and again, Welles marveled, Lincoln "declared that he, and not his Cabinet, was in fault for errors imputed to them." His refusal to let a subordinate take the blame for his decisions was never better illustrated than by his public defense of Stanton after McClellan attributed the Peninsula disaster to the War Department's failure to send sufficient troops. A vicious public assault upon Stanton ensued, with subsequent calls for his resignation. To create a dramatic backdrop that would garner extensive newspaper coverage, Lincoln issued an order to close down all the government departments at one o'clock so everyone might attend a massive Union rally on the Capitol steps. There, after the firing of cannon and patriotic music from the Marine Band, Lincoln directly countered McClellan's charge. He insisted that every possible soldier available had been sent to reinforce the general. "The Secretary of War is not to blame for not giving what he had none to give." Then, as the applause mounted, Lincoln continued: "I believe [Stanton] is a brave and able man, and I stand here, as justice requires me to do, to take upon myself what has been charged on the Secretary of War." Lincoln's spirited defense of his beleaguered secretary skillfully extinguished the campaign against Stanton.

In the end, it was Lincoln's character — his consistent sensitivity, patience, prudence, and empathy — that inspired and transformed every member of his official family. In this paradigm of team leadership, greatness was grounded in goodness.

And yet, beneath Lincoln's tenderness and kindness, he was without question the most complex, ambitious, willful, and implacable leader of them all. They could trumpet self-serving ambitions, they could criticize Lincoln, mock him, irritate him, infuriate him, exacerbate the pressure upon him; everything would be tolerated so long as they pursued their jobs with passion and skill, so long as they were headed in the direction he had defined for them and presented a united front when it counted most, as it surely did on September 22, 1862, when he issued his Emancipation Proclamation.

The hundred days between the Proclamation's publication in September and its activation on the first of January 1863 would provide a critical test of the fragile unity Lincoln had created within his cabinet. How did Lincoln weather this peculiarly distressing time?

Maintain Perspective in the Face of Both Accolades and Abuse.

Writing to Lincoln three days after the publication of the Proclamation, Vice President Hannibal Hamlin confidently predicted that it would be "enthusiastically approved and sustained" and "stand as the great act of the age." Lincoln was more realistic and skeptical about the immediate response. "While commendation in newspapers and by distinguished individuals is all that a vain man could wish," he answered Hamlin, "the stocks have declined, and troops come forward more slowly than ever. This, looked soberly in the face, is not very satisfactory."

An "ill wind" of discontent surrounded the voters as they headed to the polls for the midterm elections. "Our war on rebellion languishes," New York diarist George Templeton Strong lamented. Grandiosely satisfied with his performance at Antietam, McClellan had failed to pursue the retreating rebels and allowed Lee to cross the Potomac into Virginia. When McClellan let it be known that he would not fight for "such an accursed doctrine" as the Emancipation Proclamation, his persistent refusal to move the Army forward verged on outright insubordination.

A frustrated public blamed the administration for failure to prosecute the war more vigorously. This perception, together with conservative resentment against the Proclamation, combined to produce withering electoral results for Republicans, just as Montgomery Blair had predicted. "We have lost almost everything," Lincoln's secretary John Nicolay wrote. In Congress, the number of conservative Democrats opposed to emancipation doubled, leaving Republicans with a razor-thin majority. State legislatures in Ohio, Indiana, Pennsylvania, and New York turned heavily Democratic.

Asked how he felt about the Republican losses, Lincoln joked to burn off the gloom: "Somewhat like that boy in Kentucky, who stubbed his toe while running to see his sweetheart. The boy said he was too big to cry, and far too badly hurt to laugh."

Find Ways to Cope with Pressure, Maintain Balance, Replenish Energy.

"Most uncheerful were the so-called holidays of that season," journalist Noah Brooks wrote. "The city was filled with wounded and dying men; and multitudes of people from the North, seeking lost, missing, and wounded relatives, crowded the hotels." Following the midterm elections, Lincoln had finally removed McClellan from command after destructive procrastination. "I began to fear he was playing false," Lincoln said, "that he did not want to hurt the enemy." To replace McClellan, he chose Ambrose Burnside, known as "a fighting general," thus swinging to a temperament opposite McClellan's. Burnside's headlong spirit proved calamitous. In the middle of December, against Lincoln's counsel, he led the Army of the Potomac into the trap of "a slaughter pen" at Fredericksburg, leaving thirteen thousand Union soldiers dead or wounded.

A blizzard of recrimination beset the president from all sides. Rumors spread that the humiliating defeat at Fredericksburg would prompt England and France to side with the Confederacy, that the entire cabinet would resign, that Lincoln himself would give way to Hannibal Hamlin. The unremitting march of death and national mourning aroused fears that the war would come to a dishonorable, catastrophic conclusion, that the South would remain independent and slavery would remain intact. In this welter of worry and fear, Lincoln was tormented most of all by the appalling deaths of his soldiers, the brave men "endeavoring to purchase with their blood and their lives the future happiness and prosperity of this country." He acknowledged he was "more depressed" that terrible winter than at any time in his life, a harrowing statement given the vicissitudes of that life. "If there is a worse place than Hell," he concluded, "I am in it."

What strategies did Lincoln use to keep some kind of balance? How did he maintain sufficient stability to weather this long winter of discontent? The forms that such relief takes are as varied as the persons seeking it.

When Lincoln was under appalling duress, nothing provided greater respite and renewal than a visit to the theater. During his four years as president, he went to the theater more than a hundred times. When the gas lights dimmed, and the actors took the stage, Lincoln was able to surrender his mind "into other channels of thought." At a performance of *Henry IV Part 1,* a seatmate noted, "He has forgotten the war. He has forgotten Congress. He is out of politics. He is living in Prince Hal's time." He understood that people might think his frequent theatergoing "strange, but I must have some relief from this terrible anxiety, or it will kill me."

Nonetheless, theatergoing was not pure escapism. For though he sorely needed diversion and distraction, Lincoln was drawn to the darkest of Shakespeare's plays — *Macbeth, Lear, Hamlet* — not simply as a way out but as a way in, a way to decipher the problems confronting him. It was the philosophic depth in Shakespeare that resonated most meaningfully to the tortured leader in the midst of civil war. "It matters not to me whether Shakespeare be well or ill acted,"

Lincoln once said, "with him the thought suffices."

There remained times, however, when the burden of nightmarish days and the loneliness of his position made sleep a fugitive. Such nights, Lincoln would rise from his bed, clad in nightshirt and slippers, his well-thumbed edition of Shakespeare in his hand, and rouse John Hay from the small White House bedroom his young aide shared with John Nicolay. Still able to summon a shadow of his gifts as performer, raconteur, and mimic, Lincoln would read aloud favorite comic passages from Shakespeare. His appreciation of tragedy was matched by his appreciation of silliness, anecdote, burlesque. The narrow seam between tragedy and comedy afforded Lincoln what he called his "literary recreation." When engaged in a comic tale, his laugh, the artist Carpenter noted, resembled the "neigh of a wild horse." A friend observed that Lincoln's laugh served as a "life preserver" for him. Hay recalled that only when "my heavy eye-lids caught his considerate notice would he stop & sent me to bed." Recitation was Lincoln's way of sharing in a common humanity during an uncommon, inhumanly isolating time.

Amid the isolation of ultimate responsibility — when people were dying day after day as a consequence of his directives — Lincoln found a way to lighten his grief through the use of his pardoning power. While both his war secretary and his military officers insisted that death sentences for soldiers who ran away from battle or fell asleep on picket duty were essential to maintaining military discipline, Lincoln, on the contrary, looked "for any good excuse for saving a man's life." As he studied each petition, he tried to comprehend the soldier's perspective — the night-flight desertion of a homesick teen, a young boy "overcome by a physical fear greater than his will"; a picket so exhausted that "sleep steals upon him unawares." When he grasped a reason to reduce the sentence, he said, "I go to bed happy as I think how joyous the signing of my name will make him and his family and his friends." Momentarily, he had diverted his thoughts away from the bitterness of ubiquitous death to the jubilation of a rescued life.

Keep Your Word.

As the first of January 1863 drew near, the public displayed a "general air of doubt" as to whether the president would follow through on his September pledge to activate his Emancipation Proclamation on New Year's Day. Critics predicted that its enactment would foment race wars in the South, cause Union officers to resign their commands, and prompt 100,000 men to lay down their arms. The prospect of emancipation threatened to fracture the brittle coalition that had held Republicans and Union Democrats together. "Will Lincoln's backbone carry him through?" wondered a skeptical George Templeton Strong. "Nobody knows."

Those who knew Abraham Lincoln best would not have posed the question. All through his life, the honor and weight of his word had been ballast to his character, the "chief gem" of his pride. The breach of honor involved in his severed engagement to Mary Todd had contributed to a life-threatening depression, as had his spectacular failure to deliver on his pledge to bring Illinois an economic boom through public works. Restoration of confidence in his ability to make good on his promises and resolves had been central to his healing and the resurrection of his career. Ever since, as a family man, friend, lawyer, and politician, he had reflected carefully before setting forth his opinions and making promises. That he would hold firm to the September pledge he had made to himself and his Maker to issue the proclamation was never in question. "My word is out," Lincoln told a Massachusetts congressman, "and I can't take it back."

Though the abolitionist leader Frederick Douglass had been unsparingly critical of Lincoln's delay in issuing the Emancipation Proclamation, he fathomed Lincoln's character and the durability of his word better than most. "Abraham Lincoln may be slow," he wrote, "but Abraham Lincoln is not the man to reconsider, retract and contradict words and purposes solemnly proclaimed over his official signature." To answer those who asked if Lincoln would reconsider, Douglass gave an emphatic *no.* "Abraham Lincoln will take no step backward," he insisted. "If he has taught us to confide in nothing else, he has taught us to confide in his word."

The doors of the White House opened at noon for the traditional New Year's reception to which the general public was invited. For three hours, Lincoln stood in the Blue Room, "serene and even smiling," shaking hands with more than a thousand citizens, even though as one reporter later noted, "his eyes were with his thoughts, and they were far away." Later that afternoon, he was scheduled to sign the Proclamation.

The day before, Lincoln had reconvened the cabinet a third time for a final reading of the Emancipation Proclamation. The version he presented differed in one major respect from the latest draft in September. For months, abolitionists had argued for enlisting blacks in the armed services. Lincoln had hesitated, regarding such a radical step premature and hazardous for his fragile coalition.

Now, however, he decided the time had

come. "The dogmas of the quiet past are inadequate to the stormy present," he told Congress. "As our case is new, so we must think anew, and act anew." A new clause declaring that the Army would commence with the recruitment of blacks was inserted into the Proclamation, along with a humble closing appeal suggested by Secretary Chase asking "the considerate judgment of mankind, and the gracious favor of Almighty God."

The signing took place in a simple ceremony attended by only a dozen people, including Secretary of State Seward and his son, Fred. As the parchment was placed before the president, Fred Seward recalled, Lincoln "dipped his pen in the ink, and then, holding it a moment above the sheet, seemed to hesitate," but then began to speak in a forceful manner. "I never, in my life felt more certain that I was doing right, than I do in signing this paper," Lincoln said. "If my name ever goes down in history it will be for this act, and my whole soul is in it." His arm was "stiff and numb" from shaking hands, however. "Now, this signature is one that will be closely examined, and if they find my hand trembled, they will say 'he had some compunctions.' " So he waited for several minutes until he took up the pen once more and signed with an "unusually bold, clear, and firm" hand.

Across New England, immense crowds had gathered since early morning at churches, great halls, and theaters to await the news that the president had signed the Proclamation. In Boston's Tremont Temple and the nearby Music Hall, more than six thousand kept vigil. Orators — including Frederick Douglass, Ralph Waldo Emerson, Harriet Beecher Stowe, and Oliver Wendell Holmes — spoke as the day wore on and the suspense escalated. A "visible shadow" fell upon the crowd when it reached 10 p.m. and still no word had arrived. Finally, a man raced through the crowd. "It is coming! It is on the wires!" Douglass recorded the "wild and grand" reaction, the "Joy and gladness," the "sobs and tears," and then the singing — "Glory Hallelujah," "Old John Brown" — that united them until the first light of dawn.

The jubilation of New England in reaction to the Proclamation was not shared in the border states or, for that matter, in much of the North. If marginal victory at Antietam had muted opposition to emancipation, the humiliating defeat at Fredericksburg and the ensuing winter stalemate raised anger to full volume. In his inaugural address, Governor of Kentucky James Robinson recommended that the state legislature reject the Proclamation, warning that "the monstrous doctrine" would unify the South "into one burning mass of inextinguishable hate." In Indiana and Illinois, heavily Democratic legislatures passed resolutions calling for a compromise peace with the South that would leave slavery intact; if abolitionist New England refused to live in a country that condoned slavery, they argued, then let New England secede. In Congress, "Peace Democrats," popularly known as Copperheads, capitalizing on the protracted slough of morale, opposed the new conscription laws and even went so far as to openly encourage soldiers to desert. Anecdotal reports from the Army camps suggested that emancipation was having a negative effect upon the soldiers, numbers of whom claimed they had been deceived — they had signed up to fight for the Union, not for the Negro.

Supreme Court justice David Davis, chairman of Lincoln's nomination drive at Chicago, warned his old friend about "the alarming condition of things." Only one means remained for "saving the Country," Davis insisted: Lincoln must "alter the policy of emancipation" and reconstruct the cabinet that had mistakenly supported it. Against such defeatist counsel, Lincoln held firm. He told Davis unconditionally that his policy was "a fixed thing." When another old friend, Orville Browning, raised the specter that the North would unite behind the Democrats in their "clamor for compromise," Lincoln predicted that if the Democrats moved toward concessions, "the people would leave them." Nor was he worried that emancipation would splinter the army. While he conceded that wavering morale had inflamed tensions over emancipation and might lead to desertions, he did not believe "the number would materially affect the army." On the contrary, those inspired to volunteer as a consequence of emancipation would more than make up for those that left. Lincoln was certain, he told the swarm of doubters, that the timing was right for this repurposing of the war.

Know When to Hold Back, When to Move Forward.

From a long way off, Lincoln had seen the inexorable approach of emancipation: "Whoever can wait for it can see it; whoever stands in the way will be run over by it." Speaking in a similar vein, he said: "I claim not to have controlled events, but confess plainly that events have controlled me." Yet if events greater than the president swept him toward emancipation, the timing of the Proclamation was largely a consequence of *his* choice and *his* determination.

"It is my conviction that, had the proclamation been issued even six months earlier than it was, public sentiment would not have sustained it," Lincoln later said. "Just so, as to the subsequent action in reference to enlisting blacks in the Border States. The step, taken sooner, could not, in my judgment, have been carried out. A man watches his pear-tree day after day, impatient for the ripening of the fruit. Let him attempt to force the process, and he may spoil both fruit and tree. But let him patiently wait, and the ripe pear at length falls into his lap!"

Lincoln had carefully marked "this great revolution in public sentiment slowly but *surely* progressing." He was a careful listener and monitored the shifting opinions of his cabinet members. He was a shrewd reader, noting the direction of the wind in newspaper editorials, in the tenor of conversations among people in the North, and, most centrally, in the opinion of the troops. Although he had known all along that opposition would be fierce when the Proclamation was activated, he judged that opposition of insufficient strength "to defeat the purpose." This acute sense of timing, one journalist observed, was the secret to Lincoln's gifted leadership: "He always moves in conjunction with propitious circumstances, not waiting to be dragged by the force of events or wasting strength in premature struggles with them."

In contrast to the mental turmoil and stressful reflections Lincoln had experienced in the autumn months preceding the Proclamation, once the decision was finally made, a determined stillness descended upon him.

For Lincoln, wrestling with thought was no figure of speech; it was an exhaustive mental combat from which he emerged with confidence and clarity. It had been a tortuous ordeal to make up his mind, but he now felt confident that his lengthy decision-making process had yielded the right course and that the country would be ready and willing to follow him.

At a time when the spirits of the people were depleted and war fatigue was widespread, Lincoln had gotten a powerful second wind. Where others saw the apocalyptic demise of the founders' experiment, he saw the birth of a new freedom. This conviction of progress not only proved a correct reading of the temper of the times but was instrumental in shaping it. Just as the cabinet had cohered prior to the public issuance of the final Proclamation, so, under Lincoln's leadership, recruitments to the Army picked up, and the Congress, despite Copperhead opposition, passed all the administration's war-related bills, including financing and conscription. A further test case of the battle for northern support was met in early April when special congressional elections were held in Connecticut, Rhode Island, and New Hampshire. In all three states, Republicans and loyal Democrats soundly defeated Copperhead candidates. The Copperheads had "gone too fast and too far" in talking about a compromise peace, exactly as Lincoln had anticipated in the dark days of January.

This stunning election triumph, the *New York Times* noted, "puts the Administration safely round the cape, and insures it clear seas to the end." It was not to prove that simple, but a corner had surely been turned. Lincoln had wisely let the reaction against the defeatist sentiments grow, then worked to mobilize a renewed spirit. The story of how he was able to recognize, align, harness, and creatively shape this swelling movement toward the acceptance, incorporation, and empowerment yielded by emancipation provides a demonstration of the rare stuff of transformational leadership.

Combine Transactional and Transformational Leadership.

Among the many variants of leadership, scholars have sought to identify two seemingly antithetical types — transactional, by far the more common, and transformational. Transactional leaders operate pragmatically. They appeal to the self-interest of their followers, using quid pro quos, bargains, trades, and rewards to solicit support and influence the behavior of their followers. Transformational leaders inspire followers to identify with something larger than themselves — the organization, the community, the region, the country — and finally, to the more abstract identification with the ideals of that country. Such leaders call for sacrifice in the pursuit of moral principles and higher goals, validating such altruism by looking beyond the present moment to frame a future worth striving for.

Yet a straightforward application of these two forms of leadership fits Lincoln no better than his pants fit his long legs or his sleeves his gangling arms. For Lincoln, pragmatic, transactional strategies provided the nuts and bolts of principled, transformational leadership. Before the spring elections in Connecticut, Rhode Island, and New Hampshire, for example, Lincoln had telegraphed New York's Republican Party boss, Thurlow Weed, asking him to take the first train to Washington. "Mr. Weed, we are in a tight place," Lincoln explained over breakfast. "Money for legitimate purposes is needed immediately; but there is no appropriation from which it can be lawfully taken. I don't know how to raise it so I sent for you." Before the night had ended, Weed had delivered $15,000 to help finance a secret fund to influence the voters in the three states.

Depending on the group he was trying to persuade, Lincoln could — and often did — advocate emancipation from both transactional and transformative vantage points. In city after city, Lincoln orchestrated mass rallies designed both to invigorate the spirit of loyal Unionists and to quell Copperhead defeatism. For one such rally in his hometown of Springfield, Illinois, where Copperhead influence still exerted great force, he composed a lengthy letter to be read to the crowd. "Read it very slowly," he instructed the reader, his old friend James Conkling. "To be plain," Lincoln minced no words, "you are dissatisfied with me about the negro." He then proceeded to enumerate the reasons such dissatisfaction was both ill-placed and inappropriate. "I thought that in your struggle for the Union, to whatever extent the negroes should cease helping the enemy, to that extent it weakened the enemy in his resistance to you. Do you think differently?" he queried, challenging them on a fundamentally pragmatic basis. "I thought that whatever negroes can be got to do as soldiers, leaves just so much less for white soldiers to do, in saving the Union."

After establishing the practical benefits the black troops provided, Lincoln ventured into the transformative core of his message: "If they stake their lives for us, they must be prompted by the strongest motives — even the promise of freedom. And the promise being made, must be kept." In the end, this public letter was a skillful primer of the elevation from a practical to a moral purpose to set an inspirational charge that characterizes transformational leadership.

Nowhere was the effect of Abraham Lincoln's transformational leadership illustrated more sharply than in the changed attitudes of the soldiers toward emancipation. During the first eighteen months of the war, only three out of ten soldiers professed a willingness to risk their lives for emancipation. The majority were fighting solely to preserve the Union. That ratio shifted in the wake of the Emancipation Proclamation. Following Lincoln's lead, an overwhelming majority of the soldiers came to view emancipation and the restoration of the Union as inseparably linked. How had Lincoln's leadership set this metamorphosis in motion? How had he transferred his purpose to the soldiers?

Be Accessible, Easy to Approach.
The response of the troops was grounded in the deep trust and loyalty Lincoln had sown among the rank-and-file soldiers from the very beginning of the war. While visiting troops around Washington and on the battlefield, he shared their beans and hardtack. He inspected their sleeping quarters. He asked after their families. He chatted with fellow occupants of the Soldiers' Home and ministered to Union and Confederate wounded alike. "He cares for us," one soldier said to another, "he makes us fight but he cares."

Everywhere he went, he invited soldiers to call upon him if they felt they had been unfairly treated. And indeed, an estimated two thousand soldiers took him at his word, availing themselves of his offer to come to his office, to complain, be entertained, or simply come face-to-face with their commander in chief. This open-door policy, Lincoln explained, is the "link or cord which connects the people with the governing power." Stories of these encounters quickly circulated among the troops, as did accounts of Lincoln's clemency, his relentless efforts to find cause to stay the hand of the executioner.

In letters the soldiers wrote home, accounts of Lincoln's empathy, responsibility, kindness, accessibility, and fatherly compassion for his extended family were common. They spoke of him as "one of their own"; they carried his picture into battle. "What a depth of devotion, sympathy, and reassurance were conveyed through his smile," a Wisconsin soldier recalled. Again and again they referred to him as Father Abraham, Uncle Abe, or Old Abe. The biblical references and the filial relations connoted a reciprocal emotional charge and a shared vulnerability. The self-same mark of pain and anguish upon his face and demeanor made clear that they endured the war's toll together and suffered a shared lot. "He looks care worn," wrote a recruit from Pennsylvania. "I could not help uttering the prayer God bless Abraham Lincoln." Clearly, the sacrifice Lincoln was asking of the soldiers he had first asked of himself. Another Pennsylvania soldier told his mother he would not be returning home when his term of enlistment was up. "A country that is worth living in time of peace is worth fighting for in time of war so I am yet willing to put up with the hardships of a soldiers life."

Such was the credibility that Lincoln had established with the soldiers that it was no longer a question of fighting solely for the Union, but rather for the dual purpose of Union *and* Emancipation. "If he says all Slaves are hereafter Forever Free," wrote one soldier. "Amen." Another confessed he had "never been in favor of the abolition of slavery" but was now "ready and willing" to fight for emancipation. A new direction had been set and accepted.

Nothing would drive home the transformative power of the Emancipation Proclamation more powerfully than the recruitment and enlistment of black soldiers. As chief advocate and recruiter of black troops, Frederick Douglass sought to stir young black men in one northern city after another. "You will stand more erect, walk more assured, feel more at ease," he promised. "Once let the black man get upon his person the brass letters, U.S.; let him get an eagle on his button, and a musket on his shoulder, and bullets in his pocket, and there is no power on the earth or under the earth which can deny that he has earned the right of citizenship."

Blacks responded in thunder to the enlistment call, signing up by the tens of thousands. This initial wave of enthusiasm soon receded, however, when the black enrollees learned they would not receive pay equal to white soldiers; likewise they would neither earn an enlistment bonus nor be eligible to become officers. Feeling he could no longer in good conscience persuade soldiers to enlist, Douglass decided to call directly upon Lincoln. "I was never more quickly or more completely put at ease," Douglass recalled of their first meeting. As Douglass described how the lack of "fair play" hampered recruitment, Lincoln listened "with earnest attention and with very apparent sympathy." Although politically expedient at the time, the discriminatory policy, Lincoln now agreed, was wrong. "In the end," Lincoln promised, black soldiers "shall have the same pay as white soldiers." Douglass later related he had "never seen a more transparent countenance." A relationship of trust and decency was formed at that initial meeting which would prove instrumental in the months ahead. "He treated me as a man, he did not let me feel for a moment that there was any difference in the color of our skins!" Douglass later said. "I am satisfied now that he is doing all that circumstances will allow him to do."

Not only did blacks eventually enlist in record numbers — adding nearly 200,000 troops to the Union war effort — but, according to official testimony, they fought with striking gallantry. "I never saw such fighting as was done by the negro regiment," General James G. Blunt wrote after one early engagement. "They fought like veterans with a coolness and valor that is unsurpassed." After the battle at Fort Hudson, a white officer openly confessed: "You have no idea how my prejudices with regard to negro troops have been dispelled by the battle the other day. The brigade of negroes behaved magnificently and fought splendidly; could not have done better." Even commanders formerly opposed to his Proclamation, Lincoln stressed, now "believe the emancipation policy, and the use of colored troops, constitute the heaviest blow yet dealt to the rebellion."

Put Ambition for the Collective Interest Above Self-Interest.

In the country at large, however, approbation and acceptance of emancipation vacillated with the fortunes of the Union troops. Despite the Union victory at Gettysburg, Lee's army once again escaped, regrouped, and defeated General Ulysses S. Grant's Union forces in a nightmarish sequence of battles at Spotsylvania, Cold Harbor, and Petersburg. For both North and South, the spring of

1864 was a time of physical and spiritual depletion, darkness, and death. By summer's end, the number of dead, wounded, captured, and missing in action had reached more than 580,000 in the North and nearly 470,000 in the South. Desperation gave rise to "a mad cry" for peace at any cost.

The mood of despondency that enveloped the North threatened Lincoln's reelection. "The tide is setting strongly against us," Republican National Committee chair Henry Raymond warned Lincoln in late August. If the election were held at that moment, he would likely lose his bid for a second term. So doubtful were the Republican committee members about Lincoln's prospects for reelection that they had yet to mobilize the party machinery. The problem was not simply the lack of military success but the suspicion that Lincoln's insistence on emancipation was the main obstacle to peace. For the Republicans to have any chance of victory, Raymond told Lincoln, he must commence peace talks "on the sole condition" of re-union, leaving the issue of slavery for later consideration.

"I confess that I desire to be re-elected," Lincoln acknowledged. "I have the common pride of humanity to wish my past four years administration endorsed," and at the same time, "I want to finish this job." Nonetheless, he rejected Raymond's plea that he dispatch a commissioner to Richmond to meet with Confederate president Jefferson Davis. To sound out conditions for peace without demanding the end of slavery Lincoln considered "utter ruination." He would rather face electoral defeat than renounce emancipation. He "should be damned in time & in eternity," he vehemently declared, if he abandoned his commitment to the twin goals of Union and freedom. Moreover, those who accused him of "carrying on this war for the sole purpose of abolition" must understand that "no human power can subdue this rebellion without using the Emancipation lever." The word *firmness* is insufficient to connote the iron will with which Abraham Lincoln now stood his ground.

Overnight, the fall of Atlanta on the third of September elevated northern spirits. "Glorious news this morning," George Templeton Strong exulted. "It is [coming at this political crisis] the greatest event of the war." As celebratory headlines filled northern newspapers and throngs congregated in cities and towns to fire guns and ring bells, Lincoln's friend Leonard Swett, who only weeks before had written that Lincoln's reelection "was beyond any possible hope," now believed that God had given the Union its glorious victory to make "the ship right itself, as a ship in a storm does after a great wave has nearly capsized it."

It was clear to both parties that the massive soldier vote might well sway the election. Democrats, remembering the devotion George McClellan had once inspired among his men, had chosen the former general as their nominee on a platform that severed abolition from reunion, thereby promising an early conclusion to the war. "We are as certain of two-thirds of that [soldier] vote for General McClellan as that the sun shines," a Democratic operative jauntily predicted.

The soldiers' vote was also of paramount importance to Lincoln, but for far deeper reasons than its numerical bearing on the outcome of the election. He trusted the fellowship that he had strengthened with their common investment in the war. Such intimacy did Lincoln feel for the rank-and-file servicemen that he said that if he had to make a choice he "would rather be defeated with the soldier vote behind [him] than to be elected without it."

That circumstance never came to pass. Lincoln swept the Electoral College by a tally of 212 to 21, and captured more than seven out of ten soldiers' votes. In casting their ballots for Lincoln, the soldiers knew that in all likelihood they were prolonging their personal risk and the duration of their wartime service. They were voting against their self-interest for the greater collective interest that Lincoln had powerfully expressed in his talks with them. This contest "is not merely for to-day, but for all time to come," Lincoln had reiterated in numerous ways. "I happen temporarily to occupy this big White House. I am a living witness that any one of your children may look to come here as my father's child has. It is in order that each of you may have through this free government which we have enjoyed, an open field and a fair chance for your industry, enterprise and intelligence; that you all have equal privileges in the race of life, with all its desirable human aspirations. It is for this the struggle should be maintained." And when they went to the polls, the soldiers voted not for their own safety but for the man who had come to represent the cause they fought for together.

Winning a second term fired Lincoln's resolve to secure emancipation beyond the rebel South, to encompass the entirety of the nation. With all possible speed, he sought a formal guarantee that slavery would be abolished within the United States. Such an assurance could not rest upon an executive order but rather must be written into the law of the land by way of a constitutional amendment.

Executive war powers had enabled the circumvention of constitutionally protected slavery. Now, the supple Constitution must provide its own permanent remedy to abolish slavery in the form of the Thirteenth Amendment, introduced on January 6, 1865. Informed three weeks later that the requisite two-thirds passage was two votes short, Lincoln stridently intervened with his Capitol Hill emissaries. He made it understood that his transactional executive power extended to government jobs for relatives and friends, pardons, ministries abroad, and campaign contributions. It was not long before they had scoured up those two votes. When the final tally was announced, remarked a witness, "there was an explosion, a storm of cheers the like of which no Congress of the United States ever heard before." To a crowd of celebrants who came to serenade him the next evening at the White House, Lincoln proclaimed that the occasion was one of "congratulation to the country and to the whole world." But he reminded them that "there is a task yet before us — to go forward and consummate by the votes of the States that which Congress so nobly began."

A week later, before an immense crowd at Boston Music Hall celebrating the House passage of the Thirteenth Amendment, abolitionist William Lloyd Garrison asked the question "And to whom is the country more immediately indebted for this vital and saving amendment of the Constitution than, perhaps, to any other man? I believe I may confidently answer — to the humble rail-splitter of Illinois — to the presidential chain-breaker for millions of the oppressed — to Abraham Lincoln."

Lincoln shrank from the heroic appellation "The Great Emancipator." "I have only been an instrument," he insisted. "The antislavery people of the country and the army have done it all." Such humility did not suggest a lack of ambition. On the contrary, from the time he was a young man Lincoln had harbored a consuming ambition to make a difference in the world. During the nadir of his depression in his early thirties, he had confessed to Joshua Speed that he would gladly die but that he had "done nothing to make any human being remember that he had lived." He would be remembered now. When Speed came to the White House shortly after the signing of the Proclamation, the two old friends reminisced about that grim early period in Lincoln's life when his desire for remembrance had fueled his recovery from depression. Far beyond any grand projection when he was young, Lincoln had now rendered service to his fellow man. "I believe that in this measure," Lincoln flatly declared of the Proclamation, "my fondest hopes will be realized."

Abraham Lincoln never lived to see the completion of the task he had begun with his Proclamation — the ratification of the Thirteenth Amendment by three-quarters of the states in December 1865. Slavery, the "wen" he had spoken of cutting out of the Constitution, had been excised at terrible cost at last. "A King's cure for all the evils," he had said of the anticipated amendment. "It winds the whole thing up."

In the great convergence of the man and his times, Lincoln had driven, guided, and inspired his cabinet, the Army, and his countrymen. "Fellow citizens, we cannot escape history," he had told the Congress a month before he issued the Emancipation Proclamation. "The fiery trial through which we pass, will light us down, in honor or dishonor, to the latest generation. . . . In *giving* freedom to the slave, we *assure* freedom to the *free* — honorable alike in what we give and what we preserve. We shall nobly save, or meanly lose, the last best hope of earth."

It was through the language of his leadership that a moral purpose and meaning was imprinted upon the protracted misery of the Civil War. So surely did Lincoln midwife this process of social transformation that we look back at the United States *before* Abraham Lincoln and *after* him.

TEN:
CRISIS MANAGEMENT

Theodore Roosevelt and the Coal Strike

"It is a dreadful thing to come into the Presidency this way; but it would be a far worse thing to be morbid about it," Roosevelt wrote a friend days after President William McKinley's long-drawn death. "Here is the task, and I have got to do it to the best of my ability; and that is all there is about it."

Widespread warnings of panic swirled that the stock market might well crash unless Roosevelt provided reassurance that a steady and cautious hand had taken the helm. Accordingly, the new president immediately asked every member of McKinley's cabinet to stay on. His friends worried that some of these men might not be "loyal" to him, but he said that if those he kept "were loyal to their work," that was the loyalty for which he cared the most; "if they were not," he would swiftly change them. At the same time, he reached out to the conservative political boss Mark Hanna, McKinley's closest friend, who was now face-to-face with the situation he had dreaded when he cautioned fellow Republicans against putting "that madman" Roosevelt in the vice presidency.

"I hope you will be to me all that you have been to him," the disciplined new president now told the bereft Hanna. And furthermore, he issued a conciliating pledge: "In this hour of deep and terrible bereavement, I wish to state that I shall continue absolutely unbroken the policy of President McKinley for the peace, prosperity, and the honor of the country."

Yet, even as Roosevelt publicly promised continuity, he knew that if he pursued McKinley's conservative policies to the letter it "would give a lie to all he had stood for" in his fight to refashion the Republican Party into a progressive force. The breadth of his hands-on experience at different levels of government, from the state legislature to the police department to the governor's chair, had sensitized Roosevelt to the hidden dangers of the age: the rise of gigantic trusts that were rapidly swallowing up their competitors in one field after another, the invisible web of corruption linking political bosses to the business community, the increasing concentration of wealth and the growing gap between the rich and the poor, the squalid conditions in the immigrant slums, the mood of insurrection among the laboring classes.

So, on his first day in office, Theodore Roosevelt signaled to journalists that despite his endorsement of the status quo, a new political era was dawning. The Constitution, he reminded them, had provided for his succession as president, and he was determined "to act in every word and deed precisely as if [he] and not McKinley had been the candidate for whom the electors cast the vote for President." He had cut his political teeth in the endless crosscurrents and whiplash between machine bosses and reformers. He mistrusted and feared the former and often disappointed the latter. If it was necessary to temporarily bide his time to avoid upheavals in the market, anyone who thought he would follow the pro-business path laid out by William McKinley badly misconstrued his nature

476

and his intentions.

The impact of Roosevelt's outsized personality made it immediately clear that a new leader was in charge, one who fathomed the country's challenges in a very different way than his predecessor. "The infectiousness of his exuberant vitality made the country realize there was a new man in the White House," observed journalist Mark Sullivan, "indeed a new kind of man. His high spirits, enormous capacity for work, his tirelessness, his forthrightness, his many striking qualities, gave a lift of the spirits to millions of average men."

Throughout his political career, Roosevelt's conception of leadership had been built upon a narrative of the embattled hero (armed with courage, spunk, honor, and truth) who sets out into the world to prove himself. It was a dragon-slaying notion of the hero-leader, and Roosevelt had the good fortune to strike the historical moment in which he could prove his mettle. Under the banner of "the Square Deal," he would lead his country in a different kind of war, a progressive battle designed to restore fairness to America's economic and social life.

The Great Coal Strike of 1902 — the subject of this case study — is emblematic of the widespread mood of rebellion among the laboring classes in the wake of the Industrial Revolution. The unfolding of the president's creative handling of what was viewed as "the most formidable deadlock in the history of the country" offers a demonstration of groundbreaking crisis management.

As cold weather approached in the fall of 1902, widespread panic set in. Still, there were no signs of a settlement in the six-month-old strike between the United Mine Workers, the largest union in the nation, and a powerful cartel of railroad presidents and mine owners who monopolized anthracite (hard coal) production in Pennsylvania. The massive labor stoppage was already "the biggest and longest-running news story of the year."

The Northeast depended almost entirely on anthracite coal for winter fuel. Like a black river with myriad tributaries, coal ran from the collieries and railroad cars in Pennsylvania to the factories and mills, the hospitals, schools, and dwellings of New York and New England. Damming that river of coal would plunge the entire region into a coal famine — and like a shortage of bread, coal famine presaged suffering and violence for the populace at large.

Indeed, as this seasonal tragedy began to play out before the public and wintertime drew closer, the coal strike "assumed a shape so acute" that even conservatives warned Theodore Roosevelt that "if the situation remained unchanged we would have within a fortnight the most widespread and bloody civil disturbance we have known in our time."

What made this situation so frustrating for Roosevelt was the remarkable fact that neither legal nor historical precedent warranted presidential intervention to manage any single aspect of the crisis. So pervasive was the belief that government should refrain from interfering in the workings of an unregulated free market that quarrels between labor and management were considered wholly private matters. A chorus of voices, including Roosevelt's family, closest friends, and colleagues, advised him that unless the state of Pennsylvania requested emergency troops to quell violent disorder, he had no power whatsoever to take action.

Not only did Roosevelt have no legal authority to intervene, but from a political vantage, he was forewarned to steer clear. Meddling would poison support from the business community, the Republican Party's mainstay of support. Furthermore, if he tried and failed, the responsibility for failure would be laid at his door, damaging his party's prospects in the upcoming fall midterms and his own political future.

Roosevelt's handling of the six-month strike unfolded in three seasonal stages, beginning in the spring of the year.

The catastrophe the strike would bring on by October was nowhere to be seen in May 1902, when 147,000 miners walked out. No one conceived then that the strike would become what labor leader Samuel Gompers later deemed "the most important event in the labor movement of the United States."

The unexampled surge of industrial consolidation that produced the giant coal combination had begun a decade earlier when the coal-carrying railroads (the Reading, Lackawanna, Erie, and others) under the auspices of J. P. Morgan, Wall Street's most respected financier, had begun purchasing coalfields, using their power over freight rates to buy out one independent mine after another. The United Mine Workers had only recently gained footing in the anthracite region. Led by John Mitchell, a charismatic, conservative, articulate young leader who had worked in the mines before becoming a union official, the union had organized tens of thousands of anthracite miners.

All during the spring of 1902, Mitchell was under pressure from his rank-and-file miners to deal with a host of troubling issues, including low wages, ten-hour days, and brutal working conditions. To forestall the growing demand for a strike, which Mitchell feared would "risk everything in one great fight," the union leader went to New York to discuss potential areas of agreement with the owners. When the owners, led by George Baer, the wealthy college-educated president of the Reading Railway, flatly refused to sit at the same table with "a common coal-miner, who had worked with his hands for 15 years and was now a labor agitator," the miners voted to strike, their pride aggravated by the owners' condescension.

Though Mitchell had initially opposed the idea of a strike, fearing the new union could not sustain a major conflict during its formative time, he now assured the workers that he was committed to do everything he could to make the strike successful. He implored them to stay together: "If you stand as one man and stand long enough and strong enough, you will win; if you divide, you will lose."

Such was Mitchell's authority that at his signal, almost every miner walked out on the first day, a response far exceeding the most sanguine hopes of union organizers. Mitchell's hold on the men, many of them immigrants who barely spoke English, was legendary. Case in point: When news of President McKinley's assassination first spread to the coal region, the workmen had gathered together, openly grieving. "Who shot our President?" they cried out. Upon learning that President McKinley, not President Mitchell, had been shot, they were greatly relieved.

Calculate Risks of Getting Involved.

Even at this early stage of the strike, Roosevelt was "thoroughly awake" to the potential perils of the situation. Though repeatedly told that he had "no earthly responsibility" for the strike and should do nothing to interfere, he recognized that if the strike continued for any length of time, the public would "tend to visit upon our heads responsibility for the shortage in coal precisely as Kansas and Nebraska visited upon our heads their failure to raise good crops in the arid belt, eight, ten or a dozen years ago." In other words, if people were hurt, their leader would be held accountable whether or not he had the legal authority to act.

Furthermore, passivity ran counter to Roosevelt's disposition as well as his conception of leadership. His study of history persuaded him that there were "two schools of thought" regarding presidential power. The first, identified with James Buchanan, was a "narrowly legalistic view that the President is the servant of Congress rather than of the people, and can do nothing, no matter how necessary, unless the Constitution explicitly commands the action," thus resolving "every doubt in favor of inaction against action." A second, opposing philosophical stance, exemplified by Abraham Lincoln, considered the executive "the steward of the people." Under this conception, to which Roosevelt wholeheartedly ascribed, it was not only the executive's right but his responsibility "to do whatever the needs of the people demand, unless the Constitution or the laws explicitly forbid him to do it."

So it happened that many months before the situation had reached crisis proportions, Roosevelt was proactively seeking ways to intervene, to create a position of solid ground from which to lead. Rather than rush in, however, he demonstrated a methodical, understated, patient demeanor at odds with his storied headlong leadership style. "I am slowly going on," he told the journalist Jacob Riis, "working within my limited range of powers and endeavoring neither to shirk any responsibilities nor yet to be drawn into such hasty and violent action as almost invariably provokes reaction."

Secure a Reliable Understanding of the Facts, Causes, and Conditions of the Situation.

On June 8, a month into the strike, the president took a small, establishing step to prepare the public for future executive action. In conversation with his commissioner of labor, Carroll Wright, a provision in a law enacted years earlier came to light. This provision authorized the labor commissioner "to make special reports on particular subjects whenever required to do so by the

President or either House of Congress." Roosevelt thereby verbally directed Wright to ascertain "all facts possible relating to the present controversy." Wright, regarded as "one of the foremost statisticians in the world," was the right man for the job of conducting an evenhanded investigation into the causes and conditions underlying the strike. He had dedicated his innovative career to the study of working conditions in the new Industrial Age. And for a numbers man, he possessed an unusual sensitivity to the all-too-human elements entangled in both sides of the strike — authority and control, recognition and pride.

Roosevelt's call for the report was not simply a request for a statistical accounting. As he hoped, a report would push things forward. "The President's action in sending the Commissioner of Labor to investigate the coal strike is thought by some to forecast presidential influence," noted one editorial. "President Roosevelt evidently looks upon the strike not as a private quarrel, but as a conflict in which public interests are directly involved," remarked another. By making his directive to Wright public, Roosevelt had taken the first step, however tentative, in what would become a slow, deliberate process of seeding "a new and untried field" of presidential power.

Wright decided at the start to avoid venturing straight into the Pennsylvania coalfields, fearing that as a representative of the president, his "presence there would do more harm than good." Instead, he headed for New York, where he conducted a lengthy series of interviews with the presidents of the coal-carrying railroads, officials of the United Mine Workers union, miners, and laborers.

Wright sought to understand the pressures exerted on both sides, each answerable to its own constituency. The operators, responsible to their shareholders, claimed higher wages and shorter hours would drive several collieries out of business. "I cannot afford voluntarily to bankrupt my Company," Baer explained, "by inviting losses that any man charged with the responsibility of management would say were unnecessary and unwise." Mitchell, voice of the fledgling union, had to prove to the miners that their lives would be improved by their commitment to collective action. And beyond the specific disputes about wages, hours, and working conditions, Wright concluded, "the psychological elements must be considered" to get a true measure of the situation. "Suspicion lurks in the minds of everyone."

Commissioner Wright told Roosevelt he could not complete his report without making a few suggestions that "might lead to a more peaceful and satisfactory condition in the anthracite coal field." He proposed a six-month experimental reduction from ten to nine working hours a day to see how productivity was affected. To assuage the mistrust and ill will rippling beneath the surface, he recommended that when workers were paid by the ton, two inspectors, one representing the operators, one the miners, should be on hand to weigh the coal. And most significantly, he urged the creation of "a joint committee on conciliation, composed of representatives of the operators and the new union." These steps, Wright acknowledged, would not lead "to the millennium" but, he believed, would "allay irritation and reach the day when the anthracite coal regions" might be governed "in accordance with greater justice."

Remain Uncommitted in the Early Stages.
"This is an important report by Carroll D. Wright," Roosevelt told his attorney general, Philander C. Knox. "Will you read it over and then at cabinet we can discuss whether it shall be made public. I like its tone greatly." Knox strongly advised against its publication. He told Roosevelt that the affair was of no concern to the president, and that "he could not see what good would come of publishing the report." Elaborating further, Knox reminded the president that the report had been made for his "personal information," not because he had any responsibility for the situation. "For you to make this report public

would be construed as implying your approval of the findings of fact and the recommendations therein. I do not think you are called upon to thus commit yourself."

Roosevelt pondered the weight of this argument. To publish the report, with Wright's suggestions for improved working conditions, might seem sympathetic to the miners. If, as president, he had already "expressed an opinion" on specific issues, he would find himself in "an embarrassing and undignified position" should duty eventually require him to intervene. Yet, not to publish the report after it had been publicly announced might seem like an act of suppression, angering progressives anxiously awaiting some positive action. Caught in a crossfire, Roosevelt decided for the time being against making the report public.

SUMMER

The seasonal clock was ticking. While there was no drastic change in the daily lives of the people in the heat of summer, each passing day brought factories, schools, and hospitals, along with millions of homeowners, closer to the necessity of securing their winter's coal supply. As supplies dwindled and the dealers' bins were increasingly cleaned out, retail prices rose 50 to 60 percent — for the great majority of the people, an exorbitant burden. Reports from New England cities and towns

487

revealed that even for those able to afford the onerous prices, the scarcity of coal was such that stockpiles could be found "only here and there" in the hands of a few dealers. "Doubtless the stage is very near," the *Coal Trade Journal* predicted, "when, to all intents and purposes, supplies of anthracite will be entirely exhausted."

Use History to Provide Perspective.

That summer, with Congress in recess, Roosevelt closely monitored developments in the strike from his family's home in Oyster Bay. In the sanctuary of his library, he found what Lincoln had secured at the Soldiers' Home — the time and space in which to reflect upon the deeper roots of the struggle.

A lifelong student of history, a voracious reader, and a historian himself, Roosevelt recognized that the collision between the owners and the miners, capital and labor, the rich and the poor, had been decades in the making. "The labor problem," he comprehended, "had entered a new phase" in the wake of the Industrial Revolution. "Great financial corporations, doing a nation-wide and even a world-wide business, had taken the place of the smaller concerns of an earlier time. The old familiar, intimate relations between employer and employee were passing. A few generations before, the boss had known every man in his shop." By contrast,

Roosevelt surmised, it was unlikely that any but a random coal miner had ever laid eyes on the Reading Railroad president, much less befriended him. Furthermore, as a consequence of such consolidation, "a crass inequality in the bargaining relation between the employer and the individual employee standing alone" had developed. The miners, individually, "were impotent when they sought to enter a wage contract" with their employers; "they could make fair terms only by uniting into trade unions to bargain collectively." Labor unions, Roosevelt understood, "were bound to grow in size, in strength." And this historical inevitability "the great coal operators did not see."

Roosevelt had not only read about the Gilded Age and the growth of combinations, trusts, and labor unions, his family's history provided a singular chronicle of how wealth had accumulated in the new industrial order. From his grandfather Cornelius Roosevelt, who had become "one of the five richest men in New York" through a successful career as a merchant, banker, and real estate magnate, Theodore had inherited a family trust. From his father, who had become a pillar of the New York philanthropic world, he had developed a sense of duty and civic responsibility. From his own experiences in the woods of Maine, among the cowboys in the West, as a civil servant in Washington, a police commissioner in New York, and a soldier in Cuba, Theodore had fashioned a different path from that imagined by noblesse oblige. He had confronted a larger vision of American diversity and had developed a more complicated conception of public responsibility and leadership. The history that was being played out in the strike of 1902 was part and parcel of his knowledge of history and his own family life, his biography, and his times.

That same summer, Roosevelt embarked on completing the ten-volume biography of Abraham Lincoln by John Nicolay and John Hay. He had not only enjoyed the reading, he wrote Hay, "but I really believe I have profited." Though he understood, of course, that the task before him differed in degree from "what Lincoln saw in the supreme years of the nation's struggle," the "men and forces" at play were "yet the same in their infinite variety of kind." Furthermore, he had "a good idea of Lincoln's worry" when he was denounced by extremists on one side for not going "far enough" and on the other for going "too far." In the present coal strike, conservatives were roundly denouncing him for "showing sympathy with the miners," while progressives wanted him "to take the coal barons by the throat." Most of all, Roosevelt emphasized, Lincoln's character provided the most telling model — "to try to be good-natured and forbearing and to free myself from vindictiveness."

Be Ready to Grapple with Reversals, Abrupt Intrusions That Can Unravel All Plans.

The explosion of an anarchist's pistol had made Roosevelt president. Grappling with such sudden twists of the kaleidoscope had shaped his philosophy of life and of leadership. So now, as the relatively peaceful strike entered its twelfth week, a single violent incident at a colliery in the coal town of Shenandoah threatened to upend all hopes for a peaceful solution. From the start, Mitchell had counseled his men to avoid provocation and to keep their picket lines orderly. By late July, however, tempers were beginning dangerously to fray.

On July 30, a sheriff's deputy was escorting two men carrying "a suspicious looking bundle" into the mine. Upon the discovery that the package contained miner's gear, the union pickets turned on the "scabs," clubbing and beating them into unconsciousness. Policemen rushed to the scene. Mobs gathered in the street. "Upward of one thousand shots were fired," the *New York Times* reported. Scores of strikers and local residents were hit; "it is expected that many deaths will result." A citizen who came to the aid of the sheriff's deputy was "brutally clubbed to death." Front-page headlines across the country proclaimed "a reign of terror."

Reading the dispatches at Sagamore Hill, Roosevelt considered returning to Washington. If the violence continued, it was possible that the Pennsylvania governor would request federal troops to maintain order. "Once there is a resort to mob violence," Roosevelt later told a friend, "the only thing to do is to maintain order." While such intervention was well within his constitutional authority, Roosevelt knew from his study of history that the arrival of federal troops would be construed as a coercive action on behalf of the operators, an action that could well break the back of the strike. "It is a dreadful thing to be brought face to face with the necessity of taking measures, however unavoidable, which will mean the death of men who have been maddened by want and suffering."

Waiting to see how the situation would unfold, Roosevelt remained vigilantly but quietly at home. His patience was rewarded. The following day, John Mitchell traveled to the site of the violence. He understood that even those members of the public most sympathetic to the miners' cause would not condone a disruption of law and order. A crowd of ten thousand miners greeted the union president when he reached Scranton. The men "went fairly wild" over his appearance, one newspaper reported, but they listened soberly when he pleaded with them to refrain from violence. "The one among you who violates the law is the worst enemy you have," he warned. "I want to impress on you the importance of winning this strike. If you win . . . there will be no more strikes," but "if you lose the strike, you lose your organization."

Because Theodore Roosevelt did not rush in, because John Mitchell did swiftly and effectively respond, an uncertain peace was restored once again to the anthracite region.

Reevaluate Options; Be Ready to Adapt as a Situation Escalates.

As the strike entered its fourth month, public anxiety deepened. Both sides were replenishing their coffers to hunker down for the long haul. The strike would come to an end, the owners repeatedly emphasized, only when the miners conceded defeat and returned to work. For their part, the miners, having solicited the largest strike fund ever accumulated from fellow union members in different parts of the country, had "settled down to a long trial of endurance."

On August 21, rendered increasingly "uneasy" by this protracted stasis, Roosevelt queried his attorney general: "What is the reason we cannot proceed against the coal operators as being engaged in a trust? I ask because it is a question being continually asked of me." Indeed, reporters had suggested that the coal trust seemed in more flagrant violation of the Sherman Antitrust Act than Northern Securities, the vast transportation company against which Roosevelt had brought suit the previous February. Northern Securities, forged under the auspices of J. P. Morgan during Roosevelt's watch in late 1901, had consolidated three rival rail and shipping lines into one giant company, creating (behind Morgan's U.S. Steel) "the second largest corporation in the world." The new holding company had absolute power to determine freight rates within its domain. The unforeseen announcement of the government's suit to "test the validity of the merger," had staggered the financial world.

"If we have done anything wrong," Morgan had informed Roosevelt in a White House meeting three days later, "send your man to my man and they can fix it up." Morgan's attitude, Roosevelt later said, was "a most illuminating illustration of the Wall Street point of view," which regarded the president as simply "a rival operator." With the Northern Securities suit, the first of a series that would establish for Roosevelt the moniker "trust-buster," the president intended "to serve notice on everybody that it was going to be the Government," not Wall Street, "who governed these United States."

In answer to the president's query concerning an antitrust suit against the coal operators, however, Knox argued that they were not combined in such a manner as to fit the legal definition of a trust. Furthermore, he reminded Roosevelt that even if a suit against the coal owners should eventually prevail, the slow workings of the court machinery would deliver no remedy for the crisis at hand. After seven months, the Northern Securities suit was still in the first stage of argument in the federal courts; nearly three years would pass before the Supreme Court finally decided the case in the government's favor.

Troubled by the attorney general's objections, Roosevelt contemplated a different, less controversial step. Perhaps, he suggested to Knox, the time had come to reevaluate his earlier decision to withhold the Wright Report. Knox reiterated that he had "never thought it wise for you to give it out, and have no reason now to change my opinion." This time, however, after consulting with additional advisers, Roosevelt chose to move ahead and release the report to the press. Let the case be laid before the public! In the appendix of the report, which included the letters exchanged between the operators and the miners, the virulent animosity of the operators toward their employees spoke loud and clear. Again and again, the operators had refused to meet with Mitchell. As for the idea of ensuring every miner a minimum daily wage, the owners countered that it was "patent to anyone" who had any knowledge of the differing conditions in different mines that "such an idea can be but the product of an ignorant and diseased mind."

Most significantly, the report revealed that the operators did not in any way feel answerable to the public. When Wright asked them if there were "any sort of suggestion" the president might make to help resolve the strike, the owners bluntly replied that if he and everyone else simply got out of the way, "it will do more to end it than anything else."

When Roosevelt released the report, he was careful to include Knox's opinion that the president had neither authority nor responsibility in the matter. But increasingly, Roosevelt felt otherwise. As representative of the public, he had substantial influence, if not the power of explicit law. And, slowly, the idea that the public — whose lives and livelihoods hung in the balance of this increasingly bitter struggle — had a role to play was beginning to take a firm hold. The seeds that Roosevelt had planted early in the struggle had begun to grow, nurtured by the expectations and needs of the public. Incrementally, the president had constructed a new kind of platform from which he could speak. And now the time had come to build a foundation of support among the citizenry in the eye of the coming storm — the people of New England.

Be Visible. Cultivate Public Support Among Those Most Directly Affected by the Crisis.

Even before the coal strike approached an acute stage, Roosevelt had planned a late-summer speaking tour through New England and the Midwest to generate enthusiasm for Republicans in the upcoming fall elections. The mounting concerns of New Englanders about the prolonged strike gave the barnstorming venture a decided political jolt and accent. Traveling by train and open carriage from Rhode Island, Connecticut, and Massachusetts to Vermont, New Hampshire, and Maine, Roosevelt attracted massive throngs every place he went. "The booming of cannon, the clanging of church bells, the tooting of whistles, the braying of brass bands and the cheering of thousands" signaled his progress. "Factories shut down," the *Boston Daily Globe* reported, "stores put up their shutters, flags were hoisted and the people were out in their holiday clothes." It struck one journalist that "small towns turned out their entire population." Roosevelt understood that people were drawn "to see the President much as they would come to see a circus." His energy never flagged: he smiled, gesticulated, radiated good humor, absorbed and reciprocated affection. At every stop, he delivered extemporaneous remarks about citizenship, character, and "a square deal for every man, great or small, rich or poor."

While he deliberately avoided speaking about the coal strike during set speeches, he lent "a sympathetic ear" to the "unfocused discontent" he encountered about the growing consolidation of industry and the growing gap between the rich and the poor. He understood that many looked back with nostalgia upon the preindustrial era, "when the average man lived more to himself." He challenged them to look forward, not backward — to a time when public sentiment was ready for the national government to find constructive ways to intervene in the workings of the economic order, to regulate the trusts, stimulate competition, and protect small companies. He agreed with Lincoln about the essential role that public sentiment plays when a leader hopes to move his countrymen in a different direction.

As the summer days were coming to a close, Roosevelt was stirring up that public sentiment. More frequently, the pressure of public opinion was being heard and the eyes of the people were looking to the White House for help. "We have endured patiently," came one message. But now "it is time for the people to speak. It is time that their voice should be heard." We appeal "to the president of the people" to "use your influence to stay the juggernaut which crushes us." The power of public sentiment was creating space for the president to act.

Clear the Deck to Focus with
Single-mindedness on the Crisis.

As the coal strike began to flare into an acute phase at the beginning of the fall, Theodore Roosevelt was halfway through barnstorming, raising his political stock and his visibility. Once again chance bolted into his life with terrible violence. The horse-driven carriage transporting the president's party from Pittsfield, Massachusetts, to Lenox for a speaking engagement was crossing trolley tracks when rammed at full speed by an onrushing trolley car.

"With a crash that echoed through the hills the car ploughed through the landau," witnessed a reporter, "overturning it and smashing wheels and body into bits." The president's favorite secret service agent, William Craig, was cast under the wheels of the trolley car and killed. Amid this carnage, Roosevelt himself was catapulted some thirty feet, suffering bruises to his jaw and eye and a deep bone contusion on his left shin. "I felt sure," he remembered, "all in the carriage would be killed."

With characteristic bravado, he sloughed off his injuries, determined to proceed with the next part of his scheduled speaking tour in the Midwest. By the time he reached Indiana, his leg was badly swollen, the result of a developing abscess. When the pain became severe and his temperature rose, he finally consented to hospitalization. Doctors decided to operate immediately. Refusing anesthesia, Roosevelt joked with the surgeons, "Gentlemen, you are formal; I see you have your gloves on," referring to their antiseptic gloves. "Mr. President," said one surgeon. "It is always in order to wear gloves at a president's reception."

The abscess was successfully drained, but the doctors insisted that he cancel the rest of his tour and stay off his foot for at least two weeks to avoid what could be serious complications. Returning to Washington, Roosevelt was carried by stretcher to the temporary White House at 22 Jackson Place, the executive mansion being renovated to separate the living quarters from a new West Wing of executive offices.

This man of action who had always dealt with private tragedy and adversity with a flurry of distracting motion was now incapacitated. Ironically, his lingering injuries would provide the occasion for a single-minded focus on the coal strike at the very moment when the worsening consequences of that strike were about to burst into public consciousness. He did not need to clear the deck of all superfluous matters; the accident had cleared the deck for him. "I do not have to see the innumerable people whom there is no object in seeing, but whom I would have to see if I were not confined to my room with my leg up," he told Connecticut senator Orville Platt, "and I am able to do all the important work, like that affecting the coal strike, just exactly as well as if I were on two legs."

In the course of two weeks of convalescence, Roosevelt would make a precedent-breaking decision to intervene in the coal strike. "I had as yet no legal or constitutional duty — and therefore no legal or constitutional right in the matter," he acknowledged. "I knew I might fail; but I made up my mind that if I did fail it should at least not be because of adopting the Buchanan-like attitude of fearing to try anything." What had transpired during his immobility that emboldened Roosevelt's decision?

Scarcely had he settled into his bedroom overlooking Lafayette Park when he was pelted by a veritable nor'easter of alarming forecasts. Urgent pleas came from mayors of big cities in the path of the storm. "I cannot emphasize enough injustices of the existing coal situation," New York mayor Seth Low wired, "millions of innocent people . . . will endure real suffering if present conditions continue." From Maine came reports that the coal shortage would soon result in the closing of the mills: "Thousands of operatives are in danger of being thrown out of employment. Hotels and railroads are also short of fuel." In Connecticut, lack of fuel had already forced factories and small businesses to shut down. Workers were being laid off at an alarming, accelerating clip. Hospitals throughout the region reported a rise in tuberculosis and diphtheria. Damp and frigid schoolhouses were compelled to send children home to houses with empty coal stoves. Most troubling, the threat of violence filled the air. Mobs commandeered coal cars as they moved heavily through villages and towns; bombs were detonated at bridges and railway lines.

The time left on the clock before this fuel famine spread "untold misery" and spilled blood had nearly run out. Whether or not he had a clear legal mandate, this was not a normal course of events. The time of appraisal was over; the time of decision had come. Theodore Roosevelt would find or force a way in.

Assemble a Crisis Management Team.
There was nothing haphazard about the crisis management team Theodore Roosevelt assembled from both outside and inside his administration. Each of the seven men he gathered for consultation had a particular vantage from which to view the strike; each was aligned to a different aspect of the stalemated contest. And all these lines converged in Roosevelt and his own overlapping

fields of experience and expertise. He knew who they were, what they knew, and what they knew how to do. If he could bring their intelligence, perspectives, and influence together on a team, they would figure out how to proceed with a shared objective. Indeed, the decisions he made in the weeks ahead would directly spring from this assembled team.

The first person Roosevelt summoned was Governor Winthrop Crane of Massachusetts, a state in the crosshairs of the coal famine. The two men had bonded during the president's recent trip to Massachusetts. Seated next to Roosevelt when the rushing trolley cleaved the presidential carriage, Crane, too, had escaped death by being thrown to the ground. Roosevelt trusted the conservative businessman, surely "no alarmist," to provide a firsthand view of the situation. Crane lost no time providing urgent advice. "Unless you end this strike," Crane warned Roosevelt in a tone so strident it could not be ignored, "the workers in the North will begin tearing down buildings for fuel. They will not stand being frozen to death." Delay was not an option.

Crane remained in Washington in the days that followed while Roosevelt conducted a series of daylong meetings with his newly assembled team, which brought together the worlds of big business, labor, politics, and law. Secretary of War Elihu Root's lifelong ties to Wall Street made him a reliable liaison to the financial world and a conduit to J. P. Morgan, the unmoved mover of the financial reservoir behind the operators of the railroads and the mines. Postmaster General Henry Payne understood the mind-set of the railroad owners, having been president of the Chicago and Northern Railroad before joining the administration. To represent the union's perspective, Roosevelt consulted Frank Sargent, his commissioner of immigration, who had formerly served as chief of the Brotherhood of Locomotive Firemen and was a respected cohort of Samuel Gompers and, most importantly, a friend of John Mitchell. Pennsylvania's senior senator, Matthew Quay, had a deep familiarity with the operation of the anthracite mines. Labor Commissioner Wright, Roosevelt's invaluable statistician, fairly represented both sides. And of course, there was Attorney General Knox, who had consistently counseled him to keep his hands off the whole matter.

Crane proposed a course of action based on his recent experience with a teamsters' strike in Massachusetts in which neither side would meet with the other. As their governor, Crane had invited the employers and the union members to take separate suites in the same hotel. He then traveled back and forth between the two suites and eventually brought them to a compromise settlement.

What if the president invited the coal owners and the union representatives to meet with him in Washington?

Roosevelt immediately grasped the potential of Crane's concept; the team was less certain, preferring the strike be settled without presidential interference. Finally, everyone except Knox concurred that the president must act. Knox continued to fear that a precedent was being set that would involve the chief executive in every future labor struggle. Once the policy was determined, however, Knox "acted as he always does in such cases," Roosevelt approvingly said, "he did his very best to make it successful."

Identical telegrams were sent to union president John Mitchell and the six presidents of the anthracite coal companies. "I should greatly like to see you on Friday next, October 3d, at eleven o'clock a.m., here in Washington in regard to the failure of the coal supply, which has become a matter of vital concern to the whole nation." This ostensibly straightforward yet unprecedented invitation captured headlines across the nation. "For the first time in the history of the country," a writer in *Collier's Weekly* exclaimed, great corporate leaders and union representatives would join "the President of the United States to talk over their differences face-to-face."

At once, a din of protest sounded in the conservative press, which characterized the intervention as a dangerous "un-American" experiment. "Worse by far than the strike is Mr. Roosevelt's seemingly uncontrollable penchant for impulsive self-intrusion," complained the *Journal of Commerce.*

Frame the Narrative.
"It was very kind of you to come here at my invitation," Roosevelt hailed his guests as they filed into the second-floor parlor room of the temporary White House. "You will have to excuse me, I can't get up to greet you." Seated in a wheelchair in the corner of the room, Roosevelt was dressed in a "blue-striped bathrobe belted around him." Covered with a soft white blanket, his "wounded leg stuck out straight in front of him."

Roosevelt opened the meeting by reading a carefully scripted statement laying out the ground rules for their discussion: "There are three parties affected by the situation in the anthracite trade — the operators, the miners, and the general public." He assured them that he championed "neither the operators or the miners." He spoke for "the general public." While disclaiming any legal "right or duty to intervene," Roosevelt considered the current situation so "intolerable" that he felt compelled to use whatever personal influence he had to bring the parties together. "I do not invite a discussion of your respective claims and positions. I appeal to your spirit of patriotism, to the spirit that sinks personal considerations and makes individual sacrifices for the general good."

No sooner had the president finished than John Mitchell, seated in the back row of chairs beside three of his district presidents, "literally jumped to his feet." In a dramatic bid to frame the narrative, Mitchell pledged that "the miners should immediately go back to work and that all questions between the operators and miners should be left to the decision of a commission appointed by [the president], each side agreeing to abide by this decision." Mitchell's opening salvo took both the operators and the president by surprise. Turning to the operators, Roosevelt asked: "What have you gentlemen to say to this proposition?" After hastily conferring with his fellow owners, George Baer rose: "We cannot agree to any proposition advanced by Mr. Mitchell," he categorically proclaimed. "Very well," said the president. "I shall ask you, then, to return at three o'clock and I wish you would present at that time your various positions in writing."

When the group reconvened, Baer presented a written statement designed to reframe the story to the owners' advantage. Twenty thousand workers, he maintained, "stood ready" to return to the mines and secure the needed coal, but were prevented "by Mitchell and his goons" from doing so. "The duty of the hour is not to waste time negotiating with the fomenters of this anarchy and insolent defiance of the law," he argued, "but to do as was done in the war of the rebellion, restore the majesty of law, the only guardian of a free people." Looking directly at the president, he charged that if the administration refused to send federal troops to protect the destruction of private property and end the strike, then "government is a contemptible failure."

They not only "insulted me for not preserving order," Roosevelt later wrote of the mine owners, but they "attacked Knox for not having brought suit against the miners' union as violating the Sherman antitrust law." Tension escalated when coal owner John Markle advanced into the space of the confined president and shouted: "Are you asking us to deal with a set of outlaws?"

Keep Temper in Check.

From start to finish, Roosevelt later wrote, the operators "did everything in their power to goad and irritate Mitchell, becoming fairly abusive in their language to him, and were insolent to me. I made no comment on what they said, for it seemed to me that it was very important that I should (keep my temper and be drawn into no squabble)." Rupture nearly

508

came at the moment when Markle chastised him for dealing with "a set of outlaws." Roosevelt later admitted that he wanted to take him "by the seat of his breeches and nape of the neck and chuck him out of the window." By grabbing the edge of the wheelchair and biting his lip, however, Roosevelt managed to tamp down his anger.

The president was impressed and astonished by John Mitchell's discipline: how, regardless of provocation, "Mitchell behaved with great dignity and moderation," never once losing his temper. In so doing, he "towered above" them all. When Roosevelt asked the union leader to respond to the charge the owners had made of wanton violence and murder, Mitchell acknowledged straight off that seven deaths had occurred. "No one regrets them more than I do. However, three of these deaths were caused by management's private police forces, and no charges have been leveled in the other four cases. I want to say, Mr. President that I feel very keenly the attack made upon me and my people, but I came here with the intention of doing nothing and saying nothing that would affect reconciliation."

A sense of failure pervaded the room. Roosevelt tried one final time to resolve the conflict, asking the owners once again if they would submit the conflict to a presidential tribunal. "NO," they chimed in unison.

Adamantly, they refused "to have any dealings of any nature with John Mitchell." And with that, the conference came to an abrupt close. As the conferees filed out, the coal barons provided their own account to the press, reveling "in the fact that they had 'turned down' both the miners and the President." In a note to Mark Hanna, Roosevelt acknowledged: "Well, I have tried and failed. I feel downhearted over the result." Yet if the conference had failed, a plan to salvage something from that failure was already under way.

Document Proceedings Each Step of the Way.

Earlier that morning, before the start of the meeting, Roosevelt had obtained the permission of the conferees, given the gravity of the circumstances, to bring in his stenographer to make a record of the entire proceeding. This would be "the first time since the foundation of the Republic," one journalist remarked, that a verbatim report of a presidential meeting had ever been recorded.

No sooner had the conference ended than Roosevelt's office staff began typing up the stenographer's shorthand. The transcript was then rushed to the Government Printing Office, which produced a small pamphlet containing all that was said, representing, one journalist marveled, "one of the quickest pieces of work ever turned out by that establishment." Pamphlets were handed to the press in time for the papers to meet their midnight deadline for publication in the morning edition.

Control the Message in the Press.

As the press exposed the narrative of the conference in front-page stories across the country the next morning, Roosevelt's sense of failure quickly dissipated. The majority of the press contrasted the president's patient, courteous, dignified, and evenhanded behavior with the surly demeanor of the coal barons, "who resented in unmistakable terms his interference in what they claimed to be their own business." As Roosevelt's opening statement was read in city homes and country farms, the idea that a third party had rights and interests in this "private struggle" gained a powerful grasp on the public. "The President did both a brave and wise thing," *The Outlook* editorialized, by bringing the public into the strike as a third party, thus giving "official recognition" to the idea that "its interests are more important than those of either labor or capitalist."

Furthermore, as the contrasting tones of John Mitchell and George Baer were read and reread, public sentiment canted overwhelmingly in favor of the miners. With a public relations canniness equal to that of

Roosevelt himself, John Mitchell appeared eminently reasonable at all times, exhibiting a willingness to abide by arbitration, demonstrating heartfelt concern over the scattered outbreaks of violence, knowing that in a single day of bloody riot he could forfeit all public sympathy. By contrast, the coal owners appeared intransigent and oblivious to the public welfare.

In the days that followed, a simplified morality play was enacted in real time before the eyes of the American public: A standoff between the oppressor and the oppressed began to emerge, between the coal barons who arrived at the conference in elaborate carriages staffed by footmen in "plum-colored livery" and the miners who trudged down the street carrying their own grips.

Certainly, the statements of George Baer did little to bolster the owners' cause. At one point he even insisted that the rights of the working men would be better protected not by labor agitators but by "Christian men to whom God in his infinite wisdom has given control of the property interests of the country." His statement, which was reproduced in the press, created widespread condemnation and mockery. "The divine right of kings was bad enough," scoffed one Boston paper, "but not so intolerable as the doctrine of the divine right of plutocrats."

Even if Roosevelt's decision to hold the

conference met with broad public approval, future action was anything but clear. "All Washington is waiting with bated breath to see what the President will do next," the *Washington Times* reported, "and undoubtedly the whole country is in the same state of painful suspense."

Find Ways to Relieve Stress.

"I find it pleasant when I have been hard at work at some big state question," Roosevelt told a friend, "to entirely change the current of my thoughts." Though possessed of no surpassing athletic gifts, robust activity was his way of keeping mental balance. His letters abound with accounts of raucous tennis matches, strenuous hikes in the wooded cliffs of Rock Creek Park, and numerous efforts to scour up sparring partners to box with him. He regaled his children with comic tales of being "thrown about" by two Japanese wrestlers: "I am not the age or build one would think to be whirled lightly over an opponent's head and batted down on a mattress without damage but they are so skillful that I've not been hurt at all." Similarly, he relished jousting with his helmeted and armored friends in a game called Singlestick.

Deprived of such zany exertions by his infected leg, Roosevelt turned with a vengeance to his most reliable recreation — books. From his earliest days, young Roosevelt had found in literature not only diversion but an escape into the lives of others, allowing him to embark vicariously on thrilling adventures, to breathe free, and accomplish great deeds. It is hardly an exaggeration to say that books were the chief building blocks of his identity.

So now, confined to his wheelchair, he appealed to the librarian of Congress, Herbert Putnam, for "some books that would appeal to my queer taste" — histories of Poland or the early Mediterranean races. Two days later, fully gratified, he wrote to Putnam. "I owe you much! You sent me exactly the books I wished. I am now reveling in Maspero and occasionally make a deviation into Sergis' theories about the Mediterranean races. . . . It has been such a delight to drop everything useful — everything that referred to my duty — everything, for instance, relating to the coal strike . . . and to spend an afternoon in reading about the relations between Assyria and Egypt; which could not possibly do me any good and in which I reveled accordingly."

Be Ready with Multiple Strategies; Prepare Contingent Moves.

In the wake of the failed conference, Roosevelt's activity markedly quickened. If the several plans he now contemplated differed in the degree and severity of executive interference (ranging from demonstration to persuasion to coercion), they all shared the same goal: to protect the public from the lack of fuel once plummeting temperatures enveloped the region. The situation that had troubled him in both spring and summer had come to pass in a full-blown crisis.

"There was beginning to be ugly talk of a general sympathetic strike," Roosevelt recalled in a letter to Senator Crane, "which would have meant a crisis only less serious than the civil war." The entire nation would come to a standstill. Roosevelt confided to Knox and Root that he was contemplating a far-reaching action that "would form an evil precedent." He would take this radical action "most reluctantly," but he was determined to do whatever was necessary to protect the citizens from "suffering and chaos." This plan must remain secret until he was ready to set it in motion. At that point, just as Lincoln had readily permitted his cabinet officials to file written objections to his Emancipation Proclamation, so Roosevelt instructed both Knox and Root, the only two cabinet members apprised of the plan, to "write letters of protest against it if they wished, so as to free themselves from responsibility." He would act on his own as commander in chief, "just as if we were in a state of war."

As Roosevelt figured out details of his radical plan, he pressed ahead on two less extreme fronts. "It is never well to take drastic action," he liked to say, "if the result can be achieved with equal efficiency in less drastic fashion." His crisis management team suggested that pressure be brought to bear on Pennsylvania governor William A. Stone to send state troops into the coalfields to test the operators' claim that tens of thousands of miners would "flock back to the mines" if protected from union intimidation. While the operators' inflexibility had inflamed public sentiment, this one claim had "made quite an impression throughout the country." Because he represented and advocated for the public rather than for either capital or labor, Roosevelt recognized the importance of verifying the operators' contentions.

Governor Stone agreed to deploy the state troops, and within thirty-six hours the entire body of the Pennsylvania State Guard reached the coalfields. The days that followed loudly demonstrated the fallacy of the operators' claim. No more than "a trifling" number of miners showed up to work; the overwhelming majority decided to remain on strike until a decent settlement was reached.

With "not the slightest sign of an end to the strike," Roosevelt readied a second plan — the creation of a Blue Ribbon Commission to investigate the causes of the strike and make recommendations for both executive and legislative action. Scrambling once again to find warrant for such intervention, he argued he was empowered by his constitutional duty to report to Congress on the state of the Union. To lend the prospective commission gravity, he needed distinguished names. "In all the country," he flatteringly confided to former Democratic president Grover Cleveland, "there is no man whose name would add such weight to this inquiry as would yours."

In truth, the proposed commission possessed more ribbons than authority, for there was no means to enforce its findings. Nonetheless, the prospect of a Blue Ribbon Commission was more than a simple replication of Wright's earlier investigation, for it signaled bipartisan support at the approach of the midterm elections and, most importantly, supplied a persuasive instrument to build "the strongest possible bulwark of public opinion" should Roosevelt find it necessary to deploy the harshest, most problematic, and least desirable of his plots to compel the ending of the strike.

Don't Hit Unless You Have to, but When You Hit, Hit Hard.

It was now mid-October. Weeks would pass before the Blue Ribbon Commission could be assembled, conduct and complete an investigation, and issue its findings. By then, it might well be too late. Roosevelt knew that even after the strike ended, it would take time

517

for coal to be mined and the supply restocked. Urgently needful action was no longer counted in weeks or even days, but in hours. "Wherever the fault might lie the present system of management had failed," Roosevelt asserted, "and the needs of the country would brook no delay in curing the failure." His strategy of "last resort" was to organize an invasion of the coalfields with ten thousand regular army troops under "a first-rate general." The troops would "dispossess the operators" and run the mines as a receiver for the government until such time as a settlement could be reached.

For this formidable task, he summoned retired general John M. Schofield, the right mixture of "good sense, judgment, and nerve to act." Roosevelt secured the general's agreement to pay "no heed to any authority, judicial or otherwise," except his own as "Commander-in-Chief." In the event "the operators went to court and had a writ served on him, [Schofield] would do as was done under Lincoln, and simply send the writ on to the President." If the strikers tried to prevent coal from being mined, he would bring the full weight of federal force to bear upon them. Simultaneously, the federal troops would maintain law and order among the miners and divest the operators of their property.

To create the chain of communications

required to activate such a strategy, Roosevelt brought Pennsylvania senator Matthew Quay to the temporary White House. Without divulging details of the seizure portion of the plot, he asked Quay to arrange with Pennsylvania's Governor Stone that whenever the president "gave the word," the governor should formally request federal troops, thus triggering the sole constitutional power a president had to intervene — the power to keep order. The signal to start the chain of communications would come in the form of a presidential telegram with the inconspicuous message: "The time for the request has come." Roosevelt assured Quay that once federal troops were deployed, he, himself, would take full responsibility for all that subsequently transpired. Indeed, the senator should feel "perfectly welcome" later on, if the ensuing action sufficiently vexed him, to institute impeachment proceedings! The audacious plan exemplified one of Roosevelt's favorite maxims: "Don't hit till you have to, but, when you do hit, hit hard."

Was Roosevelt bluffing? Some believe that Roosevelt never intended to carry out his radical plan. After all, the far less invasive measures already taken had provoked shrill charges of the "usurpation of power." Nor was it clear how the coal would actually be mined. Would the miners return once the government acted as receiver? If not, would the government attempt to mobilize non-union miners? If the owners of the coal-carrying railroads were dispossessed, how could coal be transported to the eastern seaboard? There is no evidence that any work had been done to determine exactly how to prime the great machinery of coal production and distribution.

Yet, everything we know about Roosevelt's temperament suggests that he was not bluffing. Although he had exhibited an exemplary caution and patience throughout the strike, the situation had reached a state of acute danger to the people he was pledged to protect. When the people needed help, Roosevelt's spirit could not tolerate "any implication that the government of the United States was helpless." This was the motive heart of his iconoclasm. For this, he was ready and willing to break precedents. For this, he would risk his leadership. "I am Commander in Chief of the Army," he flatly declared. "I will give the people coal."

Theodore Roosevelt later contended that his scheme of military seizure of the coal mines provided the long-sought key to the resolution of the strike. Threat of "the intervention that never happened" provided the "big stick" that Elihu Root carried with him to New York, where he met with J. P. Morgan for five hours aboard his private yacht, the *Corsair*. If anyone could bring the operators to the table before the launch of a massive military invasion that nobody wanted, it was J. P. Morgan, the original architect of the powerful coal trust.

Find Ways to Save Face.
Before taking the midnight sleeper to New York, Secretary of War Root told Roosevelt he had figured out a way for the operators "to get out of the impasse without humiliation," but needed "entire freedom" to negotiate with Morgan. That would be possible only if he went to New York as a private citizen, "an interloper" on his own behalf, rather than the president's official representative. Roosevelt gave his blessing. Despite Root's conditions, he was clearly no ordinary citizen on this visit, but the president's most intimate cabinet adviser, imbued with the aura of Roosevelt's leadership.

Root had parsed the stenographer's notes from the October 3 conference at which the cadre of operators had flatly refused to consider Mitchell's suggestion of a presidential commission to arbitrate the issues. Beneath the downright negativity of the operators, Root detected not an opposition to arbitration per se, but an unwillingness to accept any suggestion put forth by Mitchell himself. The union leader represented a frontal challenge to their authority, a threat to the basic assumptions of their financial worldview. "There cannot be two masters in the management of the business," George Baer repeatedly said.

"The bones of it struck you in the eye for anyone who has been in litigation of this description," Root later said. What if the owners themselves advocated the idea of arbitration, allowing them to maintain the fiction they were not dealing directly with Mitchell? Anchored aboard the *Corsair,* Root and Morgan drafted a memorandum to be signed by the operators. "We suggest," the draft memo proposed, "a commission be appointed by the President (if he is willing to perform that public service) to whom shall be referred all questions at issue," and "the decision of that commission shall be accepted by us." Root later acknowledged that "it was a damn lie" to attribute ownership of the originating arbitration idea to the operators when it was clearly Mitchell's idea. It "looked fair on paper," however, and somewhat soothed the operators' egos.

That evening, Root took the return train to Washington while Morgan brought the memorandum to a meeting of owners at the Union Club. The situation was about to boil over, Morgan warned. A military plan for taking over their mines was well in the works. Agreement to arbitrate would derail that plan. Reluctant, but fully aware of the consequences of further delay, the owners grudgingly signed the agreement with the added stipulation that the Anthracite Coal Strike Commission be comprised of five members chosen from specific categories: a military officer, an expert mining engineer, a Pennsylvania judge, a businessman familiar with mining and selling coal, and an eminent sociologist.

Upon receiving the signed agreement from Morgan, Roosevelt immediately spotted a glaring, crippling absence of any category representing labor. Nonetheless, "in view of the great urgency of the case," Roosevelt sought to persuade Mitchell to accept, trusting that as president of the commission, he would choose first-class, exceptionally fair-minded men to fill each of the five categories. Mitchell had indeed come to trust the president but argued that he could never gain the miners' approval without a labor man on the commission. In a dispute between labor and capital, labor self-evidently must have a seat at the table. Mitchell also requested that the commission be expanded to include a Catholic bishop, since the majority of the miners were Catholic.

Through Root, Roosevelt sent word to Morgan that he needed someone from the House of Morgan to come to Washington posthaste to reopen negotiations. That same evening, with Roosevelt now hobbling around on crutches, two of Morgan's young partners arrived at the temporary White House with full authority to negotiate for the owners, who had convened at Morgan's office. For a frantic three hours over an open phone line, the young partners tried to extract the owners' consent to add the two extra men. While the owners might consider adding a Catholic prelate, under no circumstances would they acquiesce to a labor man.

"It looked as if a deadlock were inevitable," Roosevelt recalled. "They had worked themselves into a frame of mind where they were prepared to sacrifice everything and see civil war rather than back down." Then, as midnight drew nigh, imminent tragedy turned to farce. "Suddenly it dawned on me," Roosevelt said, "that they were not objecting to the thing, but to the name. I found they did not mind my appointing any man, whether he was a labor man or not, so long as he was not appointed as a labor man," so long as the appointment somehow fell under one of the five agreed-upon titles. To fill the "eminent sociologist" slot, Roosevelt promptly suggested labor leader E. E. Clark, the head of the Order of Railway Conductors. "I shall never forget the mixture of relief and amusement I felt when I thoroughly grasped the fact that while they would heroically submit to anarchy rather than have Tweedledum, yet if I would call it Tweedledee they would accept with rapture."

At the Wilkes-Barre convention several days later, the miners voted as one to return to work. Headlines blazoned the news: "Anthracite Miners Decide to Have Their Issues and Interests Determined by President's Commission. New Era Marked in the Affairs of Labor."

Thus, after 163 days of deadlock, the potentially most devastating strike in American history reached a peaceful conclusion. Acting as "the people's attorney," Roosevelt had defined the public interest in the hitherto private struggle between labor and capital. He had waited patiently through five months of the strike, moving one step at a time, until the "steady pressure of public opinion" created space for bringing the two sides together in a first-ever federal binding arbitration. "The child is born," Carroll Wright wrote, "and I trust will prove a vigorous . . . member of society."

Share Credit for the Successful Resolution. An ebullient Roosevelt generously shared paternity of this child, first off with J. P. Morgan. "If it had not been for your going into the matter, I do not see how the strike could have been settled at this time," he wrote Morgan. "I thank you and congratulate you with all my heart." Then, in a string of letters written in the aftermath of the strike, Roosevelt attributed to each member of his team —

Root, Knox, Quay, Sargent, Wright, Crane, and Payne — a significant role. If "defeat is an orphan," the old saying goes, "victory has a thousand fathers," and in this case, Roosevelt was delighted to let the world know of the unique contribution of each of the fathers. Privately, however, he let off steam against the coal operators. "May heaven preserve me for ever again dealing with so wooden-headed a set," he vented in a letter to his sister Bamie.

If he liberally broadcast praise, newspapers across the nation and the world poured accolades back upon Roosevelt. "His injury and his bravery, and then his part in resolving the strike," wrote the *North American Review,* "have given the color of romance and knight errantry to the prosaic office and heightened the appeal of his character." Upon hearing the news, the members of the French Parliament cheered and the London *Times* recognized that "in the most quiet and unobtrusive manner, President Roosevelt has done a very big and entirely new thing."

Furthermore, though the miners had immediately returned to work, the plaudits Roosevelt heaped upon others and reaped himself served to point everyone in the same direction as the binding arbitration hearings got under way. The hearings lasted more than three months. Each side put forth its best case, and in the end the commission unanimously agreed to award the miners a retroactive wage increase of 10 percent, a reduction in the daily work schedule from ten to nine hours, and a board of conciliation to resolve matters of future contention. It did not address the miners' desire for formal recognition of their union.

So, while not a blanket solution or an unqualified victory for labor or for capital, the binding arbitration resulted in a durable adjustment in the power relationship between capital, labor, and the federal government. "We are witnessing not merely the ending of the coal strike," the London *Times* remarked, "but the entry of a powerful government upon a novel sphere of operation."

Leave a Record Behind for the Future.
In the aftermath of this trailblazing event, Theodore Roosevelt wanted to set the record straight, to write a history of the crisis for the future. He had broken long-established precedents by intervening directly in a private quarrel between labor and management. His actions had provoked both outrage and approbation. Once the crisis was resolved, he wanted to clarify the nature of this unusual event, to define and restrict what he had done, to make clear the unique circumstances that compelled him to intervene. This was of paramount importance in order to avoid a carte blanche for an alarming, even despotic expansion of executive power.

The day after the strike ended, Roosevelt composed an astonishingly complete three-thousand-word letter to Massachusetts senator Crane detailing his actions from the start of the struggle the previous May. "I think it well that a full account of the whole affair should be on file," he told Crane. He then set forth the rationale behind each of his decisions — his calculation of the risks, his search for a reliable understanding of the facts, his initial decision not to publish the Wright Report, the change in circumstances that finally led to its publication, his unprecedented call for a face-to-face meeting with the opposing sides, his refusal to "sit supinely by" after the conference failed, his readiness to take drastic action even though he knew it would produce a serious backlash, the involvement of J. P. Morgan that made the invasion moot, the absurdity of the struggle over nomenclature, until, finally, resolution was reached.

He followed his letter to Crane with another, explaining further how the unique nature of the coal crisis forced him to take actions that were "not strictly legal." If the strike had been one of ironworkers, for instance, he told the celebrated historian William Roscoe Thayer, "he would have held himself aloof, but the coal strike affected a product necessary to the life and health of the people." Moreover, "if the President of the United States may not intervene to prevent a widespread calamity, what is his authority for?"

In the years that followed, Roosevelt told audiences that he wished the "clear and masterful" report of the Anthracite Coal Strike Commission "could receive the broadest circulations as a tract wherever there exists or threatens to exist trouble in any way akin to that with which the commissioners dealt." The commission members "did not speak first as capitalist or as laborer, did not speak first as judge, as army man, as church man, but all of them signed that report as American citizens anxious to see right and justice prevail."

With the coal strike, Theodore Roosevelt had grasped the historical moment that signaled the clear emergence of a domestic purpose for his young administration — to restrain the rampant consolidation of corporate wealth that had developed in the wake of the Industrial Revolution. The speed and size of that consolidation, Roosevelt powerfully felt, "accentuates the need of the Government having some power of *supervision and regulation* over such corporations." At the height of the crisis, he acknowledged that he "would like to make a fairly radical experiment on the anthracite coal business to start with!"

Theodore Roosevelt's leadership during the

experimental resolution of that crisis would prove to be the dawn of a new era. Under the banner of his Square Deal, a mood of progressive reform swept the country, creating a new vision of the relationship between labor and capital, between government and the people. As he explained to his friend Bill Sewall of Maine, "Now I believe in rich people who act squarely, and in labor unions which are managed with wisdom and justice; but when either employee or employer, laboring man or capitalist, goes wrong, I have to clinch him, and that is all there is to it."

ELEVEN:
TURNAROUND LEADERSHIP

Franklin Roosevelt and the Hundred Days

"Looking back on those days, I wonder how we ever lived through them," Secretary of Labor Frances Perkins said of the deepening Depression. "It is hard today to reconstruct the atmosphere of 1933 and to evoke the terror caused by unrelieved poverty and prolonged unemployment." The economy had reached "rock bottom." American industry was paralyzed; a quarter of the labor force was unemployed, and the hours of those who were working had been radically reduced. People had lost farms, homes, and small businesses that had been in their families for generations. Thousands of banks had collapsed, taking with them the deposits and savings of millions of people. The relief funds of cities and states were exhausted. Starving people wandered the streets. Food riots broke out. The future of capitalism, indeed of democracy itself, appeared grim. "We are at the end of our string," President Herbert Hoover despaired.

"No cosmic dramatist could possibly devise a better entrance for a new President — or a new Dictator, or a new Messiah — than that accorded to Franklin Roosevelt," White House aide Robert Sherwood observed, aligning himself with those who believe that a leader is summoned to the fore by the needs of the time. "When the American people feel they are doing all right for themselves they do not give much thought to the character of the man in the White House; they are satisfied to have a President 'who merely fits the picture frame,' as Warren Harding did." However, "when adversity sets in and problems become too big for individual solution," then, Sherwood argued, the people start looking anxiously for guidance, calling for a leader to "step out of the picture frame and assert himself as a vital, human need."

Mere opportunity is not enough, however, as we have seen. The scorched landscape that confronted Franklin Roosevelt presaged great failure just as easily as great success. The leader must be ready and able to meet the challenges presented by the times. And no leader was more prepared to diagnose the national malady correctly and assert himself as "a vital human need" than "old Doc Roosevelt," as he had been affectionately called at Warm Springs, where he had directly engaged with his fellow polio patients as architect, developer, program director, head counselor, therapy director, and spiritual adviser, "all rolled into one."

"Doc" Roosevelt was ready to minister with frankness, affability, near-mystical confidence, and an unshakable resolve to take whatever actions were necessary to transfuse the nation. He was prepared to administer a sustained, reanimating jolt of new leadership to his paralyzed and despondent nation. After all, in a searing and personal way, he had been through all this before.

One week before the March 4, 1933, inauguration of Franklin Delano Roosevelt, the journalist Agnes Meyer had entered into her diary, "the world literally rocking beneath our feet." Following three years of precipitous decline, the "vital organs" of the financial system, the nation's banks, were shutting down. The economic system of the nation had entered a physical and spiritual state akin to death throes.

Such extreme language depicting the nation as a gravely ill *body politic* was hardly an exaggeration. Indeed, beneath what Roosevelt called "the immediate material illness of the moment" — the acute circulatory crisis of the tottering banks — remained the far more pernicious condition of "the sore spots which had crept into our economic system." Hanging in the balance was nothing less than what kind of government and country we were and might continue to be.

"Panic was in the air," Roosevelt's incoming cabinet member Harold Ickes recalled of this frightening, terminal stage of the Great Depression. In the countryside, millions of families had lost their farms to foreclosure. A rural lawyer from Iowa asserted that no experience of his professional life had prepared him for the desolating experience of watching "men of middle age, with families, go out of bankruptcy court with furniture, team of horses, a wagon and a little stock as all that is left from twenty-five years of work." In the cities, more than one in four people had lost their jobs, the remainder working for diminished wages. Soup kitchens were running out of food, leaving tens of thousands of Americans starving and millions more ill-fed.

Nowhere was a safety net in evidence.

In mid-February, "the full brunt of the Depression" struck when banks in one state after another began to bolt their doors. During the early years of the economic downturn, some five thousand small, mostly rural banks had collapsed, wiping out the savings of millions of Americans, ransacking not only their security but their hopes for the future. In the winter of 1933, with no recovery in sight, rumors of fatal vulnerability in the entire banking system began to spread. People in villages and cities all over the country rushed to withdraw their savings, standing in long lines with satchels in their hands, demanding the immediate release of funds which they planned to stash under mattresses or bury on their property.

Banks rarely had deposits on hand to meet sudden, overwhelming demand. During the speculative fever that gripped the nation in the Roaring Twenties, banks had used depositors' money to buy stocks, most of which were now worthless. As the banks' cash and assets diminished, minuscule limits on withdrawals were set. Soon, even these limits began to stretch the resources the banks had on hand. Faced with increasingly unruly customers lining up at bank doors, governors in one state after another ordered all the banks in their states closed for an indefinite period.

For millions of people, such hard times were reckoned as end times. The great city of Chicago "seemed to have died," one resident recalled as she walked through the once swarming shopping district on the Loop. "The few people I saw seemed to be walking in a trance. There was something awful — abnormal — in the very stillness of those streets." The pulse of the nation could hardly be detected.

If proof were needed that the terrible drama had reached a terminal state, the very dawn of Inauguration Day brought the news that the governor of New York, the state wielding a commanding influence over the wealth and financial resources of the nation, had suspended all banking operations. Now, more than half the states had shut their doors. The remainder operated only on a limited basis. And a few hours later, as brokers awaited the signal to start trading, Richard Whitney, president of the New York Stock Exchange, took his place at the rostrum to announce that the Exchange was closing for the *indeterminate* future.

To President-elect Roosevelt, it appeared "that the whole house of cards" might fall before he had a chance to be sworn in. An old poker player, Roosevelt knew something about cards, just as he knew about faith, poise, hope, and action in the face of devastating illness. Many times in the months and years ahead Roosevelt would resort to extended metaphors of doctors and patients to explain the sickness of the body politic. Often, he would stretch such metaphors into full-blown allegories to describe the experimental treatments "Dr. New Deal" would administer, not only to break the acute circulatory crisis of the financial system, but to remedy the conditions from which the illness had arisen.

Doc Roosevelt knew at once that three lines of attack were necessary. First, the feelings of helplessness, impotence, dread, and accelerating panic had to be reversed before any legitimate recovery could commence; then, without delay, the financial collapse had to be countered; and finally, over time, the economic and social structure had to be reformed.

The steps Roosevelt took during the next hundred days to stem the immediate banking crisis set in motion a turnaround that would forever alter the relationship between the government and the people.

THE FIRST DAY
Draw an Immediate Sharp Line of Demarcation Between What Has Gone Before and What Is about to Begin.

The Inauguration Day of Franklin Delano Roosevelt began in prayer and ended in action. His every word and deed communicated the clear vision that this day represented no mere changing of the guard from one party to another. Something vast and debilitating had come to an end; something new and hopeful was beginning. The centerpiece of this carefully constructed day of political theater was the assertion of an intrepid and long-abandoned leadership, coupled with an assault on both the deflated psychological and the economic condition of the country.

Early that Saturday morning, accompanied by his entire cabinet, staff, family, and friends, Roosevelt attended a special prayer session at St. John's Episcopal Church. "A thought to God is the right way to start off my Administration," he told them. "It will be the means to bring us out of the depths of despair." After the twenty-minute service came to an end, Roosevelt remained on his knees, "his face cupped in his hands." Later that morning, as he waited at the Capitol for the ceremony to begin, the president-elect improvised a new opening sentence to his address: "This is a day of national consecration." Clearly, the address he was about to deliver was a civil sermon designed to provide "the larger purposes" that would bind the people together "as a sacred obligation."

Roosevelt's inspired resolve was glimpsed by the wife of Alabama senator Joseph Hill, who observed the president-elect as he slowly maneuvered himself to the rostrum. "I had not realized then," she said, "what a tremendous effort it was for him to manipulate his crippled legs. It gave me a feeling of his greatness that he could conquer such a physical handicap. Never have I seen an expression as he wore on his face — it was faith, it was courage, it was complete exultation!"

On this day of defining separation from the past, he asked the chief justice if, instead of simply saying "I do" after the oath was read — as thirty-one presidents had done before him — he could repeat every phrase of the presidential oath (I, Franklin Delano Roosevelt, do solemnly swear and . . .). He sought to invest a more personal affirmation in every syllable of the vow he was taking. In ways large and small Roosevelt loved to surprise, to break precedent, to transmit an inspiriting readiness to assume responsibility before a single word of the inaugural address was delivered.

Restore Confidence to the Spirit and Morale of the People. Strike the Right Balance of Realism and Optimism.

Roosevelt began by directly facing the facts of the dire situation. "This is preeminently the time to speak the truth," he declared, to address "honestly" the situation in our country. "Only a foolish optimist can deny the dark realities of the moment." But, he famously asserted, "the only thing we have to fear is fear itself." This phrase has gained such iconic stature as to eclipse the rest of the inaugural. Its provenance remains murky: Roosevelt speechwriter Ray Moley attributed it to longtime aide Louis Howe; Eleanor thought it was inspired by a passage by Thoreau found at the Mayflower Hotel in Washington in the days before the inauguration. Whatever the phrase's origin, Roosevelt gave the statement power, providing the spike to nail hysteria to the spot at the opening of his address.

Roosevelt's understanding of and empathy for the ordinary man suffused every aspect of the speech. Intuitively, he fathomed that what the people needed to hear was that they were not to blame for the misery of their individual circumstances. "The people of the United States have not failed," he insisted. Nor, he said, alluding to the Book of Exodus, had the country been "stricken by a plague of locusts." Failure of the economic system was neither due to the visitation of divine punishment, nor natural decline in the business cycle, nor lack of resources. To the contrary, he maintained, "plenty is at our doorstep." Failure, he insisted, was due to a lack of leadership. That void had left people unprotected against "unscrupulous money changers." Then, as the downward spiral deepened, leadership refused to take sufficient remedial measures, remaining passive at the very time robust leadership was needed most. Restoration would come through "a leadership of frankness and vigor," just as such leadership had carried the people through "every dark hour of our national life." With such a renewal, he was certain that the American people would once again rise.

Infuse a Sense of Shared Purpose and Direction.

As befitted this grave moment of communal bonding, Roosevelt's language was perfectly pitched to the occasion, elevated and religious, yet without affectation. At the center of his speech, he called for a new contract between the leader and the people, a contract built upon the recognition of our dependence on one another. We must move forward "as a trained and loyal army willing to sacrifice" for the common good, displaying "a unity of duty hitherto evoked only in time of armed strife." He considered his election by the people their gift to him; in return, he would work to fulfill their request "for discipline and direction under leadership." And in the spirit of that bequest, he pledged, "On *my* part and *yours we* face *our* common difficulties."

Foremost, he understood that "the Nation asks for action, and action now." Accordingly, he promised that he would put people back to work, provide a sound currency, prevent foreclosures of homes and farms, and "put an end to speculation with other people's money." As ever, immediately beneath the skin of vision lay the sinew and bone of pragmatic action.

Tell People What They Can Expect and What Is Expected of Them.

He told the country he was prepared to recommend to Congress a series of measures that "a stricken Nation" required. If the members should fail to respond "to the unprecedented need for undelayed action," however, he would ask Congress "for the one remaining instrument to meet the crisis — broad Executive authority to wage a war against the emergency, as great as the power that would be given to me if we were in fact invaded by a foreign foe." Here he harked back to the tradition of Abraham Lincoln, who issued the Emancipation Proclamation as an executive order based on his powers as commander in chief, and to Theodore Roosevelt who saw himself as "steward of the people," an office giving him the warrant to do whatever the people needed unless expressly forbidden by the Constitution or the laws. This was no dictator or Messiah holding forth. Franklin Roosevelt spoke in the name of the people for a resurgence of the strength of democracy, for a constitutional system capable of meeting "every stress" without losing its essential form.

To emphasize that each of his cabinet appointees was part of an ensemble, he gathered them together at the White House that evening — nine men and one woman — to be sworn in by Supreme Court justice Benjamin Cardozo. "Never before has the Cabinet been sworn in at the same time and in the same place and by the same official administering the oaths," the *New York Times* observed. Postmaster General James Farley would remember the scene in detail: "The new President sat at his desk, a beaming smile on his face, and read out one by one the name of each member of his official family." After each member was sworn in, he extended an exuberant handshake and handed over the commission. "This is a strictly family party," he said when the communal oath-taking was completed. He trusted that they "would all be able to pull together without friction and to work shoulder to shoulder for the common good and the best interests of the nation." With this "informal little touch," Farley recalled, "the Chief Executive had successfully converted what is usually a stiff and pompous ceremonial into a friendly, happy occasion."

The day's work was not yet done, however. By that evening, Roosevelt had reached two significant decisions. If a constitutional method could be discovered for "obtaining jurisdiction over the entire banking system of the Nation," he would, as his first act, declare a uniform shutdown of the banks, ironically called "a bank holiday." He asked his attorney general and treasury secretary to be ready the next day at the first formal cabinet meeting "to outline a constitutional method of closing all banks." With this power in hand, he would then convene a special session of Congress both to validate his action and to craft a legislative plan for reopening banks "in an orderly manner," depending on their degree of solvency. There would be no sleep that night for the members of Roosevelt's team.

In a way that defies all probability and logic, this man who had arduously rebuilt his own body and regained a spirit of confident optimism was chosen to rebuild the entire body politic and endeavor to resuscitate its spirit. That such a man was suited for such a task at such a time informed his leadership with something ineffable, something approaching enchantment. That magic of leadership was contagious, a young lawyer who had joined the administration remembered, as if "the air suddenly changed, the wind blew through corridors." A half a million letters of encouragement and support were on their way to the White House. "It seemed to give the people, as well as myself hope," one citizen wrote, "a new hold on life." This atmospheric change, "the sense that life was resuming," was reiterated in headlines and commentary across the country:

THE ERA OF INACTION HAS COME TO AN END. THE GOVERNMENT STILL LIVES. PERHAPS A LEADER HAS COME!

Lead by Example.

Franklin Roosevelt's compelling and authentic performance on Day One had been decades in the making. The young boy who had concealed an ugly gash on his forehead beneath his cap so as not to worry his ailing father, the polio victim who conveyed relentless good cheer to shield his family, had fashioned no mere mask but an outward demeanor of serenity, confidence, and relaxation, however grave the maelstrom that encircled him.

Because strenuous thought and anxiety were not etched into Roosevelt's features, as with Abraham Lincoln, people confused the projected surface for the interior. "How does your husband think?" reporter John Gunther asked Eleanor Roosevelt. "My dear Mr. Gunther, the President never thinks. He decides." Yet, the picture of Roosevelt as a prodigy, a natural, a purely instinctive leader belies the long periods of hard thought and preparation that went into everything he said or did. "Nobody knows how that man

545

worked," Eleanor's friend Marion Dickerman had said after watching him struggle for hours in his library rehearsing the short distance he would have to traverse in order to reach the stage at the Democratic National Convention for his first public speech after having contracted polio. "I never saw a man who worked harder," Sam Rosenman said of Roosevelt during his years as governor, recalling the long sessions at Hyde Park when he would shoot questions at a rapid clip at experts in various fields, absorbing vast stores of information, deepening his knowledge of every policy area.

"The remarkable thing about him," California senator Hiram Johnson observed of Franklin Roosevelt, "was his readiness to assume responsibility and his taking that responsibility with a smile." If the new president had long since learned to make himself appear confident in order to become confident, might not the characteristic uplifted tilt of his head, the sparkle of his eye, his dazzling smile, and his assured, calm voice soothe and embolden the fragile nerves of the country at large? In a time of ubiquitous loss and uncertainty, such a halcyon projection was no small gift to the people of America.

Forge a Team Aligned with Action and Change.

That Franklin Roosevelt had assembled no team of rivals was abundantly clear when his cabinet held its first formal meeting on Sunday afternoon. Without doubt and by design, the president was the patriarch of this official family. Where, critics asked, were the "big" men, the luminaries with familiar names and large reputations, the likely presidential possibilities? On first blush, it seemed as if the members had been selected "on the basis of loyalty from among those who had supported him for the nomination"; most of them were friends he had worked with over the years.

On closer inspection, the pattern behind Roosevelt's cabinet emerges. The obvious cabinet choices, the persons of distinction in the Democratic Party, were affiliated with the old order, "set in party lines, set against change." In the face of worsening crisis, they had tread water too long, mired in orthodoxy, waiting for the economic down cycle to peter out and the wheel to turn. The family team Roosevelt needed must be open to whatever shifts and exigencies the future might bring.

However various the geographic and political composition of the cabinet, they shared a common trait. Whether Democrats or Republicans, liberals or conservatives, easterners or westerners, they manifested a decided bias for action, an allegiance to whatever might be deemed necessary to get the country out of its misery. Through this "gallery of associates," Roosevelt hoped to introduce "a new mind into the government," a new adventurous spirit. And unquestionably, he was the "boss on this adventure."

Slated for attorney general until his sudden death from a heart attack on his way to the inauguration was Montana's Thomas Walsh, the liberal crusader who had exposed the Teapot Dome scandal. Connecticut lawyer Homer Cummings, strongly in favor of federal relief for the unemployed, took his place. For Treasury, Roosevelt selected Republican businessman William Woodin, a fellow trustee of the Warm Springs Foundation, a man of teeming energy and possessed of an unusually fertile mind. To fill Interior and Agriculture, he chose two progressive Republicans — Harold Ickes and Henry Wallace.

For labor secretary he picked liberal Democrat Frances Perkins, his industrial commissioner in New York, whose positive, innovative spirit, intelligence, and work ethic he had witnessed firsthand during his two terms as New York's governor. When first approached, Perkins hesitated: "Labor had always had, and would expect to have, one of its own people as Secretary." Roosevelt replied that "it was time to consider all working people, organized and unorganized." So Perkins became the first female cabinet officer in history, allowing Roosevelt to break yet another convention.

The question arose: What should she be called? Was there a female title corresponding to Mr. Secretary? *Robert's Rules of Order* suggested "Madam Secretary," which was fine with Perkins, although she cringed when reporters occasionally referred to her as "The Madam." Within the cabinet, Perkins happily recounted, she never experienced "any suggestion of a patronizing note," though at one point when the secretary of the navy was about to tell a story, he held back, wondering if it were appropriate for a lady to hear. "Go on," said the president, "she's dying to hear it."

Create a Gathering Pause, a Window of Time.

At the first formal cabinet meeting that Sunday afternoon, Perkins recalled, "the President outlined, more coherently than I had heard it outlined before, just what this banking crisis was and what the legal problems involved were." Turning to his attorney general (who had spent the entire night searching for a constitutional method that would allow the federal government to take over the banks), Roosevelt was delighted to hear that an obscure 1917 precedent had been unearthed, authorizing the president to investigate and regulate hoarding of currency. Upon this sliver of authority, the *New York Times* observed, was built "the most drastic" peacetime exercise of presidential power "ever taken." Without a note of dissent, the cabinet fell in line and work began at once on a presidential proclamation establishing a four-day bank holiday that would eventually stretch into a week.

The holiday provided a window of time, "an anesthetic before the major operation," a breathing space to devise a plan to reopen the banks in an orderly way. The coordinated closing, historian Arthur Schlesinger remarked, gave the long economic slide "the punctuation of a full stop, as if this were the bottom and hereafter things could only turn upward."

Bring All Stakeholders Aboard.

Midway through the cabinet meeting, Roosevelt brought in congressional leaders from both parties to solicit their support for his plan to call the 73rd Congress into special session to enact emergency banking legislation. In the era before the inaugural date was changed from March 4 to January 20, Congress would not ordinarily have been called into session until the following December. The singular exception was July 1861, when Lincoln called a special session to deal with the outbreak of civil war. To accommodate the return of far-flung members to the capital, Roosevelt set Thursday, March 9, as the date for Congress to convene.

That same Sunday, at Roosevelt's invitation, a group of prominent bankers from New York, Philadelphia, Richmond, and Chicago arrived in Washington to lend the administration a hand in the drafting of the bill. Progressives, who had hoped for radical action, even nationalization of the banks, were disturbed by the administration's decision to consult the very men impugned as "unscrupulous money changers" in the inaugural speech. But Roosevelt knew that he needed the technical expertise and support of the banking community and felt it important to include them in the process of drafting the bill. The search for technical knowledge also led him to heed members of former president Hoover's Treasury Department. While this, too, "ran counter to the spirit of the moment," these staffers had wrestled for months with various plans for saving the banks. Repeatedly frustrated by Hoover's inaction, they were eager to contribute.

To round out his search for consensus, Roosevelt invited the nation's governors to meet with his entire cabinet at the White House the following morning. He wanted to provide them "a complete picture of the banking situation," in the hope of securing their "help and cooperation." Acting swiftly, the governors passed a series of resolutions, pledging their full support.

And so, layer by layer, stitch by stitch, Roosevelt gathered into his materializing contingency plans not only his executive team but congressional leaders, leading bankers, and state governors — a consensus of various levels of leadership, public and private. And all the while he was planning novel ways to appeal, appease, and encourage the most important stakeholders of all — the American people.

Set A Deadline And Drive Full-Bore To Meet It.

The new president had promised action. Only a single week separated the proclamation of the national bank holiday on Monday morning, March 6, and the scheduled reopening of the banks on Monday, March 13. In that brief space his team had to prepare, rehearse, and produce what would amount to the staging of a national drama aimed at restoring public confidence in the nation's failed banking system. The entire country would be in attendance when the production had its debut on March 13, and their response that single day would determine success or failure. What if the emergency legislation were not completed and enacted in time? What if the people did not believe in the soundness of the plan? What if on Monday morning mobs of depositors all over the country stormed their banks? The outcome was anything but certain for both the banking system and the fledgling administration.

An enormous mountain of data had to be sifted and organized, pressing decisions made and funneled into a comprehensible language for an emergency banking bill ready for Congress. A preliminary decision was made to reopen banks in stages dependent upon their financial stability. But who should make those determinations? What if banks had solid assets but insufficient currency to meet demand? Should the federal government provide additional currency against those assets? If so, should it be scrip or newly printed money? How could such currency be printed and distributed in time? If insolvent banks with impaired assets had to be closed, how could depositors be treated in a just and orderly way? "Everyone was aware that in the rush serious mistakes might be made," Roosevelt adviser Raymond Moley acknowledged, "some banks would be reopened that should have remained closed, and others would be closed that might have weathered the storm." One thing was incontestable — under the new legislation, it would be necessary to concede a massive consolidation of power to the executive branch.

The marathon week called for a military-style operation complete with coordinating deadlines. The emergency bill had to be ready by noon on Thursday when Congress assembled. Night after night, Roosevelt was still in his office after midnight struck, conferring with Moley, Treasury Secretary Bill Woodin, old Hooverites, bankers, and legislative draftsmen. The team worked around the clock, stealing time only to eat a sandwich, snooze on a couch, or take a shower.

Early on, the decision was made to shore up weaker banks with federal funds. The Bureau of Engraving was ordered to begin printing new currency posthaste, and a fleet of airplanes was commandeered to stand by, ready to carry the money to banks across the country.

By Wednesday, a first draft of the bill went to the White House. With the help of bank examiners and the Federal Reserve, Treasury officials had prepared a map with multicolored pins to differentiate a bank's status according to its soundness. Always partial to maps as a way of visually clarifying problems for himself or teaching others, Roosevelt was "delighted with it," Moley reported. Later that evening the draft was presented to the majority and minority leaders in both houses. After small changes, congressional leaders pledged their full support. Not until three o'clock in the morning was the bill sent to the printer. When asked if the bill was finished, the puckish Bill Woodin said: "Yes, it is finished. My name is Bill and I'm finished too."

The bill was essentially a conservative endeavor, designed "to patch up failings and shortcomings," to stabilize, not alter, the existing structure. While Roosevelt was already contemplating far-reaching structural changes in the banking community, it was necessary first "to clear the financial arteries of the economy." Only if this opening gambit was successful could momentum be gained to address systemic problems. Unless this crisis was resolved, there could be no turn-around.

Roosevelt was busy in conferences on Wednesday night until past midnight. While the details of the bill had been agreed upon, one further task remained — a presidential message to be sent to Congress prior to the bill's introduction. Rising at 7 a.m. Roosevelt began composing that message in longhand. As each page was completed, the *New York Times* reported, "it was copied on the type-writer and sent immediately to the executive office for stenciling."

"I cannot too strongly urge upon the Congress the clear necessity for immediate action," Roosevelt began. "Our first task is to reopen all sound banks. This is an essential preliminary to subsequent legislation directed against speculation with the funds of depositors and other violations of positions of trust." First things must be first. "In the short space of five days it is impossible for us to formulate completed measures to prevent the recurrence of the evils of the past." But together they had set out, and soon, he pledged, he would propose action on a "rounded program of national restoration" that would "mark the beginning of a new relationship between the banks and the people." For recovery without reform would only temporarily disguise, not remove, the original causes of the financial collapse.

With thirty minutes to spare, the new administration met the first deadline. They delivered the prospective bill (or at least a single copy of it) before Congress gathered at noon on Thursday, March 9. "Here's the bill," Congressman Henry Steagall, chairman of the House Banking Committee, said, waving the single copy over his head. "Let's pass it." House leaders ruled that no amendments could be offered and that debate would be restricted to forty minutes. Republican minority leader Bertrand Snell urged his colleagues to give the president carte blanche: "The House is burning down and the President of the United States says this is the way to put out the fire." With shouts of "Vote, Vote" rising from the floor, a voice vote was taken. Not one voice of dissent broke the silence.

By the time the Senate commenced its own

debate, the newly printed copies of the bill were fully circulated. The few amendments offered by progressives to strengthen national regulation of the banks were swiftly shouted down. The final tally was seventy-three ayes, seven nays, the latter mainly from agrarian progressives. Twenty-two minutes later, the bill was shuttled to the White House for Roosevelt's signature. The signing ceremony took place in the Oval Room on the second floor that would become the president's study, but was presently a disheveled space with half-unpacked boxes and paintings waiting to be hung. Prior to the signing, Eleanor prompted her husband to comb his hair for the camera. Their Scottish terrier barked, and a clerk handed Roosevelt a pen to sign the first bill of his presidency. Less than nine hours had passed since the special session of what would become the famous Hundred Day Congress had opened. Such congressional dispatch had no equal.

The president expressed his gratitude to Congress for the passage of the bill, particularly citing "the unity that prevailed." While the Democrats now had huge majorities in both houses, the Republicans had backed every step of the rapidly evolving process. Still, Roosevelt understood that nothing yet had been accomplished. The true test would come on Monday morning when the banks reopened. Then the American public would determine the fate of the financial system. Would they feel confident enough in the banks to redeposit their savings? If not, if they continued to further withdraw and hoard, the situation might well stampede into chaos. Roosevelt had three days left to present and solidify his case before the public. The time had come for the impresario who had co-ordinated a multilayered team to prepare the bill and plan for its implementation to step from behind the curtain and assume the leading role in persuading the American people.

Set Forth and Maintain Clear-cut Ground Rules with the Press.

As a first step in educating the public during those critical days, Roosevelt held two free-flowing press conferences that little resembled those held by earlier administrations. "I am told that what I am about to do will become impossible," he told the 125 members of the press crammed in his office, "but I am going to try it."

The stakes of this experiment were high. Roosevelt's secretary noted that he was "unusually nervous" before starting. "His hand was trembling and he was wet with perspiration." Once the buzzer sounded and the members of the press filed into his office, however, there was no sign of the enormous pressure he was under. Amazingly, he looked "fresh and fit," the *New York Times* reported.

Former presidents had conducted irregular, often awkward meetings, relying upon previously submitted questions. Roosevelt proposed to discard written questions, hopeful for a semblance of give-and-take to establish an arena where actual interchange might occur, a stage for genuine improvisation and even whimsy — yet all within carefully prescribed ground rules. Direct quotations must be cleared with Press Secretary Steve Early. Background information could be used on the reporters' own authority but not attributed to the White House. Off-the-record information must remain confidential, not even to be revealed to an editor or colleague, "because there is always the danger that, while you people may not violate the rule, somebody may forget."

Roosevelt envisioned regular biweekly press conferences as settings for mutual education, not confrontation. A former editor of the *Harvard Crimson* himself, he respected journalists and understood that they had jobs to do, just as he had his. They wanted access to ascertain what was happening. He wanted to disseminate his own narrative in his own way. The style of his press conferences reflected the style of the man. This was no forum for heated debate, confrontation, or any manner of aggression. There prevailed only the simple demand for a cordial, good-humored, and civil exchange.

Roosevelt was well-acquainted with the novel ways in which his cousin Theodore had engaged and entertained the press. Every day at one o'clock, reporters were invited to the former president's midday shave, the "barber's hour," when they were permitted to question, or more accurately, listen, as Theodore expounded upon any number of subjects while the barber desperately tried to ply his trade. Later in the day, reporters were welcomed back when the president began his daily task of sorting correspondence. A quarter of a century later, Franklin Roosevelt proposed to formalize these encounters through the invention of a new manner of press conference, one that would reconceive the relationship between press and president.

If the ground rules were not respected, he half-jokingly threatened to revive the Ananias Club, an institution established by Theodore Roosevelt to which journalists who printed untruthful or fabricated items were banished from the proceedings. The name was chosen to commemorate a disciple of Jesus who was struck dead after lying to Peter the Apostle. In the nearly one thousand press conferences Franklin Roosevelt held after these first two, violations of the basic ground rules rarely occurred. "We were antagonists," one journalist remarked, "but we liked each other and we laughed and we had a perfect understanding of what each was trying to do."

After setting out the rules, Roosevelt generated the first round of laughter by announcing, "Now as to news. I don't think there is any!" The genial tone was sustained throughout the entire conference as he responded to questions "simply and unhurriedly as if he were sitting at a table talking to an old friend." If he didn't "know enough" to provide an answer, he would simply say so; but "Oh," he exclaimed, "I am learning a lot about banking." The *Baltimore Sun* reporter designated it "the most amazing performance of its kind the White House has ever seen." Roosevelt relished the rough-and-tumble of the initial experiment, and when it concluded, the press corps, transformed into an appreciative audience, applauded.

To compound the innovative nature of the new administration, Eleanor Roosevelt held her own first press conference at the same time that day. She made a rule that only female reporters could attend, which meant that all over the country conservative publishers had to hire their first female reporters. Indeed, because of Eleanor Roosevelt's weekly press conferences, an entire generation of female journalists got their start.

The *New York Times* characterized this first week as "so swift-moving and momentous that it contained as many major events as have occurred in the entire administrations of some Presidents," little knowing that the momentum gained had just begun.

Tell the Story Simply, Directly to the People.
On the Sunday eve of the decisive Monday morning of the bank reopenings on March 13, Roosevelt delivered the first of what became known as his "fireside chats." At various times throughout the previous week, he had sketched out and rehearsed the story of the banking crisis. At the initial gathering of the cabinet, he had outlined the banking dilemma in what seemed to Frances Perkins remarkably lucid and straightforward terms. Subsequently, the narrative was further pruned, revised, and simplified for the members of Congress and the assembled press. Now he was finally ready to go before the American people.

Roosevelt had earlier perused the draft provided by the Treasury Department and tried to demystify the language of the legal and banking community. He sought to translate their specialized language into words of one syllable that could be better understood by himself and the average citizen — by "a mason at work on a new building," he said, "a girl behind a counter, a farmer in his field." At last, seated at a desk before six microphones and a small assemblage of family and colleagues, he imagined the American people listening in their parlors or kitchens. "My friends," he opened, striking an immediate intimacy. As he spoke, Perkins recalled, "his face would smile and light up." He was not merely "talking directly to the people of the nation," observed Rosenman, but rather, "to each person in the nation."

"I want to tell you *what* has been done in the last few days, *why* it was done, and *what* the next steps are going to be," he began. Abraham Lincoln had provided a similar roadmap of orientation when he set out to tell the story of how the "house divided" had come about and how the people could come together to reunify that house: "If we could first know *where* we are and *whither* we are tending, we could then better judge *what* to do and *how* to do it." So Roosevelt, like Lincoln, sought to communicate with and guide his audience by telling a story.

"When you deposit money in a bank," Roosevelt explained, "the bank does not put the money into a safe deposit vault." It invests your money in bonds, loans, and mortgages "to keep the wheels of industry and of agriculture turning around." In normal times, the cash on hand is sufficient to cover the needs of depositors. "What then, happened?" A number of banks had "used the money entrusted to them in speculations and unwise loans." When the market crashed and these banks collapsed, confidence in the entire banking system was undermined. A general rush to withdraw took place — "a rush so great that the soundest banks could not get enough currency to meet the demand." Now, backed by the new federal pledge to provide loans and additional currency if necessary, approved banks could safely begin to open their doors again. "I can assure you," he reasoned, "that it is safer to keep your money in a reopened bank than under the mattress."

He identified the very questions the people asked themselves and urgently needed answering. "A question you will ask is this: why are all the banks not to be reopened at the same time? The answer is simple." The process of determining which banks could open immediately and which needed help would take time. "A bank that opens on one of the subsequent days," he assured them, "is in exactly the same status as the bank that opens tomorrow." He would not promise that no individual would be subject to losses, but if the country had "continued to drift," far greater losses would have been suffered. Again, as in the inaugural, he asked the people for courage and faith. "Let us unite in banishing fear. We have provided the machinery to restore our financial system; it is up to you to make it work."

The man and the moment had converged. Roosevelt had grasped the revolutionary opportunity radio presented, that "marvelous twentieth century invention which has all but annihilated time, distance, and space." An estimated sixty million people listened to the president's radio chat. His soft, relaxed, and modulated speaking voice was naturally attuned to the conversational style of the new radio age. This fireside chat was precisely that, an interchange rather than an oration. Most importantly, his voice projected empathy, confidence, and warmth that made one believe and trust in his words.

As the White House nervously apprehended, however, the true test would be the people's reaction when banks reopened. Early reports suggested long lines at teller windows, but "it was a run to make new deposits, not to take money out." Headlines in city after city told the self-same story. "City Recovers Confidence," the *Chicago Tribune* proclaimed. "Rush to Put Money Back Shows Restored Faith as Holiday Ends," declared the *New York Times*. Many depositors cited the renewed confidence the president's radio chat had given them. A bank president in San Antonio noted that the customers seemed to be "an entirely different list of people" than those who had scrambled to remove their money weeks before. "Their names and signatures are the same, but their frame of mind is as different as day and night."

With simple, plain language devoid of metaphors or eloquence, Roosevelt had accomplished his purpose of explanation and persuasion. The banking crisis that had gripped the country with fear and panic subsided. When trading resumed on Wednesday, the stock market registered a 15 percent jump, its largest rise in years. By the standard of its impact on events, this first fireside chat, one historian noted, ranks "as one of the most important speeches in U.S. history." The patient had survived the acute crisis. Only now, to prevent relapse, could the doctor propose a regimen to treat the sources of that disease.

Address Systemic Problems. Launch Lasting Reforms.

Roosevelt had initially planned for Congress to adjourn after the emergency banking legislation had passed. He soon realized, however, that the momentum generated from the first victory should not be squandered. Accordingly, he asked congressional leaders to remain in continuous session, a request that would beget the historic turnaround that would become known as "the hundred days."

"The process of recovery," Roosevelt understood from the start, would require the removal of "the destructive influences of the past," the uprooting of "old abuses" so "they could not readily grow again." Over and over he spoke of the condition the country faced as an organic disease, an affliction with multiple sites. What were these "old abuses," these "destructive influences of the past," these "sore spots" that hindered prospects for a lasting cure?

To Roosevelt's thinking, the essential obstacle lay in an industrial capitalism that had remained largely unregulated save for brief spates of progressive legislation under Theodore Roosevelt and Woodrow Wilson. Systemic problems had festered "for a whole generation" before the Great Depression exposed their catastrophic effects. The pathology Franklin Roosevelt diagnosed entailed the entire economic and social structure; it went to "the roots of our agriculture, our commerce, our industry." It was his conviction that recovery demanded nothing less than "a complete reorganization and a measured control of the economic structure." This could only be attained by supplanting the old pyramidal order of "special privilege" with a "new order of things designed to benefit the great mass of our farmers, workers and business men."

As Roosevelt had anticipated, no sooner was the banking crisis resolved than "a vocal minority began to cry out that reform should be placed on a shelf and not taken down until after recovery progressed." That minority offered growing resistance to the far-flung activist plans contemplated by the New Deal. Those at the pyramid's apex still believed that by saving the banks and bailing out corporations, prosperity would "trickle down" to the benefit of the people at large. They refused, Roosevelt said, "to realize that recovery and reform must be permanent partners in permanent well-being." If recovery of the banks had been a decisive initiating battle, reform would be a widespread, protracted war.

Roosevelt decided to unveil his vision for systematic economic and social reform in a second fireside chat on May 7, 1933. So sweeping were the changes he intended to espouse that his speechwriter Moley called his attention to the fact that he was taking a giant step away from the laissez-faire philosophy that kept private enterprise free from government intrusion and considered all regulation anathema. "Roosevelt looked graver than he had been at any moment since the night before his inauguration," Moley remembered. "And then, when he had been silent a few minutes, he said, 'If that philosophy hadn't proved to be bankrupt, Herbert Hoover would be sitting here right now.' "

Roosevelt began his second radio conversation building upon his first fireside chat on the banking crisis eight weeks before. "In the same spirit and by the same means," he would discuss general plans to remedy deeply implanted problems and to sketch the purpose behind the specific policies. Never should the American people try to revert to the old order. The emergent order Roosevelt had in mind was not the coercive imposition of government control but the concept of a partnership between government, farming, industry, and transportation. At the center of this new collaboration stood a revolutionary bond between the president and the great rank and file of the people as his partners in the government.

Comfort did not reside in bombast: "We cannot ballyhoo ourselves back to prosperity," he cautioned. The country's descent could be reversed only by coordinated action. He asked Congress for a staggering array of governmental programs, which, taken together, would redefine the role of the federal government to regulate the economy and secure the lives of the American people from the bottom to the top. His purpose — to rebuild the social system "on sounder foundations and on sounder lines" — sprang from what Frances Perkins called "his general attitude that *the people mattered.*"

Before Congress adjourned on its hundredth day, fifteen major pieces of legislation had been passed and signed into law. Billions of dollars were appropriated to undertake massive public works, provide direct work relief, ease mortgage distress, safeguard investors, guarantee bank deposits, ensure decent wages, provide collective bargaining, raise agricultural prices, generate public power. *Relieve, ease, safeguard, guarantee, ensure:* all words designed to bring comfort to those who were suffering, words that connoted policies that had begun to weave the vast safety net of protection and regulation that would eventually become the New Deal.

Contemporaries were boggled, filled with a sense of wonder upon witnessing the leadership exercised by Franklin Roosevelt during the hundred-day turnaround and beyond. Then, as now, one asks: How was it possible for a single man to give coherence to multiple layers of new programs cutting across the entire economic and social spectrum?

Be Open to Experiment. Design Flexible Agencies to Deal with New Problems.

First off, Roosevelt stressed the improvisational, experimental nature of the New Deal. Confronting the unmapped ocean of human distress the Depression had wrought, Roosevelt had "little in the way of precedent" to guide either the formulation or the execution of policies. With a bewildering array of sweeping laws to execute, he had no choice, he believed, but to experiment with unorthodox administrative practices. "We have new and complex problems," Roosevelt explained. "We don't really know what they are. Why not establish a new agency to take over the new duty rather than saddle it to an old institution?" Old-line departments were inevitably accustomed to familiar routines, established ways of thinking and acting. New agencies would be free to create new cultures built around innovation, vitality, and speed. In the course of his first eighteen months, Roosevelt would create twenty new agencies from "the alphabet soup" and give them names that would become known by their acronyms.

Roosevelt's first venture — the Civilian Conservation Corps, popularly called the CCC — bore the signature of his personal invention. Frances Perkins once remarked that "every now and then" Roosevelt would have flashes "of almost clairvoyant knowledge and understanding." The CCC, which linked all kinds of disparate things together in an original, romantic, yet practical program, was just such a concept. The program, when initially announced in March, aimed to provide work and purpose for 250,000 young men by mid-July. Most lived in cities, had recently left school, and were seeking "an opportunity to make their own way." Nowhere could jobs be found, and they were listless and depressed. At the same time, dozens of national forests had fallen into "a sad state of neglect" over the years, to become choking third- and fourth-growth tracts of scrubland. Dead trees and shrubs had to be cleared, new trees planted, firewalls built, paths cleared.

The CCC would heal the forests while healing the young men. Since the greater portion of the wages would be sent home, earnings would simultaneously help families and stimulate local economies adjacent to the camps. A practical measure for the present and a material investment in the future, the CCC, as envisioned by Roosevelt, planted trees while more importantly planting "a moral and spiritual value" to uplift and sustain a generation of young men adrift.

When Roosevelt first described the plan to the cabinet, Perkins considered it "a pipedream." How would a quarter of a million young men be recruited? How would they be transported to the forests, clothed, fed, and housed? Who would design and supervise the work projects? How could the program possibly be up and running in three months' time? The answers to all such questions lay in Roosevelt's leadership style: *Establish a clear purpose; challenge the team to work out details; traverse conventional departmental boundaries; set large short-term and long-term targets; create tangible success to generate accelerated growth and momentum.*

Over the course of several cabinet discussions, an overall method to actualize Roosevelt's conception took shape. Four departments would contribute to this unique collaboration. The Labor Department was to select and enroll the young men from the relief rolls. Interior and Agriculture would recommend the work sites and design site-appropriate projects. The Army was to construct camps, transport, feed, clothe, house, and pay the men. Reserve Army officers would return to active duty to run the camps; the Interior Department was to select civilian foremen to oversee the work. To lead the CCC and coordinate the interdepartmental operations, Roosevelt shrewdly selected Robert Fechner, a union leader whose career had begun as a machinist. When Roosevelt asked him how long he needed to set up his first camp, Fechner replied, "a month." Roosevelt countered, "Too long"; at once, Fechner halved the estimate. "Good," Roosevelt said simply.

By calling for a quarter of a million men to occupy the forest camps by mid-July, Roosevelt challenged his team to exceed normal standards by setting a target beyond all conventional expectations. "Do it now and I won't take any excuses," he told them. "It was characteristic of him that he conceived the project boldly, rushed it through, and happily left it to others to worry about the details," Perkins later said. "He put the dynamite under the people who had to do the job and let them fumble for their own methods." And his entire team responded. By early July, Roosevelt proudly declared, more than 250,000 men were at work in 1,500 camps, "the most rapid large-scale mobilization of men in our history." The Labor

Department had managed to enroll ten thousand men daily until the target was reached. A cadre of talented officers, including Colonel George Marshall, had erected camps to accommodate more men than had been deployed in the Spanish-American War. The corps members, deeply engaged in a wide variety of conservation tasks, had found "a place in the world" — they were to make an enduring transformation of the infrastructure of public lands, improving timberland, securing flood and fire control, managing and conserving forestland for generations to come.

The CCC proved to be among the most popular of the New Deal programs. More than two and a half million young men would pass through the camps before the program was discontinued after the outbreak of World War II. Many of these men had never seen a forest before, let alone dwelled in a natural setting. Few had performed arduous manual labor. But, as Roosevelt had hopefully foreseen, they developed a broad range of job skills and learned to labor alongside others from different, hitherto unknown parts of the country. "I weighed about 160 pounds when I went there, and when I left I was 190," said one boy, filled with a newfound sense of self-respect. "It made a man of me all right."

Roosevelt understood, of course, that the CCC was not "a panacea," for despite its initial success, the quarter of a million CCC jobs comprised but one-sixtieth of the problem of fifteen million unemployed Americans. To better illustrate the situation, he reverted to a sports analogy. He likened himself to the quarterback of a football team who "has a general plan of game in mind." He knew what his first play was going to be but could not tell you the play after that "until the next play is run off. If the play makes ten yards, the succeeding play will be different from what it would have been if they had been thrown for a loss." The resounding success of the CCC had provided an enabling first play in the intricate game plan that was just beginning to unfold for dealing with the colossal unemployment problem.

Stimulate Competition and Debate. Encourage Creativity.

Roosevelt worked most productively, Sam Rosenman believed, when "ideas and arguments, pro and con, would be 'batted out' before him, discussed and debated." He surrounded himself with strong personalities who fought hard for their own ideas, and then he deliberately contrived situations that challenged them to defend their opposing positions. Finally, of great importance, he steered them into reconciliation. Time and again, defying orthodox administrative protocol, he would give the same assignment to different people in the same agency or allocate the same project to different agencies. "There is something to be said for having a little conflict," Roosevelt observed. "A little rivalry is stimulating, you know. It keeps everybody going to prove that he is a better fellow than the next man."

While Roosevelt himself never felt threatened by multiplicity and confusion, the "inherently disorderly nature" of his administration frequently disgruntled subordinates. At times, morale was threatened and feelings were rankled. "The maintenance of peace in his official family," Roosevelt's secretary Grace Tully remarked, "took up hours and days of Roosevelt's time." When he determined that a member of his team was feeling undervalued or under pressure, he sprang into action. He would invite the aggrieved aide to the White House for a "hand-holding session." One administrator observed that Roosevelt "had a rare capacity for healing the wounded feelings which he had inadvertently caused."

"In a quieter time, when problems were routine, there would have been every reason to demand a tight and tidy administration," Schlesinger remarked. "But a time of crisis placed a premium on initiative and innovation and on an organization of government which gave these qualities leeway and reward." By leaving lines of authority ambiguous, Roosevelt could simultaneously move in different directions; he could allow members of his spirited team to run, never doubting his ability to rein them in. Moreover, by refusing to delegate or consolidate too much power in a single person, he kept the ultimate decisions just where he wanted them — in his own hands.

Nowhere was Roosevelt's competitive theory of administration illustrated more revealingly than in the struggle between two extremely able men — Harold Ickes and Harry Hopkins — for control of the billions of dollars allocated to relieve unemployment through public works.

As secretary of interior and director of the Public Works Administration (PWA), Ickes had the perspective of a progressive businessman. The best way to attack unemployment, he believed, was to "prime the pump" by subsidizing private contractors to construct immense projects that would take an extended period of time to complete, but once accomplished, would endure. Such projects included the Bonneville Dam, the Lincoln Tunnel, LaGuardia Airport, and the Great Smoky Mountains National Park.

Harry Hopkins, a former social worker who headed the Civil Works Administration (CWA) and later the Works Progress Administration (WPA), favored a multifarious range of smaller and decentralized projects deliberately designed to get as many people off the relief rolls and into actual jobs as quickly as possible. Such speedily mobilized community-centered projects included many hundreds of schools, libraries, firehouses, playgrounds, skating rinks, and swimming pools. The Federal Arts Project sponsored painted murals for public buildings; the Federal Theatre Project enabled live productions of classical works to reach people in far-flung regions.

The contrasting administrative styles of the two men mirrored their differing philosophies and temperaments. Known as "Honest Harold," Ickes was a seasoned administrator determined to restore the reputation of an Interior Department badly damaged by the Teapot Dome scandal during the Harding administration. Ickes insisted on meticulous planning; he micromanaged every contract, ever-watchful for waste or scandal. A scrupulous disciplinarian, he arrived early and remained late at his desk in the ornate Interior building. Until the voice of public disapproval was raised, he locked the front doors at 8:35 a.m. to prevent employees from wandering in late, and even removed bathroom stall doors to discourage employees from reading newspapers.

Hopkins, "a chain smoker and black coffee drinker" who occupied "the shabbiest building in Washington," often looked as if he had slept at his desk, wearing "the same shirt three or four days at a time." Impatient with bureaucracy and averse to organizational charts, he focused obsessively on "the physical, mental and spiritual suffering" caused by the dearth of jobs. He believed that direct relief in the form of the dole undermined character and independence and that men and women desperately wanted and needed the dignity of work and the discipline labor gave to one's life. When critics complained that the CWA jobs were often of short duration with little impact on the long-run economy, he countered, "People don't eat in the long run — they eat every day."

Franklin Roosevelt valued, needed, and would utilize and reconcile the philosophies of both men. He sought both short- and long-term benefits — decentralized immediate work projects and centralized durable improvements — to help heal the nation. He participated directly in the allocation of funds by sitting on the committee that evaluated the competing projects submitted by the two men. He listened attentively when Hopkins argued that the heavy projects Ickes favored took too much time to develop, that with the higher cost of materials a lower percentage of dollars went directly into the pockets of people. He shared Ickes's concern that Hopkins could not carefully oversee the tens of thousands of small projects he had initiated, exposing them to the risk of inefficiency, potential graft, and diminished congressional support.

As the Depression continued month after month, however, Roosevelt found himself siding more frequently with Hopkins. Roosevelt had always been susceptible to the stories of people's lives rather than statistically driven macro-projects. Hopkins had a host of such stories for Roosevelt — how the provision of a government job had "rehabilitated" an entire family or how a WPA project had delivered a playground, park, or swimming pool to a grateful community. As appropriations tilted more to favor Hopkins's myriad projects, Roosevelt was forced to placate Ickes. In his diary, Ickes records numerous occasions when he had resolved to resign, only to be reeled back into the fold by "the unaffected simplicity and personal charm of the man." Here was the president of the United States, patiently listening to his side of the story, all the while being "dressed with the help of his valet," yet remaining relaxed, focused, and empathetic to his personal grievances. "What could a man do with a President like that?" Ickes later said.

Long-smoldering antagonisms eventually ignited in public view. Ickes referred to WPA projects as "make-work" and "leaf raking." Hopkins counterpunched, railing against the constant delays in the interior secretary's construction projects. While the president valued, even fomented such arguments within his official family, he was less than pleased when feuds surfaced in newspapers. Within short order, he invited both Ickes and Hopkins to accompany him on a speaking tour across the country, followed by a cruise through the Panama Canal. The two men spent days and nights together with the president, game-fishing in the shoals off Mexico, palavering, playing poker, drinking martinis. Both men thoroughly enjoyed the intimacy of the unusual monthlong trip. Once again Ickes marveled at the "high cheer" of Roosevelt's disposition as he was "being carried up and down like a helpless child when he went fishing." Hopkins told his brother he had "a perfectly grand time" and felt "really rested."

In the ship's daily newspaper, *The Blue Bonnet,* a curious news item appeared, entitled "Buried at Sea." Its sprightly style pointed directly to the old newspaperman, Roosevelt himself.

The feud between Hopkins and Ickes was given a decent burial today. With flags at half mast . . . the President officiated at the solemn ceremony which we trust will take these two babies off the front page for all time.

Hopkins expressed regret at the unkind

things Ickes had said about him and Ickes on his part promised to make it stronger — only more so — as soon as he could get a stenographer who would take it down hot.

The President gave them a hearty slap on the back — pushing them both into the sea. "Full steam ahead," the President ordered.

Open Channels of Unfiltered Information to Supplement and Challenge Official Sources. Don't confuse what people in Washington are saying for what people in the country are feeling, Roosevelt repeatedly counseled his aides: "Go and see what's happening. See the end product of what we are doing. Talk to people; get the wind in your nose." If the unprecedented conditions demanded the creation of "new and untried" programs, Roosevelt, as chief administrator, had to figure out which of these programs were working, which were not. Such evaluations were not likely to bubble up through formal channels. To prevent imprisonment within the official pipelines of information, Roosevelt set in motion a nationwide reconnaissance. He tapped all manner of unorthodox sources of intelligence that allowed him to alter, discard, or revamp existing programs on the fly.

Although he began his day by consuming a half-dozen metropolitan papers "like a combine eating up grain," he relied on his long-time secretary Louis Howe to cut-and-paste a digest of articles and editorials culled from newspapers from small villages and towns across the country. Through this *Daily Bugle,* as it was called, Roosevelt absorbed a more personalized sounding of what people were feeling about individual New Deal programs. Similar clippings were compiled from the torrent of letters that reached the White House — somewhere between six and eight thousand letters every day after Roosevelt let it be known that he wanted to hear directly from the people. Eleanor also asked people to write her, citing the danger that a public figure "may be set apart from the stream of life affecting the country." Her daily column not only dispensed advice but received opinions and suggestions from the people. She, like her husband, had opened two-way communications.

More than any other source, Roosevelt counted on Eleanor to provide "the unvarnished truth." He called her his "will o' the wisp" wife, for she traveled hundreds of thousands of miles around the country, spending weeks and months at a time talking with a great variety of people from every region, listening to complaints, examining New Deal programs, amassing an anthology of stories. Each time she returned, she arranged "an uninterrupted meal" with her husband so the anecdotes would be "fresh and not dulled by repetition." Roosevelt had absolute trust in the dependability and accuracy of her observations. "She saw many things the president could never see," Frances Perkins said. "Much of what she learned and what she understood about the life of the people of this country rubbed off onto the president." Cabinet secretaries often heard Roosevelt's refrain: "My missus gets around a lot," he would say. "My missus says that people are working for wages way below the minimum set by NRA in the town she visited last week."

Eleanor's reports mobilized Roosevelt to streamline programs, sharpen their effectiveness, and sometimes create altogether new agencies. The Agricultural Adjustment Administration (AAA) had begun paying farmers to destroy their crops and slaughter animals in an attempt to raise the depressed farm prices that had created untold suffering in rural areas. "Why do you dump all these little pigs into the Mississippi when there are thousands of people in the country starving?" Eleanor pointedly asked an administrator. Her appalled observations about the wasteful aspects of the AAA program led to the creation of a new agency (the Federal Surplus Relief Corporation). The government purchased surplus wheat, corn, meat, and cotton and then distributed the excess commodities to relief agencies to feed and clothe the unemployed.

While bringing fresh sources of information from *outside,* Franklin Roosevelt churned up the normal flow of information from *inside* as well. Told about an interesting young subordinate in a bureau, he was likely to invite that employee to the White House, disrupting the chain of command and often irking the department's chief. Roosevelt habitually read more deeply into people than in books. Conversation afforded him the occasion to work out his own thoughts. "In the course of the average day," Roosevelt said, "I come in contact with representatives of about half the Federal relief agencies personally, or by telephone, or by correspondence. I try to keep in touch with the coordinating of all our work as much as is humanly possible." Memos were tailored to winnow down the mountains of data that piled up every hour. "I learned to prepare material so that it would photograph itself upon his memory," Frances Perkins said. Recommendations for action should be short, "preferably one page," presented in outline form, revealing who was in favor, who opposed, and why. But what he wanted most of all, she knew, were the particular stories of ordinary people. These stories indelibly tattooed his memory.

Adapt. Be Ready to Change Course Quickly When Necessary.

"I do not deny that we may make mistakes of procedure," Roosevelt had said when he first outlined plans for systemic changes in his second fireside chat. "I have no expectation of making a hit every time I come to bat. What I seek is the highest possible batting average, not only for myself, but for the team." Repeatedly, he told staffers prone to stress about the magnitude of the tasks before them that so long as they considered every angle as best they could in the time they had, there was no use agonizing over whether they were right or wrong. "You and I know people who wear out the carpet walking up and down worrying whether they have decided something correctly," Roosevelt confided to Rosenman. "Do the very best you can in making up your mind, but once your mind is made up go ahead."

Such adaptability, the willingness to shift ground, revise, and accommodate the contours of changing circumstances, can be discerned as an animating principle threading through the scores of programs set forth during the hundred days and beyond. Some of these programs would remain a permanent part of the federal government, including the TVA (Tennessee Valley Authority), FHA (Federal Housing Administration), and FCC (Federal Communications Commission).

Others would be disbanded once the mobilization for war rendered them unnecessary — among them the CWA (Civil Works Administration), PWA (Public Works Administration), WPA (Works Progress Administration), NYA (National Youth Administration).

Readiness to adapt played a central role in enabling Roosevelt to fulfill the pledge he had made at the height of the banking crisis — to follow recovery with reform, to uproot "old abuses" in both the unregulated stock market and the banking system so they would not reoccur. He took his first stab at regulating the stock market with the Truth in Securities Act, designed, he said, "to guard investors against false information in the selling of securities." Having seen "so much misery come to honest families who had been persuaded to invest their savings in speculative securities masquerading under the name of investments and sold by high pressure methods," he had come to the conclusion, Roosevelt said, "that national legislation was a necessity." The act required issuers of new securities to file complete registration statements with the Federal Trade Commission. Deliberate misrepresentation would be subject to up to five years' imprisonment. The bill angered people on both the right and the left. While businessmen warned that the "draconian" punishments, determined by amateurs at the Federal Trade Commission, would so restrain brokers that the market would be stalled, further retarding recovery, reformers were profoundly disappointed that all stocks and bonds already issued were exempted from regulation.

Realizing within six months that the bill was "unworkable," Roosevelt set out immediately "to loosen up the constrictions" and to extend federal regulation over the whole field of stocks and bonds, not simply new issuances. The act called for a wide range of specific prohibitions against all forms of stock manipulation. It proposed the creation of a new regulatory body, the Securities and Exchange Commission (SEC), to be comprised of five commissioners appointed for five years. Business leaders reacted with outrage at the idea of putting a government "cop on their corner." The New York Stock Exchange threatened to move to Montreal. Roosevelt sent a special letter to Congress warning that a "more highly organized drive" had formed against this bill than any other New Deal legislation. If any attempt were made to weaken or scuttle the bill, he warned, the members would have to answer to the American people, who were fully aware that "unregulated speculation" had helped precipitate "the unwarranted boom" and the "terrible" years that followed the crash. The bill easily passed. And eventually, the SEC became one of the most admired of the New

Deal agencies.

Legislation to regulate the banking community was finally signed into law on Day ninety-nine of the hundred days. The Glass-Steagall Act offered prophylactic reforms to check the signal abuses contributing to the banking crisis. That crisis had arisen, Roosevelt believed, when banks were unable to meet withdrawal demands because they had used depositors' funds to speculate in an overheated stock market. The new bill required banks to make a choice. They could pursue either commercial activities or investment banking, but henceforth, they were forbidden to do both.

During the debate on the bill, the Senate added an amendment calling for the federal government, in conjunction with insurance premiums placed on banks, to guarantee deposits up to a certain limit, which would shift over time. Roosevelt strongly objected to this guarantee. In a written note, he asked the members of the House-Senate conference committee to reject the amendment. "It won't work," he insisted, convinced that "the weak banks will pull down the strong." He even threatened to veto the entire bill unless the amendment to guarantee deposits was defeated. Nonetheless, after a contentious debate, the bill finally passed with the amendment intact. Roosevelt at once telephoned congratulations to Senator Glass and at the signing ceremony joked that the bill had more lives than a cat. "A good natured admission," Moley observed, "of his ultimate defeat on deposit insurance."

Yet, within a matter of months, Roosevelt realized that his staunch opposition to guaranteed deposits had been wrongheaded. The creation of the Federal Deposit Insurance Corporation (FDIC) gave depositors the security they needed. Over 90 percent of banks purchased the insurance by 1934, and within five years deposits had increased by nearly 50 percent. According to monetary historians, "federal insurance of bank deposits was the most important structural change to result from the 1933 panic, the most conducive to monetary stability."

In both these cases, Roosevelt tinkered with his original proposals and proved willing to compromise. The Securities and Exchange Act softened the severity of penalties while widening the field that would constitute transgression. After opposing the FDIC, Roosevelt gracefully accepted it, and, in the end, embraced it as his own successful and legitimate child. Nothing was set in stone. Nothing was final. For FDR, decision making and administration were parts of a living process. "We have to do the best we know how to do at the moment. If it doesn't work out," he assured Perkins, "we can modify it as we go along."

Given this penchant for improvisation, alteration, and modification, given the imaginative and proliferating nature of this template of supple leadership, it is unsurprising that Roosevelt is so often likened to a creative artist — "a real artist in government," according to the playwright Robert Sherwood. As an artist of the turnaround, Roosevelt had no finished model or maquette before him to enlarge and then impose upon the country. Rather, Perkins observed, he "worked with the materials and problems at hand, and as he worked with one phase the next evolved." And as one project after another took shape, so his deftness and skill continued to flourish. His intuitive touch became more confident and refined just as the country's confidence and trust in him and in themselves grew stronger.

At the close of the hundred days, when the special session of the 73rd Congress finally adjourned on June 16, Roosevelt let his gratitude be known. He spoke in praise of "this spirit of teamwork" that had "transcended party lines." He paid tribute to "the whole-hearted cooperation between the legislative and executive branches" that had embraced a "new approach to problems both new and old" and "has proven that our form of government can rise to an emergency and can carry through a program in record time."

When war came, Roosevelt liked to say that Dr. New Deal had metamorphosed into Dr. Win the War. While the two doctors faced different challenges, they shared the same practice, as well as the same DNA of leadership — a temperament that did not wear out the carpet worrying, that relaxed and thought out problems while conversing, that relished the joy of exercising leadership itself. When something desperate needed doing, both doctors leapt into the fray.

The doctor who set a target of enrolling a quarter of a million young people in the CCC in but three months' time made a dramatic call seven years later for a staggering annual productive capacity of fifty thousand planes to put America ahead of Germany within a single year. What at first seemed a preposterous goal proved "a psychological target to lift sights," fire the imagination of team members, and galvanize the home front into accomplishing the unobtainable. The educator who had lucidly explained the labyrinthine complexity of the banking crisis in his first fireside chat would later ask the nation to spread a global map of the theater of war upon their tables so he could point out "something about geography — what our problem is, and what the overall strategy of the war has to be — how each battle fits into the picture."

Roosevelt's gift of communication proved

the vital instrument of his success in developing a common mission, clarifying problems, mobilizing action, and earning the people's trust. His faith never foundered that if the people "were taken into the confidence of their government and received a full and truthful statement of what was happening, they would generally choose the right course." This reciprocal connection between Roosevelt and the people he served lay at the heart of his leadership.

Indeed, if ever an argument can be made for the conclusive importance of the character and intelligence of the leader in fraught times, at home and abroad, it will come to rest on the broad shoulders of Franklin Delano Roosevelt.

TWELVE:
VISIONARY LEADERSHIP

Lyndon Johnson and Civil Rights

"Everything was in chaos," Lyndon Johnson recalled of the hours and days following Kennedy's assassination. One shocking event cascaded into the next as the country watched in real time, aghast — the announcement that shots had been fired at Kennedy's motorcade, confirmation of the president's death, the arrest and subsequent murder of Lee Harvey

594

Oswald, the identification of Dallas nightclub owner Jack Ruby as the murderer, the speculation that both murders were part of a larger conspiracy related to Russia, Cuba, or the Mafia. For four days, from the assassination to the funeral, Americans remained transfixed before television screens as the three networks canceled all regular programming to cover the news.

This unfolding tragedy presented Lyndon Johnson with extreme danger yet also an unprecedented opportunity for action and judgment. A successful transition called for both the establishment of immediate command and the symbolic assurance of continuity. "The times cried out for leadership," Johnson later said. "A nation stunned, shaken to its very heart had to be reassured that the government was not in a state of paralysis." And beyond the nation, "the whole world would be anxiously following every move I made — watching, judging, weighing." As such, "it was imperative that I grasp the reins of power and do so without delay. Any hesitation or wavering, any false step, any sign of self-doubt, could have been disastrous."

"We were all spinning around and around, trying to come to grips with what had happened, but the more we tried to understand it, the more confused we got. We were like a bunch of cattle caught in the swamp, unable to move in either direction, simply circling round and round." With this imagery, Johnson harked back to his childhood in the Texas Hill Country, to the stories his grandfather told. "I knew what had to be done," Johnson continued. "There is but one way to get the cattle out of the swamp. And that is for the man on the horse to take the lead, to assume command, to provide direction. In the period of confusion after the assassination, I was that man."

Even as he showed strength and assurance to the public at large, however, he exhibited modesty and deference to Kennedy's inner circle. In contrast to Theodore Roosevelt, who, in the wake of McKinley's assassination, had three years to gain his footing before facing the electorate in his own right, Johnson had less than a year before the next election. There was no time to build a new team from scratch. Furthermore, the retention of the important Kennedy men signaled respect and steadiness. In this contradictory role of beseeching power, as humble apprentice striving gradually to attain mastery, Johnson had long excelled.

Johnson approached each of the Kennedy men: "I know how much *he* needed you. I need you that much more and so does our country." Never once did he suggest that however things were done before, this was now *his* White House. "I knew how they felt," he later said. "Suddenly *they* were outsiders just as I had been for almost three years, outsiders on the inside." Checking his storied arrogance, softening his tone, he conveyed a deep humility, sharing his doubts, continuously requesting patience, advice, and assistance. "There is much I don't know," he would say. "You must teach me." That so many key figures of Kennedy's cabinet and White House staff remained during the transition testified to the perfect pitch he displayed during this fraught transition.

So faultless was Johnson's performance upon his assumption of leadership that it appeared as if he had long rehearsed what he would do if he held the power and the time were ripe. Suddenly, the time was right. He chanced to hold the power and he intended to use it.

Everyone agreed that Lyndon Johnson was a master mechanic of the legislative process. What became apparent from the first hours of his presidency, however, was that he meant to use these unparalleled skills in the service of a full-blown vision of the role government should play in the lives of the people. From the outset, he knew exactly where he wanted to take the country in domestic affairs and he had a working idea of how to get there.

After landing in the nation's capital at 6 p.m. of the day of the assassination, he reached out by phone to scores of people, including former presidents Harry Truman and Dwight Eisenhower, and met with a delegation of congressional leaders in his vice presidential office in the Executive Office Building. At 10 p.m., he returned to "The Elms," his three-story residence in Spring Valley, Washington, with a small group of advisers and friends. "Spend the night with me," he entreated three close aides, Jack Valenti, Cliff Carter, and Bill Moyers. More than ever, he did not want to be alone. After this cataclysmic day, he especially needed an intimate circle of listeners to sort out his thoughts and to get his bearings. An hour later, after Lady Bird went to sleep in her own bedroom, Johnson put on his pajamas, and with the three men propped beside him on his immense bed, held forth as they all watched the nonstop reportage of the world-riveting story on the television.

In the early morning hours, Valenti recalled, "the new president began to ruminate aloud about his plans, his objectives, the great goals he was bound to attain." In his mind's eye he could already envision a future in which all of Kennedy's progressive legislation, then deadlocked in Congress, had become law: "I'm going to get Kennedy's tax cut out of the Senate Finance Committee, and we're going to get this economy humming again. Then I'm going to pass Kennedy's civil rights bill, which has been hung up too long in the

Congress. And I'm going to pass it without changing a single comma or a word. After that we'll pass legislation that allows everyone anywhere in the country to vote, with all the barriers down. And that's not all. We're going to get a law that says every boy and girl in this country, no matter how poor, or the color of their skin, or the region they come from, is going to be able to get all the education they can take by loan, scholarship, or grant, right from the federal government. And I aim to pass Harry Truman's medical insurance bill that got nowhere before."

The somnolent vice president seemed magically reawakened as he revealed a rudimentary sketch of what would become the Great Society. This might seem an apocryphal tale had not three aides been there until 3 a.m. to witness his fierce resolve not simply to dislodge Kennedy's stalled agenda but to realize a society built on racial and economic justice far beyond the dreams of the New Deal and the New Frontier.

The vision Johnson traced in those predawn hours had been incubating for many decades. From his populist father he had inherited the belief that the role of government was to look after those who needed help. "That's what we're here for," his father had repeatedly reminded his son. The seminal concept that government should use its power to better the lives of others had been consolidated during his work in Roosevelt's New Deal. It was further enumerated in his "call to arms" speech in the wake of his near fatal heart attack, and informed his maneuvers to pass the 1957 civil rights bill.

"That whole night," Moyers recalled of Johnson's musings at The Elms, "he seemed to have several chambers of his mind operating simultaneously. It was formidable, very formidable."

How was Johnson able to actualize this vision?

Make a Dramatic Start.

Lyndon Johnson's most important task, the necessary condition upon which all else hinged, was to convince his countrymen that he was capable of filling the brutally sudden vacuum of leadership. He had to dispel doubts, quell suspicions, and allay fears.

In this time of dark national emergency, the new president was inclined by temperament to act quickly. At each new position in his long career he had sought a quick, sure start, an attention-fastening moment. Now, the day after Kennedy's burial, he chose to make a major speech to the nation. This choice was not without risk, for, with few exceptions, Johnson had revealed an inability to speak persuasively in large, formal settings. The man who could exercise instant command over any small gathering had tended to stiffen when forced to stand behind a podium. And this address would be the most important he had ever delivered. "He knew," Moyers said, "that the people watching it were burning with questions, wondering, 'Who is that man?'" When he stepped off the podium, "they would either have confidence in him — or not."

Lead with Your Strengths.

From the start, Johnson made two important decisions. First, he would deliver his speech before a live audience at a Joint Session of Congress rather than before a television camera in the empty Oval Office. Congress had been his home for more than three decades, the source of his security, achievement, and power. Many in the audience would be longtime friends and colleagues. Also in attendance would be the Supreme Court justices and the members of the cabinet, the full panoply of legitimate succession.

Second, he would use the occasion to call upon his former colleagues to break the total legislative gridlock that had prevented every one of Kennedy's major domestic initiatives from becoming law. A month before the assassination, columnist Walter Lippmann had written that there was "reason to wonder whether the Congressional system as it now operates is not a grave danger to the Republic." Indeed, as an editorial in *Life* magazine had pointed out, this Congress had sat longer than any previous body "while accomplishing practically nothing." The inability of Congress to move legislation forward, Johnson agreed, was "developing into a national crisis," exposing America's democratic system to widespread criticism at home and abroad.

In choosing to focus on Kennedy's blocked domestic agenda, Johnson settled on the field where he felt most deeply involved, most confident of his knowledge, most comfortable in dealing with policy details. The arenas of foreign and military affairs, which had been the specialty and focus of the Kennedy administration, were uncongenial to him. And he was fortunate to come into office at an ostensibly tranquil moment in international affairs.

"If any sense were to come of the senseless events which had brought me to the office of the Presidency," he later said, "it would come only from my using my experience as a legislator to encourage the legislative process to function." Believing that Kennedy's death had created "a sympathetic atmosphere" for the passage of the stalled New Frontier agenda, Johnson planned to turn the "dead man's program into a martyr's cause." But the window of opportunity was very small. If he had any chance of succeeding, he had to move ahead at warp speed before the supportive mood began to dissipate.

Simplify the Agenda.

From the outset, Johnson decided to pare down Kennedy's domestic agenda to two essential items: the civil rights bill designed to end segregation in the South and the tax cut intended to stimulate the economy. Over many hours of conversation at The Elms, Johnson's advisers debated the wisdom of these choices. "At one point," attorney Abe Fortas recalled, one of the men spoke up forcefully against recommending "congressional action on civil rights," and most particularly against making it his "number one" priority. "The presidency has only a certain amount of coinage to expend," he warned Johnson, "and you oughtn't to expend it on this. It will never get through."

"Well," Johnson replied with an unambiguous answer, "what the hell's the presidency for?"

When Johnson entered the House chamber at noon of November 27, 1963, a hush came over the audience. "All that I have," he began, "I would have given gladly not to be standing here today." With simple eloquence, he set a tone of sorrowful humility that would blend a funeral oration with an inaugural call for action.

On the 20th day of January, in 1961, John F. Kennedy told his countrymen that our national work would not be finished "in the first thousand days, nor in the life of this administration, nor even perhaps in our lifetime on this planet. But," he said, "Let us begin." Today, in this moment of new resolve, I say to all my fellow Americans, let us continue.

In contrast to the Kennedy inaugural, however, which presaged a resurgent America in the world's eye with no mention of domestic affairs, Johnson outlined his hopes for domestic policy with hardly a nod to foreign policy.

First, no memorial oration or eulogy could more eloquently honor President Kennedy's memory than the earliest possible passage of the civil rights bill for which he fought so long. We have talked long enough in this country about equal rights. We have talked for one hundred years or more. It is time now to write the next chapter and to write it in the books of law.

And second, no act of ours could more fittingly continue the work of President Kennedy than the early passage of the tax bill for which he fought all this long year.

He firmly believed, Johnson said, "in the ability of the Congress, despite the divisions of opinions which characterize our Nation, to act — to act wisely, to act vigorously, to act speedily when the need arises. The need is here. The need is now. I ask your help."

In his call for action to fill the leadership vacuum, one journalist noted, Johnson appeared to have "modeled" himself "after the man he has most admired in his political career — Franklin D. Roosevelt." Just as Roosevelt had called "for action, and action now" to carry the people through a "dark hour" in their national life, so Johnson had exhorted us to show the world that "we can and will act and act now." Both men addressed a volatile, depressed, and fearful nation. Both men countered despondency and confusion and sought to give hope, confidence, and renewed direction. And both men ministered to a stricken nation and uplifted the country's morale.

By the time Johnson finished, the applauding audience was on its feet, many in tears. "It was a remarkable performance," critics agreed, "perfectly suitable to the most difficult circumstances, directly calculated to get results." Equal to the words of the address, his demeanor, measured pace, solemnity, and determination all conveyed that a genuine transference of power and purpose from the slain president to his successor had taken place. Headlines told the story:

Through this single speech, delivered to a nation still in mourning, Lyndon Johnson bridged what had seemed an impossible span. He had seized the reins of power and established a shared sense of direction and purpose for his sudden presidency.

Establish the Most Effective Order of Battle. While passage of the civil rights bill was the foremost of Lyndon Johnson's two objectives, the tortuous legislative path to get there resembled a maze filled with false corridors, pitfalls, and dead ends. After speaking with congressmen and senators on the Hill, Johnson concluded that he should first push for the tax cut before contending with the far more divisive issue of civil rights. Kennedy's aide Theodore Sorensen disagreed with this order of battle. Sorensen reminded Johnson that as vice president, he had been absent from the last Congressional Leadership Breakfast, where the decision had been made to move first on civil rights. Johnson listened respectfully to Sorensen, but on this procedural issue, he trusted his own instincts and experience rather than that of the Kennedy team. A straightforward charge for civil rights would prevent both the civil rights bill and the tax cut from succeeding.

Even if the civil rights bill could get through the southern-dominated committee structure in the House, it would be stopped in the Senate, where southern leaders were fully prepared to mount a filibuster, shutting down all other business until either the bill was withdrawn or its proponents managed to secure a two-thirds cloture vote to bring debate to an end. As long as the filibuster endured, no other piece of legislation could reach the floor. Such prolonged deadlock would only deepen the national crisis and severely wound the new administration's prospects. If the tax cut could be passed first, however, traction might beget a sense of momentum. With actual evidence of progress, the administration could then single-mindedly address civil rights.

Yet success in enacting the tax bill was by no means certain. The bill had lingered in Congress for thirteen months before its passage in the House and was now firmly mired in the Senate Finance Committee, whose chairman, conservative Virginia senator Harry Byrd, was guardian of the gate. The genteel southerner had the power either to keep the bill locked in committee or to release it to the floor. At the time of Kennedy's death (in a reversal of future roles) support for corporate and individual tax cuts came from liberals and opposition from conservatives. Kennedy's young economic advisers argued that tax cuts would stimulate the economy and expand tax revenues, which could then fund a range of social programs. Conservatives, preaching the gospel of the balanced budget, were ideologically committed to the fight against deficits. And no one represented this Old Guard frugality more categorically than Harry Byrd, who had elevated reduction of government spending into a crusade.

Searching for whatever might pry the bill from Byrd's clutches, Johnson ceaselessly worked the phone with various members of the Finance Committee. From Florida's George Smathers he gleaned that Byrd was determined to hold the bill in hearings until he could carefully evaluate the upcoming budget due on January 9. If that budget exceeded $100 billion, a "magic" line for him, he would prevent the bill from leaving his committee. With this knowledge, Johnson suddenly saw the glimmer of an opening. If he could shave the budget below the psychological barrier of $100 billion, perhaps a deal could be made that might allow the bill to come to the floor, even if Byrd would eventually vote against it.

In his courtship of Byrd, Lyndon Johnson spared nothing. On December 4, less than two weeks after Kennedy's assassination, Johnson invited Byrd to the White House: "Harry, why don't you come down here and see me tomorrow. I want to get some of your wisdom." A presidential limousine met the senator outside the Senate office building. The president personally greeted him upon his arrival and then played tour guide through the West Wing, the swimming pool, and the massage room until they settled down in the small room adjoining the Oval Office for an intimate lunch over Byrd's favorite potato soup and vanilla ice cream.

After reminiscing about old Senate days, the mannerly haggling began. "Harry, that tax cut is important to me, mightily important," Johnson began. "You know that we cannot have a tax cut without serious decreases in the budget," Byrd countered. "Yes," Johnson agreed, "but my latest studies tell me that I would be fortunate, really fortunate, if I could get it down below $105 or $107 billion." Both men knew he was starting high in the manner of all country dickering. (The working Kennedy budget was $103 billion, leaving a deficit of more than $10 billion.) "Too big, Mr. President, too big," said Byrd. "Well Harry, just suppose, and I say just suppose because I don't think it can realistically be done, just suppose I could get the budget down somewhere under $100 billion, what would you say then?" In that case, Byrd answered, "we might be able to do some business." Knowing that Byrd was a man of his word, Johnson summarily stood up and offered his hand. "Harry, you have made a deal. It's been good seeing you. I don't see enough of you." He then gently ushered Byrd to the door.

Honor Commitments.
Now the hard work of budget paring commenced. Members of Kennedy's team told him they had whittled it down as far as they could. There was no fat left, they warned; any more cutting would hit muscle and bone. But Johnson was adamant. "Unless you get to $100 billion," Johnson warned everyone, "you will not pee one drop."

"I worked as hard on that budget as I have worked on anything," Johnson recalled. "I studied almost every line, nearly every page, until I was dreaming about the budget at night." He recognized that to the ordinary citizen the federal budget was a boggling compilation of statistics — "thicker than a Sears-Roebuck catalog and duller than a telephone directory" — but to a president responsible for setting priorities, it was "a human document affecting the daily lives of every American." For Lyndon Johnson, as for Franklin Roosevelt, people lived behind the figures, people hoping for some form of aid from their government.

The campaign Johnson launched to reduce government expenditures cast a wide net. He consolidated federal buildings upon land the government already owned, ordered agencies to buy in bulk, and turned out lights in the White House, earning him the nickname "Lightbulb Lyndon." More significantly, he sent memos to each department, including the Pentagon, demanding lists of cuts. So intent was he to jump-start his domestic agenda that the largest cuts — more than $1 billion — came from the Defense Department under Secretary Robert McNamara.

Byrd had told the president he would have to see the budget in writing and have sufficient time for his staff to analyze it before he allowed the tax bill to move forward. Fully aware that Byrd's team would spot any gimmicks, Johnson reduced the budget down to $97.5 billion, leaving plenty of room for argument. "You can tell your grandchildren you were the senator who finally got a President to cut his budget." He wanted Byrd to understand that future judgment would be rendered upon this achievement, and he was more than willing to share the credit if it would enhance and speed along the present objective.

All along, Johnson knew that reciprocal trust was of paramount importance. So long as he fulfilled his promise, Byrd would keep his end of the deal. And in early February, the chairman finally released the bill from his committee to the floor. Still, time remained of the essence. The ordinary legislative process to move the bill forward through debate on the Senate floor, on to a vote, and then to the conference committee with the House, might take weeks, or even months. If this lengthy pace of business prevailed, if, as Johnson worried, "they just procrastinate, and put off, and shimmy around," then the window of opportunity to harness public sentiment for the martyred president would surely close.

Drive, Drive, Drive.

"No detail of the legislative process eluded him," White House aide Larry O'Brien said of Lyndon Johnson. "Every day, every hour, it was drive, drive, drive." No sooner had Byrd's committee voted to send the bill to the floor than Johnson called the chief committee clerk, Elizabeth Springer, to urge her to make all haste writing the majority and minority reports to send to the floor. How soon could the report be completed? he inquired. Told it would take about a week, Johnson asked, "Are they working any at night?" Tell everyone, he said, he would provide overtime. Thrilled by hearing directly from the president, Springer called back to promise that the report would be completed in three days. "Oh that's wonderful, I love you," Johnson told her. Immediately, he placed a call to the Government Printing Office to rush the printing of the report.

"There's a crew working tonight," the printer assured Johnson, "we'll keep the plant open and get the job done."

Once the bill reached the floor, Johnson worked with individual senators to hold the line against the attachment of a single amendment, which would "open the floodgates" and delay the process. He pushed all his cabinet officers to lean on wavering senators. To those who had planned to attend a foreign policy conference on NATO, he made it clear that he didn't "look with very much favor on their hightailing it around the world." The job they needed to focus upon was on Capitol Hill, not in Europe. Once the bill passed the Senate, he turned to the chairman of the House Ways and Means Committee, Wilbur Mills, urging him to use his powerful influence to speed the bill through the conference committee.

On February 26, three short months after Kennedy's assassination, the tax bill passed both houses. At the signing ceremony, Johnson lavished praise on Senator Byrd, chief among the half dozen men he had termed his "partner" during negotiations. That Byrd had allowed the majority to work its will despite his continued opposition to the bill was the mark of "a gentleman and a scholar, and a producer."

To sweep away stagnation, to get things moving in this lethargic Congress, Lyndon

Johnson had used every straw of the broom. Furthermore, he made it clear to Congress and his administration that he was now prepared to brush aside all other pending legislation to clear space for a single-minded focus on civil rights.

Master the Power of Narrative.
Lyndon Johnson, like Abraham Lincoln and Franklin Roosevelt, knew that people were "more easily influenced" by stories "than any other way," that stories were remembered far longer than facts and figures. So now, when talking with civil rights leaders and diehard southerners, Johnson told variations of the same personal story to underscore his conviction that the ironclad system of segregation that had governed daily life in the South for three-quarters of a century — the Jim Crow laws that prevented blacks from entering white-only public restaurants, bathrooms, hotels, motels, lunch counters, movie theaters, sports arenas, and concert halls — must stand no longer.

Every year, Johnson related, his longtime black employees — his housemaid and butler, Helen and Gene Williams, and his cook, Zephyr Wright — would drive his extra car from Washington back to Texas. On one of these arduous three-day journeys, Johnson asked Gene if he would take along the family beagle. Johnson was surprised when Gene balked. "He shouldn't give you any trouble, Gene. You know Beagle loves you." Gene was reluctant.

"Well, Senator," Gene explained, "it's tough enough to get all the way from Washington to Texas. We drive for hours and hours. We get hungry. But there's no place on the road we can stop and go in and eat. We drive some more. It gets pretty hot. We want to wash up. But the only bathroom we're allowed in is usually miles off the main highway. We keep going 'til night comes — 'til we get so tired we can't stay awake any more. We're ready to pull in. But it takes us another hour or so to find a place to sleep. You see, what I'm saying is that a colored man's got enough trouble getting across the South on his own, without having a dog along." At that juncture, Johnson had confessed, "there was nothing I could say to Gene."

He told another variant of this anecdote to segregationist John Stennis of Mississippi after the senator vehemently denounced the public accommodations section of the civil rights bill. "You know, John," Johnson said, "that's just bad. That's wrong. And there ought to be something to change that. And it seems to me if the people in Mississippi don't change it voluntarily, that it's just going to be necessary to change it by law."

Still another version of this story was told to civil rights advocates when asked why he was so passionate about ending Jim Crow. It was just plain wrong, he told James Farmer, leader of the Congress of Racial Equality, that Zephyr Wright, his college-educated cook, had to "go squat in the middle of the field to pee." It was humiliating. Something had to be done about it.

And now, for the first time, Johnson concluded, the country finally had the makings of a real answer for Gene and for all black Americans. If the civil rights bill currently stonewalled in Congress could become the law of the land, blacks would no longer have to suffer the indignities of an outmoded and cruelly unjust system of segregation.

Know for What and When to Risk It All.

The proposed bill surely contained the most flammable social, political, and moral issues — and the most deeply personal ones — Johnson had ever taken on. The chances of failure were large. "My strength as President was then tenuous — I had no strong mandate from the people. I had not been elected to that office." The next presidential election was only eleven months away. Nor was the decision taken without a tremendous sense of personal loss: "It was destined to set me apart forever from the South, where I had been born and reared. It seemed likely to alienate me from some of the Southerners in Congress who had been my loyal friends for years."

And yet, "there comes a time in every leader's career," Johnson said, quoting Franklin Roosevelt's poker-playing vice president, John Nance Garner, "when he has to put in all his stack. I decided to shove in all my stack on this vital measure." As a consequence of the civil rights movement, the country was changing and so was he. Johnson intended to use "every ounce of strength" he possessed to achieve passage of the civil rights bill. Civil rights leader Roy Wilkins was immediately "struck by the enormous difference between Kennedy and Johnson." Where Kennedy was "dry-eyed, realistic," Johnson was passionate. Both Martin Luther King and Whitney Young also came away from their first meetings with the new president profoundly impressed by his "deep convictions" and "the depth of his concern" for civil rights. Indeed, Martin Luther King told friends that "it just might be that he's going to go where John Kennedy couldn't."

Rally Support Around a Strategic Target.
In the House of Representatives, the civil rights bill was stuck in procedural limbo by Virginia's eighty-year-old autocrat, Judge Howard Smith. A defiant Smith had predictably used his authority as Rules Committee chair to prevent his committee from holding hearings to establish the rules of debate — without which no bill could even proceed to

the floor. Meanwhile, the frustration of civil rights leaders mounted, and in the streets tensions escalated.

As Johnson analyzed the situation, he concluded that only one option remained — a rarely used House procedure known as a discharge petition. If a majority of the members (218) signed the petition, a bill bottled up in committee would be blasted onto the floor. Since House members generally felt protective of seniority and the traditional committee system, however, only a handful of discharge petitions had ever become law.

Johnson acknowledged that it was "a mighty hard route," but at the same time he understood that the fight for 218 signatures would give civil rights supporters a specific target to consolidate what was otherwise an ill-organized campaign. And he knew that for Judge Smith, no charm offensive would work; without coercion, Smith would "piddle along," delaying hearings all through winter and spring until summer came and it was time for Congress to adjourn.

Johnson understood that direct presidential meddling on a question of internal House proceedings might compromise the chances for the discharge petition. So instead, he worked to pressure members from the outside in. During his first two weeks in office, he met with civil rights leaders, liberal groups, union leaders, church groups, and members of the Business Council. He reasoned, prodded, pleaded, and, in the end, inspired them to make the discharge petition their priority. Then, day after day, he followed up with dozens of phone calls, which, fortunately for history, he secretly taped. These recordings reveal the conversational dexterity of a master strategist at work, providing a far more complex portrait of leadership than the bullying transgression of others' personal space, the jabbing index finger, and the simple-minded quid pro quo generally described as the "Johnson treatment."

He began with civil rights leaders A. Philip Randolph, Martin Luther King, and Roy Wilkins. He didn't want to be quoted, he told them, but he suggested that they concentrate all their focus on getting "every friend to sign that petition the moment it's laid down." Call on your supporters in Congress. Go to see them. Create a sense of momentum. "This ought to be your-all's strategy. And I want you to be thinking about it." He reached out to liberal groups who had long been skeptical of his leadership. "If I've done anything wrong in the past," Johnson told Americans for Democratic Action founder Joe Rauh, "I want you to know that's nothing now — we're going to work together." He told David McDonald, head of the United Steelworkers of America, that "if there's ever a time when you really need to talk to every human being you could," this is the time. "They'll be saying they don't want to violate procedure," he warned everyone, and offered the talking point: "Just say that the humblest man anywhere has a right to a hearing."

The drive for Democratic signatures from the North and West quickly totaled 150, but to reach the magic number of 218, 50 or 60 Republicans would be needed. Talking with members of the Business Council and with former officials in Eisenhower's cabinet, Johnson disclosed a dramatic new line of argument. He told them to tell their Republican friends there was no longer a place to hide behind procedure: "You're either for civil rights or you're not. You're either the party of Lincoln or you ain't — by God, put up or shut up!"

In private phone calls to prominent journalists and editors, he laid out an attack against those unwilling to sign. "Point them up," he told the *Washington Post*'s Katharine Graham, "and have their pictures, and have editorials." Ask them, "Why are you against a hearing?" Whatever man is against a hearing to bring the bill to the floor where it can be voted on its merits, "is not a man that believes in giving humanity a fair shake." A few days later the *Washington Post* published an editorial, "Friend or Foe," which made the precise argument Johnson had outlined. "Let the members of the House make no mistake about it: the test is at hand. They will determine the fate of the civil rights bill by their willingness to sign the discharge petition before they go home for Christmas." This is no less than "a test of the capacity of Congress to meet an inescapable and historical challenge."

When, after two weeks, the number of signatures had climbed to 209 and was still rising, a ranking Republican member of the House Rules Committee approached Howard Smith. "I don't want to run over you, Judge, but . . ." Nothing more needed to be said. Smith capitulated, avoiding "the indignity of being relieved of responsibility for the bill." On December 9, he promised to hold hearings as soon as Congress reconvened after Christmas. When the hearings concluded, the bill was finally brought before the floor on January 31. The majority succeeded in striking down every amendment that would have substantially weakened the bill.

Between the moral force of the civil rights movement and Johnson's skillful use of the bully pulpit, a consensus had been built. While "to some people," Johnson noted in his memoirs, the word *consensus* meant "a search for the lowest common denominator," that definition belied the "prime and indispensable obligation of the Presidency" — to decide first what needs "to be done regardless of the political implications" and then to "convince the Congress and the people to do it." For Johnson, a successful consensus was the consequence of effective persuasion.

On February 10, by a clear margin, the House of Representatives passed the strongest civil rights bill since Reconstruction. The wheels of democratic government were at last beginning to turn.

Draw a Clear Line of Battle.

As Johnson prepared for the Senate fight, he made it absolutely clear that this time, unlike 1957, he would allow no significant compromises. "I knew that the slightest wavering on my part would give hope to the opposition's strategy of amending the bill to death." Uncharacteristically, the master bargainer and wheeler-dealer had drawn a line in the sand. And upon that outcome Lyndon Johnson's relationship to his heritage, to his political career, and most of all to his vision for the country's future, hung in the balance.

To make his position transparent, he invited Richard Russell, leader of the southern opposition, to join him in the White House for a Sunday morning breakfast. In less august circumstances they had established this intimate tradition many years before. "Dick, I love you and I owe you," he began. "I wouldn't have been leader without you. I wouldn't have been vice-president, and I wouldn't have been president. So everything

I am, I owe to you, and that's why I wanted to tell you face to face, because I love you: don't get in my way on this civil rights bill, or I'm going to run you down."

"Well, Mr. President, you may very well do that. But if you do, I promise, you'll not only lose the election, but you'll lose the South forever."

"Dick, you may be right. But if that's the price I've got to pay, I'm going to gladly do it."

"These few words shaped the entire struggle," Johnson later wrote. The two old friends knew each other intimately. It would be a fight to the end. Russell would do everything in his power to hold on to his region's historic past, to prevent the federal government from forcibly changing the local laws and the customs that governed daily life. "It's too late in life for me to change," he said. For his part, Johnson saw beyond the present struggle to a time when the old South would be freed from "old hostilities" and "old hatreds," when a new South would rise, "growing every hour," joined "in single purpose" with "every section of this country."

Russell told a reporter in early January that he "would have beaten President Kennedy," or at least forced him to make substantial concessions, but now, with Johnson, it would be "three times harder." Kennedy "didn't have to pass a strong bill to prove anything on civil rights. President Johnson does." The moment a son of the South begins to compromise, Russell explained, his credibility among northerners would be shattered. Both men understood that "it would be a fight to total victory or total defeat without appeasement or attrition."

Impose Discipline in the Ranks.

So, even before the House bill reached the Senate, Russell had begun mobilizing his troops for what would become the longest filibuster in American history. He prepared a tag team of senators to talk for four or five hours at a time, reading the Constitution, reciting poetry, excoriating provisions of the bill. While Russell feared Johnson's mastery of the process, he knew that history was on his side. Never had advocates for a civil rights bill been able to achieve the two-thirds vote necessary to invoke cloture and bring debate to a close. Even senators who supported civil rights were reluctant to cut short a procedure that held an honored place in the Senate, especially among senators from smaller, less populous states who considered the filibuster a final defense against being bullied by the majority.

From the outset, Johnson understood that Russell's objective was "to talk the bill to death," or at least prolong its consideration until adjournment for the Republican convention in July, when public events might well change the configuration of things. Johnson also feared that the longer the bill was kept from reaching the floor, the greater the frustrations of the civil rights movement, the more likely the chance that any flaring violence in the cities might stoke white backlash against civil rights.

The battle thereby became a tug-of-war over time. Civil rights supporters aimed to compress time, opponents to extend it. Frequent quorum calls were a favorite southern tactic to prolong time. If fewer than fifty-one senators were on the floor, any member could request a quorum call. The day's activity would be interrupted while senators were rounded up. If a quorum could not be reached, the Senate would be compelled to adjourn. The current legislative day would cease, giving southerners a rest until the following morning. If these quorum calls resembled a child's game of musical chairs, it was deadly competition, providing the means for stretching time until the Senate adjourned without ever engaging the bill.

When only thirty-nine of the fifty-one senators showed up for a quorum call one Saturday in early April, Johnson angrily reacted, telling floor manager and civil rights champion Hubert Humphrey that liberals had to learn the rules, that they couldn't be "off making speeches when they ought to be in the Senate. I know you've got a great opportunity here but I'm afraid it's going to fall between the boards." At Johnson's insistence, Humphrey created "a corporal's guard," a team of ten civil rights supporters responsible for mustering five or six colleagues to answer the quorum call. The duty list changed daily, Humphrey recalled, "recognizing that some senators had to be away part of the time," especially those up for reelection.

That civil rights supporters never afterward missed a quorum call was theatrically apparent during the Washington Senators' opening day baseball game. President Johnson had invited dozens of senators to join him. A small group of southerners who had stayed behind to continue the filibuster took advantage of the absence and called for a quorum. "Attention please! Attention please!" the public address system blared, carrying the message through D.C. Stadium. "All senators must report back to the Senate for a quorum call!" A fleet of limousines pulled up to the park and carried the senators back to the Senate floor to meet the quorum call in twenty-three minutes. For the first time in the long struggle to pass meaningful civil rights legislation, the parliamentary skill and discipline of the southern contingent was met by the equally organized ranks of civil rights supporters.

Identify the Key to Success. Put Ego Aside.

A legendary nose-counter, Lyndon Johnson was certain "that without Republican support" (given the sectional split in the Democratic Party) "we'd have absolutely no chance of securing the two-thirds vote to defeat the filibuster. And I knew there was but one man who could secure us that support, the senator from Illinois, Everett Dirksen." Just as he had identified Senate finance chair Harry Byrd as the key to success in the tax struggle, so now he saw that Republican minority leader Dirksen was the one man able to corral the twenty-five or so Republicans needed to invoke cloture.

"The bill can't pass unless you get Ev Dirksen," Johnson instructed Humphrey. "You and I are going to get Ev. It's going to take time. But we're going to *get* him. You make up your mind now that you've got to spend time with Ev Dirksen. You've got to let him have a piece of the action. He's got to look good all the time. Don't let those bomb throwers talk you out of seeing Dirksen. Yet get in there to see Dirksen. You drink with Dirksen! You talk with Dirksen! You listen to Dirksen!"

Johnson told Humphrey that civil rights leaders, who might be chary of working with the conservative Dirksen, must understand that "unless we have the Republicans joining us," unless we "make this an American bill and not just a Democratic bill," there will be "mutiny in this goddamn country." Bipartisan unity was essential to placate the turbulence that would likely follow if the bill passed. To NAACP leader Roy Wilkins, Johnson made a similar plea: "I think you're all going to have to sit down and persuade Dirksen this in the interest of the Republican Party and I think that he must know that if he helps you then you're going to help him." This issue at hand transcended party politics.

If letting Dirksen take center stage, even to the point of eclipsing both his own role and that of his Democratic colleagues, was essential to achieve effective harmony between the unfolding events in the political arena and in the volatile cities across the country, Johnson was more than ready to oblige.

Take the Measure of the Man.
Like a tailor stitching a bespoke suit, Lyndon Johnson took the measure of Everett Dirksen, just as he had of Harry Byrd, Judge Smith, and indeed, most of the other senators. A decade of experience with the Illinois Republican had taught Johnson that Dirksen had no hesitation asking for "a laundry list" of favors in return for his support on legislation. Now that pattern only accelerated as the filibuster droned on. Johnson would sit with Dirksen over drinks in the White House dispensing all manner of quid pro quos: a

judgeship in the 5th District, a post office in Peoria, a promised presidential speech in Springfield, an ambassadorial appointment, a federal project in Chicago. A thick pile of memos in the Johnson Library attests to their copious swappings and dealings over the years.

But this time, Johnson offered Dirksen something far more important than tangible favors. Beneath the flamboyant minority leader's penchant for grandstanding, Johnson detected a genuine idealism and patriotism. He appealed to Dirksen's hunger to be remembered. "I saw your exhibit at the World's Fair, and it said, 'The Land of Lincoln,' " Johnson pointed out. "And the man from Lincoln is going to pass this bill and I'm going to see that he gets proper credit." With a gift for flattery equal to Dirksen's vanity, he assured the senator, "if you come with me on this bill, two hundred years from now there'll be only two people they'll remember from the state of Illinois: Abraham Lincoln and Everett Dirksen!"

As the filibuster dragged on week after week, Dirksen began to play what might have become a "dangerous game." Unless he could thumbprint the language of the final measure with some amendments of his own, Dirksen could not bring his fellow Republicans along. Although Johnson appreciated Dirksen's dilemma, he balked at any public discussion of amendments, relegating the process of negotiation with Dirksen to Humphrey, Attorney General Robert Kennedy, and the civil rights leaders. In the end, the civil rights coalition reached an agreement on several amendments that did not alter the fundamental integrity of the bill. "We've got a much better bill than anyone dreamed possible," Humphrey assured Johnson. Once that agreement was reached, Dirksen took to the floor to announce his support for the bill. Quoting Victor Hugo, Dirksen said: "Stronger than an Army is an idea whose time has come." With the Senate minority leader fully on board, a cloture petition was filed, setting June 9 as the date for the vote. Dirksen's support notwithstanding, the civil rights forces appeared a half-dozen votes short.

The time had come for both the president and the civil rights coalition to shift into overdrive. In the waning hours, Johnson personally recruited several western senators, while clerics of all denominations reached out to their congregations. On June 9, after more than five hundred hours of talk stretched over seventy-five days, Humphrey was finally convinced he had secured the requisite sixty-seven votes. After a high-voltage, questioning phone call from Johnson, Humphrey stayed up all night to make sure.

When the Senate convened at 10 a.m. on June 10 for the final hour of debate before the cloture vote would be taken, every seat was filled and the walls of the Senate gallery were lined with people standing to witness the grand event. "I say to my colleagues of the Senate," Hubert Humphrey said, "that perhaps in your lives you will be able to tell your children's children that you were here for America to make the year 1964 our freedom year."

Tension rose as the clerk began the roll call. No sound was heard when California's senator Clair Engle's name was called. The fifty-two-year-old Engle had been hospitalized since April following surgery for a malignant brain tumor. The night before, after speaking with Engle's wife and doctor, Johnson had arranged for an ambulance to transport Engle to the Senate. Seated in a wheelchair, unable to speak, Engle slowly lifted his hand and pointed to his eye. "I guess that means 'aye,' " the clerk said, as the chamber erupted in applause. When the clerk reached the Ws, Delaware's John Williams recorded the 67th vote, shutting off the filibuster. Finally the majority could register its vote. There was nothing now to stop the passage of the sweeping bill that would vanquish legal segregation in the United States at last.

"Although I differ — and differ vigorously — with President Johnson on this so-called civil rights question," Russell said, "I expect to support the President just as strongly when

I think he is right as I intend to oppose him when I think he is wrong." For his part, Johnson had approached Russell from the beginning with affection and sensitivity and without a trace of vindictiveness. Clearly, both men loved the South, but Russell clung to its past while Johnson nurtured a different economic and social vision for its future, a vision stillborn without the changes this bill promised to deliver.

On July 2, after the House accepted the Senate's version, Lyndon Johnson signed the Civil Rights Act of 1964 before members of Congress and the civil rights coalition at a memorable ceremony in the East Room of the White House. He gave the first of seventy-five signing pens to Everett Dirksen, followed by Hubert Humphrey, the House leaders, and leaders of the civil rights movement. During the reception, Johnson reminded Lady Bird that this was the ninth anniversary of his heart attack, the profound experience that had altered his outlook on power and purpose. "Happy anniversary," she told him with a laugh.

And a joyous day it was. After the signing, Johnson's thoughts returned "to that afternoon a decade before when there was absolutely nothing I could say to Gene Williams or to any black man, or to myself. That had been the day I first realized the sad truth that to the extent Negroes were imprisoned, so was I. On this day, July 2, 1964, I knew the positive side of that same truth: that to the extent Negroes were free, really free, so was I. And so was my country."

Set Forth a Compelling Picture of the Future.

With the passage of the two top items on Kennedy's agenda — the tax cut and the civil rights bill — the prologue of what would become Johnson's signature program, the Great Society, had begun in earnest. Kennedy's stalled intentions had served their purpose as a springboard; now the time had come for Johnson to spell out his own progressive vision for America.

For that purpose, Johnson chose a May commencement at the University of Michigan, the place where Kennedy had called for a Peace Corps to lay out his own expansive picture of a future in which every person would share in the progress of the country. By building on the strengths of prosperity rather than on the necessities of Depression, the Great Society would exceed the New Deal. "For a century we labored to settle and to subdue a continent," Johnson told the graduates. "For half a century we called upon unbounded invention and untiring industry to create an order of plenty for all our people. The challenge of the next half century is whether we have the wisdom to use that wealth to enrich and elevate our national life."

From its first declaration, the Great Society was presented in philosophical, qualitative, and visionary terms. At the heart of his vision, Johnson later explained, was "an extension of the Bill of Rights," an enlarged definition of freedom requiring that every American have "the opportunity to develop to the best of his talents." To reach this goal he intended to wage a war on poverty, provide economic aid for both inner-city slums and distressed rural areas, make medical care available for the elderly and the poor, conserve natural resources, and much more. "We have enough to do it all," he said. "We are the wealthiest nation in the world."

"These are the goals toward which I will lead, if the American people choose to follow," Johnson had pledged when he accepted the Democratic Party's nomination in August 1964. In the service of this projected vision, he asked the people for "a mandate to begin." A mandate was necessary to harness the moment, to help direct and implement its possibilities, to give legitimacy to Johnson's mammoth aspirations. The true contest in this election, he declared, "is between those who welcome the future and those who turn away from its promise."

That election, which pitted Johnson against Barry Goldwater (viewed by many as an extremist who would dismantle the New

Deal's social network), yielded the sweeping mandate Johnson sought. His landslide victory brought liberal majorities into the House and Senate for the first time since Roosevelt's smashing victory in 1936.

The Readiness Is All.
While propitious circumstances — the sympathetic reaction to Kennedy's death, the landslide election, the strength of the civil rights coalition, a booming economy, and a seemingly peaceful world — created the context for the historic success of the 89th Congress, Johnson's gargantuan ambition, driving temperament, and unique legislative experience all converged to make the most of this rare moment of opportunity. To this day, the lightning pace of the 1965 congressional session, the quality and quantity of the landmark laws it would produce, glazes the mind. And without question, the generator at the core of this high-speed process was Lyndon Johnson.

For this moment, Johnson had long been in readiness. Even before the election and its decisive mandate he had begun constructing a legislative assembly line as original and daring as the assembly line that built Henry Ford's Model T automobiles. At the christening speech of the Great Society, he had promised to "assemble the best thought and the broadest knowledge" into task forces unbound by conventional thinking. "The standard method of developing legislative programs," he explained, "had consisted of adopting proposals suggested by the departments and agencies of the government." He had "watched this process for years" and "was convinced that it did not encourage enough fresh and creative ideas." Government bureaucracy was "too preoccupied with day-to-day operations," too "dedicated to preserving the status quo." What is more, as Johnson had gathered from his mentor, Franklin Roosevelt, "the cumbersome organization of government is simply not equipped to solve complex problems that cut across departmental jurisdictions."

By early summer of 1964, fourteen such task forces were already under way. Johnson had made it clear to each of the chairmen that he wanted them to set their sights "too high rather than too low," and that he expected their work to be kept top secret until, by Election Day, their completed reports were on his desk. Those reports were then distilled into special messages to Congress that recommended specific legislation. Ordinarily, a president might send one or two special messages each month to Congress. So comprehensive was Lyndon Johnson's preparation process, however, that in January alone he sent six messages to the new Congress. And in the following months, on a wide variety of issues, nearly sixty additional messages requested legislative action.

Hardly a week after the inauguration, haunted by an inordinate sense of how fleeting and fragile was this moment of opportunity, Johnson convened the congressional liaison officers from every department in the Fish Room for a discussion of his plans for implementing the Great Society. "I was just elected by the biggest popular margin in the history of the country, fifteen million votes," Johnson noted to the gathered crowd. "Just by the natural way people think and because Barry Goldwater scared hell out of them, I have already lost about two of these fifteen and am probably getting down to thirteen. If I get in any fight with Congress I will lose another couple of million and if I have to send any more of our boys into Vietnam I may be down to eight million by the end of the summer." Such shrinkage, he explained, was "in the nature of what a president does. He uses up his capital." All this subtraction added up to one gigantic goad: "So I want you guys to get off your asses and do everything possible to get everything in my program passed as soon as possible before the aura and the halo that surround me disappear."

"Momentum is *not* a mysterious mistress," Johnson liked to say. "It is a controllable fact of political life that depends on nothing more exotic than preparation." The separation of powers ordained that Congress held the power to decide what bills to consider and in what order to consider them. The executive prerogative, however, could influence and reformulate the legislative calendar by the order the president chose and the rate of delivery of the messages he sent to the Hill. To avoid crippling opposition to particular bills, he could withhold messages until problems were resolved. He could seek out desirable sponsors in advance. He could steer each bill to the most responsive subcommittee.

In pursuit of federal aid to education, for example, Kennedy had used up an entire legislative year. He had not preaddressed the central problem of how to include parochial schools in the prospective program without running afoul of the separation of church and state. That dilemma unresolved, Johnson would never have sent the measure to the House. Because of Johnson's utilization of the task forces, however, a remedy was devised beforehand whereby federal aid was dispersed not to P.S. 210 or St. Joseph's, but to impoverished school districts in general. Similarly, the task force on health care untangled the "Gordian knots" relating to doctor's fees. Only then did Johnson proceed with his first two messages — Medicare, designated as HR 1 in the House and S 1 in the Senate, and federal aid to elementary and secondary education. Both initiatives had developed substantial support over the years; and with time-consuming controversies now averted, they could easily pass, making room on the assembly line for dozens of additional bills.

Much as Henry Ford's streamlined production methods, conveyor belts, and moving chassis assembly lines had initiated a new era, so Lyndon Johnson's construction of an overflowing cornucopia of legislation (the ever-moving steps, the dramatically increased productivity) ushered in a new era of modern lawmaking.

Give Stakeholders a Chance to Shape Measures from the Start.

"My experience in the NYA," Johnson recalled, "taught me that when people have a hand in shaping projects, these projects are more likely to be successful than the ones simply handed down from the top." As president, "I insisted on congressional consultation at every single stage, beginning with the process of deciding what problems and issues to consider for my task forces right up to the drafting of the bills." Not only did Johnson put congressmen and senators onto his secret task forces, but he dispatched aides to the Hill for secret sessions with key members to determine what should be in both his messages and the drafts of his bills. Then, the night before each message was sent, he invited members of Congress to dine at the White House mess. There cabinet officials provided background information and fielded questions. Such a preview might have seemed "like nothing," Johnson commented, "but, in fact, it was everything." These preliminary briefings "put them in good shape the next day when reporters and cameramen began pounding the Hill for reactions." The members "looked smart before their constituents and that made an enormous difference in their attitude toward the bill."

The significance of briefings was underscored by his experience as a young congressman. "I was standing in the back of the House behind the rail as Speaker Sam Rayburn listened to the House clerk read an important new administration message President Roosevelt had just sent to the Hill. Several dozen Democrats were gathered around him. As he finished, a unanimous chorus of complaints rushed forth: 'Why, that message is terrible, Mr. Sam — we can't pass that' . . . 'Why in the world did you let the President send one up like that?' . . . 'Why didn't you warn us?' " After the crowd dispersed, Rayburn turned to Johnson. "If only the President would let me know ahead of time when these controversial messages are coming up. I could pave the way for him.

I could create a base of support. I could be better prepared for criticism." That Rayburn's "pride was hurt" Johnson immediately understood. "I never forgot that lesson."

Nor did Johnson's executive micromanagement cease when the messages reached the Hill. The assembly line he had created was not a mechanized process; it was made of individual people and required tending and consideration at every step along the way. An extended family of legislators, constituents, and lobbyists surrounded each bill, all demanding his personal attention. In the spring and summer of 1965 — before Vietnam spread its pall upon the Great Society — Johnson devoted most of his waking hours to the legislative process. A summary of the *Congressional Record* appeared at his bedside table each morning. Nightly memos from his White House staff detailed every legislative contact of the previous day, flagging special problems. "Pending legislation" headlined the agenda of every cabinet meeting. Each secretary was expected to report on the progress of his department's legislative program.

Nothing mattered more to the president than the passage of his Great Society program. An oversized chart rested on an easel in the corner of the Cabinet Room, illustrating the journey of individual bills: which ones were still in subcommittee, which were ready for mark-up or poised for debate on the floor.

Such information allowed Johnson and the members of his team to exert the necessary pressure at the right moment upon the right person to keep the process steadily advancing.

During the first ten months of his presidency, Johnson invited every member of Congress to the White House. Couples came in groups of thirty to be treated to festive dinners, complete with wine and cocktails, all at Johnson's expense. Afterward, while the men smoked cigars and drank bourbon with the president, Lady Bird escorted the women on a private tour of the mansion. These small dinners allowed the president and the members to relax, tell stories, enjoy each other's company. "There is but one way for a President to deal with Congress," Johnson explained at one point, "and that is continuously, incessantly, and without interruption. If it's really going to work, the relationship between the President and the Congress has to be almost incestuous."

At another point, Johnson likened the Congress to "a dangerous animal that you're trying to make work for you. You push him a little bit and he may go just as you want but you push him too much and he may balk and turn on you. You've got to sense just how much he'll take and what kind of mood he's in every day. For if you don't have a feel for him, he's liable to turn around and go wild."

Know When to Hold Back, When to Move Forward.

After the long struggle to secure the Civil Rights Act of 1964, Johnson felt that the dust had to settle before pressing for the next item on the agenda of the civil rights coalition — a vastly strengthened voting rights bill. Congress, he adjudged, needed time to heal the wounds of division. On a practical level, federal agencies needed time to develop enforcement procedures to integrate public restaurants, bathrooms, and theaters. And the American people needed a period of calm without renewed discord in order to assimilate the vast political and social impact of the earlier bill.

Johnson's commitment to the objective of voting rights was never in question. He told Martin Luther King at the start of the 1965 congressional session that passage of a strong voting rights bill would be "the greatest breakthrough" for African Americans, more vital than the Civil Rights Act of 1964. "Once the black man's voice could be translated into ballots," he maintained, "many other breakthroughs would follow, and they would follow as a consequence of the black man's own legitimate power as an American citizen, not as a gift from the white man." For the present, he entreated King to work with him on the rest of the Great Society legislation. Both Medicare and aid to education were at critical stages, and both were vital to the quality of black as well as white lives. Queued behind these bills on the prospective assembly line awaited a public works bill for economically distressed communities, a nationwide job training act, a revitalization of inner cities, expanded poverty relief, and much more. Let this agenda get through to help all Americans, Johnson promised, and voting rights would be the absolute number one priority in 1966.

Events in Selma, Alabama, would alter the entire landscape. An added cog was driven into the orderly timetable of Lyndon Johnson's projected order of legislation. In early March 1965, King and civil rights activists had taken independent action to mobilize support for a voting rights bill that would eliminate the exclusionary and punitive tests southern officials required African Americans to pass before allowing registration. Such sham tests included quoting the first ten amendments, reciting sections of the Constitution, or explaining the Fourteenth Amendment. The discriminatory system worked precisely as southern officials planned: of fifteen thousand voting-age African Americans in Selma, only 335 were registered to vote.

On March 7, an infamous day that came to be known as "Bloody Sunday," more than six hundred civil rights activists gathered at Brown Chapel in Selma to begin a peaceful fifty-four-mile march to Montgomery, the state's capital. When they reached the narrow Edmund Pettus Bridge, they walked side by side, singing "We Shall Overcome," the anthem of the civil rights movement. At the top of the bridge, they were met by state troopers and Sheriff Jim Clark's mounted posse, armed with pistols, nightsticks, bullwhips, and billy clubs. As television cameras recorded the scene, "the mounted men charged. In minutes it was over, and more than sixty marchers lay injured, old women and young children among them. More than a score were taken to the hospital." As the marchers retreated toward Brown Chapel, the mounted posse pursued them. The carnage, which was witnessed by millions of television viewers, mobilized the conscience of the nation.

"It was important to move at once if we were to achieve anything permanent from this transitory mood," Johnson recalled. "It was equally important that we move in the right direction." As demonstrations across the country spread in size and intensity, massive pressure was brought to bear on Johnson to mobilize the National Guard to protect the marchers who planned to resume their walk to Montgomery. Pickets surrounded the White House carrying placards designed to shame the president into action: "LBJ, open your eyes, see the sickness of the South, see the horrors of your homeland." Despite the terrible pressure, Johnson deemed the moment had not yet come. He feared "that a hasty display of federal force at this time would destroy whatever possibilities existed for the passage of voting rights legislation." As a southerner, he knew well that the sending of federal troops would revive bitter memories of Reconstruction and risk transforming Alabama's governor George Wallace into a martyr for states' rights. "We had to have a real victory for the black people," he insisted, "not a psychological victory for the North."

As people from all over the country streamed into Selma to join the march, Johnson reached out to Governor Wallace. He understood that Wallace was caught in a bind. As governor, he was responsible for maintaining law and order. Continued bloodshed would damage his national standing and hopes for higher office. Yet if Wallace deployed the Alabama State Guard to protect black citizens, his white political base would turn on him. "It's his ox that's in the ditch," Johnson figured. At a hastily arranged private meeting at the White House, Johnson suggested a deal. If Wallace *requested* help because the state could not properly protect the marchers with its own resources, Johnson would at once federalize the Alabama National Guard. Of utmost importance was at whose request federal force was brought to bear. When the troops went in, Johnson later explained, "they were not intruders forcing their way in," and "that made all the difference in the world."

With the immediate problem of law and order held in abeyance, Johnson focused on the major underlying issue — how best to utilize the Selma atrocity and the ensuing national humiliation to expedite passage of a voting rights bill. On Bloody Sunday, Johnson had directed Attorney General Nicholas Katzenbach to work nonstop to draft the strongest possible bill. By the following Sunday morning, the draft was completed. Through seven crisis-filled days, Johnson had outwaited critics and let the horrific events in Selma reverberate through the American people.

Now the time to push for voting rights had come. The question arose: how best to transmit the message and the bill to Congress. It had been nearly twenty years since a president appeared before Congress to deliver a legislative message. It was full of risk to bypass Congress and appeal directly to the people. Regardless, Johnson chose to seize this moment for executive advocacy with all the might of the bully pulpit. On Sunday evening, he summoned the leaders of Congress to the White House and asked to address a Joint Session at 9 p.m. on Monday night.

"I speak tonight for the dignity of man and the destiny of democracy," Johnson began, speaking with extreme deliberation. "At times history and fate meet at a single time in a single place to shape a turning point in man's unending search for freedom. So it was at Lexington and Concord. So it was a century ago at Appomattox. So it was last week in Selma, Alabama.

There is no Negro problem. There is no Southern problem. There is only an American problem. And we are met here tonight as Americans — not as Democrats or Republicans — we are met here as Americans to solve that problem.

There is no issue of States rights or national rights. There is only the issue of human rights. But even if we pass this bill, the battle will not be over. What happened in Selma is part of a far larger movement which reaches into every section and State of America. It is the effort of American Negroes to secure for themselves the full blessings of American life.

Their cause must be our cause too. Because it is not just Negroes, but really it is all of us, who must overcome the crippling legacy of bigotry and injustice.

Here Johnson stopped. He raised his arms and repeated the words of the old Baptist hymn. "And we . . . shall . . . overcome."

"There was an instant of silence," one White House staffer recalled, "the gradually apprehended realization that the president had proclaimed, adopted as his own rallying cry, the anthem of black protest, the hymn of a hundred embattled black marches." Then, in a matter of seconds, "almost the entire chamber — floor and gallery together — was standing, applauding, shouting, some stamping their feet."

The power of the speech was found not simply in its graceful rhetoric, but in its demonstration of consummate leadership at a critical juncture. Importantly, Johnson declared that "the real hero of this struggle is the American Negro," whose actions had "awakened the conscience of this Nation." Yet, he refused to scapegoat the South, making it clear that no part of the country was immune from responsibility for failing to accord justice to black citizens. "In Buffalo as well as Birmingham, in Philadelphia as well as Selma, Americans are struggling for the fruits of freedom." He reminded his countrymen that while the bill he was sending to Congress was designed for black Americans, civil rights was one part, albeit a keystone, of his vision for a Great Society in which *all* Americans would have "a decent home, and the chance to find a job, and the opportunity to escape from the clutches of poverty."

As he neared the close of his speech, Johnson returned to his own seminal experience as a teacher in the poor Mexican American community of Cotulla, Texas — the place where his ambitions for power were first joined with a deep sense of purpose.

> Somehow you never forget what poverty and hatred can do when you see its scars on the hopeful face of a young child. I never thought then, in 1928, that I would be standing here in 1965. It never occurred to me in my fondest dreams that I might have the chance to help the sons and daughters of those students and to help people like them all over this country.
>
> But now I do have that chance — and I'll let you in on a secret — I mean to use it. And I hope that you will use it with me.

The applause swelled to a crescendo, ignited by the manifest emotional conviction of this moment. "What convinces is conviction," Johnson liked to say. "You simply have to believe in the argument you are advancing." In this instance, Johnson spoke directly from the heart.

Even from his old friend and mentor Richard Russell came words that brought a gratifying smile to Johnson's face. While he couldn't vote for the bill, Russell told Johnson, "it was the best speech he ever heard any president give." More telling for the nation at large, there came a telegram from Martin Luther King: "Your speech to the Joint Session of Congress was the most moving, eloquent and passionate plea for human rights ever made by any President of the Nation."

Let Celebrations Honor the past and Provide Momentum for the Future.

Johnson orchestrated the signing ceremonies for each of his Great Society programs with the same concentrated care and intensity that he had bestowed upon every step of their march through the legislative process.

To sign the Elementary and Secondary Education Act, which Congress had passed in early April after years of wrangling, he traveled back to the one-room schoolhouse, the Junction School, where he had started school at the age of four. From California, he had transported his former teacher, Miss Katie Dietrich, who had taught all eight grades. By returning to the beginning of his own education, he wanted to remind others "of that magic time when the world of learning" begins to open before a child's eye. "As the son of a tenant farmer," he said, "I know that education is the only valid passport from poverty." Outside of a consuming career in politics, only the teaching profession had ever beckoned to Johnson. To honor that vital element of his past, he had brought former students from both Cotulla Elementary and Sam Houston High to the ceremony. To have the privilege as president of signing "the most sweeping educational bill ever to come before Congress" was, he said, the fulfillment of a dream. "A pattern had come full circle in the course of fifty years."

It was not sentimentality but Johnson's sense of history and gratitude that led him to abruptly reschedule the signing of Medicare from Washington, D.C., to Independence, Missouri. He felt it was an honor earned and due to former president Harry Truman in his hometown. Johnson wanted to remind the country that the battle for health care had really begun with the man from Independence. Congressional leaders and cabinet officials, including Undersecretary of Health, Education and Welfare Wilbur Cohen, resisted, citing the confusion resulting from so many people shuffled from the nation's capital to Missouri on the spur of the moment. Confusion notwithstanding, Johnson held firm. "Why, Wilbur, don't you understand? I'm doing this for Harry Truman. He's old and he's tired and he's been left all alone down there. I want him to know that his country has not forgotten him. I wonder if anyone will do the same for me." Johnson's instincts were right. Truman was deeply touched. "You have done me a great honor in coming here today," Truman said. "It is an honor I haven't had for, well, quite a while."

For the signing of the voting rights bill on August 6, Johnson chose the President's Room off the Senate chamber where Abraham Lincoln, on that same August day a little more than a century earlier, had signed a bill that freed fugitive slaves pressed into service by the Confederates. "Today is a triumph for freedom as huge as any victory that has ever been won on any battlefield," he told the gathering of civil rights leaders, cabinet officials, White House staff, senators, and congressmen. In just four months' time, "this good Congress" worked together to pass "one of the most monumental laws in the entire history of American freedom." Yet, even as he heralded the collapse of "the last of the legal barriers," Johnson insisted that the fight for freedom had only just begun. To achieve true social and economic opportunity, "the struggle for equality must move toward a different battlefield. It is nothing less than granting every American Negro his freedom to enter the mainstream of American life."

In each of these three ceremonies, far more than self-congratulatory fanfare was taking place. In Johnson's hands, they offered occasions to give credit to others, to survey the past and look forward to the future, to mark the moment when a legislative process was completed and the process of implementation had begun.

When Lyndon Johnson signed the Voting Rights Act, only 623 days had passed since Kennedy's assassination, since the night Johnson shared his prospective vision for his unforeseen presidency with three sleep-deprived aides. What was most astounding, exceeding the breadth and coherence of that vision, was that in a year and three-quarters Lyndon Johnson had accomplished everything he set out to do that night — tax reduction, civil rights, federal aid to education, Medicare, and voting rights. Moreover, the impact of these five landmark bills was greatly enhanced by their deep interrelationships. The tax cut helped generate three years of phenomenal growth, providing fuel for the Great Society programs without inciting "a class struggle between the haves and the have-nots." To receive Medicare funds, hospitals had to comply with the nondiscrimination provisions of the Civil Rights Act. Before long, all segregated hospitals in the South had vanished. The Voting Rights Act led to an exponential increase in the registration of black voters — which, in turn, led to a tenfold increase in black elected officials. Head Start programs widened horizons and increased the health of millions of underprivileged young children, expanding their chances to graduate from high school, enter the job market, and become productive citizens. With the help of Medicare, life expectancy was actually increased by five years.

And more sweeping bills followed in the three remaining months of the 89th Congress: a higher education act to provide scholarships, loans, and work study programs for needy students; a public works and economic development act; a national foundation of the arts and humanities to ensure that art, music, dance, and culture were not limited to metropolitan areas; a public broadcasting network; a housing and urban development act to expand federal housing programs and reinvigorate the inner cities. And finally, he signed into law a major immigration bill that abolished the discriminatory national origins quota system that favored whites from western and northern Europe. By opening America's doors to immigrants on the basis of their merits as individuals without reference to the country of their birth, and by adding a preference for family unification once the first members arrived, the new law shifted the immigration stream to Africa, Asia, and Latin America, dramatically expanding American diversity.

For nearly two years, under Lyndon Johnson's domestic leadership, Republicans and Democrats had toiled together to engineer the greatest advances in civil rights since the

Civil War and to launch a comprehensive, progressive vision of American society that would leave a permanent imprint on the national landscape. When Congress adjourned in late October 1965, the *New York Times* hailed the restoration of productive "relations between the executive branch and the legislative branch that had been missing for years." Columnists noted the unusual concatenation of circumstances that led to "the legislative harvest," including the emotional consequences of Kennedy's death, sustained economic growth, and huge liberal majorities in the Congress. All these factors notwithstanding, it was generally agreed that the prodigious record of the 89th Congress was "above all the record of a great legislative leader who had suddenly become President of the United States."

The right man at the right time in the right place had come as close as any president to envisioning and pursuing what Abraham Lincoln had once defined as the object of a free government — to provide all its citizens with "an open field and a fair chance" to use their "industry, enterprise and intelligence" to compete "in the race of life."

At this glorious summit of achievement, it would have been inconceivable to imagine that this president's consummate exercise of leadership was drawing to a close. Yet, as the terrain shifted from domestic politics to the war in Vietnam, Lyndon Johnson demonstrated an epic failure of leadership that would compromise his credibility and trust, forever scar his legacy, and nearly tear the country apart.

CODA

How did the visionary leadership Lyndon Johnson exhibited from the day of Kennedy's assassination come to abandon him so utterly when he dealt with foreign affairs and Vietnam?

From the first day of his presidency, when engaging domestic affairs and civil rights, Johnson had a concrete vision of the goals he wanted to achieve and a clear strategy for how to rouse Congress and the people to attain those goals. By contrast, when he drew his countrymen into a ground war in Vietnam he was motivated less by a set of positive goals than by a powerful sense of what he wanted to avoid — failure, loss, and a humiliating defeat for himself and his country.

Only weeks after becoming president, while focused full-bore on Kennedy's stalled legislative program, Johnson was warned by his military advisers that unless the tide of the war was reversed by greater involvement on America's part, South Vietnam might succumb to communism within a matter of months. "It just worries the hell out of me,"

Johnson told his national security adviser, McGeorge Bundy, explaining, "I don't think it's worth fighting for and I don't think we can get out. And it's just the biggest damn mess I ever saw." However troublesome Vietnam was for his military advisers in those early days, for Johnson the war was on the back burner of an enormous stove. What he initially wanted was simply containment of the problem, protection against making a serious error that might in any way compromise the momentum of his domestic vision.

What emerged was an incremental decision-making process, a course predicated as much on what *not* to do as on what to do. The leader whose entire persona was built upon an aura of "can do," found himself in a reactive posture at odds with his active, driving temperament. Lacking the self-confidence he radiated in domestic affairs, the judgment that allowed him to override domestic advice that contradicted his own instincts born of long experience, Johnson heeded the counsel of a small circle of holdover cabinet members and advisers — "the best and the brightest." By and large, that cadre represented the established wisdom, the shared generational predisposition that the war was a struggle between communism and democracy, that losing the struggle would incite the falling dominoes of communist aggression and profoundly weaken America in the Cold War.

While in the domestic arena he had called upon task forces outside of government to solicit new ideas and approaches unbound by conventional thinking, here he failed to reach out either to dissenters within his own administration or to Southeast Asia scholars in universities and think tanks. He ignored those who argued that South Vietnam was not vital to America's national security, that its loss at that moment, before major U.S. escalation, would likely be interpreted as a setback to the Free World rather than solely an American defeat.

Piecemeal, without a clear strategic agenda or narrative, Johnson's decision making lacked both coherence and conviction. After Viet Cong guerrillas raided the barracks of U.S. advisers in February 1965, he approved retaliatory air strikes against targets in North Vietnam. Next, he added troops to protect the air bases from which the air raids were launched. Shortly thereafter, he sent more troops to protect the marines — the same marines who were there to protect the air bases. By April, more than fifty thousand troops were in South Vietnam. The mission was no longer to protect the air bases but to permit participation in active combat if nearby Vietnamese units were in trouble. By June, permission had been granted to commit American troops to combat, in conjunction with Vietnamese forces or on their own.

All his life Johnson had believed that every man had his price, that if he could sit down and look that man in the eye, he would figure the cost of compromise. If he could only get into a room with Ho Chi Minh, he was sure he could convince him to recognize the strength of the forces against him. The war, Johnson said, would be "like a filibuster — enormous resistance at first, then a steady whittling away, then Ho hurrying to get it over with." Holding fast to the belief that this was a battle between two antagonistic groups with negotiable interests, Johnson never recognized that the war in Vietnam was a civil war, a social revolution, and that the will of the North Vietnamese, fighting in and for their own country, was stronger than that of their American-bolstered counterparts in the South.

When bombing failed to bring the uncompromising North to the table, the baffled Johnson offered to transplant a benevolent American dream onto Vietnamese soil. The terrible paradox of his position cannot escape notice: While his left hand continued to raze the Vietnamese landscape, his right hand proposed a billion-dollar project for the social and economic betterment of both Vietnams. He would dam the Mekong River to generate such vast amounts of power as to overshadow the New Deal's Tennessee Valley Authority. He had seen it all before in miniature with the electrification of the Hill Country. He would establish new schools, new roads, new houses and bring "the wonders of modern medicine" to small villages. From mounting destruction and desolation would come the reconstruction of a Vietnamese Great Society.

By July 1965, it was clear that neither the sustained bombing nor the promises of development would bring North Vietnam to halt their infiltration of the South. Johnson's inner circle of advisers told him once more that the South was in danger of collapse. To "stave off defeat," they recommended a massive expansion of American troops (eventually reaching more than 500,000), and once more he capitulated. They urged him to order the mobilization of 235,000 reservists, declare a "state of emergency," put the economy on a wartime footing, ask Congress for higher taxes to pay for the war, and let the people know that we were embarked upon a major war.

Nowhere is the failure of leadership more pronounced than in decisions made that July. While accepting recommendations for a major war expansion, Johnson simultaneously rejected counsel to inform Congress and country of the likelihood of a protracted and costly struggle. Thereafter, Lyndon Johnson unquestionably owned the war. Determined to keep voting rights, immigration reform, and prospective Great Society legislation moving forward, he decided instead to tell Congress and the public no more about the war than was absolutely necessary. "I could see and almost touch my youthful dream of improving life for more people than any other leader including FDR," he later said. "I had no choice but to keep my foreign policy in the wings. I knew the Congress as well as I know Lady Bird, and I knew that the day it exploded into a major debate on the war, that day would be the beginning of the end of the Great Society."

In sum, all the skills Johnson had utilized to construct the Great Society were now employed with negative force to conceal the full extent and nature of the war from the American people. To avoid a dramatic announcement of the need for more men, he increased draft calls and extended enlistments rather than mobilize reserves. He folded the announcement of an additional fifty thousand troops into a crowded midday press conference. He refused to ask Congress for a war tax. While formerly he had toiled to shave the budget in order to dislodge the tax cut from legislative limbo, he now adroitly manipulated the budget to obscure rising defense costs, a decision that eventually stoked inflation and squeezed the very domestic programs he sought to protect.

As the war dragged on month after month, year after year — from 1965 to 1968 —

public dissatisfaction deepened. Demonstrations that began on American campuses spilled onto the streets, with crowds reaching tens of thousands in city after city. When Arkansas senator J. William Fulbright initiated hearings that provided public debate on the conduct of the war, Johnson was unwilling to listen. Ravenous for information in favorable times, he hunkered down, further narrowing his circle of advisers to those who agreed with his policy of slowly mounting escalation. Unwilling to shoulder responsibility when support for his leadership began to shrink, he found ubiquitous scapegoats — the press, the intellectuals, the ultraliberals, outside agitators. And all the while, he continued to deceive the public about the toxic slough the war had become.

Glaring evidence that Johnson had broken faith with the American people came in early 1968, when North Vietnam and the Viet Cong launched their Tet offensive deep within South Vietnam. Though the incursion was ultimately blunted, the televised films of captured cities and bloody skirmishes belied the administration's repeated assurances that the war was going well, that there was light at the end of the tunnel. It was too late now to placate or level with the public. A sense of betrayal had descended upon the country, the commencement of a terminal disconnect between Johnson and his countrymen. His credibility, already suspect, entered into free fall. A majority of people had come to believe that he had systematically misled them. Most pervasive and damaging, the loss of faith in this president would initiate a lingering mistrust in government and in leadership itself.

A central measurement of a democratic regime can be gauged by questions its leaders share with the public, how important decisions are explained and defined for the country at large. The business of war entails the severest sacrifices that can fall on ordinary men and women. In war, more than at any other time, the people must be sufficiently informed to understand the choices that are being made. In the end, no statesman can successfully pursue a war policy unless he has instilled a sense of shared direction and purpose, unless people know what to expect and what is expected of them. By all these standards of candor and collaboration between a leader and the people in the critical time of war, Lyndon Johnson had failed.

Finally aware of the full measure of public dissatisfaction with his conduct of the war, Lyndon Johnson struck upon a way to extricate the country, as well as himself, from the punishing bind of war. In a televised address on March 31, 1968, he announced that he was unilaterally de-escalating the war by halting the bombing in North Vietnam. He then startled the nation by stating categorically that he would neither seek nor accept the nomination of his party for another term as president. The reasons for his surprising withdrawal were, in Shakespeare's words, "as plentiful as blackberries." The public's affection and support — the life-blood of his career — were gone. Success in the upcoming primaries was anything but assured. He felt he had used up "every ounce" of the substantial political capital he had possessed at the time of his landslide election. His personal capital of vitality, energy, and resilience was dangerously depleted. And given his family's history of heart disease, he did not believe he "could survive another four years of the long hours and unremitting tensions."

Yet, beyond these political and personal reasons, Johnson's eyes were fixed on the verdict of history. By renouncing his candidacy, he sought to address seemingly intractable problems from above the fray. Perhaps, then, without the taint of self-serving motives, Hanoi might credit his peace initiative. Freedom from partisanship would also strengthen his hand in securing a tax increase, which by now had become absolutely essential to the nation's health. And closest to his heart, his removal from the race might successfully prod the passage of a third major civil rights law which had been stalled in

Congress for two years — a fair housing act designed to prohibit discrimination in the sale or rental of any dwelling on the basis of race, color, religion, or national origin.

The immediate response of the press seemed to justify Johnson's aspirations. Headlines trumpeted "Lyndon Johnson's finest hour," calling his withdrawal "an act of political selflessness unexceeded in American political history." Even his harshest critics, like Senator Fulbright, viewed his withdrawal as "an act of a great patriot." When North Vietnam expressed a willingness to come to the table, Johnson's popularity soared. In a matter of weeks, Congress passed both the tax surcharge and the Civil Rights Act of 1968, known as the Fair Housing Act. With this housing bill, Johnson proudly noted, "the voice of justice speaks again." For a time, the president looked and acted, one journalist noted, "like a man who had just invented peace of mind, peace of soul, or both." Johnson's euphoria did not last. The initial flurry of peace talks petered out. The war that had ravaged both Vietnam and America continued its ruinous course. The fault line through Lyndon Johnson's presidency would split his legacy and haunt him for the rest of his life.

EPILOGUE:
OF DEATH AND REMEMBRANCE

Just as there was no single path that four young men of different background, ability, and temperament followed to the leadership of the country, so toward the end of their lives they harbored different thoughts about the afterlife of leadership, of death and remembrance.

While their personal stories came to very different ends, they were all looking beyond their own lives, hopeful that their achievements had shaped and enlarged the future. The fame they craved, the recognition they sought, bears little resemblance to today's cult of celebrity. For these leaders, the final measure of their achievements would be realized by their admittance to an enduring place in communal memory.

Two of the four men died in office. Abraham Lincoln, at the time of his murder, was fixed upon the task of healing the gravely wounded nation. Franklin Roosevelt was mustering his ebbing strength for the prospect of tying up the war and preparing for the complicated peace in its wake.

Theodore Roosevelt and Lyndon Johnson both survived beyond their presidencies to experience the problematic aftermath of leadership. Theodore Roosevelt was never able to surrender his dream of returning to power. On the day he died, he was making plans to run for president again in 1920. By contrast, Lyndon Johnson knew, with a consuming sadness, that his days of active leadership had come to an end. The four years left to him were more bitter than sweet — as I was there to witness.

During his last months in the White House, Johnson had often spoken with me about going to Texas to work full time on his memoirs and the establishment of his presidential library in Austin. I was looking forward to returning to Harvard, where I was scheduled to begin teaching. When I hesitated and asked if we could work out something on a part-time basis, Johnson replied with an emphatic "No. Either you come or you don't."

On his last day in the White House, Johnson called me into the Oval Office. "I need help," he said quietly, "part-time as you wish, on weekends, during vacation, whatever you can give." This time I had no hesitation. "Of course I will," I said. "Thanks a lot," he replied, adding, "Now you take care of yourself up there at Harvard. Don't let them get at you, for God's sake, don't let their hatred for Lyndon Johnson poison your feelings about me."

I turned to go, but he called me back to say one more thing. "It's not easy to get the help you need when you're no longer on top of the world. I know that and I won't forget what you're doing for me."

So, in the months and years that followed, while beginning my teaching career at Harvard, I spent academic breaks and parts of summer vacations in Austin and at the ranch. I became part of a small team of former speechwriters, aides, and staff members assisting Johnson in the process of writing his memoirs. Happily, I was assigned to the chapters on civil rights and the Congress, but we all worked together, combing through files, preparing questions for recorded conversations with the president that were designed to serve as the basis for the book.

During discussions about the Vietnam War he would invariably stiffen, shuffling through his papers before uttering a word, his voice hardening and dropping to a whisper. Unlike Franklin Roosevelt or Harry Truman, Johnson was the type who would "wear out the carpet walking up and down worrying whether they had decided something correctly." Truman, Johnson once wistfully explained to me, "never looks back and asks,

'Should I have done it? Oh! Should I have done it!' No, he just knows he made up his mind as best he could and that's that. There's no going back. I wish I had some of that quality, for there's nothing worse than going back over a decision made, retracing the steps that led to it, and imagining what it'd be like if you took another turn. It can drive you crazy." Though rarely voiced, Johnson's regrets over Vietnam were turned over in his mind every day.

By contrast, when he recounted stories about work with Congress on domestic issues, his vitality filled the room. He would rise from his desk and stride up and down, employing his masterful gifts for mimicry and storytelling while impersonating Harry Byrd, Richard Russell, Hubert Humphrey, or Everett Dirksen, rendering vivid snatches of dialogue on the budget and civil rights. These were full-blown theatrical performances, the language enhanced by his facial expressions and extravagant gestures. His spirits aroused, Johnson was able to tap once more the positive energy of the early days of his presidency.

In preliminary drafts of the two chapters I was working on, I quoted directly from the arresting stories Johnson told, hoping to capture something of his natural speaking style, his wide-ranging insights, impersonations, and bawdy humor. "God damn it, I can't say this," he instructed me after perusing the pages. "It's a presidential memoir, damn it, and I've got to come out looking like a statesman, not some backwoods politician!" No amount of argument could persuade him that his repertoire of stories was appropriate for a dignified memoir. Consequently, his vernacular voice, outlandish depictions, and the swiftness of his mind were left on the cutting-room floor — only to reemerge when the recordings Johnson secretly made during his private telephone conversations from the White House were finally released to the public.

Johnson was never fully engaged in his memoirs. He repeatedly addressed the idea that history's judgment was already stacked against him. "All the historians are Harvard people. It just isn't fair. Poor old Hoover from West Branch, Iowa, had no chance with that crowd. . . . Nor does Lyndon Johnson from Stonewall, Texas." If such statements contained more than a habitual strain of self-pity, they also signified that he knew that his presidency had not been all he had hoped. His aversion to the memoir project also represented an antipathy to the completeness, the final tying up of his life's work. Finishing his memoirs meant that his long public service, his usefulness, was done with. "There's nothing I can do about it," he said. "So I might as well give up and put my energies in the one thing they cannot take away from me — and that is my ranch."

During these years, Johnson's altered appearance was striking. Gone was the slicked, groomed hair which, over time, grew into long white curls over his collar. His dark presidential suit and polished oxfords had been traded in for short sleeves and work boots. An informal atmosphere prevailed in the place Lady Bird called "our heart's home." Family dinners often took place in the small kitchen or, as in so many homes in Middle America, on trays before the television in the comfortable living room.

Even a cursory inspection, however, suggested anything but a conventional middle-class existence. A massive communications network enabled Johnson instantaneously to receive and transmit information to the world at large. In that era before cell phones, telephones floated on a special raft in the swimming pool. Phones were handy when sitting on the toilet, riding in any of his cars, or cruising on his motorboat. A three-screen television console allowing him to watch all three networks at the same time was built into a cabinet in his bedroom. If necessary, Johnson's voice could be broadcast on thirteen loudspeakers installed at strategic points on the ranch.

I would sometimes accompany Johnson on his early-morning drives to inspect his fields and give instructions to the workers. The grand disparity of power between the White House and the ranch lent an inherent pathos, even comedy, to the urgency with which Johnson conducted briefings with his ranch hands. "Now," he would begin, "I want each of you to make a solemn pledge that you will not go to bed tonight until you are sure that every steer has everything he needs. We've got a chance of producing some of the finest beef in the country if we work at it, if we dedicate ourselves to the job."

No detail was too small to warrant the label "HP," high priority. "Get some itch medicine for the sore eye of that big brown cow in Pasture One. Start the sprinklers in Pasture Three. Fix the right wheel in the green tractor." Status reports on legislation that had been staples of Johnson's night reading in the White House were replaced by reports of how many eggs had been laid that day. "Monday (162) Tuesday (144) . . . Thursday (158) . . . Saturday (104)." He initialed these daily memos and made further inquiries. "Only 104 on Saturday? Out of 200 hens? What do you reckon is the matter with those hens?"

When I think back over these years, my most vivid memories were the walks we took in the late afternoons after the day's work on the memoirs was done. Those walks, setting out from the ranch, traversed the actual way stations of Johnson's childhood. Less than a mile down the road was the house where he was born, painstakingly restored as a public museum. He liked to check the variety of license plates in the parking lot and track the attendance sheets to see how many people had visited that week, a gauge of how the winds of historical judgment might blow. Across the field, hardly a throw from his birth house, was the cottage site where his grandfather had once lived. There, Lyndon could find refuge; there, he would revel in his grandfather's vast world of cowboy tales and ancestral lore. On a rise further down the road stood the Junction School, where his formal learning had commenced.

Clustered along this road was the nucleus of his life: ranch, birth house, grandfather's cottage, school — and finally, across the road, beneath enormous pin oaks overlooking the meandering Pedernales River, the Johnson family cemetery. "Here's where my mother lies," he would say, pointing to her grave in the small burial plot. "And here's where my daddy is buried. And here is where I'm gonna be too."

Rarely was there a moment of silence on our walks, a moment not filled with the sound of Johnson's voice. He found comfort and relief in moving backward in time from his tumultuous presidency to the early years of his upward climb. He spoke with pride of his teaching days in the impoverished town of Cotulla, of the work he had done to introduce all manner of activities to his Mexican American students. He relished memories of working under Franklin Roosevelt, putting thousands of needy young people to work in the National Youth Administration, building roadside parks, school gyms, and swimming pools. He returned again and again to the story of how he had brought electric power to the Hill Country, and how electricity had changed the daily lives of thousands of farm families, letting them enjoy such modern conveniences as electric lights, refrigerators, and washing machines for the first time. He spoke of the joy he took in the passage of the 1957 Civil Rights Act, which, despite the weakness of its enforcement procedures, had opened the door to the far larger achievements of the 89th Congress during his first eighteen months as president.

"Those were the days when we really got something done," he said, "the days when my dream of making life better for more people than even FDR truly seemed possible. Think of how far we might have reached if things had gone differently." He sucked in a deep breath, shook his head, and exhaled, his expression revealing a deep and unsettling well of sadness.

Returning that night to my room at the ranch, making notes on what he had said, I asked myself a question I would ask many times in the years to follow: Why was he telling me all these things? Why was he allowing me to see his vulnerability and sorrow? Perhaps it was because I was a young woman and aspired to become a historian, two constituencies he badly wanted to reach, to persuade, to shape, and to inspire. Perhaps, to a lesser extent, it was because I possessed an Ivy League pedigree, which he both held in contempt and coveted. Or maybe it was simply that I listened with sleepless intensity as he strove to come to terms with the meaning of his life.

For the more we talked, the more it seemed to me that he believed his life was drawing to a close. Indeed, I later found out that he had commissioned an actuarial table while still in the presidency which statistically predicted, based on his family history of heart failure, that he would likely die at sixty-four. Only a little more than a year into his retirement, in the spring of 1970, severe chest pains sent him to Brooke Army Medical Center in San Antonio, where he was diagnosed with angina. He embarked on a strict regime of diet and exercise, but it was not long before he resumed eating rich foods, drinking Cutty Sark scotch, and chain-smoking. "I'm an old man so what's the difference?" he said. "I don't want to linger the way Eisenhower did. When I go, I want to go fast."

In April 1972, Johnson suffered a massive

heart attack while staying at the Virginia home of his daughter Lynda. Against doctor's orders, he insisted on returning to Texas to recuperate. Reprising his father's dying wish, he wanted to return to a place where "people know when you're sick and care when you die." Though he managed to survive his second heart attack, his remaining time was filled with pain. "I'm hurting real bad," he told friends. Mornings would begin fairly well, but by afternoon, he often experienced "a series of sharp, jolting pains in the chest that left him scared and breathless." A portable oxygen tank beside his bed provided only temporary relief.

Nine months later, on December 11, 1972, Johnson was scheduled to speak at a civil rights symposium at the LBJ Library. All the leaders of the civil rights community would be present: Roy Wilkins, Clarence Mitchell, Hubert Humphrey, Julian Bond, Barbara Jordan, Vernon Jordan, former chief justice Earl Warren, among many others. On the Sunday night before the symposium's opening, however, a treacherous ice storm had descended on Austin. It was unclear if the event would even proceed. "So cold and icy was it," library director Harry Middleton recalled, "that we got word that the plane carrying many of the participants from Washington couldn't land at the Austin airport, and they would have to come here by bus."

"Lyndon had been quite sick the night before and up most of the night," Lady Bird remembered. "The doctor insisted that he absolutely, positively could not go." Nevertheless, wearing "a dark-blue presidential suit" and "flawlessly polished oxfords," he headed out over the icy roads on the seventy-mile trek to Austin. Though he had given up driving in recent months, he became so agitated by the driver's slow pace that he took the wheel himself.

Those who watched the ailing former president ascend the steps to the stage knew that determination alone drove him. He struggled noticeably to reach the lectern. The pains in his chest were such that he paused to place a nitroglycerin tablet in his mouth. If this effort was to cost him his life, so be it. He spoke haltingly, acknowledging that he no longer spoke in public "very often" or for "very long," but, he emphasized, there were now things that he wanted to say.

"Of all the records that are housed in this library, 31 million papers over a 40-year period of public life," he began, the record relating to civil rights "holds the most of myself within it, and holds for me the most intimate meanings." While admitting that civil rights had not always been his priority, he had come to believe that "the essence of government" lay in ensuring "the dignity and innate integrity of life for every individual"

— "regardless of color, creed, ancestry, sex, or age."

Continuing, Johnson insisted, "I don't want this symposium to come here and spend two days talking about what we have done, the progress has been much too small. We haven't done nearly enough. I'm kind of ashamed of myself that I had six years and couldn't do more than I did."

The plight of being "Black in a White society," he argued, remained the chief unaddressed problem of our nation. "Until we address unequal history, we cannot overcome unequal opportunity." Until blacks "stand on level and equal ground," we cannot rest. It must be our goal "to assure that all Americans play by the same rules and all Americans play against the same odds."

"And if our efforts continue," he concluded, "and if our will is strong, and if our hearts are right, and if courage remains our constant companion, then, my fellow Americans, I am confident *we shall overcome.*"

This would be Lyndon Johnson's last public statement. By going to this symposium, Lady Bird later said, "he knew what he was spending, and had a right to decide how to spend it." The choice he made that day represented his hope that history would recall the time when he had been willing to risk everything for civil rights, to push in all the chips, the entire capital of his presidency. "If I am ever to be remembered," Johnson wistfully told me, "it will be for civil rights."

Five weeks after this keynote address on civil rights, he suffered a fatal heart attack. The man who needed to be surrounded by people all his life was alone. At 3:50 p.m., he called the ranch switchboard for the Secret Service. By the time they reached his bedroom, Lyndon Johnson was dead. As he had long foretold, he was sixty-four years old. Three days later, he was buried in the family cemetery, in the sheltering shade of the massive oak trees.

Whenever Theodore Roosevelt held forth upon leadership, death, and remembrance (which was often), he sprayed sparks in every direction, like a man sharpening his blade on a grindstone. At times, he seemed to scorn the vainglory of posthumous fame. "As the ages roll by," he suggested, it was only a matter of time "before the memory of the mighty fades." It might take a hundred, a thousand years, or even ten thousand years, but eventually "the inevitable oblivion, steadily flooding the sands of time, effaces the scratches on the sand we call history." Yet, on other occasions, Roosevelt replaced this dismissive perspective toward personal remembrance with the romantic heroism of dying "in the harness at the zenith of one's fame" with the consciousness of having "work worth doing" and doing it well. "In the days and hours before dying," he speculated, "it must be pleasant to feel that you have done your part as a man and have not yet been thrown aside as useless."

For such an aggressive, self-propelled spirit, a tranquil retirement was out of the question. A restless and frantic search for meaning, service, duty, and adventure would haunt Theodore Roosevelt for the remainder of his days. The youngest man to ascend to the presidency, he was only fifty years old when his seven-and-a-half-year tenure was done. He was the youngest former president in our history. Anathema was a life without a definitive and challenging task to perform and a spotlight in which to perform it. His daughter Alice quipped that he so fiercely craved being at the center of action that he wanted to be the baby at the baptism, the bride at the wedding, and the corpse at the funeral.

He had savored "every hour" of being president, "the greatest office in the world." He had been fortunate, he realized, having chanced to lead the nation at a time when his dragon-slaying, trust-busting, crisis-management leadership style found an answering chord in the public. He frequently spoke of the zeitgeist, and how it shifted like a kaleidoscope to attract or discard particular capacities at particular times. The harmonic congruence between the times and Theodore

Roosevelt reached a pinnacle in 1904, when, after serving out three and a half years of President William McKinley's term, he had won election in his own right by what was then "the greatest popular majority and the greatest electoral majority ever given to a candidate for President."

Nonetheless, at the moment of this great victory, he had stunningly announced that he would not run for the presidency again, citing "the wise custom which limits the President to two terms," a duration which he would have essentially completed by 1908. He feared that even his most fervent supporters would be disappointed by the unseemly ambition to hold office "longer than it was deemed wise for Washington to hold it." With unusual care for a sitting leader, he picked and groomed a successor, his friend and cabinet member William Howard Taft. Furthermore, he worked assiduously to engineer Taft's nomination at the head of the Republican ticket. No sooner had the Republican convention opened, however, than remorse settled upon him. "I would cut my hand off right there," he told a friend, pointing to his wrist, "if I could recall that written statement." Had Roosevelt given the slightest indication to the delegates that he had changed his mind, the nomination would have been his. He felt, however, that he must honor the pledge he had made. "The people think that my word is good," he explained to his friend Bill Sewall, "and I should be mighty sorry to have them think anything else." Reiterating his unconditional support for Taft, he insisted that there was no man in the country "so well fitted to be president."

Immediately after Taft's inauguration, Roosevelt set sail for a year-long safari in Africa. "It will let me down to private life without that dull thud of which we hear so much," he reasoned; it would "break his fall" into life as a citizen. No sooner had he come home, however, than his characteristic restlessness returned. His agitation and fidgetiness flared when one progressive delegation after another journeyed to Sagamore Hill, urging him to run for president in 1912. Under Taft, they argued, old-line conservatives were once more in the ascendant, threatening the advances of past years. "Like a war horse scenting the sniff of distant battles," Roosevelt eventually threw his hat in the ring, challenging the incumbent he had once nurtured for the Republican nomination. Then, when Taft defeated him at the convention, he consented to lead the progressive forces on a third party ticket.

With the Republican Party split in two, "the only question now," Senator Chauncey Depew aptly remarked, "is which corpse would get the most flowers." From the start, Democrat Woodrow Wilson was the prohibitive favorite. In mid-October, however, a chance event threatened to upend the race. While Roosevelt stood in an open car in front of a Milwaukee hotel waiting to depart for a speech venue, an assassin raised a pistol and fired at "point blank range" at Roosevelt's chest. Had the bullet not been deflected by the metal eyeglass case in Roosevelt's pocket, it would have gone "straight into his heart." Defying the doctor's order that he be taken straight to the hospital emergency room, Roosevelt proceeded to the venue. Somewhat unsteadily, color drained from his face, Roosevelt delivered his entire speech before consenting to hospitalization. His stalwart response to the attempt upon his life brought a surge of support for his candidacy. "The bullet that rests in Roosevelt's chest has killed Wilson for the Presidency," one Democratic speaker suspected.

A week before the election Roosevelt had sufficiently recovered to deliver his final speech of the campaign at Carnegie Hall. In contrast to the caustic tone toward opponents that had marked his campaign, he now focused solely on the principles for which the Progressive Party stood. He believed, he told his spellbound audience, that "perhaps once in a generation" the time comes for the people to enter the battle for social justice. If the continuing problems created by the Industrial Age were not addressed, he warned, the country would eventually be "sundered by those dreadful lines of division" that set "the haves" and the "have-nots" against one another. "Win or lose I am glad beyond measure that I am one of the many who in this fight have stood ready to spend and be spent."

Though Roosevelt garnered far and away the largest percentage of votes any third party candidate had ever received, Woodrow Wilson carried the election. More damaging still, the split party had hurt the very progressive cause Roosevelt championed. In one state after another, Republican progressives, victorious two years earlier, were now defeated.

As had been true throughout his life when beset by political loss, personal grief, or depression, Roosevelt sought relief from pain in physical challenge, motion, and adventure. Just as his African hunting trip had cushioned his fall after leaving the presidency, so now, the fifty-five-year-old defeated candidate sailed to South America for an expedition to the unmapped River of Doubt in the heart of the inaccessible Brazilian rain forest — "his last chance to be a boy." This time he nearly died from a life-threatening infection, combined with a severe bout of malaria, which left him debilitated for the rest of his life. "The Brazilian wilderness," Roosevelt told a friend, "stole away ten years of his life."

Still, Roosevelt's impassioned supporters

refused to believe that his political star had set, pressing him to run for president in 1916. Roosevelt rebuffed their entreaties, casting a realistic eye on the temper of the times. "For a dozen years I held a great place in the confidence and good will of the American people and I was able to do many things which I fervently believed ought to be done." His great "usefulness," he felt, had come particularly in the settlement of the coal strike, in the national parks and wilderness reserves that he had set apart for future generations, and in the busting of trusts and the regulatory legislation that had created a fairer economic playing field. "While I have in no manner changed," he believed, "there have been such changes in the currents of thought" that it would be senseless to imagine that the Republicans, who "seem to be sinking back into a kind of inert and dangerous conservatism," would even consider nominating him. Indeed, "it would be an entirely unwise thing to nominate me, unless this country is in something of the heroic mood that it was in the time of the Revolution and again in the time of the Civil War."

So Roosevelt bided his time, feeling superfluous, frustrated, and depressed until a chance for vigorous action arrived in April 1917 with America's entry into the First World War. Roosevelt immediately sought permission to raise and command a division of volunteers. Long before, as a young man in the Badlands when border tensions with Mexico had begun to boil over, he had offered to raise a company of horse riflemen. He told his friend Henry Cabot Lodge, "There is some good fighting stuff among these harum-scarum rough riders out here." Later, he had famously succeeded in mobilizing the Rough Riders during the Spanish-American War. So now, he beseeched President Woodrow Wilson to allow him to raise a volunteer division. Applications for his division poured in by the thousands, but Wilson denied his request.

All his life, Roosevelt had displayed a disturbing, romantic grandiosity about combat. "The great prize of death in battle" was a reward he "ranked above all others." Once before he had even threatened to abandon his wife Edith's bedside when she was seriously ill, if given the opportunity to engage in battle. He claimed at one point that "all who feel any joy in battle know what it is like when the wolf rises in the heart"; in another instance he argued that the victories of war were greater than the victories of peace. His disappointment over Wilson's refusal developed into a serious depression when his four sons were deployed overseas while he remained in "do-nothing ease and safety" at home. When his youngest son, Quentin, was killed in battle, his grief was so deep that he felt the world had "shut down" upon him, finally acknowledging "a sickening feeling" that he had inspired his boys to take undue risks.

His fiery will rekindled more quickly than his body recovered. In speeches and articles, he challenged his countrymen to honor those who had died by working together to make the country a fairer and more equitable place, by setting in motion sweeping reforms "to bring justice under new conditions in a new world." Once again, his knight-errant style of leadership found a response, and before long Roosevelt was again the most popular man in the country.

Though he was urged to run for governor in 1918, he declined. "I have only one fight left in me," he told his sister Corinne, "and I think I should reserve my strength in case I am needed in 1920." The malaria he had contracted in Brazil had left him prone to fever, infection, and sporadic invalidism. A severe attack of rheumatoid arthritis sent him to the hospital for six weeks at the end of 1918. Cautioned that he might be required to use a wheelchair for the remainder of his days, he said, "All right! I can work that way, too." There were too many things he wanted to accomplish before he died. Still in considerable pain when he returned home on Christmas Day, he acknowledged that he would be unable to get out much for a couple of months, but he set to work drafting articles and editorials, talking with party officials, and, most importantly, making plans for the next presidential election.

He spent Sunday, January 5, 1919, dictating letters and proofreading a piece for *Metropolitan Magazine* that outlined a full-scale domestic agenda that foreshadowed elements of Franklin Roosevelt's New Deal. He called for old age pensions, unemployment insurance, an eight-hour workday, and collective bargaining. He insisted that it was "an absurdity longer to higgle" over the women's vote. He argued that government had a responsibility to ensure returning soldiers access to land and jobs. He proposed a universal national service program to mobilize young men and women from different backgrounds "to work in a spirit of brotherhood for the common good." Long before, he had predicted that the "rock of class hatred" was "the greatest and most dangerous rock in the course of any republic," that disaster would follow when "two sections, or two classes are so cut off from each other that neither appreciates the other's passions, prejudices, and, indeed, point of view."

At ten o'clock that night, after a packed day of brooding over plans for social and industrial reforms, he told Edith that he felt a curious "sensation of depression about the chest," as if his heart was about to stop. "I know it is not going to happen," he assured her, "but it is such a strange feeling." The family physician was called but found nothing indicative of heart trouble, so Roosevelt settled into bed. He never woke up. He was sixty years old. A blood clot had reached his lungs and stopped his heart.

A note was found beside the bed to remind himself to get together with Republican Party chair Will Hays. At Roosevelt's direction, Hays was planning a ten-day trip to Washington to bring Republican conservatives and progressives together around domestic issues. The split of 1912 had caused lingering distrust and antipathy on both sides. If Roosevelt were given another chance to lead the country, he intended to make the Republican Party once more the progressive party of Abraham Lincoln, to restore "the fellow feeling, mutual respect, the sense of common duties and common interests which arise when men take the trouble to understand one another, and to associate for a common object."

His last waking dream, the expression of his powerful will, had looked forward to 1920, when the kaleidoscope might turn and things align, enabling him once more to grasp the reins of the leadership that he so loved.

That death stalked Franklin Roosevelt in the last year of his life is clear, but only in retrospect. Certainly, by 1944, Roosevelt appeared far older than his sixty-two years. Many noted his gray pallor, the darkened hollows beneath his eyes, how his hand shook as he attempted to light a cigarette. While he attributed this condition and his nagging cough to the combination of influenza and bronchitis he had contracted that winter, his daughter, Anna, was deeply worried. She had grown accustomed to his amazing physical resilience, but when spring arrived, fatigue continued to dog him and his strength seemed to be failing. She asked her father's personal physician, Admiral Ross McIntire, to arrange a thorough checkup at Bethesda Naval Hospital.

"I suspected something was terribly wrong as soon as I looked at him," recalled the young cardiologist Howard Bruenn. "His face was pallid and there was a bluish discoloration of his skin, lips and nail beds." The simple act of moving from one side of the table to the other caused significant breathlessness. His heart was enlarged, there was fluid in his lungs, and his blood pressure was dangerously high. Bruenn's diagnosis revealed that the president was suffering from acute congestive heart failure. Throughout the exam, Roosevelt chatted amiably about a wide range of topics, repelling any serious inquiry with a shield of talk. Not once did he question the doctor. Nor did Bruenn feel at liberty to impose his findings upon the patient; he had been forewarned by McIntire not to volunteer information. When the examination was completed, Roosevelt flashed his celebrated smile, thanked the doctor, and left, cheerfully greeting patients and members of the staff as he made his way to the car.

Later that same afternoon, Roosevelt conducted his 945th press conference. Asked how he felt, he coughed and admitted he had bronchitis and had gone to the hospital earlier to have X-rays taken. Was he alarmed? Not at all, he retorted. He had heard that bronchitis developed into pneumonia in one case out of 48,500 so he figured his prognosis was good! Laughter filled the room and the reporters went on to their regular sequence of policy questions. "Not only were the President's color and voice better," the New York Times noted, "but his spirits were good, too." A week later, Dr. McIntire casually assured the press that the president simply suffered a lingering case of bronchitis. All he required was "some sunshine and exercise."

Concealment of personal matters had been a major motif throughout Roosevelt's life. He had been trained from boyhood to present a consistently confident and encouraging demeanor before his invalid father. During the six agonizing weeks he spent in the hospital after contracting polio, he had projected a

693

uniformly optimistic image. By buoying up others, he had learned to uplift himself. In his mother's family, Franklin's cousin Laura Delano recalled, "You just never said you were sick." Similarly, in the weeks and months that followed during the spring of 1944, Roosevelt chose to ignore his illness, always keeping the potential gravity of his condition at arm's length. He simply did what Dr. Bruenn's new regimen required without asking questions. He took digitalis every day and displayed no interest in his blood pressure readings. Religiously, he followed the prescribed low-salt/low-fat diet and shed so much weight that he quipped proudly, "I'm a young man again. Look how flat my stomach is," at which point "he slapped himself with a sense of glee."

Roosevelt's steadfast heartiness proved infectious. Innumerable accounts from his closest colleagues reveal that he was invariably able to rouse himself and focus on the task at hand. Even on days when he admittedly felt "like hell," he remained, according to one aide, so "cheerful in spirit" and "good natured" that he did not seem seriously ill. While Frances Perkins had been initially appalled by his appearance early that spring, she was so relieved at the vitality he exhibited when he returned at the end of April from a two-week rest at financier Bernard Baruch's South Carolina plantation that she "did not have another moment's concern about him until very near the end."

Yet no matter how much he tried to ignore the state of his health, no matter how brightly he burnished his image, Roosevelt knew that on bad days willpower alone kept him going. Why, then, did he decide to run for a fourth term in 1944? Four years earlier, in the spring of 1940, Hitler's invasion of Holland, Luxembourg, Belgium, and France had created a crisis for Western civilization that warranted breaking the cherished two-term tradition — in Roosevelt's mind and in public opinion. By the spring of 1944, he had already been in office for twelve years, the longest presidential service in American history. Should he attempt, he asked friends, to extend the shattered precedent once more and run for a fourth term?

In late May 1944, seven weeks before the Democratic convention, Roosevelt's indecision continued. The gargantuan jobs of ending the war and envisioning the peace to follow were far from a fait accompli. Hanging in the balance was nothing less than the survival of our nation and of democracy itself. A million men and supplies had been transported to embarkation posts in southern England, awaiting the signal to begin the invasion of Normandy. All the major European capitals remained in German hands, including Paris, Amsterdam, Warsaw, and

Athens. Japan controlled the Philippines. "Terrible decisions to have to make," Roosevelt's cousin Margaret Suckley recorded in her diary. In private conversations with Suckley, Roosevelt disclosed his dilemma. On the one hand, the future being so challenging, he felt a profound sense of "duty to carry on, as long as he was able." On the other hand, if he knew that he was "not going to be able to carry on for another four years, it wouldn't be fair to the American people to run for another term." The conclusive factor would be the condition of his health in the weeks ahead.

So immersed was he in the tasks at hand that events seemed to determine the state of his health and the level of the energy he had so carefully husbanded. His spirits rose with the news on D-Day, June 6, 1944, that the beach landings had been successful and that the troops, taking fewer casualties than expected, were advancing up the hills. In the late afternoon, Roosevelt held a press conference. "A great moment in history," one reporter observed. "The President sat back in his great green chair calm and smiling." His cigarette "was cocked at the angle they say he always has it when he is pleased with the world." Throughout the proceedings, another reporter noted, "he seemed happy and confident," though he warned against overconfidence. "You just don't land on a

696

beach and walk through — if you land successfully without breaking your leg — walk through to Berlin. And the quicker this country understands it the better." That evening, Eleanor observed, her husband "looked very well and seemed himself again, full of plans for the future."

Two weeks later, circumstances once more provided a tonic. Roosevelt looked "in the pink of condition" when he signed the G.I. Bill of Rights, the massive program of education and training for returning soldiers that would broaden the educational horizons of an entire generation. That Roosevelt had conceived the program eighteen months earlier, that he had begun postwar planning so long before the cross-channel invasion, was deemed, in speechwriter Sam Rosenman's judgment, "one of the greatest examples of statesmanlike vision." It was that vision, Perkins concluded, Roosevelt's uncanny ability "to keep his head above the welter of administrative problems," to see "the whole picture" and "keep his eye on the objectives of highest importance," that persuaded all the key members of the cabinet and White House staff that the president, regardless of diminished energy and health, was the superior man to lead.

Five days before the Democratic convention was set to open, Roosevelt finally offered himself for a fourth term. His decision was driven primarily by his considered belief — given his long experience and wide-ranging knowledge of the central players and the stakes involved — that he was the best man to carry the war to its conclusion and lay the foundation for peace. He announced he would accept his party's nomination a fourth time and serve as president if "so ordered by the Commander in Chief of us all — the sovereign people of the United States." A week later, the delegates to the Democratic National Convention nominated Franklin Roosevelt by acclamation as their candidate, a fourth time, for president of the United States.

In the fall, Roosevelt had to demonstrate that he had the stamina to compete with his young Republican challenger, New York governor Thomas E. Dewey. Roosevelt knew that his opponents were circulating a whispering campaign that he was no longer physically or mentally competent. "People have been asked to believe that I am all worn out and sick," he said. There was but one sure method to disprove such gossip. He had to put himself before the people and let them make up their own minds about his capacities. He had to conduct "an old-fashioned, rough-and-tumble campaign."

On a single day in New York City, three million people lined the streets as the president was driven fifty miles in an open car through

Brooklyn, Queens, and the Bronx, across Harlem, down Broadway, and into the Garment District. The tail of a hurricane had produced bone-chilling rains that pelted down upon the multitudes. Rain soaked the president's suit, beaded his glasses, and trickled down his cheeks. The miserable weather neither quenched his smile nor stopped his progress, and the crowds loved him for it. The energy of the crowd gave him "a sense of belonging, gave him happiness." They kept him so "warm," he afterward told Perkins, that he didn't realize he was "wet through." Throughout the rest of the campaign, he was "full of fight," and at the end he looked healthier than when he began. He had gained twelve pounds as well as gained election to a fourth consecutive term.

When Roosevelt was inaugurated on January 20, 1945, he had eighty-two days to live. From hindsight, critics would debate whether he was too debilitated to function effectively in his final months — whether, during the grueling marathon of diplomacy with Joseph Stalin and Winston Churchill at Yalta, he had given too much for too little. At Yalta, his strength was manifestly waning; his physical condition was deteriorating. Yet, in the end, Roosevelt achieved his two foremost objectives. He secured Russia's commitment to join the invasion of Japan, a struggle that was expected to cost a million American casualties. And he also secured Russia's support for the creation of a new world organization for peace that would arise from the wreckage of the most destructive war in history.

Finishing the war and preparing for peace were the twin goals that propelled Roosevelt through his final days. Everything else was put on the back burner. Never did he take the time to share confidential briefings about the war with his vice president, Harry Truman. Nor — an appalling lapse — did he brief his successor on the existence of the atomic bomb. When asked later if he "might have been better prepared for the presidency," Truman generously replied, Roosevelt "did all he could."

Roosevelt reserved what strength remained for the "great unfinished business" of his administration: He was planning to go to San Francisco in late April, where representatives from fifty Allied nations were to convene in order to establish the framework for the United Nations. After San Francisco, Roosevelt planned to go to England for a state visit. So excited was he at the prospect that he was unable to keep it a secret. He brought it up in conversation with Canada's prime minister, Mackenzie King, and again with Perkins. His eyes sparkled with anticipation when he told Perkins that Eleanor would accompany him to England and that he had urged her to order some fine clothes so she would "make a really handsome appearance."

The future promised to hold a crowded and jubilant itinerary. They would journey by ship to Southampton and then by rail to London, where they would stay at Buckingham Palace with the king and queen. He would drive with the king through the streets of London, address Parliament, and then spend several days with Churchill at his estate, Chequers. Churchill predicted that the "genuine and spontaneous" reception the president would receive from the British people would be "the greatest reception ever accorded to any human being since Lord Nelson made his triumphant return to London."

"But the war!" Perkins protested. "I don't think you ought to go. It is dangerous." Roosevelt cupped his hand over his mouth and whispered in her ear, "The war in Europe will be over by the end of May." It greatly comforted Perkins, she later said, "that he was so sure, two weeks before his death, that the end of the war was at hand."

His excitement over these future travels notwithstanding, Roosevelt could not conceal the depth of his exhaustion. To recover and prepare his speech to inaugurate the United Nations, Roosevelt departed the White House at the end of March for a fortnight's vacation in Warm Springs, hopeful that this place of almost preternatural rejuvenation for him would once more do its work. "It wasn't just a matter of our hoping the trip would help the Boss," Secret Service agent Mike Reilly said, "we just naturally assumed it would." This assumption was shared by everyone. For more than a dozen years Franklin Roosevelt had been a national emblem of resilience, his confidence in recovery and victory infusing and infused by the people.

"The thought never occurred to me," White House speechwriter Robert Sherwood later wrote, "that this time he might fail to rally as he always had." On the morning of April 12, Roosevelt's color seemed "exceptionally good" as he went through his mail and sat for a portrait. "He looked smiling and happy & ready for anything," his cousin Margaret observed. Suddenly then, his head slumped forward and he collapsed from a cerebral hemorrhage, never to regain consciousness.

Franklin Roosevelt had died as Theodore Roosevelt had once yearned he might die himself, as a leader in harness in the midst of battle, his life dissolving into the task before him. At his death, he was endeavoring to gain victory in a war to save democracy and to lay the groundwork for global peace. That he was listed as a casualty of war is a simple statement of fact. It was not the grandeur of a knight-errant's death, but his quiet heroism — the willingness to persevere as long as he was able — that was so telling.

Though he rarely spoke of his legacy, Roosevelt had "a keen sense of history and his own place therein." An inveterate collector, he had directed his White House staff to save every document, every letter, every scrap of paper that came into his office. Six years before his death, he had bequeathed his papers to the government and pledged part of his Hyde Park estate for the building of a library and museum, a formal act that initiated the system of presidential libraries. A confident Roosevelt wanted to give historians full access to his personal and professional papers to make their own evaluations of his leadership.

In his own judgment, as Roosevelt made clear when he laid the cornerstone of his library, the key to that leadership could be found in the dependable, reciprocal relationship he had established with the people he served: "Of the papers which will come to rest here I personally attach less importance to the documents of those who have occupied high public or private office, than I do the spontaneous letters which have come to me and my family and my associates from men, from women, and from children in every part of the United States, telling me of their conditions and problems, and giving me their opinions."

So unique was the tender intimacy of Franklin Roosevelt's leadership that in the days after his death, the *New York Times* reported, "in the streets of every American town, strangers stopped to commiserate with one another. Over and over again one heard the same lament: 'We have lost our friend.' "

"The greatest human tribute," one citizen from Trenton wrote, "is that because one man died 130 millions feel lonely."

On Good Friday, April 14, 1865, Abraham Lincoln rose with great and unaccustomed cheer to greet the final day of his life.

The evening before, the city of Washington had been in dazzling holiday illumination. At long last, the punishing Civil War was coming to an end. The Republic had been saved. Candles glinted in the windows of every building, gorgeous lanterns swayed along the walls, and flags flew from the roofs of every housetop. The streets were filled with people "drunk with joy," strolling arm in arm, talking, laughing, singing. Ten days earlier, the Confederate capital at Richmond had been evacuated. The following week, General Robert E. Lee had surrendered his army to General Ulysses Grant at Appomattox. Each passing night, it seemed, brought new reasons to celebrate: a suspension of the draft had been announced by the War Department, purchases of military supplies had been halted, ports opened for trade, and Grant himself was coming to the White House.

Lincoln had breakfast that morning with

his wife, Mary, and their oldest son, Robert, a captain in the army and a member of Grant's staff, who had just returned from the front. Word came to the breakfast room that House Speaker Schuyler Colfax had arrived. Colfax was planning a cross-country trip to California and wanted to confirm that Lincoln had no plans to call an extra session of Congress. Lincoln assured him that he did not. "How I would rejoice to make that trip!" Lincoln told Colfax. "I can only envy you its pleasures."

And then, rising from his chair, Lincoln outlined a message that he wanted Colfax to deliver to the gold and silver miners in the West. He had been thinking about the hundreds of thousands of returning veterans who would be looking for jobs. He believed that in the great western country, "from the Rocky Mountains to the Pacific," lay an "inexhaustible" supply of mineral wealth, the surface of which had hardly been scratched. In that vast mining region, there was "room enough for all" — for returning soldiers and new immigrants alike. Tell the miners that "I shall promote their interests to the utmost of my ability, because their prosperity is the prosperity of the nation, and we shall prove in a very few years that we are indeed the treasury of the world."

At 11 a.m. Lincoln headed for his regularly scheduled Friday cabinet meeting. The forbidding war room of maps, battle planning, and military paraphernalia that had characterized cabinet meetings for longer than four years had on this day acquired a brighter mood and a serious new subject — how best to proceed with reconciliation and reconstruction. "This is the great question before us," Lincoln announced, "and we must soon begin to act."

From the outset, Lincoln wanted to establish the healing tone that must prevail in the months to come. "Enough lives have been sacrificed," he said. "We must extinguish our resentments if we expect harmony and union." Indeed, Lincoln considered it auspicious that Congress had adjourned on March 4, the day of the second inauguration, for there were men there "who, if their motives were good, were nevertheless impracticable, and possessed feelings of hate and vindictiveness in which he did not sympathize and would not participate."

To the question of what to do with the rebel leaders, Lincoln made clear that "none need expect he would take any part in hanging or killing those men, even the worst of them." He understood that their continued presence might hobble the process of healing, but he would prefer to simply "frighten them out of the country, open the gates, let down the bars, scare them off," emphasizing his intentions with a gesture of uplifted palms as if shooing sheep from the paddock. They should be informed, however, that while "no attempt will be made to hinder them" if they voluntarily chose to leave, "if they stay, they will be punished for their crimes."

General Grant, having just returned from Appomattox, joined the cabinet meeting and related the story of General Lee's surrender. "What terms did you make for the common soldiers?" Lincoln asked. "I told them to go back to their homes and their families," Grant responded, "and they would not be molested, if they did nothing more." As for the officers, they could keep their private horses and their sidearms; Grant believed it would be an unnecessary humiliation to call upon them to deliver up their personal property. Hearing this, the president's "face glowed with approval."

For three hours and more, the cabinet members hashed out problems of communication and commerce, reopening post offices and federal courts, reestablishing connections to allow for commercial and social intercourse — the nuts-and-bolts needed to suture relations with the defeated rebels and begin the re-creation of a unified country. Lincoln found any simple imposition of federal power upon the states abhorrent. "Let 'em up easy," Lincoln repeated on several occasions, "let 'em up easy." He felt strongly that it was not his executive prerogative to "undertake to run State governments in all these southern states. Their people must do that — though I reckon at first some of them may do it badly." The process of reconstruction must be built step by step and remain sensitive to unfolding events. Of utmost importance, the process must be flexible.

"Didn't our Chief look grand today!" Secretary of War Edwin Stanton remarked to a colleague after the meeting drew to a close. "That's the most satisfactory cabinet meeting I have attended in many a long day." There was general agreement among the members of the cabinet that Lincoln had never seemed "more glad, more serene." The "indescribable sadness, which had previously seemed to be an adamantine element of his very being," one member observed, "had been suddenly changed to an equally indescribable expression of serene joy, as if conscious that the great purpose of his life had been achieved."

At three o'clock that afternoon, Lincoln and Mary took a leisurely carriage drive. "You almost startle me by your great cheerfulness," Mary told Lincoln. He replied, "and well I may feel so, Mary, I consider *this day,* the war has come to a close." And then he added, "I have never felt better in my life."

As the carriage rolled toward the Navy Yard, they spoke of their future together once his presidency was over. They were both relatively young. Lincoln was fifty-six, Mary forty-six.

They hoped to travel with their sons — to journey through Europe, visit the Holy Land, cross the Rocky Mountains and see California and the West Coast for the first time. Finally they would come full circle to Illinois, where their marriage had begun.

The carriage returned to the White House just as a group of old friends, including Illinois governor Richard Oglesby, were taking their leave. "Come back, boys, come back," Lincoln implored them. He had been through a long, starving time and badly wanted to relax, chat, perform, and especially read aloud from one of his humorous books. "They kept sending for him to come to dinner," Oglesby recalled. "He promised each time to go, but would continue reading the book. Finally he got a peremptory order that he must come to dinner at once."

An early dinner was required, for the Lincolns had evening plans to go to Ford's Theatre to see a light comedy, *Our American Cousin.* After dinner, Lincoln entertained another small group of friends, including Massachusetts congressman George Ashmun. As the hour reached eight o'clock, Lincoln stood up: "I suppose it's time to go, though I would rather stay," he said, the note of reluctance clear. "It had been advertised that we will be there and I cannot disappoint the people." His word was out; his promise must be kept.

Lincoln's assassin, the actor John Wilkes Booth, was a familiar figure in the theater world. Having learned by midday of the president's plans, Booth had decided that this night would provide the optimal chance to kill the man he considered an "even greater tyrant" than Julius Caesar. He believed posterity would honor him for the deed, and he would thereby achieve immortality. Thus was set in motion the most iconic moment of tragic horror in the history of the American presidency.

Booth was already inside the theater when the Lincolns took their seats in the comfortable presidential box. At twelve minutes past ten, Booth's calling card gained him access to the rear of the executive box. The president was leaning forward in his rocking chair, his right hand on his chin, his arm on the railing. Booth moved silently forward to within two feet of Lincoln. He raised his derringer, pointed it behind Lincoln's left ear, and fired. In a white fog of smoke, Lincoln slumped forward. Leaping from the box to the stage, Booth caught the spur of his riding boot on a regimental flag decorating the box. His awkward fall broke his leg, but before hobbling off the stage and escaping into the alley, he raised his dagger and shouted the words "Sic semper tyrannis" (Thus always to tyrants).

There was a savage, terrible irony in these

words. The dying president had warned long before that lawlessness, murder, and mob rule would create fertile ground for a Caesar or a Napoleon, men of towering egos who would seek distinction by "pulling down" rather than "building up." The dying president, who had worked much of his life to counter extremism, hate, and vindictiveness — who, that very afternoon, had counseled his colleagues against exercising arbitrary power over the vanquished southern states — was himself the victim of a racist extremist who would be remembered in infamy only for the man he killed.

"Mr. Lincoln had so much vitality," doctors reported, that for nine hours after sustaining the wound that "would have killed most men instantly," he continued to struggle. At 7:22 the following morning, that struggle came to an end. Abraham Lincoln was pronounced dead. "Now," Stanton said, "he belongs to the ages." Stanton's tribute proved not merely poetic but an accurate description of the fame and influence that connects the moment of Lincoln's death to the living values he passed on to us and to all succeeding generations.

What are the components of this legacy of living values — and how do they get passed on over time?

From the very moment he first appeared before the people as a twenty-three-year-old in Sangamon County, Lincoln connected education and history, remembrance of the past and freedom. He singled out education "as the most important subject which we as a people can be engaged in," so that every man could "thereby be enabled to read the histories of his own and other countries to appreciate the value of our free institutions."

As a twenty-nine-year-old, Lincoln worried that memories of the Revolution and the ideals for which it stood were growing "more and more dim by the lapse of time." Through history, he had hoped that the story of our country's founding would be "read of, and recounted, so long as the bible shall be read." He considered history, an understanding of how we came to be, the best vehicle for understanding who we are and where we are going.

The master story Lincoln told grew deeper and simpler throughout his life. It was the narrative of our country, the birth of our democracy, and the development of freedom within our Union. At the time of his great debates with Stephen Douglas, Lincoln invited his audiences on a communal storytelling journey so they might collectively understand the dilemma of slavery in a free country and, together, fashion a solution. At Gettysburg, he challenged the living to finish "the unfinished work" for which so many soldiers had given their lives — that "government of the people, by the people, for the people, shall not perish from the earth." At the Second Inaugural, Lincoln asked his countrymen "to strive on to finish the work we are in, to bind up the nation's wounds." These same words nourished Franklin Roosevelt. He drew upon them, he said, because Abraham Lincoln had set goals for the future "in terms of which the human mind cannot improve."

Lincoln never forgot that in a democracy the leader's strength ultimately depends on the strength of his bond with the people. In the mornings he set aside several hours to hear the needs of the ordinary people lined up outside his office, his time of "public opinion baths." Kindness, empathy, humor, humility, passion, and ambition all marked him from the start. But he grew, and continued to grow, into a leader who became so powerfully fused with the problems tearing his country apart that his desire to lead and his need to serve coalesced into a single indomitable force. That force has not only enriched subsequent leaders but has provided our people with a moral compass to guide us. Such leadership offers us humanity, purpose, and wisdom, not in turbulent times alone, but also in our everyday lives.

ACKNOWLEDGMENTS

Simon & Schuster has been my publishing home for nearly four decades. I cannot imagine publishing a book without the team of Carolyn Reidy, Jonathan Karp, Alice Mayhew, Richard Rhorer, Jackie Seow, Stephen Bedford, Stuart Roberts, Julia Prosser, Lisa Healy, Kristen Lemire, Lisa Erwin, and Lewelin Polanco.

I am thankful once again to Jackie Seow, who patiently worked through countless jacket designs to create this final one; and to Julia Prosser and Stephen Bedford, whose expertise, keen insights, and tenacity have helped connect my books to my readers. To Stuart Roberts, who with such care shepherded the manuscript through every stage; and to my copy editor, Fred Chase, who was with me at my Concord home during a difficult time and with warmth and patience completed the project.

I am especially grateful to Jonathan Karp whose creative vision helped me think about the structure of this book in a different way, including the use of case studies of the four leaders at pivotal moments.

On this book, as on so many others, Alice Mayhew provided masterly judgment, peerless editorial skills and steadfast support. For better than twenty years, I've been fortunate to have the unrivaled strength of Binky Urban as my literary agent.

And for almost forty years Linda Vandegrift has been my gifted research assistant. All my books have been informed by her extraordinary talent and incomparable investigative skills. Together, we have grown as storytellers.

For help with finding the daguerreotypes and photographs I thank my friend Michelle Krowl, as well as the talents of Bryan Eaton, Jay Godwin, and Matthew Hanson.

For critical artistic input on the book's jacket, I thank Juliana Rothschild; and for providing perceptive structural judgment and precision of language on every chapter, I am indebted to Ida Rothschild.

It is hard to describe the role my manager and cherished friend Beth Laski played in this book or indeed plays in my life. For me she is absolutely indispensable. For two decades her stunning talents, ingenuity, and imagination, loyalty, and her passion have sustained me and given me balance. As she knows, she is my "Harry."

And first and last, my late husband, Richard Goodwin, and Michael Rothschild.

Our three lives and our families have been intertwined for more than forty years. Michael is a brilliant writer, sculptor, apple orchardist, and farmer — the closest to Thomas Jefferson, Dick once told me, whom he had ever met. Year after year, the three of us worked together on writing projects. We read the same books, debated ideas, and fought over language. In Dick's memory and to Michael's presence, this book is dedicated.

BIBLIOGRAPHY

Alter, Jonathan. *The Defining Moment: FDR's Hundred Days and the Triumph of Hope.* New York: Simon & Schuster, 2006.

Angle, Paul M., ed. *Abraham Lincoln by Some Men Who Knew Him.* Chicago: Americana House, 1950.

Arenberg, Richard A., and Robert B. Dove. *Defending the Filibuster: The Soul of the Senate.* Bloomington: Indiana University Press, 2012.

Armstrong, Louise Van Voorhis. *We Too Are the People.* Boston: Little, Brown, 1938.

Asbell, Bernard. *The F.D.R. Memoirs.* Garden City, N.Y.: Doubleday, 1973.

———. *When F.D.R. Died.* New York: Holt, Rinehart & Winston, 1961.

Badger, Anthony J. *FDR: The First Hundred Days.* New York: Hill & Wang, 2008.

Baringer, William Eldon. *Lincoln's Rise to Power.* Boston: Little, Brown, 1937.

Barnes, Thurlow Weed, ed. *Memoir of Thurlow Weed.* Boston: Houghton Mifflin, 1884.

Barry, David S. *Forty Years in Washington.* Boston: Little Brown, 1964.

Basler, Roy P., ed. *The Collected Works of Abraham Lincoln.* 8 vols. New Brunswick, N.J.: Rutgers University Press, 1953.

Bates, Ernest Sutherland. *The Story of the Congress: 1789–1935.* New York: Harper & Brothers, 1936.

Beasley, Maurine H. *Eleanor Roosevelt: Transformative First Lady.* Lawrence: University Press of Kansas, 2010.

Benjamin, Walter. *Illuminations: Essays and Reflections.* New York: Schocken, 1969.

Beschloss, Michael, ed. *Reaching for Glory: Lyndon Johnson's Secret White House Tapes, 1964–65.* New York: Touchstone, 2001.

Beveridge, Albert J. *Abraham Lincoln, 1809–1858.* 2 vols. Boston: Houghton Mifflin, 1928.

Bishop, Joseph Bucklin. *Theodore Roosevelt and His Time, Shown in His Letters.* 2 vols. New York: Charles Scribner's Sons, 1920.

Boettiger, John R. *A Love in Shadow.* New York: W. W. Norton, 1978.

Bolden, Tonya. *FDR's Alphabet Soup: New Deal America, 1932–1939.* New York: Alfred A. Knopf, 2010.

Boritt, Gabor S. *Economics of the American Dream.* Urbana: University of Illinois Press, 1994.

———., ed. *The Lincoln Enigma: The Chang-*

ing *Faces of an American Icon.* New York: Oxford University Press, 2001.

Boutwell, George S. *Speeches and Papers Relating to the Rebellion and the Overthrow of Slavery.* Boston: Little, Brown, 1867.

Brands, H. W. *Selected Letters of Theodore Roosevelt.* New York: Cooper Square Press, 2001.

———. *T.R.: The Last Romantic.* New York: Basic Books, 1997.

Brinkley, Douglas. *The Wilderness Warrior: Theodore Roosevelt and the Crusade for America.* New York: HarperCollins, 2009.

Brooks, Noah. *Washington in Lincoln's Time.* New York: Century, 1895.

Browne, Francis Fisher. *The Every-Day Life of Abraham Lincoln: A Narrative and Descriptive Biography.* Chicago: Browne & Howell, 1914.

Burlingame, Michael. *Abraham Lincoln, a Life.* 2 vols. Baltimore: Johns Hopkins University Press, 2008.

———. *The Inner World of Abraham Lincoln.* Chicago: University of Illinois Press, 1994.

———., ed. *An Oral History of Abraham Lincoln: John Nicolay's Interviews and Essays.* Carbondale: Southern Illinois University Press, 1996.

———., ed. *With Lincoln in the White House: Letters, Memoranda, and Other Writings of John G. Nicolay, 1860–1865.* Carbondale:

Southern Illinois University Press, 2000.

Burlingame, Michael, and John R. Turner Ettlinger, eds. *Inside Lincoln's White House: The Complete Civil War Diary of John Hay.* Carbondale: Southern Illinois University Press, 1997.

Burns, James MacGregor. *Roosevelt: The Lion and the Fox.* Old Saybrook, Conn.: Konecky & Konecky, 1970.

Burns, James MacGregor, and Susan Dunn. *The Three Roosevelts: Patrician Leaders Who Transformed America.* New York: Grove, 2001.

Butt, Archie, and Lawrence F. Abbott, ed. *The Letters of Archie Butt, Personal Aide to President Roosevelt.* New York: Doubleday, Page, 1924.

Califano Jr., Joseph A. *The Triumph & Tragedy of Lyndon Johnson: The White House Years.* New York: Touchstone, 2015.

Carmichael, Donald Scott, ed. *FDR, Columnist.* Chicago: Pellegrini & Cudahy, 1947.

Caro, Robert. *The Years of Lyndon Johnson: Master of the Senate.* New York: Vintage, 2003.

―――. *The Years of Lyndon Johnson: Means of Ascent.* New York: Vintage, 1991.

―――. *The Years of Lyndon Johnson: The Passage of Power.* New York: Vintage, 2013.

―――. *The Years of Lyndon Johnson: The Path to Power.* New York: Vintage, 1990.

Carpenter, Francis B. *Six Months at the White House with Abraham Lincoln.* Lincoln: University of Nebraska Press, 1995.

Chanler, Winthrop, and Margaret Chanler. *Winthrop Chanler's Letters.* Privately printed, 1951.

Churchill, Winston S. *The Second World War,* Vol. 4: *The Hinge of Fate.* Boston: Houghton Mifflin, 1950.

Cohen, Adam. *Nothing to Fear: FDR's Inner Circle and the Hundred Days That Created Modern America.* New York: Penguin, 2009.

Colfax, Schuyler. *The Life and Principles of Abraham Lincoln.* Philadelphia: Jas. R. Rodgers, 1865.

Cordery, Stacy A. *Alice: Alice Roosevelt Longworth, from White House Princess to Washington Power Broker.* New York: Viking, 2007.

Cornell, Robert J. *The Anthracite Coal Strike of 1902.* Washington, D.C.: Catholic University of America, 1957.

Cornish, Dudley Taylor. *The Sable Arm: Black Troops in the Union Army, 1861–1865.* Lawrence: University Press of Kansas, 1956.

Cornwell Jr., Elmer E. *Presidential Leadership of Public Opinion.* Bloomington: Indiana University Press, 1965.

Cowger, Thomas W., and Sherwin J. Markman, eds. *Lyndon Johnson Remembered: An Intimate Portrait of a Presidency.* Lanham,

Md.: Rowman & Littlefield, 2003.

Crook, Col. William H.; Margarita Spaulding Gerry, ed. *Through Five Administrations: Reminiscences of Colonel William H. Crook.* New York: Harper & Brothers, 1910.

Dallek, Robert. *Flawed Giant: Lyndon Johnson and His Times, 1961–1973.* New York: Oxford University Press, 1998.

———. *Lone Star Rising: Lyndon Johnson and His Times, 1908–1960.* New York: Oxford University Press, 1991.

Dalton, Kathleen Mary. "The Early Life of Theodore Roosevelt." PhD diss., Johns Hopkins University, 1979.

———. *Theodore Roosevelt: A Strenuous Life.* New York: Vintage, 2004.

Davis, Kenneth S. *FDR: The Beckoning of Destiny, 1882–1928.* New York: G. P. Putnam's Sons, 1972.

Davis, Oscar. *Released for Publication: Some Inside Political History of Theodore Roosevelt and His Times, 1889–1919.* Boston: Houghton Mifflin, 1925.

Davis, Richard Harding. *The Cuban and Puerto Rican Campaigns.* New York: Charles Scribner's Sons, 1898.

Davis, William C. *Lincoln's Men: How President Lincoln Became Father to an Army and a Nation.* New York: Touchstone, 2000.

de Kay, James Tertius. *Roosevelt's Navy: The Education of a Warrior President, 1882–1920.*

New York: Pegasus, 2012.

DeRose, Chris. *Congressman Lincoln: The Making of America's Greatest President.* New York: Threshold, 2013.

Donald, David Herbert, ed. *Inside Lincoln's Cabinet: The Civil War Diaries of Salmon P. Chase.* New York: Longmans, Green, 1954.

———. *Lincoln.* New York: Simon & Schuster, 1995.

Douglass, Frederick. *The Life and Times of Frederick Douglass.* Mineola, N.Y.: Dover, 2003.

Dugger, Ronnie. *The Politician: The Life and Times of Lyndon Johnson.* New York: W. W. Norton, 1982.

Eaton, John. *Grant, Lincoln, and the Freedman: Reminiscences of the Civil War.* New York: Longmans, Green, 1907.

Edwards, George C. *The Strategic President: Persuasion and Opportunity in Presidential Leadership.* Princeton: Princeton University Press, 2009.

Ellis, Sylvia. *Freedom's Pragmatist: Lyndon Johnson and Civil Rights.* Tallahassee: University Press of Florida, 2013.

Emerson, Ralph Waldo. *The Journals and Miscellaneous Notebooks of Ralph Waldo Emerson,* Vol. 11, *1848–1851,* Cambridge, Mass.: Belknap Press of Harvard University Press, 1975.

Emerson, Ralph, and Adaline Emerson. *Mr. &*

Mrs. Ralph Emerson's Personal Recollections of Abraham Lincoln. Rockford, Ill.: Wilson Brothers, 1909.

Evans, Rowland, and Robert Novak. *Lyndon B. Johnson: The Exercise of Power.* New York: Signet, 1966.

Farley, James A. *Behind the Ballots: The Personal History of a Politician.* New York: Harcourt, Brace, 1938.

————. *Jim Farley's Story: The Roosevelt Years.* New York: McGraw-Hill, 1948.

Faust, Drew Gilpin. *Republic of Suffering.* New York: Vintage, 2009.

Fenster, Julie M. *FDR's Shadow: Louis Howe, the Force That Shaped Franklin and Eleanor Roosevelt.* New York: St. Martin's Griffin, 2009.

Flower, Frank Abial. *Edwin McMasters Stanton: The Autocrat of Rebellion, Emancipation, and Reconstruction.* Akron, Ohio: Saalfield, 1905.

Freidel, Frank. *Franklin D. Roosevelt: The Apprenticeship.* Boston: Little, Brown, 1952.

————. *Franklin D. Roosevelt: Launching the New Deal.* Boston: Little, Brown, 1952.

————. *Franklin D. Roosevelt: The Ordeal.* Boston: Little, Brown, 1954.

————. *Franklin D. Roosevelt: A Rendezvous with Destiny.* Boston: Little, Brown, 1990.

Furman, Bess. *Washington By-line; The Personal Story of a Newspaper Woman.* New

York: Alfred A. Knopf, 1949.

Gallagher, Hugh Gregory. *FDR's Splendid Deception.* New York: Dodd, Mead, 1985.

Gillette, Michael. *Lady Bird: An Oral History.* New York: Oxford University Press, 2012.

Goldberg, Richard Thayer. *The Making of Franklin D. Roosevelt: Triumph over Disability.* Cambridge, Mass.: Abt Books, 1981.

Goldman, Eric. *Rendezvous with Destiny: A History of Modern American Reform.* Chicago: Ivan R. Dee, 2002.

———. *The Tragedy of Lyndon Johnson.* New York: Alfred A. Knopf, 1969.

Goodwin, Doris Kearns. *The Bully Pulpit: Theodore Roosevelt, William Howard Taft, and the Golden Age of Journalism.* New York: Simon & Schuster, 2013.

———. *Lyndon Johnson and the American Dream.* New York: Harper & Row, 1976.

———. *No Ordinary Time: Franklin and Eleanor Roosevelt: The Home Front in World War II.* New York: Simon & Schuster, 1994.

———. *Team of Rivals: The Political Genius of Abraham Lincoln.* New York: Simon & Schuster, 2005.

Goodwin, Richard. *Remembering America: A Voice from the Sixties.* New York: Little Brown, 1988.

Gould, Lewis L. *The Presidency of Theodore Roosevelt.* New York: Oxford University Press, 2012.

————., ed. *Bull Moose on the Stump: The 1912 Campaign Speeches of Theodore Roosevelt.* Lawrence: University Press of Kansas, 2008.

————. *The Presidency of Theodore Roosevelt.* New York: Oxford University Press, 2012.

Graham, Jr., Otis L., and Meghan Robinson Wander, eds. *Franklin D. Roosevelt: His Life and Times: An Encyclopedic View.* New York: Da Capo, 1990.

The "Great Strike": Perspectives on the 1902 Anthracite Coal Strike. Easton, Penn.: Canal History & Technology Press, 2002.

Greenstein, Fred I. *The Presidential Difference: Leadership Styles from FDR to Clinton.* New York: Free Press, 2000.

Grondahl, Paul. *I Rose Like a Rocket: The Political Education of Theodore Roosevelt.* Lincoln: University of Nebraska Press, 2004.

Gunther, John. *Roosevelt in Retrospect.* New York: Harper & Brothers, 1950.

Hagedorn, Hermann. *The Boy's Life of Theodore Roosevelt.* New York: Harper & Brothers, 1941.

————. *Roosevelt in the Badlands.* New York: Houghton Mifflin, 1921.

Halberstam, David. *The Best and the Brightest.* New York: Ballantine, 1993.

Halstead, Murat; William B. Hesseltine, ed.

Three against Lincoln: Murat Halstead Reports the Caucuses of 1860. Baton Rouge: Louisiana State University Press, 1960.

Hamby, Alonzo. *Man of Destiny: FDR and the Making of the American Century.* New York: Basic Books, 2015.

Harbaugh, William Henry. *Power and Responsibility: The Life and Times of Theodore Roosevelt.* New York: Farrar, Straus & Cudahy, 1961.

Hassett, William D. *Off the Record with F.D.R.* New Brunswick, N.J.: Rutgers University Press, 1958.

Helm, Katherine. *The True Story of Mary, Wife of Lincoln: Containing the Recollections of Mary Lincoln's Sister Emilie (Mrs. Ben Hardin Helm), Extracts from Her War-time Diary, Numerous Letters and Other Documents Now First Published by Her Niece, Katherine Helm.* New York: Harper & Brothers, 1928.

Hendrick, Burton J. *Lincoln's War Cabinet.* Boston: Little, Brown, 1946.

Herndon, William H., and Jesse W. Weik; Douglas L. Wilson and Rodney D. Davis, eds. *Herndon's Lincoln.* Urbana: University of Illinois Press, 2006.

Herndon, William H., and Jesse W. Weik. *Herndon's Life of Lincoln: The History and Personal Recollections of Abraham Lincoln.* New York: Cleveland, Ohio: World Publishing, 1949. https://archive.org/details/

herndonslifeoflinco00hern./

Hollister, O. J. *Life of Schuyler Colfax.* New York: Funk & Wagnalls, 1886.

Holzer, Harold, and Sara Vaughn Gabbard, eds. *Lincoln and Freedom: Slavery, Emancipation, and the Thirteenth Amendment.* Carbondale: Southern Illinois University Press, 2007.

Hull, Henrietta McCormick. *A Senator's Wife Remembers: From the Great Depression to the Great Society.* Montgomery, Ala.: New South Books, 2010.

Ickes, Harold. *The Autobiography of a Curmudgeon.* New York: Quadrangle, 1969.

———. *The Secret Diary of Harold L. Ickes: The First Thousand Days, 1933–36.* Vol. 1. New York: Simon & Schuster, 1953.

Jackson, Robert H. *That Man: An Insider's Portrait of Franklin D. Roosevelt.* New York: Oxford University Press, 2003.

Jeffers, H. Paul. *Colonel Roosevelt: Theodore Roosevelt Goes to War, 1897–1898.* New York: John Wiley & Sons, 1996.

Jessup, Philip C. *Elihu Root.* 2 vols. New York: Dodd, Mead, 1938.

Johnson, Lyndon Baines. *The Vantage Point: Perspectives of the Presidency, 1963–1969.* New York: Holt, Rinehart & Winston, 1971.

Johnson, Lyndon Baines; Max Holland, ed. *The Presidential Recordings: Lyndon B. Johnson,* Vol. 1: *Nov. 22–30, 1963.* New York: W.

W. Norton, 2005.

Johnson, Lyndon Baines; Robert David Johnson and David Shreve, eds. *The Presidential Recordings: Lyndon B. Johnson*, Vol. 2: *December 1963*. New York: W. W. Norton, 2005.

Johnson, Lyndon Baines; Kent B. Germany and Robert David Johnson, eds. *The Presidential Recordings: Lyndon B. Johnson*, Vol. 3: *January 1964*. New York: W. W. Norton, 2005.

Johnson, Lyndon Baines; Robert David Johnson and Kent B. Germany, eds. *The Presidential Recordings: Lyndon B. Johnson*, Vol. 4: *February 1–March 8, 1964*. New York: W. W. Norton, 2005.

Johnson, Lyndon Baines; Guian A. McKee, ed. *The Presidential Recordings: Lyndon B. Johnson*, Vol. 6: *April 14–May 31, 1964*. New York: W. W. Norton, 2007.

Johnson, Rebekah Baines. *A Family Album*. New York: McGraw-Hill, 1965.

Kearney, James R. *Anna Eleanor Roosevelt: The Evolution of a Reformer*. Boston: Houghton Mifflin, 1968.

Kiewe, Amos. *FDR's First Fireside Chat: Public Confidence and the Banking Crisis*. College Station: Texas A&M University Press, 2007.

Kilpatrick, Carroll. *Roosevelt and Daniels, a Friendship in Politics*. Chapel Hill: University of North Carolina Press, 1952.

Kleeman, Rita Halle. *Gracious Lady: The Life of Sara Delano Roosevelt.* New York: D. Appleton-Century, 1935.

Knokey, Jon A. *Theodore Roosevelt and the Making of American Leadership.* New York: Skyhorse, 2015.

Kohlsaat, Herman H. *From McKinley to Harding: Personal Recollections of Our Presidents.* New York: Charles Scribner's Sons, 1923.

Kohn, Edward P. *Heir to the Empire City: New York and the Making of Theodore Roosevelt.* New York: Basic Books, 2014.

Kotz, Nick. *Judgment Days: Lyndon Baines Johnson, Martin Luther King Jr., and the Laws That Changed America.* New York: Houghton Mifflin, 2005.

Lang, Louis J., ed. *The Autobiography of Thomas Collier Platt.* New York: B. W. Dodge, 1910.

Lash, Joseph P. *Eleanor and Franklin: The Story of Their Relationship.* New York: W. W. Norton, 1971.

Lee, Elizabeth Blair; Virginia Jeans Laas, ed. *Wartime Washington: The Civil War Letters of Elizabeth Blair Lee.* Urbana: University of Illinois Press, 1999.

Lehrman Lewis E. *Lincoln at Peoria: The Turning Point.* Mechanicsburg, Penn.: Stackpole Books, 2008.

Leuchtenburg, William E. *Franklin D. Roo-*

sevelt and the New Deal, 1932–1940. New York: Harper Perennial, 2009.

———. In the Shadow of FDR: From Harry Truman to Barack Obama. Ithaca: Cornell University Press, 2009.

———. The White House Looks South: Franklin D. Roosevelt, Harry S. Truman, Lyndon B. Johnson. Baton Rouge: Louisiana State University Press, 2005.

Levin, Linda Lotridge. The Making of FDR: The Story of Stephen T. Early, America's First Modern Press Secretary. New York: Prometheus, 2007.

Lewis, William Draper. The Life of Theodore Roosevelt. Chicago: John C. Winston, 1919.

Lindley, Ernest K. Franklin D. Roosevelt: A Career in Progressive Democracy. Indianapolis: Bobbs-Merrill, 1931.

———. The Roosevelt Revolution: First Phase. London: Victor Gollancz, 1934.

Lodge, Henry Cabot. Selections from the Correspondence of Theodore Roosevelt and Henry Cabot Lodge: 1884–1918. Vol. 1. New York: Charles Scribner's Sons, 1925.

Loevy, Robert D., ed. The Civil Rights Act of 1964: The Passage of the Law That Ended Racial Segregation. Albany: State University of New York Press, 1997.

Lorant, Stefan. The Life and Times of Theodore Roosevelt. Garden City, N.Y.: Doubleday, 1959.

Louchheim, Katie, ed. *The Making of the New Deal: The Insiders Speak.* Cambridge, Mass.: Harvard University Press, 1983.

Lowitt, Richard, and Maurine Beasley, eds. *One Third of a Nation: Lorena Hickok Reports on the Great Depression.* Urbana: University of Illinois Press, 2000.

Lubow, Arthur. *The Reporter Who Would Be King: A Biography of Richard Harding Davis.* New York: Scribner, 1992.

Lucks, Daniel S. *Selma to Saigon: The Civil Rights Movement and the Vietnam War.* Lexington: University Press of Kentucky, 2014.

Marshall, Edward. *The Story of the Rough Riders, 1st U.S. Volunteer Cavalry: The Regiment in Camp and on the Battle Field.* New York: G. W. Dillingham, 1899.

Martin, George Whitney. *Madame Secretary, Frances Perkins.* New York: Houghton Mifflin Harcourt, 1983.

Matthews, Donald R. *U.S. Senators and Their World.* New York: W. W. Norton, 1973.

McFeeley, William S. *Frederick Douglass.* New York: W. W. Norton, 1995.

McPherson, James M. *Abraham Lincoln and the Second American Revolution.* New York: Oxford University Press, 1991.

———. *Battle Cry of Freedom: The Civil War Era.* New York: Oxford University Press, 1988.

Millard, Candice. *The River of Doubt: Theodore Roosevelt's Darkest Journey.* New York: Broadway Books, 2005.

Miller, Merle. *Lyndon: An Oral Biography.* New York: G. P. Putnam's Sons, 1980.

Miller, Nathan. *FDR: An Intimate History.* New York: Madison Books, 1983.

———. *The Roosevelt Chronicles.* New York: Doubleday, 1979.

Miller, Randall M., ed. *Lincoln and Leadership: Military, Political, and Religious Decision Making.* New York: Fordham University Press, 2012.

Miller, William L. *Lincoln's Virtues: An Ethical Biography.* New York: Vintage, 2003.

Moley, Raymond. *After Seven Years.* New York: Harper & Brothers, 1939.

———. *The First New Deal.* New York: Harcourt, Brace & World, 1966.

Moody, Booth. *The Lyndon Johnson Story.* New York: Avon, 1964.

Morel, Lucas E. *Lincoln and Liberty: Wisdom for the Ages.* Lexington: University Press of Kentucky, 2014.

Morris, Edmund. *The Rise of Theodore Roosevelt.* New York: Modern Library, 2001.

———. *Theodore Rex.* New York: Modern Library, 2001.

Naylor, Natalie A., Douglas Brinkley, and John Allen Gable, eds. *Theodore Roosevelt: Many-Sided American.* Interlaken, N.Y.:

Heart of the Lakes, 1992.

Neustadt, Richard E. *Presidential Power and the Modern Presidents.* New York: Free Press, 1980.

Nevins, Allan, and Milton Halsey Thomas, eds. *The Diary of George Templeton Strong,* Vol. 3: *The Civil War, 1860–1865.* New York: Macmillan, 1952.

Nicolay, Helen. *Personal Traits of Abraham Lincoln.* New York: Century, 1912.

Nicolay, John G. *A Short Life of Abraham Lincoln.* New York: Century, 1909.

Nicolay, John G., and John Hay. *Abraham Lincoln: A History.* Vol. 1. New York: Century, 1890.

Niven, John, ed. *The Salmon P. Chase Papers,* Vol. 1: *Journals, 1829–1872.* Kent, Ohio: Kent State University Press, 1983.

Oldroyd, Osborn H., comp. *The Lincoln Memorial: Album-Immortelles.* New York: G. W. Carleton, 1882.

O'Toole, Patricia. *When Trumpets Call: Theodore Roosevelt after the White House.* New York: Simon & Schuster, 2005.

Parsons, Frances Theodora. *Perchance Some Day.* Privately printed, 1952.

Pease, Theodore Calvin, and James G. Randall, eds. *Diary of Orville Hickman Browning,* Vol. 1: *1850–1864.* Springfield: Illinois State Historical Library, 1925.

Perkins, Frances. *The Roosevelt I Knew.* New

York: Penguin, 2011.

Phillips, Donald. *Lincoln on Leadership*. New York: Warner Books, 1992.

Phipps, Joe. *Summer Stock: Behind the Scenes with LBJ in '48*. Fort Worth: Texas Christian University Press, 1992.

Pink, Daniel. *Drive: The Surprising Truth about What Motivates Us*. New York: Riverhead Books, 2011.

Pinsker, Matthew. *Lincoln's Sanctuary: Abraham Lincoln and the Soldiers' Home*. New York: Oxford University Press, 2003.

Pool, William C., Emmie Craddock, and David E. Conrad. *Lyndon Baines Johnson: The Formative Years*. San Marcos: Southwest Texas State College Press, 1965.

Potiker, Jan. *Sara and Eleanor: The Story of Sara Delano Roosevelt and Her Daughter-in-Law, Eleanor Roosevelt*. New York: St. Martin's Griffin, 2005.

Potter, David. *The Impending Crisis: America before the Civil War, 1848–1861*. New York: Harper & Row, 1976.

Pringle, Henry. *Theodore Roosevelt: A Biography*. New York: Harcourt, Brace, 1931.

The Public Papers of the Presidents of the United States: Lyndon B. Johnson, 1963–64, Book I. Washington, D.C.: Office of the Federal Register, National Archives and Records Service, General Services Administration, 1965.

The Public Papers of the Presidents of the United States: Lyndon B. Johnson, 1963–64, Book II. Washington, D.C.: Office of the Federal Register, National Archives and Records Service, General Services Administration, 1965.

The Public Papers of the Presidents of the United States: Lyndon B. Johnson, 1965, Book I. Washington, D.C.: Office of the Federal Register, National Archives and Records Service, General Services Administration, 1966.

The Public Papers of the Presidents of the United States: Lyndon B. Johnson, 1965, Book II. Washington, D.C.: Office of the Federal Register, National Archives and Records Service, General Services Administration, 1966.

Purdum, Todd S. *An Idea Whose Time Has Come: Two Presidents, Two Parties, and the Battle for the Civil Rights Act of 1964.* New York: Picador, 2015.

Putnam, Carleton. *Theodore Roosevelt: The Formative Years, 1858–1886.* New York: Charles Scribner's Sons, 1958.

Rappleye, Charles. *Herbert Hoover in the White House: The Ordeal of the Presidency.* New York: Simon & Schuster, 2016.

Rawley, James A. *Turning Points of the Civil War.* Lincoln: University of Nebraska Press, 1989.

Reedy, George. *Lyndon B. Johnson: A Memoir.* New York: Andrews and McMeel, 1982.

Remini, Robert Vincent. *Henry Clay: Statesman of the Union.* New York: W. W. Norton, 1991.

Rice, Allen Thorndike, ed. *Reminiscences of Abraham Lincoln by Distinguished Men of His Time.* New York: North American, 1886.

Riis, Jacob. A. *How the Other Half Lives: Studies among the Tenements of New York.* New York: Charles Scribner's Sons, 1914.

————. *The Making of an American.* New York: Macmillan, 1904.

————. *Theodore Roosevelt, the Citizen.* New York: Outlook, 1904.

Rixey, Lilian. *Bamie: Theodore Roosevelt's Remarkable Sister.* New York: D. McKay, 1963.

Robinson, Corinne Roosevelt. *My Brother, Theodore Roosevelt.* New York: Charles Scribner's Sons, 1921.

Rollins Jr., Alfred B. *Roosevelt and Howe.* New York: Alfred A. Knopf, 1962.

Roosevelt, Eleanor. *This I Remember.* New York: Harper & Brothers, 1949.

————. *This Is My Story.* New York: Harper & Brothers, 1937.

Roosevelt, Eleanor, and Helen Ferris. *Your Teens and Mine.* Garden City, N.Y.: Doubleday, 1961.

Roosevelt, Elliott, ed. *F.D.R.: His Personal Let-*

ters: *Early Years.* New York: Duell, Sloan & Pearce, 1947.

—————., ed. *F.D.R.: His Personal Letters, 1905–1928.* New York: Duell, Sloan & Pearce, 1948.

—————., ed. *F.D.R.: His Personal Letters, 1928–1945.* 2 vols. New York: Duell, Sloan & Pearce, 1950.

Roosevelt, Elliott, and James Brough. *A Rendezvous with Destiny: The Roosevelts in the White House.* New York: G. P. Putnam's Sons, 1975.

Roosevelt, Franklin D. *On Our Way.* New York: John Day, 1934.

—————. *The Public Papers and Addresses of Franklin D. Roosevelt.* Vol. 1: *The Genesis of the New Deal, 1928–1932.* New York: Random House, 1938.

—————. *The Public Papers and Addresses of Franklin D. Roosevelt.* Vol. 2: *The Year of Crisis, 1933.* New York: Random House, 1938.

—————. *The Public Papers and Addresses of Franklin D. Roosevelt.* Vol. 3: *The Advance of Recovery and Reform, 1934.* New York: Random House, 1938.

—————. *The Public Papers and Addresses of Franklin D. Roosevelt.* Vol. 5: *The People Approve, 1936.* New York: Random House, 1938.

—————. *The Public Papers and Addresses of*

Franklin D. Roosevelt, 1944–45: Victory and the Threshold of Peace. Compiled with special material and explanatory notes by Samuel I. Rosenman. Book 1. New York: Harper & Brothers, 1950.

Roosevelt, James, and Sidney Schalett. *Affectionately FDR: A Son's Story of a Lonely Man.* New York: Harcourt Brace, 1959.

Roosevelt, Sara Delano. As told to Isabel Leighton and Gabrielle Forbush. *My Boy Franklin.* New York: Ray Long & Richard R. Smith, 1933.

Roosevelt, Theodore. *Addresses and Presidential Messages of Theodore Roosevelt, 1902–1904.* New York: G. P. Putnam's Sons [The Knickerbocker Press], 1904.

———. *An Autobiography.* New York: Charles Scribner's Sons, 1925.

———. *Letters from Theodore Roosevelt to Anna Roosevelt Cowles, 1870–1918.* New York: Charles Scribner's Sons, 1924.

———. *The New Nationalism.* New York: Outlook, 1909.

———. *The Rough Riders.* New York: P. F. Collier & Sons, 1899.

Roosevelt, Theodore, Hermann Hagedorn, and G. B. Grinnell. *Hunting Trips of a Ranchman: Ranch Life and the Hunting Trail.* New York: Charles Scribner's Sons, 1927.

Roosevelt, Theodore; Lewis L. Gould, ed. *Bull Moose on the Stump: The 1912 Cam-*

paign Speeches of Theodore Roosevelt. Lawrence: University Press of Kansas, 2008.

Roosevelt, Theodore; Hermann Hagedorn, ed. *The Works of Theodore Roosevelt.* 24 vols. New York: Charles Scribner's Sons, 1923–1926.

Roosevelt, Theodore; Alfred Henry Lewis, ed. *A Compilation of the Messages and Speeches of Theodore Roosevelt, 1901–1905.* New York and Washington, D.C.: Bureau of National Literature and Art, 1906.

Roosevelt, Theodore; Elting E. Morison, John M. Blum, and John J. Buckley, eds. *The Letters of Theodore Roosevelt.* 8 Vols. Cambridge, Mass.: Harvard University Press, 1951–1954.

Rosenman, Samuel I. *Working with Roosevelt.* New York: Harper & Brothers, 1952.

Ross, Laura, ed. *A Passion to Lead: Theodore Roosevelt in His Own Words.* New York: Sterling Signature, 2012.

Rothman, Hal. *LBJ's Texas White House: "Our Heart's Home."* College Station: Texas A&M University Press, 2001.

Russell, Jan Jarboe. *Lady Bird: A Biography of Mrs. Johnson.* Waterville, Maine: Thorndike Press, 2000.

Sandburg Carl. *Abraham Lincoln: The Prairie Years.* Vol. 1. New York: Charles Scribner's

Sons, 1943.

————. *Abraham Lincoln: The Prairie Years.* Vol. 2. New York: Charles Scribner's Sons, 1943.

————. *Abraham Lincoln: The War Years.* Vol. 3. New York: Charles Scribner's Sons, 1943.

————. *Abraham Lincoln: The War Years.* Vol. 6. New York: Charles Scribner's Sons, 1943.

————. *Mary Lincoln: Wife and Mother.* Bedford, Mass.: Applewood Books, 1995.

Sargent, James E. *Roosevelt and the Hundred Days: Struggle for the Early New Deal.* New York: Garland, 1981.

Schlesinger Jr., Arthur M. *The Age of Roosevelt,* Vol. 1: *The Crisis of the Old Order, 1919–1933.* New York: Mariner, 2003.

————. *The Age of Roosevelt,* Vol. 2: *The Coming of the New Deal, 1933–1935.* New York: Mariner, 2003.

————. *The Age of Roosevelt,* Vol. 3: *The Politics of Upheaval, 1935–1936.* New York: Mariner, 2003.

Sears, Stephen W., ed. *The Civil War Papers of George C. McClellan: Selected Correspondence, 1860–1865.* New York: Ticknor & Fields, 1989.

Segal, Charles M., ed. *Conversations with Lincoln.* New York: G. P. Putnam's Sons, 1961.

Sewall, William Wingate. *Bill Sewall's Story of Theodore Roosevelt.* New York: Harper & Brothers, 1919.

Seward, Frederick William. *Reminiscences of a War-Time Statesman and Diplomat: 1830–1915.* New York: G. P. Putnam's Sons [Knickerbocker Press], 1916.

————. *Seward at Washington as Senator and Secretary of State: A Memoir of His Life, with Selections from His Letters, 1861–1872.* New York: Derby and Miller, 1891.

Shenk, Joshua Wolf. *Lincoln's Melancholy: How Depression Challenged a President and Fueled His Greatness.* New York: Mariner, 2006.

Sherwood, Robert E. *Roosevelt and Hopkins: An Intimate History.* New York: Harper & Brothers, 1948.

Shoumatoff, Elizabeth. *FDR's Unfinished Portrait.* Pittsburgh: University of Pittsburgh Press, 1990.

Smith, Jean Edward. *FDR.* New York: Random House, 2007.

Staudenraus, P. J., ed. *Mr. Lincoln's Washington: Selections from the Writings of Noah Brooks Civil War Correspondent.* South Brunswick, N.J.: Thomas Yoseloff, 1967.

Steffens, Lincoln. *The Autobiography of Lincoln Steffens.* 2 vols. New York: Harcourt, Brace & World, 1931.

Steinberg, Alfred. *Sam Johnson's Boy: A Close-up of the President from Texas.* New York: Macmillan, 1968.

Stiles. Lela. *The Man behind Roosevelt: The

Story of Louis McHenry Howe. New York: World, 1954.

Stoddard, William O. *Abraham Lincoln: The True Story of a Great Life.* New York: Fords, Howard, & Hulbert, 1884.

————. *Inside the White House in War Times.* Lincoln, Neb.: Bison, 2000.

Stone, I. F. *The War Years, 1939–1945.* Boston: Little, Brown, 1990.

Straus, Oscar S. *Under Four Administrations: From Cleveland to Taft.* Boston: Houghton Mifflin, 1922.

Strock, James M. *Theodore Roosevelt on Leadership.* Roseville, Calif.: Prima Publishing, 2001.

Strozier, Charles B. *Lincoln's Quest for Union: Public and Private Meanings.* Chicago: University of Illinois Press, 1987.

Sullivan, Mark. *Our Times: The United States, 1900–1925,* Vol. 2: *America Finding Herself.* New York: Charles Scribner's Sons, 1927.

————. *Our Times: The United States, 1900–1925,* Vol. 4: *The War Begins, 1909–1914.* New York: Charles Scribner's Sons, 1927.

Tarbell, Ida M. *The Life of Abraham Lincoln.* 4 vols. New York: Lincoln Historical Society, 1903.

————. *A Reporter for Lincoln: Story of Henry E. Wing, Soldier and Newspaperman.* New York: Macmillan, 1927.

Tarbell, Ida M. Assisted by McCan Davis.

The Early Life of Abraham Lincoln. New York: S. S. McClure, 1896.

Thayer, William Roscoe. *Theodore Roosevelt: An Intimate Biography.* Boston: Houghton Mifflin, 1919.

Thomas, Evan. *The War Lovers: Roosevelt, Lodge, Hearst, and the Rush to Empire, 1898.* Boston: Little, Brown, 2014.

Thwing, Eugene. *The Life and Meaning of Theodore Roosevelt.* New York: Current Literature, 1919.

Tobin, James. *The Man He Became: How FDR Defied Polio to Win the Presidency.* New York: Simon & Schuster, 2013.

Tugwell, Rex W. *The Democratic Roosevelt.* Baltimore: Penguin, 1957.

Tully, Grace. *F.D.R. My Boss.* New York: Charles Scribner's Sons, 1949.

Turgenev, Ivan. *Sketches from a Hunter's Album,* translated with an introduction and notes by Richard Freeborn. New York: Penguin, 1990.

Turner, Justin G., and Linda Levitt Turner. *Mary Todd Lincoln: Her Life and Letters.* New York: Alfred A. Knopf, 1972.

Usher, John P. *President Lincoln's Cabinet.* New York: Nelson H. Loomis, 1925.

Valenti, Jack. *A Very Human President.* New York: Pocket Books, 1977.

Wagenknecht, Edward. *The Seven Worlds of Theodore Roosevelt.* Guilford, Conn.: Lyons Press, 2009.

Walker, Turnley. *Roosevelt and the Warm Springs Story.* New York: A. Wyn, 1953.

Ward, Geoffrey C. *Before the Trumpet: Young Franklin Roosevelt, 1882–1905.* New York: Vintage, 2014.

———. *Closest Companion: The Unknown Story of the Intimate Friendship between Franklin Roosevelt and Margaret Suckley.* New York: Simon & Schuster, 1995.

———. *A First-Class Temperament: The Emergence of Franklin Roosevelt, 1905–1928.* New York: Vintage, 2014.

Ward, Geoffrey C., and Ken Burns. *The Vietnam War: An Intimate History.* New York: Alfred A. Knopf, 2017.

Warren, Louis. *Lincoln's Youth: Indiana Years, Seven to Twenty-one, 1816–1830.* Indianapolis: Indiana Historical Society, 1959.

Washburn, Charles Grenfell. *Theodore Roosevelt: The Logic of His Career.* Boston: Houghton Mifflin, 1916.

Weik, Jesse W. *The Real Lincoln: A Portrait.* Boston: Houghton Mifflin, 1922.

Weintraub, Stanley. *Young Mr. Roosevelt: FDR's Introduction to War, Politics, and Life.* New York: Da Capo, 2013.

Welles, Gideon; Howard K. Beale, ed. *Diary of Gideon Welles: Secretary of the Navy under Lincoln and Johnson,* Vol. 1: *1861–*

March 30, 1964. New York: W. W. Norton, 1960.

White, Horace. *Abraham Lincoln in 1854: An Address delivered before the Illinois State Historical Society, at its 9th Annual Meeting at Springfield, Illinois, Jan. 30, 1908.* Springfield: Illinois State Historical Society, 1908.

Whitney, Henry C. *Life on the Circuit with Lincoln.* Boston: Estes and Lauriat, 1892.

————. *Lincoln, The Citizen.* New York: Baker & Taylor, 1908.

Wiley, Bell. *The Life of Billy Yank.* Baton Rouge: Louisiana State University Press, 1979.

Wilson, Douglas L. *Honor's Voice: The Transformation of Abraham Lincoln.* New York: Vintage, 1999.

————. *Lincoln before Washington: New Perspectives on the Illinois Years.* Urbana: University of Illinois Press, 1998.

Wilson, Douglas L., and Rodney O. Davis, eds. *Herndon's Informants: Letters, Interviews, and Statements about Abraham Lincoln.* Chicago: University of Illinois Press, 1998.

Winik, Jay. *April 1865: The Month That Saved America.* New York: Harper Perennial, 2002.

Wister, Owen. *Roosevelt: The Story of a Friendship, 1880–1919.* New York: Macmillan, 1930.

Wood, Frederick S. *Roosevelt as We Knew Him.* Philadelphia: John C. Winston Co., 1927.

Woods, Randall B. *LBJ: Architect of American Ambition.* Cambridge, Mass.: Harvard University Press, 2006.

Wordsworth, William. *The Complete Poetical Works of William Wordsworth, Together with a Description of the Country of the Lakes in the North of England, Now First Published with His Works,* Henry Reed, ed. Philadelphia: James Kay, Jun. and Brothers, 1837.

Zinsser, William, ed. *Extraordinary Lives: The Art and Craft of American Biography.* Winter Park, Fla.: American Heritage Press, 1986.

BUSINESS BOOKS ON LEADERSHIP SKILLS

Harvard Business Review's 10 Must Reads Series

On Collaboration. Boston: Harvard Business Review Press, 2013.
On Communication. Boston: Harvard Business Review Press, 2013.
On Emotional Intelligence. Boston: Harvard Business Review Press, 2015.
On Leadership. Boston: Harvard Business Review Press, 2011.
On Managing People. Boston: Harvard Business Review Press, 2011.
On Managing Yourself. Boston: Harvard Business Review Press, 2011.
On Teams. Boston: Harvard Business Review Press, 2013.

Other Business Books on Leadership Skills

Bennis, Warren. *On Becoming a Leader.* New York: Basic Books, 2009.
Bennis, Warren, and Burt Nanus. *Leaders:*

Strategies for Taking Charge. New York: Harper Business Essentials, 2003.

Bennis, Warren, and Robert J. Thomas. *Geeks and Geezers.* Boston: Harvard Business School Press, 2002.

———. *Leading for a Lifetime: How Defining Moments Shape Leaders of Today and Tomorrow.* Boston: Harvard Business School Press, 2007.

Burns, James McGregor. *Leadership.* New York: Harper & Row, 1978.

———. *The Power to Lead: The Crisis of the American Presidency.* New York: Simon & Schuster, 1994.

———. *Transforming Leadership.* New York: Grove Press, 2003.

Champy, James, and Nitin Nohria. *The Arc of Ambition: Defining the Leadership Journey.* Cambridge, Mass.: Perseus, 2000.

Collins, Jim. *Good to Great.* New York: HarperCollins, 2001.

Covey, Stephen R. *The 7 Habits of Highly Effective People: Restoring the Character Ethic.* New York: Free Press, 2004.

Crandall, Major Doug. *Leadership Lessons from West Point.* San Francisco: Jossey-Bass, 2007.

Drucker, Peter F. *The Essential Drucker: The Best of Sixty Years of Peter Drucker's Essential Writing on Management.* New York: HarperCollins, 2001.

Duhigg, Charles. *The Power of Habit: Why We Do What We Do in Life and Business.* New York: Random House, 2014.

Ferguson, Alex. With Michael Ortiz. *Leading: Learning from Life and My Years at Manchester United.* New York: Hachette, 2015.

Fink, Steven. *Crisis Management: Planning for the Inevitable.* Lincoln, Neb.: iUniverse, 2002.

Fullan, Michael. *Turnaround Leadership.* San Francisco: Jossey-Bass, 2016.

Gardner, Howard. With Emma Laskin. *Leading Minds: An Anatomy of Leadership.* New York: Basic Books, 1995.

Gardner, John W. *On Leadership.* New York: Simon & Schuster, 1990.

Gates, Robert M. *A Passion for Leadership: Lessons on Change and Reform from Fifty Years of Public Service.* New York: Vintage, 2017.

George, Bill. With Peter Sims. *True North: Discover Your Authentic Leadership.* San Francisco: Jossey-Bass, 2007.

Gladwell, Malcolm. *David and Goliath: Underdogs, Misfits, and the Art of Battling Giants.* New York: Little, Brown, 2013.

Goleman, Daniel. *Emotional Intelligence: Why It Can Matter More than IQ.* New York: Bantam, 1995.

———. *Social Intelligence: The New Science of Human Relationships.* New York: Bantam

Dell, 2006.

Goleman, Daniel, Richard Boyatzis, and Annie McKee. *Primal Leadership: Unleashing the Power of Emotional Intelligence.* Boston: Harvard Business Review Press, 2013.

Gottschall, Jonathan. *The Storytelling Animal: How Stories Make Us Human.* New York: Mariner, 2013.

Harvard Business Essentials: Business Communication. Boston: Harvard Business Review Press, 2003.

Harvard Business Essentials: Crisis Management: Master the Skills to Prevent Disasters. Boston: Harvard Business Press, 2014.

Heifetz, Ronald A. *Leadership Without Easy Answers.* Cambridge: Harvard University Press, 1998.

Heifetz, Ronald, Alexander Grashow, and Marty Linsky. *The Practice of Adaptive Leadership: Tools and Tactics for Changing Your Organization and the World.* Boston: Harvard Business Press, 2009.

Heifetz, Ronald, and Marty Linsky. *Leadership on the Line: Staying Alive Through the Dangers of Change.* Boston: Harvard Business Review Press, 2002.

Kanter, Rosabeth Moss. *The Change Masters: Innovation & Entrepreneurship in the American Corporation.* New York: Simon & Schuster, 1993.

————. *Confidence: How Winning Streaks and*

Losing Streaks Begin and End. New York: Green River Press, 2004.

————. *On the Frontiers of Management.* Boston: Harvard Business Review Press, 2005.

Kotter, John P. *Leading Change.* Boston: Harvard Business Review Press, 2012.

Maxwell, John C. *The 5 Levels of Leadership.* New York: Center Street, 2011.

Mayo, Anthony, and Nitin Nohria. *In Their Time: The Greatest Business Leaders of the Twentieth Century.* Boston: Harvard Business Review Press, 2005.

Mayo, Anthony, Nitin Nohria, and Laura G. Singleton. *Paths to Power: How Insiders and Outsiders Shaped American Business Leadership.* Boston: Harvard Business School Press, 2006.

Moss, David. *Democracy: A Case Study.* Cambridge, Mass.: The Belknap Press of Harvard University Press, 2017.

Nanus, Burt. *Visionary Leadership.* San Francisco: Jossey-Bass, 1992.

Nohria, Nitin, and Rakesh Khurana, eds. *Handbook of Leadership Theory and Practice.* Boston: Harvard Business Press, 2010.

O'Loughlin, James. *The Real Warren Buffet: Managing Capital, Leading People.* Yarmouth, Me.: Nicholas Brealey Publishing, 2004.

Peters, Thomas J., and Robert H. Waterman.

In Search of Excellence: Lessons from America's Best-Run Companies. New York: HarperCollins, 2004.

Silver, A. David. *The Turnaround Survival Guide: Strategies for the Company in Crisis.* Dearborn, Mich.: Dearborn Trading Pub., 1992.

Weinzweig, Ari. *A Lapsed Anarchist's Approach to Being a Better Leader (Zingerman's Guide to Good Leading).* Ann Arbor, Mich.: Zingerman's Press, 2012.

Welch, Jack. With Suzy Welch. *Winning.* New York: HarperCollins, 2005.

ABBREVIATIONS
USED IN NOTES

AL Abraham Lincoln

ARC Anna Roosevelt Cowles

BP Doris Kearns Goodwin. *The Bully Pulpit.* New York: Simon & Schuster, 2013.

CRR Corrine Roosevelt Robinson

CW Roy P. Basler, ed. *The Collected Works of Abraham Lincoln.* 8 vols. New Brunswick, N.J.: Rutgers University Press, 1953.

DKG Doris Kearns Goodwin

DKG/LBJ Conversations between the author and LBJ, in the possession Conversations of the author.

ER Eleanor Roosevelt

FDR Franklin D. Roosevelt

FDRL Franklin D. Roosevelt Library, Hyde Park, New York

HCL Henry Cabot Lodge

HI Douglas L. Wilson and Rodney O. Davis, eds. *Herndon's Informants: Letters, Interviews, and Statements about Abraham Lincoln.* Chicago: University of Illinois Press, 1998.

LBJ Lyndon Baines Johnson

LBJOH LBJ Library Oral History

LC Library of Congress

LJAD Doris Kearns Goodwin. *Lyndon Johnson and the American Dream.* New York: Harper & Row, 1976.

LTR Theodore Roosevelt; Elting E. Morison, John M. Blum, and John J. Buckley, eds. *The Letters of Theodore Roosevelt.* 8 vols. Cambridge, Mass.: Harvard University Press, 1951–1954.

Nicolay Papers Papers of John J. Nicolay, Manuscript Division, Library of Congress.

NOT Doris Kearns Goodwin. *No Ordinary Time: Franklin and Eleanor Roosevelt: The Home Front in World War II.* New York: Simon & Schuster, 1994.

NYT New York Times

OHRO/CUL Oral History Research Office Collection of the Columbia University Libraries

PPA Franklin D. Roosevelt. *The Public Papers and Addresses of Franklin D. Roosevelt.* Vols. 1–5. New York: Random House, 1938.

PPP Lyndon Baines Johnson. *Public Papers of the Presidents of the United States.* Washington, D.C.: Government Printing Office, 1964–1970.

PRLBJ The Presidential Recordings: Lyndon B. Johnson. 7 vols. New York: W. W. Norton, 2005.

SDR Sara Delano Roosevelt

Steffens Papers Lincoln Steffens Papers. Rare Books and Manuscript Library, Columbia University

TOR Doris Kearns Goodwin. *Team of Rivals.* New York: Simon & Schuster, 1994.

TR Theodore Roosevelt

TRC Theodore Roosevelt Collection, Houghton Library, Harvard University

TRP Theodore Roosevelt Papers, Manuscript Division, Library of Congress

VP Lyndon Baines Johnson. *The Vantage Point: Perspectives of the Presidency, 1963– 1969.* New York: Holt, Rinehart & Winston, 1971.

WTR Theodore Roosevelt; Hermann Hagedorn, ed. *The Works of Theodore Roosevelt.* 24 vols. New York: Charles Scribner's Sons, 1923–1926.

NOTES

Foreword

"I have often thought . . . 'real me!' ": William Zinsser, ed., *Extraordinary Lives: The Art and Craft of American Biography* (Winter Park, Fla.: American Heritage Press, 1986), pp. 181–82.

"If there is not the war . . . have known his name now": TR, "The Conditions of Success," May 26, 1910, WTR, 13:575.

"It is not in the still calm . . . out great virtues": Abigail Adams to John Quincy Adams, Jan. 19, 1780, *The Adams Papers, Adams Family Correspondence,* Vol. 3, April 1778–September 1780, ed. L. H. Butterfield and Marc Friedlaender (Cambridge, Mass.: Harvard University Press, 1973), pp. 268–69.

"Rarely was man so fitted to the event": Abraham Lincoln eulogy by Ralph Waldo Emerson, April 15, 1865, http://www.rwe.org/abraham-lincoln-15-april-1865-eulogy-by-

ralph-waldo-emerson/.

"greater than that which rested upon Washington": AL, "Farewell Address at Springfield, Illinois," [A. Version], Feb. 11, 1861, *CW,* 4:190.

"I have only . . . army have done it all": Michael Burlingame, *Abraham Lincoln, A Life* (Baltimore: Johns Hopkins University Press, 2008), pp. 750–51.

"With public sentiment . . . nothing can succeed": AL, "Fragment: Notes for Speeches [Aug. 21, 1858], *CW* 2:553.

Chapter One

Abraham: "Every man is said to have his peculiar ambition"

"Every man is . . . many of you": AL, "Communication to the People of Sangamon County," March 9, 1832, *CW,* 1:8.

"I was born . . . much chagrined": Ibid., p. 9.

"strong conviction . . . even possible": Joshua Wolf Shenk, *Lincoln's Melancholy: How Depression Challenged a President and Fueled His Greatness* (New York: Mariner, 2006), p. 17.

"condensed into . . . of the poor": John L. Scripps, in *HI,* p. 57.

"more in the way . . . his own name": AL, "Autobiography Written for John L. Scripps" [c. June 1860], *CW,* 4:61.

"she was superior . . . in Every way": Nathaniel

Grigsby, *HI,* p. 113.

"keen — shrewd — smart": Dennis F. Hanks, ibid., p. 37.

"All that I am . . . my mother": Michael Burlingame, *The Inner World of Abraham Lincoln* (Chicago: University of Illinois Press, 1994), p. 42.

milk sickness: HI, p. 40; Philip D. Jordan, "The Death of Nancy Hanks Lincoln," *Indiana Magazine of History* (June 1944), pp. 103–10.

"a wild region": AL, "Autobiography written for Jesse W. Fell," Dec. 20, 1859, *CW,* 3:511.

"the panther's . . . on the swine": "The Bear Hunt," [Sept. 6, 1846?] *CW,* 1:386.

"wild — ragged & dirty": Quoted by Dennis Hanks, *HI,* p. 41.

"snug and comfortable" . . . clothing for the children: A. H. Chapman, *HI,* p. 99.

"He was the learned . . . unlearned folks": Anna Caroline Gentry, *HI,* p. 132.

"He carried away . . . equal": David Herbert Donald, *Lincoln* (New York: Simon & Schuster, 1995), p. 32.

"the best": Louis Warren, *Lincoln's Youth: Indiana Years, Seven to Twenty-One, 1816–1830* (Indianapolis: Indiana Historical Society, 1959), p. 80.

"marvelously retentive": Allen C. Guelzo, "Lincoln and Leadership: An Afterword," in Randall M. Miller, ed., *Lincoln and Leader-*

ship: Military, Political, and Religious Decision Making* (New York: Fordham University Press, 2012), p. 100.

"a wonder . . . rub it out": Joshua Speed, *HI*, p. 499.

"When he came . . . rewrite it": Sarah Bush Lincoln, *HI*, p. 107.

"When a mere child . . . bounded it west": Ida M. Tarbell, *The Life of Abraham Lincoln*, 4 vols. (New York: Lincoln Historical Society, 1903), Vol. 1, pp. 43–44.

"The ambition . . . whilst we played": Grigsby, *HI*, p. 114.

"letters, words . . . could be drawn": Warren, *Lincoln's Youth*, p. 24.

"the best penman . . . neighborhood": Joseph C. Richardson, *HI*, pp. 473–74.

"their guide and leader": Grigsby, *HI*, p. 114.

"great pains" . . . not the moon: Anna Caroline Gentry, *HI*, p. 132.

"When he appeared . . . what he said": Grigsby, *HI*, pp. 114–15.

"no small part . . . up and down": AL, quoted in Francis B. Carpenter, *Six Months at the White House with Abraham Lincoln* (Lincoln: University of Nebraska Press, 1995), pp. 312–13.

"the Style & tone" . . . Baptist preachers: Chapman, *HI*, p. 102.

additional material for his storytelling . . . the nearest courthouse: Chapman, *HI*, p. 102;

Tarbell, *The Life of Abraham Lincoln,* Vol. 1, p. 36.

"winning smile": Horace White, *Abraham Lincoln in 1854* (Springfield: Illinois State Historical Society, 1908), p. 19.

"there was not a corn blade . . . on a stalk": Oliver C. Terry, *HI,* p. 662.

"Josiah blowing his bugle": AL, "Chronicles of Reuben," in Carl Sandberg, *Abraham Lincoln: The Prairie Years,* vol. 1 (New York: Charles Scribner's Sons, 1943) p. 55.

"it was wrong . . . cruelty to animals": Grigsby, *HI,* p. 112.

"pulled a trigger on any larger game": Tarbell, *The Life of Abraham Lincoln,* Vol. 1, p. 25.

"It was a man" . . . *to warm him up:* David Turnham, *HI,* p. 122.

pig caught: Helen Nicolay, *Personal Traits of Abraham Lincoln* (New York: Century, 1912), p. 81.

"ready to out-run . . . out-lift anybody": Leonard Swett, in Allen Thorndike Rice, ed., *Reminiscences of Abraham Lincoln by Distinguished Men of His Time* (New York: North American, 1886), p. 71.

"could carry . . . & sweat at": Joseph C. Richardson, *HI,* p. 120.

"sufficient to make . . . doubly wasted": John B. Helm, *HI,* p. 48.

"he could lay his hands on": Dennis Hanks, *HI,* p. 41.

"When I read aloud . . . remember it better": Robert L. Wilson, *HI,* p. 207.

father's treatment of AL: Dennis Hanks, *HI,* p. 41.

"I tried to stop . . . be got out": Douglas L. Wilson, *Honor's Voice: The Transformation of Abraham Lincoln* (New York: Vintage, 1999), p. 57.

"His melancholy dript . . . as he walked": William H. Herndon, "Analysis of the Character," *Abraham Lincoln Quarterly* (1941), p. 339.

"No element . . . melancholy": Henry C. Whitney, *Life on the Circuit with Lincoln* (Boston: Estes and Lauriat, 1892), p. 146.

"necessary to his very existence": Robert Rutledge, *HI,* p. 409.

"to whistle off sadness": David Davis, *HI,* pp. 348, 350.

"that he was going to be something": Burlingame, *The Inner World of Abraham Lincoln,* p. 237.

"a vision of an alternative future": John Kotter, "What Leaders Really Do," *Harvard Business Review* (May–June 1990), p. 47.

"intend to delve . . . will come": Burlingame, *The Inner World of Abraham Lincoln,* p. 237.

"Seeing no prospect . . . the broad world": AL to Joshua Speed, Aug. 24, 1855, *HI,* p. 52.

"supplied a large . . . flour and lumber": Rutledge, *HI,* p. 382.

Description of New Salem: Tarbell, *The Life of Abraham Lincoln,* Vol. 1, pp. 59–60.

"Gawky and rough-looking": Carl Sandburg, *Abraham Lincoln: The Prairie Years,* Vol. 1 (New York: Charles Scribner's Sons, 1943), p. 161.

"the most ludicrous . . . a pair of socks": Clipping from *Menard Axis* (Illinois), Feb. 15, 1862, *HI,* p. 24.

"open — candid . . . loved him": Henry Mc-Henry, *HI,* p. 14.

"spontaneous, unobtrusive": Tarbell, *The Life of Abraham Lincoln,* Vol. 1, p. 108.

"filled a unique place . . . intellectual and social center": Ida M. Tarbell, Assisted by J. Mc-Can Davis, *The Early Life of Abraham Lincoln* (New York: S. S. McClure, 1896), p. 119.

general store as meeting place: Ibid.

farmers traveling: Sandburg, *The Prairie Years,* Vol. 1, p. 134.

"a Center of attraction": Mentor Graham, *HI,* p. 9.

"among the best clerks . . . great tenderness": William G. Greene, *HI,* p. 18.

"unabashed eagerness to learn": Donald, *Lincoln,* p. 41.

"a fire of shavings sufficiently bright": Tarbell, *The Early Life of Abraham Lincoln,* p. 125.

"When he was ignorant . . . to acknowledge it": Speed, *HI,* p. 499.

Kirkham's English Grammar: Herndon and Weik, *Herndon's Lincoln,* p. 65.

"understood by all classes": Joseph Gillespie, *HI,* p. 508.

"If elected . . . my support": AL, "Communication to the People of Sangamon County," March 9, 1832, *CW,* 1:7.

"I can only say . . . free institutions": Ibid., 1:8.

"the humble walks of life": Burlingame, *The Inner World of Abraham Lincoln,* p. 238.

"ready to renounce them": AL, "Communication to the People of Sangamon County," March 9, 1832, *CW,* 1:8.

"too familiar with . . . never to try it again": J. Rowan Herndon, *HI,* p. 7.

"success in life . . . much satisfaction": AL, "Autobiography Written for John L. Scripps," *CW,* 4:64.

"vandoos . . . get the news": Tarbell, *The Early Life of Abraham Lincoln,* p. 155.

"did not follow . . . other Speakers": Robert L. Wilson, *HI,* p. 204.

"drawn from all classes of Society": William L. Miller, *Lincoln's Virtues: An Ethical Biography* (New York: Vintage, 2003), p. 8.

"either the argument . . . or the author": Wilson, *HI,* pp. 204–5.

"did not dampen . . . his ambition": Herndon and Weik, *Herndon's Life of Lincoln,* p. 76.

"body and soul together": AL, "Autobiography Written for John L. Scripps," *CW,* 4:65.

"men and boys . . . and jokes": Tarbell, *The Life of Abraham Lincoln,* Vol. 1, p. 132.

"with perfect ease": J. Rowan Herndon, *HI,* p. 8.

"Can't the party . . . put together": Ibid.

"suitable clothing . . . maintain his new dignity": Herndon and Weik, *Herndon's Life of Lincoln,* p. 104.

"anything but . . . in the background": Ibid., pp. 110–11.

(including two future . . . State Supreme Court justices): Tarbell, *The Life of Abraham Lincoln,* Vol. 1, p. 132.

"studied with nobody": AL, "Autobiography Written for John L. Scripps," *CW,* 4:65.

After finishing each book . . . another loaner: Herndon and Weik, *Herndon's Life of Lincoln,* p. 91.

"Get the books . . . any other one thing": AL to Isham Reavis, Nov. 5, 1855, *CW,* 2:327.

"They say I tell . . . than any other way": Donald Phillips, *Lincoln on Leadership* (New York: Warner Books, 1992), p. 155.

"crowning gift . . . diagnosis": Helen Nicolay, *Personal Traits of Abraham Lincoln,* p. 77.

"From your talk . . . that way themselves": Ibid., p. 78.

"his thorough knowledge . . . have ever known": Herndon and Weik, *Herndon's Life of Lincoln,* p. 118.

"We followed . . . ordinary argument": Henry

C. Whitney, *Lincoln, the Citizen* (New York: The Baker & Taylor Co., 1908), p. 140.

"roused the lion within him": Herndon and Weik, *Herndon's Life of Lincoln,* p. 115.

"The gentleman . . . offended God": AL, quoted in ibid., pp. 115–16.

"indulged in some fun . . . with the deepest chagrin": Ibid., p. 130.

"we highly disapprove . . . property in slaves": Resolutions by the General Assembly of the State of Illinois, quoted in note 2 of "Protest in Illinois Legislature on Slavery," March 3, 1837, *CW,* 1:75.

"the institution of slavery . . . and bad policy": "Protest in Illinois Legislature on Slavery," March 3, 1837, *CW,* 1:75.

"if slavery is not wrong, nothing is wrong": AL to Albert Hodges, April 4, 1864, *CW,* 7:281.

"pruned of any offensive allusions": Herndon and Weik, *Herndon's Life of Lincoln,* p. 145.

"a bold thing . . . political pariah": William O. Stoddard, *Abraham Lincoln: The True Story of a Great Life* (New York: Fords, Howard, & Hulbert, 1884), p. 116.

"DeWitt Clinton of Illinois": Burlingame, *The Inner World of Abraham Lincoln,* p. 239.

promise of the American dream: This point is developed by Gabor S. Boritt, *Economics of the American Dream* (Urbana: University of Illinois Press, 1994).

"in the middle of a river . . . it would go down":

AL, "Remarks in the Illinois Legislature Concerning the Illinois and Michigan Canal," Jan. 22, 1840, *CW,* 1:196.

"If you make a bad bargain, hug it the tighter": AL to Joshua F. Speed, Feb. 25, 1842, *CW,* 1:280.

"peculiar ambition": AL, "Communication to the People of Sangamon County," March 9, 1932, *CW,* 1: 8.

"something of ill-omen . . . the bible shall be read": AL, "Address before the Young Men's Lyceum of Springfield, Illinois," Jan. 27, 1838, *CW,* 1:109–14.

"proud fabric of freedom": Ibid., p. 108.

Chapter Two
Theodore: "I rose like a rocket"

"run on his own hook": John T. Stuart, *HI,* p. 77.

"Having been nominated . . . Election Day": TR, "To the Voters of the 21st Assembly District," Nov. 1, 1881, in *LTR,* 1:55.

"picked me . . . for myself": TR, *An Autobiography* (New York: Charles Scribner's Sons, 1925), pp. 59–60.

"one of the most . . . honored name": New York *Daily Tribune,* Nov. 6, 1881.

"no wealthy or popular relations": AL, "Communication to the People of Sangamon County," March 9, 1832, *CW,* 1:8.

"the element of chance . . . to take advantage":

TR, "The Conditions of Success," May 26, 1910, *WTR,* 13:575.

"I put myself . . . and they happened": James M. Strock, *Theodore Roosevelt on Leadership* (Roseville, Calif.: Prima, 2001), p. 43.

"no simple thing . . . any other club": TR, *An Autobiography,* pp. 55–56.

"men of cultivated . . . rough and tumble": Ibid., p. 56.

"who has in him . . . success himself": TR, *An Autobiography,* pp. 51–52.

"the gospel of will": Jacob Riis, *Theodore Roosevelt, the Citizen* (New York: Outlook Co., 1904), p. 15.

"I like to believe that . . . to Americans": Eugene Thwing, *The Life and Meaning of Theodore Roosevelt* (New York: Current Literature, 1919), p. 1.

"Nobody seemed to think I would live": The *World* (New York), Nov. 16, 1902.

"My father . . . lungs, strength — life": Lincoln Steffens, *The Autobiography of Lincoln Steffens,* 2 vols. (New York: Harcourt, Brace & World, 1931), Vol. 1, p. 350.

"From the very fact . . . power of concentration": William Draper Lewis, *The Life of Theodore Roosevelt* (Chicago: John C. Winston, 1919), p. 36.

"Do I know them? . . . and weaknesses": Riis, *Theodore Roosevelt, the Citizen,* p. 19.

"need more than . . . prose or of poetry": TR,

An Autobiography, p. 334.

"the greatest of companions": Edward Wagenknecht, *The Seven Worlds of Theodore Roosevelt* (Guilford, Conn.: Lyons Press, 2009), p. 50.

prodigious memory: H. W. Brands, *T.R.: The Last Romantic* (New York: Basic Books, 1997), p. 62.

"a piece of steel . . . to rub it out": Speed, *HI,* p. 499.

"wax to receive . . . everything he read": William Wingate Sewall, *Bill Sewall's Story of Theodore Roosevelt* (New York: Harper & Brothers, 1919), p. 39.

TR at center of play group: Corinne Roosevelt Robinson, quoted in Lewis, *The Life of Theodore Roosevelt,* p. 35.

"unreconstructed" southerner: TR, *An Autobiography,* p. 11.

"a purposeful . . . were concerned": Carleton Putnam, *Theodore Roosevelt: The Formative Years, 1858–1886* (New York: Charles Scribner's Sons, 1958), p. 99.

"Roosevelt Museum of Natural History": TR, *An Autobiography,* p. 14.

Elliott to beg for a separate room: Hermann Hagedorn, *The Boy's Life of Theodore Roosevelt* (New York: Harper & Brothers, 1941), p. 45.

"And of course . . . in our lives": CRR, *My Brother, Theodore Roosevelt* (New York:

Charles Scribner's Sons, 1921), p. 80.

"Theodore, you have . . . I'll make my body": Ibid., p. 50.

"They found that . . . helpless position": TR, *An Autobiography,* p. 52.

"The young man . . . natural history in his hands": Putnam, *Theodore Roosevelt,* p. 127.

"the house . . . not be diverted": Charles Grenfell Washburn, *Theodore Roosevelt: The Logic of His Career* (Boston: Houghton Mifflin, 1916), p. 3.

"The story . . . to be like them": Hagedorn, *The Boy's Life of Theodore Roosevelt,* p. 1.

"My father was the best . . . than did my father": TR, *An Autobiography,* pp. 7, 9.

"his best and most intimate friend": TR to TR Sr., Oct. 22, 1876, *LTR,* 1:18.

"It seems perfectly . . . my own fault": Ibid., p. 19.

"studious, ambitious . . . appeal at first": Henry Pringle, *Theodore Roosevelt: A Biography* (New York: Harcourt, Brace, 1931), p. 33.

"never conquered asthma completely": CRR in Kathleen Mary Dalton, *Theodore Roosevelt: A Strenuous Life* (New York: Vintage, 2004), p. 420.

"just as you'd expect . . . he hopped": Putnam, *Theodore Roosevelt,* p. 106.

"broadened every interest . . . his own age": Ibid.

"I fear for your future . . . any length of time": Kathleen Mary Dalton, "The Early Life of Theodore Roosevelt.," PhD diss., Johns Hopkins University, 1979, p. 282.

"I felt as if I . . . taken away": Theodore Roosevelt Private Diary, Feb. 12, 1878, Series 8, Reel 429, TRP.

"If it were not . . . almost perish": Putnam, *Theodore Roosevelt,* p. 148.

"Every now . . . companion, friend": TR, Private Diary, March 29, 1878, Series 8, Reel 429, TRP.

"The death . . . him to the grave": *NYT,* Feb. 13, 1878.

"Oh, how little worthy . . . keep up his name": TR, Private Diary, Feb. 22, 1878, Series 8, Reel 429, TRP.

"leading the most . . . a bit of an optimist": Ibid., March 29, 1879.

"No one but my wife . . . [my father's] place": Dalton, "The Early Life of Theodore Roosevelt," p. 300.

"It was a real case . . . my first love too": TR, Private Diary, Jan. 30, 1880, TRP.

"everything subordinate to winning her": TR to Henry Davis Minot, Feb. 13, 1880, *LTR,* 1:43.

"nearly crazy . . . my own happiness": TR, Private Diary, Jan. 25, 1880, TRP.

"I do not believe . . . than I love her": Ibid., March 11, 1880.

"that he had made . . . the microscope": TR,

An Autobiography, p. 24.

"I want you to take . . . unless by his demerit": Sewall, *Bill Sewall's Story of Theodore Roosevelt,* p. 2.

"I tried faithfully . . . to work in his own way": Riis, *Theodore Roosevelt, the Citizen,* pp. 36–37.

"I'm going to try . . . I don't know exactly how": William Roscoe Thayer, *Theodore Roosevelt: An Intimate Biography* (Boston: Houghton Mifflin, 1919), p. 21.

"what law is, not what it ought to be": Robert Charles, "Legal Education in the Late Nineteenth Century, through the Eyes of Theodore Roosevelt," *American Journal of Legal History* (July 1993), p. 247.

"talk glibly": TR, *An Autobiography,* p. 23.

"When I went into politics . . . with other people": Ibid., p. 61.

"lack of interest . . . young men especially": James MacGregor Burns and Susan Dunn, *The Three Roosevelts: Patrician Leaders Who Transformed America* (New York: Grove, 2001), p. 25.

"greenhorn": Caleb Carman, *HI,* p. 429.

"Who's the dude? . . . tailor could make them": Recollections of John Walsh, quoted in *Kansas City Star,* Feb. 12, 1922.

"I went around . . . 'being a stranger' ": TR, *An Autobiography,* p. 57.

"a paternal interest": Ibid., p. 60.

"a personal canvass" . . . *Valentine Young's bar:* Riis, *Theodore Roosevelt, the Citizen,* p. 51.

"not high enough": TR, *An Autobiography,* p. 60.

"owned by no man": Paul Grondahl, *I Rose Like a Rocket: The Political Education of Theodore Roosevelt* (Lincoln: University of Nebraska Press, 2004), p. 65.

"untrammeled and unpledged . . . serve no clique": Putnam, *Theodore Roosevelt,* p. 248.

"We take much . . . honesty and integrity": Thayer, *Theodore Roosevelt,* p. 30.

"Men worth millions . . . glad to get them": Riis, *Theodore Roosevelt, the Citizen,* p. 51.

"brownstone vote": Ibid.

"My first days . . . wealthiest district in New York": TR, *An Autobiography,* p. 63.

"How do you do . . . ninety percent": Hermann Hagedorn, Isaac Hunt, and George Spinney, "Memo of Conversation at Dinner at the Harvard Club," Sept. 20, 1923, p. 41, TRC.

"very good men . . . nor very bad": TR, "Phases of State Legislation" (Jan. 1885), *WTR,* 13:47.

"the most talked . . . in fitting terms": NYT, April 8, 1882.

"so corrupt a government": Dalton, "The Early Life of Theodore Roosevelt," p. 282.

"black horse cavalry": Edmund Morris, *The Rise of Theodore Roosevelt* (New York: Modern Library, 2001), p. 179.

"There is nothing . . . thing, I act": Grondahl, *I Rose Like a Rocket,* p. 61.

"a dreadful misfortune . . . holding office": TR, *An Autobiography,* p. 56.

"I rose like a rocket": TR to TR Jr., Oct. 20, 1903, *LTR,* 3:635.

"if they do shoot . . . down like sticks": Riis, *Theodore Roosevelt, the Citizen,* p. 54.

"was swelled": Ibid., p. 58.

"There is an increasing . . . on his person": Quoted in Putnam, *Theodore Roosevelt,* p. 288.

"a perfect nuisance": Hagedorn, Hunt, and Spinney, "Memo of Conversation at Dinner at the Harvard Club," p. 26.

"He was just like . . . of a box": Ibid., p. 16.

"rotten": TR, "True Americanism," April 1894, *WTR,* 13:16–17.

"to sit on his coat-tails": O'Neill, quoted in Putnam, *Theodore Roosevelt,* p. 255.

"everybody else . . . indiscreet": Hagedorn, Hunt, and Spinney, "Memo of Conversation at Dinner at the Harvard Club," p. 19.

"would listen . . . no advice": Riis, *Theodore Roosevelt, the Citizen,* p. 58.

"was absolutely deserted . . . was not all-important": Putnam, *Theodore Roosevelt,* p. 290.

"that cooperation . . . all he could": Hagedorn, Hunt, and Spinney, "Memo of Conversation at Dinner at the Harvard Club," p. 19.

He turned to help others . . . gave him a hand: Riis, *Theodore Roosevelt, the Citizen,* p. 59.

"biased . . . laborers": TR, "A Judicial Experience," *The Outlook,* March 13, 1909, p. 563.

"beyond a shadow . . . and hygienic": Ibid.

"The real things of life . . . more and more": Riis, *Theodore Roosevelt, the Citizen,* p. 60.

"A man who conscientiously . . . point of view": TR, "Fellow-Feeling as a Political Factor" (Jan. 1900), *WTR,* 13:368, p. 355.

"had the reins": TR to Alice Lee Roosevelt, Jan. 22, 1884, *LTR,* 1:64.

Chapter Three
Franklin: "No, call me Franklin"

Springwood: Geoffrey C. Ward, *Before the Trumpet: Young Franklin Roosevelt, 1882–1905* (New York: Vintage, 2014), p. 90.

"the right person for the job": John Mack Interview, Feb. 1, 1949, Oral History Collection, FDRL.

"Nothing would please . . . to seek out": Ibid.

"with class lines . . . hands outside": James MacGregor Burns, *Roosevelt: The Lion and the Fox* (Old Saybrook, Conn.: Konecky & Konecky, 1970), p. 9.

"tipped their hats": Ward, *Before the Trumpet,* p. 121.

"There's a Mr. Franklin . . . topic of politics": Tom Leonard Interview, Jan. 11, 1949, Oral History Collection, FDRL.

"On that joyous . . . ever since": FDR, "The Golden Rule in Government — An Extemporaneous Address at Vassar College, Poughkeepsie, N.Y.," Aug. 26, 1933, *PPA,* 2:338.

"I'm dee-lighted . . . all my relatives": Poughkeepsie Eagle-News, Sept. 12, 1910.

"Temperament . . . great separator": Richard E. Neustadt, *Presidential Power and the Modern Presidents* (New York: Free Press, 1980), p. 153.

"A second-class . . . temperament": Geoffrey C. Ward, *A First-Class Temperament: The Emergence of Franklin Roosevelt, 1905–1928* (New York: Vintage, 2014), p. xv.

"All that is in me . . . to the Hudson": Joseph P. Lash, *Eleanor and Franklin: The Story of Their Relationship* (New York: W. W. Norton, 1971), p. 116.

"a very nice child . . . and happy": Ward, *Before the Trumpet,* p. 145.

"Never . . . with itself": Sara Delano Roosevelt, *My Boy Franklin* (New York: Ray Long & Richard R. Smith, 1933), pp. 19–20.

"pain-killing can . . . conflicting interests": John R. Boettiger, *A Love in Shadow* (New York: W. W. Norton, 1978), p. 29.

"We coasted! . . . out for tomorrow!!": FDR to

SDR [1888], in Elliott Roosevelt, ed., *F.D.R.: His Personal Letters: Early Years* (New York: Duell, Sloan & Pearce, 1947), p. 6.

"Went fishing . . . dozen of minnows": FDR to SDR, May 18, 1888, ibid., p. 8.

"Then . . . back to his routine": SDR, *My Boy Franklin,* pp. 5–6.

"We never subjected . . . kind of handling": Ibid., p. 33.

"a very nice child": Ward, *Before the Trumpet,* p. 145.

stamp collection: Otis L. Graham Jr. and Meghan Robinson Wander, eds., *Franklin D. Roosevelt: His Life and Times: An Encyclopedic View* (New York: Da Capo, 1990), p. 400.

"the thrill of acquisition": Walter Benjamin, *Illuminations: Essays and Reflections* (New York: Schocken, 1969), pp. 60–61.

"in its proper place . . . cares of State": Winston S. Churchill, *The Second World War,* Vol. 4, *The Hinge of Fate* (Boston: Houghton Mifflin, 1950), p. 712.

"feeling of calm . . . beset him": Grace Tully, *F.D.R. My Boss* (New York: Charles Scribner's Sons, 1949), p. 7.

"he lay sprawled . . . two things at once": SDR, *My Boy Franklin,* p. 34.

"There was something . . . playful moods": Frances Perkins, *The Roosevelt I Knew*

(New York: Penguin, 2011), p. 32.

"generally preferred . . . gist right away": Samuel I. Rosenman, *Working with Roosevelt* (New York: Harper & Brothers, 1952), p. 17.

"a gentleman . . . boy's companion": Ward, *Before the Trumpet,* p. 173.

"unorthodox" manner: Ibid., p.174.

"when he became . . . issuing country": Robert H. Jackson, *That Man: An Insider's Portrait of Franklin D. Roosevelt* (New York: Oxford University Press, 2003), p. 12.

"almost halfway through": Rita Halle Kleeman, *Gracious Lady: The Life of Sara Delano Roosevelt* (New York: D. Appleton-Century, 1935), p. 190.

"The other boys . . . friendships": Eleanor Roosevelt, *This I Remember* (New York: Harper & Brothers, 1949), p. 43.

"They knew things he didn't; he felt left out": Bess Furman, *Washington By-line: The Personal Story of a Newspaper Woman* (New York: Alfred A. Knopf, 1949), p. 272.

"felt hopelessly out of things": John Gunther, *Roosevelt in Retrospect* (New York: Harper & Brothers, 1950), p. 173.

"both mentally and physically": FDR to SDR and James Roosevelt, Sept. 18, 1896, Elliott Roosevelt, ed., *F.D.R.: His Personal Letters: Early Years,* p. 35.

"getting on . . . with the fellows": FDR to SDR,

Oct. 1, 1896, ibid., p. 42.

49 *"an interloper . . . school activity"*: SDR, *My Boy Franklin,* pp. 39–40.

"Over 30 votes . . . given this year": FDR to SDR and James Roosevelt, March 24, 1897, Elliott Roosevelt, ed., *F.D.R.: His Personal Letters: Early Years,* pp. 78–79.

"immensely proud": SDR, *My Boy Franklin,* p. 49.

"I have served . . . school-spirit before": FDR to SDR and James Roosevelt, May 14, 1897, Elliott Roosevelt, ed., *F.D.R.: His Personal Letters: Early Years,* p. 97.

"There has been . . . slight for success": Elliott Roosevelt, ed., *F.D.R.: His Personal Letters: Early Years,* p. 34, note.

"Never, no never! . . . upstanding American": SDR, *My Boy Franklin,* p. 4.

"unthinkable": Ibid., p. 56.

"She was an indulgent . . . his soul his own": Ward, *Before the Trumpet,* p. 245.

"The competition was . . . time exhausting": Philip Boffey, "FDR at Harvard," *Harvard Crimson,* Dec. 13, 1957.

"My Dearest . . . quite a strain": FDR to SDR, April 30, 1901, Elliott Roosevelt, ed., *F.D.R.: His Personal Letters: Early Years,* p. 456.

"kept the whole . . . for an hour": FDR to SDR and James Roosevelt, June 4, 1897, ibid., p. 110.

"Young man . . . tomorrow morning": Boffey, "FDR at Harvard."

"I don't want to go . . . out of ourselves": FDR to SDR, April 30, 1901, Elliott Roosevelt, ed., *F.D.R.: His Personal Letters: Early Years,* pp. 456–57.

"in one day . . . election and legislature": Editorial, *Harvard Crimson,* Oct. 8, 1903, ibid., p. 509.

"read Kant . . . best teacher": Bernard Asbell, *The F.D.R. Memoirs* (Garden City, N.Y.: Doubleday, 1973), p. 85.

"conceited" and *"cocky":* Frank Oilbert, "FDR Headed Crimson," *Harvard Crimson,* Dec. 11, 1950.

"quick-witted . . . frictionless command": Rev. W. Russell Bowie, quoted in ibid.

"I know what pain . . . to love you": FDR to SDR, Dec. 4, 1903, Elliott Roosevelt, ed., *F.D.R.: His Personal Letters: Early Years,* p. 518.

"a new life": Eleanor Roosevelt, *This Is My Story* (New York: Harper & Brothers, 1937), p. 65.

"everything . . . comes in contact with": Lash, *Eleanor and Franklin,* p. 74.

"The surest way . . . for others": Ibid., p. 87.

"I had a great . . . every experience": ER, *This Is My Story,* p. 111.

"featherduster": Arthur Schlesinger Jr., *The Age of Roosevelt,* Vol. 1: *The Crisis of the*

Old Order, 1919–1933 (New York: Mariner, 2003), p. 323.

"broad human contact": Nathan Miller, *FDR: An Intimate History* (New York: Madison Books, 1983), p. 51.

"My God . . . lived like that": Eleanor Roosevelt and Helen Ferris, *Your Teens and Mine* (Garden City, N.Y.: Doubleday, 1961), p. 181.

"he would amount to something someday": Lash, *Eleanor and Franklin,* p. 107.

"It is impossible . . . absolutely happy": Ibid., p. 109.

FDR admiration of TR: Ward, *A First-Class Temperament,* p. 86.

"We are greatly . . . open before you": Lash, *Eleanor and Franklin,* p. 138.

"Well, Franklin . . . name in the family": Ibid., pp. 138, 139, 141.

"to take advantage" of it: TR to Francis Markue Scott, Oct. 30, 1884, *LTR* 1:84.

"fell into discussion . . . entirely reasonable": *Harvard Alumni Bulletin,* April 28, 1945, pp. 451–52.

Feeling "snakebitten": Jean Edward Smith, *FDR* (New York: Random House, 2007), p. 64.

"It was made . . . of the third": John Mack Interview, Feb. 1, 1949, Oral History Collection, FDRL.

"I'll take it . . . no hesitation": Ibid.

"I'll win the election": SDR, *My Boy Franklin,* p. 70.

"not intend to sit still": Poughkeepsie-Eagle News, Oct. 7, 1910.

"had a distinct . . . available voter": SDR, *My Boy Franklin,* pp. 73–74.

"The automobile . . . occasional injuries": The Franklin D. Roosevelt Collector (May 1949), p. 4.

designed his own posters and buttons . . . direct contact with people: Smith, *FDR,* p. 66.

"spoke slowly . . . never go on": ER, *This Is My Story,* p. 167.

"that smile of his . . . as a friend": Tom Leonard Interview, Jan. 11, 1949, Oral History Collection, FDRL.

"but none of his . . . campaign of 1910": The *FDR Collector* (May 1949), p. 3.

"be a real . . . chance to fill it": Ward, *A First-Class Temperament,* p. 122.

"I know I'm no orator . . . like to hear": Frank Freidel, *Franklin D. Roosevelt: The Apprenticeship* (Boston: Little, Brown, 1952), p. 92.

winning by the largest margin: Poughkeepsie Eagle-News, Nov. 19, 1910.

"I never had . . . the bivouac fire": NYT, Jan. 22, 1911.

"disagreeable": "Notable New Yorkers," Reminiscences of Frances Perkins (1951–

1955), Part 1, Session 1, p. 240, OHRO/ CUL.

"I can still see . . . an awfully mean cuss": Perkins, *The Roosevelt I Knew,* p. 11.

"O'Gorman . . . better than Sheehan": Edmund R. Terry, "The Insurgents at Albany," *The Independent* (July–September 1911), p. 115.

"converted defeat . . . taken an upward step": Burns and Dunn, *The Three Roosevelts,* p. 121.

"How would I like it . . . would love to hold": Carroll Kilpatrick, *Roosevelt and Daniels, a Friendship in Politics* (Chapel Hill: University of North Carolina Press, 1952), p. xii.

"always thrilled to tales of the sea": SDR, *My Boy Franklin,* p. 30.

"man-to-man". . . career would demand: Ward, *A First-Class Temperament,* p. 173.

collection of . . . naval history: Graham and Wander, eds., *Franklin D. Roosevelt,* p. 280.

"It is interesting . . . to the full": TR to FDR, *LTR,* 7:714.

"an old fuddy duddy": Gunther, *Roosevelt in Retrospect,* p. 211.

"was too damn slow for words": Blaine Taylor, "Rehearsal of Glory: FDR as Assist. Sec. of the U.S. Navy," *Sea Classics* 33, no. 7 (July 2000).

"You should be . . . should resign": James Tertius de Kay, *Roosevelt's Navy: The Educa-*

tion of a Warrior President, 1882–1920 (New York: Pegasus, 2012), p. 55.

FDR duties: Ibid., p. 53.

"A man with a flashing mind . . . complicated subjects": Ernest K. Lindley, Franklin D. Roosevelt: A Career in Progressive Democracy (Indianapolis: Bobbs-Merrill, 1931), p. 124.

"dead wood": Ibid., p. 117.

"second to none": Rex W. Tugwell, The Democratic Roosevelt (Baltimore: Penguin, 1957), p. 100.

"economizer": Lindley, Franklin D. Roosevelt, p. 126.

"It is only a big man . . . handled yourself": Freidel, Franklin D. Roosevelt: The Apprenticeship, pp. 322–23.

"gnome-like": ER, This Is My Story, p. 192.

"a singed cat": James Tobin, The Man He Became (New York: Simon & Schuster, 2013), p. 55.

"luminous eyes": Lela Stiles, The Man behind Roosevelt: The Story of Louis McHenry Howe (New York: World, 1954), p. 24.

seldom spent more than a couple days apart: Ward, A First-Class Temperament, p. 199.

"deflate Roosevelt's pride, prod his negligence": Alfred B. Rollins Jr., Roosevelt and Howe (New York: Alfred A. Knopf, 1962), p. 75.

"He was a great trial and error guy": Taylor, "Rehearsal of Glory: FDR as Assist. Sec. of the U.S. Navy."

"a suitable bond" . . . World War II: Kilpatrick, *Roosevelt and Daniels,* p. 31.

"to go to jail for 999 years": Gunther, *Roosevelt in Retrospect,* p. 211.

"with a twinkle . . . with the Army": Lindley, *Franklin D. Roosevelt,* p. 140.

"We want to get . . . talk things over": Stanley Weintraub, *Young Mr. Roosevelt: FDR's Introduction to War, Politics, and Life* (New York: Da Capo, 2013), p. 25.

"My dear chief . . . about to skyrocket": Elliott Roosevelt, ed., *F.D.R.: His Personal Letters: 1905–1928* (New York: Duell, Sloan & Pearce, 1947), Vol. 2, p. 489.

FDR not listed as one of thirty-nine vice presidential candidates: Gunther, *Roosevelt in Retrospect,* p. 216.

"Return to normalcy": Stiles, *The Man behind Roosevelt,* p. 68.

"had everything . . . nothing to lose": Frank Freidel, *Franklin D. Roosevelt: The Ordeal* (Boston: Little, Brown, 1954), p. 70.

"We really had trouble . . . what they're hiring": Stiles, *The Man behind Roosevelt,* p. 70.

"once he met a man . . . circumstances": Linda Lotridge Levin, *The Making of FDR: The Story of Stephen Early, America's First Modern Press Secretary* (New York: Prometheus, 2008), p. 61.

eight hundred speeches: Gunther, *Roosevelt*

in Retrospect, p. 216.

"the driest subjects from seeming heavy": Freidel, *Franklin D. Roosevelt: The Ordeal,* p. 77.

"it is becoming almost impossible . . . I yank his coattails!": Julie M. Fenster, *FDR's Shadow: Louis Howe, the Force That Shaped Franklin and Eleanor Roosevelt* (New York: St. Martin's Griffin, 2009), p. 121.

"had something . . . good constitution": Freidel, *Franklin D. Roosevelt: The Ordeal,* p. 81.

"A darn good sail": Levin, *The Making of FDR,* p. 59.

"Curiously enough . . . during the campaign": Freidel, *FDR: The Ordeal,* p. 90.

"a fraternity in spirit": Fenster, *FDR's Shadow,* p. 122.

"Cuff-Links Club": Ogden [Utah] Standard-Examiner, May 16, 1934.

"At that very first meeting . . . President of the United States": NYT, Nov. 27, 1932.

Chapter Four
Lyndon: "A steam engine in pants"

daylong "speaking": Robert Caro, *The Years of Lyndon Johnson: The Path to Power* (New York: Vintage, 1990), p. 202.

vandoos: Tarbell, *The Early Life of Abraham Lincoln,* p. 155.

"I saw coming . . . behalf of Pat Neff": Welly Hopkins Interview, May 11, 1965, LBJOH.

"I'm a prairie dog lawyer": Robert Dallek, *Lone Star Rising: Lyndon Johnson and His Times, 1908–1960* (New York: Oxford University Press, 1991), p. 86.

"so wrapped . . . pleasantly received": Hopkins Interview, May 11, 1965, LBJOH.

"the hit of the Henly picnic": Dallek, *Lone Star Rising,* p. 87.

LBJ listening to his father and political cronies: DKG, *LJAD,* p. 35.

"I loved going . . . what was going on": The author's conversations with LBJ during time spent at the LBJ ranch between 1968 and 1971 (DKG/LBJ Conversations) and quoted extensively in DKG, *LJAD.*

"If you can't come . . . no business in politics": Alfred Steinberg, *Sam Johnson's Boy: A Close-up of the President from Texas* (New York: Macmillan, 1968), p. 26.

"was very friendly . . . doing something nice": Dallek, *Lone Star Rising,* p. 46.

"We've got to . . . we're here for": Caro, *The Path to Power,* p. 82.

"They walked the same . . . talked to you": Ibid., p. 76.

Cecil Maddox's barbershop: Ibid., p. 71.

"We drove in the Model T . . . could go on forever": DKG/LBJ Conversations.

"My mother . . . worst year of her life": Ibid.

"a two-story . . . broad walks": Rebekah Baines Johnson, *A Family Album* (New York:

McGraw-Hill, 1965), p. 29.

"dashing and dynamic": Dallek, *Lone Star Rising,* p. 27.

"whirlwind courtship": Rebekah Baines Johnson, *A Family Album,* p. 25.

"the problem of adjustment . . . new way of life": Ibid., p. 30.

"piled high": Dallek, *Lone Star Rising,* p. 28.

"Then I came along . . . she never did": DKG/LBJ Conversations.

"never seen such a friendly baby": Dallek, *Lone Star Rising,* p. 32.

"I'll never forget . . . strangled to death": DKG/LBJ Conversations.

"I remember playing . . . in the world": Ibid.

"For days after . . . my father and sisters": Ibid.

the Johnson *"freeze-out"*: DKG, LJAD, p. 25.

"perfect escape . . . life imaginable": DKG/LBJ Conversations.

"very brilliant . . . faster than they did": Caro, *The Path to Power,* p. 71.

"smothered . . . force feedings": Larry King, "Bringing up Lyndon," *Texas Monthly,* January 1976, http://www.texasmonthly.com/issue/january-1976.

"Is it true?" . . . history or government: Time, May 21, 1965.

"the self-confidence . . . his intellectual equal": Donald, *Lincoln,* p. 32.

"My daddy . . . I never could": DKG/LBJ Conversations.

"The way you get ahead . . . Evans, for ex-

ample": Alfred B. Johnson "Boody," quoted in Merle Miller, *Lyndon: An Oral Biography* (New York: G. P. Putnam's Sons, 1980), p. 28.

"there was only . . . for him directly": DKG/LBJ Conversations.

"kowtowing . . . brown nosing": Mylton Kennedy, quoted in Caro, *The Path to Power,* p. 153.

"ruthless": Steinberg, *Sam Johnson's Boy,* p. 41.

"to cut your throat . . . you wanted": Helen Hofheinz, in Caro, *The Path to Power,* p. 194.

"didn't just dislike . . . despised him": Henry Kyle, in ibid., p. 196.

"Ambition is . . . pressing forward": LBJ, *College Star,* June 19, 1929, quoted in William C. Pool, Emmie Craddock, and David E. Conrad, *Lyndon Baines Johnson: The Formative Years* (San Marcos: Southwest Texas State College Press, 1965), pp. 131–32.

"the somebody . . . wanted to be": Caro, *The Path to Power,* p. 170.

"My students were poor . . . pain of prejudice": LBJ, "Presidential News Conference," March 13, 1965, *PPP,* 1:286.

"He respected . . . do your work": *Time,* May 21, 1965, p. 60.

"down-to-earth and friendly": They Remember LBJ at Cotulla," *South Carolina News* (Flor-

ence, S.C.), Jan. 27, 1964, p. 12.

"he didn't give . . . a blur": Dallek, *Lone Star Rising,* p. 79.

"I was determined . . . care of itself": DKG/LBJ Conversations.

"I can still see . . . who sat in my class": Caro, *The Path to Power,* p. 170.

"Even in that day . . . political lore": Hopkins Interview, May 11, 1965, LBJOH.

"gifted with a very . . . greet the public": Welly Hopkins, quoted in Caro, *The Path to Power,* p. 203.

"We worked . . . I'd be elected": Hopkins Interview, May 11, 1965, LBJOH.

"wonder kid . . . in the area": Steinberg, *Sam Johnson's Boy,* p. 53.

"won anything": Gene Latimer Interview, Oct. 5, 1979, LBJOH.

"rather vigorous . . . extremely aggressive": Luther Jones Interview, June 1, 1969, LBJOH.

"could get people . . . think of doing": Latimer Interview, Oct. 5, 1979, LBJOH.

"a human dynamo . . . a steam engine in pants": Jones Interview, June 13, 1969, LBJOH.

"He had a variety . . . another one in the eye": Latimer Interview, Oct. 5, 1979, LBJOH.

"we were . . . football team": Latimer Interview, Oct. 5, 1979, LBJOH.

"All that day . . . was behind me": DKG/LBJ Conversations.

"I would not say . . . Power I mean": LBJ, quoted in Merle Miller, *Lyndon,* p. 38.

"This skinny boy . . . here twenty years": Arthur Perry, in Booth Moody, *The Lyndon Johnson Story* (New York: Avon, 1964), p. 38.

"a hard man . . . way he wanted it": Jones Interview, June 13, 1969, LBJOH.

"We've been relaxing . . . your own time?": Dallek, *Lone Star Rising,* p. 101.

"a bluff and good" . . . delighted: Jones Interview, June 13, 1969, LBJOH.

"every problem had a solution": Caro, *The Path to Power,* p. 235.

"extraordinarily direct . . . of his capabilities": Eric F. Goldman, *The Tragedy of Lyndon Johnson* (New York: Alfred A. Knopf, 1969), p. 343.

"very, very . . . wavy hair": Caro, *The Path to Power,* p. 299.

"sheer lunacy": Merle Miller, *Lyndon,* p. 52.

"I'm ambitious . . . never will": Caro, *The Path to Power,* pp. 300–301.

"Texas yip": LBJ, quoted in ibid.

"I don't think . . . set eyes on her": Latimer Interview, Aug. 17, 1971, LBJOH.

"balancing wheel": Jones Interview, June 13, 1969, LBJOH.

NYA . . . "a lost generation": "Saving a 'Lost Generation' through the National Youth Administration," Roosevelt Institute, May

19, 1911, http://rooseveltinstitute.org/sav
ing-lost-generation-through-national-youth-
administration/.

"He wanted me . . . a mistake had been made":
Tom Connally, quoted in ibid., p. 340.

*"I'm not the assistant type . . . I'm the executive
type":* Dallek, *Lone Star Rising,* p. 120.

"We gathered . . . and go to work": W. Sherman
Birdwell Jr. Interview, April 1, 1965,
LBJOH.

"start the ball rolling": Jones Interview, June
13, 1969, LBJOH.

roadside parks: Willard Deason Interview,
April 11, 1969, LBJOH.

"beside himself with happiness": Luther Jones,
quoted in Caro, *The Path to Power,* p. 348.

"a model for the nation": Suggested by Joe B.
Frantz, interviewer, in Deason Interview,
April 11, 1969, LBJOH.

Eleanor Roosevelt: Dallek, *Lone Star Rising,*
p. 143.

*"Everything had to be done . . . be done im-
mediately":* Ibid., p. 130.

*"couldn't wait" . . . midstream from the type-
writer:* Mary Henderson, quoted in Caro,
The Path to Power, p. 351.

"The hours were long and hard": Deason
Interview, May 7, 1965, LBJOH.

The lights: Jesse Kellam Interview, April
1965, LBJOH.

"clockwatchers" . . . "never heard of a clock":
Willard Deason, in NYA Group, "Discus-

sion Days in NYA: William Deason, J. J. Pickle, Ray Roberts, Fenner Roth, Albert Brisbin, C. P. Little," taped in 1968 at William S. White's house, LBJL.

"He would pair . . . was always behind": Ray Roberts, in ibid.

"God, he could rip a man up and down": Ernest Morgan, quoted in Caro, *The Path to Power,* p. 352.

pitting workers against one another: Daniel Pink, *Drive: The Surprising Truth about What Motivates Us* (New York: Riverhead Books, 2011), p. 174.

"Now, fellows . . . wheel and pitch in": Brisbin, "Discussion Days in NYA," LBJL.

"We weren't like boarders . . . member of the family": Jones Interview, June 13, 1969, LBJOH.

"paragraph . . . cake for us": Birdwell Interview, April 1, 1965, LBJOH.

"to work harder . . . be more effective": Brisbin, "Discussion Days in NYA," LBJL.

"the greatest organizer": Roberts, in ibid.

"to put first things . . . one at a time": Deason, in ibid.

"see around corners": White, in ibid.

"we made no bones . . . going somewhere": Roberts, in ibid.

"I just couldn't keep . . . bottled up inside": DKG/LBJ Conversations.

"She's an old woman . . . she won't run": Caro, *The Path to Power,* p. 399.

"Wirtz had a wife . . . as a son": Ibid., p. 393.

he would need at least $10,000: DKG/LBJ Conversations.

"the die was cast . . . got to his car": Jones Interview, June 13, 1969, LBJOH.

"My father became . . . the Johnson family": DKG/LBJ Conversations.

"total Roosevelt man": Jones Interview, June 13, 1969, LBJOH.

"I don't have . . . way to duck": Steinberg, *Sam Johnson's Boy,* p. 110.

"he could get . . . anybody else": Birdwell Interview, April 1965, LBJOH.

campaigning: Sam Fore, in Merle Miller, *Lyndon,* p. 61.

"A five minute speech . . . minutes for handshaking": DKG/LBJ Conversations.

"a phenomenal memory . . . names and faces": Joe B. Frantz, interviewer, in Willard Deason Interview, April 11, 1969, LBJOH.

"It was like he . . . relatives were": Carroll Keach in Caro, *The Path to Power,* p. 426.

"a mental imprint . . . of his mind": Deason Interview, April 11, 1969, LBJOH.

"discussions with himself . . . 'have to do better, that's all' ": Carroll Keach, quoted in Caro, *The Path to Power,* p. 426.

"I've just met . . . anything you can": Tommy Corcoran, quoted in ibid., p. 448.

"He was very much . . . depended on": Elizabeth Wickendham Goldschmidt Interview,

Nov. 6, 1974, LBJOH.

"The lack of electric . . . the country folk": William E. Leuchtenburg, *Franklin D. Roosevelt and the New Deal, 1932–1940* (New York: Harper Perennial, 2009), p. 157.

"Did you ever see . . . all over again": LBJ, quoted in Merle Miller, *Lyndon,* p. 70.

"the bigger the better . . . show him": Tommy Corcoran, quoted in Dallek, *Lone Star Rising,* p. 180.

"city big shots": LBJ, quoted in Merle Miller, *Lyndon,* p. 70.

"I have never . . . these rural rivers!": Ronnie Dugger, *The Politician: The Life and Times of Lyndon Johnson* (New York: W. W. Norton, 1982), p. 212.

"a mental picture . . . milking machines": Michael Gillette, *Lady Bird: An Oral History* (New York: Oxford University Press, 2012), pp. 101–2.

"John, I have a young . . . of my life": LBJ, quoted in Merle Miller, *Lyndon,* pp. 70–71.

"home to that little . . . I carried him home": DKG/LBJ Conversations.

"Because . . . and so overwhelming": Merle Miller, *Lyndon,* p. 72.

"Now, look, I want us . . . Negroes and the Mexicans": Dugger, *The Politician,* pp. 209–10.

"one dreary room . . . ill-nourished and sordid": Ibid., p. 210.

"the government is competing . . . That's how": Merle Miller, *Lyndon,* p. 72.

"a consensus about the boy": Tommy Corcoran, in Dallek, *Lone Star Rising,* p. 162.

"marvelous stories": Elizabeth Rowe Interview, June 6, 1975, LBJOH.

"greatest stories": Elizabeth Rowe, quoted in Caro, *The Path to Power,* p. 453.

"If Lyndon Johnson . . . would take fire": Ibid., p. 454.

"special interest": Elizabeth Wickendham Goldschmidt Interview, Nov. 6, 1974, LBJOH.

"if he . . . first Southern president": Elliot Janeway, quoted in Caro, *The Path to Power,* p. 449.

Chapter Five
Abraham Lincoln: "I must die or be better"

"Why some people . . . are not": Warren Bennis and Robert J. Thomas, "Crucibles of Leadership," *Harvard Business Review,* Sept. 2002, https://hbr.org/2002/09/crucibles-of-leadership.

Some people lose . . . greater resolve and purpose: Jim Collins, *Good to Great* (New York: HarperCollins, 2001), p. 82.

"Lincoln's roseate hopes . . . no financier": Whitney, *Lincoln, The Citizen,* p. 142.

"unladylike": Mary Lincoln to Mercy Levering, Dec. [15?], 1940, quoted in Justin Tur-

ner and Linda Levitt Turner, *Mary Todd Lincoln: Her Life and Letters* (New York: Alfred A. Knopf, 1972), p. 516.

"in the winter of 40 & 41 . . . so well as myself": Speed, in *HI,* p. 430.

"his ability . . . support a wife": Douglas L. Wilson, *Lincoln before Washington: New Perspectives on the Illinois Years* (Urbana: University of Illinois Press, 1998), p. 105.

"I am so poor . . . in a year's rowing": AL to Speed, July 4, 1842, *CW,* 1:289.

"breach of honor": Tarbell, *The Life of Abraham Lincoln,* Vol. 1, p. 174.

"kills my soul": AL to Joshua Speed, July 4, 1842, *CW,* 1:282.

"resolves when . . . much importance": Ibid., 1:289.

"more than any one dead or living": Wilson, *Lincoln before Washington,* p. 101.

"I shall be verry [sic] lonesome . . . pained by the loss": AL to Joshua Speed, Feb. 25, 1842, *CW,* 1:281.

"indifferent . . . desert her throne": Shenk, *Lincoln's Melancholy,* p. 19.

"I am now the most . . . write no more": AL to John T. Stuart, Jan. 23, 1841, *CW,* 1:229–30.

"Lincoln went Crazy . . . it was terrible": Speed, in *HI,* p. 474.

"delirious to the extent . . . to talk incoherently": Michael Burlingame, ed., *An Oral History of*

Abraham Lincoln: John Nicolay's Interviews and Essays (Carbondale: Southern Illinois University Press, 1996), p. 2.

"like the same person": Wilson, *Lincoln before Washington,* p. 110.

"He is reduced . . . is truly deplorable": Carl Sandburg, *Mary Lincoln: Wife and Mother* (Bedford, Mass.: Applewood Books, 1995), p. 39.

"within an inch . . . lunatic for life": Wilson, *Lincoln before Washing* ton, p. 110.

"done nothing . . . his fellow man": Speed, in *HI,* p. 197.

"a friendless . . . working on a flatboat": AL to Martin S. Morris, March 26, 1843, *CW,* 1:320.

"one of the finest . . . legal mind": Michael Burlingame, *Abraham Lincoln, a Life,* 2 vols. (Baltimore: Johns Hopkins University Press, 2008), Vol. 1, p. 185.

"would work hard . . . almost a father to me": Ibid., p. 186.

"how to prepare . . . until middle life": Burlingame, ed., *An Oral History of Abraham Lincoln,* p. 38.

"dreams of Elysium . . . can realize": AL to Joshua F. Speed, Feb. 25, 1842, *CW,* 1:280.

"resolves . . . the chief gem": AL to Joshua F. Speed, July 4, 1842, *CW,* 1:289.

"It is my pleasure . . . child to its parent": Mary Todd Lincoln, in *HI,* p. 357.

"Now if you should . . . to go very much": AL to Richard S. Thomas, Feb. 14, 1843, *CW*, 1:307.

"as ambitious . . . man in the world": Burlingame, *The Inner World of Abraham Lincoln*, p. 236.

"trusting to escape . . . burning surface": AL, "Speech in United States House of Representatives: The War with Mexico," Jan. 12, 1848, *CW*, 1:438–41.

"a very able . . . upright young man": Tarbell, *The Life of Abraham Lincoln*, Vol. 2, p. 11.

"the crack speech . . . talking, gesticulating": Ibid.

"Abe Lincoln . . . in the House": Burlingame, *Abraham Lincoln, a Life*, Vol. 1, p. 279.

"I had been chosen . . . lessons in deportment": Chris DeRose, *Congressman Lincoln: The Making of America's Greatest President* (New York: Threshold, 2013), p. 203.

"replete with good sense . . . the western orators": Ibid., p. 206.

"neither slavery . . . of said territory": David Potter, *The Impending Crisis, America before the Civil War, 1848–1861* (New York: Harper & Row, 1976), p. 21.

"at least forty times": AL to Joshua Speed, Aug. 24, 1855, *CW*, 2:323.

"the time had come . . . we have been doing": DeRose, *Congressman Lincoln*, pp. 206–7.

address slavery within the District of Columbia:

AL, "Remarks and Resolution Introduced in United States House of Representatives Concerning Abolition of Slavery in the District of Columbia," January 10, 1849, *CW*, 2:20.

"that slave hound from Illinois": Wendell Phillips, quoted in Albert J. Beveridge, *Abraham Lincoln, 1809–1858,* 2 vols. (New York: Houghton Mifflin, 1928), Vol. 2, p. 185.

"despaired of . . . had never lived": Burlingame, *The Inner World of Abraham Lincoln,* pp. 4–5.

"I hardly ever felt . . . failure in my life": Francis Fisher Browne, *The Every-Day Life of Abraham Lincoln: A Narrative and Descriptive Biography* (Chicago: Browne & Howell, 1914), p. 107.

"was losing interest in politics . . . than ever before": AL, "To Jesse W. Fell, Enclosing Autobiography," Dec. 20, 1859, *CW,* 3: 511–12.

"I am not an accomplished lawyer": AL, "Fragment: Notes for a Law Lecture" [July 1, 1850?], *CW,* 2:81.

"a broad knowledge of the principles": Herndon and Weik, *Herndon's Life of Lincoln,* p. 248.

"a certain lack of discipline . . . or disturb him": Ibid., pp. 247–48.

"the circuit": Tarbell, *The Life of Abraham Lincoln,* Vol. 2, pp. 36–38.

"almost to the point of exhaustion": Jesse W.

Weik, *The Real Lincoln: A Portrait* (Boston: Houghton Mifflin, 1922), p. 240.

"nearly mastered the Six Books of Euclid": AL, "Autobiography Written for John L. Scripps," *CW,* 4:62.

"would read . . . could ever solve": Herndon and Weik, *Herndon's Life of Lincoln,* p. 248.

"he was in the habit . . . ponder, and soliloquize": Lawrence Weldon, quoted in Tarbell, *The Life of Abraham Lincoln,* Vol. 2, p. 6.

"muttering to himself": Ibid., Vol. 1, p. 120.

"he had suddenly . . . listened and laughed": Sandburg, *The Prairie Years,* Vol. 1, p. 474.

"the largest trial . . . central Illinois": Charles B. Strozier, *Lincoln's Quest for Union: Public and Private Meanings* (Chicago: University of Illinois Press, 1987), pp. 172–73.

"into its simplest elements": Tarbell, *The Life of Abraham Lincoln,* Vol. 2, p. 43.

"on his well-trained memory": Ibid., p. 45.

"logical and profound . . . without adornment": Whitney, *Life on the Circuit with Lincoln,* p. 114.

"He had the happy . . . trying the case": Tarbell, *The Life of Abraham Lincoln,* Vol. 2, p. 49.

"His power of mimicry . . . heartier than his": Herndon and Weik, *Herndon's Life of Lincoln,* pp. 249–50.

"No lawyer . . . member of the bar": Tarbell, *The Life of Abraham Lincoln,* Vol. 2, pp. 40–41.

"You're in the wrong place . . . I'll stay here": Ibid., p. 38.

"He was remarkably . . . young lawyers": Ibid., p. 41.

"kindly and cordially": Whitney, *Life on the Circuit with Lincoln,* p. 30.

"Lincoln was the . . . on his election": Tarbell, *The Life of Abraham Lincoln,* Vol. 2, p. 40.

"is the lawyer's . . . done to-day": AL, "Fragment: Notes for a Law Lecture," [July 1, 1850?], *CW,* 2:81.

"work, work, work": AL to John M. Brockman, Sept. 25, 1860, *CW,* 4: 121.

"workshop . . . self introspection": Henry Whitney, in Sandburg, *The Prairie Years,* Vol. 1, p. 475.

"brilliant military manoeuvers . . . not be scared": AL, "Eulogy of Zachary Taylor," XIV. *CW,* 2:83–90.

"enduring spell . . . the whole country": AL, "Eulogy of Henry Clay," July 6, 1852, *CW,* 2:125–26.

"knocked at the door": AL, "Eulogy of Henry Clay," July 6, 1852, *CW,* 2:127.

"If by your legislation . . . I am for disunion": Debate in the House of Representatives, Dec. 13, 1849, *Congressional Globe,* 31st Cong., 1st Sess., p. 28.

"The Great Pacificator": Robert Vincent Remini, *Henry Clay: Statesman of the Union* (New York: W. W. Norton, 1991), p. 192.

"Devotion to the Union . . . so inclined them":

AL, "Speech at Peoria, Ill.," *CW,* 2: 253.

"apparent conservatism . . . were so great": Herndon and Weik, *Herndon's Life of Lincoln,* p. 292.

"The time is coming . . . Abolitionists or Democrats": Ibid.

"Popular sovereignty": Herndon and Weik, *Herndon's Life of Lincoln,* p. 294.

"fixed, and hopeless of change for the better": John G. Nicolay and John Hay, *Abraham Lincoln: A History* (New York: Century, 1890), Vol. 1, p. 392.

"inside . . . and downside": Herndon and Weik, *Herndon's Life of Lincoln,* p. 478.

"such a hunt . . . caught it": Tarbell, *The Life of Abraham Lincoln,* Vol. 1, p. 43.

"If A. can prove . . . superior to your own": AL, "Fragment on Slavery," [April 1, 1854?], *CW,* 2: 222.

"We were both . . . fills the nation": AL, "Fragment on Stephen A. Douglas," [Dec. 1856?], *CW,* 2:382–83.

"at the head . . . band of music": Lewis E. Lehrman, *Lincoln at Peoria: The Turning Point* (Mechanicsburg, Penn: Stackpole Books, 2008), p. 53.

"I wish you . . . him skin me": AL, "Speech at Peoria, Ill.," Oct. 16, 1854, *CW,* 2:247–48.

"What do you say . . . demonstrations of approval": James M. Rice, quoted in Lehrman, *Lincoln at Peoria,* p. 59.

"the plain, unmistakable . . . end of a given time": AL, "Speech at Peoria, Ill.," Oct. 16, 1854, *CW,* 2:275, 274.

"But now . . . 'God speed you' ": Ibid., p. 275.

"You rascal . . . their own way": AL, "Editorial on the Kansas-Nebraska Act," Sept. 11, 1854, *CW,* 2:230.

"they — and not he *— were trying the case"*: Tarbell, *The Life of Abraham Lincoln,* Vol. 2, p. 49.

"The doctrine of self government . . . our fathers gave it": AL, "Speech at Peoria, Ill.," Oct. 16, 1854, *CW,* 2:265, 272, 276.

"no prejudice . . . give it up": Ibid., p. 255.

"we shall not only . . . worthy of the saving": Ibid., p. 276.

"The whole . . . continued huzzas": Tarbell, *The Life of Abraham Lincoln,* Vol. 2, p. 75.

"The inspiration . . . his hearers also": Burlingame, *Abraham Lincoln, a Life,* Vol. 1, p. 387.

"His speaking went . . . speaker himself": White, *Abraham Lincoln in 1854,* p. 10.

"When . . . completely?": Tarbell, *The Life of Abraham Lincoln,* Vol. 2, p. 75.

"Nothing so much marks . . . reputation of a man": The Journals and Miscellaneous Notebooks of Ralph Waldo Emerson, *Vol. 11, 1848–1851* (Cambridge, Mass.: Belknap Press of Harvard University Press, 1975), p. 341.

"A great storyteller . . . life is wisdom": Walter

Benjamin, "The Storyteller," in Dorothy J. Hale, ed., *The Novel: An Anthology of Criticism and Theory, 1900–2000* (Malden, Mass.: Blackwell, 2006), pp. 364, 378.

"first choice": Gillespie, in *HI*, p. 182.

"the 47 men . . . agony is over at last": AL to Elihu B. Washburne, Feb. 9, 1855, *CW*, 2:304.

"gives me more pleasure . . . gives me pain": Ibid., 2:306.

"If we could first know . . . against itself cannot stand": AL, "Speech at Springfield, Illinois," June 16, 1858, *CW*, 2:461.

"Who is this man . . . his style inimitable?": Tarbell, *The Life of Abraham Lincoln*, Vol. 2, p. 116.

"the emotions of defeat . . . fresh": Sandburg, *The Prairie Years*, Vol. 2, p. 167.

"I am glad I made . . . other way": AL to Anson G. Henry, Nov. 4, 1858, *CW*, 3:335–36.

"You will soon feel better . . . shall have fun again": AL to Charles H. Ray, Nov. 20, 1858, *CW*, 3:342.

"No man of this . . . in this canvass": Tarbell, *The Life of Abraham Lincoln*, Vol. 2, p. 116.

"were so much better . . . its present status": AL, quoted by Jesse W. Fell, in Osborn Oldroyd, comp., *The Lincoln Memorial: Album-Immortelles* (New York: G. W. Carleton & Co., 1882), p. 474.

"in a mood . . . their first love": AL to James

Berdan, Jan. 15, 1879, *CW,* 4:33–34.

"No man knows . . . he has tried it": Tarbell, *The Life of Abraham Lincoln,* Vol. 3, p. 188.

"as an evil not . . . protection a necessity": AL, "Address at Cooper Institute, New York City," Feb. 27, 1860, *CW,* 3:535.

"avoidance of extremes . . . never off its balance": Chicago Daily Press and Tribune, May 16, 1860.

"I am not in a position . . . of the vineyard?": AL to Norman B. Judd, Feb. 9, 1960, *CW,* 3:517.

"vote as a unit": William Eldon Baringer, *Lincoln's Rise to Power* (Boston: Little, Brown, 1937), p. 186.

"most of them . . . political morality": Whitney, *Lincoln, the Citizen,* p. 266.

"the defeat of Seward . . . nomination of Lincoln": Murat Halstead; William B. Hesseltine, ed., *Three against Lincoln: Murat Halstead Reports the Caucuses of 1860* (Baton Rouge: Louisiana State University Press, 1960), p. 159.

"especial assistance": AL to Salmon P. Chase, May 26, 1860, *CW,* 4:53.

"chances were more . . . very slim": AL to Anson G. Henry, July 4, 1860, *CW,* 4:82.

"a hired laborer . . . any man's son!": AL, "Speech at New Haven, Conn.," March 6, 1860, *CW,* 4:24.

"a man of the people": Jacob Bunn quoted in

Paul M. Angle, ed., *Abraham Lincoln by Some Men Who Knew Him* (Chicago: Americana House, 1950), p. 108.

"so thoroughly interwoven . . . become part of them": Herndon and Weik, *Herndon's Life of Lincoln,* p. 372.

"man for a crisis": AL, "Eulogy on Henry Clay," July 6, 1852, *CW,* 2:129.

Chapter Six
Theodore Roosevelt: "The light has gone out of my life"

"There is a curse . . . Alice is dying too": Putnam, *Theodore Roosevelt,* p. 386.

"The light has gone out of my life": TR, Private Diary, Feb. 14, 1884, TRP.

"We spent three years . . . been lived out": Feb. 16, 1884, ibid.

"wholly unprecedented . . . annals": TR, *In Memory of My Darling Wife Alice Hathaway Roosevelt and of My Beloved Mother Martha Bulloch Roosevelt who died in the same house and on the same day on February 14, 1884* (New York: G. P. Putnam's Sons, n.d.), TRP.

"in a dazed stunned state . . . he does or says": Sewall, *Bill Sewall's Story of Theodore Roosevelt,* p. 11.

"peculiar" . . . long ministry: The Sun (New York), Feb. 17, 1884.

"It was a grim . . . from working": Sewall, *Bill*

Sewall's Story of Theodore Roosevelt, pp. 11–12.

"I think I should . . . not employed": TR to Carl Schurz, Feb. 21, 1884, *LTR,* 1:66.

"a changed man . . . his own soul": Hagedorn, Hunt, and Spinney, "Memo of Conversation at Dinner at the Harvard Club."

"We are now holding . . . the better I like it": TR to ARC, March 26, 1884, quoted in Putnam, *Theodore Roosevelt,* p. 395.

"the bitter and venomous hatred": TR to Simon Dexter North, April 30, 1884, *LTR,* 1:66.

"seemed to incarnate . . . brighter and better": Undated speech, Charles Evans Hughes, Houghton Library, TRC.

"Our defeat . . . mass of my party": TR to ARC, June 8, 1884, *LTR,* 1:70.

"I was at the birth . . . witness its death": Morris, *The Rise of Theodore Roosevelt,* p. 258.

"hearty support": *NYT,* quoted in Putnam, *Theodore Roosevelt,* p. 464.

"by inheritance . . . Republican convention": TR, interview in the *Boston Herald,* July 20, 1884, quoted in *WTR,* 14:40.

"Theodore Beware . . . promising as you": *Boston Globe,* June 11, 1884, quoted in Putnam, *Theodore Roosevelt,* p. 463.

"I have very little . . . keep in politics": TR to Simon North, April 30, 1884, *LTR,* 1:66.

"I can not regret . . . part in the fray": TR to HCL, Aug. 24, 1884, *LTR,* 1:80.

"I think it will . . . back into politics": TR to

Bamie, Aug. 12, 1884, in Theodore Roosevelt, *Letters from Theodore Roosevelt to Anna Roosevelt Cowles, 1870–1918* (New York: Charles Scribner's Sons, 1924), p. 61.

"I am going . . . I cannot tell": Putnam, *Theodore Roosevelt,* p. 444.

"No ranch or other hiding . . . man like Blaine": Ibid., p. 468.

"Punching cattle . . . avoid campaigning": Hermann Hagedorn, *Roosevelt in the Badlands* (New York: Houghton Mifflin, 1921), p. 165.

"the most important educational asset": Theodore Roosevelt, *The New Nationalism* (New York: Outlook, 1909), p. 106.

"I would take . . . who lived nearest her": TR, quoted by Albert B. Fall, in Frederick S. Wood, *Roosevelt as We Knew Him* (Philadelphia: John C. Winston, 1927), p. 12.

trust them with $40,000 . . . a thousand head of cattle: Morris, *The Rise of Theodore Roosevelt,* pp. 209–10.

"a share of anything": Sewall, *Bill Sewall's Story of Theodore Roosevelt,* p. 12.

"He never was . . . make a decision": Ibid., p. 92.

"a streak of honor": A. T. Packer, "Roosevelt's Ranching Days," *Saturday Evening Post,* March 4, 1905, p. 13.

"was very melancholy . . . well off without me": Sewall, *Bill Sewall's Story of Theodore Roo-*

sevelt, p. 47.

"was not playing cowboy — he was a cowboy": Edward Schapsmeier and Frederick H. Schapsmeier, "TR's Cowboy Years," in Natalie Naylor, Douglas Brinkley, and John Allen Gable, eds., *Theodore Roosevelt: Many-Sided American* (Interlaken, N.Y.: Heart of the Lakes, 1992), p. 148.

able to sleep at night: TR to ALC, Sept. 20, 1884, *LTR,* Vol. 1, p. 82.

"Black care . . . pace is fast enough": Theodore Roosevelt, Hermann Hagedorn, and G. B. Grinnell, *Hunting Trips of a Ranchman: Ranch Life and the Hunting Trail* (New York: Charles Scribner's Sons, 1927), p. 329.

"We only knew . . . ever to be the guide": Undated speech, Charles Evans Hughes, Houghton Library, TRC.

suffer from asthma the rest of his life: CRR, in Dalton, *Theodore Roosevelt,* p. 52.

"he was a frail young man . . . for his livelihood": Sewall, *Bill Sewall's Story of Theodore Roosevelt,* p. 41.

gained thirty pounds: Putnam, *Theodore Roosevelt,* p. 530.

"was clear bone, muscle and grit": Sewall, *Bill Sewall's Story of Theodore Roosevelt,* p. 41.

"failed to make . . . to drive oxen": From *Pittsburgh Dispatch,* Aug. 23, 1885, quoted in Putnam, *Theodore Roosevelt,* p. 530.

"nervous and timid": TR, *An Autobiography,* p. 27.

"there were all kinds . . . soul and spirit": Ibid., p. 52.

"constantly forcing himself . . . even dangerous thing": Frances Theodora Parsons,

Perchance Some Day (Privately printed, 1952), p. 28.

"a matter of habit . . . of will-power": TR, *An Autobiography,* p. 32.

"mean" horses: Jon A. Knokey, *Theodore Roosevelt and the Making of American Leadership* (New York: Skyhorse, 2015), pp. 144–45.

"Perseverance": TR, quoted in Douglas Brinkley, *The Wilderness Warrior: Theodore Roosevelt and the Crusade for America* (New York: HarperCollins, 2009), p. 161.

"as something to be . . . practicing fearlessness": TR, *An Autobiography,* pp. 52–53.

"the indomitable courage . . . ingrained in his being": NYT editorial, quoted in Strock, *Theodore Roosevelt on Leadership,* p. 50.

"he would never . . . West as he did": CRR, *My Brother, Theodore Roosevelt,* p. 150.

"I would not . . . experience in North Dakota": "Roosevelt National Park, North Dakota," National Park Service, Gohttps://www.nps.gov/nr/travel/presidents/t_roosevelt_park.html.

"Baby Lee . . . both weak and morbid": TR to

CRR, March 7, 1908, *LTR,* 6:966.

"falling out . . . very intimate relations": Putnam, *Theodore Roosevelt,* p. 170.

"with all the passion . . . never loved before": EKR to TR, June 8, 1886, Derby Papers, TRC.

"I would like a chance . . . I could really do": TR to HCL, Aug. 20, 1886, *LTR,* 1:109.

"a perfectly hopeless contest": TR to HCL, Oct. 17, 1886, *LTR,* 1:111.

"would bury him in oblivion": Grondahl, *I Rose Like a Rocket,* p. 212.

felt *"below"* what he deserved: TR to HCL, Dec. 9, 1896, *LTR,* 1:570.

"careful . . . in word and act": Steffens, *The Autobiography of Lincoln Steffens,* Vol. 1, p. 260.

"Do what you can . . . where you are": TR, *An Autobiography,* p. 337.

"genius . . . readiness to learn": Riis, *Theodore Roosevelt, the Citizen,* p. 154.

"It treats all offices . . . party leaders": TR, "The Merit System versus the Patronage System," *Century Magazine* (Feb. 1890), p. 628.

"a living force": TR to HCL, June 29, 1889, *LTR,* 1:167.

"everything in their power": WP, May 17, 1889.

"the progress . . . execution of the law": TR, "The Merit System versus the Patronage System," p. 629.

"a hard row to hoe": TR to HCL, June 29,

1889, *LTR,* 1:167.

three guilty employees: Edward P. Kohn, *Heir to the Empire City: New York and the Making of Theodore Roosevelt* (New York: Basic Books, 2014), p. 132.

"going to be . . . fear or favor": TR to HCL, June 29, 1889, *LTR,* 1:167.

"so-called voluntary contributions": Galveston Daily News, Jan. 27, 1890.

"the difference between . . . dress for his wife": Riis, *Theodore Roosevelt, the Citizen,* p. 105.

"His colleagues . . . consequent attack": Quoted in William Henry Harbaugh, *Power and Responsibility: The Life and Times of Theodore Roosevelt* (New York: Farrar, Straus & Cudahy, 1961), p. 80.

"My two colleagues . . . more decided steps": TR to ARC, May 24, 1891, in Theodore Roosevelt, *Letters from Theodore Roosevelt to Anna Roosevelt Cowles, 1870–1918,* p. 117.

"He came into official office . . . Government": Washington Post, May 6, 1890.

"put a padlock . . . uncontrollable jaws": Ohio Democrat, Nov. 27, 1890.

"Mr. Roosevelt is a young Lochinvar . . . in a good cause": Boston Evening Times, Oct. 29, 1890, TR scrapbook, TRC.

"the fellow with no pull . . . social prestige": Riis, *Theodore Roosevelt, the Citizen,* p. 106.

"I have the most . . . on my hands": TR to

ARC, May 19, 1895, *LTR,* 1:458.

"Six Years' War" as Civil Service commissioner: Riis, *Theodore Roosevelt, the Citizen,* p. 122.

"It was all breathless . . . What do we do first?": Steffens, *The Autobiography of Lincoln Steffens,* Vol. 1, pp. 257–58.

"unmitigated mischief . . . power by the people": TR, *An Autobiography,* pp. 170–71.

"Thinks he's the whole board": Steffens, *The Autobiography of Lincoln Steffens,* Vol. 1, p. 257.

"He talks, talks . . . in the papers": Joseph Bucklin Bishop, *Theodore Roosevelt and His Time, Shown in His Letters,* 2 vols. (New York: Charles Scribner's Sons, 192), Vol. 1, p. 63.

"I've come to help . . . really worth living": Riis, *Theodore Roosevelt, the Citizen,* p. 131.

"from top to bottom": Knokey, *Theodore Roosevelt and the Making of American Leadership,* p. 186.

"utterly demoralized": Avery Andrews, "Citizen in Action: The Story of TR as Police Commissioner," unpublished typescript, n.d., p. 8, TRC.

forced the resignations: Morris, *The Rise of Theodore Roosevelt,* pp. 506–7.

"would spare no man": Lincoln Steffens, Scrapbook 1, Lincoln Steffens Papers.

"midnight rambles": TR to ARC, June 23, 1895, *LTR,* 1:463.

"What is that . . . his teeth and glasses?": Andrews, "Citizen in Action," TRC.

"Sly Policemen Caught By Slyer Roosevelt": Knokey, *Theodore Roosevelt and the Making of American Leadership*, p. 193.

"Roosevelt on Patrol . . . for Sleepy Policemen": *New York Sun*, June 8, 1895, Clipping Scrapbook, TRC.

"the most interesting man in America": Knokey, *Theodore Roosevelt and the Making of American Leadership*, p. 194.

"However amusing . . . entirely serious": Andrews, "Citizen in Action," TRC.

"the beginning of a new epoch": *New York Sun*, June 8, 1895, Clipping Scrapbook, TRC.

"naturally first-rate men": Knokey, *Theodore Roosevelt and the Making of American Leadership*, p. 195.

"You are to be congratulated . . . well-patrolled": Morris, *The Rise of Theodore Roosevelt*, p. 510.

"courage and daring" . . . everyday duties: TR, *An Autobiography*, pp. 176–77.

"men with the nightsticks": Riis, *Theodore Roosevelt, the Citizen*, p. 139.

technological improvements: Dalton, *Theodore Roosevelt*, p. 157.

"one body . . . summary fashion": Ibid., p. 159.

"my whole work . . . work possibly could": TR to Anna Roosevelt, June 23, 1895, *LTR*, 1:463.

"One might hear . . . single midnight inspection": Riis, *Theodore Roosevelt, the Citizen,* p. 144.

"caught off its guard . . . true grain of the thing": Jacob A. Riis, *The Making of an American* (New York: Macmillan, 1904), p. 235.

the worst tenements were razed: Ibid., p. 343.

"the tap-root": Riis, *Theodore Roosevelt, the Citizen,* p. 138.

"The result . . . network of crime": TR, *An Autobiography,* p. 189.

"fairly and squarely": TR to Carl Schurz, Aug. 6, 1895, *LTR,* 1:472.

"against some and not others": Andrews, "Citizen in Action," TRC.

"no honorable . . . to enforce it": TR to Anna Roosevelt, June 30, 1895, *LTR,* 1:463.

"never been . . . more savage fight": TR to HCL, July 20, 1895, *LTR,* 1:469.

"driving and walking . . . most limited extent": TR to HCL, Aug. 22, 1895, in Henry Cabot Lodge, *Selections from the Correspondence of Theodore Roosevelt and Henry Cabot Lodge: 1884–1918* (New York: Charles Scribner's Sons, 1925), Vol. 1, p. 164.

"furious rage": TR to ARC, June 30, 1895, *LTR,* 1:463.

"You are the biggest fool . . . made of yourself": Andrews, "Citizen in Action," TRC.

"A less resolute man . . . was sworn to do":

Jacob A, Riis, *How the Other Half Lives: Studies among the Tenements of New York* (New York: Charles Scribner's Sons, 1914), p. 241.

"the howl": Riis, *Theodore Roosevelt, the Citizen,* p. 142.

"the Police Czar . . . Roosevelt's Razzle Dazzle Reform Racket": NYT, Sept. 26, 1895.

"Bully for Teddy!": Ibid.

"Teddy, you're a man!": Daily Republican (Decatur, Ill.), Sept. 27, 1895.

"Cheered by Those Who Came to Jeer": Chicago Evening Journal, reprinted in ibid.

"let up on the saloon": TR to HCL, Oct. 11, 1895, *LTR,* 1:484.

"He was terribly angry . . . I would not change": TR to HCL, Oct. 15, 1895, *LTR,* 1:486.

"Reform was beaten": Steffens, *The Autobiography of Lincoln Steffens,* Vol. 1, p. 181.

"Just at present . . . profound depression": TR to ARC, Nov. 19, 1895, TR, *Letters from Theodore Roosevelt to Anna Roosevelt Cowles,* p. 164.

"He seems . . . much lowered": HCL to ARC, [Dec. 1895], quoted in Lilian Rixey, *Bamie: Theodore Roosevelt's Remarkable Sister* (New York: D. McKay, 1963), p. 89.

"I do not deal . . . with the law": Knokey, *Theodore Roosevelt and the Making of American Leadership,* p. 199.

"on each side . . . course to follow": Sewall, *Bill*

Sewall's Story of Theodore Roosevelt, p. 105.

"jammed, people . . . in the aisles": TR to ARC, Oct. 4, 1896, TR, *Letters from Theodore Roosevelt to Anna Roosevelt Cowles,* p. 194.

"all of his time . . . work of the campaign": Albert B. Cummins, in Wood, *Roosevelt as We Knew Him,* p. 42.

lobbied on his behalf: TR to HCL, Dec. 4, 1896, *LTR,* 1:568.

"I want peace . . . is too pugnacious": H. Paul Jeffers, *Colonel Roosevelt: Theodore Roosevelt Goes to War, 1897–1898* (New York: John Wiley & Sons, 1996), p. 22.

friends cautioned Roosevelt not to settle for this lesser post: TR to HCL, Dec. 4, 1896, *LTR,* 1:568.

"a reserve of good feeling": Stephen R. Covey, *The 7 Habits of Highly Effective People: Restoring the Character Ethics* (New York: Free Press, 2004), p. 188.

"dry docks . . . torpedo boats": Jeffers, *Colonel Roosevelt,* p. 31.

"He is full . . . careful as I am": John D. Long Diary, Feb. 26, 1897, quoted in Knokey, *Theodore Roosevelt and the Making of American Leadership,* p. 238.

"broke the record . . . and rivets": Jeffers, *Colonel Roosevelt,* p. 42.

"A century has passed . . . menace to peace": TR, "Address to Naval War College," June 2, 1897, in Bishop, *Theodore Roosevelt and*

His Time, Vol. 1, pp. 74–75.

"I have always . . . translated into deeds": Laura Ross, ed., *A Passion to Lead: Theodore Roosevelt in His Own Words* (New York: Sterling Signature, 2012), p. 66.

"The Secretary is away . . . running the Navy": TR to Bellamy Storer, Aug. 19, 1897, *LTR,* 1:655.

"As I am given . . . a great deal": TR to ARC, Aug. 1, 1897, TR, *Letters from Theodore Roosevelt to Anna Roosevelt Cowles,* p. 208.

"hot-weather": TR to HCL, July 22, 1891, *LTR,* 1:256.

"I knew that . . . should be done": TR, *An Autobiography,* p. 213.

"You must be tired . . . an entire rest": TR to John D. Long, Aug. 9, 1897, *LTR,* 1:642.

"If things go . . . back for six weeks more": TR to Long, Aug. 15, 1897, *LTR,* 1:651.

"I am very glad . . . weather we have had": TR to Long, Sept. 15, 1897, *LTR,* 1:676.

"ohastened": TR to Long, Aug. 15, 1897, *LTR,* 1:651.

"beguilingly honest and open": Burns and Dunn, *The Three Roosevelts,* p. 47.

"was just what you . . . letter and spirit": TR to Long, Sept. 18, 1897, *LTR,* 1:681.

"generous . . . every possible way": TR to Long, Jan. 3, 1898, *LTR,* 1:751.

"it should come finally . . . made long before": TR to Long, Jan. 14, 1898, *LTR,* 1:759.

"an act of friendly courtesy": Pringle, *Theodore Roosevelt,* p. 176.

"I have been through . . . want to see another": Knokey, *Theodore Roosevelt and the Making of American Leadership,* p. 210.

"Do not take any step . . . sensation in the papers": Bishop, *Theodore Roosevelt and His Time,* Vol. 1, p. 86.

"peremptory orders . . . number of seamen": John D. Long Diary, Feb. 26, 1897, in Stefan Lorant, *The Life and Times of Theodore Roosevelt* (Garden City, N.Y.: Doubleday, 1959), p. 390.

"keep full of coal . . . not leave the coast": TR to George Dewey, Feb. 25, 1898, *LTR,* 1:784.

"Roosevelt, in his precipitate . . . yesterday afternoon": Long Diary, Feb. 26, 1898, quoted in Knokey, *Theodore Roosevelt and the Making of American Leadership,* p. 238.

"just recovering . . . moment have taken": Long Diary, Feb. 26, 1898, quoted in Lorant, *The Life and Times of Theodore Roosevelt,* p. 390.

"If it had not been . . . energy and promptness": Ray Stannard Baker, "TR," *McClure's* (Nov. 1890), p. 23.

"few men would . . . he took it": Quoted in Knokey, *Theodore Roosevelt and the Making of American Leadership,* p. 239.

"I really think . . . political career for good": Win-

throp Chanler to Margaret Chanler, April 29, 1898, in Winthrop Chanler and Margaret Chanler, *Winthrop Chanler's Letters* (Privately printed, 1951), p. 68.

"more important work . . . Navy Department": Sewall, *Bill Sewall's Story of Theodore Roosevelt,* p. 102.

"lost his head . . . utterly unaware": Long Diary, April 25, 1898, quoted in Lorant, *The Life and Times of Theodore Roosevelt,* p. 293.

"usefulness . . . largely disappear in time of war": TR to Alexander Lambert, April 1, 1898, *LTR,* 2:807.

"My work here . . . using the tools": Sewall, *Bill Sewall's Story of Theodore Roosevelt,* p. 103.

"You know what . . . answered that call": Lawrence Abbott, ed., *The Letters of Archie Butt, Personal Aide to President Roosevelt* (New York: Doubleday, Page, 1924), p. 146.

"composed exclusively . . . horsemen and marksmen": Morris, *The Rise of Theodore Roosevelt,* p. 613.

"I told [Alger] . . . it into action": TR, *An Autobiography,* p. 218.

"Alger considered this . . . I could have performed": Ibid., p. 219.

"possessed in common . . . thirst for adventure": Theodore Roosevelt, *The Rough Riders* (New York: P. F. Collier & Sons, 1899), p. 22.

"swells": Evan Thomas, *The War Lovers: Roosevelt, Lodge, Hearst, and the Rush to Empire, 1898* (Boston: Little, Brown, 2014), p. 263.

"fellow feeling": TR, "Fellow-Feeling," Jan. 1900, *WTR,* 13:355.

He assigned Knickerbocker Club members to wash dishes for a New Mexico company: TR to HCL, May 18, 1898, in Lodge, *Selections from the Correspondence of Theodore Roosevelt and Henry Cabot Lodge,* 1:298.

"When we got down . . . slept out in the open": TR, *The Rough Riders,* p. 178.

"The men can go in . . . miles of the camp": Pringle, *Theodore Roosevelt,* pp. 186–87.

"When things got easier . . . not enforce discipline": TR, *The Rough Riders,* pp. 178–79.

"Instead of falling back . . . closer at every volley": Richard Harding Davis, *The Cuban and Puerto Rican Campaigns* (New York: Charles Scribner's Sons, 1898), p. 170.

propelled his troops toward the enemy: Ibid., p. 170.

"up and down" . . . bewilderment, and excitement: Edward Marshall, *The Story of the Rough Riders, 1st U.S. Volunteer Cavalry: The Regiment in Camp and on the Battle Field* (New York: G. W. Dillingham, 1899), p. 104.

"What to do next I had not an idea": TR, *An Autobiography,* p. 242.

"the most magnificent . . . Americans in Cuba":

Marshall, *The Story of the Rough Riders,* p. 104.

"great day": Pringle, *Theodore Roosevelt,* p. 181.

"to see our commanding . . . enjoyable camping trip": Knokey, *Theodore Roosevelt and the Making of American Leadership,* p. 341.

"We must advance . . . Come on": TR, *An Autobiography,* p. 249.

"No one who saw . . . of the rifle pits": Arthur Lubow, *The Reporter Who Would Be King: A Biography of Richard Harding Davis* (New York: Scribner, 1992), p. 185.

"If you don't wish . . . pass, please": Richard Harding Davis, *The Cuban and Puerto Rican Campaigns,* p. 30.

"Up, up they went . . . an awful one": Riis, *Theodore Roosevelt, the Citizen,* p. 167.

"shouting for his men to follow": Thomas, *The War Lovers,* p. 325.

"cheering and filling . . . with cowboy yells": Richard Harding Davis, *The Cuban and Puerto Rican Campaigns,* p. 170.

"had single-handedly crushed the foe": Lubow, *The Reporter Who Would Be King,* p. 185.

"You are the next governor of New York!": Lincoln Steffens, "Theodore Roosevelt, Governor," *McClure's* (May 1899), p. 57.

"In my regiment . . . them as I could": TR to Theodore (Ted) Roosevelt, Jr., Oct. 4, 1903, container 7, TR Jr. Papers, LC.

"stumped the State . . . towns and cities": Steffens, "Theodore Roosevelt, Governor," p. 60.

"electrical, magnetic": TR to HCL, Oct. 16, 1898, *LTR*, 2:885.

"that indefinable 'something' . . . hill of San Juan": *Commercial Advertiser* (Chicago), Oct. 26, 1898.

"I have played it . . . hold another office": TR to Cecil Spring Rice, Nov. 25, 1898, *LTR*, 2:888.

"the dignity of the office . . . instead of a green chair": TR to Seth Low, Aug. 3, 1900, *LTR*, 2:1372.

"No man resolved . . . personal contention": AL to Capt. James M. Cutts, Oct. 26, 1863, *CW*, 6:538.

"I am delighted . . . under advisement": "A Day with Governor Roosevelt," *NYT, Illustrated Magazine*, April 23, 1899.

"Speak softly and carry a big stick": "Roosevelt 'Big Stick' Speech at State Fair," Sept. 3, 1901, reprinted in *Star Tribune* (Minneapolis), Sept. 2, 2014.

"continually blusters . . . of that softness": Ibid.

"gentlemen's understanding": TR, *An Autobiography*, p. 275.

"It was a matter of plain decency": Ibid., p. 308.

"pay their fair share of the public burden": TR to Thomas Collier Platt, May 8, 1899, *LTR*, 2:1004.

"storm of protest": TR, *An Autobiography,* p. 308.

"the big mistake": Thomas Platt to TR, May 6, 1899, TRC.

"right-hand . . . ultimatum": TR, *An Autobiography,* p. 300.

"I persistently . . . not be retained": TR, *An Autobiography,* p. 291.

"a list of four good machine men": Morris, *The Rise of Theodore Roosevelt,* p. 728.

"yelled and blustered" . . . gotten behind him: TR to Henry Sprague, Jan. 26, 1900, *LTR,* 2:1141.

"by the simple process . . . disagreeable to him": TR to Josephine Shaw Lowell, Feb. 20, 1900, *LTR,* 2:1197.

"I have ever preferred . . . then to not do it": Louis J. Lang, ed., *The Autobiography of Thomas Collier Platt* (New York: B. W. Dodge, 1910), pp. 274–75.

"served notice . . . the Vice-Presidency": Lincoln Steffens, "Governor Roosevelt," *McClure's* (June 1900), p. 112.

"Don't you know . . . and the White House?": TR to William McKinley, June 21, 1900, quoted in note, *LTR,* 2:1337.

"figurehead": TR to HCL, Feb. 2, 1900, *LTR,* 2:1160.

"Roosevelt has a big head . . . Vice-President": TR, quoted in *The World* (New York), June 18, 1900.

"His enemies triumphed . . . they wanted him": Riis, *Theodore Roosevelt, the Citizen,* p. 235.

"useless and empty position": Edith Carow Roosevelt, quoted in Stacy A. Cordery, *Alice: Alice Roosevelt Longworth, from White House Princess to Washington Power Broker* (New York: Viking, 2007), p. 40.

"I am not doing any . . . then to do it well": TR to Taft, March 12, 1901, *LTR,* 3:11.

"the kaleidoscope will . . . victory will be in order": TR to Charles Wood, Oct. 23, 1899, *LTR,* 2:108.

"shot into the presidency": H. H. Kohlstat, *From McKinley to Harding: Personal Recollections of Our Presidents* (New York: Charles Scribner's Sons, 1923), p. 101.

Chapter Seven
Franklin Roosevelt: "Above all, try something"

"like some amazing stag": Gunther, *Roosevelt in Retrospect,* p. 201.

"It was the most wonderful athletic feat": Perkins, Part 2, p. 69, OHRO/CUL.

"bleary with smoke": Ward, *A First-Class Temperament,* p. 583.

"I'd never felt . . . way before": Ibid., p. 584.

"Not improving": Burns and Dunn, *The Three Roosevelts,* p. 79.

"Death": Ivan Turgenev, *Sketches from a Hunter's Album,* translated with an introduc-

tion and notes by Richard Freeborn (New York: Penguin, 1990), p. 227.

"The psychological factor . . . utterly crushing him": Ward, *A First-Class Temperament,* p. 604.

"bright and happy": Ward, *Before the Trumpet,* p. 145.

"rebellious" body: TR to Walter Camp, Sept. 28, 1921, in Elliott Roosevelt, ed., *F.D.R.: His Personal Letters, 1905–1928* (New York: Duell, Sloan & Pearce, 1947), p. 530.

"a trapeze-like contraption . . . a goner": Gunther, *Roosevelt in Retrospect,* p. 229.

"win . . . happy over little things": ER, Introduction, in Elliott Roosevelt, ed., *F.D.R.: Personal Letters, 1905–1928,* p. xviii.

"If you spent two years . . . seem easy!": Schlesinger, *The Crisis of the Old Order,* p. 405.

"trial and error": Gunther, *Roosevelt in Retrospect,* p. 229.

"a number of mechanical" . . . to reach his library books: Tobin, *The Man He Became,* p. 171.

"fellow polios": Ward, *A First-Class Temperament,* p. 729.

"serving his purposes": ER, *This I Remember,* p. 349. Actual wording is "served his purposes."

"If he didn't have . . . in his personality": Perkins, Part 2, p. 463, OHRO/CUL.

"a deep . . . and tenderness": James Roosevelt and Sidney Schalett, *Affectionately FDR: A Son's Story of a Lonely Man* (New York: Harcourt Brace, 1959), p. 313.

"changed everything": NYT, Nov. 27, 1932.

"He had one loyalty . . . Roosevelt": Rosenman, *Working with Roosevelt*, p. 24.

a newspaper designed for a readership of one: Fenster, *FDR's Shadow*, p. 200.

"Father was too busy . . . his shoulders": Ibid., pp. 146–48.

Franklin would be president of the United States: Ibid., p. 147.

"leg muscles responded . . . from about 5 p.m. on": FDR to Paul Hasbrouck, in Ward, *A First-Class Temperament*, p. 668.

"Water got me . . . will get me out again!": Gunther, *Roosevelt in Retrospect*, p. 229.

other "wife": Asbell, *The F.D.R. Memoirs*, p. 249.

Missy gave "Effdee": Ward, *A First-Class Temperament*, p. 679.

"sense of nonsense": Asbell, *The F.D.R. Memoirs*, p. 245.

"There were days . . . light-hearted façade": Ibid., p. 241.

"probably said . . . position longer": Rosenman, *Working with Roosevelt*, p. 25.

"never hesitating . . . about his work": Ward, *A First-Class Temperament*, p. 710.

"By this time . . . the grandstand": Rosenman,

Working with Roosevelt, p. 113.

"He might have . . . able to be": ER, *This I Remember,* p. 349.

"I sometimes acted . . . wanted or welcomed": Ibid.

"We're not going . . . about that anymore": Anna Rosenberg Hoffman, OH, FDRL.

"Nothing to worry about . . . Let's go": Turnley Walker, *Roosevelt and the Warm Springs Story* (New York: A. Wyn, 1953), pp. 8–9.

"Nobody knows . . . struggled and struggled": Fenster, *FDR's Shadow,* p. 204.

"like pincers": James Roosevelt and Schalett, *Affectionately FDR,* p. 205.

a friend to shake the rostrum: Gunther, *Roosevelt in Retrospect,* p. 246.

"There was a hush . . . holding their breath": Perkins, Part 2, p. 325, OHRO/CUL.

"across his face . . . world-encompassing smile": Hugh Gregory Gallagher, *FDR's Splendid Deception* (New York: Dodd, Mead, 1985), p. 62.

"unfortunate habit": Perkins, *The Roosevelt I Knew,* p. 11.

"from the great cities . . . political battlefield": Burns and Dunn, *The Three Roosevelts,* p. 188.

"doomed to go in company . . . glorious gain": Henry Reed, ed., William Wordsworth, *The Complete Poetical Works of William Wordsworth, Together with a Description of the*

Country of the Lakes in the North of England, Now First Published with His Works (Philadelphia.: James Kay, Jun. and Brothers, 1837), p. 339.

"trembling . . . true and vigorous": Perkins, Part 2, p. 325, OHRO/CUL.

"just went crazy" . . . hour-long demonstration: Ward, *A First-Class Temperament*, p. 696.

"They howled, yelled . . . crowded galleries": *Morning Herald* (Hagerstown, Md.), June 26, 1924.

"I have witnessed . . . display of mental courage": *Syracuse Herald,* June 27, 1924.

"the real hero": Kenneth S. Davis, *FDR: The Beckoning of Destiny, 1882–1928* (New York: G. P. Putnam's Sons, 1972), p. 757.

"Adversity has lifted . . . sectional prejudices": Elliott Roosevelt, ed., *F.D.R.: His Personal Letters, 1905–1928,* note, p. 563.

"been physically . . . I have ever met": Ward, *A First-Class Temperament*, p. 699.

"he held out . . . 'I did it!' ": Fenster, *FDR's Shadow,* p. 206.

"discovery of a place": FDR to ER [Oct. 1924], in Elliott Roosevelt, ed., *F.D.R.: His Personal Letters, 1905–1928,* p. 565.

"Almost everything was falling to pieces": Donald Scott Carmichael, ed., *FDR, Columnist* (Chicago: Pellegrini & Cudahy, 1947), p. 9.

"Every morning I spend . . . pool in the world": Ibid., p. 10.

"There is no question . . . put together": FDR to James R. Roosevelt, April 30, 1925, Elliott Roosevelt, ed., *F.D.R.: His Personal Letters, 1905–1928,* p. 580.

"a hunch": Richard Vervill and John Ditrunno, "FDR, Polio, and the Warm Springs Experiment: Its Impact on Physical Medicine and Rehabilitation," *American Academy of Physical Medicine and Rehabilitation* (Jan. 2013), p. 5, http://www.pmr journal.org/article/S1934-1482(12)01714-5/fulltext.

"a great 'cure' . . . be established here": FDR to SDR, Sunday [Autumn 1924], in Elliott Roosevelt, ed., *F.D.R.: His Personal Letters, 1905–1928,* p. 568.

"live normal lives . . . science at the time": Vervill and Ditrunno, "FDR, Polio and the Warm Springs Experiment," p. 6.

"there were times . . . see it all": George Whitney Martin, *Madame Secretary, Frances Perkins* (New York: Houghton Mifflin Harcourt, 1983), p. 435.

decided to invest $200,000: Ward, *A First-Class Temperament,* p. 715.

to buy the hotel, the springs, and the cottages along with twelve hundred acres of land: Elliott Roosevelt, ed., *F.D.R.: His Personal Letters, 1905–1928,* p. 609.

"consulting architect . . . landscape engineer": Ward, *A First-Class Temperament,* p. 724.

He staffed the facility with great care: Vervill

and Ditrunno, "FDR, Polio and the Warm Springs Experiment," p. 6.

"a research protocol": Ibid., p. 5.

"Vice-President in charge . . . rolled into one": Ward, *A First-Class Temperament*, p. 724.

"there were bridge . . . amateur theatricals": Gallagher, *FDR's Splendid Deception*, p. 57.

"We mustn't let . . . alive every day": Walker, *Roosevelt and the Warm Springs Story*, p. 101.

"a remarkable spirit . . . their self-consciousness": Ernest K. Lindley, *The Roosevelt Revolution: First Phase* (London: Victor Gollancz, 1934), p. 214.

"spiritual transformation . . . us by humiliation": Perkins, Part 2, p. 78, OHRO/CUL.

"purged . . . a deeper philosophy": Perkins, *The Roosevelt I Knew*, p. 29.

"It was a place . . . possible": Vervill and Ditrunno, "FDR, Polio and the Warm Springs Experiment," p. 8.

As soon as the campaign was done: Lindley, *Franklin D. Roosevelt*, pp. 16–20.

"When you're in . . . play the game": Asbell, *The F.D.R. Memoirs*, p. 253.

Often speaking fourteen times a day: Richard Thayer Goldberg, *The Making of FDR: Triumph over Disability* (Cambridge, Mass.: Abt Books, 1981), p. 105.

"It was a dreadful . . . kind of scared": Perkins, Part 2, p. 559, OHRO/CUL.

"a perilous, uncomfortable": Frances Perkins, quoted in Burns, *Roosevelt,* p. 103.

"My God, he's got nerve": Perkins, Part 2, p. 559, OHRO/CUL.

"humiliating entrance": Frances Perkins, quoted in Burns, *Roosevelt,* p. 103.

"good-natured . . . and drink it": Perkins, Part 2, p. 564, OHRO/CUL.

Stunned by the devastating loss, Smith retreated: Gunther, *Roosevelt in Retrospect,* p. 256.

"Al came to see me . . . was nearly finished": FDR to Adolphus Ragan, April 6, 1938, unsent, *LTR,* 2:772–73.

"I realized that I've got . . . but here I am": Perkins, *The Roosevelt I Knew,* p. 52.

"I created you . . . doing to me!": Gunther, *Roosevelt in Retrospect,* p. 256.

"ended the close . . . Governor Smith": ER, *This I Remember,* p. 51.

"eyes and ears": Kathleen McLaughlin, "Mrs. Roosevelt Goes Her Way," *NYT,* July 5, 1936.

"At first my . . . actually getting that food?": ER, *This I Remember,* p. 56.

"educable": Perkins, Part 2, p. 232, OHRO/CUL.

He filled the Governor's Mansion: Gallagher, *The Splendid Deception,* p. 77.

Sam Rosenman: Burns, *Roosevelt,* p. 101.

"I made up your . . . careful investigation": Rosenman, *Working with Roosevelt,* p. 31.

"brain trust": Graham and Wander, eds., *Franklin D. Roosevelt,* p. 55.

"The routine was simple": Raymond Moley, *After Seven Years* (New York: Harper & Brothers, 1939), p. 20.

"nothing was so important . . . all day for this hour": Rosenman, *Working with Roosevelt,* p. 24.

"random talk came . . . into the evening": Moley, *After Seven Years,* p. 20.

"was at once . . . and a judge": Asbell, *The F.D.R. Memoirs,* p. 86.

"irregularity . . . than was comfortable": Perkins, *The Roosevelt I Knew,* p. 89.

"infinitely better . . . the descending spiral": Ibid., pp. 93–95.

"What was clear . . . immediate activities": Ibid., p. 89.

"assume leadership . . . for the State of New York": Rosenman, *Working with Roosevelt,* p. 49.

"we are trying to construct . . . no one is left out": Perkins, *The Roosevelt I Knew,* p. 109.

"What is the State? . . . and well-being": FDR, "New York State Takes the Lead in the Relief of the Unemployed. A Message Recommending Creation of Relief Administration," Aug. 28, 1931, *PPA,* 1:457.

"provide public work . . . from public funds": Rosenman, *Working with Roosevelt,* p. 50.

"wishy-washy": Ibid., p. 51.

"the bottom up . . . was a living person": Ibid., pp. 61–62.

"absurd . . . in professed ignorance": FDR, "Address Accepting the Presidential Nomination for the Presidency," July 2, 1932, *PPA,* 1:647.

"I pledge you . . . it is a call to arms": Ibid.

"nearer to the final . . . the history of any land": Burns and Dunn, *The Three Roosevelts,* p. 209.

At the slightest uptick in the stock market . . . the worst was over: Ibid.

"The country needs . . . try something": FDR, "Address at Oglethorpe University," May 22, 1932, *PPA,* 1:646.

Chapter Eight
Lyndon Johnson: "The most miserable period of my life"

"he could get . . . anybody else": Birdwell Interview, April 1965.

"wunderkind": Dallek, *Lone Star Rising,* p. 113.

"familiar with disappointments": AL, "Communication to the People of Sangamon County," March 9, 1832, *CW,* 1:9.

"a darn good sail": Levin, *The Making of FDR,* p. 59.

"the most miserable period of my life": DKG/LBJ Conversations.

"immediately interested": Dallek, *Lone Star Rising,* p. 207.

"Lyndon Johnson . . . things together!": April 22, 1941, Press Conferences of President Franklin D. Roosevelt, 1933–1945, FDRL.

"If you really . . . and Lyndon B.": Harfield Weedin Interview, Feb. 24, 1983, LBJOH.

"tremendously commanding presence": Ibid.

"When my mother . . . days in the hospital": Merle Miller, *Lyndon,* p. 84.

"nervous exhaustion": Dallek, *Lone Star Rising,* p. 213.

"He was depressed and it was bad": Jan Jarboe Russell, *Lady Bird: A Biography of Mrs. Johnson* (Waterville, Maine: Thorndike Press, 2000), p. 252.

"legal fees" or "bonuses": Robert Caro, *The Years of Lyndon Johnson: Master of the Senate* (New York: Vintage, 2003), p. 685.

"shed his coat . . . talked turkey": Brownsville Herald (Texas), June 19, 1941.

raffle ticket: Caro, *The Path to Power,* p. 710.

a photograph appeared: El Paso Herald Post, June 30, 1941.

"Lyndon Johnson . . . Election": McAllen [Texas] *Daily Press,* June 29, 1941.

"Only Miracle . . . Anointed Out": Caro, *The Path to Power,* p. 733.

"We gave him . . . he didn't win": Merle Miller, *Lyndon,* p. 106.

"I felt that . . . in my face": Dallek, *Lone Star Rising,* p. 226.

"Lyndon . . . sit on ballot boxes": Merle Miller,

Lyndon, p. 88.

"I always believed . . . make him my friend": DKG/LBJ Conversations.

"Some of us . . . very, very silent": Robert Caro, *The Years of Lyndon Johnson: Means of Ascent* (New York, Vintage, 1991), p. 77.

"I always had . . . worlds to conquer": O. C. Fisher Interview, May 8, 1969, LBJOH.

"Fits of depression . . . him after that": Randall B. Woods, *LBJ: Architect of American Ambition* (Cambridge, Mass.: Harvard University Press, 2006), p. 158.

"had to get . . . devoured": Dugger, *The Politician,* p. 216.

"I was literally working . . . I never took a breath": Caro, *The Path to Power,* p. 494.

"Like two young oaks . . . intertwining": Louis Kohlmeier, Ray Shaw, and Ed Cony, "The Johnson Wealth," *Wall Street Journal,* March 23, 1964.

"I think the term . . . out of business": Wichita *Daily Times,* April 9, 1947.

"I just could not bear . . . losing everything": DKG/LBJ Conversations.

"You have to realize . . . election rolls around": Joe Phipps, *Summer Stock: Behind the Scenes with LBJ in '48* (Fort Worth: Texas Christian University Press, 1992), pp. 117–18.

"even worked . . . never stopped": Dallek, *Lone Star Rising,* p. 306.

"This is Lyndon . . . all of you": Woods, *LBJ,* p. 204.

"Hello there, Mr. Jones . . . at election time": Merle Miller, *Lyndon,* p. 120.

"In 1948 . . . sort of fraud": Dallek, *Lone Star Rising,* p. 327.

"They were stealin' . . . actually won it": Ibid., p. 347.

"folkways . . . norms of behavior": Donald R. Matthews, *U.S. Senators and Their World* (New York: W. W. Norton, 1973), p. 92.

"the right man . . . the right time": George Reedy, *Lyndon B. Johnson: A Memoir* (New York: Andrews & McMeel, 1982), p. 89.

"The way you get . . . heads of things": Merle Miller, *Lyndon,* p. 28.

"there was only . . . request was granted": DKG/LBJ Conversations.

"Russell found . . . care of him": Ibid.

"one of the most . . . of his life": DKG, *LJAD,* p. 107.

"they feared . . . older people": DKG/LBJ Conversations.

"When you're . . . particular senator": Ibid.

Knowledge of the minutiae: Rowland Evans and Robert Novak, *Lyndon B. Johnson: The Exercise of Power* (New York: New American Library, 1966), pp. 113–15.

"the biggest . . . of the Senate": Stewart Alsop, "Lyndon Johnson: How Does He Do It?," *Saturday Evening Post,* Jan. 24, 1959, p. 14.

"a magnificent . . . lives in his interests": Reedy, *Lyndon B. Johnson,* pp. 130, xiii.

"superb . . . forgot his grievances": Ibid., p. xiv.

"sitting on the top of the world": LBJ, "My Heart Attack Taught Me How to Live," *American Magazine* (July 1956), p. 17.

"blew his stack . . . hell out of here": Caro, *Master of the Senate,* p. 621.

"my chest really began to hurt": Merle Miller, *Lyndon,* p. 181.

"as though I had . . . crushed my chest in": Samuel Shaffer, "Senator Lyndon Johnson: 'My Heart Attack Saved My Life,' " *Newsweek,* Nov. 7, 1955, p. 35.

"My God . . . heart attack": Woods, *LBJ,* p. 293.

"It was a very hectic . . . serious thing": Caro, *Master of the Senate,* p. 622.

"undertake any . . . period of months": Ibid., p. 625.

"Heart Attack . . . Hopefuls": Ibid., p. 626.

"He'd just sort . . . going full speed": George Reedy Interview, Aug. 16, 1983, LBJOH.

"He'd read them . . . in those letters": Caro, *Master of the Senate,* p. 630.

"got to the point . . . room for him": Reedy quoted in Woods, *LBJ,* p. 295.

"everybody loves Lyndon": Caro, *Master of the Senate,* p. 630.

"Time is the most . . . spend it well": Gillette, *Lady Bird,* p. 162.

healthy diet: Newsweek, Nov. 7, 1955, p. 36.

"My Heart Attack Taught Me How to Live":

American Magazine, July 1956.

"sprawled on . . . into the air": Newsweek, Nov. 7, 1955, p. 35.

"the brink of death": William Deason Interview, April 11, 1969, LBJOH.

"a matter of honor for everybody": Merle Miller, *Lyndon,* p. 184.

"back in the saddle again": George Reedy, quoted in Caro, *Master of the Senate,* p. 647.

"We've got to look . . . we're here for": Caro, *The Path to Power,* p. 82.

"every three minutes . . . were still flying": George Reedy Interview, Aug. 16, 1983, LBJOH.

"He even rewrote . . . the last minute": Merle Miller, *Lyndon,* p. 184.

"call to arms . . . Program with a Heart": Woods, *LBJ,* p. 299.

"I had never . . . of an audience": George Reedy Interview, Aug. 16, 1983, LBJOH.

"leapt to their feet . . . their approval": The Baytown (Texas), Nov. 23, 1955.

"sounded like . . . it and the fire": Reedy Interview, Aug. 16, 1983, LBJOH.

"affected every newspaperman . . . and one strike out": Ibid.

"A very fine batting average . . . at last": NYT, Nov. 23, 1955.

he would carry a civil rights bill: NYT, Sept. 2, 1957.

"ran his pen . . . be it in the end!": Ibid.

"there'll be . . . wild legislation": DKG/LBJ Conversations.

"I want to see . . . in a long time": Clinton Anderson, in "Congress Approved Civil Rights Act of 1957," *Congressional Quarterly,* https://library.cqpress.com/cqalmanac/document.php?id=cqal57-1345184.

"by the standards . . . old national wound": NYT, Sept. 1, 1957.

"A man with . . . own hands": DKG/LBJ Conversations.

"We've shown . . . couple of years": Harry McPherson, in Sylvia Ellis, *Freedom's Pragmatist: Lyndon Johnson and Civil Rights* (Tallahassee: University Press of Florida, 2013), p. 98.

"without the Democratic . . . been expected": Raymond Lahr, "Political Winds: This Year Has Been Lyndon's Year," *Delta Democrat-Times* (Greenville, Miss.), Sept. 2, 1957.

"to leave the Confederacy voluntarily": LBJ, Speech before the Democratic Caucus, Sept. 15, 1957, quoted in DKG, *LJAD,* p. 151.

"the most dramatic moment": Henry Graff, quoted in Robert Caro, *The Years of Lyndon Johnson: The Passage of Power* (New York: Vintage, 2013), p. 343.

"The Democratic Party . . . close to Appomattox": Dallek, *Lone Star Rising,* p. 541.

"the best qualified . . . a Southerner": Woods,

LBJ, p. 573.

"the balance . . . and west": Caro, *The Path to Power,* p. 449.

"never said a word . . . in the Senate": Robert Dallek, *Flawed Giant: Lyndon Johnson and His Times, 1961–1973* (New York: Oxford University Press, 1998), p. 7.

"A vice president . . . he resides": Dallek, *Lone Star Rising,* p. 567.

"evangelical . . . Attorney General": Quoted in Woods, *LBJ,* p. 411.

"appeared almost a spectral presence": Caro, *The Passage of Power,* p. 226.

"made to be Vice President": Dallek, *Flawed Giant,* p. 34.

"trips around . . . every minute of it": DKG/LBJ Conversations.

"He felt . . . political road": Ed. Weisl Sr. Interview, May 13, 1969, LBJOH.

"engines in pants": Robert Woods, *LBJ,* p. 11.

Chapter Nine
Transformational Leadership: Abraham Lincoln and the Emancipation Proclamation

"I consider the central idea . . . to govern themselves": AL quoted, "7 May Tuesday," in Michael Burlingame and John R. Turner Ettlinger, eds., *Inside Lincoln's White House: The Complete Civil War Diary of John Hay* (Carbondale: Southern Illinois University Press, 1997), p. 20.

"I began at once . . . with me the burden": AL, quoted in entry for Aug. 15, 1862, in Gideon Welles; Howard K. Beale, ed., *Diary of Gideon Welles: Secretary of the Navy under Lincoln and Johnson,* Vol. 1: *1861–March 30, 1864* (New York: W. W. Norton, 1960), p. 159.

"No one, not in my situation . . . I may return": John G. Nicolay, *A Short Life of Abraham Lincoln* (New York: Century, 1909), p. 169.

"They were so great . . . possible to survive them": Memo, July 3, 1861, quoted in Michael Burlingame, ed., *With Lincoln in the White House: Letters, Memoranda, and Other Writings of John G. Nicolay, 1860–1865* (Carbondale: Southern Illinois University Press, 2000), p. 46.

"differences in . . . measure was his": Gideon Welles, "The History of Emancipation," *Galaxy* (Dec. 1872), p. 844.

"We are in . . . gloomy thinking": Allan Nevins and Milton Halsey Thomas, eds., *The Diary of George Templeton Strong* (New York: Macmillan, 1952), Vol. 3, p. 241.

"Things had gone . . . change our tactics": Carpenter, *Six Months at the White House with Abraham Lincoln,* p. 20.

Slaves' war work: Welles, entry for October 1, 1862, *Diary of Gideon Welles,* p. 159; Burton J. Hendrick, *Lincoln's War Cabinet* (Boston: Little, Brown, 1946), p. 355.

"The slaves . . . with us or against us": Welles, "The History of Emancipation," p. 843.

"he had literally to run the gantlet": John Hay, "Life in the White House in the Time of Lincoln," *Century* (Nov. 1890), p. 34.

Soldiers' Home: Matthew Pinsker, *Lincoln's Sanctuary: Abraham Lincoln and the Soldiers' Home* (New York: Oxford University Press, 2003).

"earnestly on the . . . and delicacy": Welles, *Diary of Gideon Welles,* p. 70.

"a military . . . of the Union": James A. Rawley, *Turning Points of the Civil War* (Lincoln: University of Nebraska Press, 1989), p. 134.

"otherwise unconstitutional": AL to Albert G. Hodges, April 4, 1864, *CW,* 7:281.

"the weapon of emancipation": James M. McPherson, *Abraham Lincoln and the Second American Revolution* (New York: Oxford University Press, 1991), p. 85.

"You can not . . . embrace it?": AL, "Proclamation Revoking General Hunter's Order of Military Emancipation of May 9, 1862," May 19, 1862, *CW,* 5:222.

"emancipation in any form": AL, "Appeal to Border State Representatives to Favor Compensated Emancipation," July 12, 1962, *CW,* 5:319, note 1.

"I am a patient . . . card unplayed": AL to Reverdy Johnson, July 26, 1862, *CW,* 5:343.

"that band . . . never before": Carpenter, *Six*

Months at the White House with Abraham Lincoln, p. 11.

"As a fit . . . be free": AL, "Emancipation Proclamation — First Draft," [July 22, 1862], *CW,* 5:336.

"first the one side . . . question arising": Tarbell, *The Life of Abraham Lincoln,* Vol. 3, p. 115.

"immediate promulgation": Burlingame, *Abraham Lincoln, A Life,* Vol. 2, p. 363.

"magnitude . . . and weight": Welles, "The History of Emancipation," p. 848.

"an extreme . . . War powers": Hendrick, *Lincoln's War Cabinet,* p. 359.

"desperation . . . slave-owners": Welles, "The History of Emancipation," p. 848.

"resign and . . . Administration": John P. Usher, *President Lincoln's Cabinet* (New York: Nelson H. Loomis, 1925), p. 17.

Blair position: Welles, "The History of Emancipation," p. 847.

"It went beyond . . . on the other": Ibid.

"No commanding general . . . my responsibility": AL to Salmon P. Chase, May 17, 1962, *CW,* 5:219.

"feel justified . . . in the field": "Proclamation Revoking General Hunter's Order of Military Emancipation of May 9, 1862," May 19, 1862, *CW,* 5:222.

"The depression . . . on the retreat": Frederick William Seward, *Seward at Washington as Senator and Secretary of State: A Memoir of*

His Life, with Selections from His Letters, 1861–1872 (New York: Derby and Miller, 1891), p. 121.

"until the eagle . . . its neck": Frances Carpenter, "A Day with Govr. Seward," Seward Papers, LC.

"It was an aspect . . . of events": Carpenter, *Six Months at the White House with Abraham Lincoln,* p. 22.

"the bloodiest . . . history": Drew Gilpin Faust, *Republic of Suffering* (New York: Vintage, 2009), p. 66.

"arson in the third degree": Retold in *Cincinnati Enquirer,* Nov. 23, 1869.

"I wish it were . . . driven out": John Niven, ed., *The Salmon P. Chase Papers,* Vol. 1: *Journals, 1829–1872* (Kent, Ohio: Kent State University Press, 1983), p. 394.

"fixed and unalterable . . . were his alone": Welles, "The History of Emancipation," p. 848.

"pondered . . . passed on": Ibid., p. 847.

"very emphatic . . . opinion": Ibid., p. 846.

"fully" satisfied . . . with all my heart": Entry for Sept. 22, 1862, in Niven, ed., *The Salmon P. Chase Papers,* Vol. 1, pp. 394–95.

"an arbitrary . . . of freedom": Hendrick, *Lincoln's War Cabinet,* p. 359.

"to assent . . . the measure": Welles, "The History of Emancipation," p. 846.

Caleb Smith: Hendrick, *Lincoln's War Cabinet,*

pp. 356, 347.

"afraid of the . . . on the army": David Herbert Donald, ed., *Inside Lincoln's Cabinet: The Civil War Diaries of Salmon P. Chase* (New York: Longmans, Green, 1954), p. 152.

"but the difficulty . . . forward movement": Welles, "The History of Emancipation," p. 847.

"to recognize and to maintain": William Henry Seward, quoted in entry for Sept. 22, 1862, in Niven, ed., *The Salmon P. Chase Papers,* Vol. 1, p. 394.

"So long as . . . man's bosom": AL, "Response to Serenade," Nov. 10, 1864, *CW,* 8:101.

"greatly pained . . . to the country": AL, "Memo to Cabinet," July 14, 1864, *CW,* 7:439.

"too vast for malicious dealing": Randall Miller, ed., *Lincoln and Leadership,* p. 98.

"The pressure . . . is immeasurable": Frank Abial Flower, *Edwin McMasters Stanton: The Autocrat of Rebellion, Emancipation, and Reconstruction* (Akron, Ohio: Saalfield, 1905), pp. 369–70.

"Every one likes a compliment": AL to Thurlow Weed, March 15, 1865, quoted in Phillips, *Lincoln on Leadership,* p. 18.

"Neptune": Welles, entry for July 14, 1863, *Diary of Gideon Welles,* Vol. 1, p. 370.

"that you have been remiss . . . success": AL to GW, July 25, 1863, *CW,* 6:349.

"the President . . . still work on": SPC to James

Watson Webb, Nov. 7, 1863, reel 29, Chase Papers.

"by his like . . . his friend": Leonard Swett, *HI,* p. 166.

"principle of . . . wrong hereafter": AL to Stanton, Feb. 5, 1864, *CW,* 7:169.

"Why did you . . . you no good": William Henry Herndon to James Watson Webb, Jan. 6, 1887, reel 10, Herndon-Weik Collection, Manuscript Division, LC.

"seen anything . . . thoroughly prepared": Ralph and Adaline Emerson, *Mr. & Mrs. Ralph Emerson's Personal Recollections of Abraham Lincoln* (Rockford, Ill.: Wilson Brothers, 1909), p. 7.

"when convinced . . . the appointment": William L. Miller, *Lincoln's Virtues,* p. 424.

"No two men . . . each other": New York Evening Post, July 13, 1891.

"never sent and never signed": AL to Major General Meade, "never sent or signed," July 14, 1863, *CW,* 6:328.

"I would like . . . in the basket": William H. Crook, "Lincoln as I Knew Him," *Harper's Monthly* (May–June 1907), p. 34.

"Forget it . . . of it again": Elizabeth Blair to Samuel Lee, March 6, 1862, in Elizabeth Blair Lee; Virginia Jeans Laas, ed., *Wartime Washington: The Civil War Letters of Elizabeth Blair Lee* (Urbana: University of Illinois Press, 1999), p. 109.

"declared that . . . to them": Welles, *Diary of Gideon Welles,* Vol. 1, pp. 23–25.

"The Secretary of War is not . . . of War": AL, "Address to Union Meeting at Washington," Aug. 6, 1862, *CW,* 5:388–89.

"enthusiastically . . . very satisfactory": Welles, "The History of Emancipation," p. 483.

"ill wind": Seward, *Seward at Washington as Senator and Secretary of State,* p. 141.

"Our war on . . . languishes": Entry for Oct. 23, 1862, in Nevins and Thomas, eds., *The Diary of George Templeton Strong,* Vol. 3, p. 267.

"such an accursed doctrine": McClellan letter to his wife, Sept. 25, [1862], in Stephen W. Sears, ed., *The Civil War Papers of George C. McClellan: Selected Correspondence, 1860–1865* (New York: Ticknor & Fields, 1989), p. 481.

"We have lost almost everything": Oct, 16, 1862, Burlingame, ed., *With Lincoln in the White House,* p. 89.

"Somewhat like . . . hurt to laugh": Carl Sandburg, *Abraham Lincoln: The War Years,* Vol. 3 (New York: Charles Scribner's Sons, 1943), p. 611.

Most uncheerful . . . crowded the hotels": Noah Brooks, *Washington in Lincoln's Time* (New York: Century, 1895), p. 44.

"I began to fear . . . hurt the enemy": AL, quoted in "25 Sept. 1863, Sunday," in Bur-

lingame and Ettlinger, eds., *Inside Lincoln's White House,* p. 232.

"a fighting general": DKG, *TOR,* p. 485.

"a slaughter pen": Noah Brooks, in P. J. Staudenraus, ed., *Mr. Lincoln's Washington: Selections from the Writing of Noah Brooks, Civil War Correspondent* (South Brunswick, N.J.: Thomas Yoseloff, 1966), p. 155.

Rumors spread: James M. McPherson, *Battle Cry of Freedom: The Civil War Era* (New York: Oxford University Press, 1988), p. 574.

"endeavoring to purchase . . . of this country": AL, "Reply to Serenade in Honor of Emancipation Proclamation," Sept. 24, 1862, *CW,* 5:438.

"more depressed": Nancy F. Kohen, "Lincoln's School of Management," *NYT,* Jan. 26, 2013.

"If there is . . . I am in it": Burlingame, *The Inner World of Abraham Lincoln,* p. 105.

"into other channels of thought": William O. Stoddard, *Inside the White House in War Times* (Lincoln, Neb.: Bison, 2000), p. 191.

"He has forgotten . . . it will kill me": AL, quoted in Schuyler Colfax, *The Life and Principles of Abraham Lincoln* (Philadelphia: Jas. R. Rodgers, 1865), p. 12.

"It matters not . . . thought suffices": Francis Carpenter, quoted in Charles M. Segal, ed., *Conversations with Lincoln* (New York: G. P.

Putnam's Sons, 1961), pp. 302–3.

"literary recreation": William Kelley, in Rice, ed., *Reminiscences of Abraham Lincoln by Distinguished Men of His Time,* p. 270.

"neigh of a wild horse": Carpenter, *Six Months at the White House with Abraham Lincoln,* p. 51.

"life preserver": Isaac N. Arnold, quoted in ibid., p. 150.

"my heavy eye-lids . . . me to bed": Burlingame and Ettlinger, eds., *Inside Lincoln's White House,* p. 76.

"for any good excuse for saving a man's life": Carpenter, *Six Months at the White House with Abraham Lincoln,* p. 172.

"overcome by . . . than his will": Helen Nicolay, *Personal Traits of Abraham Lincoln,* p. 280.

"sleep steals upon him unawares": John Eaton, *Grant, Lincoln, and the Freedman: Reminiscences of the Civil War* (New York: Longmans, Green, 1907), p. 180.

"I go to bed . . . and his friends": Carpenter, *Six Months at the White House with Abraham Lincoln,* p. 172.

"general air of doubt": NYT, Dec. 27, 1862.

"Will Lincoln's . . . Nobody knows": Entry for Dec. 30, 1862, in Nevins and Thomas, eds., *The Diary of George Templeton Strong,* Vol. 3, p. 284.

"chief gem": AL to Joshua Speed, July 4,

1842, *CW*, 1:289.

"My word . . . take it back": Quoted in George S. Boutwell, *Speeches and Papers Relating to the Rebellion and the Overthrow of Slavery* (Boston: Little, Brown, 1867), p. 392.

"Abraham Lincoln . . . confide in his word": *Douglass' Monthly* (Oct. 1862).

"serene and even . . . were far away": Brooks, *Washington in Lincoln's Time,* p. 42.

"The dogmas . . . and act anew": AL, "Annual Message to Congress," Dec. 1, 1862, *CW,* 5:537.

"the considerate judgment . . . Almighty God": Brooks, in Staudenraus, ed., *Mr. Lincoln's Washington,* p. 57.

"dipped his pen . . . bold, clear, and firm": Seward, *Seward at Washington as Senator and Secretary of State,* p. 151.

"visible shadow . . . sobs and tears": Frederick Douglass, *The Life and Times of Frederick Douglass* (Mineola, N.Y.: Dover, 2003), p. 255.

"Glory . . . John Brown": William S. McFeeley, *Frederick Douglass* (New York: W. W. Norton, 1995), p. 237.

"the monstrous doctrine . . . inextinguishable hate": *Journal of the House of Representatives of the Commonwealth of Kentucky* (Frankfort: John B. Major, 1863), p. 1126.

"the alarming . . . a fixed thing": Quoted in entry for Jan. 19, 1862, in Theodore Calvin

Pease, and James G. Randall, eds., *Diary of Orville Hickman Browning,* Vol. 1: *1850–1864* (Springfield: Illinois State Historical Library, 1925), p. 616.

"clamor for . . . leave them": Ibid., Jan. 26, 1862, p. 620.

"the number . . . affect the army": William C. Davis, *Lincoln's Men: How President Lincoln Became Father to an Army and a Nation* (New York: Touchstone, 2000), p. 101.

"Whoever can wait . . . run over by it": Swett, *HI,* p. 164.

"I claim not to . . . controlled me": AL to Albert G. Hodges, April 4, 1864, *CW,* 7:281.

"It is my conviction . . . into his lap!": Carpenter, *Six Months at the White House with Abraham Lincoln,* p. 77.

"this great revolution . . . to defeat the purpose": Ibid.

"He always moves . . . struggles with them": John W. Forney, quoted in "31 December 1863, Thursday," in Burlingame and Turner, eds., *Inside Lincoln's White House,* p. 135.

"gone too fast and too far": Brooks, in Staudenraus, ed., *Mr. Lincoln's Washington,* p. 138.

"puts the Administration . . . to the end": NYT, April 9, 1863.

"Mr. Weed . . . sent for you": Thurlow Weed Barnes, ed., *Memoir of Thurlow Weed* (Boston: Houghton Mifflin, 1884), pp. 434–35.

"Read it very slowly": AL to James C. Conkling, Aug. 27, 1863, *CW*, 6:414.

"To be plain . . . in saving the Union": AL to James C. Conkling, Aug. 26, 1863, *CW*, 4:407.

"If they stake . . . must be kept": Ibid.

"He cares for us . . . he cares": Tarbell, *The Life of Abraham Lincoln*, Vol. 3, p. 150.

"link or cord . . . governing power": Davis, *Lincoln's Men*, p. 130.

"one of their own": Ibid., p. 95.

"What a depth . . . his smile": Ibid., p. 69.

"He looks . . . bless Abraham Lincoln": Ibid., p. 142.

"A country that is worth . . . a soldiers life": Ibid., p. 108.

"If he says . . . Amen": Ibid., p. 91.

"never been in favor . . . ready and willing": Bell Wiley, *The Life of Billy Yank* (Baton Rouge: Louisiana State University Press, 1979), p. 44.

"You will stand . . . right of citizenship": *Douglass' Monthly* (Aug. 1862).

"I was never . . . fair play": Douglass, *The Life and Times of Frederick Douglass*, pp. 784–85.

"with earnest attention . . . apparent sympathy": Frederick Douglass, in Rice, ed., *Reminiscences of Abraham Lincoln by Distinguished Men of His Time*, p. 187.

"In the end . . . as white soldiers": Ibid., p. 188.

"never seen a more transparent countenance": Douglass, *The Life and Times of Frederick Douglass,* p. 485.

"He treated me . . . will allow him to do": Douglass, in Rice, ed., *Reminiscences of Abraham Lincoln by Distinguished Men of His Time,* p. 320.

"I never saw . . . is unsurpassed": Dudley Taylor Cornish, *The Sable Arm: Black Troops in the Union Army, 1861–1865* (Lawrence: University Press of Kansas, 1956), pp. 146–47.

"You have no . . . done better": Ibid., pp. 142–43.

"believe the . . . the rebellion": AL to James C. Conkling, Aug. 26, 1863, *CW,* 6:408–9.

"a mad cry": Browne, *The Every-Day Life of Abraham Lincoln,* p. 486.

"The tide is setting . . . on the sole condition": Henry J. Raymond to AL, Aug. 22, 1864, Lincoln Papers, Manuscript Division, LC.

"I confess that . . . finish this job": "The interview between Thad Stevens & Mr. Lincoln as related by Colonel R. M. Hoe," compiled by John G. Nicolay, container 10, Nicolay Papers.

"utter ruination": Nicolay, in Burlingame, ed., *With Lincoln in the White House,* p. 152.

"should be damned . . . Emancipation lever": "Interview with Alexander W. Randall and Joseph T. Mills," Aug. 19, 1864, *CW,* 7:507.

"*Glorious news . . . event of the war*": Sept. 3, 1864, in Nevins and Thomas, eds., *The Diary of George Templeton Strong,* Vol. 3, pp. 480–81.

"*was beyond any possible hope*": Burlingame, *Abraham Lincoln, a Life,* Vol. 2, p. 668.

"*the ship right . . . capsized it*": Tarbell, *The Life of Abraham Lincoln,* Vol. 3, p. 203.

"*We are as certain . . . the sun shines*": *The World* (New York), Oct. 14, 1864.

"*would rather be . . . elected without it*": Ida M. Tarbell, *A Reporter for Lincoln: Story of Henry E. Wing, Soldier and Newspaperman* (New York: Macmillan, 1927), p. 70.

"*is not merely . . . should be maintained*": AL, "Speech to One Hundred Sixty-Sixth Ohio Regiment," Aug. 22, 1864, *CW,* 7:512.

"*there was an . . . heard before*": Brooks, *Washington in Lincoln's Time,* p. 187.

"*congratulation to the country . . . nobly began*": AL, "Response to a Serenade," Feb. 1, 1865, *CW,* 8:254.

"*And to whom . . . to Abraham Lincoln*": Burlingame, *Abraham Lincoln, a Life,* Vol. 2, p. 749.

"*I have only . . . done it all*": Ibid., p. 751.

"*done nothing . . . will be realized*": Speed, *HI,* p. 197.

the "*wen*": AL, "Speech at Peoria, Ill.," Oct. 16, 1854, *CW,* 2:274.

"*A King's cure . . . whole thing up*": AL, "Response to a Serenade," Feb. 1, 1865, *CW,* 8:254.

"*Fellow citizens . . . hope of earth*": AL, "Annual Message to Congress," Dec. 1, 1862, *CW,* 5:537.

Chapter Ten
Crisis Management: Theodore Roosevelt and the Coal Strike

"*It is a dreadful thing . . . that is all there is about it*": TR to HCL, Sept. 23, 1901, in Lodge, *Selections from the Correspondence of Theodore Roosevelt and Henry Cabot Lodge,* Vol. 1, p. 506.

"*were loyal to their work . . . if they were not*": TR, *An Autobiography,* p. 350.

"*that madman*": TR to William McKinley, June 21, 1900, quoted in note, *LTR,* 2:1337.

"*I hope you will be . . . have been to him*": Mark Sullivan, *Our Times: The United States, 1900–1925,* Vol. 2; *America Finding Herself* (New York: Charles Scribner's Sons, 1927), p. 392.

"*In this hour of deep . . . honor of the country*": *New York Tribune,* Sept. 17, 1901.

"*would give a lie to all he had stood for*": Rixey, *Bamie,* p. 172.

"*to act in every word . . . vote for President*": David S. Barry, *Forty Years in Washington* (Boston: Little Brown, 1964), p. 268.

"*The infectiousness . . . of average men*": Sullivan, *Our Times: America Finding Herself,* Vol. 2, p. 399.

"the most formidable . . . of the country": Walter Wellman, "The Progress of the World," *American Monthly Review of Reviews* (Oct. 1902).

"the biggest . . . of the year": Joseph P. McKerns, "The 'Faces' of John Mitchell: News Coverage of the Great Anthracite Strike of 1902 in the Regional and National Press," in *The "Great Strike": Perspectives on the 1902 Anthracite Coal Strike* (Easton, Penn.: Canal History & Technology Press, 2002), p. 29.

"assumed a shape . . . in our time": TR to Carl Schurz, Dec. 24, 1903, *LTR,* 3:379–80.

"the most important . . . United States": Joseph Gowaskie, "John Mitchell and the Anthracite Strike of 1902," in *The "Great Strike,"* p. 129.

"risk everything . . . great fight": Robert J. Cornell, *The Anthracite Coal Strike of 1902* (Washington, D.C.: Catholic University of America, 1957), p. 92.

"a common . . . labor agitator": Walter Wellman, "The Inside History of the Coal Strike," *Collier's,* Oct. 18, 1902, p. 7.

"If you stand . . . you will lose": Cornell, *The Anthracite Coal Strike of 1902,* p. 94.

"Who shot our President?": Lincoln Steffens, "A Labor Leader of Today: John Mitchell

and What He Stands For," *McClure's* (Aug. 1902), p. 355.

"thoroughly awake": TR to Lodge, Sept. 30. 1902, in Lodge, *Selections from the Correspondence of Theodore Roosevelt and Henry Cabot Lodge,* Vol. 1, p. 535.

"no earthly . . . dozen years ago": TR to Marcus Hanna, Sept. 27, 1902, *LTR,* 3:329–30.

"two schools . . . against action": TR, *An Autobiography,* pp. 362, 365.

"the steward of the people": Ibid., p. 357.

"to do whatever . . . to do it": Ibid., p. 464.

"I am slowly . . . provokes reaction": Riis, *Theodore Roosevelt, the Citizen,* p. 375.

"to make special . . . House of Congress": Carroll D. Wright, "Report to the President on Anthracite Coal Strike" (Nov. 1902), Bulletin: Department of Labor, No. 43, p. 1147. (Hereinafter Wright Report.)

"all facts . . . present controversy": Ibid.

"one of the foremost . . . the world": *Defiance Express,* June 27, 1902.

"The President's . . . directly involved": *Literary Digest,* June 21, 1902, p. 826.

"a new and untried field": Riis, *Theodore Roosevelt, the Citizen,* p. 373.

"presence there . . . harm than good": Jonathan Grossman, "The Coal Strike of 1902 — Turning Point in U.S. Policy," *Monthly Labor Review,* Oct. 10, 1975, p. 23.

"I cannot afford . . . and unwise": Richard G.

Healey, "Disturbances of the Peace: The Operators' View of the 1902 Anthracite Coal Strike," in *The "Great Strike,"* p. 100.

"the psychological . . . minds of everyone": Wright Report, p. 1151.

"might lead . . . accordance with greater justice": Ibid., pp. 1166–67.

"This is an important . . . publishing the report": Grossman, "The Coal Strike of 1902 — Turning Point in U.S. Policy," p. 23.

"personal information . . . undignified position": Philander Knox to TR, Aug. 23, 1902, Theodore Roosevelt Papers. Library of Congress Manuscript Division. http://www.theodorerooseveltcenter.org/Research/Digital-Library/Record?libID=039143. Theodore Roosevelt Digital Library. Dickinson State University.

"only here and there . . . entirely exhausted": *Literary Digest,* Aug. 9, 1902, p. 152.

"The labor problem . . . operators did not see": TR, *An Autobiography,* pp. 470–72.

"one of the five richest men in New York": Nathan Miller, *The Roosevelt Chronicles,* (New York: Doubleday, 1979), p. 117.

"but I really . . . variety of kind": TR to John Hay, July 22, 1902, *LTR,* 3:300.

"a good idea . . . by the throat": TR to William Allen White, Oct. 6, 1902, *LTR,* 3:343.

"to try to be . . . from vindictiveness": AL to John Hay, July 22, 1902, *LTR,* 3:300.

"a suspicious . . . scabs": Edmund Morris,

Theodore Rex (New York: Modern Library, 2001), p. 134.

"Upward of one . . . were fired": *NYT,* July 31, 1902.

"it is expected . . . clubbed to death": New York Tribune, July 31, 1902.

"a reign of terror": Ibid.

"Once there is . . . want and suffering": TR to Robert Bacon, Oct. 5, 1902, *LTR,* 3:340.

"went fairly wild": McKerns, "The 'Faces' of John Mitchell," p. 39.

"The one among . . . your organization": Morris, *Theodore Rex,* p. 135.

"settled down . . . of endurance": *Literary Digest,* August 2, 1902.

"uneasy . . . asked of me": TR to Philander Chase Knox, Aug. 21, 1902, *LTR,* 3:323.

"the second largest corporation in the world": Ray Stannard Baker, "The Great Northern Pacific Deal," *Collier's,* Nov. 30, 1901.

"test the validity of the merger": New York Herald, Feb. 20, 1902.

"If we have done . . . can fix it up": Bishop, *Theodore Roosevelt in His Own Time,* Vol. 1, pp. 184–85.

"a most illuminating . . . rival operator": Ibid.

"to serve notice . . . governed these United States": Owen Wister, *Roosevelt: The Story of a Friendship, 1880–1919* (New York: Macmillan, 1930), p. 210.

"never thought . . . my opinion": Philander C.

Knox to TR, Aug. 23, 1902, Theodore Roosevelt Digital Library, Dickinson State University, http://www.theodorerooseveltcenter.org/Research/Digital-Library/Record?libID=o39143.

"patent to anyone . . . diseased mind": Wright Report, p. 1192.

"any sort . . . anything else": Ibid., p. 1212.

"The booming . . . their holiday clothes": The Daily Times (New Brunswick, N.J.), Aug. 27, 1902.

"small towns . . . entire population": Galveston Daily News, Aug. 24, 1902.

"to see the President . . . see a circus": TR to John Hay, Aug. 9, 1903, LTR, 3:549.

"a square deal . . . rich or poor": Boston Globe, Aug. 26, 1902.

"a sympathetic ear . . . more to himself": Leroy Dorsey, "Reconstituting the American Spirit: Theodore Roosevelt's Rhetorical Presidency," PhD diss., Indiana University, 1993, pp. 181–82.

public sentiment: Allen C. Guelzo, " 'Public Sentiment Is Everything': Abraham Lincoln and the Power of Public Opinion," in Lucas E. Morel, ed., Lincoln and Liberty: Wisdom for the Ages (Lexington: University Press of Kentucky, 2014), p. 171.

"We have endured . . . which crushes us": Little Falls Herald, Sept. 5, 1902.

"With a crash . . . body into bits": The World

(New York), Sept. 4, 1902.

"I felt sure . . . would be killed": Ibid.

"Gentlemen . . . president's reception": *The World* (New York), Sept. 25, 1902.

"I do not have . . . were on two legs": TR to Orville Platt, Oct. 2, 1902, *LTR,* 3:335.

"I had as yet . . . in the matter": TR to Winthrop Murray Crane, Oct. 22, 1902, *LTR,* 3:360.

"I knew I might . . . to try anything": TR to Carl Schurz, Dec. 24, 1903, *LTR,* 3:679.

"I cannot . . . conditions continue": Telegram from Seth Low to TR, Theodore Roosevelt Papers. Library of Congress Manuscript Division. http://www.theodoreroosevelt center.org/Research/Digital-Library/ Record?libID=o284062. Digital Library, Dickinson State University.

"Thousands . . . short of fuel": *New York Tribune,* Sept. 27, 1902.

Workers were being laid off: Ibid.

"untold misery": TR to Crane, Oct. 22, 1902, *LTR,* 3:360.

"no alarmist": Ibid.

"Unless you end . . . frozen to death": Morris, *Theodore Rex,* p. 151.

Crane . . . compromise settlement: Cornell, *The Anthracite Coal Strike of 1902,* p. 176.

"acted as he always . . . make it successful": TR to Crane, Oct. 22, 1902, *LTR,* 3:360.

"I should . . . whole nation": TR to John Mitchell, Oct. 1, 1902, *LTR,* 3:334.

"For the first time . . . face-to-face": Walter Wellman, "The Inside History of the Great Coal Strike," *Collier's Weekly,* Oct. 18, 1902, p. 6.

"un-American": Cornell, *The Anthracite Coal Strike of 1902,* p. 180.

"Worse by far . . . self-intrusion": Sullivan, *Our Times: America Finding Herself,* Vol. 2, p. 430.

"It was very kind . . . straight in front of him": The World (New York), Oct. 4, 1902.

"There are three . . . for the general good": Ibid.

"literally jumped to his feet": Ibid.

"the miners . . . positions in writing": Letter from TR to Seth Low, not sent, Theodore Roosevelt Papers. Library of Congress Manuscript Division. http://www.theodore rooseveltcenter.org/Research/Digital-Library/Record?libID=0266115. Digital Library, Dickinson State University.

"stood ready . . . and his goons": The World (New York), Oct. 4, 1902.

"The duty of the hour . . . of a free people": Public Policy, Oct. 25, 1902, p. 261.

"government is a contemptible failure": Ibid.

"insulted me . . . the Sherman antitrust law": Theodore Roosevelt to Mark Hanna, October 3, 1902, container 77, Theodore Roosevelt Jr. Papers, LC.

"Are you asking . . . set of outlaws?": Morris, *Theodore Rex,* p. 160.

"did everything . . . out of the window": The *World* (New York), Oct. 4, 1902.

"Mitchell behaved . . . moderation": TR to Crane, Oct. 22, 1902, *LTR*, 3:360.

"towered above": TR to Robert Bacon, Oct. 5, 1902, *LTR*, 3:340.

"No one regrets . . . affect reconciliation": Morris, *Theodore Rex*, p. 160.

"NO . . . with John Mitchell": The *World* (New York), Oct. 4, 1902.

"in the fact that . . . and the President": TR, *An Autobiography*, p. 466.

"Well, I have tried . . . over the result": TR to Mark Hanna, Oct. 3, 1902, *LTR*, 3:337.

"the first time . . . of the Republic": The *Independent* [New York City], Oct. 30, 1902, p. 2563.

"one of the quickest . . . that establishment": *Washington Times*, Oct. 4, 1904.

"who resented . . . own business": *Plain Dealer* (Cleveland), Oct. 17, 1902, quoted in *Public Policy*, Nov. 15, 1902, p. 315.

"The President did . . . either labor or capitalist": The *Outlook*, Oct. 11, 1902, p. 345.

"plum-colored livery": The *World* (New York), Oct. 4, 1902.

"Christian men . . . of the country": Baer to W. I. Clark, July 17, 1902, quoted in Cornell, *The Anthracite Coal Strike of 1902*, p. 170.

"The divine right . . . right of plutocrats": *Boston Watchman*, quoted in Sullivan, *Our Times:*

America Finding Herself, Vol. 2, p. 426.

"All Washington . . . painful suspense": Washington Times, Oct. 4, 1904.

"I find it pleasant . . . my thought": TR to Henry Beach Needham, July 19, 1905, *LTR,* 4:1280.

"thrown about . . . hurt at all": TR to Kermit Roosevelt, March 5, 1904, *LTR,* 4:744.

"some books . . . queer taste": TR to Herbert Putnam, Oct. 6, 1902, *LTR,* 3:343.

"I owe you . . . reveled accordingly": TR to George Frisbie Hoar, Oct. 8, 1902, *LTR,* 3:344.

"There was beginning . . . the civil war": TR to Crane, Oct. 22, 1902, *LTR,* 3:362.

"would form . . . suffering and chaos": TR to Crane, Oct. 22, 1902, *LTR,* 3:362.

"write letters . . . state of war": Ibid.

"It is never well . . . drastic fashion": TR, *An Autobiography,* p. 476.

"flock back to the mines": The American Monthly Review of Reviews (Nov. 1902).

"made quite . . . the country": Chicago Record-Herald, Oct. 5, 1902.

"a trifling": The World (New York), Oct. 4, 1902.

"not the slightest . . . the strike": TR to Crane, Oct. 22, 1902, *LTR,* 3, p. 361.

"In all the country . . . as would yours": Morris, *Theodore Rex,* p. 164.

"the strongest . . . public opinion": Sullivan,

Our Times: America Finding Herself, Vol. 2, p. 437.

"Wherever the fault . . . curing the failure": TR to Crane, Oct. 22, 1902, *LTR,* 3:362–63.

"last resort": Morton Gitelman, "The Evolution of Labor Arbitration," *DePaul Law Review* (Spring–Summer 1960), p. 182.

"a first-rate general . . . Commander-in-Chief": TR, *An Autobiography,* p. 474.

"the operators . . . to the President": Sullivan, *Our Times: America Finding Herself,* Vol. 2, p. 436.

"gave the word": TR, *An Autobiography,* p. 475.

"The time . . . has come": Sullivan, *Our Times: America Finding Herself,* Vol. 2, p. 437.

"perfectly welcome": Cornell, *The Anthracite Coal Strike of 1902,* p. 211.

"Don't hit till . . . hit hard": Walter Wellman, "The Settlement of the Coal Strike," *American Monthly Review of Reviews* (Nov. 1902).

"usurpation of power": The American, Oct. 6, 1900, p. 485.

"any implication . . . was helpless": Sullivan, *Our Times: America Finding Herself,* Vol. 2, p. 437.

"I am Commander in Chief . . . give the people coal": James E. Watson in Wood, *Roosevelt as We Knew Him,* p. 112.

scheme of military seizure: TR, *An Autobiography,* pp. 475–76.

"the intervention . . . happened": Ibid., p. 473.

"to get out . . . an interloper": Root to TR, Oct. 11, 1902, in Philip C. Jessup, *Elihu Root,* 2 vols. (New York: Dodd, Mead, 1938), Vol. 1, p. 275.

"There cannot be . . . of the business": Wright Report, p. 1177.

"The bones of it . . . this description": Jessup, *Elihu Root,* Vol. 1, p. 276.

"We suggest . . . accepted by us": "Operators statement," Oct. 14, 1902, quoted in Sullivan, *Our Times: America Finding Herself,* Vol. 2, p. 440.

"it was a damn lie . . . fair on paper": Jessup, *Elihu Root,* Vol. 1, p. 276.

"in view . . . of the case": TR quoted in Morris, *Theodore Rex,* p. 167.

"It looked . . . accept with rapture": TR, *An Autobiography,* pp. 468–69.

"Anthracite Miners . . . Affairs of Labor": Bisbee [Arizona] *Daily News,* Oct. 21, 1902; *Butler County* [Hamilton, Ohio] *Democrat,* Oct 23, 1902; *New York Tribune,* Oct. 22, 1902.

"the people's attorney": SEP, April 4, 1903, p. 4.

"steady pressure of public opinion": Public Opinion, Oct. 23, 1902.

"The child is born . . . member of society": Carroll D. Wright to Dr. Graham Brooks, Oct. 18, 1902, in Jonathan Grossman, "The Coal Strike of 1902 — Turning Point in U.S. Policy," *Monthly Labor Review,* Oct.

10, 1975, p. 25.

"If it had not been . . . all my heart": TR to J. P. Morgan, Oct. 16, 1902, *LTR,* 3:353.

"May heaven preserve . . . wooden-headed a set": TR to ARC, Oct. 16, 1902, in TR, *Letters from Theodore Roosevelt to Anna Roosevelt Cowles,* p. 252.

"His injury . . . appeal of his character": Lewis Gould, *The Presidency of Theodore Roosevelt* (New York: Oxford University Press, 2012), p. 71.

"in the most quiet . . . entirely new thing": Riis, *Theodore Roosevelt, the Citizen,* p. 378.

Each side put forth its best case: Sullivan, *Our Times: America Finding Herself,* Vol. 2, p. 445.

"We are witnessing . . . sphere of operation": Morris, *Theodore Rex,* p. 169.

"I think it well . . . should be on file": TR to Crane, Oct. 22, 1902, *LTR,* 3:359.

"sit supinely by" . . . resolution was reached: Ibid., p. 362.

"not strictly legal . . . his authority for?": Thayer, *Theodore Roosevelt,* pp. 245–46.

"clear and masterful . . . justice prevail": TR, *Addresses and Presidential Messages of Theodore Roosevelt, 1902–1904* (New York: G. P. Putnam's Sons [The Knickerbocker Press], 1904), p. 165.

"accentuates the . . . to start with!": TR to Mark Hanna, Oct. 3, 1902, *LTR,* 3:337.

"Now I believe . . . all there is to it": Sewall, *Bill Sewall's Story of Theodore Roosevelt,* p. 112.

Chapter Eleven
Turnaround Leadership: Franklin Roosevelt and the Hundred Days

"Looking back . . . lived through them": Perkins, *The Roosevelt I Knew,* p. 203.
"It is hard today . . . prolonged unemployment": Ibid., p. 174.
"rock bottom": Alonzo Hamby, *Man of Destiny: FDR and the Making of the American Century* (New York: Basic Books, 2015), pp. 169–70.
"We are at the end of our string": Eric Goldman, *Rendezvous with Destiny: A History of Modern American Reform* (Chicago: Ivan R. Dee, 2001), p. 323.
"No cosmic dramatist . . . accorded to Franklin Roosevelt": Robert E. Sherwood, *Roosevelt and Hopkins: An Intimate History* (New York: Harper & Brothers, 1948), p. 40.
"When the American . . . vital, human need": Ibid., p. 39.
"all rolled into one": Jonathan Alter, *The Defining Moment: FDR's Hundred Days and the Triumph of Hope* (New York: Simon & Schuster, 2006), p. 61.
"the world literally . . . our feet": Leuchtenburg, *Franklin D. Roosevelt and the New Deal, 1932–1940,* p. 39.

"vital organs": Alter, *The Defining Moment,* p. 1.

"the immediate . . . our economic system": FDR, "Introduction," *PPA,* 2:3.

"Panic was in the air": Adam Cohen, *Nothing to Fear: FDR's Inner Circle and the Hundred Days That Created Modern America* (New York: Penguin, 2009), p. 15.

"men of middle age . . . twenty-five years of work": Ibid., p. 16.

"the full brunt of the Depression" . . . bolt their doors: NYT, March 19, 1933.

"seemed to have died . . . stillness of those streets": Louise Van Voorhis Armstrong, *We Too Are the People* (Boston: Little, Brown, 1938), p. 50.

"that the whole house of cards": Ernest Sutherland Bates, *The Story of the Congress, 1789–1935* (New York: Harper & Brothers, 1936), p. 408.

"A thought to God . . . depths of despair": James A. Farley, *Jim Farley's Story: The Roosevelt Years* (New York: McGraw-Hill, 1948), p. 36.

"his face cupped in his hands": "National Affairs: We Must Act," *Time,* March 13, 1933, p. 11.

"This is a day of national consecration": Rosenman, *Working with Roosevelt,* p. 91.

"the larger purposes . . . as a sacred obligation": FDR, "Introduction," *PPA,* 2:13–14.

"I had not realized . . . complete exultation!": Henrietta McCormick Hull, *A Senator's Wife Remembers: From the Great Depression to the Great Society* (Montgomery, Ala.: New South Books, 2010), p. 34.

chief justice: Frank Freidel, *Franklin D. Roosevelt: Launching the New Deal* (Boston: Little, Brown, 1952), p. 202.

"This is preeminently . . . fear itself": FDR, "Inaugural Address," March 4, 1933, *PPA,* 2:11.

"The people . . . national life": Ibid., pp. 11–12.

"as a trained and loyal . . . other people's money": Ibid., p. 13.

"a stricken Nation . . . by a foreign foe": Ibid., p. 15.

"steward of the people": TR, *An Autobiography,* p. 464.

"every stress": FDR, "Inaugural Address," March 4, 1933, *PPA,* 2:15.

"Never before has . . . the oaths": NYT, March 5, 1933.

"The new . . . his official family": James A. Farley, *Behind the Ballots: The Personal History of a Politician* (New York: Harcourt, Brace, 1938), p. 209.

"This is a strictly family party": NYT, March 5, 1933.

"would all be able . . . happy occasion": Farley, *Behind the Ballots,* p. 209.

"obtaining jurisdiction . . . bank holiday": FDR, "The President Proclaims a Bank Holiday. Gold and Silver Exports and Foreign Exchange Transactions Prohibited. Proclamation No. 2039," March 6, 1933, *PPA,* 2:26, note.

"to outline a . . . closing all banks": Franklin D. Roosevelt, *On Our Way* (New York: John Day, 1934), p. 3.

"in an orderly manner": FDR, "The President Proclaims a Bank Holiday. Gold and Silver Exports and Foreign Exchange Transactions Prohibited. Proclamation No. 2039," March 6, 1933, *PPA,* 2:28.

"the air suddenly . . . corridors": Katie Louchheim, ed., *The Making of the New Deal: The Insiders Speak* (Cambridge, Mass.: Harvard University Press, 1983), p. 121.

"It seemed to . . . hold on life": Freidel, *Launching the New Deal,* p. 206.

"the sense that life was resuming": Louchheim, ed., *The Making of the New Deal,* p. 121.

"THE ERA . . . TO AN END": Oelwein Daily Register (Iowa), March 11, 1933.

"THE GOVERNMENT STILL LIVES": NYT, March 19, 1933.

"PERHAPS A LEADER HAS COME!": Southwest Times (Pulaski, Va.), March 10, 1933.

"How does your husband . . . He decides": Alter, *The Defining Moment,* p. 235.

"Nobody knows . . . man worked": Fenster,

FDR's Shadow, p. 216.

"I never saw . . . worked harder": Rosenman, *Working with Roosevelt,* p. 37.

"The remarkable . . . responsibility with a smile": Freidel, *Launching the New Deal,* p. 215.

"big" men . . . "for the nomination": NYT, March 19, 1933.

"set in party . . . against change": Ibid.

"gallery of associates": NYT, Nov. 20, 1932.

"a new mind . . . on this adventure": NYT, March 19, 1933.

"Labor had . . . and unorganized": Perkins, *The Roosevelt I Knew,* p. 144.

"The Madam": Cohen, *Nothing to Fear,* p. 199.

"any suggestion . . . dying to hear it": Perkins, *The Roosevelt I Knew,* pp. 145–46.

"the President outlined . . . involved were": Perkins, Part 1, Session 1, p. 75, OHRO/ CUL.

"the most drastic . . . ever taken": Cohen, *Nothing to Fear,* p. 73.

"an anesthetic before the major operation": Ibid., p. 76.

"the punctuation . . . turn upward": Arthur M. Schlesinger, *The Age of Roosevelt,* Vol. 2: *The Coming of the New Deal, 1933–1935* (New York: Mariner, 2003), p. 6.

a group of prominent bankers . . . a hand in the drafting of the bill: Freidel, *Launching the New Deal,* pp. 214–15.

"unscrupulous money changers": FDR, "Inau-

gural Address," March 4, 1933, *PPA*, 2:12.

"ran counter . . . of the moment": Cohen, *Nothing to Fear*, p. 67.

"a complete picture . . . help and cooperation": FDR, *On Our Way*, p. 8.

"Everyone was . . . weathered the storm": Raymond Moley, *The First New Deal* (New York: Harcourt, Brace & World, 1966), p. 191.

"delighted with it": Ibid., p. 177.

"Yes, it is finished . . . I'm finished too": Schlesinger, *The Coming of the New Deal*, p. 7.

"to patch up failings and shortcomings": George C. Edwards, *The Strategic President: Persuasion and Opportunity in Presidential Leadership* (Princeton: Princeton University Press, 2009), p. 114.

"to clear the financial arteries of the economy": Schlesinger, *The Coming of the New Deal*, p. 4.

"it was copied . . . stenciling": NYT, March 10, 1933.

"I cannot too strongly urge . . . banks and the people": FDR, "Recommendation to the Congress for Legislation to Control Resumption of Banking," March 9, 1933, *PPA*, 2:45–46.

"Here's the bill . . . Let's pass it": Cohen, *Nothing to Fear*, p. 79.

"The House is burning . . . Vote, Vote": Edwards, *The Strategic President*, p. 112.

"the unity that prevailed": NYT, March 10, 1933.

"I am told that . . . I am going to try it": Elmer E. Cornwell Jr., *Presidential Leadership of Public Opinion* (Bloomington: Indiana University Press, 1965), p. 143.

"unusually nervous": James E. Sargent, *Roosevelt and the Hundred Days: Struggle for the Early New Deal* (New York: Garland, 1981), p. 100.

"His hand was trembling . . . with perspiration": Anthony J. Badger, *FDR: The First Hundred Days* (New York: Hill & Wang, 2008), p. 40.

"fresh and fit": NYT, March 9, 1933.

"because there is . . . somebody may forget": FDR, "The First Press Conference," March 8, 1933, *PPA,* 2:32.

"barber's hour": Steffens, *The Autobiography of Lincoln Steffens,* Vol. 2, p. 509.

"We were antagonists . . . was trying to do": Smith, *FDR,* p. 310.

"Now as to news . . . there is any!": FDR, "The First Press Conference," March 8, 1933, *PPA,* 2:32.

"simply and unhurriedly . . . an old friend": Schlesinger, *The Coming of the New Deal,* p. 561.

"know enough": FDR, "The First Press Conference," March 8, 1933, *PPA,* 2:30.

"Oh . . . a lot about banking": FDR, "Press Conference of President Franklin D. Roo-

sevelt, 1933–1945," March 10, 1933, Digital Collection, FDRL.

"the most amazing . . . has ever seen": Cohen, *Nothing to Fear,* p. 78.

"so swift-moving . . . of some Presidents": NYT, March 12, 1933.

outlined the banking dilemma . . . straightforward terms: Freidel, *Launching the New Deal,* p. 215.

"a mason at work . . . My friends": Amos Kiewe, *FDR's First Fireside Chat: Public Confidence and the Banking Crisis* (College Station: Texas A&M University Press, 2007), p. 82.

"his face would . . . light up": Perkins, *The Roosevelt I Knew,* pp. 69–70.

"talking directly . . . each person in the nation": Rosenman, *Working with Roosevelt,* p. 92.

"I want to tell you . . . are going to be": FDR, "The First 'Fireside Chat' — An Intimate Talk with the People of the United States on Banking," March 11, 1933, *PPA,* 2:61.

"If we could first . . . to do it": AL, "A House Divided Speech, Springfield, Ill.," June 16, 1858, *CW,* 2:461.

"When you deposit . . . under the mattress": FDR, "The First 'Fireside Chat,' " 2:61–64.

"A question you will ask . . . make it work": Ibid., 2:63, 65.

"marvelous twentieth century . . . distance, and

space": *The News Herald* [Spencer, Ill.], May 12, 1933.

"*it was a run . . . take money out*": *Olean* [NY] *Times Herald,* March 15, 1933.

"*City Recovers Confidence*": *Chicago Tribune,* May 14, 1933, quoted in William L. Silber, "Why Did FDR's Bank Holiday Succeed?," *Federal Reserve Bank of New York Economic Policy Review* (July 2009), p. 27.

"*Rush to Put . . . as Holiday Ends*": *NYT,* March 14, 1933.

"*an entirely different . . . day and night*": *San Antonio Express,* March 15, 1933.

15 percent jump: Silber, "Why Did FDR's Bank Holiday Succeed?," p. 27.

"*as one of . . . in U.S. history*": Kiewe, *FDR's First Fireside Chat,* p. 9.

"*The process of recovery . . . sore spots*": FDR, "Introduction," 1933, *PPA,* 2:3–4.

"*for a whole generation . . . special privilege*": FDR, *On Our Way,* pp. 35, x.

"*new order . . . business men*": FDR, "Introduction," *PPA,* 2:5.

"*a vocal minority . . . permanent well-being*": Ibid., *PPA,* 2:6.

"*Roosevelt looked . . . here right now*": Moley, *After Seven Years,* p. 189.

"*In the same spirit . . . ourselves back to prosperity*": FDR, "The Second 'Fireside Chat' — 'What We Have Been Doing and What We Are Planning to Do,' " May 7, 1933,

PPA, 2:160, 164.

"on sounder foundations and on sounder lines": FDR, "Introduction," 1933, *PPA,* 2:6.

"his general attitude . . . mattered": Perkins, *The Roosevelt I Knew,* p. 165.

"little in the way of precedent": FDR, "Three Essentials for Unemployment Relief (C.C.C., F.E.R.A., P.W.A.)," March 21, 1933, *PPA,* 2:82.

"We have new . . . to an old institution?": Schlesinger, *The Coming of the New Deal,* p. 534.

"the alphabet soup": See Tonya Bolden, *FDR's Alphabet Soup: New Deal America, 1932–1939* (New York: Alfred A. Knopf, 2010).

"every now and then . . . knowledge and understanding": Fred I. Greenstein, *The Presidential Difference: Leadership Styles from FDR to Clinton* (New York: Free Press, 2000), p. 24.

"an opportunity to make their own way": NYT, March 21, 1933.

"a sad state of neglect": FDR, "Three Essentials for Unemployment Relief (C.C.C., F.E.R.A., P.W.A.)," March 21, 1933, *PPA,* 2:80, note.

"a moral and spiritual value": Ibid., p. 81.

"a pipedream": Cohen, *Nothing to Fear,* p. 210.

"a month . . . Good": Ibid., p. 219.

"Do it now and I won't take any excuses": Alter, *The Defining Moment,* p. 293.

"It was characteristic . . . about the details": Cohen, *Nothing to Fear*, p. 209.

"He put the dynamite . . . their own methods": Alter, *The Defining Moment*, p. 293.

"the most rapid . . . in our history": FDR, "The Civilian Conservation Corps Is Started. Executive Order No. 6101," April 5, 1933, *PPA*, 2:110, note.

A cadre of talented officers . . . Marshall: Schlesinger, *The Coming of the New Deal*, p. 339.

camps to accommodate . . . the Spanish-American War: Cohen, *Nothing to Fear*, p. 225.

"a place in the world": FDR, "Three Essentials for Unemployment Relief (C.C.C., F.E.R.A., P.W.A.)," March 21, 1933, *PPA*, 2:81, note.

"I weighed about 160 . . . a man of me all right": Schlesinger, *The Coming of the New Deal*, p. 339.

"a panacea": FDR, "Three Essentials for Unemployment Relief," March 21, 1933, *PPA*, 2:80.

"has a general plan . . . thrown for a loss": FDR, "The Thirteenth Press Conference," April 19, 1933, *PPA*, 2:139.

"ideas and arguments . . . discussed and debated": Rosenman, *Working with Roosevelt*, p. 63.

"There is . . . than the next man": Schlesinger, *The Coming of the New Deal*, pp. 534–35.

"inherently disorderly nature": Ibid., p. 535.

"The maintenance of . . . Roosevelt's time": Tully, *F.D.R. My Boss,* p. 170.

"hand-holding . . . inadvertently caused": Schlesinger, *The Coming of the New Deal,* p. 540.

"In a quieter time . . . leeway and reward": Ibid., p. 536.

"Honest Harold": Harold Ickes, *The Autobiography of a Curmudgeon* (New York: Quadrangle, 1969), p. x.

"a chain smoker . . . coffee drinker": Sherwood, *Roosevelt and Hopkins,* p. 29.

"the shabbiest building in Washington": Cohen, *Nothing to Fear,* p. 268.

"the same shirt three or four days at a time": Sherwood, *Roosevelt and Hopkins,* p. 29.

"the physical, mental and spiritual suffering": *NYT,* Nov. 19, 1933.

"People don't eat . . . eat every day": Cohen, *Nothing to Fear,* pp. 267–68.

"rehabilitated" . . . grateful community: Perkins, *The Roosevelt I Knew,* p. 179.

"the unaffected simplicity . . . the help of his valet": Aug. 23, 1935, in Harold L. Ickes, *The Secret Diary of Harold L. Ickes: The First Thousand Days, 1933–36* (New York: Simon & Schuster, 1953), Vol. 1, p. 423.

"What could a man do . . . President like that": Arthur M. Schlesinger Jr., *The Age of Roosevelt: The Politics of Upheaval, 1935–36*

(New York: Mariner, 2003), p. 351.

Long-smoldering antagonisms eventually ig-nited in public view: NYT, Sept. 11, 1935.

"make-work": Cohen, *Nothing to Fear,* p. 112.

"leaf raking": Sherwood, *Roosevelt and Hop-kins,* p. 71.

"high cheer . . . he went fishing": Oct. 27, 1935, in Ickes, *The Secret Diary of Harold L. Ickes,* Vol. 1, p. 449.

"a perfectly grand time . . . really rested": Sherwood, *Roosevelt and Hopkins,* p. 79.

"Buried at Sea": Ibid., pp. 78–79.

Roosevelt repeatedly counseled his aides: Schlesinger, *The Coming of the New Deal,* p. 525.

"Go and see what's happening . . . wind in your nose": Ibid.

"new and untried": FDR, "New Means to Rescue Agriculture — The Agricultural Adjustment Act," March 16, 1933, *PPA,* 2:77, note.

"like a combine eating up grain": Asbell, *The F.D.R. Memoirs,* p. 84.

Daily Bugle . . . *clippings:* Stiles, *The Man behind Roosevelt,* p. 249.

"may be set apart . . . the country": ER, radio speech for Pond's Co. (March 3, 1933), ER, Speeches and Articles, Box 3, FDRL.

"the unvarnished truth": Richard Lowitt and Maurine Beasley, eds., *One Third of a Na-tion: Lorena Hickok Reports on the Great*

Depression (Urbana: University of Illinois Press, 2000), p. xxiii.

"will o' the wisp": Elliott Roosevelt and James Brough, *A Rendezvous with Destiny: The Roosevelts in the White House* (New York: G. P. Putnam's Sons, 1975), p. 71.

"an uninterrupted meal . . . not dulled by repetition": ER, *This I Remember*, p. 125.

"She saw many things . . . off onto the president": Frances Perkins Interview, Graff Papers, FDRL.

"My missus says . . . last week": Perkins, *The Roosevelt I Knew*, p. 70.

"Why do you dump . . . the country starving?": Lash, *Eleanor and Franklin*, pp. 383–84.

"In the course . . . is humanly possible": FDR, "Informal Extemporaneous Remarks to the New Jersey State Emergency Council," Jan. 18, 1936, *PPA*, 5:60.

"I learned to prepare . . . preferably one page": Perkins, *The Roosevelt I Knew*, p. 153.

"I do not deny . . . but for the team": FDR, "The Second 'Fireside Chat': What We Have Been Doing and What We Are Planning to Do," May 7, 1933, *PPA*, 2:165.

"You and I know . . . up go ahead": Rosenman, *Working with Roosevelt*, p. 36.

"old abuses": FDR, "Introduction," *PPA*, 2:4.

"to guard investors . . . was a necessity": FDR, *On Our Way*, p. 44.

"draconian": Cohen, *Nothing to Fear*, p. 151.

"unworkable . . . the constrictions": Moley, *The First New Deal,* p. 315.

to extend federal regulation: Joplin Globe (Missouri), March 30, 1933.

"cop on their corner": Schlesinger, *The Coming of the New Deal,* p. 464.

"more highly organized drive" . . . "terrible" years that followed the crash: "The President insisted upon Federal Supervision of the Sale of Securities," March 26, 1934, *PPA,* 4:169.

"It won't work . . . on deposit insurance": Cohen, *Nothing to Fear,* p. 277.

Over 90 percent of banks: Graham and Wander, eds., *Franklin D. Roosevelt,* p. 132.

within five years deposits had increased by nearly 50 percent: Anthony J. Mayo and Nitin Nohria, *In Their Time: The Greatest Business Leaders of the Twentieth Century* (Cambridge, Mass.: Harvard Business Review Press, 2005), p. 108.

"federal insurance . . . monetary stability": Milton Friedman and Anna J. Schwartz, quoted in Moley, *The First New Deal,* p. 320.

"We have to do . . . as we go along": Perkins, *The Roosevelt I Knew,* p. 156.

"a real artist in government": Sherwood, *Roosevelt and Hopkins,* p. 73.

"worked with . . . the next evolved": Perkins, *The Roosevelt I Knew,* p. 155.

"this spirit of teamwork . . . in record time":
FDR, "A Letter of Appreciation to the
Congress," June 16, 1933, *PPA,* 2:256.
"a psychological target to lift sights": Irving
Holley Jr., *Buying Aircraft: Materiel Procure-
ment for the Armed Forces* (Washington,
D.C.: Office of the Chief of Military History, 1964), p. 228.
"something about . . . fits into the picture": *NYT,*
Feb. 24, 1942.
"were taken into . . . the right course": Rosenman, *Working with Roosevelt,* p. 92.

Chapter Twelve
Visionary Leadership: Lyndon Johnson and
Civil Rights

"Everything was in chaos": Caro, *The Passage
of Power,* p. 353.
"The times cried . . . been disastrous": LBJ,
VP, pp. 12, 18.
"We were all spinning . . . I was that man":
Ibid., p. 172.
"I know how much . . . does our country":
Goldman, *The Tragedy of Lyndon Johnson,*
p. 26.
"I knew how they felt . . . on the inside": DKG/
LBJ Conversations.
"There is much . . . teach me": Walter Heller,
quoted in Evans and Novak, *Lyndon B.
Johnson,* p. 360.
"Spend the night with me": Discussion with

Harry McPherson and Jack Valenti, "Achilles in the White House," *Wilson Quarterly* (Spring 2000), p. 90.

"the new president . . . got nowhere before": Jack Valenti, "Lyndon Johnson: An Awesome Engine of a Man," in Thomas W. Cowger and Sherwin J. Markman, eds., *Lyndon Johnson Remembered: An Intimate Portrait of a Presidency* (Lanham, Md.: Rowman & Littlefield, 2003), p. 37.

"That's what we're here for": Caro, *The Path to Power,* p. 82.

"That whole night . . . very formidable": Merle Miller, *Lyndon,* p. 325.

"He knew . . . him — or not": Caro, *The Passage of Power,* p. 426.

"reason to wonder . . . to the Republic": LBJ, *VP,* p. 3.

"while accomplishing practically nothing": Life, Dec. 13, 1963, p. 4.

"developing into a national crisis": LBJ, *VP,* p. 21.

"If any sense were . . . process to function": Ibid., p. 35.

"a sympathetic atmosphere": Caro, *The Passage of Power,* p. 435.

"dead man's program into a martyr's cause": DKG/LBJ Conversations.

"At one point . . . hell's the presidency for?": Merle Miller, *Lyndon,* p. 337.

"All that I have . . . I ask your help": LBJ, "Ad-

dress before the Joint Session of Congress,"
Nov. 27, 1963, *PPP*, 1:8–10.

"modeled . . . Roosevelt": San Antonio Express,
Dec. 1, 1963.

"for action, and action now . . . dark hour":
FDR, Inaugural Address, March 4, 1933,
PPA, 2:12, 11.

"we can . . . act now": LBJ, "Address before
the Joint Session of Congress," Nov. 27,
1963, *PPP,* 1:9.

*"It was a remarkable performance . . . get
results": Anniston Star* (Ala.), Dec. 1, 1963.

*"LEADERSHIP IN GOOD HANDS": Sheboygan
Press* (Wisc.), Nov. 29, 1963.

*"JOHNSON EMERGES GRAVE AND
STRONG":* Caro, *The Passage of Power,*
p. 433.

"NEW CHIEF MET THE TEST": Anniston Star
(Ala.), Dec. 1, 1963.

*Theodore Sorensen disagreed with this order
of battle: PRLBJ,* Vol. 2, pp. 38–39.

"magic" line: Ibid., p. 123.

"Harry, why don't you . . . of your wisdom":
Caro, *The Passage of Power,* p. 475.

potato soup: Ibid., p. 476.

vanilla ice cream: Jack Valenti, *A Very Human
President* (New York: Pocket Books, 1977),
p. 153.

"Harry, that tax cut . . . enough of you": Ibid.,
pp. 153–54.

no fat left: PRLBJ, Vol. 1: pp. 167–68.

"Unless you get . . . pee one drop": Caro, *The Passage of Power*, p. 423.

"I worked as hard . . . lives of every American": LBJ, *VP*, p. 36.

"Lightbulb Lyndon": *Globe Gazette* (Mason City, Iowa), Aug. 17, 1964.

"You can tell your grandchildren . . . President to cut his budget": Caro, *The Passage of Power*, p. 482.

"they just procrastinate . . . shimmy around": PRLBJ, Vol. 2, p. 371.

"No detail of the legislative . . . drive, drive, drive": Edwards, *The Strategic President*, p. 122.

"Are they working any at night?": PRLBJ, Vol. 3, p. 855.

"Oh that's wonderful, I love you": Ibid., p. 878.

"There's a crew . . . get the job done": Ibid., p. 886.

"open the floodgates": PRLBJ, Vol. 4, p. 159.

"look with very . . . around the world": PRLBJ, Vol. 2, p. 373.

Wilbur Mills: PRLBJ, Vol. 4, pp. 291–96.

"a gentleman and a scholar, and a producer": Dallek, *Flawed Giant*, p. 74.

"more easily influenced" . . . "than any other way": Phillips, *Lincoln on Leadership*, p. 158.

"He shouldn't give . . . nothing I could say to Gene": LBJ, *VP*, pp. 153–54.

"You know, John . . . change it by law": Merle Miller, *Lyndon*, p. 367.

"go squat . . . the field to pee": Nick Kotz, *Judgment Days: Lyndon Baines Johnson, Martin Luther King Jr., and the Laws That Changed America* (New York: Houghton Mifflin, 2005), p. 22.

"My strength as President . . . to that office": LBJ, *VP*, p. 157.

"It was destined . . . friends for years": Ibid., p. 37.

"there comes a time . . . this vital measure": Ibid., p. 38.

"every ounce of strength": Ibid., p. 157.

"struck by the enormous . . . deep convictions": Caro, *The Passage of Power*, p. 90.

"the depth of his concern": NYT, Dec. 3, 1963.

"it just might . . . John Kennedy couldn't": Caro, *The Passage of Power*, p. 491.

"a mighty hard route": Ibid., p. 490.

"piddle along" . . . Congress to adjourn: PRLBJ, Vol. 1, p. 381.

"Johnson treatment": Merle Miller, *Lyndon*, p. 411.

"every friend to sign that . . . be thinking about it": PRLBJ, Vol. 1, p. 301.

"If I've done anything wrong . . . to work together": Todd S. Purdum, *An Idea Whose Time Has Come: Two Presidents, Two Parties, and the Battle for the Civil Rights Act of 1964* (New York: Henry Holt, 2015), p. 176.

"if there's ever a time" . . . is the time: PRLBJ, Vol. 1, p. 263.

"They'll be saying . . . violate procedure": Purdum, *An Idea Whose Time Has Come,* p. 164.

"Just say that . . . a right to a hearing": PRLBJ, Vol. 1, p. 71.

"You're either for . . . put up or shut up!": Ibid., p. 382.

"Point them up . . . humanity a fair shake": PRLBJ, Vol. 2, p. 43.

"Friend or Foe": William Pool, Dec. 8, 1963.

"Let the members . . . and historical challenge": Ibid.

"I don't want to run . . . but . . .": Purdum, *An Idea Whose Time Has Come,* p. 166.

"the indignity . . . responsibility for the bill": NYT, Dec. 8, 1963.

"to some people . . . the people to do it": LBJ, VP, p. 28.

"I knew that the slightest . . . the bill to death": Ibid., p. 157.

"Dick, I love you . . . to gladly do it": Discussion with Harry McPherson and Jack Valenti, "Achilles in the White House," *Wilson Quarterly* (Spring 2000), p. 94.

"These few words . . . entire struggle": LBJ, VP, p. 157.

"It's too late in life for me to change": William E. Leuchtenburg, *The White House Looks South: Franklin D. Roosevelt, Harry S. Truman, Lyndon B. Johnson* (Baton Rouge:

Louisiana State University Press, 2005), p. 303.

"old hostilities . . . every section of this country": LBJ, "Remarks in Atlanta at a Breakfast of the Georgia Legislature," May 8, 1964, *PPP,* 1:648.

"would have beaten . . . Johnson does": *NYT,* Jan. 12, 1964.

"it would be a fight . . . appeasement or attrition": LBJ, *VP,* p. 15.

"to talk the bill to death": *Lake Charles American Press* [La.], April 7, 1964.

"off making speeches . . . between the boards": Merle Miller, *Lyndon,* p. 368.

"a corporal's guard": Kotz, *Judgment Days,* p. 122.

"recognizing that . . . part of the time": Robert D. Loevy, ed., *The Civil Rights Act of 1964: The Passage of the Law That Ended Racial Segregation* (Albany: State University of New York Press, 1997), p. 82.

"Attention please!" . . . quorum call in twenty-three minutes: Ibid., p. 68.

"that without Republican . . . Everett Dirksen": DKG/LBJ Conversations.

"The bill can't pass . . . listen to Dirksen!": Kotz, *Judgment Days,* p. 115.

"unless we have . . . this goddamn country": *PRLBJ,* Vol. 6, p. 696.

"I think you're all going . . . going to help him": *PRLBJ,* Vol. 3, p. 192.

"a laundry list": Kotz, *Judgment Days,* p. 117.

"I saw your exhibit . . . proper credit": PRLBJ, Vol. 6, p. 662.

"if you come with me . . . and Everett Dirksen!": Joseph A. Califano Jr., *The Triumph & Tragedy of Lyndon Johnson: The White House Years* (New York: Touchstone, 2015), p. xxvi.

"dangerous game": Kotz, *Judgment Days,* p. 136.

"We've got a much better bill . . . possible": PRLBJ, Vol. 6, p. 696.

"Stronger than an Army . . . time has come": *Jefferson City Daily Capital News* (Missouri), May 20, 1964.

"I say to my colleagues . . . 1964 our freedom year": Purdum, *An Idea Whose Time Has Come,* p. 316.

"I guess that means 'aye' ": Richard A. Arenberg and Robert B. Dove, *Defending the Filibuster: The Soul of the Senate* (Bloomington: Indiana University Press, 2012), p. 65.

"Although I differ . . . I think he is wrong": Merle Miller, *Lyndon,* p. 369.

"Happy anniversary": NYT, July 3, 1964.

"to that afternoon . . . was my country": LBJ, *VP,* p. 160.

"For a century . . . our national life": LBJ, "Remarks at the University of Michigan," May 22, 1964, *PPP,* 1:407.

"*an extension . . . best of his talents*": LBJ, *VP*, p. 104.

"*We have enough . . . nation in the world*": DKG/LBJ Conversations.

"*These are the goals . . . away from its promise*": "Remarks before the National Convention upon Accepting the Nomination," Aug. 27, 1964, *PPP*, 1964, 2:1010, 1012.

"*assemble the best . . . departmental jurisdictions*": LBJ, *VP*, pp. 326–27.

"*too high rather than too low*": Ibid., p. 327.

"*I was just elected . . . up his capital*": Evans and Novak, *Lyndon B. Johnson*, pp. 514–15.

"*So I want you guys . . . me disappear*": Merle Miller, *Lyndon*, p. 408.

"*Momentum is* not . . . *exotic than preparation*": DKG/LBJ Conversations.

"*Gordian knots*": Greenstein, *The Presidential Difference*, p. 88.

"*My experience in the NYA . . . drafting of the bills*": DKG/LBJ Conversations.

"*like nothing* . . . *attitude toward the bill*": Ibid.

"*I was standing in the back . . . I never forgot that lesson*": LBJ, *VP*, pp. 447–48.

During the first ten months . . . enjoy each other's company: Post-Herald and Register (Beckley, W.V.), Oct. 24, 1965.

"*There is but one way . . . be almost incestuous*": DKG/LBJ Conversations.

"*a dangerous animal . . . wild*": Goldman, *The

Tragedy of Lyndon Johnson, p. 60.

"the greatest breakthrough": Michael Beschloss, ed., *Reaching for Glory: Lyndon Johnson's Secret White House Tapes, 1964–65* (New York: Touchstone, 2001), p. 159.

"Once the black man's . . . from the white man": LBJ, *VP,* p. 161.

The discriminatory system worked: Califano, *The Triumph & Tragedy of Lyndon Johnson,* p. 44.

"the mounted men . . . taken to the hospital": *Independent Press Telegram* (Long Beach, Calif.), March 14, 1965.

"It was important to move . . . the right direction": LBJ, *VP,* p. 162.

"LBJ, open your eyes . . . your homeland": Ibid., p. 228.

"that a hasty display . . . victory for the North": Ibid., p. 161.

"It's his ox that's in the ditch": Kotz, *Judgment Days,* p. 303.

"they were not . . . difference in the world": LBJ, *VP,* p. 163.

"I speak tonight . . . And we . . . shall . . . overcome": "Special Message to the Congress: The American Promise," March 15, 1965, *PPP,* 1965, 1:281, 284.

"There was an instant . . . stamping their feet": Richard Goodwin, *Remembering America: A Voice from the Sixties* (New York: Little,

Brown, 1988), p. 334.

"the real hero . . . clutches of poverty": PRLBJ, Vol. 1, p. 285.

"Somehow you never . . . will use it with me": Ibid., p. 286.

"What convinces . . . you are advancing": DKG/LBJ Conversations.

"it was the best . . . president give": Richard Goodwin, *Remembering America,* p. 237.

"Your speech . . . President of the Nation": Daniel S. Lucks, *Selma to Saigon: The Civil Rights Movement and the Vietnam War* (Lexington: University Press of Kentucky, 2014), p. 142.

"of that magic time . . . course of fifty years": LBJ, *VP,* p. 212.

"Why, Wilbur . . . same for me": DKG, *LJAD,* p. 250.

"You have done me . . . quite a while": *NYT,* July 31, 1965.

"Today is a triumph . . . of American life": LBJ, "Remarks in the Capitol Rotunda at the Signing of the Voting Rights Act," Aug. 6, 1965, *PPP,* 2:840–42.

"a class struggle between the haves and the have-nots": *Hamilton Daily News Journal* (Ohio), Oct. 23, 1965.

"relations between . . . missing for years": *NYT,* Oct. 25, 1965.

"the legislative harvest . . . President of the United States": *Hamilton Daily News Journal*

(Ohio), Oct. 23, 1965.

"an open field . . . in the race of life": Independent *Press Telegram* (Long Beach, Calif.), March 14, 1965.

"It just worries the hell . . . damn mess I ever saw": Geoffrey C. Ward and Ken Burns, *The Vietnam War: An Intimate History* (New York: Alfred A. Knopf, 2017), p. 104.

"the best and the brightest": David Halberstam, *The Best and the Brightest* (New York: Ballantine, 1993).

"like a filibuster . . . get it over with": Goldman, *The Tragedy of Lyndon Johnson,* p. 404.

"the wonders of modern medicine": LBJ, "Address at Johns Hopkins: 'Peace without Conquest,' " April 7, 1965, *PPP,* 1: 397.

"stave off defeat . . . state of emergency": LBJ, *VP,* p. 281.

"I could see and almost . . . Great Society": DKG/LBJ Conversations.

"as plentiful as blackberries": Shakespeare, *Henry IV, Part 2.*

"every ounce": LBJ, *VP,* p. 157.

"could survive another . . . unremitting tensions": Ibid., p. 426.

"Lyndon Johnson's finest hour": Oakland *Tribune,* April 1, 1968.

"an act of political selflessness . . . political history": Roscoe Drummond, quoted in *Fairbanks Daily News-Miner* (Alaska), April 6, 1968.

"an act of a great patriot": Oakland Tribune, April 1, 1968.

"the voice of justice speaks again": NYT, April 12, 1968.

"like a man who . . . peace of soul, or both": Winona [Minn.] Daily News, April 2, 1968.

Epilogue
Of Death and Remembrance

"No. Either you come or you don't": DKG/LBJ Conversations.

"I need help . . . feelings about me": Ibid.

"It's not easy . . . you're doing for me": Ibid.

"wear out the carpet . . . something correctly": Rosenman, Working with Roosevelt, p. 36.

"never looks back . . . It can drive you crazy": DKG/LBJ Conversations.

"God damn it . . . backwoods politician!": Ibid.

"All the historians . . . from Stonewall, Texas": Ibid.

"There's nothing I can . . . and that is my ranch": Ibid.

"our heart's home": Hal Rothman, LBJ's Texas White House: "Our Heart's Home" (College Station: Texas A&M University Press, 2001), p. 264.

"Now . . . matter with those hens?": DKG/LBJ Conversations.

"Here's where my mother . . . I'm gonna be too": Leo Janos, "The Last Days of the President: LBJ in Retirement," The Atlantic (July

1973), https://www.theatlantic.com/maga
zine/archive/1973/07/the-last-days-of-the-
president/376281/.

"Those were the days . . . had gone differently":
DKG/LBJ Conversations.

"I'm an old man . . . I want to go fast": Janos,
"The Last Days of the President."

"people know when . . . when you die": DKG/
LBJ Conversations.

*"I'm hurting real bad . . . scared and breath-
less":* Janos, "The Last Days of the President."

"So cold and icy . . . come here by bus": Merle
Miller, *Lyndon,* p. 559.

*"Lyndon had been quite sick . . . positively could
not go":* Ibid., p. 560.

"a dark-blue . . . polished oxfords": Hugh Sidey,
"The Presidency," *Life,* Dec. 29, 1972,
p. 16.

"very often" or for "very long": "Lyndon Baines
Johnson Civil Rights Symposium Address,"
December 12, 1972, "American Rhetoric,"
Online Speech Bank, Lyndon Baines Johnson Library, Austin, TX, http://www
.americanrhetoric.com/speeches/lbjfinal
speech.htm.

"Of all the records . . . we shall overcome":
Ibid.

"he knew what he was . . . how to spend it":
Sidey, "The Presidency," p. 16.

"If I am ever . . . for civil rights": DKG/LBJ
Conversations.

"As the ages roll by . . . we call history": TR to William Allen White, Nov. 28, 1906, *LTR,* 5:516.

"in the harness . . . of one's fame": TR to Henry Cabot Lodge, July 18, 1905, *LTR,* 4:1279.

"work worth doing": TR to William Howard Taft, March 12, 1901, *LTR,* 3:12.

"In the days . . . aside as useless": TR to Cecil Arthur Spring Rice, July 24, 1905, *LTR,* 4:1282–83.

"every hour . . . office in the world": Oscar S. Straus, *Under Four Administrations: From Cleveland to Taft* (Boston: Houghton Mifflin, 1922), p. 251.

"the greatest popular . . . candidate for President": TR to Kermit Roosevelt, Nov. 10, 1904, *LTR,* 4:1024.

"the wise custom . . . to two terms": Herman A. Kohlsaat, *From McKinley to Harding: Personal Recollections of Our Presidents* (New York: Charles Scribner's Sons, 1923), pp. 137–38.

"longer than it was . . . Washington to hold it": TR to George Trevelyan, June 19, 1908, *LTR,* 6:1089.

"I would cut my hand . . . recall that written statement": Kohlsaat, *From McKinley to Harding,* p. 137.

"The people think that my word . . . think anything else": Sewall, *Bill Sewall's Story of*

Theodore Roosevelt, p. 112.

"so well fitted to be president": Boston Daily Globe, June 19, 1908.

"It will let me down . . . break his fall": Abbott, ed., *The Letters of Archie Butt,* p. 41.

"Like a war horse . . . distant battles": Ray Stannard Baker, Notebook, Dec. 8, 1911, Ray Stannard Baker Papers.

"the only question now . . . get the most flowers": Mark Sullivan, *Our Times: The United States 1900–1925,* Vol. 4: *The War Begins* (New York: Charles Scribner's Sons, 1927), p. 531.

"point blank range . . . into his heart": Oscar Davis, *Released for Publication: Some Inside Political History of Theodore Roosevelt and His Times, 1889–1919* (Boston: Houghton Mifflin, 1925), pp. 381–82.

"The bullet that rests in . . . Wilson for the Presidency": NYT, Oct. 27, 1912.

"perhaps once in a generation . . . lines of division": TR, "Address at Madison Square Garden," Oct. 30, 1912, in Lewis L. Gould, ed., *Bull Moose on the Stump: The 1912 Campaign Speeches of Theodore Roosevelt* (Lawrence: University Press of Kansas, 2008), p. 187.

"the haves . . . spend and be spent": Ibid., pp. 191–92.

"his last chance to be a boy": Candice Millard, *The River of Doubt: Theodore Roo-*

sevelt's Darkest Journey (New York: Broadway Books, 2005), p. 61.

"The Brazilian wilderness . . . ten years of his life": Thayer, Theodore Roosevelt, p. 130.

"For a dozen years . . . ought to be done": TR to John Callan O'Laughlin, Aug. 27, 1914, LTR, 7:813.

"usefulness": TR to Edwin Van Valkenburg, Sept. 5, 1916, LTR, 8:1114.

"While I have . . . dangerous conservatism": TR to John Callan O'Laughlin, Aug. 27, 1914, LTR, 7:813.

"it would be . . . of the Civil War": TR to Gifford Pinchot, Feb. 8, 1916, LTR, 8:1016.

"There is some good . . . riders out here": TR to HCL, Aug. 10, 1886, LTR, 1:108.

"The great prize . . . above all others": Wood, Roosevelt as We Knew Him, p. 480.

"all who feel any . . . in the heart": Wagenknecht, The Seven Worlds of Theodore Roosevelt, p. 247.

"do-nothing ease and safety": TR to Quentin Roosevelt, Sept. 1, 1917, LTR, 8:1232.

"shut down": Bishop, Theodore Roosevelt and His Time, Vol. 2, p. 468.

"a sickening feeling": Patricia O'Toole, When Trumpets Call: Theodore Roosevelt after the White House (New York: Simon & Schuster, 2005), p. 398.

"to bring justice . . . in a new world": TR, "Eyes

to the Front," *Metropolitan Magazine* (Feb. 1919).

"I have only one . . . in case I am needed in 1920": CRR, *My Brother, Theodore Roosevelt,* p. 345.

"All right! I can work that way, too": Harbaugh, *Power and Responsibility,* p. 489.

"an absurdity longer to higgle": TR, "Eyes to the Front," *Metropolitan Magazine* (Feb. 1919).

"to work in a spirit . . . the common good": Matthew J. Glover, "What Might Have Been: Theodore Roosevelt's Platform for 1920," in Naylor, Brinkley, and Gable, eds., *Theodore Roosevelt,* p. 489.

"rock of class hatred . . . course of any republic": TR at Banquet of the Iroquois Club, Chicago. May 10, 1905, in TR; Alfred Henry Lewis, ed., *A Compilation of the Messages and Speeches of Theodore Roosevelt, 1901–1905* (Washington, D.C.: Bureau of National Literature and Art, 1906), p. 620.

"two sections, or two classes . . . point of view": TR, "Fellow Feeling as a Political Factor" (Jan. 1900), *WTR,* 13:355.

"sensation of depression about the chest": New York Tribune, Jan. 9, 1919.

"I know . . . such a strange feeling": DKG, *BP,* p. 746.

"the fellow feeling . . . for a common object": TR, "Fellow Feeling as a Political Factor"

(Jan. 1900), *WTR,* 13:355.

"I suspected something . . . lips and nail beds": DKG, *NOT,* p. 494.

FDR examination: Ibid., pp. 494–95.

945th press conference: March 28, 1944, transcript, FDRL.

"Not only were . . . spirits were good, too": NYT, March 29, 1944.

"some sunshine and exercise": NYT, April 5, 1944.

"You just never said you were sick": Ward, *A First-Class Temperament,* p. 607.

"I'm a young man again . . . a sense of glee": Perkins, *The Roosevelt I Knew,* p. 374.

"like hell": William D. Hassett, *Off the Record with F.D.R.* (New Brunswick, N.J.: Rutgers University Press, 1958), p. 239.

"cheerful in spirit" and "good natured": Ibid., p. 240.

"did not have . . . until very near the end": Perkins, *The Roosevelt I Knew,* p. 374.

"Terrible decisions to have to make": Margaret Suckley, in Geoffrey C. Ward, *Closest Companion: The Unknown Story of the Intimate Friendship between Franklin Roosevelt and Margaret Suckley* (New York: Simon & Schuster, 1995), p. 316.

"duty to carry on, as long as he was able": Ibid., p. 316.

"not going to be able . . . to run for another term": Ibid., p. 302.

"A great moment in history . . . pleased with the world": Letter from "B" to "Mom," June 6, 1944, Reminiscences by Contemporaries, FDRL.

"he seemed happy and confident": I. F. Stone, *The War Years, 1939–1945* (Boston: Little, Brown, 1990), p. 236.

"You just don't land . . . understands it the better": FDR, "The Nine Hundred and Fifty-Fourth Press Conference — D Day," June 6, 1944, *PPA,* 1:159.

"looked very well . . . plans for the future": DKG, *NOT,* p. 510.

"in the pink of condition": Ward, *Closest Companion,* p. 254.

"one of the greatest . . . vision": Rosenman, *Working with Roosevelt,* p. 394.

"to keep his head . . . of highest importance": Perkins, *The Roosevelt I Knew,* p. 371.

"so ordered by . . . of the United States": Official announcement letter, FDR to Robert Hannegan, July 11, 1944, FDR, *PPA, 1944–45,* p. 197.

"People have been asked . . . wet through": Perkins, *The Roosevelt I Knew,* p. 116.

"full of fight": Ward, *Closest Companion,* p. 340.

gained twelve pounds as well as gained election to a fourth consecutive term: Perkins, *The Roosevelt I Knew,* p. 372.

Yalta: DKG, *NOT,* pp. 573–85.

"might have been better . . . did all he could":

William E. Leuchtenburg, *In the Shadow of FDR: From Harry Truman to Barack Obama* (Ithaca: Cornell University Press, 2009), p. 7.

"great unfinished business": Anne O'Hare McCormick, " 'His Unfinished Business' and Ours," *NYT,* April 22, 1945.

"make a really handsome appearance": Frances Perkins, "The Roosevelt I Knew: the War Years," *Collier's,* Sept. 21, 1946, p. 103.

"genuine and spontaneous . . . triumphant return to London": Rosenman, *Working with Roosevelt,* p. 546.

"But the war! . . . the war was at hand": Perkins, *The Roosevelt I Knew,* p. 380.

"It wasn't just a matter . . . assumed it would": Ibid.

"The thought never . . . to rally as he always had": Sherwood, *Roosevelt and Hopkins,* p. 880.

"exceptionally good": Elizabeth Shoumatoff, *FDR's Unfinished Portrait* (Pittsburgh: University of Pittsburgh Press, 1990), p. 108.

"He looked smiling . . . ready for anything": Ward, *Closest Companion,* p. 417.

"a keen sense . . . own place therein": Gunther, *Roosevelt in Retrospect,* p. 80.

"Of the papers . . . giving me their opinions": FDR, Nov. 19, 1939, quoted in *Oil City Derrick* (Penn.), Nov. 20, 1939.

"in the streets . . . 'lost our friend' ": Anne

McCormick, "A Man of the World and the World's Man," *NYT,* April 14, 1945.

"The greatest human tribute . . . 130 millions feel lonely": Ben Vine, April 13, 1945, in "Tributes to the Late President," *NYT,* April 17, 1945.

"drunk with joy": Montgomery C. Meigs Diary, quoted in Segal, ed., *Conversations with Lincoln,* p. 393.

"How I would rejoice . . . envy you its pleasures": O. J. Hollister, *The Life of Schuyler Colfax* (New York: Funk & Wagnalls, 1886), p. 252.

"from the Rocky Mountains . . . treasury of the world": Segal, ed., *Conversations with Lincoln,* pp. 392–93.

"This is the great question . . . begin to act": Jay Winik, *April 1865: The Month That Saved America* (New York: Harper Perennial, 2002), p. 208.

"Enough lives . . . the worst of them": Gideon Welles, "Lincoln and Johnson," *Galaxy* (April 1872), p. 526.

"frighten them . . . for their crimes": Winik, *April 1865,* p. 208.

"What terms did you make . . . glowed with approval": Frederick William Seward, *Reminiscences of a War-Time Statesman and Diplomat: 1830–1915* (New York: G.P. Putnam's Sons [Knickerbocker Press], 1916), pp. 256, 255.

"Let 'em up easy" . . . "let 'em up easy": Carl

Sandburg, *Abraham Lincoln: The War Years,* Vol. 6 (New York: Charles Scribner's Sons, 1943), p. 227.

"undertake to run . . . may do it badly": Seward, *Reminiscences of a War-Time Statesman,* p. 256.

"Didn't our Chief . . . in many a long day": Burlingame, *Abraham Lincoln, A Life,* Vol. 2, p. 806.

"more glad, more serene": Tarbell, *The Life of Abraham Lincoln,* Vol. 4, p. 29.

"indescribable sadness . . . life had been achieved": Katherine Helm, *The True Story of Mary, Wife of Lincoln* (New York: Harper & Brothers, 1928), p. 253.

"You almost startle me . . . felt better in my life": Winik, *April 1865,* p. 220.

"Come back, boys, come back": Helm, *The True Story of Mary, Wife of Lincoln,* p. 255.

"They kept sending . . . come to dinner at once": Ibid., p. 256.

"I suppose it's time . . . would rather stay": Hollister, *The Life of Schuyler Colfax,* p. 253.

"It had been advertised . . . disappoint the people": Col. William H. Crook; Margarita Spaulding Gerry, ed., *Through Five Administrations: Reminiscences of Colonel William H. Crook* (New York: Harper & Brothers, 1910), p. 67.

"even greater tyrant" . . . achieve immortality: Donald, *Lincoln,* p. 597.

"pulling down" . . . *"building up"*: AL, "Address before the Young Men's Lyceum of Springfield, Illinois," Jan. 27, 1838, *CW*, 1:114.

"Mr. Lincoln had . . . most men instantly": Dr. Charles Sabin Taft, quoted in *The Diary of Horatio Nelson Taft*, Vol. 3, Manuscript Division, LC.

"Now" . . . *"he belongs to the ages"*: Quoted by Robert V. Bruce, "The Riddle of Death," in Gabor S. Boritt, ed., *The Lincoln Enigma: The Changing Faces of an American Icon* (New York: Oxford University Press, 2001), p. 144.

"as the most important subject . . . our free institutions": AL, "To the People of Sangamon County," March 9, 1832, *CW*, 1:8.

"more and more dim . . . bible shall be read": AL, "Address before the Young Men's Lyceum of Springfield, Illinois," Jan. 27, 1838, *CW*, 1:115.

"the unfinished work . . . perish from the earth": AL, "Address Delivered at the Dedication of the Cemetery at Gettysburg," Nov. 19, 1963, [final text], *CW*, 7:23.

"to strive on . . . the nation's wounds": AL, "Second Inaugural Address," March 4, 1865, *CW*, 8:333.

"in terms of which the human mind cannot improve": Rosenman, *Working with Roosevelt*, p. 452.

"public opinion baths": Helen Nicolay, *Personal*

Traits of Abraham Lincoln (New York: Century, 1912), p. 258.

ILLUSTRATION CREDITS

Chapter One
Abraham Lincoln at 48, *Courtesy of the Chicago History Museum*

Chapter Two
Theodore Roosevelt at 23, *Courtesy of the Library of Congress*

Chapter Three
Franklin Roosevelt at 28, *Courtesy of the Library of Congress*

Chapter Four
Lyndon Johnson at 23, *Courtesy of the University Archives, Texas State*

Chapter Five
The Fourth Great Lincoln-Douglas Debate, *Courtesy of Heather Hayes, Illinois Secretary of State's Office*

Chapter Six
Theodore Roosevelt in the Badlands, *Courtesy of the Library of Congress*

Chapter Seven
Franklin Roosevelt swimming at Warm Springs, *Courtesy of the FDR Presidential Library and Museum*

Chapter Eight
Rally opening Lyndon B. Johnson's 1941 U.S. Senate Campaign, *Courtesy of the LBJ Presidential Library and Museum*

Chapter Nine
A reading of the Emancipation Proclamation, *Courtesy of the Library of Congress*

Chapter Ten
Strike Arbitration Commission appointed by President Theodore Roosevelt, *Courtesy of the Library of Congress*

Chapter Eleven
Irate customers at the closed doors of the Bank of United States, New York, *Courtesy of the Associated Press*

Chapter Twelve
The march from Selma to Montgomery, Alabama, *Courtesy of the Library of Congress*

Epilogue

Abraham Lincoln, 1865, *Courtesy of the Library of Congress*

Theodore Roosevelt, 1918, *Courtesy of the Library of Congress*

Franklin Roosevelt, 1945, *Courtesy of the FDR Presidential Library and Museum*

Lyndon B. Johnson, 1972, *Courtesy of the LBJ Presidential Library and Museum*

ABOUT THE AUTHOR

Doris Kearns Goodwin's interest in leadership began more than half a century ago as a professor at Harvard. Her experiences working for LBJ in the White House and later assisting him on his memoirs led to the bestselling *Lyndon Johnson and the American Dream*. She followed up with the Pulitzer Prize–winning *No Ordinary Time: Franklin and Eleanor Roosevelt: The Home Front in World War II*. She earned the Lincoln Prize for the runaway bestseller *Team of Rivals*, the basis for Steven Spielberg's Academy Award–winning film *Lincoln*, and the Carnegie Medal for *The Bully Pulpit*, the *New York Times* bestselling chronicle of the friendship between Theodore Roosevelt and William Howard Taft. She lives in Concord, Massachusetts.

www.DorisKearnsGoodwin.com
@DorisKGoodwin